John James Audubon's
Journal of 1826

John James Audubon's Journal of 1826

The Voyage to *The Birds of America*

JOHN JAMES AUDUBON

Edited & with an introduction by Daniel Patterson

Patricio J. Serrano, Assistant Editor

Foreword by John R. Knott

University of Nebraska Press ⟩ *Lincoln and London*

Library of Congress Cataloging-in-Publication Data

Audubon, John James, 1785–1851.
John James Audubon's journal of 1826: the voyage
to the Birds of America / John James Audubon;
edited and with an introduction by Daniel Patterson;
Patricio J. Serrano, assistant editor; foreword
by John R. Knott.
    p. cm.
Includes bibliographical references and index.
ISBN 978-0-8032-2531-2 (cloth: alk. paper)
1. Audubon, John James, 1785–1851—Diaries.
2. Naturalists—United States—Diaries.
3. Ornithologists—United States—Diaries.
4. Artists—United States—Diaries.
5. Audubon, John James, 1785–1851. Birds of America.
I. Patterson, Daniel, 1953– II. Serrano, Patricio J.
III. Title. IV. Title: Voyage to The Birds of America.
QL31.A9A3   2011
508.092—dc22   2011004500

Set in Arno Pro by Kim Essman.
Designed by A. Shahan.

For Alison

[I]f my work deserves the attention of the Public, it will stand on its own legs as firm as if joined to those of men who are no doubt far my superiors in point of education and literary acquirements, but not so in the actual courses of observations of Nature at her Best — in her Wilds! — as I positively have done.

John James Audubon to Thomas Stuart Traill,
OCTOBER 28, 1826

Contents

Illustrations

Foreword

John James Audubon's 1826 journal offers rare insights into the life of one of the most fascinating and elusive characters in American cultural history. Audubon sailed for England with his portfolio of drawings at a critical point in his career, when he had failed to find a publisher for his immensely ambitious *The Birds of America* in the United States and was forced to gamble his future livelihood and that of his family on succeeding abroad. As Daniel Patterson shows in the introduction to his definitive new edition, the 1826 journal reveals Audubon's vulnerability to periods of doubt and anxiety about his chances of winning support from the moneyed elite upon whom he would depend for subscriptions and even greater anxiety about the continuing affection of his absent wife, Lucy, left behind to support their two sons. We see his emotional volatility as he responds to successes and rebuffs on his way from Liverpool to Manchester and finally to Edinburgh. In that intellectual center, his art quickly earns him the respect of leading naturalists, and he finds a congenial environment in which to work on the bird biographies that he has become convinced he must write as a companion to the fascicles of engravings that will make up *The Birds of America*. The journal gradually turns into a story of triumph, revealing Audubon's growing confidence as his drawings amaze viewers who see them in exhibitions or private showings, as he gets the advice that enables him to clarify a plan for his work, and as he discovers that he can charm his hosts by playing on their fascination with frontier America.

Patterson's introduction and his extensive notes re-create the social, intellectual, and political contexts of Audubon's initial experience of England and Scotland. He brings into critical focus ways in which Audubon's encounters with the social constraints and class consciousness of his hosts deepen his commitment to American freedoms and democratic ways, showing how the journal becomes an outlet for political feelings that Audubon struggles to keep to himself when he is in public. We see, with Patterson's help, how the journal illuminates Audubon's interior life, including his susceptibility to depression when letters from Lucy are delayed and the irrepressible admiration of beautiful women that complicates his relationship to his "dearest Friend," particularly when he feels compelled to describe their beauty in detail in letters to her. By paying careful attention to shifts in tone, Patterson also shows how playful, witty, and satiric Audubon could be in writing for his journal.

Audubon was insecure enough about his ability to write acceptable English prose to seek out editorial help with writing that he intended for the public, most notably, the five volumes of his *Ornithological Biography*. In this case he trusted a young Edinburgh naturalist, William MacGillivray, to smooth the "asperities" of his prose and make it fit for Victorian readers. We are likelier to find Audubon's authentic voice in the few journals that have survived, although until Christoph Irmscher published a new transcription of the 1820–21 journal in his 1999 edition of Audubon's works for the Library of America, editors had been preoccupied with improving Audubon's prose to make it conform to current standards of correctness and taste. Maria Audubon's 1897 edition of Audubon's journals is notoriously unreliable because of "improvements" that include not only revisions of the prose but additions and omissions intended to sanitize the image of her grandfather. Modern readers of Audubon's 1826 journal have relied primarily upon Alice Ford's 1967 edition. Patterson convincingly demonstrates that this edition is also flawed by numerous revisions and additions that subtly and sometimes not so subtly distort the original and that constitute a form of interpretation. By examining Ford's papers as well as her published work, he is able to show that this respected Audubon scholar, author of one of the most important biographies, had her own assumptions about how Audubon's prose needed to be improved to be suitable for modern readers.

One of the strengths of Patterson's edition is his determination to preserve what Audubon actually wrote, except in cases where his prose would be unintelligible without emendation. He makes an unusual effort to present Audubon's authentic voice in its spontaneity, its sometimes awkward syntax, and its hybridity. Patterson recognizes more than previous editors that to experience this voice fully we need to hear its French accents in

Audubon's choice of words and expressions and sometimes in his syntax. The voice that one encounters in the manuscripts reflects Audubon's French upbringing as well as his experience of listening to the voices of the American frontier. In his writing Audubon ranges from the colloquial to the grandiloquent as he reaches for a more literary style inspired by his reading, and he can stumble over idiom and syntax in his rush to record his observations and express his enthusiasms. Yet Audubon's prose is invariably lively, reflecting his mercurial temperament, his candor, and the freshness of his perceptions. Daniel Patterson's edition of the 1826 journal reflects his commitment to enabling the reader to experience this liveliness directly. He performs a major service by restoring Audubon's authentic and original voice and by making what may be his most important surviving journal available in an edition that one can trust.

John R. Knott

Acknowledgments

This project has, indeed, been a labor of love, and I have been the beneficiary of much welcome assistance, guidance, and support.

Patricio J. Serrano and I learned to read Audubon's hand together over the two semesters he worked as my research assistant. I am grateful to Patricio for many hours of cordial work together and to Lorena, his wife, and their sons, Fernando and Felipe, for making room in their family life for Patricio's dedicated work on Audubon's manuscript journal. Patricio is now director of the Applied Linguistics Career and professor of TESOL at his home institution, Escuela Politécnica del Ejército, in Quito, Ecuador.

I am grateful to Christoph Irmscher for showing me the way to this project. While transcribing selected pages from the microfilm of the 1826 journal for his Library of America edition of Audubon's writings and drawings, Christoph discovered surprising discrepancies between Alice Ford's edition and the manuscript. It was only after he informed me of this problem that I undertook the investigation and labor that have produced this volume.

I am also grateful to John Knott. At the request of the University of Nebraska Press, John carefully read through the entire manuscript of this work and made numerous suggestions, which have made this a better book than it otherwise would have been. At a conference in the summer of 1997, it was John who first kindled an interest in me to read Audubon more seriously when he talked about his study of the differences between the bird biographies published in *Ornithological Biography* and the manuscript versions. John's *Imagining Wild America* is a model of scholarly writing about some of our common interests, including the authentic voice of Audubon that can be found in the surviving manuscripts. It is no small honor for me to share a title page with John.

My academic home, Central Michigan University, supplied various forms of institutional support, including a research assistant, travel funds, and a sabbatical. I would have needed another full year to complete this project without this assistance.

Two colleagues at CMU very kindly answered my queries in their respective fields of expertise. I thank Amy J. Ransom, assistant professor of French, for helping me learn to hear the French accent of Audubon's prose and for tenaciously disentangling several French words in the manuscript that were nearly illegible, including what I consider her masterpiece: *démangeaison*. I also thank Professor Gregory Smith, a classicist in CMU's history department, for his insights into Audubon's unschooled Latin.

I am grateful for permission to quote from Alice Ford's papers, housed at the John James Audubon Center at Mill Grove. I wish to thank specifically Jill Dixon, Michelle Harris, Carl Klase, and Nancy Powell for their helpful communications and for setting up a work space for me in the fine old great room of the Old Mill House overlooking the Perkiomen Creek.

For collegial interest and clarifying conversations, I thank John Fierst, librarian at CMU's Clarke Historical Library, and Steve Arch and Ned Watts of Michigan State University's English department. Andrew Hook, Emeritus Bradley Professor of English Literature at the University of Glasgow, graciously answered questions about Edinburgh and the border villages of Scotland. Eugene Beckham, naturalist-illustrator and professor of natural science at Northwood University, kindly read the introduction and offered significant suggestions for improving it, for which I thank him.

Ron Tyler, director of the Amon Carter Museum in Fort Worth, Texas, generously brought his broad expertise to bear on the introduction to this edition and noted several misstatements, for which I am grateful.

The New-York Historical Society provided a copy of its microfilm copy of Audubon's 1826 journal. At Yale University's Beinecke Rare Book and Manuscript Library, Adrienne Sharpe arranged to send me a copy of the fragment of Audubon's 1826 journal in its holdings. Alexandra Mazzitelli, research associate at the New-York Historical Society, helped identify Audubon's sketch of John Cleves Symmes. My thanks, of course, for all their help.

To Matt Bokovoy of the University of Nebraska Press I owe the very survival of this project. At a moment when I thought the project was dead, he showed me the way through some institutional obfuscations, and I pressed forward. Later, when I rather airily suggested that it would be helpful if Alice Ford had left her research papers and correspondence behind, he said, "Go find them." More than an acquisitions editor, Matt has proven to be an able advisor, for which I am grateful.

Also at the University of Nebraska Press I wish to thank Heather Lundine, editor in chief, for helping arrange a welcome for this project at the press. All my correspondence with Elisabeth Chretien, associate acquisitions editor, and Sabrina Stellrecht, associate project editor, assured me that this book was being ushered, watched, and fretted over by caring professionals who express their utter competence most graciously. My debt to Mary M. Hill, who copyedited the manuscript of this book, is great, but I incur the debt happily because of the expert eye she brought to this work, improving it significantly. Finally, the care and intelligence with which Sarah Statz Cords prepared the index contribute a welcome degree of coherence to the entire volume.

I thank Bill Steiner for passing my query on to an Audubon family descendant when I asked him whether he knew of any papers Alice Ford might have deposited somewhere. This descendant had heard that Ford's papers were at the Mill Grove Museum, Audubon, Pennsylvania, where I was pleased to find them.

My gratitude to Alice Ford is that of a scholar whose work is built on that of another. The qualities of the present edition stand in direct relation to those of her edition. As I explain later in the introduction, her edition is flawed, but she is the scholar who succeeded in locating the forgotten manuscript of the 1826 journal and in making a much more accurate edition than had existed before.

I have dedicated this volume to Alison Miller, my wife and companion. Every aspect of this work from inception to completion has been shaped by the ongoing conversation that is our life together. For so fulfilling and inspiring a conversation, I am grateful beyond words.

Introduction

*The History and Significance of
Audubon's Journal of 1826*

As the record of the interior story of the making of *The Birds of America*
and of the motives and yearnings of its maker, Audubon's manuscript
journal for 1826 is one of the richest documents in the history of American culture. Because most of his other journals were destroyed, the 1826
journal is valuable also as a rare record of Audubon's authentic voice, a
voice whose expressive qualities have not been fully valued. It is the primary source for all we know about Audubon's unlikely success, and it has
never been reliably and accurately edited.

When Audubon embarked for Liverpool from New Orleans on April
26, 1826, his forty-first birthday, he carried with him more than 250 of his
"*watter coloured <u>Drawings</u>*" in a heavy case, a packet of letters of introduction, and good reason to believe that he was a fool to be gambling his family's future prosperity on so risky and grandiose a venture. Having failed to
find a publisher in the United States, he was sailing to England in search
of the engraver and printer who could do justice to his bird drawings and
publish what eventually became the 435 prints comprising *The Birds of
America*, one of the largest and most expensive books ever published up
to that time. It is a monumental achievement in the history of natural history illustration.

The prose companion to *The Birds of America* plates is the three-thou-
sand-page, five-volume *Ornithological Biography*, which he composed (at
a pace nearly manic at times) from field notebooks, journals, and memory.
For each species depicted in the plates, Audubon wrote a "bird biography,"
a blend of field observations, natural history, travel writing, anecdote, and
anatomy. These essays, together with the tales of frontier life and further
travels placed throughout the first three volumes, comprise the bulk of
Audubon's descriptive prose, for which he was universally praised. But

the 1826 journal, more so than any other surviving document, gives us the mind and heart of the man who created *The Birds of America*.

The first leg of this journey, from New Orleans through the seemingly endless, calm Gulf, was tedious. The artist was often seasick, but he drew some birds, marine life, and deck scenes, described his observations of the same, enjoyed the company of the captain and others onboard, read a few books a few times, and drank some port. The thirty-seven days from May 18 to June 23 were spent slowly lumbering toward the Atlantic, upon entering which Audubon celebrated with a statement of his resolve:

> We at last Entered the Atlantic Ocean this morning, 23$^{\underline{d}}$, with a propitious Breese — The Land Birds have left us and, I — I leave my Beloved America, my Wife, Children and acquaintances — The purpose of this voyage is to Visit not only England but all Europe with the intention of Publishing my work of the Birds of America; if not sadly disapointed, my return to these happy shores will be the brightest Birth day I shall have ever enjoyed: Oh, America, Wife, Children and acquaintances, Farewell!

Audubon was a natural showman, and here he writes like a stage director preparing his audience to anticipate the rising action of the success story to follow.

Upon his arrival in Liverpool on July 21, he was quickly in the sooty streets to deliver his letters of introduction and begin to advance his purpose, but in this strange land he was at first avoided by his wife's sister Ann Gordon and her husband and troubled by doubts at night that he might be a fool to have gambled so much on this venture. Nevertheless, Audubon's irrepressible enthusiasm and confidence in his work never faded for long, even after a fit of *mauvaise honte*, a feeling of embarrassment and unworthiness he regularly experienced when he was anticipating meeting accomplished and wealthy people upon whose approval he depended. Nearly five months later, on December 12, Audubon would write to his wife, Lucy, of a similar moment in Edinburgh, "Thou art probably the only one, sweet wife, that ever analised them as I felt them [. . .] a man who has allways felt awkward and very shy in the presence of a stranger." Audubon would soon be well known for his charisma, confidence, and social graces, but this journal reveals his vulnerable side and Lucy's intimate knowledge of her husband's personality.

Within the first week of his arrival in Liverpool, however, his reception by several leading families gave him good reason to expect success. The letter of introduction that Audubon's German friend Vincent Nolte wrote for him to present to Richard Rathbone became perhaps the most consequential of all the numerous letters of introduction he carried with him from the United States. Upon their first meeting, Richard Rathbone invited Audubon to dine with his family at their home. That same evening and over the next few days, Rathbone introduced Audubon to the influential persons in Rathbone's wide social circle, with the result that ladies and gentlemen began calling on Audubon in his lodgings to meet him and see his drawings. Several times during that first week, the shy, charming "American woodsman" narrated the moment of opening his folio, turning the tissue paper over, and hearing the praise of these kind people. Audubon soon felt befriended by the families of Richard and William Rathbone and of their mother, Hannah Mary Reynolds Rathbone, whom Audubon would come to call the "Queen Bee." Her daughter and namesake, the thirty-five-year-old unmarried Hannah Mary, sister of Richard and William, became a close friend, receiving and returning considerable affectionate regard. Away from his adopted country and from his wife and sons, he found much comfort among his new Rathbone friends, comfort much needed as ship after ship arrived bearing no letter from Lucy.

Within this first week also, however, Audubon realized that he must be disciplined and diligent. Things were beginning to go his way, but he must not become complacent: "As my Business Increases here so much, the more must my exertions and Industry be called on and employed to meet all demands." He must make himself available to meet anyone who might be able to help him, he must turn down no dinner invitation, and he must show his drawings whenever possible. From this point in the journal, the plot takes on a distinctly upward movement; to a great extent, it becomes a success story, the tale of an unknown but talented autodidact who succeeds through hard work, the persuasiveness of his character, the passion that drives him, and the artistic merit of his paintings. "What many reflections encumber my mind," he wrote to Lucy at the end of his eighth day in Liverpool, so encouraged by events, " — Would it be possible that I should not in any Degree Succeed, I can scarcely think so. Ah,

Delusion Hope, how much further wilt thou lead me?" But there is also a downward movement: as the weeks pass with no letter from his wife or sons, his loneliness and anxiety grow ever more palpable until he begins to grow emotionally distant from Lucy as if to protect himself.

An important aspect of Audubon's success would be the gradual accretion of a new identity as a gentleman artist-naturalist accepted into Europe's institutions of natural history. This transformation began for him in Liverpool, where on July 31 he opened the doors of the Royal Institution on the first European exhibition of his paintings of the birds of America. His dilemma became whether to charge a fee for admission, which a gentleman would not do. When the suggestion was made that he charge admission, he wrote, despite his poverty, "but my heart revolted at the thought and although I am poor Enough, God Knows, I could not think of doing such a thing consistantly with the Station that I wish to preserve." In America, wherever he was known, it was as a failed businessman who could not support his wife and children. In England, because of the drawings he had produced in the American wilds over the preceding twenty years and more, he could remake himself as a gentleman naturalist. But he did need the "needful," and, after allowing himself to be tossed briefly on the horns of this dilemma, he accepted the opinion of his supporters who believed that he could make some money from his exhibition and still be "*J. J. Audubon Naturalist.*"

With attendance strong at the exhibition, Audubon was making money for the first time from his bird drawings. He was also spending increasing amounts of time among the Rathbones at their family seat, Green Bank, where he was received as an intimate family friend and where his comfort far from home began to exacerbate the lengthening silence from Lucy. He concluded every long day of activity in Liverpool and outlying areas with a session of reporting to Lucy in the journal the progress he was making and the many observations of English life he had made. But the absence of letters from Lucy — together with his planned removal to Manchester to exhibit his drawings there, even farther from Lucy — affected him so powerfully by August 11 that he was unable to write for two nights. On the evening of August 13, he explained that his spirits had been too low and his worries about Lucy too acute to write:

[A]fter having thrown off my Coat, open^d my watch to Judge of the Time, and hung my Cravat on the arm^d chair on which I allways

set to write this pitifull Book; my Ideas flew sudenly to America
so forcibly that I saw thee, dearest Friend!! — Ah, yes, saw thee:
covered with such an attire as completly destroyed all my powers
— The Terror that ran through my blood was chilling and I was
like stupified for a full hour — No — I could not have made a pen
had the Universe been at stake. Both nights I undressed slowly,
mour[n]fully, and bedewed my pillow with bitterest tears — Is
it not strange — Not a Line from thy pen has yet reach^d me —
Vessels one after one have arrived from the Dear Country that
Bears thee, and not a consolatory Word has yet reach[ed] my ear to
assure thee [art] — Well and Happy. —

This is the downward movement of the journal's narrative. As he found
encouragement, assistance, and genuine friendship from the leading citizens of Liverpool and could for the first time imagine that he would manage to make his family's fortune from his drawings, he was tormented by
worries about his family. On this same night, he was moved to plead with
Lucy, "Oh, do write or *I shall not be able to write at all.*"

Like his identity, Audubon's politics were inchoate and conflicted.
Despite an oath he and Lucy made early on in their relationship "[n]ever
to open our Lips (or write) either on religion" or politics (July 17), he regularly felt the tension between his dependence on the wealth of Europe's
aristocrats and his affinity for the democratic freedoms and independence
afforded by his American wilds. Clearly, though, not all aristocrats were
the same in his eyes. Among the Rathbones and his other chief supporters,
the Roscoes, were men who had made their fortunes through trade and
banking, often complicit in the transatlantic slave trade, but who also were
intellectuals with developed interests in literature, the natural sciences, the
arts, and civic improvements. Their mothers, wives, and daughters were
all trained in the arts, languages, and music. His admiration for this class
of England's wealthy was consistent.

The journal shows that he had to craft a middle political or ethical
ground. At Green Bank on August 15, when a walk was suggested, Audubon expressed dismay at the confinement of the lanes and paths to which
they had to limit themselves: "[W]e were forced to walk in files on the
narrow portion of a wall fearing the rebuke of the Landlord around the
grounds of which we had a desire to ramble." He managed to accommodate

this restriction by conceiving of British culture as existing on two planes, interior and exterior: "It is not very Shocking that whilst in England, all is Hospitality within, all is Aristocratic without their Dwellings — No one dare *trespass*, as it is called, one foot on the Grass." While he pursued his and his family's interests, he would focus on the "Hospitality within" and hold his tongue about the geography of aristocracy.

Between August 21 and September 6, Audubon interrupted his habit of writing to Lucy at the end of every day. He was working diligently on oil paintings that he intended as recompense for the Rathbones' hospitality and for the Royal Institution's gratis use of its rooms for his exhibition. Every day that passed made Lucy's apparent silence ever more inexplicable and foreboding for Audubon, and now with his acceptance of the Rathbones' invitation to join them at Green Bank to continue his work before proceeding to Manchester, the next planned stop on his exhibition tour, his attention seems to have turned more and more fully to his friends, his work, and his plans at Green Bank. Advice he received here at this time and further discussions and advice he would receive later in September and early October from the London bookseller Henry George Bohn while at Green Bank helped Audubon complete the design for *The Birds of America* and lay out the more specific plans for its publication. This country seat, then, three miles outside of Liverpool, can be seen as the nest where he incubated his *Birds*.

The confidence and thoroughness of Bohn's advice impressed Audubon, as did the vision Bohn provided of Audubon's future as the successful publisher of his *Birds*. Bohn's advice was practical and, despite his relatively young age, based soundly on an experiential knowledge of the European book market. Audubon should proceed immediately to London, publish a prospectus and the first number of *The Birds of America*, make himself known among the leading natural history societies, and then proceed to Brussels and Paris to learn where the engraving and printing of the rest of his work could be best accomplished. But he must compromise by publishing his birds smaller than "the size of life," certainly no larger than twice the size of Alexander Wilson's *American Ornithology*. Otherwise, only a few institutions and noblemen would purchase it. The many other potential buyers would find the grand scale of Audubon's work disproportionately larger than the other books they wished to show off:

[A]t Present, Productions of Taste are purchased with delight by
Persons who receive company particularly, and that to have Your
Book, to be laid on the table as a Past time Piece of Entertainment
is the principal use made of it, and that if in Compass it needs so
much room as to bring shame on other works, or encumber the
table, it will not be purchased by this set of People who now are
the very life of the trade.

Bohn's vision must have been spellbinding for the still-unknown American, who resolved in his journal on the same night (September 29) to follow Bohn's advice, accepting even the compromise on size. At this time,
however, Bohn had not seen Audubon's drawings. On October 10 in Manchester, as Audubon explained to the physician and naturalist Thomas Stuart Traill on October 28, when Bohn was able to examine them closely, the
bookseller was persuaded to the artist's view: "What will you think and
say when you read here that he is of opinion now that the work ought (if
at all) to come forward, *The Size of Life*? — He said more, for he offered
to publish it himself if no one else would undertake it."

Audubon's meetings with Bohn crystallized the scattered array of wishes,
motives, and goals in his mind. In his October 1 letter to Lucy, he attributed to Bohn's influence also his need to become a writer:

[S]o full of prudence, care, and knowledge have I found that
Gentleman to be possessed of, that, I now will proceed with a firm
resolution to attempt the *Being an Author*. It is a Terrible thing
to me, far better fitted to study & delineate in the Forests than to
arrange phrases with sensible gramarian skill == However, my
efforts will only equal my faculties, and with this I must & will be
satisfied if remunerated suficiently to enhance thy Comfort and
that of our Dear Boys.

Thus it was three days after receiving his vision from Bohn that Audubon
saw the necessity to become a writer, and it was on the night before Bohn
saw Audubon's drawings for the first time (October 9) that it became clear
to the naturalist the kind of writer he must become: a writer of America's
natural history. He realized this in the course of a pleasant evening spent
with the Gregs of Manchester when a "Map of the U. S. was laid before me,

and they all were astonished to discover how Little the Particular[i]ties of that country have been mentioned by Writers." Audubon had always been attracted to published accounts of expeditions, voyages, and travels, but only a handful of books about travel in the United States had been published at this time, and even fewer titles of American natural history. So here was his opportunity: "I wish[d] I could write. I would delight at giving my Country Fair Play."

Two letters from Lucy reached Audubon in Manchester on September 16. They were dated May 28 and June 3, and while Audubon expressed great relief, his journal entries for September 16 and 17 do not reveal much about the content of the letters that brought him the relief. He would receive no other letters from Lucy until two arrived for him in Edinburgh on December 11; they were dated August 14 and 27.

After meeting Bohn in Liverpool and Manchester, Audubon saw his work clearly laid out before him. He must find an engraver and printer to publish the plates of his life-size *Birds*, and he must transform his numerous notebooks of field observations into the "letterpress" that would accompany the images, the natural history work that would become the five-volume *Ornithological Biography*. And he would go to Edinburgh to do this.

When Audubon crossed from England into Scotland, like most romantic American travelers to Scotland in the early nineteenth century, he was well prepared for what he would see, the landmarks he would look for. The novels of Walter Scott had made of Scotland a "modern classic ground," displacing the history and literature of Italy and Greece (see Andrew Hook's chap. 6). In his heightened excitement, Audubon noted the precise time of his border crossing: "[P]assed thro a Village Called Longtown and entered Scotland at 10 minutes before 10" (October 25). He was genuinely thrilled to be passing near to Scott's Abbotsford House at Melrose: "I past so near Sir Walter Scot's place or seat that I raised from my seat and streched my neck some Inches to see it, but it was all in vain." But he was also approaching a renowned European seat of natural history, where the University of Edinburgh had become a nourishing ground for many of Europe's greatest naturalists, and his *mauvaise honte* returned, but briefly this time: "I thought so much of the multitude of Learned Men that abound in this Place that I dreaded the delivering my Letters tomorow."

The next night, the first he spent alone in his new lodgings, 2 George

Street, was a melancholy evening. Having largely failed that afternoon on his first attempt to deliver his letters of introduction, he opened his folio to view his drawings and wondered whether they ever would be published. Dining alone, he felt lonely, even gloomy, missing his country and his wife and having visions of his father and adoptive mother: "My Dinner was there cooling fast whilst each part I swallowed went down slowly as if choaking. I felt frequently tears about my eyes, and I forced myself out of the Room to destroy this painfull Gloom that I dread at all times and that sometime I fear may do more" (October 26). But his reception in Liverpool and Manchester had nourished a deeply rooted confidence, and his unease in Edinburgh lasted but one night. His first few days in Edinburgh saw a minor turning point in Audubon's life, for thereafter his self-doubts would never seriously trouble him again.

The journal allows us to witness as Audubon articulates the sources of his confidence in himself and his work. The first was his talent for drawing and painting, which he relied upon nearly completely after his business ventures failed and he found that his only means to generate an income was to travel the Ohio and Mississippi rivers drawing portraits of citizens who had some money to spare. From Edinburgh on October 28, he encouraged his son John, then not quite fourteen, to enhance his chances for future success by developing his talents for music and drawing: "Draw [a] Great Deal and study Music also, for men of talents are wellcome all over the world."

Audubon's extensive field observations contributed to his confidence as well. Among the elite of Europe's naturalists, Audubon was constantly aware that he lacked the formal education and cultural pedigree that most of them felt made them superior to American naturalists, but Audubon knew that over the past twenty-some years in the American woods, swamps, rivers, and fields he had come to know more about bird behavior than anyone else. On the same day that he wrote to John, he explained the value of his field observations to Thomas Traill: "[I]f my work deserves the attention of the Public, it will stand on its own legs as firm as if joined to those of men who are no doubt far my superiors in point of education and literary acquirements, but not so in the actual courses of observations of Nature at her Best — in her Wilds! — as I positively have done." He does not wish to offend, however, so he does not use the derogatory term "closet naturalist" here: "Yet, as I am but an Infant entering the Great

World of Man, I wish to be submissive to its ways and not stubornly raise mountains betwen my connections with it and my own Interests." This "infant" is certainly circumspect and has become quite savvy about how to plot his success in "the Great World of Man."

Throughout this journal, Audubon's profound sense of personal liberty is evident, and the confidence in his ability to see *The Birds of America* through to publication that fully emerged in Edinburgh was cultivated by his long years of difficult travel across American landscapes. If he failed as a businessman, which he never tried to deny or excuse, he also succeeded in becoming one of the most accomplished and formidable wilderness travelers of his century. The freedom to pursue such travels — all devoted to finding, observing, and drawing America's birds — had transformed the eighteen-year-old fop of Millgrove, his first home in the United States, into a rugged naturalist of incredible endurance and little appreciation for confined, tame game animals, such as he observed several times in England and Scotland. This sense of personal freedom is almost physical and may appear as cockiness in some moments, but it provided a concrete base on which grew the confidence he needed to see his life's work to its completion. His free spirit was evident on the evening of October 29, when he expressed some concern that the eminent naturalist Professor Robert Jameson and others he had just met in Edinburgh might become his competitors for recognition as ornithologists: "[N]ever the less I will have fair Play if I deserve it, for although there exists heavy taxes on Windows in this Country, still I, being a free man, will have my share of the Sun when shining."

The journal shows that for the rest of 1826 in Edinburgh, the rate of Audubon's acceleration toward success increased almost daily. His unavailing trips to the post office were the only source of worry or sadness. His journal writings in November and December enact an entire gamut of expressions of surprise, disbelief, joy, and antic jubilation at his rising success, but speckling his success story are his concerns about Lucy. Is she still in for the duration? Do they still share common goals? On a few occasions Audubon's patience and anxiety seem stretched to the snapping point. An awkward and revealing moment occurs in the December 5 entry. On this evening, weeks since he had had any word from Lucy and seven months since he last saw her, the image of a lady's hand serving him coffee put him in mind of the hand of his favorite, Hannah Mary, serving him wine. As if momentarily forgetting that he was talking to Lucy, he slipped into a private reverie, remembering Hannah's hands and eyes, but then abruptly and awkwardly rushed to cover his *faux pas*: "I saw the Friends Lizars and took my usual Cup of Coffee from the hands of Lady № 1, as I liked so much to do from those of that delightfull Girl Hannah Rathbone a Glass of Wine — How much I would like to see her fine eyes just now or thine, or hear thee or her talk and her dear mother, or my Johny or Victor or thy sweet lovely sister Eliza." After he heard himself express a desire to see Hannah's eyes again, as if to say, "Oh, but you too, Lucy," he quickly tossed in "or thine" and followed that with several other distracting references to talking with Hannah or her mother, the Queen Bee, or to his sons or to Lucy's sister. While this can be seen as an amusing moment in the journal, it also shows that Audubon's feelings about his wife had become genuinely troubled and quite mixed.

His hopes with regard to Lucy took a grim turn over the next few days. He concluded the entry for December 7 with this abrupt complaint: "I am positively quite done, Harassed about thee. So apprehensive am I that I cannot enjoy any thing, not even a few hours repose at night." By December 10 he had withdrawn emotionally and issued clear instructions to Lucy in the tone of an ultimatum: "It is now about time to know from thee what thy future Intentions are — I wish thee to act according to thy Dictates but wish to know what those dictates are." He still wanted her as his partner, but in the absence of letters from her, he had lost his faith in their future together: "Cannot we move together, and feel and enjoy the mutual need of each other? Lucy, my Friend, think of all this very seriously. Not a portion of the Earth exists but will support us amply, and we may feel Happiness any where if Carefull. When you receive this, set and Consider well. Consult N. Berthoud, Thy son Victor, or such a Person as Judge Mathews, then Consult *thyself* and in a long plain, explanatory letter, give me thy own kind Heart entire!" A few hours after reaching this chilly, frightening low point, Audubon received two letters from his wife, dated August 14 and 27: "How I read them! Perhaps never in my Life were Letters so well wellcome — and they were such sweet Letters, My Lucy!" Before beginning his account of that day's developments, he made it clear that he had needed those words from Lucy: "I felt a new life, and braced to encounter any dificulties."

Nevertheless, with letters from Lucy arriving so erratically and the travel distance between them so great, Audubon continued to struggle to know Lucy's — and even his own — desires. A large question before them was whether Lucy and their son John would join Audubon in London the following summer. In the entry for December 22, Audubon expressed some joy about this possibility, but a lingering doubt caused him to express only a cautionary approbation: "Since I received thy letters [. . .] I have felt delighted at the idea of thy probably coming to Europe sometime next summer — But, my Lucy, we must not hurry too much. I wish to found all well and be perfectly assured of the general ultimate success of my work." He was not being disingenuous; he maintained an awareness that his fortune could turn without warning. In the final entry of the journal, December 31, he characterized the world he was venturing forward into as "yet unknown, and dangerous to be known. A World wherein I may prosper but wherein it is the easiest thing to sink into compleat oblivion."

Audubon's move from England to Edinburgh comprised a general change of cultural context from philanthropy to science, and the types of demands placed upon him to advance his cause in the context of Scotland's eminent seat of learning changed accordingly. In two months in Edinburgh, Audubon achieved three goals crucial to the eventual completion of *The Birds of America*. He won the support and endorsements of the leading naturalists there, including even Robert Jameson, "The first Professor of this Place"; and this is what had eluded his grasp in America's seat of learning, Philadelphia, two years earlier. He found the engraver and printer who could and would publish his drawings. And through some rather intense work he managed to become the *"Author"* he declared to Lucy on October 1 that he then knew he must.

After delivering his letters of introduction, Audubon regularly received visitors in his rooms between 10:00 a.m. and 2:00 p.m., where time after time he opened his folio to the astonished delight of Edinburgh's elite. Professor Jameson called on Audubon on November 1 and offered his assistance. By November 19 Audubon had the invitation he sought to exhibit his drawings in the rooms of the Royal Institution. Notes of praise for his work began appearing in the newspapers, and by December 2 Audubon had learned that an important article about him and his work would appear in *Blackwood's Edinburgh Magazine*. At the end of his entry for December 4, he could only shake his head rhetorically over his "very Extraordinary Situation at present in Edinburgh, look^d upon with respect, receiving the attentions of the most distinguished Caracters and support by all men of Science — It is really Wonderfull. Am I really deserving all this?" On December 20, still dizzy from the rapidity of developments, he revealed how hopeful he had allowed himself to become: "The Professors of all classes are pleased to call me a valuable man to Society. I am Courted by the Nobility, and if I do not become a proud fool (and God forbid) I cannot help but succeed."

The engraver and printer William Home Lizars became crucial to Audubon's Edinburgh success. On October 30, shortly after Audubon was introduced to Lizars, the two walked together to his rooms, Lizars praising along the way the work of Prideaux John Selby that he was currently printing, but when "his Eye fell on my Port folio," Audubon wrote, it "gave him some other thoughts, I am quite sure = It is a doubt with me if I open^d my Lips at all during all this; I slowly unbuckled the straps, and putting a chair for him to set, without uttering a Word, I turned up a Drawing! — Now, Lucy, poor Mr Selby was the suferer by that movement — Mr Lizars, quite surprised, exclaimed, 'My God, I never saw any thing like this before.'" By November 19, Lizars and Audubon had finalized their negotiations, and Lizars was committed to publishing the first "number" (consisting of the first five plates) of Audubon's *The Birds of America*. From that day forward, Audubon seems to have made regular stops at Lizars's print shop to watch the progress of the engravers and colorists as they transformed his drawings into prints. The first two completed, colored prints were displayed at his exhibition in the Royal Institution a few days before December 10, just over forty days after Audubon's arrival in "Fair Edina." Lizars expected to have the first number completed and ready for distribution to subscribers by mid-January. Audubon was pleased with Lizars's work and planned, upon completion of the first number, to "travel with it over all England, Ireland & Scotland & then over the European Continent, taking my Collection with me to exibit it in all principal Cities" and make his family's fortune.

Just as rapidly as Audubon gained the support of the leading lights of Edinburgh and successfully employed an engraver, he also moved with surprising quickness to the difficult work of writing the essays that would comprise, in their final form, his *Ornithological Biography*. Before *The Birds of America* could be considered complete, the illustrator had to compose a natural history essay on each of the bird species included. His journals and other records of field observations would be his primary source. Since French was his first language and he had no formal education in English, he felt some trepidation about exposing himself to yet another set of critics: "It is a Terrible thing to me, far better fitted to study & delineate in the Forests than to arrange phrases with sensible gramarian skill" (October 1).

Nevertheless, the journal shows that on November 20, Audubon had written a draft of his first bird biography, that of the wild turkey. His friend David Bridges advised him to take it to John Wilson (a.k.a. Christopher North) of *Blackwood's* "to have it put in English," which he did. He soon planned to begin reading essays on American wildlife at the regular meetings of the Wernerian Society, which elected him as a member later that month. He was quite nervous on December 12 when he read his essay on the black vulture (or "carrion crow") to the natural history editor David Brewster, seeing himself as "a man who never look[d] into an English Grammar, and very seldom, unfortun[a]tely, in a French or a Spanish One" and therefore as unqualified to write for learned readers. Brewster helped Audubon correct this draft, which was then read at the Wernerian Society on December 16. Audubon soon found, however, that he was not completely passive in this author-editor relationship. On December 19, when Audubon read his essay on the black vulture to a group of friends, he found that Brewster had made even further changes to the text, which "made me quite sick — He had Improved the style and destroyed the matter." Audubon would continue to seek help with his prose, and he would often defer to the literary taste and judgment of his editors, but he did not want his voice entirely obliterated. In any case, the journal shows that in his first two months in Edinburgh, Audubon made long strides toward becoming a naturalist publishing his own natural history essays. His first two would be published shortly after the new year, and Professor Jameson solicited more letters on American birds from Audubon for his *Edinburgh Philosophical Journal.*

Audubon's "voyage" to *The Birds of America* was complete in a sense at this point. His great work would be published. Because of a strike by Lizars's colorists, Audubon contracted with the London engraver Robert Havell, Jr., to take over the printing and publishing of his plates in 1827. With the printing continuing, Audubon returned to the United States in May 1829 to collect and draw more birds and to convince Lucy to return to England with him, which she did the following spring. *The Birds of America* was completed in 1838, eleven years after the first plates were produced. In the following year, the fifth and final volume of *Ornithological Biography* appeared.

THE PROSE STYLE OF THE 1826 JOURNAL

It would be surprising if the voice of Audubon's prose were less passionate, impetuous, and colorful than the man himself was known to be. Audubon was naturally charismatic and engaging, always a presence and a personality that attracted attention whether he wanted it or not. And just as his *mauvaise honte* attended him as he presented himself socially and professionally, so too did he doubt the strengths and decorum of his own prose. Because of these doubts, he invited and allowed editors to tame and homogenize his writing, but an authentic early American voice was obscured in this process that the 1826 journal allows us to hear. When he embarked for England, he had been speaking primarily English for some twenty-three years, but his English was still colored by French intonation, words, expressions, and syntax, and his erratic and somewhat harried existence on the American frontier all those years had not prepared him to write the proper formal prose he thought the publishers and reading public would demand. One goal of this edition is to restore Audubon's authentic voice in order to understand and appreciate its qualities.

In the final entry of the 1826 journal, Audubon acknowledges, "I like to put down my opinions as they come at once fresh from the active mind." Anyone who reads his original, unaltered prose will see the truth of this statement, for he rarely wrote a dull or listless sentence. One of his extreme stylistic behaviors was bombast, and he shared the view of some of his friends that he ought to rein in that tendency: "I leaped from the downy bed at dawn of day. I had then, Impatiently been lo[u]nging (for a long time) for!!! ~~~~ the sweet voice of the Lark at the window nearly opposite mine = Its melow throat reached my ear and followed the rotary movements of *my system* with electric swiftness. — I thought imediatly of England, but wished myself in America = I would have wrote *heaven* but *some of my Friends* having once told me that I was nearing the Bombastick I did not" (July 23). Since he was aware of the tendency, occurrences of bombast are always self-consciously playful, never intended to impress with obfuscation or a false display of erudition. Such moments generally reveal an agility of intellect: "I reach[ed] the rail way and saw the Brigg *Homer* 26 days Less from New Orleans than we are — (a mere Moment in the life of man and scarce an attom in eternal calculations)" (July 17). In the December 8 entry, Audubon confesses to Lucy that he is aware that some of his analogies may seem distracting or puzzling to her: "Now I run into one of those curious aerial flights of the mind that puzles thee quite, I know." But his was an active mind that he preferred to indulge rather than to oppress or curb, and his prose reflects that aesthetic.

The dominant mode of his voice in the journal, however, is playfulness. Whether he is bored in the cabin of the becalmed *Delos* and complaining about the quality of the air between his nose and the captain's hammock above him (July 17), frustrated by being unable to find a particular street in unfamiliar Liverpool (July 24), or delighted by the attention of a room full of phrenologists (November 27), he renders the moments with a touch of levity: "There's Phrenology for Thee, sweet Wife!" His humor is often recognizably Shandyesque. While returning to Green Bank on September 6, for example, he is moved to emphasize an irrelevant observation he made of their driver's *ass* from his perspective within the carriage: "The Postilion raises as the Horse he rides trots each step and I can see the Landscape as his xxx escapes the bounce it would receive was he to ride solidly between his sadle and his well rounded, well formed and well buff leather covered xxx." Even a state of extreme annoyance could evoke a witty and well-paced lashing-out. On September 11 Audubon wrote about the man who attended him that day a bit too closely, "I wished him at Hanover or in Congo or New Zealand or at Bombay or in a Bomb Shell in his route to Eternity." Just as he could feign cruelty to humorous effect, so could he joke about self-destruction: "I would not have wrote so much about a morning, the like of which I have had for full 30 Years, but I had nothing else to do and to have been Idle might have created evil wishes, ending probably by hanging myself, as many [a] man has certainly done for want of other much better employment" (October 6). The master stroke here is the cold sure-handedness of "probably." The journal also shows that he was quite the skilled, wry satirist from time to time. Following the lead of Lord Stamford's gamekeeper, Audubon's hunting party apparently transgressed: "Pheasants are not to be touched in this Land of Freedom untill the 1st of October, and I dare venture to say that, had we seen none, we would not have infringed the Laws of the goodly Country, but somehow or other (as a Kentuckian would say it) I positively saw one tilt over tail after head untill down to the earth he came, I believe, as dead as if shot any time next month" (September 20). And nearly pervasive throughout the journal are moments of sheer delightful lightheartedness. In describing a brief, pleasant visit with Mr. and Mrs. Lizars on the evening of November 1, he wrote in well-balanced clauses, "Mr Lizars uncorked a bottle of warm^d London Porter, Lady N° 1 handed it me with a smile, and I handed it to my mouth with thanks!" Of all the surviving documents, the 1826 journal shows the most evidence of Audubon's talent for verbal wit and humor.

While most of Audubon's editors have thought it appropriate to anglicize his francophone phrasing, I think it is important to hear the French accent of his prose. In the first half of the nineteenth century, America was a "melting pot" not only of European nationalities but also of languages and accents. Up and down the Ohio and Mississippi river watersheds, every European language was spoken by immigrants and their descendants, all of whom were contributing to an emerging new American language. Since no other American writer of this time wrote as much about as many American places or bore such prolific witness to the new culture that was emerging as Audubon, we misinform ourselves about this time if we erase his particular expression. Audubon's voice is the voice of Europeans coming to North America and reinventing themselves in active engagement with American places and environments.

The French influence is evident on several levels. On the level of diction, one finds "relatif" for "relative," "compt" for "count," "portefeuille" for "portfolio." His December 27 use of "démangeaison" for an itch or urge shows his delight in play between the two languages. Various phrases or usages contribute to the uniqueness of his voice. He regularly referred to blind persons in the plural as "the blinds," echoing the French usage "les aveugles." Rather than "day after day," Audubon wrote "day following day," after the French idiom "jour après jour." Audubon's word for the garment worn on the head in church, "coverhead," strikes an English speaker as odd, but in his search for the English word, he simply built one on analogy with "couvrechef." His phrase for "foreign travelers," "Travellers Strangers," similarly transliterates the French. When he felt "under the guard of three promisses," he was calling on the French idiom "garder une promesse." Beneath the syntax of some of his more awkward expressions can be heard the background noise of French syntax. Two examples are

"We are seated and feasting on the rarefied Breese our lungs" and "to stop the Breese from disturbing of my Black Lead the Touches."

Audubon knew that part of his appeal, beyond the persona of the American woodsman that he cultivated, was his peculiar manner of expression, as he reveals in the September 20 entry after an evening spent with a number of ladies: "I know that I astonished the Ladies with my odd ways and my curious expressions." His conversation, especially among ladies, was typically animated and playful, occasionally by his own testimony pushing the limits of social decorum. On the evening of July 29, while visiting at the home of Lucy's sister in Liverpool, Audubon received a bit of advice about his manner of conversation and responded to Lucy, "[B]ut I watch[d] my *slipery Tongue* that Doctor Pascallis called *Candid* but the word is very unfashionable I am assured. Indeed, to be Candid is quite *Burlesque I am also Told*, so that I tried to be somewhat fashionable also — much, I assure thee, against my Heart = but the World Dictates and man must follow the mandate." If we are to come nearer to a true understanding of Audubon, his prose should be allowed to reflect this aspect of the man's unique character.

WHAT WE LEARN HERE AND NOWHERE ELSE

The 1826 journal is uniquely valuable for much that we know and think about Audubon's life and character and is yet to be mined for all that we can learn from it. Apart from the main story, that is, the making of *The Birds of America*, the journal sheds significant light on Audubon's politics, his thoughts on women, and what I would call his quality of mind. Reflecting aspects of that mind, on numerous occasions Audubon creates powerful moments of pathos and hints enticingly at secrets of his life that he was loath to disclose.

The journal shows that his political profile looks much like his preference for American wildness and freedom over the cultivated tameness of Europe. After a tour of Lord Stanley's hunting grounds near Manchester on September 10, Audubon objected viscerally to the European practice of raising game animals in captivity to be released for the gunning pleasure of property owners and their guests: "I thought it more Cruel to permit them to grow gentle, nay, quite tame and sudenly and by Frisks murder them by Thousands than to give them the Fair Play that our Game has with us in our Forests of being Free." "Frisks" place the European hunter in a dishonest relation with the game animals, which his hunting ethic, briefly characterized in what follows, condemns: "ah yes, Free and as Wild as Nature made them to Excite the active healthfull pursuer to search after it and pay for it thro the pleasure of Hunting it downe against all dificulties." Many readers who learn of the multitudes of birds Audubon killed are repulsed by what they regard as the hypocritical, unworthy behavior of a sport-killer. Statements in this journal, however, show that he followed an ethic that he could articulate. And whether a reader today agrees with the ornithologist's ethic of 1826 or not, this journal helps to show the way to a constructive, specific discussion of the issue his gunning raises.

Following dinner at a new friend's home in Liverpool on August 19, Audubon parsed the political implications of the game birds roasted for that occasion: "The *Moore Game*, however, was highly tainted, the True Flavour for the Lords of England = Common people, or persons who have no title *Hereditary*: Those who are not *Heritics by Birth* have to write a very particular note of thanks for every paire of Rotten Grous they receive from a Fatten^d Friend." Apart from being superb, acerbic prose, this passage shows Audubon's awareness of his complicated political situation. He is the freedom-loving American woodsman come to Europe to curry favor and support from the privileged classes, who are complicit in slavery, imperialism, and other forms of political oppression, no matter how pious and kind they might be at dinner. By pulling and twisting "Heritics" out of "Hereditary," he insinuates that the ruling class stands in unnatural relation to the orthodoxy of the natural law of liberty. He continues by contrasting the political situation in his adopted country: "Now in America *Freedom is Hereditary*!!! — Grous and Turkey, the Elk, the Bufaloe or the *Venaison* reach^d the palate of all Individuals without a Sigh of Oppression." Certainly on a practical level it is convenient that Lucy and her husband had vowed to one another not to discuss politics, a vow Audubon reminds himself of in the ensuing statement, which he casts as a gentle reminder from his spouse: "'Politics again — I would be enclined to believe that thou hast a Tendency towards such matters.'" No other document makes Audubon's tendency toward political analysis as clear as does the journal he kept while pursuing the publication of his greatest work.

The 1826 journal also testifies abundantly to the fact that John James Audubon liked women. He commented on September 14 that "without female society I am like a Herring on a Gridle." Indeed, he sometimes appears to have written about women and their eyes in the 1826 journal more than any other topic except *The Birds of America*. When readers today see how frequently the traveling artist-naturalist expected his wife at work in Louisiana to somehow appreciate or enjoy his descriptions of the beautiful eyes of ladies he met or of her own sister's lips, simple incredulity is the typical response. Statements in this journal, however, offer insights into what the man must have been thinking. Perhaps disingenuously at times, Audubon nonetheless offered explanations of why he so admired and wrote about attractive women, and these statements have a bearing on any assessment of Lucy's place in Audubon's life.

As I noted above, Audubon valued free expression "fresh from the active mind." Nevertheless, he was occasionally aware that his effusive descriptions of women could be misconstrued. Following the free expression of his August 7 admiration of his host Edward Roscoe's daughter ("the fine Eyes, the fine mouth — the fine form — aye! the sentiment of her grand Father exists Throw out her expressions, her look, her movements! She is a beautifull child"), he acknowledges that a reader of his journal might accuse him of finding too many women beautiful, but he would reject the criticism and "[c]ontinue with pleasure to Write of Nature Naturally, i.e. as I meet it!" Thus, he treats the beauty of a woman as another wonder of nature and grants himself the license to admire it as such without embarrassment. On October 7 a "Tall female figure" he encountered, who stood in telling contrast to the several paintings of women he had been viewing, reinforced the same principle by giving him "a powerfull Idea of the Inferiority of Art when in contact with beautifull Nature." License or not, one must wonder how his distant wife responded when she read his next observation: "She, Lucy, has blue eyes and is very aimiable and, I doubt not, very Clever, but I really Like the fair Helen of Quarry Bank better, and the Dark eyes of Miss Hannah also." A certain inability to understand how others might interpret his eager appreciation of women may be revealed in the following passage from September 10: "I went to bid adieu to thy Sister Ann, and shamefull as it is for me to say it, she for several Minutes refused to Kiss Me — My Mortification was extreme — I cannot bear Prudery — To be *Simple, Natural, truthfully Kind* is my Motto — and I cannot well bear any other Conduct." Audubon undoubtedly intended many of his statements about women in his characteristic spirit of playfulness, but he at least believed that Lucy would understand them as essentially innocent. After eighteen years of marriage, she would have known that her husband believed that "Women were most undoutedly Intended for the comfort of Men" (October 29) and would have known how he meant that. Of all Audubon's manuscripts that survive, only this journal is so revealing of his view of womankind.

Audubon also created numerous moments of profound pathos in the journal, many of which reflect his quality of mind. Several cryptic references to vows of silence or to secrets he could not reveal certainly deepen the pathos of his journal persona. At the end of the long entry written at sea on July 17, for example, he nearly violated a silence he and Lucy seem to have agreed to keep: "I recollect just now that when I first knew thee, Dearest friend: Frequently I was asked if this *Passion* of mine would be of Lasting Duration — Hush, I am now Entering on a sacred Subject." Clearly, his passion for drawing birds had endured, but the subject may be "sacred" because of the great risk he had run and the extreme cost to his wife, whose voice he evoked to close this day: "'Husband — Shut thy Book, pray.'" On December 21, in a letter to William Rathbone, one of his principal supporters, he alluded to secrets he had kept from him and his family: "Twenty times at least when with Your Brother Richard, yourself & excellent Mother, has my heart been on the eve of opening itself entire to you all and let you enter into secrets that would probably make you look at me with astonishment, but sensations that I cannot describe did Keep me silent and I cannot now confide to paper what I regret I have not said to you on the subjects I now allude to." As loquacious and gregarious as Audubon was, the persona that emerges in this journal kept a large, complicated interior life to himself, allowing only occasional and brief glimpses of a somehow problematic past that he clearly yearned to reveal to his most trusted friends.

At some moments in the journal we are able to see Audubon's apperception of the real strangeness of his world and of his bartered place therein. He regularly rose early, and on December 19 the sunrise seen from the Old Town of Edinburgh was especially affecting: "The morning was pure and beautifull — The sun was about raising higher than the line of the Old Town — The horizon was all like burnished Gold — The walls of the castle, white in the light and allmost black in their shade, along with many of the detached buildings in the distance, had a surprising effect on my feelings." He was moved to think of "the Grandeur of the scene = of that

Power of the great Creator that formed it all with a thought, of the Power of Imitative Man [. . .] when a child, bear footed, ragged and apparently on the eve of starvation, shook my views and altered my whole devotion." Just as romantic "Edina" awash in this sunrise led him to contemplate the affinity of God and humankind in their shared creative powers, the sublime spell was broken by the critical needs of the city's disenfranchised. After giving the child a shilling and realizing the inadequacy of so small a gift, he thought to take "it" with him to the hotel where he was to meet Sir William Jardine for breakfast. But "thinking how Novel such an act might appear, how little I yet knew Sir W., and how strange the world is, I told him to come with me." Audubon walked with the child to his rooms, where he made him a gift of all his linen clothes and five more shillings. He concluded, "I gave it my blessings and I felt — oh, my Lucy, I felt such pleasure — I felt as if God smiled on me!" This is an extraordinary passage for the window it offers onto Audubon's habit of reading the moments of his life deeply. He begins with an observation of nature, the sunrise, then contemplates the place of humans in the context of a "strange" world created by a god, then shifts focus to the problematic class divisions that insulate the wealthy from the poor, leaving the day-to-day fate of destitute children in the hands of random acts of small charity, from which a benefactor can return to his god with comfort. This is Audubon the romantic artist ensconced in the burnished gold and filthy streets of the seat of science: "white in the light and allmost black in their shade."

On an earlier morning in Liverpool, the recent arrival from America was at the Mersey River with a book before sunrise, and he reported this quiet, bucolic, but somewhat active and engaging scene: "This morning I was quite surprised to see Persons out so early = I saw Two men hunting with a Dog without Guns — The Dog was a Shabby looking setter but moved well — I thought the men redened as I approached them, but they stood Still and saw me go bye = Another man was Catching Linnets with Bird Lime — Others were Searching Clams and other Shell Fish along the Shores = I also examined some Large Baskets with mouths up Stream to Catch Fish as the River flows toward the Sea" (August 20). He had risen long before the Rathbones would be awake and dressed to receive him, so he took a book with him and explored the river culture on his way to Green Bank, which was some three miles from Liverpool's center. Audubon's image of himself as the solitary traveler across this silent landscape arriving and waiting to be greeted by this family that had welcomed him so warmly is quite affecting: "It was 8 o'clock but no sound was heard. All were yet reposing — I read on the Grass — and the sweet Children soon came to me to be kissed and to wish me well." This is a painter's scene, narrating his restoration by placing the artist in the foreground reading on the pastoral grass and being embraced by the innocent love of the children of a benefactor. Everything begins anew from this moment. This quality of Audubon's mind, this deep comprehension of the challenged and challenging world, is another of the reasons the 1826 journal is so valuable.

THE PUBLICATION HISTORY OF THE 1826 JOURNAL

Audubon's manuscript journal for 1826 has made several and varied appearances, partial and full, in the century and a half since his death in 1851. The first two were based on a large manuscript prepared by Lucy Audubon and the Reverend Charles Coffin Adams from Audubon's voluminous journals and other documents in the summer of 1867. When the London publisher Sampson Low agreed to hire an editor to turn Lucy's manuscript into a book, she shipped it to him, and Low hired Robert Buchanan, who characterized the manuscript as "chiefly consisting of extracts from the diary of the great American naturalist." Characterizing his role as "subeditorial rather than editorial," he explained, "I have had to cut down what was prolix and unnecessary, and to connect the whole in some sort of a running narrative,—and the result is a volume equal in bulk to about one-fifth of the original manuscript" (v). In Buchanan's published volume, *The Life and Adventures of John James Audubon, the Naturalist* (1868), material taken from the 1826 journal occupies only pages 100–115 and is heavily edited. For the American edition, Lucy, with aid from a friend, James G. Wilson, worked from a copy of the Buchanan volume, since the original manuscript remained in London. In her volume, *The Life of John James Audubon, the Naturalist* (1869), Lucy reproduced precisely the text of the 1826 material edited by Buchanan, including several of Buchanan's parenthetical explanations (118–34).

The first full edition of the 1826 journal was prepared by one of Audubon's granddaughters, Maria Rebecca Audubon, daughter of John Woodhouse Audubon, and published in 1897 in her *Audubon and His Journals*. This two-volume work became widely available in a Dover Press edition in 1960 and subsequent reprints of that edition. This granddaughter, however, was motivated by a desire to preserve the reputation of her famous grandfather and of the Audubon family name by manufacturing a gentleman naturalist who would meet late Victorian American standards of refinement and decorum. Her agenda is quite apparent in her claim that, in all of Audubon's journals, "there is not one sentence, one expression, that is other than that of a refined and cultured gentleman" (1:ix–x). To be sure of this, she revised her grandfather's prose freely, omitted material inconsistent with the image of the man she hoped to create, and presented passages she wrote as part of the original journals. This edition is therefore fundamentally unreliable, and because Maria Audubon apparently subsequently destroyed most of the journals in her possession, the unreliability of her edition was not known for decades.

Each of the first two thoroughly researched biographies of Audubon makes some use of the original 1826 journal. Francis Hobart Herrick reproduced in facsimile the first page of the journal entries (dated April 26, 1826) in his two-volume *Audubon the Naturalist* in 1917 (1:349), thanking Maria Audubon for permission to examine the journal and publish some material from it. His transcription of that page is verbatim, but his treatment of the year 1826 is so brief (1:347–55) that only very little of the manuscript material is presented directly. Stanley Clisby Arthur reproduced Herrick's transcription of the journal's first page verbatim in his *Audubon: An Intimate Life of the American Woodsman* (1937), but for any further material from the journal, he cited Maria Audubon's edition (311–34).

In the context of Audubon studies, the next public appearance of the 1826 manuscript journal was a sensational one. While researching and writing her full biography of Audubon, *John James Audubon* (1964), the independent scholar Alice Ford, after three years of searching, located and transcribed the 1826 journal, which family descendant Victor Morris Tyler had apparently sold to the book collector Henry Bradley Martin in the mid-1940s (at about which time the New-York Historical Society microfilmed the manuscript). It would not have taken long in comparing her transcription against Maria Audubon's edition to see just how unreliable *Audubon and His Journals* was. In the foreword to her edition of the 1826 journal (University of Oklahoma Press, 1967), Ford announced that Maria Audubon had "cut, censored, paraphrased, bowdlerized, and even [rewritten] at will, until her misguided striving for an image relieved of imperfections sacrificed typical effusiveness and candor and many engagingly human touches" (*Journal*, vi). Ford would later characterize Maria Audubon as "prim" and as a "censor" who subsequently destroyed all but a few of her grandfather's journals because she "did not intend to leave them 'for daws to peck at'" (AFP). In the foreword to her edition, Ford gives her readers the following assurance: "The following pages are scrupulously faithful to the original manuscript, except of course where failure to transpose a phrase, or add and bracket a word, would mean certain confusion for the reader" (*Journal*, vi).

The main reason for the present new edition of the journal, however, is that that claim is not true. Alice Ford's edition is much more reliable than Maria Audubon's, but it is not "scrupulously faithful to the original." Christoph Irmscher was the first to discover discrepancies between Ford's edition and the text of the manuscript. While transcribing numerous pages from the New-York Historical Society's microfilm of the manuscript for his Library of America volume, *John James Audubon: Writings and Drawings* (1999), Irmscher saw that the differences between Ford's edition and the manuscript were not insignificant. I investigated further and was surprised by the range and extent of the unacknowledged revisions, additions, and omissions in Ford's edition. Ford's prose is more polished than Audubon's, but it is not Audubon's authentic voice that comes through.

ALICE FORD'S EDITORIAL PRINCIPLES AND PRACTICES

Alice Ford was a devoted, assiduous Audubon scholar and editor. She read and made notes about everything published about Audubon; over several decades she actively tracked down Auduboniana in public and private collections in the United States, England, and France; she published numerous books on Audubon and his work; she sought out and transcribed many hundreds of letters to, from, and about Audubon and his family members; upon her death at approximately ninety years of age, she left behind several book manuscripts for which she had been actively seeking publishers (a biography of young Audubon in France, a biography of the Audubon family she considered a sequel to her earlier biography of Audubon, a three-volume edition of letters to and from Audubon family members, and new editions of Audubon's 1820–21 journal and the Labrador journal); and she had in her possession a photocopy of an apparently forgotten partial copy of Audubon's Upper Missouri River journal of 1843. She studied and wrote about Audubon for nearly fifty years.

Among Audubon scholars she had no peer, and this is why her biography of Audubon (University of Oklahoma Press, 1964; Abbeville, 1988) superseded all others.

As I learned more about Ford by reading through her papers at Mill Grove (in May 2008), the liberties she took with Audubon's manuscript seemed ever more anomalous, puzzling, and — I soon came to believe — personal. Because my respect for this accomplished scholar was genuinely profound, I needed to understand the kinds of changes she made to the text in the context of her motives and justifications, if I could discover or infer those. I believed that the editorial license she granted herself was not simply gratuitous or arbitrary.

The following discussion of paired passages will illustrate the types of changes Ford made to Audubon's text. Practically every paragraph of Ford's edition contains such unacknowledged alterations.

Here is one sentence as it appears in Ford's text:

> For if I have not ran off from my mother and friends and farm, I have from the country that has nourished me and brought me up with all the feelings I now profess. (*Journal*, 70)

Here is the sentence as it appears in the present edition:

> for if I have not ran off from my mother & friends: I {am} sure, I have from the Country that has nourished me and brought me up with all the feelings I now possess. == (July 1826)

Ford's "profess" is possibly a simple misreading of Audubon's long *s*, a simple enough error. Her omission of "I {am} sure," however, seems capricious, and her addition of "and farm" is a misrepresentation of what Audubon wrote.

On the next page, where Audubon is diminishing the importance of a ship's late arrival, Ford claims he uses the following phrase: "a more normal calculation" (*Journal*, 71). The actual manuscript reading, however, shows Audubon's clearer and much more characteristically passionate style: "a mere Moment in the Life of Man and scarce an Attom in eternal Calculations." The two phrases do not correspond in any way, and Ford does not acknowledge her change.

While many of Ford's bracketed comments and revisions are helpful, the editorial license she granted herself was far too generous. The following is a substantive example. On Sunday evening, July 23, Audubon drank an unspecified quantity of "*Claret* call$\underline{d}$ here *Port*," and while he brought his day to a close with a session of writing to Lucy, he grew ever more verbally playful, while his handwriting grew increasingly larger and his use of dashes all the freer. He was clearly under the influence. But he was coherent, and as he wrote, he developed a recurring leitmotif of "It was Sunday" in order to complain self-mockingly about how dull the day was. Here is a brief passage from the day's entry as it appears in Ford's edition:

> Now [to] the dullness of the day. — I needed shaving but I did not shave — no! — why? Because it was Sunday. Sunday is a sacred day with me. I like to spend it dully — soberly and — I will not say another word. Oh! that oath of mine, never to tell a politician, or a priest, no, [that] I am — what? What? [Illegitimate.] No one knows, not even my poor self. I have frequently believed myself a fool; but the opinion has been variously received, and it was Sunday, this very morning, when I thought so again as much as I ever did in my life. (*Journal*, 86)

Here is my transcription of the passage from the manuscript:

> Now the dullness of the day — I needed shaving but I did not shave — no! — why? — because it was Sunday. = Sunday is a sacred day with me. I like to spend it duly — soberly and — I will not say another word. Oh! that oath of mine *Never* to be a Politician or a — Priest — no. I am — what? What? — No one knows, not even My Poor self. I have frequently believed myself a Fool, but the Opinion has been variously received and — it was Sunday this very morning when I thought so again, as much as I Ever did in my Life.

In square brackets Ford adds three words, "to," "that," and "Illegitimate." She also misreads an important verb, reporting "tell" where Audubon wrote "be" in darker ink over an original four-letter word ending in "ill" (see fig. 14). Ford apparently believed Audubon was suddenly troubled by his illegitimate birth, so she answered his question "What?" for him by inserting "[Illegitimate]." Her reading of the verb as "tell" (from Audubon's revision of the original "*ill" to "be") does serve to heighten the mysteriousness of her passage: "never to *tell* a politician, or a priest"; however, she allowed to stand the absurdity she created by having Audubon go on to write that not even he knows that he is illegitimate: "not even my poor self." Audubon did keep mum about his parentage problem, but there is no evidence here or elsewhere that he was concerned about it on this night. On July 18 Audubon mentioned this oath he once made not to become a politician ("I have now to regret that I am *by Oath* no Politicician"), the thought of which on this night leads him to consider just what he *is*: "I am — what?" He is risking his family's entire future on this trip to England to find the support he needs to make one of the largest and most expensive books in the history of the world, and he wakes on this his second day in England on a lonely, dull Sunday morning worried that he just might be a fool. Ford's rendering of this passage significantly misinforms the reader.

In the following example, Ford's edition misrepresents not only Audubon's journal but the man himself. Audubon is in Liverpool and has been away from his wife, Lucy (whom he always addressed in his letters to her as "my dearest friend"), for three months. At a dinner party, the sight of a particularly happy couple causes him to miss Lucy and recall a cherished memory of an evening when Lucy swam before her husband. This is Ford's version:

> The calmness of the countryside soon reached my heart, and soon did I contemplate [American] scenery in imagination. I thought of an evening when we were walking, gently arm-in-arm together, towards the waters of the Bayou Sara, and I watched thee bathe thy gentle form in its current. I thought of the happiness [we] have enjoyed while [I] gazed on the happy couple before me. I thought — ah, my dearest friend — ! (*Journal*, 113)

Here is what Audubon actually wrote:

> The calmness existing in the Country soon reach[d] my heart and soon did I contemplate such Scenery in Imagination in America = I thought of such an Evening walking gently arm in arm

together towards the watters of the Bayou Sarah to watch thee
Bathe thy gentle form in its current. I thought of the Happiness
I have enjoyed whilst gazing on the Happy Couple before me. I
thought! — ah, my Dearest Friend. (July 31, 1826)

Ford's bracketed "[American]" is an innocuous enough change, and she
acknowledges it. But her other changes radically alter the meaning of the
original passage. Where Ford's version has Audubon and Lucy walking
to the bayou "*and* I watched thee bathe," Audubon himself is telling his
wife that he recalled walking with her "*to* watch thee Bathe." Ford's "and"
makes the husband's watching his wife bathe incidental to their evening
stroll; the husband's actual "to" with the later "I have enjoyed" make clear
that his pleasure is the purpose of the stroll. Alice Ford clearly knew the
difference a word can make, and she decided she would tone down the
amorousness of the couple's relationship without acknowledging her
misrepresentations. While the brackets enclosing the two pronouns that
follow look like editorial honesty, the altered pronouns prevent readers
from understanding what Audubon is telling his wife: "While I gazed on
the happy couple before me," he tells her, "I thought of the happiness *I*
have enjoyed" on those evenings when she would bathe for him. And "I
thought! — ah, my dearest friend." Lucy Audubon and her husband, at
the time of his departure in 1826, had been enjoying an erotic, loving marriage, and this passage is one of the clearest indications of that aspect of
their lives together. The fullness of both Audubon's and Lucy's humanity
is diminished by Ford's alterations.

The 1826 journal reveals the extent to which Audubon shared his observations of feminine loveliness with his wife, an extent that surprises most
readers. One wonders how the young wife left behind to work and raise
the children would have received such news. Alice Ford seems to have
drawn the line at the extremity of flirtatiousness he reported to Lucy in
the entry for October 8 by omitting the entire passage:

I went to church at M.ʳ Gregg's chapel, sat by the side of his Fair
Daughter and prayed that she may be as Happy as she is Beautifull
= The Sermon was good, delivered by a Young Man. I sung
amongst the Rest — and when service [was] over took Miss

Helen under my arm and had a long ramble thro the Gardens. She presented me with flowers and I wore them for her sake =

"My Dear Laforest [Lucy's pet name for Audubon], thou speaks as if positively thou wert about falling in Love with the Fair female."

My Dear Lucy, I have already done so, I positively do Love Miss Helen, I admire her most sincerely; she is fair, young, & kind to me, and I will promiss that if *thou* dost not Love her as much as I do when you meet, I will abandon all claims of the knowledge I have of thee =

This husband knows he is pushing the limits of his wife's tolerance for his oft-expressed appreciation of women, but he is too impetuous to move toward restraint. By voicing Lucy's complaint and answering it, he bets the farm with blustery confidence: if Lucy does not love the kind, young, fair Ellen when she meets her, he does not know his own wife. No reference to this entry appears in Ford's edition.

There has never been any mystery surrounding Maria Audubon's motives for altering her grandfather's journals for publication, but as I became aware of alterations Alice Ford made even while claiming scrupulous fidelity to the original, I wanted an explanation not from idle curiosity but because so excellent a scholar would not make such unacknowledged changes inadvertently. A fair assessment of her edition of the 1826 journal depends upon an understanding of her motives. I found some answers and explanations in the papers Ford bequeathed to the Audubon Center at Mill Grove, Audubon's first home in the United States.

Among the Alice Ford Papers are statements and other evidence of a set of motives that seem to have moved Ford to dress up her Audubon and tone him down a bit. She wanted to present Audubon's "typical effusiveness and candor and many engagingly human touches," but she believed that Audubon would have acquiesced to her suggestions for the improved public image Ford thought appropriate.

Over a period of some forty-two years, Ford repeatedly described an approach to editing Audubon's writings that justified significant editorial changes to what Audubon wrote without specific notations of those changes. She published three volumes in which she edited Audubon's writings, some of which had been edited previously, and among her papers at Mill Grove are two further proposed editions of Audubon's previously published journals, for which she wrote editorial introductions. Throughout these works, Ford consistently characterized Audubon's unedited prose as problematic and in need of improvement, although she valued "the vitality and charm of the irrepressible style of the originator" to some degree (*Himself*, vi). As his editor, Ford saw herself as serving Audubon much as did William MacGillivray, the Scottish naturalist Audubon hired to edit his *Ornithological Biography*, except that she reveals a sense of greater license since she did not work in physical proximity to the author. She characterizes her edition of one of Audubon's "episodes" as follows:

> It is true that the present rendering differs a little from that of Macgillivray [*sic*], who had to groom copy only a few doors away from Audubon and the latter's amanuensis and wife, Lucy. Yet it no more diminishes the vitality and charm of the irrepressible style of the originator than did a virtual palimpsest of nineteenth-century hands that bore down on the often wayward grammar, punctuation, paragraphing, spelling and syntax. It may conceivably come closer, than any attempt thus far, to the way in which Audubon would have written if English had been his native tongue. (*Himself*, v–vi)

Later in the same work (published two years after the first appearance of her edition of the 1826 journal), Ford disagrees with MacGillivray's decision to allow much of Audubon's voice through:

> Why did Macgillivray permit the words *muffle, flapper, hulk* and other lapses stand, when Audubon meant to say *muzzle, flipper,* and *hull*? Why did he pass over the cascading redundancies, *non sequiturs*, misleading allusions, indefinite antecedents, and desperate participles? Perhaps because of the sheer magnitude of the task before him, and the fact that he himself was a writer only of necessity. Whatever the answer, there seemed no reason to preserve them here. Macgillivray barred a cruel passage that appeared in the manuscript of "The Opossum," but, unaccountably, he did not censor those in "The Raccoon Hunt" and "Scipio [and] the Bear." Present-day champions of the cause of conservation and wildlife will not find them here. (*Himself*, vi)

These two passages reveal several important differences between Ford's editorial principles and those of the present edition (whose guiding purpose is to present what Audubon wrote except where that is unintelligible, which rarely occurs). In the first of the two passages above, it seems clear that Ford believed the highest editorial goal would be to make Audubon's prose read like that of a native English speaker. Thus, she devalues the authentic voice of the man whose mind we strive to understand. The second passage goes much farther, however. It is a declaration that she will "censor" Audubon. Various characteristics or peculiarities of his prose she finds "no reason to preserve," and she questions MacGillivray's judgment again where he, "unaccountably," "did not censor" cruel passages. In 1952 Ford made a strikingly similar statement in her very first published statement about editing Audubon:

> Passages from Audubon were slightly edited in the interest both of readability and taste. Pleonastic sentences and endless paragraphs were converted to a series. Parenthetical effusions and period mannerisms were here and there deleted. More than a century of intensive alteration of the naturalist's published prose preceded this comparatively modest and restrained activity. Much of the original editing went on with the naturalist's personal approval and direction; but, even so, signs of his century's curious admixture of the unconsciously cruel and the errantly sentimental persisted. The paradox was a Romantic and Victorian characteristic, to be witnessed in the vast painted and literary output of that era. Squeamish though he was, William MacGillivray, scientific ghost writer who edited Audubon's "episodes" and *Ornithological Biography*, suffered much to be printed toward which today's reader might well exhibit slight tolerance. (*Audubon's Butterflies*, 8)

In the early 1990s Ford prepared new editions of Audubon's 1820–21 journal and the Labrador journal of 1833, both of which show her exercising a similar editorial license. In the foreword to the 1820–21 journal, Ford once again criticizes Maria Audubon's edition as designed to please a socially conservative readership and notes that Howard Corning's edition of 1929 was prepared "for a like membership" (AFP). Her approach to editing this journal she characterizes (in a letter to the director of the

University of Oklahoma Press dated July 17, 1993) as "to render it in lucid English" (AFP). For her proposed new edition of the Labrador journal, she will simply work from Maria Audubon's edition, as she explains in a diary entry for January 18 or 19, 1992: "The English is good enough, on the whole, as is, but much paragraphing would render it far more vivid & readable. I shall not offer it until I have redone the 100 or so pp. of *Audubon & His Journals*, removed from my battered 2-vol set" (AFP).

Clearly, Alice Ford believed her duty was to craft an Audubon who wrote standard English and who would not offend her readers' sensibilities. Preserving his authentic voice was, for her, a minor and occasional concern. Given Ford's consistent editorial philosophy, it seems anomalous that for the "rarest and the most important" of all Audubon's surviving journals she would adopt a different editorial approach — at least nominally — to claim that her edition was, this time, "scrupulously faithful to the original."

As I read through Alice Ford's papers, another motivation for some of the changes she made to the text of Audubon's journal began to come into view. There is clear evidence that she sympathized with Lucy Audubon's plight (as does anyone who learns about her life) of supporting her husband through all the years of difficulty and uncertainty, through even the final, brief success, and through the twenty-three years she lived beyond his death struggling to survive economically. But there is also evidence that Alice Ford identified with Lucy significantly, so much, her papers suggest, that she was moved to present the world with an Audubon that from her point of view would have been worthier of Lucy's devotion and loyalty.

Alice Ford left behind a typescript of a biography of the Audubons entitled "Dearest Friends" in which Ford brings Lucy into the foreground. (While the typescript of this work, which a note by Ford says was 352 pages in length, does not appear in AFP, there is a 306-page typescript of a biography entitled "The Audubons: Portrait of a Family," which may be a different draft of "Dearest Friends.") In a synopsis of the work, Ford characterizes her treatment of Lucy in the new biography: "The marriage is under high magnification for the first time. Lucy ceases to be one-dimensional at last. Her telling share in *The Birds of America* comes clear. High time" (AFP). In the following passage from the synopsis, one sees Ford's emphasis on Lucy's role in Audubon's ultimate success:

She encourages his desire to reach England with his portfolio and find a publisher, not long after his failure to find a way for it in Philadelphia and New York City. [...] She persuades Audubon to teach, save money with her help, and sail for England in spring 1826: of course, alone and without her. Thanks, in great part, to her coaching as to the importance of letters of introduction he begins to ride high in Liverpool — then in Manchester — and, finally, in Edinburgh where he launches *The Birds of America*. (AFP)

In a diary entry for November 14, 1986, Ford notes that she began this work on Lucy's story nearly thirty years before: "In January 1959 I was [...] revising a draft of *Lucy*, the very first stage of what is now *Dearest Friends*. So I began in 1958?" (AFP). From this it seems that her original intent was to tell Lucy's less-known story, not the monumental story of Audubon. Ford's sympathy for Lucy is also evident in her characterization of "Dearest Friends" in a diary entry for October 10, 1989:

One becomes conscious not so much of one towering figure, as of the aspirations and ironies engendered by the pursuit of fame, & its subjection of other lives to its demands. Would that the story from first to last — "the realization of a dream" — were one of far less pathos. As narrator I had a script to follow, left behind in elusive collections, one more often bitter than sweet. (AFP)

Ford wished that Lucy's life had been sweeter than it was, that the subjugation of her life to Audubon's had not been necessary to the larger plotline.

Ford gives fullest expression of her identification with Lucy in her diary entry for November 13, 1986, when, while recovering from illness, she is preparing to submit her manuscript to Putnam's:

Tonight I am better again, especially after having done a 2800-word synopsis of *Dearest Friends*. I shall send it, with a letter, to the Senior editor at Putnam's, a firm that long ago passed from the family of George Putnam who published the USA edition of Lucy's *Life of Audubon*, & who was a friend to her in other ways. Surprisingly, the publisher, the V-P, and the chief editor are all women, which should help Lucy obtain a wedge against sexism prejudice. (AFP)

Ford appears to have felt a sense of sisterhood with Lucy, with whom she bonds in this passage in a struggle against "sexism prejudice," a prejudice she felt contributed to the numerous rejections she received from publishers in the 1980s. Much of Ford's unacknowledged revision of Audubon's prose is no doubt a matter of taste, but much of it also is motivated by the editor's perception that Lucy deserved a husband more attentive to her wishes, less flirtatious, and a bit more anglophone. Ford strove for another chance to tell the Audubons' story in order to give Lucy a more emphatic place, but she found that, just as in Audubon's day, the charismatic artist-naturalist held the gaze.

One last feature of Ford's edition should be noted. Numerous lines or portions of lines that are clearly in the manuscript do not appear in either of the two printings of the Ford edition. This indicates that, after having prepared her edited transcription of the manuscript journal, Ford did not proof that edited text against the manuscript at a later stage, such as a copyedited typescript or galley proofs. These are inadvertent errors that, if the editor had checked her text against the manuscript, she would have seen and corrected. Several dozen such errors occur. They range from the omission of phrases to the omission of a five-line paragraph (from the entry for August 17).

An error of a different sort also indicates that a final proofreading did not occur. In the entry for September 19, Ford reports the manuscript "7 miles" as "several miles." This could occur if the editor initially recorded the numeral as a word, "seven," and later mistakenly copied "seven" as "several." A subsequent check against the original would have exposed the error.

Because it is inevitable that an editor will omit manuscript material during transcription, multiple proofreadings against the manuscript are necessary. It is possible that, after gaining permission from the book collector Henry Bradley Martin to prepare a transcription of the manuscript in his possession, Ford's access to the manuscript for later proofreading was limited or inconvenient. Whatever the explanation, the textual evidence suggests that a needed stage of correction did not occur.

BIBLIOGRAPHY

Arthur, Stanley Clisby. *Audubon: An Intimate Life of the American Woodsman*. New Orleans: Harmanson, Publisher, 1937.

Audubon, John James. *The Birds of America*. London: Published by the Author, 1827–38.

———. *Ornithological Biography*. 5 vols. Edinburgh: Adam Black, 1831–39.

Audubon, Lucy. *The Life of John James Audubon, the Naturalist*. New York: G. P. Putnam's Sons, 1869.

Audubon, Maria Rebecca, ed. *Audubon and His Journals*. 2 vols. New York: Charles Scribner's Sons, 1897.

Buchanan, Robert, ed. *The Life and Adventures of John James Audubon, the Naturalist*. London: Sampson Low, Son and Marston, 1868.

Corning, Howard. *Letters of John James Audubon, 1826–1840*. 2 vols. Boston: Club of Odd Volumes, 1930; repr., New York: Kraus Reprint Company, 1969.

DeLatte, Carolyn E. *Lucy Audubon: A Biography*. Baton Rouge: Louisiana State University Press, 1982.

Ford, Alice, ed. *Audubon, by Himself: A Profile of John James Audubon from Writings Arranged, Selected, and Edited by Alice Ford*. Garden City NY: Natural History Press, 1969.

———, ed. *Audubon's Butterflies, Moths, and Other Studies*. New York: Studio Publications, in Association with Thomas Y. Crowell Company, 1952.

———, ed. *The 1826 Journal of John James Audubon*. Norman: University of Oklahoma Press, 1967; repr., New York: Abbeville Press, 1987.

———. *John James Audubon: A Biography*. Norman: University of Oklahoma Press, 1964; repr., New York: Abbeville Press, 1988.

———. Papers. Audubon Collection — Archival Record Group 1. John James Audubon Center at Mill Grove, Montgomery County, Pennsylvania.

Herrick, Francis Hobart. *Audubon the Naturalist: A History of His Life and Time*. 2 vols. 1917; repr., New York: D. Appleton-Century Company, 1938.

Hook, Andrew. *Scotland and America: A Study of Cultural Relations, 1750–1835*. 2nd ed. Glasgow: Humming Earth, 2008.

Irmscher, Christoph, ed. *John James Audubon: Writings and Drawings*. New York: Library of America, 1999.

Wilson, Alexander. *American Ornithology*. 9 vols. Philadelphia: Bradford and Innskeep, 1808–14.

Editorial Principles and Procedures

The guiding principles of this edition of Audubon's journal of 1826 are accuracy, accountability, readability, and restraint. The text of this edition accurately represents what Audubon wrote. Since the author was not preparing a carefully written text for publication, however, many of his manuscript practices are not reproduced here. My attempt throughout is to produce a readable text with the fewest changes possible. In order to produce a text that is free of distracting features (such as no punctuation between sentences or confusing use of lowercase letters), the editorial principles explained below have been employed to present a text that is both reliable and readable.

To establish the text of this edition, the editors first prepared a complete unedited transcription from the microfilm of the manuscript held at the New-York Historical Society. The manuscript was microfilmed in 1946, when it was owned by Victor Morris Tyler of East River, Connecticut. Two sets of eyes pored over the journal pages in the preparation of the transcription. When we disagreed about a letter, word, or phrase, we scrutinized the manuscript carefully until we reached agreement. Whenever readings are questionable (either illegible or anomalous), it is because of Audubon's formation of letters, not because of problems with the microfilm. The next step was to edit the transcription according to the editorial principles explained below.

The manuscript of Audubon's 1826 journal is held by the Field Museum, Chicago, Illinois. The director of education and library collections at the Field Museum denied my request for an opportunity to examine the manuscript, giving as her reason the museum's intention to publish its own edition of the journal.

SPELLING

This edition retains the manuscript spelling except where it would likely distract or confuse a reader. In all cases, however, any emendation of the manuscript spelling is documented. For example, Audubon's "profission" is an attempt at "provision" that might stump a reader, but it also is evidence of Audubon's accent. In such cases, I give Audubon's spelling in square brackets following the emended reading; thus, "allured by false provision [MS: profission]." Any letter that I add to a word appears in brackets as well. Because Audubon often spelled persons' names and place-names incorrectly and inconsistently, I give the correct spelling at the first occurrence of the name in the journal and in the explanatory note for the person or place. Thereafter this edition reports the manuscript spelling except when that spelling is so far from the original that it might confuse a reader. The index reports all references to a name or place no matter how it is spelled in the manuscript.

Audubon wrote with quills and with iron pens, and he wrote in all kinds of conditions, from turbulent seas to inebriation. It is not surprising, then, that his handwriting is not always as clear as an interested editor would like. Since he did not form every letter clearly, context is often the key to whether a tiny blot of ink is reported herein as either an *a*, an *e*, or an *o*.

SILENT EMENDATIONS

Audubon's manuscript was an informal, semiprivate document; thus, his punctuation is variable, and often a mark is so amorphous or ambiguous that it is not clearly either a period or a comma; in such cases, I use the one that is more helpful in that place. Occasionally, a pen or pencil mark between words may or may not be intended as a point of punctuation; whenever the inclusion of such a mark would unnecessarily interfere with the reader's comprehension, this edition silently omits it.

Because Audubon was not especially mindful or methodical about distinguishing uppercase and lowercase letters, this edition silently emends a lowercase letter that begins a sentence. In fact, he formed initial letters so variably that they could be aligned along a spectrum of gradations from small to large and include more than one form for any given letter. In this manuscript, Audubon frequently and inconsistently capitalized midsentence verbs, pronouns, adjectives, and adverbs. Because this distracts modern readers and because its inconsistency suggests that it does not signify, this edition does not reproduce such capitals. Since Audubon's capitalization of midsentence nouns occurs more consistently, this edition does retain these capitals. In ambiguous cases, the relative size of the letter determines whether it appears herein as lowercase or uppercase. To a limited degree, then, the pattern of capitalization herein visually reflects this feature of the manuscript orthography.

Audubon almost always wrote "whilst" as "whilt"; this edition regularly emends to "whilst."

On a few occasions Audubon used a tilde to double a consonant; such words appear herein with the consonant doubled.

Where simple scribal errors occur (e.g., "of" for "or"), I silently emend.

PUNCTUATION

Because Audubon's punctuation is inconsistent, unconventional, not evidently pertinent, and often nonexistent, I supply what I deem needed and helpful punctuation throughout the text of the journal without noting my emendations individually. I take a restrained or noninvasive approach to emending punctuation, allowing the manuscript punctuation to stand wherever that does not interfere with the reader's comprehension or present meaningless distractions. Wherever I have emended punctuation amid phrasing that is ambiguous, however, I explain that in a textual note (see, e.g., "I have shook hands with all, rather more *brotherly* than usual with kind Hanna and now God Bless Thee Good Night" [September 7], where the placement of the comma directs the reader past a momentary ambiguity). A frequent occasion for altered punctuation is the occurrence of a comma between main clauses, which this edition emends to a period in most instances, with the modern reader's comprehension in mind. Similarly, if a sentence ends inappropriately with a colon, I emend to a period. I have inserted numerous commas throughout to aid the reader in navigating Audubon's sometimes puzzling syntax.

Audubon frequently used dashes for punctuation. His dashes are of many different lengths, and no principle seems to govern how long a given dash is. This edition uses the simple em dash (with a space before and after) to represent all the various lengths of the manuscript dashes. In some cases Audubon used a double dash, which I render as = , again not indicating the length of the manuscript double dash.

Audubon was a visual artist, and he was sometimes playfully melodramatic, especially when he was bored and tipsy. Sometimes a "dash" is lower on the line than the usual dash of punctuation and seems intended to indicate a dramatic pause or ironic silence (see fig. 14). Since he often distinguishes these marks with slight squiggles, I render them herein as ~~~~.

ORTHOGRAPHY AND OTHER MANUSCRIPT FEATURES

I add a word or phrase in square brackets wherever it seems clear that Audubon intended to include that word or phrase.

Audubon occasionally struck through words or phrases in order to revise; this edition does not record the canceled words or phrases, except where the cancellation seems especially significant.

Many compound nouns appear as two words in the manuscript; this edition retains the manuscript appearance.

This edition retains Audubon's use of the ampersand and of various abbreviations (e.g., M^r, M^{rs}, Cap^e, W^{am}, and a/c for Mister, Mistress, Capitaine, William, and account); it also regularizes the underlining of the superscripted letters. This edition also retains the superscripted *d* for the past tense of weak verbs.

Where Audubon uses the letter *x* to indicate veiled letters, I render them in italics. For example, when he is angry at Captain Hatch, he refers to him as "C*xxxxxx*."

Words that Audubon underlines appear herein in italics.

Uncertain readings appear herein in curly brackets, thus, "{compound}." Asterisks in curly brackets show the approximate number of illegible letters.

Audubon's use of indentation to begin a new paragraph was not consistent. However, this edition follows Audubon's paragraphing wherever the manuscript shows an indentation. Through approximately the first third of the manuscript, double horizontal strokes seem to indicate a change of subject; each of these early double strokes occasions a new paragraph in this edition (except where the content makes the new indentation seem unnecessary). In the later portions of the manuscript, however, Audubon used double horizontal strokes much less methodically; the paragraphing herein, therefore, is based upon the editor's judgment with the reader's comprehension in mind. Wherever Audubon creates an imagined dialogue with his wife or another friend, this edition indents the beginning of each speech and supplies needed quotation marks.

In a few places, to show extreme excitement, Audubon used a double underline. This edition represents these moments with underlined italics (see the first line of the August 7 entry).

The running heads that occasionally appear in the manuscript are not reproduced herein.

Audubon underlined most of the French words and phrases he used; this edition italicizes all French and Latin words whether underlined in the manuscript or not.

TEXTUAL NOTES AND EXPLANATORY NOTES

Information about the manuscript of potential value not otherwise reported in this edition is provided in the textual notes. Other information that readers might find useful (e.g., definitions, translations, identifications, needed context) is supplied in the explanatory notes.

A superscript dagger symbol (†) in the text indicates a textual note in the rear of the volume; a superscript numeral (^{1}) in the text indicates an explanatory note.

I have drawn on numerous sources for the explanatory notes. Chief among them are the *Dictionary of National Biography*; the *Dictionary of American Biography*; biographies of Audubon by Lucy Bakewell Audubon, Stanley Clisby Arthur, Francis Hobart Herrick, and Alice Ford; editions of Audubon's journals prepared by Alice Ford and Christoph Irmscher; the *Oxford English Dictionary*; and standard encyclopedias, histories, and other reference works. References to plates from *The Birds of America* are given in parentheses.

Abbreviations and Symbols

AFP   Alice Ford Papers. Audubon Collection — Archival Record Group 1. John James Audubon Center at Mill Grove, Montgomery County, Pennsylvania.

Himself   *Audubon, by Himself: A Profile of John James Audubon from Writings Arranged, Selected, and Edited by Alice Ford.* Garden City NY: Natural History Press, 1969.

JJA   *John James Audubon: A Biography.* By Alice Ford. Norman: University of Oklahoma Press, 1964; repr., New York: Abbeville Press, 1988. All references are to the Abbeville edition.

Journal   *The 1826 Journal of John James Audubon.* Ed. Alice Ford. Norman: University of Oklahoma Press, 1967; repr., New York: Abbeville Press, 1987. All references are to the Abbeville edition.

OB   Audubon, John James. *Ornithological Biography.* 5 vols. Edinburgh: Adam Black, 1831–39.

SYMBOLS

—   A solid em dash with space before and after indicates all Audubon's various dash lengths.

=   A solid double dash with space before and after indicates all Audubon's various double-dash lengths.

~~~~   Tildes represent Audubon's squiggle dashes, placed low on the line, which indicate ironic silences or omitted indecencies.

xxx	Italicized *x*'s indicate veiled letters.
[ ]	Square brackets enclose editorial insertions, such as missing letters or words or phrases wherever it seems clear that Audubon intended to include that word or phrase.
***	Asterisks represent the approximate number of illegible letters.
{ }	Curly brackets enclose uncertain readings.
<u>*Trail*</u>	Words set in underlined italics indicate enhanced emphasis and represent words that Audubon underlined twice.

John James Audubon's
Journal of 1826

1

Departure from Bayou Sara and New Orleans; Voyage to Liverpool

26 APRIL 1826.

I left my Beloved Wife Lucy Audubon and my son John Woodhouse
on Tuesday afternoon the 26th April, bound to England, remained
at Doctr Pope at St Francisville untill Wednesday, 4 o'clock P.M.: in
the Steam Boat Red River, Cape Kimble — having for companions
[MS: compagnons] Messrs D. Holl[1] & John Holiday — reached New
Orleans Thursday 27th at 12 — Visited many Vessels for my Passage and
concluded to go in the Ship *Delos* of Kennebunk, Cape Joseph Hatch,
bound to Liverpool, Loaded with Cotton entirely —

The Red River Steam Boat left on her return on Sunday and I wrote
by her to thee, my dearest Friend,[2] and forwardd thee 2 small Boxes of
Flowering Plants —

Saw, spoke to & walked with Charles Briggs,[3] much altered young
man —

Lived at New Orleans at G. L. Sapinot's[4] in company with Costé[5] —
During my stay at New Orleans, I saw my old and friendly

---

1. This is likely Mr. Diedrich Holl, who married Lucy's student Virginia Chisholm a few days
later (DeLatte, *Lucy Audubon*, 161). Although Alice Ford identifies this man as Capt. David
Hall (*Journal*, 15), the manuscript clearly reads "Holl," both here and in the later reference to his
marriage to Chisholm.

2. Audubon's recurring greeting "my dearest friend" always refers to his wife, Lucy.

3. Charles Briggs, a merchant, had been a friend of George and John Keats since their early
schooling in England. By 1827 Briggs would be established in New Orleans.

4. Presumably a boardinghouse owned by G. L. Sapinot.

5. Napoleon L. Coste was a New Orleans acquaintance who, in 1837, as commander of the U.S.
Revenue cutter *Campbell*, would transport Audubon and his companions through the Gulf of
Mexico to collect bird specimens.

acquaintances, the familly Pamar;[6] but the whole time spent in that City was heavy & dull — A few Gentlemen call[d] to see my Drawings — I generally walked from Morning untill Dusk — my hands behind me, paying but very partially attention to all I saw — New Orleans to a man who does not trade in Dollars or any other such stuff, is a miserable spot =

Fatigued and discovering that the ship could not be ready for sea for several days, I assended the Mississipy again in the Red River and once more found myself with my Wife and Child. I arrived at M[rs] Percy[7] at 3 o'clock in the morning, having had a Dark ride through the Magnolia Woods, but the Moments spent afterwards full repaid me — I remained 2 days and 3 nights, was at a Wedding of Miss Virginia Chisholm with M[r] D. Holl &[c]. I left, in company with Lucy, M[rs] Percy's house at sun rise and went to Breakfast at my good acquaintance Bourgeat,[8] who lent me a Horse to proceed to Bayou Sarah[9] again =

At 8 o' clock I gave and received the farewell kiss to my Beloved Wife and her to me — I parted from her about 2 miles from Home =

Arrived at New Orleans, my vessel still unready — I Called on the Governor,[10] who give me a Letter bearing the seal of the State, obviatting the necessity of taking a Passport = I received several Letters of Introduction from Diferent persons, the Copies of all which will be found here in = [†]

On the 17th May my Baggage was put on Board — I had written 2 Letters to my Wife and to my Son Victor, to whom I sent as present my Pencil Case with a handsome Knife — and also to Charles

6. Audubon first met the New Orleans merchant Roman Pamar and his family in January 1821. The Pamars befriended the struggling Audubon, paying him for portraits of themselves and drawing lessons and regularly inviting him to dinner in their home.

7. The widowed Jane Middlemist Percy engaged Lucy Audubon to operate a small school on her Beech Woods plantation in West Feliciana, Louisiana, in early 1823. There Lucy taught the four Percy daughters and a few other local children until the fall of 1827, when she moved to a different school at Beech Grove, the plantation of William Garrett Johnson. Percy's brother was Charles Middlemist of London.

8. Augustin Bourgeat of Bush Hill plantation, West Feliciana Parish, Louisiana, was a friend who helped Audubon collect animal specimens and hunted with him in the swamps.

9. Bayou Sarah was a watercourse and landing near Beech Woods plantation.

10. Governor Henry Johnson (1783–1864) was a Louisiana politician, former senator, and governor from 1824 to 1828.

Bonaparte,[11] apprising him of the Box of Bird skins forward[d] to him, through M[r] Currell — The Steam Boat Hercules came along side at 7 P.M. and in 10 hours put the Delos to sea — I wrote [MS: wroth] from her another letter to Lucy and in few minut[e]s found myself severely aflicted with sea sickness =

This lasted, however, but a short time, remaining on Deck Constantly, eating and Drinking without Inclination and forcing myself to Exercise constantly — We Calculated our day of Departure from the 18[th] May at 12 o'clock, when we first made an Observation —

We are now the 27th, and having nought else to do, I put down the little incidents that have taken place between these two dates —

The weather has generally been [MS: being] fair with light winds, and the first objects that had any weight like diverting my Ideas from those left behind me was the number of Beautifull Dolphins that glided by the side of the Vessel like burnished Gold during Day and bright meteors by night — Our Cap[e] and mates proved all expert at alluring them with baited Hooks or dexterous at piercing them with a 5 prung Instrument generally called by Seamen Grains — If Hooked the Dolphin fl[o]unces desperately, slides off with all its natural swiftness, oftentimes raises perpendicularly out of this element several feet, shakes off the hook and Escapes partially hurt — if, however, the Dolphin is well hooked, he is play[d] about for a while, soon Drowned and hauled into the Vessel — Some persons prefer pulling them in at once and are seldom successful, the great vigor with which the fish Shakes sideways as he assends generally being quite suficient to extricate him — They differ very much in their sizes, being, agreably to age, smaller or Larger. I saw some 4½ feet long but a fair average could reduce them to 3 =

The paunch [MS: Punch] of all we caught contained more or less small fishes of Various species, among which the flying fish is prevalint — the latter is apparently their congenial food, and is well adapted to exercise their phisical Powers — Their flesh is firm, perhaps rather dry, yet quite acceptable at Sea[+] — Dolphins move in Companies of 4 or 5 and sometimes of 20 or more; chase the flying fish that, with

11. Charles Lucien Bonaparte (1803–57), a young ornithologist, was a nephew of one of Napoleon's brothers and son-in-law of another. Audubon often referred to him by his title, prince of Canino and Musignano. The two met in 1824 in Philadelphia, where Bonaparte was developing his supplement to Alexander Wilson's *American Ornithology*.

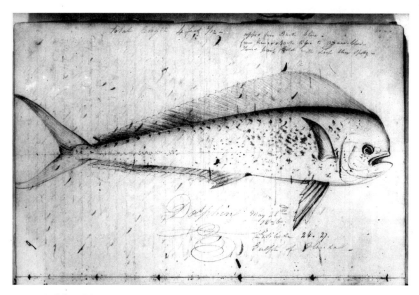

FIG. 1. Dolphin, May 28, 1826

astonishing rapidity after having avoided his sharp pursuer a while in the water, emerges and goes through the air with the swiftness of an arrow — sometime in a straight course and sometime deviating by forming part of a Circle, yet frequently the whole is unavailing. The Dolphin raises out of the sea in b[o]unces of 10, 15 or 20 feet and so rapidly moves toward his pray that oftentimes the little fish just falls to be swallowed by his antagonist —

You must not suppose[†] that the Dolphin can, however, move through the seas without risk or danger to himself — He has as well as others, valiant [MS: Valant] and powerfull Ennemies — One is the barracuda [MS: Ballocuda[†]] in shape much like a Pike, growing sometimes to a Large size — One of these Cut upwards of a foot in length off the Tail of a Dolphin as if done with an ax as this Latter made for a Baited Hook — and I may say that we about devided the Bounty — There is a degree of sympathy existing betwen Dolphins quite remarkable. The moment one of them is hooked or Grained, all those in company Imediately make up towards him and remains thus untill the unfortunate one is hoisted, and generally then all move off and seldom will bite ═ When small and in large Scools, they then bite and are caught perhaps to the last — the skin of these fish is a tissue of small scales softer in their

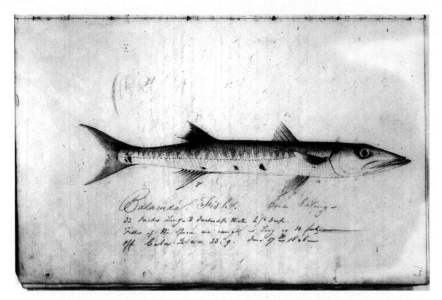

FIG. 2. Barracuda, June 17, 1826

substance than generally seen on scally fishes of such size. The skin is tough and torn off from their bodies when Cleaned =

We also Caught a Porpoise about 7 feet in length. This feat took place during the night, when the moon gave me a full view of all that happened — The Fish, contrary to Custom, was *Grained* instead of being harpooned, but grained in such a way and so effectually, through the forehead that he was thus held and sufered to fl[o]unce and beat about the bow of the Ship untill the very person that had secured it at first gave the line holding the grains to our Cap^e, and slide down along the (Bob stays) with a rope. There after some little time and perhaps some dificulties, the fish was secured imediately above its tale and hoisted with that part upwards. It arived on the Deck, gave a deep groan, much alike the last from a large dying Hog, flap^d — {severely} on the deck and Died — I had never before seen one of these annimals at hand and the Duck bill like snout along with the horizontal [ms: Orisontal] disposition of the tail with the body were new matters of observation — Their large Black, sleek body, the Imensity of warm black blood issuing from the Wound, the Blowing apperture placed over the forehead, all attracted my attention — I requested that it should remain untouch[ed] untill the next morning and this was granted =

On opening of it, the Intestine were still warm (say 8 hours after death) and resembled very much those of a Hog. They filled all the hinder [ms: Inder] Cavity. The paunch [ms: Punch] contained several *Scutle* fish partly decayed ═

The Carcass was cleaned of its flesh and left [with] the Central bone supported on its sides after the Abdomen by 2 horizontal [ms: orisontal] and one perpendicular [flange], giving it the appearance of a 4-edged cutting Instrument ═ [12]

The Lower Jaw or, as I would prefer [to] Style it, Mandible exceeds the upper about ¾ of an Inch. Both were furnish[d] with single rows of divided conical teeth about ½ Inch in leng[t]h — Just so parted as to admit those of the upper Jaw between each of those of the Lower — The fish might weigh about 200 ═

The eyes were small, proportionnally speaking, and the fish having a breathing apperture above, of Course, had no Gills. Porpoises move in Large company, and generally during Spring and Early summer close by paires coming on top to breath and playfully exibit themselves about Vessels — I have seen a parcel of them Leap perpendicularly about 20 feet and fall with a heavy dash on the sea ═ Our Cap[e] told us that small boats had been sometimes sunk by one of these fishes falling into it in one of these frisks ═

Whilst I am engaged with the finny Tribe, I may as well tell you that one morning when moving gently 2 miles per hour, the Cap[e] Call[d] me to shew me some pretty fishes just caught from our Cabin windows ═ These measured about 3 inches, thin & broad of shape and very quick through the watter; we had a pin hook and with this caught 370 in about 2 hours. They were sweet food ═ they are named generally *Rudder Fish* and allways keep in the Lee side of the Rudder, as it affords a strong Eddy to support these and enable them to follow the vessel in that situation when going doubly fast — When the sea become[s] calm, they diffuse themselves about the sides and bow and then will not bite — The least breese bring[s] the whole [ms: all] into a compact body astern again, where they seaze the baited Hook the instant it reaches the watter — By this time we have caught and eat about 500 ═

12. Audubon tries to help his reader visualize a porpoise vertebra in cross-section. In the latter portions of the spinal column, some vertebrae have three flanges, and some have four.

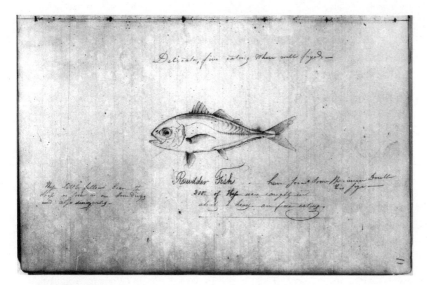

FIG. 3. Rudder fish

FIG. 4. Shark, June 18, 1826

We also have caught 2 sharks, one a female about 7 feet that had 10 young alive and able to swim well — One of them was thrown over board and made off as if accustomed to take care of himself for some time (however, it is to be remarked that these Fishes being Viviparous consequently never leave the Mother unless fully formed — Of Course, I Concluded that the young here spoken of had never Left the Dam, being yet fasten[ed] to the Womb by the feeding conduit.)† = Another was Cut in 2 and the head half swam off out of our sight — The remainder were Cut to pieces as well as the parent, for bait for Dolphins that are extremely partial to that meat.

The weather being Calm and pleasant, I felt anxious to have a view of the Ship from off her, and Capᵉ Hatch politely took me in the Yawl and had it rowᵈ all around the Delos. This was a sight I had not enjoyed for nearly 20 years and was much pleased with — Afterwards, having occasion to go out to try the bearings of the Current, I again accompanied him and Bathed in the sea, not without, however, feeling some fears =

To try the bearings of the Current, we took an Iron Pot fastened to a line of 120 fathom and made a Log Board out of a Barrel's head laden on one edge to sink it perpendicularly on its edge, and tried the velocity of the Current with it fixed to a Line by the help of a Second Glass,[13] whilst our iron Pot, Sunk at the end of our line, acted as an anchor — †

I must now change for a moment my theme and speak of Birds awhile — Mother Carey's chickens (Procellaria's)[14] came about us and I longed to have at least one in my possession — I had watched [MS: wachted] their Evolutions; their gentle patting of the sea, when on the wing with their legs hanging and webbs expanded; seen them take large and long ranges in search of food and returning still for the bits of fat thrown overboard and for them intended. I had often looked at diferent figures given by Scientific Men, but all this could not diminish for a moment the long wished for pleasure of possessing one in *Natura*

13. A second glass has the shape of an hourglass but contains only as much sand as will pour through in exactly fourteen or twenty-eight seconds. It was used in conjunction with a log line marked at lengths called "knots" to ascertain the speed, or knots per hour, of a ship's progress.

14. The genus *Procellaria* includes several species of petrels, fulmars, and shearwaters. They are often referred to by sailors as "Mother Carey's chickens," possibly derived from an epithet for the Virgin Mary, *mater cara* (dear mother). They were thought to indicate bad weather to come.

Fideli;[15] I loaded a piece and drop^d the first one that came after, along side, and the captain again desirous of pleasing, went for it ＝

I made 2 Drawings of it. It proved a female with eggs, numerous, but not larger than grains of fine powder, inducing me to think that these Birds must either breed earlier, or much latter than any others in our Southern Latitude — I would be inclined to think that the specimen I Inspected had not laid this season, although I am well satisfied that it was an old Bird —

During many Weeks following this Date, I Discovered that many flew *Mated* side by side and occasionnally, particularly in Calm pleasant weather, Caress^d each other as Ducks are known to do — †

About this time we saw a small Vessel with all sails set towards us; we were becalmed and the unknown had a light Breese. It approach^d gradually. Suspicions were intertained that it might be a Pirate as we that same day had undoutedly heard reports of Cannons from the very course she was coming; we were well manned, tolerably armed, and yet uneasiness was perceivable on every face more or less — yet we were all bent on resistance, knowing well that such Gentry, gave no quarters to Purses at least ＝

Night arrived, a small squally breese struck us, and off we moved, were out [MS: aught] of sight in a short time and resumed the Mirth and good mien that had existed among[s]t us — Two days afterwards a Brig that had been in our Wake Came near us, was hailed and found to be the Gleaner of Portland, commanded by an acquaintance of our commander and Bound also to Liverpool. This Vessel had left the City of N. Orleans 5 days before us — We kept close together, and the next day Cap^e Hatch and myself Boarded her and were kindly received; after a short stay, her Cap^e, called Jellerson, came with us and remained the day — I opened my Drawings and showed a few of them.† Mr. Swift[16] was anxious to see some, and I wanted to Examine in what state they

---

15. Audubon was no Latin scholar, so the context of "in *Natura Fideli*" is important. Literally, the phrase means "in faithful nature," but he means to contrast those "figures given by Scientific Men" with the possession of an actual bird that will enable him to make his drawing true to nature.

16. John Swift became a cordial companion to Audubon on the *Delos* and in Liverpool. He was traveling from Louisiana in the company of eleven gallons of whisky to meet his parents in Dublin.

FIG. 5. Mr. John Swift, asleep

kept — The weather being dry and clear, I feared nothing — It was agreed that Both vessels should keep Company untill *through* the Gulph Stream for security sake against *Pirates* =

So fine has the weather been so far that all belonging to the Cabin have constantly slept on Deck, over which an Awning has been extended to keep the heat of the Sun and Dampness of the atmosphere at night from us —

When full one hundred Leagues at sea, a female Rice Bunting came a Board and remain^d with us one night and part of a day — A warbler also came but remained only a few minutes and made for the Land we had left — It moved whilst on Board with great activity and sprightliness; the Bunting, to the Contrary, was exausted, panted, and I have no doubt died of Inanition —

Many Sooty terns were in sight during several days. I saw one Frigate Pelican high in air, and could only judge it to be such through the help of the telescope. Flocks of unknown Birds were also about the ship during a whole day. They swam well and prefered the watter to the air. They resembled Large Phalaropes but [I] could not be certain =

A Small alligator that I had purchased for 1 Dollar at New Orleans Died at the end of 9 Days, through my want of knowledge that salt watter was poisonous to him — In 2 days he swelled to nearly double his natural size, breathed hard and died —

In Latitude 24. 27^ds a Green Heron came on Board and remained untill frightened by me, then flew towards the Brig Gleaner. It did [MS: deed] not appear in the least fatigued.

The Cap^e of the Gleaner told me that on a preceeding Voyage from Europe to N. Orleans when about 50 Leagues from the Balize, a full grown *Hooping Crane* came on board his vessel during the night, passing over the length of his Deck close over his head, over that of the helms man, and fell in his Yawl, and that the next morning the Bird was found there completly Exausted, when every one on Board supposed that it had passed on — A Cage was made for it. It refuse[d] food and lingered a few days, when it died — When pluck^d was found sound and free from any wound, and in a good Case — a very singular case in Birds of this kind, that are inured to extensive Journies and, of Course, liable to spend much time without assistance of food —

I have not written since the 27th for reasons as natural as can be; I had scarce any new Incidents to relate — Now, however, that it is the 4$^{\underline{th}}$ of June and that at 12 o'clock I found myself a few miles south of the Line[17] for the 2$^{\underline{d}}$ time in my Life, I feel rather an Inclination — thinking daily and I might say allmost constantly of my Wife, of my familly, and Hopes all in *the Breese* (which, by the bye, is quite contrary). My time goes on Dully — Lying on the Deck on my mattress, on an hard pressed bale of cotton, having no one scarcely to talk to, only a few Books and but indiferent fare to engage me even to raise from that situation to feed myself = but to the purpose — I am really south of the Line. What Ideas it conveys to me, of my Birth, of the Expectations of my younger days, well &$^{\underline{c}}$ &$^{\underline{c}}$ —

Since I wrote last — we have parted from our Companion, the Gleaner, have had the wind constantly ahead — and are yet in the Gulph of Mexico — Here permit me to give an advise that might have been given to me: never, if you can do otherwise, sail from New Orleans for Europe, in June, July or August as, if you do, you may calculate on Delays incalculable [MS: Inculcable] in this Gulph, such as Calms, powerfull currents all contrary, and, worst of all, the *Trade Winds* so prevalent during these months, and indeed much Later — so much so that if I had this day, as I said before (I believe the 4$^{\underline{th}}$ of June), to sail from N. Orleans, I would wait untill Late in Oct$^{\underline{r}}$, but better say abandon the thought and go through to N. York and there Take a Passage —

I have now been at sea 3 Sundays and yet have not made the shores of Cuba and scarcely doubled the Florida Capes — but it is not worth while repining —

17. Audubon is apparently referring to the Tropic of Cancer as "the Line" here. Although the equator is regularly called "the Line," Audubon is, as he explains in the next paragraph, "yet in the Gulph of Mexico" and still approaching Cuba. Since his father moved him from Haiti, which is south of the Tropic of Cancer, to France when he was a child, this would indeed be "the 2$^{\underline{d}}$ time in my Life" when Audubon crossed this line.

Ford's note to this passage is perplexing for two reasons. First, she asserts that "'South of the line' means south of the Equator, a reference to passage from Haiti in childhood" (*Journal*, 30n9). Both the geography and Audubon's statements rule out the equator as a possibility; a ship would not cross the equator on its way from Haiti to Europe. Ford also claims that "Audubon (?) inked out a few lines at this point." She asserts this in her biography as well but with an emphatic difference, stating that "many lines are heavily blacked out" (*JJA*, 442n16). However, not one line is crossed out on the page in question (or on the page that follows it), as can be seen in the reproduction of the page opposite (fig. 6). The reason for Ford's erroneous report is not known.

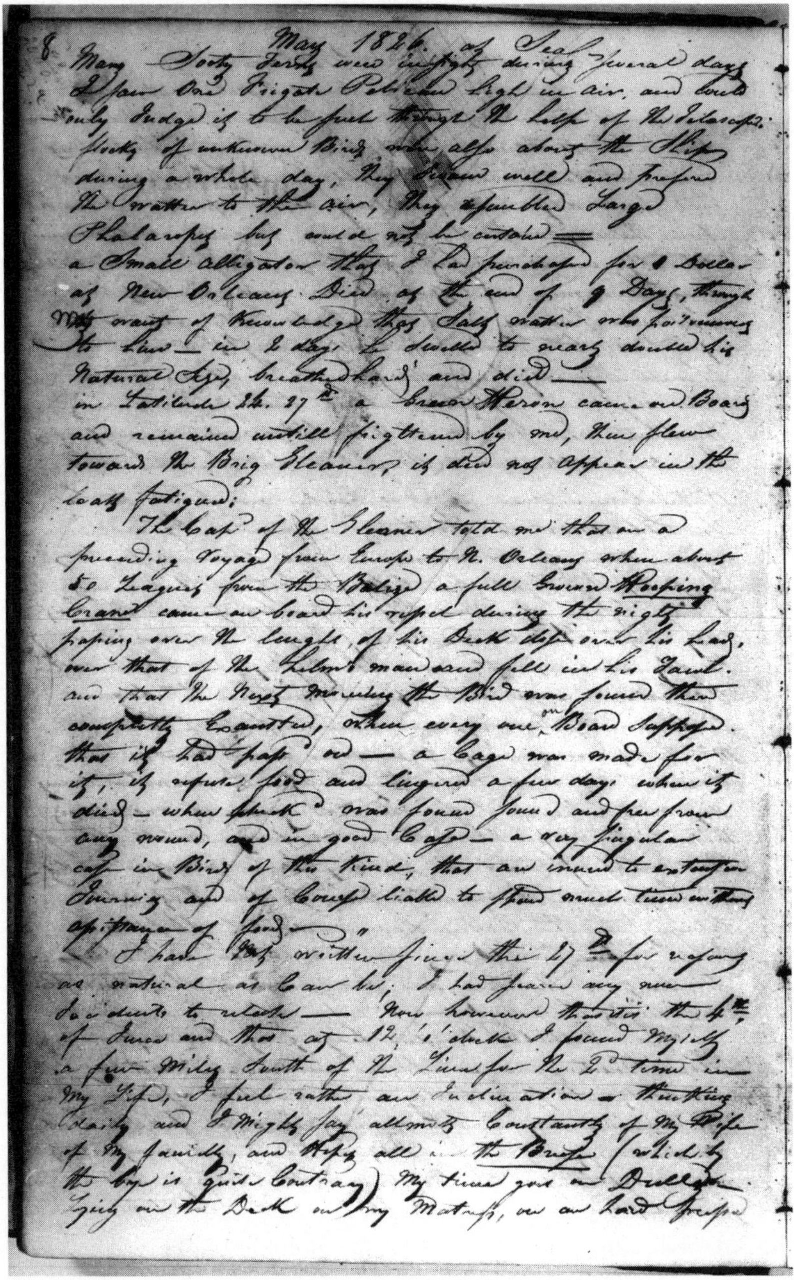
8 May 1826. at Sea
Many Sooty Terns were in sight during several days
I saw One Frigate Pelican high in air, and could
only Judge it to be such through the help of the Telescope.
flocks of unknown Birds were also about the Ship
during a whole day, they swam well and prefered
the watter to the air, they resembled Large
Phalaropes but could not be obtained =
a Small alligator that I had purchased for 1 Dollar
at New Orleans Died at the end of 9 Days, through
my want of knowledge that Salt watter was poisonous
to him — in 2 days he swelled to nearly double his
Natural Size, breathed hard' and died —
in Latitude 24. 27 m a Green Heron came on Board
and remained untill frightened by me, then flew
toward the Brig Eleanor, it did not appear in the
least fatigued;
The Capt of the Eleanor told me that on a
preceeding voyage from Europe to N. Orleans when about
50 Leagues from the Balize a full Grown Hooping
Crane came on board his vessel during the night
passing over the length of his Deck, high over his head,
over that of the helm's man and fell in his Yawl.
and that the Next morning the Bird was found there
completely Exausted, when every one on Board supposed
that it had pass'd on — a Cage was made for
it, it refused food and lingered a few days when it
died — when plucked was found sound and free from
any wound, and in good Case — a very singular
case in Bird of this kind, that are inured to extensive
Journeys and of Course liable to spend much time without
assistance of food —
I have not written since the 27th for reasons
as natural as Can be, I had seen any new
Incidents to relate — Now however that it is the 4th
of June and that at 12. o'clock I found Myself
a few Miles South of the Line for the 2d time in
My Life, I feel rather an Inclination to thinking
daily and I Might say allmost Constantly of My Wife
of My family, and Hope all in the Bruise (which by
the bye is quite Contrary) My time goes on Dully
lying on the Deck on my Matrass, or on hard presse

FIG. 6. "[S]outh of the Line for the 2d time in my Life"

I have seen since my last date a Large *Sword* Fish — but only saw it — 2 Ganets, killed a *Great footed Hawk.* (This Bird after [MS: ******d]†
having alighted several times on our Yards, made a Dash at a Warbler feeding on the flies about the Vessel, seized it and Eat it in our sight *on the wing,* much like a Mississipy Kite Devours the Red throated Lizards —).† Caught a live a Non Descript Warbler [MS: Warblers] — which I named The *Cape Florida Songster*: saw 2 Frigate Pelicans at a great hight and a Large species of Petrel entirely unknown to me — We had a severe Squall (as I call^d it) and plenty of Dull times with all — read Byron's Poems, the Corsair &^c &^c — &^c &^c — and now — I will shut my Book —

JUNE 1826 AT SEA —

The 7th of this month a Brig Bound to Boston Called the Andromache came along side, and my heart Elated at the Idea that Letters could be caried by her to America and furnish thee with Intelligence of our Passage thus far; I set to and wrote to thee and Nicholas Berthoud.[18] The weather, however, altered sudenly; we had a Light squall that separated us, and it was not untill the 9th that we Boarded her ═

Fond of all such expeditions, I went with our Captain ═ The sea ran high and the tossing of our Light Yawl was extremely disagreable to my feelings ═

The Brig Andromache was covered with Cotton, Extremely filthy, and I was glad to discover that with all our Disagreables and disappointments, we were quite Comfortable on the Delos comparatively — The passangers there were, however, extremely polite, offered us wine &^c. The Captain had our Letters put in the Post Bag and after ½ an hour Chat, we pushed for our vessel again.

The sea was extremely rough then, we took in more or Less watter from every wave that came towards us — I was glad when I found myself on the Deck of the Delos ═

Two days Elapsed and the Andromache was out of Our sight, having ran diferent tacks ═

We are the 11th of June and still are on the same Latitude and but a few miles Difering in longitude — Kitch,† Dolphins — Porpoises, —

18. Nicholas Berthoud, of Shippingport, Kentucky, was Audubon's brother-in-law by his marriage to Lucy Bakewell Audubon's sister Eliza Bakewell.

FIG. 7. The shores of Cuba, June 14 and 15, 1826

Draw a little, Read some — Sleep a good deal and with all, find the time extremely fatiguing — †

Having come into the company of a Brigg Bound to Havanna from Liverpool, called the Howard, Capᵉ Joseph Birney, I wrote to thee, Mʳ R. Currell[19] & E. Costé to give thee again an account of our slow movements. It was the 16ᵗʰ Instant and I Hoped that my Letter might reach thee in two weeks —

We have been in sight of Cuba these last 4 days — The heat excessive ⹀

I saw 3 Beautifull white headed Pigeons or Doves flying about our Ship, but after severall rounds they shaped their course towards the Floridas and disapeared — The Dolphins we catch [MS: cacth] here are suspected Poisonous and [to] assertain if they are so or not a Piece is Boiled along with a Dollar until quite cooked when, if the Piece of Silver coin is not Tarnished either black or Green, the Fish is good and safe eating. I found Bathing in sea watter extremely refreshing and therefore enjoy this Luxury every night before Lying down on my

19. Randall Currell was a wealthy merchant of New Orleans. See appendix B for his letter introducing Audubon to John Owens Johnson.

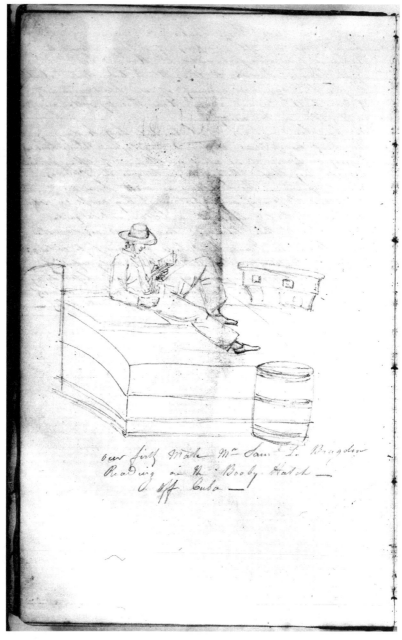

our first Mate Mr Sam L. Bragdon
Reading in the Booby Hatch —
off Cuba —

FIG. 8. First Mate Samuel L. Bragdon reading on the Booby Hatch

mattress. We have had in sight and allmost in Company 4 or 5 sails of vessel[s] for several days —

This is[†] our first Mate M[r] Sam L. Bragdon Reading on the Booby Hatch — Off Cuba

AT SEA JUNE 20TH OFF FLORIDA COAST[†]

The Birds that at diferent times during my passage thus far towards England I had taken for a Specie of Large Phalaropes, were about our vessel in great numbers, and our Mate was so forturnate as to kill four at one Shot, that were all pick[d] up by the Yawl at my Request = I was surprised and pleased at finding them belonging to the Genus *Procellarias*, or Petrel, made a sketch as usual size of Life and Preserved the Skins of all of them.

These Birds skim very low over the Sea in search of the Bunches of Floating sea weeds that abound over this Gulph, flapping their wings 6 or 7 times in quick succession and then sailing an equal Intermediate length of time, say 3 or 4 seconds, with great apparent ease, Carrying their tail much spread and long wings squarely angular with their body, Raising & falling with such beautifull ease to motions of the waves that one might suppose they receive a special power to that Effect from the Element Below them =

On approaching a Bunch of Weeds, they raise their wings obliquely, Drop their legs & feet, run apparently on the watter, and rest at last on the sea where they swim with all the ease of the Genus Anas,[20] Dive freely, at times several feet, in pursuit of the Fishes that at their approach of the weeds leave for safety, and seize them with great agility as well as voraciousness — 4 or 5 and sometimes from 15 to 20 will thus alight on and about one Bunch of weed, and during their stay about it, Diving, Flutering and swiming all in a heap, present quite agreable groupes — During this Period many Gulls of diferent kinds are hovering over and about the same spot, vociferating their anger & Disapointment as not being quite so well able to furnish themselves with the delicate fare =

No sooner have all the Fishes been [MS: being] taken or chased, that all the Birds, Raise, Diffuse, and extend their flight in search of more =

20. *Anas* is the genus of freshwater ducks.

I heard no sound Issuing from them, although many came within 20 paces of us. Consequently I suppose them endowed with excellent quick power of sight, as at the very moment that one Individual lighted, many Imediately made for the Spot and reach^d it in an instant [when distant many hundred yards]† = At Times and as if by way of reposing† themselves they alighted swiming lightly & droping their bills frequently in the water in the manner that Merganzers & some fishy Ducks do trying by tasting, if the water contains much fish. — On inspection of the Body I found the wings powerfully muscular & strong for the size of the Bird, a natural requisite for individuals that have so much extent to survey & frequently heavy (beating down) squalls, to encounter & fly against. — The stomach or paunch resembled a leather purse of 4 inches in length all much [distended]† by the contents that were comprised of fishes of different kinds more or less entire or digested — The gullet was capable of great extention, fishes 2½ inches by 1 were found nearly fresh. Their flesh smells strong, although fat, tough & not fit to eat except when destitute of better food — I tasted it & found it resembling that of a Porpoise, found no difference in the sexes either in size or color. Total length 11 inches, tail extended beyond the wings when closed 1 inch, legs ends of nearly even with the tail, Breadth 2 feet 2½ ¹⁄₁₂. General color sooty black above & snowy white below. —

I saw at the same time 2 Gulls of a large size entirely black or very deep brown with the head entirely snowy white, but could not procure one.

On the morning of the 21st We came up with the ship Thealia of Philadelphia Captn John R. Butler from Havanna to Minorca up the Mediteranean, with many Spanish passengers [MS: passengers spaniard] onboard. The Captn very politely offered ours some fruit which was accepted of course — in return we sent them a large Dolphin, they having caught none, & also one of the stuffed Petrels, as the Captn said that it was for the Philadelphia Society of science. — My friend†

CAPES OF FLORIDA JUNE 22^{D} 1826

Whilst sailing under a gentle Breese Last night, the Bird Outlined on this sheet, Commonly called by Seaman *Nody*, alighted on the boom of the Vessel and a few minutes afterward was caught by the mate. It

FIG. 9. Petrel, Capes of Florida, June 22, 1826

then Is[s]ued a rough Cry not unlike that of a young Common Crow when taken from the nest. It bit severely and with quickly renewed movements of the Bill, which, when it missed the object in view, snapp[d] Like that of our larger fly Catchers.

I found it one of the same Specie[s] that hovered over the sea weeds in company with the Large Petrels. — & that I thought then had the whole head white. Having kept it alive during the whole night, when I took it in hand to Draw it, it was Dull Looking and silent. I know nothing of this Bird more than what our Sailors say, that it is a Nody and frequently alights about Vessels in this Latitude and particularly in the neighboorhood of the Florida keys: the Bird was in Beautifull Plumage but poor. The Gullit was of great Extension, the paunch [MS: Punch] was empty, the heart Large for the Bird, but the liver [MS: Leaver] was uncommonly so: =

A short time before the Capture of the above Bird, a Vessel of war, a ship that we all supposed to be a South American Republican or Columbian, came between us and the Thalia, then distant from us about 1½ mile astern, fired a Gun, & detained her for some time. The reasons probable to us were the ships Passengers being Spaniards & Spanish property the Cargo. However, this morning Both Vessels were in view, making diferent routes. The Man of War deigned not come to us, and none on Board were much vexed at this mark of inattention [MS: Iñatation] —

This day was calm. After my Drawing finished, I caught 4 Dolphins; how much I have gaized on these beautifull Creatures, watching their last moments of Life, changing their hue in Twenty Varieties of richest arangements of Tints, from Burnished Gold to Silver Bright; mixed with touches of ultramarine spots, red & bronse & Green & quivering to death on our hard Broiling Deck. And yet I felt but a few moments before, a peculiar share of Pleasure in seizing them with a Sharp Hook, allured by false provision [MS: profission].

Two more Nodys were shot by our mate this day. They resembled in all particulars the[+] Specimen I have drawn. We saw about 20. —

We at last Entered the Atlantic Ocean this morning, 23$\underline{d}$, with a propitious Breese — The Land Birds have left us and, I — I leave my Beloved America, my Wife, Children and acquaintances — The purpose of this voyage is to Visit not only England but all Europe with the intention of Publishing my work of the Birds of America; if not sadly disapointed, my return to these happy shores will be the brightest Birth day I shall have ever enjoyed: Oh, America, Wife, Children and acquaintances, Farewell!!![+]

JULY 9$\underline{\text{TH}}$ 1826 AT SEA

My leaving the U. S. had for some time the appearance and feelings of a Dream. I could scarce make up my mind fixedly on the subject — I thought continually that I still saw my Beloved Friend, and my Dear Children. I still believed when every morning I awoke [MS: awalk^d] that the land of America was beneath me, that I would in a moment throw myself in her shady Woods, and watch for, and listen [MS: lessen], to the voice of her many Lovely Warblers, but now that I have positively been at Sea since *51 days* Tossing to & fro without the sight nor the touch of those objects so Dear to me, I feel fully convinced, and Look forward with an anxiety that I do not believe ever rufled my mind before; when I calculate that not less than 4 months (the third of a Year) must elapse, before my Friend & Children can receive any tidings of my arrival on the Distant Shores that now soon will divide us — When I think that many more months must run from the Life Sand Glass allotted to my existence, and that the time of my returning to my Country, & Friends is yet an unfolded and unknown event; my body and face feels a Sudden Glow of aprehension that I neither can describe or represent = I know only the acuteness of the feeling that cut through my whole frame Like an Ellectric Shock; I Imediately feel chilled and sullenly throw my body on my Mattrass and Cast my Eyes towards the azure [MS: asure] Canopy of Heaven, scarce able to hold the Tears from flowing —

Our 4$^{\underline{th}}$ of July was passed near the Grand Banks, how diferently from my Last, and how diferently from any that I can recollect ever having spent — The weather was thick foggy and as Dull as myself, not a sound of rejoicing did reach my ear, not once did I hear the sublime "Hail Columbia happy Land."[21] No, Nothing — perhaps nothing could have so forcibly awakened me from my Dosing situation than this lack [MS: Like] of a Pleasure so powerfully felt by me when at Home — It was then that I suddenly arose from my Lethargy and remarked the reality of my absence and present situation. The day passed [MS: past] as I conceive one spent by a General who has lost a Great advantage over an Ennemy. I complained of myself, I attributed all my disappointment to my want of foresight, but I complained to No one *else*. I felt sorrowfull in the extreme as if America had lost much this day — †

My companion [MS: Compagnon] passengers lay strewn about the Deck and on the Cotton Bales, basking like Crocodiles during all the Intervals Granted to the Sun to peep at them through the smoacky haziness that accompanied us — yet the Breese was strong, the waves moved magestically and thousands of Large Petrells Displayed their elegant aerial Movements to me — How much I envied their power of Flight to enable me to be here, there and all over the Globe, comparatively speaking, in a moment — throwing themselves Edgeways against the Breese as if a well sharpen^{d} arrow sent with the strength and grace of one Issuing from the Bow of an Appollo.

---

21. "Hail Columbia Happy Land": Philip Phile (Pfeil) composed a march tune in 1789 entitled "Washington's March" to honor Washington on his inauguration as the first president of the United States. Joseph Hopkinson wrote lyrics for the tune in 1798, when "the favorite new federal song" was first published.

I had remarked a regular increase in the number of these Petrels ever since the Capes of Florida, but here they were so numerous & for part of a Day, flew in such succession towards the West & South west that I Concluded they were migrating to some well known shore to deposit their Eggs or perhaps Leading their Young — These very seldom alighted. They were full the size of a common Gull, and as they flew they shewed in quick alternativeness the whole upper or under parts of their body — sometimes skimming Low, at other[s] forming Imense curves, then Dashing along the deep troughs of the Sea, going round our Vessel (allways out of Gun Shot reach) as if She had been at Anchor — Their Lower parts are White, a broad white patch on the rump, the head apparently all white, & the upper parts of the Body, & wings above, sooty Brown — I would conceive that one of these petrels flies [MS: fly] over as much Distance in one hour as the Little black petrels in our wake do in 12 —

Since we have left the neighborhood of the Banks, these Birds have gradually disapeared, and now in Latitude 44.53 — I see none — Our sailors and Captain speak of them as Companions in storms as much as the Little relations, the Mother Carey's Chickens —

As sudenly as if we had just Turned the Summit of a mountain Dividing a Country south of the Equator from Iceland, the weather altered — In the present Latitude & Longitude My Light Summer Clothing was not suficient. Indeed, a cloth Coat felt Light & scanty, and the Dews that fell during the Night rendered the Deck w[h]ere I allways slept too damp now to be comfortable = This, however, of two evils I preferr^d, for I could not withstand the more disagreable odor of the Cabin, where now, the Captain, officers & Mr Swift eat their meals Daily =

Setting during the day as I am now, with my poor Book in my Lap on a Parcel of Coiled Cables near the helm's man (who, by the Bye, Gazes at me as much as he looks at his Compass), I spend nearly all my Time, part of it reading; thoughtlessly leaning over the railing, Looking on the snowy braking waves that urges us on and again thinking of America. As the Sun to our eyes towards her reposing place declines, I am forced to make a bitter choice of situation and perhaps will go and Lie on the starboard side of the Long Boat, where our Cook, ready at striving to Please, will talk to me, untill wearied of this, from the spot I remove again =

Night gradually bring[s] on the *Wish to repose in sleep* when, after a few stories told, each gradually leaves the spot and goes and lays down either in his Hammock, his Birth or the Harder chicken Coop, that Line both side[s] of our Compagnion Way —

Here the days have increased astonishingly: at Nine o'clock I can easily read Large print, the Day opens at 2, and 25 minutes after 4, Phoebus enlivens the Globe and promisses a fair prosperous sixteen hours —

Our unconncerned Happy mariners, set to their daily Labour at 6 of the morn and cheerily [MS: chearly] spend the day, Improving the appearance of all about our ship, rendering her the more secure this while — Their Joviality, their Industry, their witticisms, would enable probably any other than a friend far away from his Friend to pass the Time away —

I have told you that I sat frequently on a parcel of Coiled Cables, but you are still Ignorant, that since I Left New Orleans I have sheared my Beard but once — that it now profusely expands from each ear out and from out my chin and neck around like a Crowd of stifen^d Bristles which, along with the Tawny acquired hue of my skin since on Board of this floating Prison, renders me as unlike the Daughter of Titian[22] as Satan is to God —

We had for several days a stiff propitious Breese that wafted us over the Briny deep full nine miles per hour. This was congenial to my wishes, but not to my feelings; the Vessel felt the motion before me and shifted [MS: Chifted] my Body too soon or unwar[i]ly caused me violent head aches far more distresfull than any sea sick feeling ever experienced — During this Period I found food Highly season^d and spiritous [MS: spirituo*ly] Liquors of great benefit. Here for the 3^d or 4th time, I read of Thomson's The 4 seasons, and I believe enjoyed them better than ever — When I came to his Castle of Indolence,[23] I felt

22. Titian's portrait of his daughter Lavinia (ca. 1560) depicts a young lady with a pale complexion. Part of Audubon's satire here rests on the cross-gender hyperbole.

23. Audubon has an edition of the poems of James Thomson (1700–1748), whose "Four Seasons" were originally published between 1726 and 1730 but remained extremely popular well into the nineteenth century. In Thomson's allegorical poem *The Castle of Indolence* (1748), the wizard Indolence, in whose castle many unfortunates are lulled into idleness, is finally defeated by the knight of arms and industry.

the all powerfull extent of his genius [MS: Jenius] operating on me as a Cathartic swallowed when well aware that my Body was not in a fit condition (through situation) to be benefited by it —

As we drew nearer the Shores of the far famed Spot, even the Clouds seem^d to profer a diference of consistancy and shapes; No Longer did the vivifying Orb, settle with her globular shape all fiery beyond [MS: be****] the deep. It shewed dull, pale, sickly, and as if sorry that *through diferences that for ever must exist*, the light refulgent was not to be extended over the Globe untill the omnipotent God had granted to each of all its Portions that Real sense of Fredom now only better felt in the Western Hemisphere. Here fogg suceeded foggs; the Englishmen on Board pronounced it, *Clear weather of England*, but I named it the Blasting atmosphere of Comfort —

I would continue now, but the dampness is so powerfull, although the Sun still strikes [MS: stracks] through the haze, that my Paper is Damp and receives the Ink quite too finely — Dear Friend, adieu —

Amongst the inmates composing our amount of Live Stock, we had a Large Hen; this Bird was quite familiar and allowed the privileges of the Decks; she had been Hatch^d on Board at New Orleans, and our Cook who Claimed her as private property was much attached to her, as well as our mates. One morning She imprudently flew over Board [while we] were running about 3 miles per hour. The Yawl was Imediately lowered; four men rowed her swiftly from us towards the floating Bird, that anxiously Look^d at her place of nativ abode untill picked up out of the Sea — Her return on Board appeared to please every one, and I was much gratified to discover that such kind treatment was used towards a Bird; it assured me that all exertions possible would be made to save the lives of any of our Seamen should they fall over Board = Our Hen, however, ended her Life most [MS: must] distressfully, a few weeks after this narrow escape. She again made over the sides and, the Vessel moving at 9 Knots, the sea High and rough with squally weather, the captain Thought it Imprudent to risk his men for the Bird, and we lost sight of her in a few moments —

We had our Long Boat as usual Lashed fast to the Deck, but Instead of being filled with Lumber &^c as is usually the Case, it now contained three Passengers, all Bound to Europe to visit their Friends with Intention of returning the same Autumn to America — One named

Vowles had several Books which he politely offered me — He blowed sweetly on the Flute and was a man superior to his apparent situation =

We had a Taylor also; this personage was called a Deck Passenger, but the fact is that full two Thirds of his Time was spent sleeping on the windlass = This man, however, like all others in the world, was usefull in his way; he work^d when ever called on and would with much good will, put a Button or a patch on any one's Clothing — his name was *Crow.* He Lived on Biscuit and raw Bacon the whole Voyage —

At noon one beautifull day, we discovered Two sails ahead of our ship, and our Captain renewed his exertions to overtake them. The masts were freshly greasd, all our sails brought to a nice bearing, the helms men ordered to be wary and exact, and at the brake of day next we were just betwen them — We had not, however, the contemplated pleasure of speaking to them; I discovered that as soon as the Breese became lighter, they gained away from us and vice versa —

We now saw no fish except now & then a school of Porpoises; and I frequently longed for one of the hundreds of Dolphins that we had Caught in the Gulph of Mexico —

Some w[h]ales were seen by the sailors, but I saw nothing of them —

I frequently sat during the Tedious voyage, watching our Captain at his work. I do not remember having seen many more Industrious, and apt at doing almost every thing that he needed himself — He was a good and nice Carpenter, Turner, Cooper, Black & white Smith, excellent Taylor &^{c}. I saw [him] Making a paire of Pantaloons of fine Cloth with all the neatness that a City Brother of the Cross Legged faculty could have used — He made a handsome patent swif[t]^{24} for his wife — He could also platt Straws in all sorts of ways and made excellent bearded fish Hooks out of Common Needles. At this very moment he is employed at finishing a handsome smoothing plane for his own use, manufactured out of a Piece of Beech wood that probably grew on the Banks of the Ohio — as I perceived it had belong^d to some Part of a Flat Boat, and brought on Board here to be used for fuel — I thought him an excellent sailor. The more squally it blew, the Gayer he

24. A swift is a light reel with an adjustable diameter upon which a skein of yarn or silk is placed in order to be wound off (see Audubon's illustration [fig. 11]).

FIG. 10. Capt. Joseph Hatch making powder flasks

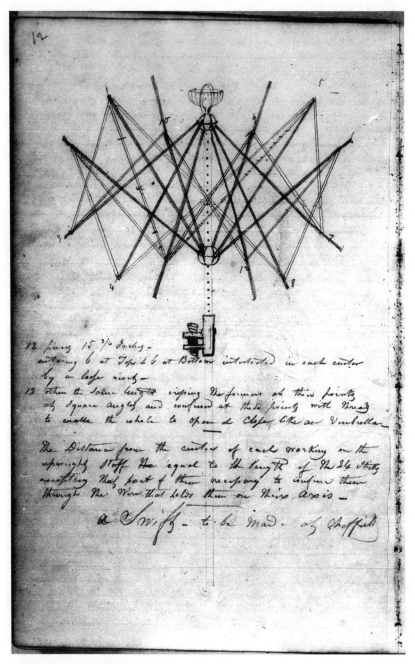

12

12 lines 15 ¾ Inches –
containing 6 at Top & 6 at Bottom interlocked in each center
by a loose rivet –
12 other the same length crossing the former at their points
at square angles and confined at these points with thread
to enable the whole to open & close like an Umbrella –

The Distance from the center of each working on the
upright Staff the equal to the length of the 24 Sticks
meeting that part of them necessary to confine them
through the wire that holds them on their axis –

a Swift – to be made of Sheffield

FIG. 11. Captain Hatch's patent swift

FIG. 12. At work on the forecastle

generally would be — and frequently during such times when drenched to the Skin, he would laugh and say "Who wouldn't sell a handsome plantation and go to Sea."

I became anxious to understand the means of assertaining the latitude on Land and also to find the true rising of the Sun whilst travelling in the uninhabited [ms: unhihabited] parts of America. This he shew^d me with pleasure, and I calculate our Latitude & Longitude from this time —

I found it necessary to employ all my time as much as possible; therefore, I frequently went about the Deck, a pencil in hand, viewing the diferent attitudes of the Sailors at Work, and made many Sketches — They frequently caused a general laugh and thus passed agreably a moment —

Our mates ex[h]ibited a kindness toward me that I would not suffer to remain un[n]oticed, under any consideration — They were all alertness at meeting all my wishes. Indeed, I often felt vexed that they should exert themselves as much, when as I was quite able to help myself; yet frequently before I was aware of it, should I walk either to the bow or stern, I would find my mattrass, Book &^{c} all carefully removed into my *Bunk*. The 1st mate was named S. L Bragdon, from Wells.[25] The 2^{d} was Hobart from Kinnebunk —

Now, I expect that you will ask what sort of a machine My *Bunk* was — The question would be natural enough, and before you make it, Like our mates I will try to surprise you = Imagine (and that I know you can easily do) a flat Box without a bed measuring 6½ feet by 3 in breadth [ms: breadth^d] and 9 Inches deep made of White Pine — Again Imagine 2 pieces of the same wood raising from the center of each end about 2½ feet, notched at their Tops to receive a light pole length ways, over which a paire of my sheets sewed [ms: sawed] together is fixed and covers the whole, representing an elongated tent, wherein my mattrass, Pillows, Coat, shoes, Books &^{c} &^{c} are snugly fitted, free from the rays of the Sun, and nearly so from the watter during rain — This is what the Sailors Call my Bunk, and so I shall call it myself —

Every Sailor or every set of Sailors have a Deity at Sea on whom they call more or less frequently for fair Wind as the case may require.

25. That is, Wells, Maine.

During our long stay in the Gulph of Mexico, from our Cap$^{\underline{e}}$ to the Cook (or as, by Courtesy, I will call him, the Stuart), this relation of Eolus was called on many times every day; it was a Saint of great renown, one whom I believe by the Bye *has stranded* as many Poor Devils as any other saint or saintess ever did, and he was hailed S$^{\underline{t}}$ Anthony — The prayers of all our Crew, those of our Cap$^{\underline{e}}$, of our Stuart, nay, even those of M$^{\underline{r}}$ Swift and mine proved unavailing. Not a breath of fair wind would he Entice his master to send us. Indeed, I became so di[s]gusted with the personage at last, that I propose[d] one morning when nature seemed all a sleep and our Vessel was so becalmed that a feather dropt$^{\underline{d}}$ from our Mast's head would scarce have deviated in its easy fall to the Deck, To abandon this renowned, fattened Saint and Call on one more in need of our regards; the proposition was unanimously accepted and Saint Mark appointted as Chief Director of the Breeses intended [MS: Intented] and much longed for to Carry our Vessel to the Shores of England —

Will you believe it — Yes, you will, as it is I that writes it. S$^{\underline{t}}$ Mark [MS: Mark^{d}] Came to our Calling under an Easy Gait; the Delos moved 3 miles per hour; all on Board begged of him to come nearer us, and in 3 days he help^{d} us on full 400 miles.

I had heard in my Youth that Saints as well as men would accept of Light gifts not to be unfashionable, and I conceived it my Duty to try the Experiment — What do you think of my *offrand*; It was not a Bull, snowy white resembling Jupiter in his pranks, No — Neither was it an Heifer snow white, for the fairest are seldom without spots —

"What then?" —

What my Dears; it was a Ram's Head — yes, a Ram's Head I promised to this Godly Saint, for a continuance of fair wind untill safely landed in Liverpool in England — I promised more: I assured the Great unknown, that it would be served up to his appetite, either raw, Boiled, Toasted, roasted, or pickled or fried or Tarred & Feathered — I have had no answer from this Genii; polite Genius's I am told never thank one [these] days — no matter how much they get when in need: This, however, does not signify. The fact is that I am well convinced he has not despised the promised Boon, for since 18 days he has procured fair winds for us to the amount of 2475 miles —

S$^{\underline{t}}$ Mark, I do hereby bind myself (no others members of my familly, recollect) to think of thee whenever I am in need and that's enough — †

Here we came in with a new set and specie of Petrels resembling those killed in the Gulph of Mexico but considerably larger — Between 50 & 60 were at one time Close to the Vessel Catching small fishes that we supposed to be Herrings — The Birds then swam swiftly over the watter, their wings partly raised and now & then diving & dipping after the fry = They flew heavily and with apparent reluctance, and alighted [MS: alitted] as soon as we passed them =

We spoke to the Brigg Albion bound to Quebec with many Passengers but only balasted; =

The little petrils had left us for 2 days. I thought that probably the cold weather had drove them away; I was satisfied that several in our wake had followed us ever since the Gulph of Mexico. Of course, the sudden diference of the weather must have been seriously felt by them; or perhaps do they not near the European coa[s]ts more =

I had a beautiful View of a whale about 500 yards from the Vessel; when we first perceived it, the watter thrown through [MS: throw] his valve had the appearance of a small thick Cloud in the hOrizon.† When near us, it dove and exibited its Tail, in appearance about 12 or 14 feet wide =

Never do I recollect having felt the weather so cold in July. Wrapt up in our Cloaks, we felt chilly and the drissle rain.

Wednesday May 17$\underline{^{th}}$ at 7$\underline{^{15}}$ o'clock P.M. left New Orleans†

Friday	19$\underline{^{th}}$	Latitude
S.	19	28.24
Sun.	20	27.28
M.	21	26.56
T.	22	25.47
W.	23	25.
Thurs.	24	24.21
F.	25	24.19
S.	26	24.21
Sunday	28	24.27
M.	29	24.42
T.	30	25.21
W.	31	

Thur June	1	24.38	
F.	2	24.24	
S.	3	23.51	
Sunday	4	23.27	
M.	5	23.37	
T.	6	24.18	
W.	7	23.38	
Thur	8	23.39	
F.	9	24.57	
S.	10	24.09	
Sunday	11	23.48	
M.	12	24.36	
T.	13		
W.	14	23.08	
Th.	15	23.20	
F.	16		
S.	17	23.09	
Sunday	18	23.12	
M.	19	23.45	
T.	20	24.45	ran up to this day 2079 Miles —
W.	21	26.11	
Th.	22	28.	
F.	23	28.25	
S.	24	29.25	86
Sunday	25	30.57	137
M.	26	180	
T.	27	33.53	152
W.	28	34.44	80
Th.	29	35.16	60
F.	30	36.24	134
S. July	1	37.26	155
Sund.	2	38.45	190
M.	3	40.09	177
T.	4	40.09	192
W.	5	40.38	170
Thur.	6	41.26	150

F.	7	42.37	170	
S.	8	43.41	161	
Sunday	9	44.53	133	
M.	10	46.08	136	
T.	11	47.25	171	
W.	12	48.50	141	
Thur	13	50.09	161	
F.	14	51.05	133	3089
S.	15	51.07	125	
Sunday	16	51.03	61	
M.	17	51.09	66	
T.	18	51.16 off Cape Clear	102	
W.	19	138		
Thur.	20	68		
F.	21			
S.				
Sunday				

AT SEA JULY 15TH 1826.

The same dull, cold, damp weather still prevails; still the wind
is northwest and propitious as can be — On a Passage like this,
how much a man may find to think upon — I am pretty sure that
few memorable events of my life (if memorable I may dare call
them or any of them) have not been [MS: be] recalled to memory,
weighed, disaranged and Improved (in thoughts only, not in action,
unfortunatly) untill the whole of my Life has been with scrutiny
surveyed and all the Lines, Land Marks, Beacons, stranding places, &ᶜ
&ᶜ, all fairly and unfairly construed, have been brought present to my
Eye sight and bodily feelings, — Yes, I have had time enough, I assure
thee, to consult on all points, and there can exist no doubts that, had
I been [MS: being] fortunate enough when ever I have erred (and I
have no doubts I erred enough), had I had such an equal opportunity
to think before I acted, I would have committed but few errors and
probably never a Sin —

These are a Curious set of thoughts, thou wilt say — Yes, I
acknowledge it, but still *thou* must acknowledge in return that those
thoughts contain much truth.

Thus my Brains were distracted, or amused, with past recollections, when all sudenly I recollected that I was still at sea, on Board of the Delos, in the very Cabin of the Delos. It made me (very naturally) Cast my Eyes a round, and they suddenly stopped their flighty course on the Looking Glass opposite me; I stopt^d short all further Inquiries about myself and determined to copy (with my pen) (which, by the Bye, is very poor when compared to my Pencil) a strict picture from Life of all the objects surrounding me — I had already cut the goose quill afresh, set my Intentions all on this picture, when I Turned disgusted from *the* thought, and thought of thee; ah, my Dearest Friend! Art thou well? Art thou Happy? The confuse[d]ness of Ideas that sudenly rushed across my mind was undescribable. I felt as if travelling through a Dismal Heavy Snow Storm, without a Compass: I could only Hope to reach the Desired spot — I sighed, my pen dropp^d, I raised my Eyes, and the Confounded Looking Glass reverberating my coarse Image destroyed *Thine*, and again, unwillingly forced me To a wish of beginning [MS: begaining] the Picture —

AT SEA JULY [17TH] 1826. — †

Mr Swift had just Left me — We had just emptied a bottle of American Porter (which, by the bye, is equal to any in the Known World) and gone to the deck to try To see the Land of his forefathers and Father Too — and where I can swear not a Potatoe will be raised this season, should this cold weather continue — when firm as a Florida Live oak, I dipt^d my Pen in the Inkhorn and swore I would describe this cabin of the Delos —

The Looking Glass is pure American Merchandize, and I Hold it more sacred because it was made (I am sure) where Tea was abhored in goodly Time — The picture or Frontispi[e]ce exemplifies the Bountifullness of God on Our gifted Land, *as it shews the Powers of Man* —

"Now, my Dear Husband, what are you going to say?" —

To say, that the Picture on the Boston made Looking Glass exibits . . . the American fair, . . . nursing the Fair American. Here I had a wish to Immortilise my Beloved Country (was it not already so) with powerfull reasonings, but I stop^d to mend my pen again —

Like an able painter I have begun by the upper and Distant part of my

Picture, as Claude Lorrain[26] would have Lightly (and more Inimitably, I am sure) thrown a Sky of azure over his better prepared Canvass = I might have brought object after objects, School Boy Like to my very Book (the nearest object to me) when following my habits I flew at once to those behind me =

"And what were they?" =

6 splendid muskets, American born, are from Harper's ferry,[27] all as bright as the Sun that sets this night over Louisianna, all in a row, and ready to defend the fair flag that now —

I was going to enter into a strain of Politics that probably might have strained all my nerves to no purpose when I recollected the promise mutually made between us Never to open our Lips (or write) either on religion or the above. There the muskets are behind me =

My Bunk Now well known on my Left, resting from my Trunk (the very one that I purchased from Capᵉ Cummings in 1820)[28] on the seat that forms a half moon fronting the Hatch way — over which I see into Mʳ Swift's Cabin (formerly mine), where it is now so Dark, that nothing could be remarkable in it of Darker hue than the Jaw Bones of a Large Shark that are hanging at the foot of it — As I Look up to see if the sun shines or not, I perceive the reversed Compass, and the Tin Lamp both to & fro moving with each motion [MS: motions] of the ship — The Bottle that containᵈ the Porter is at my right, the Tumblers & Baskets Too — The mate's Cabin still further on my right — Several mice are running about the floor picking their scanty fare. The Cocroaches began to shew from their daily retreats; my bottom is sore from sitting on the mate's hard chest. I Look at the sea through the Two windows, and Shut the Book — Why? because the Last object on which my eyes rested was the Captain's Hammock swinging so imediately over my Bunk that

26. Claude Gellée, known as Claude Lorrain (1600–1682), was a very popular and influential French landscape painter.

27. The United States Army and Arsenal at Harpers Ferry, West Virginia, was well known for its manufacture of muskets, rifles, and pistols. Beginning in 1820, the transition to mass production of firearms using interchangeable parts began there.

28. Audubon's journal of 1820–21 includes many references to Capt. Samuel Cumings, who traveled on the same flatboat as Audubon from Cincinnati to New Orleans (Irmscher, *John James Audubon*, 1–155). Beginning with his *Western Navigator* (Philadelphia: E. Littell, 1822), Cumings published numerous navigational guides for the Ohio and Mississippi rivers, revising them regularly.

it reminded [MS: remaided] me most painfully of the many hurried Times I have been obliged to put my Nostrils between my thum and Index for safe keeping from Winds neither from the South West nor Norwest but from ~~~~

Ah, my Dears, what strange incidents happen at Sea —

A Whale! A Whale! Run Mr Audubon, There's a Whale close along side — The Pen, the Book, were abandonned, the mice frightened, I ran up and Lo! There rolled most magestically the wonder of the Oceans — It was of Immense Magnitude; its dark auburn body fully overgrew the Vessel in size: One might have thought it was the God of the Seas bec[k]oning us to the Shores of Europe — I saw it and therefore believed its Existence —

Yesterday night ended the 9th Sunday spent at sea — the weather as usual, but the breese very light — Each person anxious to reach the Shore conceived a diference in the appearance of the watter — Indeed, I once thought and said that I smelt the Putrid sea weeds on the Shore. Several who had not as sensible noses thought it probable — During the afternoon all the noses were up and pointed towards Clear Cape[29] (which might have been with more propriety named Foggy) when suddenly our Captain smelt something new; it had become stronger gradually ever since the morning as the Imagined Land Smell had made its Escape from the slush [MS: Sloche] Barrel Lashed to the Camhouse,[30] and when the real cause was assertained (which now required scarce a moment), a horse laugh was raised for a while when a good share of dejection shewed on all the visages and turned nearly all the Company's noses Blue — We had many whales near us during the day and an immense number of Porpoises; our Captain, who prefers their flesh to the Best of Veal, beef or mutton, said he would freely give 5$ for one: but our Harpoon was now broken, and although several were fastened for a while to the Grains — These proved too light, and the fishes regularly after a few bounces made their Escape, probably to go and die in misery =

Two European Hawks were seen, and also 2 Curlews. This gave me some Hopes that we might see the desired object shortly —

29. Cape Clear, the southernmost Irish island and the first land sighted by many ships coming from America to England.

30. A camhouse is a box or housing built to protect people from the gears of a cam onboard.

How uncomfortable the motions of a Vessel are to a man unused to them when writing, as I am now, all cranksided with one half of my Bottom wearing fast, whilst the other in vain is seeking for support — This is not all. One, as I said before, unused to this disagreable movement may now and then slide off his seat and go and throw down a person peaceably reading three feet off; (I wish I could have said three yards, but our Cabin is hardly that wide and as I set imediatly in the center of the baseline, it could not be so). This person might conceive it an intended insult, indeed, might say so, words might arise and perhaps blows might fall when, after much trouble and hard labour on both side[s], to hold fast to attack and defend, an other heavy roll of the sea might come and force each adversary to seek diferent ways a retreat ═

Many persons speak lightly of Leaving America to go and Visit Europe; many indeed when return^d, who have not found Europe what they wished, speak lightly of the whole ═

I cannot touch the subject so superficially — I spoke for many Years of this my present Voyage; always dreaded it, before I undertook it, and now that, after being swang about, rolled, heaved, bruised and shifted probably a round half million of Times within the first 60 days of a voyage that I calculat[e] (moderatly speaking) to last full 15 months, have I not good substantial reasons to think of it prudently as I go, and to try *when I return home* again to speak of it *rationnally*?

Just as [I wrote] the word *rationnally* (which, by the bye, means much more than many rationnals conceive), our second Mate entered the Cabin and repeated the last words of the man at the Helm at the same time that he called Mr Bragdon (whom you recollect is the 1st mate), saying *Seven Bell.* — Had it not been for this hapenning at *this* very moment, I probably would have forgotten to tell you that we had a Bell on Board — It is not the *sad Curfew or Couvre feu:,*[31] it is the sounding Instrument of Joy to each man at the helm, as it is the Sorrowfull token to the sleeping one in the forecastle that he must raise, go to the relief and gaze on the sails within half an hour and the compass for full 2 hours — For we have a Bell; it sounds either 4 sharp strokes, or 4 times Twice, at four in the morning, or at 12 the meridian — I was going to

31. Curfew, or French *couvre-feu*, literally, "to cover fire." In medieval Europe a regulation was sometimes in force requiring residents to cover their fires in the evening at the sound of a bell.

describe all its usefull properties when the *Stuart* said "Sir, *permettez moi de preparer la Table pour Diner.*" I look^d at him, remark^d his Large flatened Nose, staring black eyes, beautifull Teeth and swart[h]y slick complexion untill I felt a desire to Laugh, when I shook the Ink from my Pen and again bid farewell to my Book —

Ah . . . dinner is at last over and I can return to *Thee, faithfull uncomplaining Friend*! How estimable are *such qualifications, how Noble*!!!! — The Stuart (God Bless him) has Cleared (using a sea phrase *a Propos*) the table, and I have had a full opportunity as he was thus employed to remark and examine and scrutinize the whole of his Person, from his Old Clean red Flannel Shirt rolled up to his sinewy arm joints with the shoulder blades; down to where the same red flannel Shirt shew[s] again distinctly throw a very small round apperture Looking somewhat (though very miniaturely) Like the sun setting in our Western Prairies during *The Indian Summer Evenings* — Just at the Junctions of the Two stout Pillars that support his body — Good honest fellow, how little he thought or believed that I was thus Looking at his better parts — The Bell that I had again forgotten has just struck 4; it is of course Two o'clock, — Now Let me Tell you how this very Bell saved the Lives of several seaman, a vessel and a Cargo =

All these things I would have omitted probably (had not the 2^d Mate entered the Cabin so *à point*) as I would have omitted many other incidents less alarming had I not written at the very moment they took Place (an advise I would regularly give to any person anxious to Employ his time as much as I am by writting down all *he Sees, all he thinks*; or all — yes, out with it: *all he does* —)†

A few minutes before 12, during a Dark squally night when our Vessel was running swiftly Close to the wind in the Warmer latitudes of the Gulph of Mexico, the Man at the Helm cried out "Sail Hoh"! "Close to windward." I Jumped from my Bunk where I had been thinking of thee, my Dearest Friend, and — Stared Towards the Spot like a Wild Man; the Captain had Leaped to the Deck from below in an instant [MS: anstant]. — The Vessel was small (it was a schooner running full before the wind) and the thoughts of a Pirate approaching to Board us fill^d all my Veins with fear and apprehensions — All was silent — all dreadfull suspense — when the thundering voice of our Commandant reach[ed] my Ears and, I have no doubt, those of every one on Board with "Strack the Bell there." This was done — when, all of a Sudden, the Little stranger hauled [MS: hall] to and passed so Close to our Stern that an active man, might have Leaped from one Vessel to another. Had our Bell struck one minute Latter, the Schooner would have struck our Heavy strong broad side and sunk in an Instant — Moving as fast as Both Ships then did, we had just time enough to gather from the Breese a few heavy Vociferations from the Captain of the unknown to the man at his helm — to whom he promised a good *Whaling*, and in a few moments we were far apart and thanking God that matters thus So happily ended =

The stuart is come again, and is now asking if I want "for *quelque chose*" which he is now too apt to do, because I gave him when the weather turn^d *Cold* my *Cold Breaches* (a poor gift on such an Emergency). I was ready to answer him with his own question; when, *I thought it would be unkind* to treat him that rudely: a Blush raised to my face and I said No, my good fellow — Yet as these words Isued from my Lips, I could not help looking at the Little portion of red flannel shirt Issuing from and Looking Like ~~~~

Our captain is again Turning; we have a Brigg in sight and not very far — But we have not the Land in sight: no! and God knows when we will have it —

My Time is really dull, not a Book on Board that I have not read Twice since here (I mean on Board this Ship) and I believe Twice before — thought as I said yesterday of Every thing I can well remember throw the mist of Times and feel as Dull as ever = I moved from the Deck here; from here to the deck; lay there a little, and down here longer: it is all alike; dull uncomfortable; nay: was it uncomfortable only, I do not believe I would Complain, but it is all Iddle time I spend here; all dreary Iddle time: the most miserable pitifull, sinfull way of Spending even One moment —

I have this very Instant cut the quill afresh; Now, much could be said about this goose quill: but I will not pretend to Philosophize on a goose quill — I would rather weigh the Pros & Cons of the whole [MS: all] Genus Anas — yet who knows but this single quill, now cut, and sharpen^d to a very acutte angle, did, or did not, belong to the offspring of an Egg laid as Near the North Pole [MS: Poles], as Geese Dare go — I can safely say that John Hotchkiss (a handsome youth) of the Firm

of Hochkiss & C⁰ of New Orleans, and I believe of New York, and I
believe by birth of New England: sold me this very quill for 4 cents
Lawfull money of the U. States — more or less &ᶜ &ᶜ: Now do not
think all at once, that I am Merry because we are nearing Land — No
by Heavens!! Never in my Life did I feel less concerned about Land
than I do Now, did not my Knees ache so dreadfully — and did I Not
Long as much as I do for a Large Bowl of milk and a full pound of Fresh
bread =

Ah, yes, even such a Loaf as our Franklin devoured in our
Philadelphia market, when somewhat in my situation. — for if I have
not ran off from my mother & friends: I {am} sure, I have from the
Country that has nourished me and brought me up with all the feelings
I now possess. =

What was I writing† about when this soliloquy was begun — Let
me [MS: met] Think — I begun about a quill and — This very quill
reminded me, that I saw a few minutes since, when I ran on Deck
for the purpose of disposing of a certain portion of ~~~~ a Bird that
allways resides near soundings; it looked like a small Merganser [MS:
Mergansers] — Birds that you well know are used to diving. The 1ˢᵗ
Mate callᵈ it *a Mure*!!! Linnaeus [MS: Lineus][32] never described this
Bird; neither have I nor any of my Precedents: Not Even the very highly
Celebrated and Most Conspicuous Mͬ Ord of the City of Philadelphia,
state of Pennsylvania: member of all the Societies of &ᶜ &ᶜ &ᶜ — The
perfect *academician*; they Laughed *because* a turkey could Swim! — [33]

Now, where the Devil are you running To, Audubon? — running
— why — Towards the shores of that England that Gave Birth to a
Milton!! to a Shakespeare!! — to a Driden — that raised West: that
Enableᵈ Thomson to prove his Merits = that called Goldsmith by a
well deserved name — where Johnson flourishᵈ — that gazed on the

32. Carolus Linnaeus (1707–78) was the Swedish botanist who devised the binomial
taxonomic system for classifying organisms. He was one of the most famous and influential
naturalists of his age.

33. Audubon refers to the Philadelphia ornithologist George Ord (1781–1866), who rallied
opposition in that city to Audubon's work in 1824 because he was promoting the *American
Ornithology* of Alexander Wilson. Ord and others apparently laughed derisively when Audubon
reported that turkeys could swim the remaining distance to the opposite bank of a river when
their flight falls short, as he narrates in his essay on the wild turkey (*OB*, 1:2–3).

pencil of Hogarth! with admiration — Laughed with Smollett — might have Cried with Young — was delighted of _Late_ with Scott and shed Tears for her Byron —

Oh, England! renowned Isle! how shall I Enter thee? Good God, What have I pronounced? — I am fit to enter her dominions at all? My Heart swells — The Bird seazed when sitting on her nest could not be more terrified — I look up: Yes, for mercy I look up; and Yet, how much I dread! — How far I would thus have gone when Cap^e Hatch call^d out and said the Brigg Homer was close to us — The preliminary greetings [MS: Questions] of "Brig Ho [MS: Oh]! And ship Hi [MS: I]!"† were [MS: Where] returned — whence came you? &^c &^c had been [MS: being] all Interchanged with a few Hundreds of &^c besides. I reach[ed] the rail way and saw the Brigg _Homer_ 26 days Less from New Orleans than we are — (a mere Moment in the life of man and scarce an attom in eternal calculations). _She looked well_ although her sails were patched [MS: pacthed] with Russia Duck³⁴ to save Duty on Importation —

Ah! England? is it possible that thou shouldst be {unt***ed}† by thy own sons? I can scarce believe it. Thy hoary head used and _connected_ with all Kinds of tricks ought not to suffer this — Now again — what strange itching will prevail and Lead a poor Devil to think on matters Entirely unconnected with him? — It is almost Dark. I will drink the residue in my glass and write _perhaps_ again Tomorrow —

The word _perhaps_ brings _a thousand and one_ recollections to mind = I recollect just now that when I first knew thee, Dearest friend: Frequently I was asked if this _Passion_ of mine would be of Lasting Duration — Hush, I am now Entering on a sacred Subject = "Husband — Shut thy Book, pray" =

AT SEA JULY 18TH 1826

The Sun, now, is shining clear, over Ireland: That land was seen at 3 o'clock this morning by our sailor at the helm, and our mate with a stentorial voice announced us the News =

I cannot conceive why I felt no particular pleasure, not even a diference of sensation from my feelings of Yesterday or the day

---

34. Russia duck is a strong linen or cotton fabric, lighter than canvas, used for making small sails or sailors' outerwear.

previous, or three weeks ago: — What can be the reason? When I have landed in France, or America, I allways bounced with Joy — Now I look indiferently on the shore, although it looks well — Indeed, I feel mortified that I can scarce write, for the want of better spirits — My Dear Friend, oh, it is Thee that concerns me; it is our Dear Children that fill all my thoughts: the Immense Ocean that divides us and the time that must be spent far from thee . . . I Cannot write — Oh, may God preserve you and Bless You All! —

I have come again in the Cabin; we have had Irish *Fishermen* along side (I would call them Beggars), but as they are Men like me, *brothers in blood*, I would be shocked to say so, although they acted *throw a Current of actual misfortunes* as if *they* had been {Conceived} and form^d of Inferior Materials to *Men Americans* —

Shall I tell you how they acted? —

"Yes, do, my Dear Friend."

Well, as we neared the Irish Coast, a small Boat neared us, and bye & bye came Close under our Lea; (It looked somewhat like those Boats employed in fetching Large or heavy provisions to New Orleans — Her sails were more tattered, but her men were more fair: I mean to say that they were *fairer*). They hailed us fairly too, wished to Know if we wished for fresh Fish, or New Potatoes — or Fresh Eggs — Good Fellows: They might as well have asked a sett of miserable sinners, if they would accept of Salvation = All was acceptable, I assure thee (and I will prove it in the sequel). They came along side, and threw most dexterously a light line to us — Presently they were all Busy congratulating us on the Beauty of the Vessel — her sailing &ᶜ &ᶜ (Irishmen Like), however. Fish, Potatoes, Eggs were passed from them to us: and in return we pass^d whiskey — Porter, Beef, Bread & Tabacco to them = probably as acceptable on their side as their Goods were to us —

I thought the exchange a fair one; I Expected that they were satisfied, but no — Used to diferent Ways, they called for rum, Brandy — Whisky — more of Every thing; until I really believed that if we had not ordered them to let go our Line, they would have been following us untill now and begging all the while — Their expressions struck me with wonder. It was (as they put the Liquor to their mouths —) here is to Your *Honor's health*! long life to your Honor! God Bless your Honor!

and Honors followed with such rapidity that I became [MS: becamed] quite unable to look at them any more and Turned away in Disgust —

Reflexions followed reflexions untill, I was Lost and perplexed so much I ~~~~ will drop my Pen and say no more —

However, another: and another successively came ═ to see distressed beings is really distressfull — When in thought I Compared these starved beggars with Irish Gentlemen — I could hardly conceive them as if at all Appartaining to the same race — My God, why are they not Independant? and able to scorn this miserable way of obtaining a Pittance? Oh! xxxxxxx —

The Breese has freshened. We are proceeding fast towards the Emporium of Commerce of England — Perhaps Tomorow may see me safe on land again — but perhaps Tomorow may see us all stranded; perishing where the Beautifull Albion[35] went on Shore —

Incidents *relatif* to many dull days spent on Board this Ship will be seen by you when — I Will write again —

It was my intention to commit here, (on this second rate paper) the Incidents alluded to above but as I had neither dined on Eggs to day, or am I likely to supp on Fish this Evening, I feel a certain emptiness (produced by habit) that forces me to relinquish the thought — perhaps Tomorow, or Tomorow after; when equal in disposition (if not in Power) to a Sergeant of Lieutenant Z. Pike — (now perhaps you have not read Pikes Journal — but I have, & found Page _____ (I cannot recollect the Page) that during Lieutenant Pikes expedition up the *Mississipy real* to, and across the Missoury river, and further South west; to the Colorado in Mexico) [who] refused Obedience to orders on a Cold morning: when the Lieutenant, surprised to find his best Cable (recollect, I am now on a Ship) giving way, spoke loud and remonstrated. "Lieutenant Pike (said the full blooded American soldier) feed me and I will follow you to hell."[36] The expression was

35. The *Albion* wrecked on rocks near the Kinsale Lighthouse on the shore of county Cork, Ireland, in 1822. The violent deaths of many onboard were witnessed and widely reported in newspapers.

36. Zebulon Montgomery Pike published a narrative of his explorations as *An Account of Expeditions to the Sources of the Mississippi; and through the Western Parts of Louisiana to the Sources of the Arkansaw, Kans, LaPlatte, and Pierre Juan Rivers* (Philadelphia: C. and A. Conrad and Company, 1810).

powerfull, I must allow, but the case is so connected with my present situation, that I would freely repeat the same words to *our xxxxxxx*.

We are becalmed — I mean the Delos is becalmed — not so my Bowells! — no, by heavens! — My Bowells are crying help! help! for God sake save us; take pity on us for our God's sake —

I have open^d a new theme, and I must for your Sake, my Dears, proceed to save *you* perhaps (at future times) from being as I now find myself in "*durance Vile*" — [37]

Although our *xxxxxxx* would willingly a few days since have given $5 for a sea Hog (I mean a porpoise), he would not (to save our Lifes) have killed *either* of the Two *Dear Little Piggs* that we have on Board, so heavily fat that they cannot stand up, for 10$ each! Now one would suppose that at any rate, Mr Swift and I, Lowering ourselves (*even in the eyes of The World*) to the Lowest minimum, were worth full half of that amount each =

It is all fudge, my Dears; Mr Swift would go to hell (not follow, remember, as the sergeant was willing to do his Lieutenant), and I might then also go, before our *xxxxxxx* would disturb One of the bristles of those "*Innocent, Lovely* Swains![*"*] =

"Indeed !!! Why is it possible that your Captain Hatch should have brought 2 Piggs across the Atlantic, fed you on wretched Beef — ½ a pound of Chocolate to 17 men for breakfast — Grudge you Whiskey enough to save a few small Fishes in a small bottle, when Mr Swift had brought 11 Gallons (the greatest portion of which was Drank by all hands) when you had sirups and he had porter, when you had Vinegar & oil and he a good Cheese, when you had lime juice and Gin! ~~~~ Why, Father, this is most wonderfully strange?" —

Yes, my Dears, Its the strangeness of it that renders the whole wonderfull — but, my Boys, we have in America: Yes, even on our own Dearly Beloved Land, Men of all sorts: — of Course, Men uncommon in their sorts and our C*xxxxxx* is one of them —

I would now retail; Tales of Wonders! — Yes, wonderfull Tales. I did not tell you precisely the truth when I said Two Pigs = No, I mistook; we positively had three — Ah, yes, we had three, ah! poor things — The youngest Brother of them Died one morning for want

---

37. *Durance vile* is degrading forced confinement or imprisonment.

of ~~~~ Indian Corn or other food — but he was good — yes, he was. He was murdered at the very Instant that his soul (for I believe they have souls as well as Livers) heaved out from his nearly clenched [MS: glenched] Jaws like a spirit — Some of it was roasted, some was boiled, and some was ~~~~ putrid when brought on the Table =

Now, do not think *the Dead* pig was in fault. No, No (when an Annimal is Dead, he is Innactive, and *I* Defy Innactives either to act right or wrong). *The Weather* was in fault: the thermometer might have raised [to] 90: the poor Dead Pig could not stand the Like, and during one night and a whole day of considerations, its flesh at Last gave way to *Natural Impulse* and ~~~~ stunk —

Do you prefer Magotts to Cheese?[38] Now Magots with me, have an Irrisistible, Irritating, repulsive power, and to see Two armies of those Larvas Issuing from Two opposite parts of a cheese, so much revolutionise my stomack (particularly when at sea) that, that same stomack revolutioneers again them. I feel Inclind (with a Diferent Instrument, by the bye) to exterminate Both the Nations with — the broad side of my Knife blade — I am not thinking of Philistans, not I; I am thinking of the Maggots that eat the Cheese, that *xxxxxxx*[†] was intended to go to Kennebunk again had not the Maggots, *Like overwhelming armies* <u>*on Friendly Lands*</u>, devoured (unaware [MS: unhaware]) the whole, except the Crust <u>AB</u>.[†] Well, the Crust is something! — *We* can look at it where ever the {s***er stores} flew on the table — Do you understand the allusion? — It is a query — but *Tomorow*! (I will not say precisely the day following this) I may Explain it =

What a Beautifull! True: ah, faithfull Idea! of a man *unaware of the worth of time* has the *worthy Maria of Ireland*[39] given to us — Now, it is not because I have no Inclination to write — It is not because I feel much perplexed — No, it is because I will not write more to day —

38. Not only Audubon's handwriting but also his ability to make sense are increasingly diminished through the rest of this entry, apparently because of drinking lime juice and gin while being underfed by the captain.

39. Audubon probably refers to Maria Edgeworth, the Anglo-Irish novelist whose work Audubon admired and whom he would soon hope to meet in Edinburgh. Edgeworth's *Castle Rackrent* (1801) includes a character, Sir Patrick Rackrent, who devoted much of his life to drinking heavily.

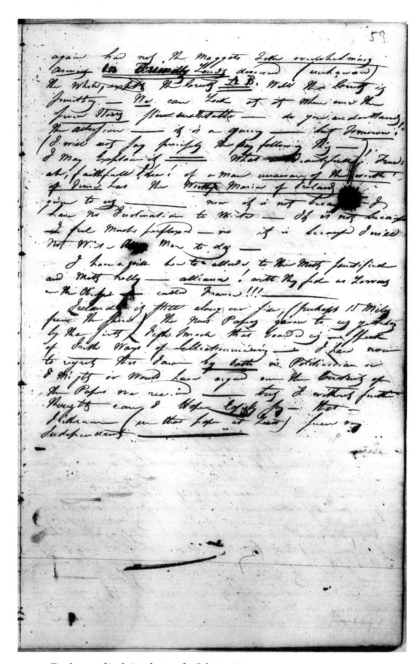

FIG. 13. Final page of inebriated entry for July 18, 1826

I have a wish here to allude to the most sanctified and most holly —
alliance! with thy {f*d} as Larvas on the Cheese called France!!! —

Ireland is still along our side, (perhaps 15 miles from the shore). The
news papers given to us yesterday by the first fish smack that boarded us
— speak of Irish ways of Ellectionneering — I have now to regret that
I am *by Oath* no Politicician or I might or would have argued on the
Contents of the Papers we received — but I without further thought
can, I Hope, Easily [MS: Easisly] say — that Irishmen (in that paper at
least) turn very Independant —

I am approaching very fast the Shores of England — Indeed, Wales
is abreast of our Ship, and we can plainly distinguish the Hedges that
devide the fields of Grain = but what nakedness the Country exibits
— scarce a patch of Timber to be seen — our fine Forests of Pines, of
Oaks, of heavy Walnut Trees, of magnific magnolias, of Hickories, or
ash, or Sugar trees; and represented here by a {diminute} growth —
named *Furze* —

Come, come no critisisms, I have not seen the country, I have not
visited any of the noble's castle's, nor any of the renowned parks — No,
I never was in England, except when I turned *page over page* with a
pleasure that I Hope I may feel again. The animating, Natural Thomson!
or the inticing Scot! — Well, then, I will look on, and think a while: =

We passed yesterday morning *The Tuscar*, a handsome light house
on a naked rock — This morning we saw *Holy Head*,[40] and now we are
not exceeding 25 miles from *Liverpool* — I feel no pleasure, my Dearest
Friend, no, and was it not for *thy* sake and the sake of *our children*, as
God Almighty was the maker of the Sun — I would readily, ah! and
most willingly: embark *to morow* to reach America's shores and — oh
[MS: ho], my Dearest Friend ~~~~

The pilot Boat that came to us this morning contained several men
— all dressd in blue, with Overcoats of *Oiled Linen*, all *good Hearty*,
Healthy *Men* — but rather too much shaped Like their boat, that
undoubtedly was very clumsy, and a miserable sailor compared to our

---

40. The Tuskar Rock lighthouse stands seven miles off Ireland's southeastern tip in St.
George's Channel. The port of Holyhead is located on the island of Anglesey, northwest Wales.

New York — Psha — I will hold my pen and — go on Deck to see if it rains still.

Now it does not rain and I may safely say (without being Jocose) that the sight, now in sight, is truly beautifull. 56 vessels with spreaden sails are in view on our Lea — and mountains after mountains fainting in the horizon [MS: orison] are on our right — Lucy, I have now cast my eyes on the *land of England* = From the Bow, it is plainly distinguishable — My Dull thoughts have all abandoned me; my Heart is elated — I see the Dear Country that gave thee Birth and I *Love it* because!! *I love thee*!!! —

What a picture could here be painted, *or Imagined*. I am not very much surprised that English artists excell (our Days) in Landscape's — The weather, the sea — the Shipping — the Land — would have given (the Long wished for view [MS: review]) to Vernet[41] — Tomorow — yes, tomorow — depend upon it, I shall not go to the Swamps below Philadelphia to Lessen to the Croakings of Frogs — No, Indeed, I shall have to Lessen to the sounds of Diferent annimals — what — ah, what — I will go on Deck again —

What a wildness of thoughts prevails on me! I wonder if any thing like the same ever prevails on men approaching Land? — For my part I am really struck with astonishment at myself — I stare with my eyes at this good Pilot's face of ours, and stare again at his words (with my ears [MS: years]) so much so that I fear he [MS: hi] remarks me in the act as the very Honorable M^{rs} xxxxxx once remark^d me at — When was it? — I have very nearly forgotten her and the spot where she remarked me, so conspicuously — that — hush, no more: M^{rs} xxxxxx is thy sister[42] and for thy sake I will hush —

Tomorow, the *Happy day of our Mind*, it is said will See us safely Landed in the city of Liverpool — and happy it may be, but with me I doubt it — Custom House officers — acceptances of Bills — hunting up of Lodgings, down in one street and up another, looking at all things

41. Claude-Joseph Vernet (1714–89) was famous for paintings of seascapes and seaports.

42. Lucy's sister is Ann Bakewell Gordon, whom Audubon is anticipating meeting in Liverpool. Her husband is the merchant Alexander Gordon, whom Audubon met in 1821 in New Orleans. Gordon extended Audubon considerable assistance at that time and married Ann Bakewell three years later.

about me, will I know so perplex *me* that *I* shall scarce know what position to lay myself in when I go to bed *Tomorow* in Liverpool =

I must on Deck again —

MERSEY RIVER OPPOSITE *LIVERPOOL* 20ᵀᴴ JULY 1826.

It is one half an hour after Nine — The night is cloudy and my Heart is — aching. Ah! I sigh really Invo[lu]ntarily — and yet we are at anchor: yes, positively at anchor opposite Liverpool — not exceeding 200 yards — The lights along the City shewed bright to my eyes a moment ago =

But let me tell you — about 3 hours since a Pilot Boat came along our Side and left on our Deck full 40 Pilots that had left Liverpool this morning, each of them in a Ship bound out; — they were all decent Looking men — all dressᵈ in blew and all, I believe — thy Country men = As soon as our anchor was dropt— Boats came along the Vessel and 3 good Loads of them delivered us of that extra Crew =

Now, my Dearest Friend, I am in England— With what success I shall go threw my undertaking I shall be sure to inform thee — Now I shall conclude with — the Tide here this day and at this hour races up the Mersey full 6 miles and raises 30 feet spring tide and 18 feet neap [MS: Nipt] tide — God Bless thee, good night! —

2

Liverpool

[LIVERPOOL, JULY 21, 1826][†]

The next morning when I landed, it was raining; yet the outward
Appearance of the City was agreable, but no sooner had I entered it
than the smoak from coal fires was so oppresive on my lungs that I
could scarcely breath[e] — I felt the same affecting my eyes also ═
All was nearly new to me: after a breakfast taken at an Inn for 2/6 —
Mr Swift accompanied me to the Exchange Buildings to the counting
House of *Gordon* & Forstall — I was anxious to deliver the letters I
had for Mr G. from Mr Briggs — After a few moments Mr G. made his
appearance but did not recollect my countenance (although I am sure
it has always been [MS: being] of the od[d] order) untill I open[ed] my
Lips to pronounce my name ═ I was coldly received (I think). I would
be very sorry to say that it was *à L'anglaise* yet it bordered on something
as *new* to me as England is this very moment — I was ask^d when I took
my leave (which was [not] long, I assure thee, after our meeting) *If* I
should not call again!!!! —

Where is that sweet Ann Bakewell that I knew when a child? that
sweet sister of thine who almost grew by my side? She is in Liverpool
and — I shall not see her. It is severe but it must be endured, and yet
what have I done — Ah, that is no riddle, my Friend. I have grown
poor. —

I presented during this morning my Bill of Exchange for acceptance
and was *somewhat mortified* that, although several vessels had arrived
from New Orleans that had all left since the Delos, that Mr Charles
Briggs had not forwarded the One I left in his charge *at his* particular
request — The rest of the day was nearly spent gazing about and
clearing (as much as possible) my Brains from a multiplicity of

Confused Ideas that filled them alternatly in the earlier part of it — I went to the Museum — I tried to see M͟r Rich͟d Rathbone[1] and some other persons but was *unfortunate* in all this —

How lonely I feel — not a soul to speak to freely — When M͟r Swift leaves me to go to his Parents in Ireland, I shall be then entirely destitute — Ah, my Victor, where art thou? What a blessing it would be for me to have thy company whilst travelling throw this world, but that is denied me and that also I must endure —

We took Lodgings & board at the Commercial Inn, not far from Exchange Buildings — We are well fed and well attended although, to my surprise, altogether (so far) by females — neatly dressed and tolerably modest —

I found to day the persons of whom I Enquired for diferent directions remarkably kind and indeed so polite that even to a man like ~~~~ me — It was real Politeness — I examined several watches at M͟r Roskell's [MS: Roschell's] and his politeness was most agreable —

I shall try to keep M͟r Swift here untill I have seen *all* that *I* can see of Liverpool — His going to London with me will be very acceptable, I assure thee —

LIVERPOOL ENGLAND JULY 22͟D 1826

The lark that sings so sweetly and that now awakened me from a Happy set of Slumbers is nearly Opposite my Table, prisonner in a cage hanging by a window where, from time to time a young person comes to look on the world below — *I look to the world above* and think of the World of the West, and — larks really sing very sweetly! delightfull creatures!! —

The custom house officers suddenly entered my Head, and after a very considerable delay *there*, I gradually returned to larks again and thought of those that I brought from America — I concluded after looking at the thousands [of] colums of Dark smoake that arised

---

1. Audubon carried with him a letter of introduction from Vincent Nolte to Richard Rathbone, who was the brother of William Rathbone (1787–1868), inheritor of the very successful Rathbone commercial interests. Four generations of Rathbones had been prominent cotton and timber merchants, ship builders and owners, and philanthropists in Liverpool since approximately 1730. Richard married Hannah Mary Reynolds (1798–1878), writer and illustrator, in 1817. He helped manage the family businesses.

allways in contact with Distant objects beyond them = (many of which I longed to see), to Call again on M: Gordon and follow the principles specified between men of Business, i.e. to take advantage of Circumstances (even with reluctance).

I saw M: G. again. He was much the same — He gave me *his card* and I now can go to see thy Sister. If I feel Inclined or think it *proper* — M: G's young Gentleman accompanied me to the Custom House — (I could here write full 6 pages). My Drawings went throw a *regular, strict,* and *complete examination* — The officers were [MS: where] all of opinion that they were free of Duty, but *the Law* was look^d at because it is not every day (*it seems*) that Such Port Folios as mine are presented at the Custom House, and I was obliged to pay 2 pence on each; being *watter coloured* <u>Drawings</u>. My Books being *American*, I paid 14 pence per pound weight. After the regular form of my having procured a *Certificate* of *my* Landing in England was over, I took my Baggage and Drawings to my Lodgings =

The noise of pattens [MS: Patins]² on the flaggs startles me very frequently. Indeed, I generally turn my head (of course, when the noise comes from behind) expecting to see a Horse full speed, with open mouth intent on taking it for fresh Grass. I am sure my Eyes are then quite full, but the moment that they meet those of a neat, plump looking maid tripping as briskly by as a killdeer [MS: keelder], they soon compose again to their regular size and — Lucy, thy Country Women are very Beautifull! Yes, Indeed, they are to my eyes very Beautifull! — It is not only the freshness of their complexion, nor added to this their lovely rosy hue — nor (continuing to add) their well shaped forms, but it is — *all about them* I admire so much. — Now, I received a Polite Note from M: R^d Rathbone this morning Inviting me to go next Wednesday to dine with him and M: Roscoe.³ I shall not forget the appointment, I assure thee =

2. Pattens worn by people were thick-soled wooden clogs; worn by horses, they were round wooden platforms fixed to the hoof to prevent sinking into soft ground.

3. William Roscoe (1753–1831) was patriarch of a prominent Liverpool family. He had a varied career: attorney, banker, patron of the arts and sciences, self-taught historian, poet, politician, abolitionist. In 1781 he married Jane Griffies, with whom he had ten children, most of whom enjoyed successes in business and/or the arts. With Thomas Stuart Traill in 1817, he cofounded Liverpool's Royal Institution as a center for adult education in the arts and sciences. He lived the final seven years of his life at 180 Lodge Lane, Liverpool.

Mr Swift took me to Dinner to Mr Lyons, and there I spent a most agreable afternoon or, say, evening rather for it was 5 P.M. [MS: A.M.] when we dined and nearly 10 when we Left — and God Bless thee. Good night —

Sunday, yes, it is Sunday: *therefore*, I must expect a long dull day. Thou wouldst again say, "Ah, my Dear Friend, how canst thou say so," and I would reply as I have done frequently before with — but Lucy; unfortunatly, I am now too far from thee to be improved by thy maxims and rendered as Happy as I have when — nearer to thee — Therefore, the day has been dull, yes, my Dearest Friend, very Dull. =

I leaped from the downy bed at dawn of day.† I had then, Impatiently been [MS: being] lo[u]nging (for a long time) for!!! ~~~~ the sweet voice of the Lark at the window nearly opposite mine = Its melow throat reached my ear and followed the rotary movements of *my system* with electric swiftness. — I thought imediatly of England, but wished myself in America = I would have wrote *heaven* but *some of my Friends* having once told me that I was nearing the Bombastick I did not —

"A word to the wise." —

Now the dullness of the day — I needed shaving but I did not shave — no! — why? — because it was Sunday. = Sunday is a sacred day with me. I like to spend it duly — soberly and — I will not say another word. Oh! that oath of mine *Never* to be† a Politi[ci]an or a — Priest — no. I am — what? What? — No one knows, not even My Poor self. I have frequently believed myself a Fool, but the Opinion has been variously received and — it was Sunday this very morning when I thought so again, as much as I Ever did in my Life. — The Weather beautifull for English Weather — thermometer in the sun 65, in the shade (and there is plenty of this about my Body) say 41 (I would have wrote forty but I Love odd numbers. I have been told that they are the fortunate ones at Loteries or at making choice among a set of females for a Wife or ~~~~ &^{c}). The fact, however, is this: that my Teeth *clattered* as I Exerted myself towards promoting reaction in my blood vessels by walking fast as I was fasting this clear, beautifull English morning before the Door of the *Commercial* Inn — Dost thou

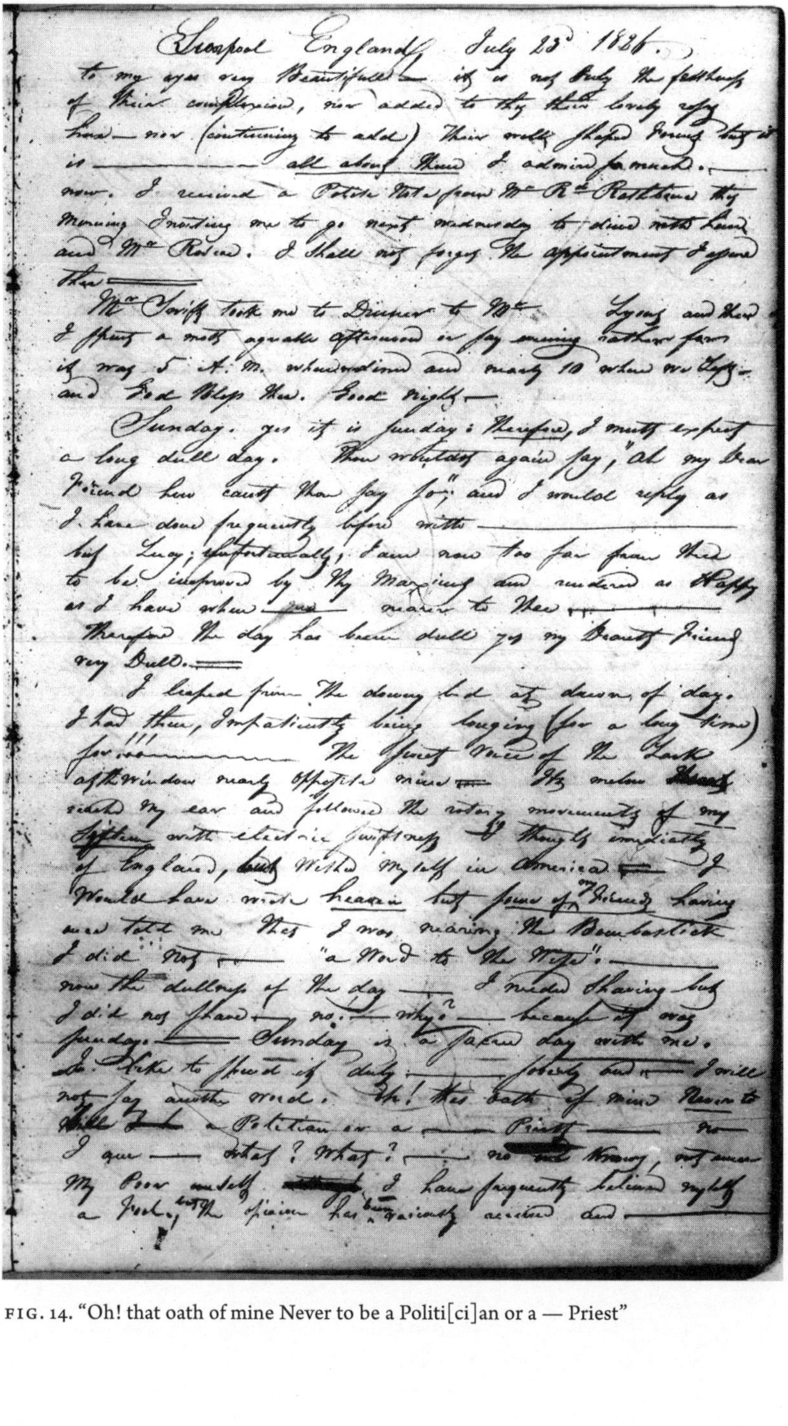

FIG. 14. "Oh! that oath of mine Never to be a Politi[ci]an or a — Priest"

remember the Wife of George Keats Esqr of London &^c &^c &^c &^c? (I will write no more of these; it dulls my German quill).

"Remember her? — I am surprised thou shouldst put such question to me" =

Well, if I did not see Mrs Keats, the wife of George Keats of London Esqr &^c &^c (confound the &^cs I say), I saw undoutedly her ghost in *Whales* this afternoon.[4]

"Why? Is it possible?"

Yes, it is possible & I will answer thy why with because it is was [*sic*] Sunday — Formerly Ghosts walk^d at Night. Now they walk on Sun-day.

"Pho! pho! What a poor Pun."

I do acknowledge that — but if I did not see Mrs George Keats, the wife of George Keats Esqr of London &^c — (Dam^d the &^c), I undoutedly saw her Ghost or a Ghost very much Like her Ghost. =

"Come, no more about this."

I am again Intruding on — what — ah, religion!! Must I put thee a side again, when thou art the Leader of all and every one of my Movements, either Mental or Phisical, either Vertical or horizontal [MS: orisontal]? — Now, Stern: yes, Stern said, I believe, (it was either Stern or some other *Merry Inclined Gentleman writer of his age*) that Horisontal [MS: Orisontal] Postures were [MS: where] most Congenial for all descriptions of feelings whatever.[5] — Now the last word *whatever* is (in my mind very strenuous). Indeed, it becomes important for persons *conceived*, but I will return to my Sunday and may God bless the *Merry Stern* = or the *Learned Stern*. Ah, Stern!!!! I am not — no = (never can I write with a worst Pen than I do now and yet I feel now as anxious as Ever I did to help To keep up Thy *Memory's Monument untill the expiring Times of ages will rise it again with thy Immortal resurection for — yes, for Ever!!! —*

I was in Wales and thereby lost my Dinner and Why? because it was *Sunday —*

---

4. George and Georgiana Keats had been paying guests in the Audubon home in Henderson, Kentucky, in 1818. Brother of poet John Keats, George had left Liverpool to travel to America to make his fortune.

5. Audubon alludes to Laurence Sterne's *Tristram Shandy* (London, 1759–67), in which Tristram explains his theory that "both man and woman bear pain or sorrow (and, for aught I know, pleasure too) best in a horizontal position" (vol. 3, chap. 29). Audubon in his cups reflects an affinity with Sterne's literary use of digressions as well.

My forenoon was spent as my afternoon was yesterday (*say last Saturday*) most agreably in the company of M̠ Lyons — He *sat* with me and *stood up* looking at my drawings for a good while = then was Kind enough to Introduce M̠ S. & myself at the Commercials reading Room of the Exchange Building where; believe me, many men read of the Distress now generally felt in England without caring a f~~~~ Will this pen of mine continue to move as much astray from the direct course as a Crab does from the unacquainted pursuer of that naturally side ways moving ~~~~ I am no concologist (although I am fond [MS: found] of eating good Crabs *out of the sea; none of our Florida Fidlers for me, I say*[)] —

I know you blushed a little when the single Letter *F* came in your sight unaccompanied. I will soon relieve you — Do not dread any Explosion from Mount Vesuvius [MS: Vesusius], for Instance, or any Mountains besides that now & then do explod most Tremendously — I intended to write *Fig* in full but my rascally pen was not suplied with materials suficient and — as I was walking very slowly towards the Mersey (for my feet are most connfoundially sore)⁺ I saw M̠ G.xxxxx⁶ passing on the opposite side of the street Looking at me between the edge of his cheek and that of his spectacles. — (He does not know how often I have Look̠ at Hawks). I made direct for him as if a Hawk my self — but *he spoke so much like a renard* that I made imediatly *Patte de Velours*,⁷ and I went — over the Mersey, Lucy. — Ah, my Dearest Friend! beloved wife! How many contrary winds we are apt to meet in our Passage throw Life — or at sea or in — a steam Boat going only over the Mersey for only 3 pence for each — Upon my word, I do not know what I can fairly or appropriatly call our specie =

The country was dull on Wales shores opposite Liverpool and duller the further we proceeded from Liverpool — Why? It was Sunday. Every object look̠ dull — The Larks, as they sprung from the Earth, felt the powerfull effect of this unacountable talisman and dropt *with powers unclosed* to the soil again as if — not one more Word. =

We returned — eat supper — drank some Claret call̠ here *Port* =

6. Mr. Gordon is Audubon's brother-in-law who has not yet invited him to visit.

7. Paws of velvet rather than with claws extended, that is, giving oneself a sweet and inoffensive appearance while remaining in fact in a position to injure.

heard of Politics in the travellers room — drank our Glass of *Pousse Caffee* and — God Bless thee — Went to bed wishing thee — my children and my country well — ah, yes, Dearest Lucy.

LIVERPOOL JULY 24TH 1826. —

Who would have thought it! I was in bed at 10 o'clock this morning! yet I was in full health — This is an occurence in a Man's Life who like me Generally has been quite *Awake* before the diurnals of the Feathered tribe retire to their rest. Here an enquiry is requested: what could the reason be? what, Indeed? — *the Influence of the Climate on Vegetables and annimals* so much adheard to by the great French Naturalist, who puzled his Brains to discover *Impossibi[li]ties,* who often repeated that, American productions were [MS: where] *all* degenerated Objects from the European *Originals.* — I wish I had known the Count de Buffon[8] — *What an original he was,* and is yet: what a *Model to copy from*! What Lights!! yes, what Lights! and what *shades* he has casted over Nature's Grand Tableau. —

Did you expect that the begaining of the last paragraph was going to trail from my raising at 10 o'clock out of my bed after Owls — Climates — anatomical parts — Impossibilities — the Count de Buffon and almost all other objects wanted to Illustrate Nature's Great Works? — No, you did not — This is not my fault but — I shaved quickly, was Dressed in a Twi[n]kling — I Bustle^d about briskly — Locked my Trunk — Took my cane, my Hat, my Gloves — all in a Hurry — ran down stairs — swallowed my breakfast without Mastication — and made as Directly as I could threw the sinuous streets of Liverpool to N° 87 Duke Street, where the Polite English Gentleman Richard Rathbone resides =

My locks flew freely from under my hat and every *Lady* that I met looked at them and then at me untill — she could see me no more —

The kind Gentleman was not in — I almost ran to his Counting house at the Salt Dock down Duke Street &^c &^c &^c — a full dozen

---

8. Georges-Louis Leclerc, comte de Buffon (1707–88), was the author and compiler of the monumental *Histoire naturelle* (44 vols., 1749–1804). Many Americans enjoyed resenting his claim that North American animal species were degenerated versions of their larger European counterparts, famously prompting Thomas Jefferson to display the complete skeleton, skin, and antlers of a moose in Paris.

[MS: doz^d] of Clerks were [MS: where] at their separate Desks — The
Ledgers — Day Books &^c &^c &^c were all under full sails — Royals —
Royals Extra — Studen sails &^c. An Immense Letter Bag belonging
to the Packet that sailed this day for the Shores where I Hope thou
art Happy (Dearest Friend) stood near the entrance — My name was
taken to the special room of Mr Rathbone, and in a moment I was met
by one who acted towards me as *a Brother ought to do*! == How truly
Kind and really polite ==

He did not give *his Card* to poor Audubon. He gave the most polite
Invitation to call at *his House* at 2 that I ever received since I left
America —

Now what an Immense Distance I had to walk to reach N° 6, Norton
Street, the house of Mrs Noble where — thy *Sister* resides with *thy*
Brother in law Mr G. in the road leading to London — full 1 and ½
mile over a pavement composed of *one peble* to each toe — Now, thou
knowest my feet and their {a*the*s} are not extravagantly large, no —
neither are the pebles here; but how much [h]arder than my Toes?

Good God! If my Toes could write as well as the Toes of a woman
now exibited here called Miss (I rather suspect throw mistake) xxxxx,
what a scientific Description the mineralogists of America would have
(when I return there) of these same small hard pebles that my Toes
have *assured me* are of the hardest Texture they have felt since they were
[MS: where] — where? Let me think a moment: tis best not to be too
rash. — since they were — ah, where? *In Liverpool!* —

Well, I trotted like a Horse string Holt,[9] street after street, allies and
Gutt[e]rs of streets untill I reach^d — no. I did not reach the desired
Object — oh!! — How is this? — what? — could not find Norton
Street? — Norton Street — Dam Norton Street. I could not find
thy Sister's lips to imprint on them an affectionate Purest Kind of a
Kiss — The Bird that once sung so sweetly unto my Ears down to my
Heart's Vitals had flown, and I Looked on the Empty Nest with more
melancholy *believe me* than ever I did when in full expectation that a
pair of [L****s]^† well known to me might be seen once more — Ah,
Delusion — I can swear that I was at the appointed moment at the

9. That is, stringhalt or stringhalted, a condition in horses that causes certain muscles to
contract spasmodically.

house of Mrs Noble — no more: I did *a Brothers part* and — I ambled off back again to Mrs Rathbone[10] in Duke Street =

See me leaning against a window from the Inside of a Handsome Dining Room — Melancholy — thoughts after thoughts rolling (like a Tormented stream over rocks all sharply angular) from my Head downwards untill I felt positively feverish over all my Body —

Le Brun[11] could not have had a better subject to Illustrate that Passion — I Leaned Heavily untill my thoughts sudenly turned to the Happy Years that I have spent with thee — Then my Life was alive again!!! Then ~~~~ Mr Rathbone entered the Room and with both arms extended advanced towards me with — "My Dear Sir, I regret I suffered you to Wait thus." I dined with ~~~~ oh, sweet children!!! Oh, Aimiable Woman — oh, Hospitable Man — I believe I said I dined — but no, I did not Dine. I feasted my Eyes, my Heart with the Delightfull picture before me = the Melow picture of a Happy familly. What a Sublime subject! Who could not study when Nature is at her Best. —

The table was left and I had the pleasure to walk by the side of this Happy Two, slowly, composedly, to a powerfull Examplification of the Powers of Genius Improved — I saw the Night scene of the Chapel of Holy Rood = Ah, Marvellous science, to what sublimity thou art raised — whilst I was willfully Inclined to Copy thy Model's {Innocent} portion =

Mrs Rathbone is, my Dearest Lucy, as aimiable a Lady and as Learned a one as ~~~~ Come — What shall I say? — Well, then, as thy sweet self!!!!!!!!

I have wrote Two full sides of my poor Book and it is only about half past three with me here [MS: hear], in the account Current of this day's transactions, but it is really 11 A.M. by the clocks that all sound for 15 minutes, one following another (Like a captain aquainted with the sounding of an harbour) and I have not reached the Exchange Buildings to where I am now going to take You (throw this medium) in company of Mr Rathbone walking fast arm in arm in order to see the American

10. That is, Mrs. Richard Rathbone (see n. 1).

11. Élisabeth Vigée-Lebrun (1755–1842) was a French portrait painter known for her pictures of two English princesses and Marie-Antoinette, among others.

Consul Maury Esq[r][12] and others = I Hope R[d] Rathbone lost nothing more by the trouble I gave him to day than the money that he Paid for my Entrance at the holy Chapel's exibition — Indeed I do, Lucy =

Introductions followed Introductions — Then I was taken throw the whole of the Exchange Buildings — the Mayor's Public Dining Hall, &[c] &[c], &[c]. I gazed on the Royal familly pictures of England by Thomas Lawrence,[13] Shea & others — mounted to the Dome and gazed on the Picture {compound} of Liverpool City with the harbour that Nature formed for her — Far — far — my eyes took my senses — I could see the Irish Chanel — a steam Boat Issuing from the River Dee in Wales — the Mersey filling the Interior with the Worlds produce — and the heavens bounding the scenery Divinely =

It was past 5. I ran to my appointment to M[r] Swift — and then went to purchase Black Chalks to — make a sketch of his physiognomy [MS: Phis.] Tomorow = I have wrote a great deal, have I not?

"Pretty well, I think."

I could write more but I am ~~~~ so distracted by the Noise of all sorts of *People below* that I will bid thee Good Night, Wish thee Blessed and ~~~~ God preserve thee, Lucy —

JULY 25TH 1826, LIVERPOOL —

Burst my Brains: Burst my coarse scull, and give the whole of _Your_ slender powers to enable me to describe my feelings this day! — I must begin slow, gradually warm my powers and — oh, poor Head; never can I Express throw thee the extent of all I saw in the Beautifull Picture surveyed during an —

"Stop — take time — consider and proceed gradually. No rashness — Recollect, thou art now going to attempt a very dificult Task — I advise thee waite." —

My Beloved Friend, I will follow thee, yes, threw Worlds of Futurity, and receive thy affectionate advises with Loyal pleasure!!! —

I waited full dressed nearly 15 minutes before the sweet lark, (my

12. James Maury (1746–1840) was the first American consul and served in Liverpool from 1790 to 1829; he was a friend of George Washington.

13. Sir Thomas Lawrence (1769–1830) was considered England's greatest portrait painter in his day; he was president of the Royal Academy from 1820.

reveille Matin) had turn^d his head from its soft pillow towards the Orb of Appolo — I wait[e]d anxiously — I felt gay and — no, not Happy, but the sweet Jinglings of Melody of the Lark help^d my spirits much $=$ Mr Swift raised and dress^d in a moment and the Black Chalk once more Touched the paper to animate it — Oh, yes, I have drawn in England. Ah, how much I have drawn in my America!! —

I finished early, so much so, Indeed, that when seven struct my ear from the clock, we were [MS: where] on the pavement bound towards the West to near thee a step: —

Naked streets look dull — We soon returned and eat a beneficial repast — Issued again and — My Dear Lucy, I bought a beautifull watch for thee from Mr Roskell's [MS: Roschell's] & Son, Church Streeet, and one also for me from the same polite Gentleman — Ten of the morning was positively past and I positively felt much ashamed when after reaching Dale Street where are our Lodgings, that a Note from Mr Rathbone had been there sometime waiting for me.

A Hackney coach was produced in a moment. I entered it with my Port Folio N° 2 and ordered quickly for Duke Street — They were gone to M^r [MS: M^rs] Rathbone's Mother — I enquired the way but before my sentence was finished; I saw their Carriage Turning back making for me — and I had once more the pleasure of being near these Kind persons — Their youngest sweet little son Bazil look^d at me and I wished him — well — Mr James Pyke was Introduced to me — We proceeded slowly and I thought of my situations — in England, in the carriage of a man Generous, and noble of heart, dressed (although perhaps queerly to them) very diferently to my Indian garb [MS: Guarb] — Gun cocked, dashing throw the deep swamps of Lower Louisiana after the Wood Ibises in company of my good friend Bourgeat. — The country open^d to our View gradually, and after having passed under a Cool arbor [MS: Harbour] of English Trees, I entered the Habitation of — Philemon & Baucis!!!^14 — Yes, a Venerable Happy pair received their children with kisses, all kindness, and bid me well come with that

---

14. Audubon alludes to the happy Phrygian couple in Jonathan Swift's poem "Baucis and Philemon" (1709). For entertaining him and Hermes hospitably, Zeus transformed their cottage into a fine temple. Audubon's August 14 references to Mr. Rathbone's mother as Baucis (see p. 118) suggest that "M^rs" here is a scribal error.

natural ease that I thought had deserted this earth [MS: hearth] with the Golden age =

I felt painfully awkward (as I allways do in new company) for a while, but so much truth was about me that I became calmer and — the good Venerable Couple walked me round a Garden transplanted from abroad, and — my Port Folio was opened in the presence of several females and a younger Rathbone — Now, I am allways in too great a Haste — I saw as I entered this happy dwelling a Beautifull Collection of the Birds of England well prepared. Yes, well prepared. — What sensations I had whilst I help^d to untie the fastening of my Folio Book. I knew by all around me that all was full of best Taste and strong judgment, but I did not know if I would at all please — A small {book} was open$^\underline{d}$. I was panting like the wing^d pheasant as he dreads the well taught Friend of Man, that may perhaps prove him too weak, to proceed in full sight of his learned Eye —

Ah, Lucy, these Kind *Friends* praised *my Birds* and I felt the praise — Yes, I breathed as if some Celestial being fanned me in Elysium —

Praises are of many kinds, but kindly praises are true, and these *good Friends* praised me kindly!!!

Farewell, venerable double one. Ah, yes, you will, must fare well in the Heavenly Gardens above —

Tender embraces were again Interchanged — I again was held by these sacred hands — again in the seat next R$^\underline{d}$ Rathbone and moved threw the avenue by the same way to Liverpool again —

I am now leaping out of the Carriage — I have bid farewell to all my Friends and — Lucy, R$^\underline{d}$ Rathbone steped towards me and in a low tone said "M$^\underline{r}$ Audubon, the coachman has been satisfied" — My blood ran high — then cold — I felt and — too much abashed, threw my self in the Vehicle that brought me to Dale Street again — Could such Incidents ever be forgotten? — No, give my Life the lasting solidity of the adamante and the Deep Touches of the Keenest Graver will be efface[d] sooner† from the Rock than from my Heart. —

The good American Consul had Called on me — I must thank him tomorow —

The reverend W. Goddard with the Rector of Liverpool and several Ladies called on me and saw some Drawings — All prais^d them —

Oh, what can I Hope? —

Beloved wife, Good night — †

As my Business Increases here so much, the more must my exertions
and Industry be called on and employed to meet all demands —

It is very late, my Beloved Wife. It is past 12 o'clock — The watchmen
below announced it some minutes ago. — I hope thou art reposing
calmly with health and Happiness on each side thy Pillow. May it be
God's will!

I felt fatigued and would soon join thee again in sleep, but the maxim
that never will cease to be good is present and I will not put untill
tomorow what can yet be performed to day.

The morning was beautifull and serene. I enjoyed it in its prime
— but no sooner had the thousands of noisy wheels began to shake
the pavement than my Heart Swelled, and involuntarily Bursted with
acute sensations of unknown sorrows accumulating so mistily fast
before my Imagination that I could not refraine from sheding an
aboundance of Tears — I felt as if some great misfortune was near^d — I
felt how much I need thee! — Yet I recollected that the Venerable M^r
Maury must not be neglected == Then I saw him == Mr Swift Left for
Dublin == I Called in vain at the Post office for news from America —
put in the Letters Mrs Percy had charge[d] me with and returned to my
Little room where my heart again was forced to discharge its burthen
and I cried — oh. ==

The soreness thus brought on to my eye lids forced me to recollect
that I was engaged to dine with Mr R^d Rathbone, that I had already too
much against me to ennable me to go throw this ceremonial Trial and
— I wash^d my Eyes — prepared my person and — waited patiently.
The Good Gentleman Called on me with his Brother William — The
latter Invited me to Dine on Friday Next with him — I accepted and
promised the former to be punctual with him also —

It is half past 6. The Coach is at 87 Duke Street — The coachman has
rung the Bell and my heart fails me. — Now this is very simple, very
foolish. Ah, yes, it is all this and more: it is a most painfull action of my
faculties —

I am in the Corridor, my Hat is taken civilly from my hand and my
Name humbly requested — I am pointed the way above and == Bear
me, my legs — I am in the Setting room of Mr Rathbone — It was time
I should have met his eye. His lively mien! What a relief it gave me. —

Now with all this I have frequently thought it strange that my *Observatory nerves* never gave way. I remarked imediately the more Polite Way of Introduction, i.e. I remark^d that no one Shook hands unless they thought fit — This pleased me — Many Pictures embellished the room and they also help to remove this misery of my life — this *Mauvaise Honte*[15] —

Mr Roscoe came in, Tall, with a good Eye under a Good eye Brow — and all mildness shook hands with me —

"Indeed!!! hast thou already seen and touch^d that renowned Citizen?" =

Yes, and Talked with him! = The Dinner is announc^d. Mr Rathbone locks in arm his Tutor — Mr Roscoe Locks in arm thy Husband — I saw not the remainder of this Friendly procession. We descended to the Room where I had Leaned some days ago against the window, and I was conduct[e]d to the seat of Honor — Mr Roscoe sat on my left next me — Mr Barclay of London Next — Mr Melly beyond — on my right R^d Rathbone next and oposite to me the Honorable Consul Maury — Mr Arnault &^c untill round the table the friends met again. —

Conviviality wafted her gentle wings full spread over the whole — I was soon less observed and it gave me the means of observing more. — I lessen^d to the mirth and *Bons sens* that allways presides in such company with pleasure Infinite.

This was a good Lesson much needed. I was glad to be assured that *Bon ton* no longer required to Drank unwillingly! — The practice of xxxxx — was, however, rejected too as we^† rose from the table and promiscuously reassend to the Parlour, where Mrs Rathbone appeared like a Diamond well set in the Circle formed about her —

T'is no wonder her husband is aimiable; they grow together. — I had the pleasure of holding for a moment her hand whilst she bid me Wellcome!! —

But, my Dear Friend, thou [h]ast not seen the beautifull set of Boxes that Mr Rathbone possesses?

---

15. Audubon uses the phrase *Mauvaise Honte* (a silly or bad shame) twice in the journal (July 26 and 28), and several other times he refers to his extreme shyness in the presence of persons of great reputation whom he needs to impress. Here he characterizes it as "this misery of my life."

"No."

I have. During the latter part of Dinner, he shew^d me several — all by Taste chosen, and all made to Improve the Taste. —

The lights are arranging: I am moving a Table — The Company is all expectation and I, oh, I — Mr Roscoe does not give me any Hopes — Neither can he destroy the feeling — I must return to "expect not too much; thou shalt not be disapointed."

"Yes, it is better so." —

The Tissue paper is Turning and Drawings one after another — The style is examined — questions answered and: Mr Roscoe is — yes, I believe rather Surprised. I sincerely Hope so. — The attractive rays of my sight prove to me that my very own head is looked at and I shrink again —

Good Mr Rathbone is all Intentness in procuring my desires. He has retired from the groupe and, Closely setting to Mr Roscoe, is Infusing his generous Heart into the mind of the Great Man. —

I am Invited to see Mr Roscoe at his seat tomorow to attend him at the Botanical Garden too — "Good night, my Dear Sir." Thus Mr Roscoe is just gone and has left me with, — the Intelligent Swiss[16] — my kind Guests and — my thoughts —

Now I see that I was not self deceived when first I saw Mrs Rathbone at Table with her lovely flock (a pleasure unfelt this Day). Some of her Drawings are before me and talent has put his undeniable stamp on each Touch! I am positively a little proud of my Judgment on this Subject. Excuse me, Dearest Friend. —

I must leave you, happy Two — Farewell! — It is not dark. The Intelligent Swiss leads me swiftly towards Dale Street — We chat very brotherly like — We arrive at^†   We part. I walk faster — I would write more but I am now safely lodged — I have bid thee again good night, and I will not, no — will not soil my Paper — with details of the last objects I saw[17] =

16. André Melly, of a patrician family in Geneva, immigrated to England in the early 1820s to set up in business; he was an amateur naturalist interested in entomology. He would marry Ellen Greg by 1828.

17. This is probably a reference to prostitutes, upon which Audubon comments with repulsion after several other nighttime returns to his quarters.

It is not twelve to night, my Dear Lucy, but it is Thrice that M^{r}
Rathbone has superceded me with the Coachman. — Yes, M^{r}
Rathbone, I began to think, has made some private Bargain with all
those fellows for as soon as I say how much? — They reply "Sir, I have
been paid." — Now this is extraordinary — What a misrepresentation
of things Mr Leecock[18] gave us at our Little Mansion of Natchez when
he said that it would require five or six years for such a man as me to be
Noticed in England — I believe that was the substance of his Speech
when I observed how much I longed to Issue in the World —

I have been only a few days in thy Country and All Smiles a welcome
to me: ah, yes, I assure thee, a Welcome. — Read and Judge —

I walked to Duke Street at 15 minutes past one, and as I entered
the House of this real Friend, Mrs R. met me — I followed her to the
parlour above and sat there a few moments — Some *English* Grapes
were presented me, refreshments were offered and I was told that I
might trust my Port Folio to the Driver, who would certainly return
[MS: returned] it safely. — I had not the pleasure of S[e]eing Mr R., but
I saw his sweet miniature and tap^{d} his fat little round arm in gratitude
as much as I did for pleasure sake — Thou knowest Best how fond [MS:
found] I am of Children —

I soon reach[ed] Mr Roscoe['s] place about one and half mile distant,
was welcome[d] at the Door and I entered a little Drawing room where
all was Nature. This Gentleman was Drawing a very handsome Plant,
very handsomely. The Cabinet was ornemented with many other
shrubs, receiving from his hands the Care that Nature had insured them
in their Native climat, for I believe they were principally Exotics from
many distant & diferent parts of the World = The youngest Daughter,
the Next and the Next were alternatively Introduced to me, and as it
was too Early to Dine, a proposition to go to the Botanic Garden was
offered and accepted Imediately. Mr Roscoe & I rode there and I was
shewn the whole with great attention — A Gentleman Botanist Guided

18. Audubon met a Mr. Leacock, a visiting English gentleman and naturalist, in Natchez on
November 3, 1822. Leacock advised Audubon to take his drawings to England but warned that
several years would pass before he could make himself known there.

us and Called name succeeding name, all we ask^d == The Hot house were in fine order and I saw here many of my Country's Growth. — This Garden is level, well Drawn and well Kept. The season is rather advanced to say that I saw it with all its advantages. —

Now Mr Roscoe is Driving me in what he Calls his Little Carr, but the Horse is so much less than what I Conceived needed to pull it along with his master in, that I was quite surprised to see the Pony trot with both of us with apparent ease — Mr Roscoe is, my Dear Friend, One of those Commatable persons that are Just what is necessary for me to have to talk to — He is plain, kind and prompt at bringing ease in his company —

Again in his charming *Laboratoire* — I look throw Windows that emcompass one full third of the oval into a neat little Garden — A Glass of good wine is offered. It is Drank and the Large Port Folio is again in sight —

I am not going to trouble thee again by enumerating — the numbers — Generas — species — varieties or Sexes. No. I will put all that aside — but I will remark to thee that one of the Daughters is an Artist herself[19] and that She examined (I thought) the form of my poor Head more Closely than Doctor Harlan[20] did when he wish[ed] to convince me that I was by no means a fool.

It is rather an uncomfortable situation for a Man to be anatomised by a handsome young Lady that has Two eyes that say more at sight than all the Books I ever read, put together — however, I found her extremely *aimiable and full of the Wish to Improve*. Now, do not think I am going to be rude — I neither mean to say her person or manners, no, merely her manner of painting flowers — She ask^d many advises and I gave them to her with all my heart —

19. Alice Ford's supposition is probably correct that this is rather Roscoe's daughter-in-law (*Journal*, 100n10). Margaret Lace Roscoe (1786/87–1840), wife of Edward Roscoe (1785–1834), was an accomplished botanical illustrator. Her *Floral Illustrations of the Seasons* was engraved by Robert Havell, Jr. (London, 1829). She dedicated this work to her father-in-law, William Roscoe, signing herself as "Your affectionate Daughter."

20. Audubon met Dr. Richard Harlan (1796–1843) in Philadelphia in 1824. Harlan tried to support Audubon there and did not join George Ord and others opposing him. Harlan's *Fauna Americana* (Philadelphia, 1825) was criticized for its errors but made original contributions to the emerging natural sciences in America. Audubon seems to allude to a moment of phrenological encouragement from the physician.

Mr Roscoe is anxious I Should do well. I handed a packet of Letters that he patiently read throw — He says that he will try to Introduce me to Lord Stanley.[21]

"Indeed."

Ah, yes, Lucy, this is nearing the Equator fast — In a word he assured me that nothing would be left untried to meet my wishes, but, said the venerable good Gentleman, "Lord Stanley is rather shy" = "however."

It was near 9 o'clock when I left my Drawings at his House and him also. I spent there what I denominate an agreable Day. The Ladies assisted all to bring me somewhat at Home — and thou Knowest well how powerfull *Ladies* are —

The old Gentleman was left alone. The Two youngest Daughters went south, and the Eldest, her husband and I West — talked of America — Localities, Improvem[ents] Politics &^{c} and I am in Dale Street again where I find the following Polite Note from —

"Mr Martin from the Liverpool Royal Institution will do himself the pleasure to wait upon Mr Ambro tomorow at 11 o'clock" —

If that Gentleman had not Missed one Letter, or if He by putting an *i* between the R and the O had made my name Ambrio, it would have been *almost Correct* — and very much more appropriate, I am sure — but no matter, I excuse the Gentleman, he means well — and I, my Beloved, Dearest Friend, wish thee well also —

LIVERPOOL JULY 28TH 1826. —

Dearest Friend, I left my lodgings this morning to ransack this City in search of *Pastells*. I have a great wish to present the Hospitable and aimiable Mrs Rathbone with a small Drawing, as a Small token of the Gratitude that I shall for ever hence feel for them — I had walk^d the principal Busy streets and Inquired at all the Booksellers I saw, for the materials wanted — had visited even what is Called here the Artist's Repository, and was returning full of Disapointment when I met ~~~~ Mr A. Gordon again = I was on the point of passing by, so shy am I of

21. Edward George Geoffrey Smith Stanley, fourteenth Earl of Derby (1799–1869), had traveled in Canada and the United States shortly before Audubon arrived in Liverpool; at this time Stanley also was serving as MP for the borough of Stockbridge but in later decades would become prime minister three times. He was a passionate sportsman and accomplished in the classical and several European languages.

those who do not meet me with open Heart and Friendship = but the thought that Ann Gordon was thy Sister — that once she resembled thee in kindness, that I had passed the Happiest portion of my Life with ye all, when yet we were all children, vibrated my Heart Strings and I presented my Hand to him; — related my having Called, — my Disapointment and, no, I did not say Surprise — the word might have been Irritation — but I repeated the great anxiety I had felt to see M͏ͬͩͫ͏ Gordon — I did not say as I allways was wont to say, *Sweet sister Ann* — and when and where could I meet her? *Tomorow*: ah, why Tomorow? Because she is engaged to go out and So am I — Shall I then see her again — look at her fair Heart throw her glowing Eyes. Oh, yes, I Hope it. —

A full Grown man with a scarlet vest & Breeches, Black stockings & shoes for the Coloring of his front, and a blue Long Coat Covering his shoulders, back & &ᶜ's reminds me somewhat of our *Summer Red Birds* (*Tanagra Rubra*).[22] Both species attract the eye a like, and since here my Eye has been by them frequently attracted — It is probable they are Tanagers but the Scientific appellation is yet unknown to me. —

There are many orange women[23] in this City. I will Describe them as quickly as possible. —

They Sell sweets during the Day, and Poison During the Night. —

At Eleven or there about Mͬ Martin (who I expect is Secretary to the Royal Institution) called and arranged in my presence a notice directed to the members &ᶜ of the Institution announcing that I would exibit them [my Drawings]⁺ There during Monday Tuesday and Wednesday following for Two hours each morning. —

The time felt heavy and I took the liberty of Calling on M͏ͬͩͫ͏ Rathbone — I knew her husband was much engaged with his Business and to have gone to his counting [MS: compting] house would have been Absurd in me — Then I paid my respects to this Lady. I found her engaged putting away in a little Square Box the parts of a Dissected

22. Audubon conflates two species that he depicted in *The Birds of America* plates: Plate XLIV, the "summer red bird," is identified as *Tanagra aestiva*; Plate CCCLIV, the scarlet tanager, is identified as *Tanagra rubra*. The scarlet tanager is the more boldly colored of the two.

23. "Orange woman" was a gentleman's euphemism for "prostitute," reflecting a common transition from poor street merchant to prostitute.

mass with which she, *Edgeworth Like*,[24] had been *transmiting knowledge with pleasure*. The Calmness of her countenance proved the ease she possesses in thus educating her children and I ~~~~ thought of thee at Henderson! M̃ʳˢ R. Imediately produced paintings on Talk — They were new. — The Port Folio of Prints was examined, but I often raised my eyes to examine the Pictures on the walls hung in chains from the ceiling. This was also new — I saw her portrait when younger — that of her good husband, Mother & Father — I saw her children coming one by one in the room and I kissed the Youngest =

"This is a minute description; however, I would not expect one more so of a non Descript Bird of thine."

This is not a Non Descript but it belongs to that rare Genus *amability real*. I would have remained longer but . . . — I returned a great round about way to this little room and found on my Table the following note —

"Mr. Rathbone[25] presents his compliments [MS: compts] to M̃ʳ A and begs leave to remind him of his engagement to dine with him to day at six o'clock. He has made an other Effort for D̃ʳ *Traill*[26] and has a Brother in law dining with him who resides in London & who he hopes may be usefull to M̃ʳ A. there. He ventures therefore to request M̃ʳ A to bring a *few* of his Drawings with him. Bedford S̃ᵗ, Abercromby Square, Friday Morning" —

So it seems that I must feel awkward once more? — Well, it is for my Friend and my Children's Sakes — From the tenor of the Note I took for granted that *Only a few* Drawings were wished to be look̃ᵈ at and fearing to act a miss I pack̃ᵈ up only a few —

24. Maria Edgeworth (1768–1849) was known as an educationist and novelist. With her father she coauthored *Essays on Practical Education* (London, 1798); her novels, for which she preferred the term "moral tales," are regularly didactic in purpose.

25. William Rathbone, the brother of Richard Rathbone, had married Elizabeth Greg, eldest child of Samuel Greg, in 1812. When Audubon first enters their home, he sees their eldest daughter, Elizabeth (who would later marry John Paget, a future magistrate of London, in 1839), and their second daughter, Hannah Mary (1816–72) (who would marry John Hamilton Thom in 1838).

26. Dr. Thomas Stuart Traill (1781–1862) was an Edinburgh-trained physician practicing in Liverpool, where he also pursued his scientific interests. He joined William Roscoe and other prominent businessmen and physicians to advance the arts and sciences in Liverpool, involving himself in both the Liverpool Literary and Philosophical Society and the Royal Institution.

I am Rolling in a Hackney Coach towards Abercromby Square. The weather is pleasant and warm for this Country —

I have entered a Parlour and find at her work a very handsome Daughter of Wm Rathbone perhaps 13 years of age and one much younger — I peep at the neat garden and at the prints beautifully framed with oak borders and Cast my Eyes from the Declaration of *Our Independence* on the good face of *Charles Fox*[27] that now fronts me and is on the Chimney mantle — Mrs Rathbone enters as if she had known me for years: "Set down. Mr R. will be here directly, how do you Like our Country" &^c &^c and she also sets at her work, how extremely Kind and Polite — I suspect that good Richard R. has told them of my *Mauvaise honte,* and she wishes to save me from the feeling — I thank them both — The Conversation opens on America — my travels &^c, Gentlemen gradually accumulate, Mr Rathbone is very kind and once more Lucy there are my Drawings —

The Dinner is announced. Mrs R. presents her hand to me (and it was fortunate that she was this kind for I was Standing Like an Ass). We walk to Dinner — The Gentlemen did not reach the Dining room for some moments and I blushed thinking that they had remained to Coment on poor me =

The Conversation was a long time kept up on the subject of *Hunter*[28] who says (and it may be very true) that he had spent nearly all his life

27. Charles James Fox (1749–1806) was a member of Parliament who switched from the Royalist Party to the Whigs and in March 1775 openly opposed the punitive taxation without representation of the American colonies. His political ideals were known to be in sympathy with those of the Declaration of Independence.

28. John Dunn Hunter (1798–1827) became internationally famous as a former white captive among Native Americans following the publication of *Manners and Customs of Several Indian Tribes Located West of the Mississippi; Including Some Account of the Soil, Climate, and Vegetable Productions, and the Indian Materia Medica: To Which Is Prefixed the History of the Author's Life During a Residence of Several Years among Them* (Philadelphia: J. Maxwell, 1823). This narrative argues for alternatives to the extirpation of Native Americans and offers detailed accounts of native culture that expose shortcomings of European and American cultures. Subsequent editions followed quickly, including translations into Dutch, German, and Swedish. Hunter was lionized in the leading cities of the United States, Britain, and France. His authenticity was passionately debated, but many of the most influential believed his story. Audubon would have been nervous in such conversations, especially just after his arrival in England, because of his problematic birth and his claim that he had studied in France under Jacques-Louis David, a claim that has been discredited by biographers.

with the Indians — The pros & cons were debated gently, but I felt very uncomfortable during the while as I dreaded that the *suspicion* that I might prove an Impostor was at hand —

M![r] Hogdson[29] to whom I had a letter from M![r] Nolte[30] was particularly kind to me and, when the Dinner was over, he took me aside, ask[d] for the Letter and spoke of doing all in his power for me — He wished me to See Lord Stanley &![c] &![c]. The Young Swiss, whom I now wish thee to know by the name of *Intelligent*, Came — The English Company appear[d] desirous I should succeed in England — The Intelligent Swiss wishes me not to Loose my Time here but proceed to Paris Imediately ═ Whilst this is going on a Number of Prints, Paintings and Books are laid on the table — Charles Bonaparte['s] Work was "much admired" (I was Politely told) "untill My Work came in sight." Every person is kind to me, particularly those who have Visited America. —

I just heard the House Clock count [MS: compt] 10 (for I dread[d] pulling out my watch) ═ My *Port feuille* is taken by a servant — M![r] James Pyke and me are moving from Mount Pleasant towards Dale Street — M![r] Pyke is a Gentleman of Merit I am sure; he speaks Well — and is altogether good Breeding —

I pull a shilling for the servant, take my *Port Feuille* — walk[d] 3 sets of stairs and here I am. —

What many reflections encumber my mind — Would it be possible that I should not in any Degree Succeed, I can scarcely think so. Ah, Delusive Hope, how much further wilt thou lead me? —

Farewell, Friend of my Heart, and ye, my Dear Sons, all good night — How I long to hear of you all —

29. Adam Hodgson was a partner in the firm Rathbone, Hodgson and Company in Manchester. Curiously, Audubon apparently confided in Hodgson that he had been born in Haiti: "He is an European by birth (or rather an Haytian of European Parents)" (see app. B).

30. Vincent Nolte (1779–1853) was a much-traveled Italian-born German merchant who lived many years in New Orleans. In his fascinating memoir, *Fifty Years in Both Hemispheres or, Reminiscences of the Life of a Former Merchant* (New York: Redfield, 1854), Nolte includes an entertaining account of his August 1811 chance meeting with Audubon at the falls of the Juniata River in Pennsylvania as well as an account of how he headed off an attempted manipulation of the cotton market in 1825–26, which much endeared Nolte to the Rathbones and Gregs of Manchester.

I arose this morning full of the Hope that I would receive a sweet Kiss from thy Sister and — no — I was not altogether Disapointed = I walked about the City a while, Visited M͟r Hunt,[31] the Best Landscape Painter of this City. I examined much of his work, found some Beautiful pieces, representations of Wales's Scenery = I visited the Royal Institution to Judge of the Light, anxious to have all the advantages necessary to a man of my humbility of Powers; and by a great round about way (to come at the precise apointed hour, say 12) I reach͟d M͟rs Noble's House, Norton Street, London Road [MS: Rode] and knock͟d — A Coarse female answered to my question that M͟rs Gordon was *In* — ah!! at Last I am again within a few Paces of — yes — of — a kind of Likeness of thee =

I sat a while *below stairs* — then a while *above stairs*, and (for time ripens all things) I saw and kiss͟d thy Syster Ann — Gordon — I kissed her I thought more than She wished; at all events, *She* did not kiss me. (I was going to write *never* but that would have been as false as any thing could possibly be.) However, she became more sensible that I was yet Audubon; perhaps too recollected that I never Injured her. Perhaps indeed she might have recollected that I allways loved her as *my Sister*: whatever might be her present reasons, she *returned* to old Times with more familiarity than I Expected = She talk[ed] a good deal — and I did also = Still I thought and think still, and perhaps may think for ever, that She had acquired a great deal of the Scotch stiffness, so well exibited *towards me* at a *Particular house in Louisianna*, that I dare say thou knowest quite as well as *I do* —

"Yes, Indeed, a hundred Times better." —

I heard a great Deal that I will not mention now — I believe thy sister, or my sister, or Our Sister, (I am a poor one at discriminating) was *rather* surprised that I should have been so well treated by Mess͟rs Rathbone, Roscoe, and Hodgson: we talk͟d altogether of *my Concept*, but I watch͟d my *slipery Tongue* that Doctor Pascallis[32] called *Candid*

---

31. Andrew Hunt (1790–1861) moved to Liverpool in 1817. He worked as a drawing instructor and was noted for his views of Cheshire and North Wales.

32. Félix Pascalis-Ouvrière (1762–1833) was a French-born physician who had practiced

but the word is very unfashionable I am assured. Indeed, to be Candid is quite *Burlesque I am also Told,* so that I tried to be somewhat fashionable also — much, I assure thee, against my Heart = but the World Dictates and man must follow the mandate —

We had in Company a Miss *Donathan.* Very Like our Jonathan, is it not? —

"No, Indeed" —

This was a good Looking young woman — Her Hair was beautifully Clean, Well put up to attract, and of a fine light tint much estimed by Sully's Pencil[33] —

"Now, what is all this Stuff about Sully's Pencil?" —

Stuff — It is hair I am speaking of — yet of that light silky hue between ~~~~ The sun is just going down beyond a church that breakes my horizon [MS: orison] most disagreably, yet the clouds about the Sun set, are much like the young Miss Donathan's Hair in Coloring. I cannot at present give any other description, the sun Dazle's me so =

Now do not stare nor start — There's no snake in thy way — I am merely Invited to dine with Mr A. Gordon and sister (yes, I will call her so) Ann — I have been 9 Days in England, slept each night within ½ mile of thy sister, and this day I first saw her. Yet Mr A. Gordon knew well where I reside — but the Scotch Caracter does not admit *Friendship Free* = No, I can swear it by a Long Course of Circumstance too Tedious to be repeated (but well known to thee in my 19th N^o of this my Poor Book) — I left after a good long visit of one and half hour — and I am again gazing to the right and left in the Streets of Liverpool. Two tall men are walking just before me — both wearing Black Epaulets made, I believe, of course Cotton yarn — They both have round Hats and a Coccade of the same materials that dance about their shoulders. — Each is tightly buttoned from the chin to the abdomen

medicine on Saint-Domingue until 1793, when a slave revolt caused him to move to Philadelphia. He published two books on the causes and treatment of yellow fever. Audubon mentions him as an acquaintance who met him in New York City upon his return to America from Europe on May 5, 1830 (Buchanan, *Life and Adventures,* 159).

33. Thomas Sully (1783–1872) was born in England and in 1792 relocated with his family to the United States, where he became one of the most accomplished portraitists of the nineteenth century. In 1824 Audubon briefly studied oil painting with Sully in Philadelphia.

in a surtout all Black that nearly reaches their heels — What corps do
they belong? — Ah! — Here is one of the same make Dressed alike
&^c Holding the Door of a Fine Carriage open whilst two handsome
females are getting out of it help^d by a Gentleman — Now I know the
regiment. —

The Carriages here are Generally handsome and Drawn by well
made fat Horses — It is not rare to see setting by the side of the
Coachman a Waiting Maid full as handsome as any portion of the
whole Establishment and Two Waiters or Vallets behind the Carriage in
a chaise attached to it —

I was shock^d this very morning to see in the Barouche of a Wealthy
Banker a young Lady tormenting a beautifull Goldfinch in chains —
How diferent the feelings of that young Lady, or the feelings of her
parents must be, from the noble sentiment of Tristram Shandy's Uncle
Toby![34] —

I have not found the population of Liverpool as dence as I expected,
and except during the Evenings (that do not commence before 8 at
this season) I have not been at all annoyd by the Elbowings of the
greater numbers that I still remember having seen in my youth in the
Largest Cities of France = Some shops [MS: chops] here (for the term
is more appropriate than in America) are beautifully supplied. They
are generally lined with two sets of purchasers, mostly Ladies, seated
and chusing the articles wanted — I compted in one of these chops 16
Gentleman attendants behind the counters [MS: Comptors] =

The New Market is in my Opinion an Object worth the attention of
all foreign travelers [MS: Travellers Strangers] — It is thus far the finest
I ever have seen — It is a large, high and Long building divided into 5
spacious avenües, each containing their specific commodities — I saw
here — Viands of all Description — Fishes, Vegetables, Game, Fruits
both Indigenous and Imported from all quarters of the World — Bird
sellers with even Little collections of stuffed specimen — cheese
of enormous Sizes, Butter in full aboundance — superior freshness
& quality along with Immense Crates of Hen's Eggs laying upon &

34. Tristram Shandy's Uncle Toby is famously the most sentimental character in Sterne's
Tristram Shandy. He would not kill a fly: "This world is surely wide enough to hold both thee and
me" (vol. 3, chap. 4).

between Layers of oats straw Imported from Ireland — 25 for one shilling.

This market is so well Lighted with Gass that at 10 o'clock this Evening I could plainly see the Colors of the Irids of Living Pigeons in Cages —

The whole City is lighted with Gass — Each shop has one of those brilliantly Illuminating fire[s], in each window and many about the Room — Fine Cambrics can be look^d at by good Judges —

Mr A. Hodgson Called on me this day and I am to Dine with him Monday — He has written to Lord Stanley about me — He very kindly ask^d if my time passed heavily, gave me a Note of admittance for the Athenium and told me that he would do all in his power for me = I saw Mr Wm Rathbone on change[35] —

I dined at the Inn to day for the second time only since my arrival here, but I imediately remarked that almost every Individual at table knew me and I was treated with attention & Respect — An American Gentleman told me this Evening that when I retired, the principal number evinced a Great desire of se[e]ing my Work and that they would go to the Royal Institution every day during my Exibition there —

I was peaceably writting all this when a knock at my Door required my ra[i]sing to go and unfasten it (a precaution I take allways when I retire for the night) and saw Cap^e Joseph Hatch of the Delos — This reminded me imediately of my having walk^d to the Vessel this afternoon and given some Silver Change to the honest Crew to Drank freely of the good Ale of England — but Cap^e Hatch told me a sad piece of news: he has lost his pocket Book this morning with about 30 £, the Register of his Vessel and sundry papers besides — He appeared much aflicted, but I could do nothing for him — He left me at Eleven o'clock — Mrs Brown of Natchez arrived this Day in the Hugh Wallace [MS: Valace] — The noise in the street is rather subsiding — Good night, Lucy. God Bless thee, Good night.

LIVERPOOL JULY 30TH 1826. SUNDAY. — ENGLAND —

It is Sunday again, but not a dull one — no. There are certainly exceptions to all rules. — I have become better acquainted here — do

---

35. "On change" was a common expression for being at the exchange.

not look on every object about me with the stranger's stare and — I went to the Church of the Asylum of the Blind[36] — I have just returned and I write because it is a pleasant Sunday altogether with me —

Follow Dale Street North E[a]st all its Length, keep Inclining to the right untill you come opposite the Islington Market and continue to where you see the asylum itself = The church is then near you — Ascend a few steps of cut stones after passing the Iron barred gate — Walk under the colonade, pay what ever you please *over* a six pence to either of the collectors at the Inner Door and if you are *a man* pull off your Hat — Then Look at the Large Picture of Christ freeing the Blind — It is the Copy of the *Great original Charity*. Follow in the midle aisle an assistant — He opens a Pew and you set on a clean well stuffed Surge Cushion — under which place your coverhead[37] — and Look around before the Service begains — A well proportioned oblong square is the structure general — A nich contains the Picture of Christ — 10 light Colums support the flat Ceiling Imitative of marble — A fine Organ with Brass Barrels is placed over the Entrance in a kind of upper Loby that also Contains the Blind Musicians — The windows are large. The glass of each pain is ground rough (not to Distract the mind by admiting of outward objects). Congregational attendants gradually fill the whole. — All is silent. Yes, silent —

The mind is filled with heavenly subjects and thoughts (I mean of Course the mind of nonsinners). The Two pulpits garnished with Purple Velvet seem to be all that is Luke warm here. — hark!!!! —

Angelically the Sound Imitative of music Sublime & Heavenly gradually glides Into your whole Composition untill by the exertive Powers of achords a general Chorus is produced Imbibing an Idea of the Sounds of the Trumpets of Resurection — My frame shook — not with fear, no — with a wish that I might feel the sensation oftenner —

The rites proceed — and female voices Divine open an Anthem Intrusted by the Creator to Hayden!! Ah, Celestial Sounds!!! — No, it is Impossible for me to describe them.

36. Liverpool's Blind Asylum, or School of Industry for the Indigent Blind, was established in 1791 and in 1826 housed approximately one hundred "blinds," as Audubon typically referred to them. Compare the French *les aveugles*. The painting titled *Charity* remains unidentified.

37. With "coverhead" Audubon once again translates literally from the French: a *couvrechef* is a head covering, typically a cap, bonnet, or piece of fabric, not a rigid hat.

A good Excellent service is mixed with this to Entice the mind and Imagination to refrain from Evil doings. Prayers are read and musically Echoed by the Blind — and — each person gently raises — walks out lightly and not untill entirely out from the Colonnade do you hear the sound of a single voice. — I give it here as my opinion of my best recollection that I never before this day saw *Devotion in a Church*. I know *Thou* understands me well —

The Reverend Wm Goddard took me to some Institutions of children on the Lancastrian System,[38] where the whole appeared well dressed, Clean, and completely systematic =

During this morning I saw long files of youths of Both sexes marching the streets on their return from devotion — Nothing except the tread of the feet on the Pavement could be heard —

I reach^d Norton Street, at half past 3 in a Coach and found Mr Gordon in the setting room upstairs — I [was] met very diferently I am sure — He praised my work and said that he was glad that I came to England — &^c

I was struct with Ann Gordon asking me if thou wert as fond as ever of Dr Dewer[39] — Our Conversation, however, was principally on science — (that is, their Conversation.) Miss Donathan reminded me much of the Eldest Daughter of Thomas Sully — We had a comfortable familly Dinner, Walk^d to the Botanic Garden with thy sister under my arm — How little did I expect when at Fatland Ford[40] in America that I should ever be in the Like situation — Mr Gordon ask^d me many questions about Charles Bonaparte and Joseph[41] — Also — offered

38. The Lancasterian system for educating young people was devised by Joseph Lancaster (1778–1838), who was born into the slums of London but in his teens demonstrated the capability of his system to educate large numbers of students efficiently and at very little cost. Eventually, the Anglican Church opposed this system because it gave children ideas above their station in life.

39. Alice Ford speculated that Dr. "Dewer" here is an error for Dr. "Dowe," to whom Audubon refers in the August 5 entry as having been a friend in Natchez. The manuscript "Dewer" is clear.

40. Fatland Ford is the name of the Bakewell family property, where Lucy Bakewell lived when Audubon first met her.

41. Following the banishment of the Bonapartes from France in 1816, Joseph Bonaparte (1768–1844), elder brother of Napoleon and one-time king of Spain, settled into the estate Point Breeze near Bordentown, New Jersey, on the Delaware River. Joseph was also the father-in-law of Charles-Lucien Bonaparte, the ornithologist, whom Audubon knew well.

me some Letters for London and we parted more as I wished than I expected — Ann recomanded my hair to be cut and a Coat Cut fashionably. Mr G. and Miss D. appear^d *brotherly* and *sisterly* kind to *each other* =

LIVERPOOL ENGLAND JULY 31$^{\underline{ST}}$ 1826. —

This day, Lucy, was one of Trial to me, believe Thy Friend — This was Monday and it was appointed to exibit partially my Collection to the Public and my kind Liverpool Friends — At 9 this morning I was quite Busy — arranging and disposing in sets my Drawings to be fairly Inspected by the Public — The Connaisseurs — the Critics — This last word has something very savage in its nature as well as in its orthography or pronunciation — I know not why — Yet, I know that I dread the very cast, askance, of a single eye of those dangerous personnages of whom I have so much heard of, but whom fortunately thus farr I have only met in scanty forms — and of little value. —

I drew my new watch and by its regular movements in 5 minutes it proved to be at the meridian — The Doors of the Royal Institution were thrown open and the Ladies flocked in. I however saw but one, Mrs R. Rathbone. There I was — all in view of the World — How many glances to meet — questions to answer and repeat = *"Ha that's Beautifull,"* again and again [re]peat^d made me wish to be in the Forests of America [MS: American] to be able myself to say at meeting a new Specimen = *Ah! how beautifull!!* — The time past, however — My Drawings were on the Floor and a Gentleman walking up directly towards me said "Sir, did you Ever reside in New York" — I answered "Yes, Sir" — "Pray, Sir, did you Mary a Miss Bakewell?" — Now, to this, answer thy own self? — This proved to be a Mr Jackson who lived at Bloomingdale near Mr Thomas Kinder[42] and who knew thee well for he said — *"Your Lady was very handsome"* — Yes, he might say that — but he said Imediately "Your Drawings are charming." — I could have slap$^{\underline{d}}$ the man for bringing my paltry Pictures with thy face all of a breath = but it is past 2 — the Doors are Closed and I run to my chamber to Dress a little, and wait for Mr Adam Hodgson. = Four o

42. The brothers Thomas and Arthur Kinder were New York merchants with whom Thomas Bakewell, Lucy's brother, occasionally had business dealings.

Clock, half past four. I am Looking from my window for his gig. — Is it him? Let me see. — Aye — that it is! = My Port Folio is under my arms and 3 by 3 I Leap down the stairs — shake the friendly hand and am seated on his left, moving toward his cottage = I am sorry I cannot paint portraits — I would represent to thee, the meekness of his Blue Eyes — his sweetness of Language — his comely movements: but, my Dear Lucy, thou knowest this: in all my attempts I never yet reach^d the original — We are going, talking about me, thee — and Ours; and — the Little poney has stop^d — I am out of the Little Chair — and conducted into a neat *English* setting Room. — Wert thou not an English Lady Born thyself, I would Describe this and, as being considered by myself a fair specimen, really scientifically. — but — I will merely say — it was beautifully snug and had Ghothic windows, throw which the Eye was freely permitted to extend its desires over an uncommon extent of Picturesque scenery. — "Mrs Hodgson, Mr Audubon, My Dear" — a fairly, Tall, Young female, with the freshness of Spring, entered the room and wish^d me welcome with an air of placid contentedness — Nay, not *even my Eye* would deny to mean, Letter *after* Letter, all that was spoken. —

We Dined! — Lucy, like at Home. — These good people gave me in perfect friendship Lessons of English Politeness = I spoke plainly about my Past diferences of Conditions to Mr H. — and moved from the Dining, into the setting room, rather after the setting of the Sun =

We had 4 Visitors: a Cap^e Somebody, his Lady and son — and a pert young Woman, the name of which I do not care half so much about as I do for those of the others, but I must let them all go bye as my poor head will not remember names (unless they may chance to be Friends names.)

The calmness existing in the Country soon reach^d my heart and soon did I contemplate such Scenery in Imagination in America = I thought of such an Evening walking gently arm in arm together towards the watters of the Bayou Sarah to watch thee Bathe thy gentle form in its current. I thought of the Happiness I have enjoyed whilst gazing on the Happy Couple before me. I thought! — ah, my Dearest Friend. Mr Hodgson asks me if I will retire to rest or Lessen to his usual habit of reading prayers to his Little Flock and servants — I prefer^d the Latter, and silently mute, each bent on Devotion prayed with this good Man. —

The "Good Night" is expressed and a sweeter *good night* I never lessen[d] to except indeed when ~~~~. Wouldst Thou like to see the little room where I am going to spend my few hours of Bodily Rest. — It also has a Ghothic Window — My Kind Host opens it at my request — Before it a Table covered with all the Implements necessary to render the Body Clean & comfortable Lay — and I can see the Particular Shape of my Poor head fully in a Large Mirrow before me —

The Bed was made as if by Thyself —

I do not remember the rest. I went to sleep thinking of thee —

I arose to listen to the Sound of an English Black Bird perhaps just as the day broke — It was a little after 3 of the morning. I dressed and as silently as in my power (carrying My Boots in one hand and the House key in another) moved down the stairs and out of the Cottage and pushed off toward the fields and meadows — I walk[d] a good Deal, went to the sea Shore, saw a Hare — and returned to M[r] A. Hodgson to Breakfast, after which and many Kind Invitations to make it my Home, I bid them farewell, and drove by their servant in the little Carriage drawn by the little poney reach[d] Dale Street a little after 8. =

I imediately went to the Institution — At 12 the Assemblage was great — I saw D[r] *Trail* and many other persons of Distinction = Several persons whom I believe are attached to that Institution wished that I should be remunera[ted] by exibiting them for Money, an offer of the Room proposed to me Gratis &[c] — but my heart revolted at the thought and although I am poor Enough, God Knows, I could not think of doing such a thing consistantly with the Station that I wish to preserve — forwarded I may say from America with Letters of our most Eminent men, to Eminent and kind persons in this Country, who all have received and honored me Highly by personnal attentions. I could not (I repeated it) think it consistant to become a mere *Show Man* and give up the Tittle of *J. J. Audubon Naturalist*: Many were in favor of my principles but more against them — I called on M[r] Gordon and was glad to see that he thought as I did. The Intelligent Swiss was also on my side. — I saw at the Institution some ladies from Natchez that had known us there but I did not —

I spent the Evening with thy sister and Mr Gordon — I felt extremely fatigued both head and Body and at 10 o'clock bid thee Good night —

AUGUST 2$^{\underline{D}}$ 1826.

I put up this Day 225 of my Drawings and the *Coup D'oeil*[43] was not bad — The Room was Crowded — Old Mr Roscoe did me the Honor to Come and presented me to Mr Sigismondé of Geneva.[44] I was Introduced to Mrs Barclay, Mrs Trail — Mrs Martin — the Miss Hodgson's, Quakeress's — and I dare say one hundred besides — *Ann*, Mr Gordon and Miss Donathan came =

I had sent a note to Mrs Rathbone to acquaint her of the extra number of Drawings in View — but she had removed to *Green Banks* and sent me a note —

I Consulted her good Husband about the Exibition. He was against it — Dr Trail in favor, Mr *Roscoe in favor* — I consulted Mr A. Hodgson, against it. — Now I concluded to drop the Idea Entirely — collect my Letters for London and go there as quick as Possible =

I remitted my Letters to Mr Ramsden of this City and saw Mr Booth of Manchester who promised me all his assistance —

I went to Mr Roscoe Cottage during a Heavy Drizle and returned by 7. An American Gentleman of Charlestown, S. C. ask^d me to go to the Theatre and I went — I was anxious to see the renowned Miss Foote[45] =

We had been seated for some time — The piece had begun when who should enter the Box — Ah, yes, who should enter the Box? — Ann. Sweet sister Ann — Mrs G. and Miss D =

Miss Foote *has been* pretty, nay handsome, nay Beautifull! but she *has been* ~~~~

The play was good, the playhouse very Bad — Thy Sister, Miss Donathan, Mr G. Shook hands with me, and my compagnion and I

43. *Coup d'oeil*, "glance," or, in this context, "appearance," "visual effect."

44. Jean-Charles-Léonard Simonde de Sismondi (1773–1842) was a Swiss historical economist whose family had fled the Continent following the French Revolution.

45. Maria Foote (1797–1867) was an actress from a theatrical family. More noted for her looks than her acting ability, she was very popular and toured widely throughout England, Scotland, and Ireland. In 1831 she married Charles Stanhope, fourth Earl of Harrington.

moved towards our lodgings — I feel very wearied. It is past 12 o'clock. God Bless Thee, good night —

My head is very much like a distracted Hornet's Nest — I am fatigued, nay, harassed — and with all satisfied and *Almost Happy*. —

Thou seest that I was not at my usual Lodgings last Night by the very date above — No, Indeed, I was not. My night was spent much more agreably, I assure thee, but before I speak of the night, it may be properer to write down an account of the day — It is long, My Dearest Friend, but not tedious — for I assure thee I shall say nought besides about Friendship like manners: —

My morning rolled off at the Institution — The Room was Crowded. 413 persons entered during Two hours — I was broke down Bowing & Scraping to all the new faces I was Introduced to — It was in a Word *a Business to Bow* =

A Certain somebody took it into its head to draw a Copy of one of my Non Descripts but the Door Keeper, an alert Scotchman, bafle[d] him in his attempt and tore his Sketch! —

M<u>r</u> A. Hodgson called on me — to Invite me to dine with Lord Stanley *tomorrow* in Companye of M<u>r</u> W<u>m</u> Roscoe S<u>r</u> — The Intelligent Swiss gave me a Letter to the Baron of Humbolt[46] from *M<u>r</u> Sismondi*, and shewed me a valuable set of Insects received from Thibet — This young Gentleman, Lucy, is Interesting beyond description. He repeated the polite Invitation of M<u>rs</u> Rathbone to go to Green Banks to spend the night — &<u>c</u> — I was engaged to take Tea at M<u>r</u> Roscoe and I went — M<u>r</u> Hodgson had Invited me to breakfast with him *this morning* so I was under the guard of three promises =

I had the pleasure of se[e]ing M<u>rs</u> W<u>m</u> Rathbone at the Institution — Perhaps never was a Woman better able to please and more disposed to do so than this very M<u>rs</u> W<u>m</u> Rathbone — I Looked at her Dark Eyes sparkling with all the Good Sense *a Man* can possess *with* a sensation the stronger felt as I was fully persuaded of the Candor that existed

46. Alexander von Humboldt (1769–1859) had become world famous for his adventurous five-year-long scientific expedition to South America (1799–1804) and for his account of it, *Relation historique du voyage aux régions équinoxiales du nouveau continent* (Paris, 1814–25).

about her. Well, I went — I mean in the afternoon, for During Dinner
Mr A. Hodgson Came to me with two Letters of recommendation *to
Two Noblemen*, the Copies of which will be Inserted here on the Day of
my Departure from Liverpool —

Well, then again I went to Mr Ed^d Roscoe[47] to drank Tea. —

"How didst Thou Go?"

How; a young son of Mrs Roscoe called in a Carr at the Institution. I
put up a few Drawings, and here we go to ~~~~ I have forgot the name
of the street and allmost the situation of the House, but, — Lucy, M^r
Ed^d Roscoe is a *Handsome* Agreable Man and his Lady is ~~~~ Come,
I dread to say too much about the Ladies of a Foreign Country, and yet
it is very hard for my slipery tongue not to say *Aimiable* after its having
Turned and Twisted itself more than Three Times I am sure within
my mouth *anxiously* bent on giving that Word — There was there
much Company, generally Ladies that draw well — also Two famous
Botanists who knew at once every plant or flower I exibited to them —
Having to walk to Green Banks (the Habitation, recollect, of Old M^{rs}
Richard Rathbone), I left Mr Roscoe at sun setting (which by the by
was Beautifull) and conducted by the young son again soon was put in
the road where we parted — The Evening was Calm and pleasant; as
I advanced into the Country Groupes of persons exercising Leisurely
met me — and some turn^d their heads to remark that Original me.
However, I passed again under the avenüe of Trees leading to Green
Banks and I am gently Knocking at one of the inner doors, my Hat
and Cane in one hand. Betwen the raps [MS: wraps] I give I pass my
Handkerchief over my face to take the Moisture occasion^d by a brisk
walk —

I can easily hear the mirth of many that I suppose on the Green
fronting the Building — I rap [MS: wrap] strong blows and the
Mother Rathbone meets me with "Oh, I am glad to see You." I was
not mistaken: the Green was Covered with beauty — Good sense and
pleasure — I was attracted mostly, however, at se[e]ing the Ladies with
bows and arrows shooting at a target perhaps 25 paces off =

It grows darker — I am seated between the Two M$^{[essrs]}$ Rathbone

47. Edward Roscoe, son of William Roscoe, was a merchant married to the illustrator
Margaret Lace Roscoe (see n. 19).

— I am sorry that my little friend Bazil has retired to repose — I would
have liked to Kiss him very much = The Father of Mrs Rathbone
ask^d many questions respecting the Religious Inclinations and rites of
Indians — spoke a good deal about American Trees — things quite
unknown here where there are no Trees larger than Common sapplings
in Louisiana — The Good Rich^d brings me a glass of wine. Miss Hanna
Maria Rathbone[48] has Just entered the saloon and comes towards me
with open hand and I press That hand with pleasure, I assure thee —
Yes, the Hospitable hand out to be pressed — The table was covered
with a profusion of Fruits and refreshments and every one amicably
help^d themselves. Ah! I hear the Clock strack 10: the Company leave
for their own Habitation and I am with the familly only = I wish to
see the New Work on the Birds of England[49] — I am guided into a
Drawing room and shewn it — Mr R^d R. ask^d if I am a musician — I
answer that I am fond [MS: found] of music — and my ear Is pleased in
a moment =

Now, Lucy, what thinks thou of all this? Is it not delightfully kind in
these good people to treat me so? — Oh, my Beloved Wife, my Eyes
were often on the eve of Sheding Tears of Gratitude and pleasure the
purest! —

I did not like the work I saw on Birds. I prefer greatly Thomas
Bewick[50] — *Bewick, Lucy, is the Willson of England.* I do not know how
to call the other — Indeed I find no name for him yet =

It is late. We all return^d to the parlour or Saloon = We are standing
up — A servant comes and offers to Draw my Boots — Draw my
Boots, yes — I could no more have [MS: has] sufered it than I could
have restrained from Estiming the familly Rathbone = not because I
had holy stockings on, no. My Stockings were not holy — but I thought
rude in their presence. —

Good night — Good night — to each and from each — R^d R.

48. The father of Mrs. Rathbone is Joseph Reynolds (b. 1768, d. after 1857), an ironmaster.
Miss Hannah Maria Rathbone is the sister of William and Richard Rathbone, daughter of the
elder Mrs. Rathbone, the "Queen Bee."

49. Prideaux John Selby (1788–1867) published his *Illustrations of British Ornithology* between
1821 and 1833. The 222 plates were mostly drawn and etched by Selby himself.

50. Thomas Bewick (1753–1828) was a wood engraver whose *History of British Birds* was
published in two parts, 1797 and 1804.

precedes me and I follow the gentle flights of stairs to a chamber where I am again shewn comfort — Mr R. takes me by both hands, desires me to make myself at home, and bids me good night — I wished to return his adieu with a "God Bless Thee, Good Man," but the words did not reach my lips in time — He was gone — and my heart felt the value of my wish as the wish returned to it to rest there forever! =

Farewell, Dearest Friend. To thee also I send from my heart a "God Bless thee" —

I hear the Clattering of Rain against my window — I am up, Dress^d and Walking throw the wet fields any where, every where — I see the Mersey, I reach it — The carriage is to be ready for me by 8 to go to A. Hodgson. I returned and the first object I see in the walk is Elder Mrs Rathbone reading a pamphlet of Sismondi on Religion. I accost her and she smiles Hapiness = I could have had hundred breakfasts had I accepted of one half of what was offered to me =

The Carriage is at the Door. I bid farewell and — "Mr Audubon, my Daughter will be glad of the pleasure of accompanying you if you have no Objection!" Objections! In a moment I see her Dark Eyes throw her veil, give her my hand and we are both seated in the Little carriage Called her own — The Mother smiles again, I bow — we are rolling off =

Two little Welch poneys that two common men could take up on their backs draw us beautifully — They are beautifully Grey and very well match[ed] — I examine the large buttons on the Livery Coat of the Driver, but I soon turn [from] them to remark the brillancy of Miss Rathbone's Eyes = She is very aimiable, indeed. ~~~~

"Now, Laforest, I never knew thee say that a Lady was not aimiable" —

No. Oh, I beg thy pardon, recollect Miss XX, Miss XX, Miss X, &^{c} &^{c}

"Ah, yes, I now remember well. What of Miss Rathbone?" —

She Inquires after thee and our children, talk of America again and again — and having reach^d the House of A. Hodgson, I press her hand again and she returns to Green Banks whilst I proceed into the Cottage (I speak, recollect, in England).

In a few minutes I see my kind Friends again — Enter the Breakfast Room and ~~~~ Mr Hodgson is reading Prayers — Breakfast^d —

Wrote a note to Wm Roscoe Esqr about [the] Lord Stanley meeting —
and towards Liverpool we are rattling at about a rate of 7 miles per hour.
It rains a little — I hold the umbrella — "Good bye." *Good bye* — I have
arrived and Mr H. goes to his compting house — He will call for me at
the Institution Tomorow at 12 precisely =

    I dined to day with Sister Ann and Miss Donathan, the Time there
quite agreable — Ann dislikes England and I Like it — I saw Dr Trail
at his House — Mr Hinks and perhaps 200 persons at the Institution
— bought an Umbrella for 16 shillings — saw a Boxing match — and
Good night, my Lucy — God Bless thee, good night —

LIVERPOOL AUG^T 5TH 1826. —

Fine Clear morning, weather somewhat resembling the 10th of March
with us — took my beneficial walk — and breakfasted as usual before
every one at the Inn, say 8 o'clock — Two hours Latter than we were
[MS: where] in the habit of doing at Natchez when the Good old Doct^{rs}
Dowe and Provan were pleased to Drank of our Coffee and eat of *Thy*
Toast — ah, America! —

    From the time I was up this morning untill the moment I reached
the Institution, my head was full of Lord Stanley and indeed so much
so that I believe thy sweet name did not come forth to my senses for
perhaps an hour at a Time — I am a very poor Fool, to be sure — to
be troubled and disturbed in mind at the Idea of meeting *an English
Gentleman* called *more over a Lord*! Yes, and particularly the biger
fool am I, as the English Lords are not only men Like others, but
are superior men, in manners, in Interests, in Kindness, to strangers
and generally the upholders of Science in their Country, but that
confounded feeling is too deeply rooted ever to be extricated from my
nature, and with a sense of Pity towards myself I must get more and
more accustomed to the disagreable thought of Dying with it —

    The Miss Roscoe's were at the Institution. I tell thee that because they
have spent 2 or perhaps 3 hours looking at my Drawings every day, I
believe, since exibiting. — How diferently they view them from what I
do. I wish to do more and am sick of those [al]ready made —

    Lucy, a lady came in (I mean at the Institution) having her younger
self at her side and handed me a parcel directed outside "Mr Audubon"
= Her eyes sparkled. They were Dark, and yet mild. —

"Ah, then, it was Mrs Wm Rathbone."

Yes, Lucy, it really was. It could be no other with such looks, believe me — I received the Packet with thanks for she told me it contained letters from her Husband for Persons in Manchester and other parts — I put it up and bid her farewell for the present — took a few rounds round the rooms and thought of opening the Parcel to read the names of the persons to whom the letters were directed to =

The parcel is open^{d}: a Pocket Book!! — My Heart Shook and the slenderest trendrels of it filld my Frame and Judgment with aprehensions — I trembled as I examined each Compartment Least it should contain more than Letters.

Gradually these feelings subsided and others Warmed me again — I Look^{d} on this Kindly token with affectionnate regard and Kissed it — in Devotion! — Ah, England, tis no wonder thy renown is spread afar, possessed as thou art of such real, Intri[n]sic worth: Lucy, I Kissed the Token again and I Hope thou shalt do the same =

Those are the moments of my Life, Dearest Friend, when filled with reciprocating Desire to please that I suffer so violently throw want of means — I would have given all I had to be so situated as to enable me to return something as Kind to this aimiable, accomplished Lady — There was *a Note* in the Book, yes, Lucy, a Note — beautifully written, well lettered and Dearer to me at that moment than all the Notes on the Bank of England! I Look^{ed} at the Book again and Twice again — and now that I am writting, it is so fixed on the Table before me that I can easily see it and guide my Penn. —

12 o'clock came. I was dressed according to my means i.e. Clearly decent — Mr A. Hodgson is come, the Port Folio N° 2 is pack^{d} up and not one Drawing is to be publickly seen at Liverpool — We are off towards the Cottage again — filled again with the Ideas of meeting a Lord (now, I would rather have been engaged in a Bear Hunt). I asked many questions to Mr H. to Enable me not to be too Rude to Lord Stanley — He very Kindly gave me all the information requisite and required — I am again setting just opposite his sweet Consort and he is tapping her rosy cheek amourously =

Thou knowest how? dost not thou? =

"Ah now, my Dear Laforest, Proceed" —

I wish I could but — well, I will proceed —

M⸢r⸣ H. requests me to Drank Two Glasses of wine — This good man enters in my feelings and down goes the wine —

"Sir, Lord Stanley"

Now, I have not the least doubt that if my head had been looked at, it would have been thought the Body Globularly Closed of one of our Largest Porcupines — All my Hair (and I have enough) stood straight on end [ms: hand] — Here he Comes! —

Tall — Well formed — formed for activity — simply dressed — well dressed — "Sir, I am glad to see You" =

Now, believe me, I was the glader of the Two to hear Lord Stanley thus adress Poor Audubon =

Drawings again — Lord Stanley is a great naturalist and it is Audubon who says it — "Fine" — "That is beautifull" — I saw Lord Stanley on his Knees looking at my Work! — There's for You, my Countrimen!! — What an Enormous Stupid Idea we have of an English Lord in America — Lucy, Lord Stanley is very Like Thomas Sully — He spoke the Truth, I mean — He remarked *a fault* in one of my Drawings and I thank⸢d⸣ him for that — He praised my Drawings highly and I bowed to him =

We are at Dinner and I Look at him closely, depend upon it — His Large undiscovered forehead would have suited D⸢r⸣ Harlan precisely to assure the Philadelphia Academy (of which I never will be a member)[51] that a conceptive natural power existed within that Cranium, and the acquired Protuberances over his Eye brows would also have proved to those same academician[s] (if they are not what I fear they are) the extent of his readings — speculative scientific powers and powers of exertions to acquire knowledge — I was friendlily requested to call on him in Grosvenor Street in Town (thus he Call⸢d⸣ London) — He shook hands in a friendly way Twice with me and mounting an Elegant Hunter moved off at the rate of 12 miles per hour! — I follow the Ridder — The Horse is Lost by the hight of the Hedges — I have Lost the sight of his white Hat — The servant is entirely lost to my View. =

"My Dear Friends, I must loose sight of you also" — I gaze upon

51. Audubon was, nevertheless, elected to membership in the Philadelphia Academy of Natural Sciences in 1831.

them — feel the pressure of their warm hearted hands and walk towards Liverpool —

I reached a New Cut street and Enquired to Know if it would lead towards Abercromby Square — "Yes, Sir" — Then I go, anxious as I am to thank Mrs Wm Rathbone for her Letters and Book =

I did reach her House — but having found her employed with her handsome Daughter, my Powers proved Inadequate and I stood or sat just like a fool again —

Oh, that I had been flogged out of this miserable way of feeling and acting when young —

Mr Rathbone came — Tea was on the Table — Cap^{e} Kirkland was announced and I look^{d} at the sweet children that were gamboling there in the Little Garden — Here enters the *Intelligent Swiss* — I take a full pinch of his Improved Snuff and we are all talking about Interesting Subjects (*of Course, not all at once as is done in some Countries, Latitude 30.*[52] *I will not mention the Longitude because from where I am it would require some calculation.*)

I must leave you all — Yes, I must — I must call on sweet Sister Ann — Good night — down Mount Pleasant — down Rodney Street — down Norton Street — It is Dark. I am obliged to walk up to the Door and seek with my Eye for the Numbers. = 4 — Two doors below — Here it is — I Knock — Now I know nothing about the proper ways of Knocking — but I Knock^{d} as properly as I knew how —

I found sweet sister Ann and her sweet companion busily engaged at *Saturday nights Work*. Lucy, Dear Friend, *Guess like a Yankee* what they are at — Cannot, hey! — Ah, Indeed! — Well be it so — I left them, went home — found my Birds in my Room sent from A. Hodgson = found my Eye lids drooping fast — wrote this in a Hurry and wish^{d} thee good night —

LIVERPOOL AUGUST 6TH SUNDAY 1826. —

When I arrived in this City, I felt dejected, yes, miserably so — The uncertainty of being Kindly received, of having my works approved of were all acting on Both my Physical and Mental Powers — I felt as

---

52. While latitude 30 passes, like all the others, around the planet, it is not insignificant that it passes directly through Bayou Sara in Louisiana, where Lucy Audubon was living.

if nutritive food was within my sight not to be touched — Now how diferently my sensations — I am well received where ever I am Known — Every object known to me smiles as I meet it — and my poor heart is at least relieved from the great anxiety that has for so many Years agitated it by thinking now that I have not work^d altogether in vain — That I may no Longer be postitively ashamed of the Productions of my Pencil (whatever may become of those of my Pen are yet very far in the distant ground, and I dread will never produce an Effect unless, indeed, it be a bad one, and then I doubt if speaking like an artist it would be effect at all) —

"Well, my Dear Laforest, these thoughts of Thine have been known to me these 10 Years at least. Give me, pray, thy day's Expenditure" —

Ah, Expe[n]diture — Let us see — Bed Last night 1 shilling, Breakfast 2 — Dinner 3. — Boots 6 pence — maids 6 pence — waiter nothing this day — wine Extra 3 shillings and 6 pence at the Blind asilum's church — That makes 10/6 — within 6 pence sterling of Two Dollars. I will manage Diferently when I reach *Town*, speaking as Lord Stanley and, I dare venture to say, many more Lords do without enumerating the Gentlemen that do so also — It is rather a High way of Living for *a Naturalist*; nay, Let me fully write *an author*! However, it is about the rate we pay at the Mansion house in Philadelphia — and the City Hotel in New York — It is, Indeed, less than in Washington City — [(]but to return to the true meaning of thy question for which I would give half my authorship to have it *Natura personnalis*)[53] I will say! Up early as usual and will not mention it again — Indeed, I must beg thy Pardon for thus miserably tormenting thy kind patience — Well, I went to church as thou seest per *Bill annexed*. Now there's mercantile stuff for thee — Bill annexed. Yes, many could I bring forward as *Living specimens*, I assure thee — but Let [us] go to church —

It was filled to a Crany — I had drop^d my six pence in the silver plate and had walk^d with that natural awkwardness that I possess so very Iminently smack into the Middle of the Centerial aisle, when so many female Constellations flashed on my staring Eyes that I stop^d — droop^d my head and waited patiently for events. — Now, do not believe that I was thoughtless [MS: thouthless], no Indeed — I really then thought

53. By *Natura personnalis* Audubon means of a personal nature or in person.

of thee, Dearest Wife — and wish^d thee at my Elbow to urge me and to, To — The Conductor walks up — takes Hold of my soiled Glove with his snow white hand and Leads me politely in the Pew Next to the Priest — The Music was exquisitely fine — I am rather a Judge, Thou Knowest that by my Ears. — but the sermon was not so — It was delivered by a *Closet Priest*. I mean by one who had not studied *Nature herself*, Beautifull Nature devoid of art — however, I understood that he was a young man of great promiss.

I Called on sister Ann and chatted some there. I understood she was writting to sister Eliza Berthoud[54] and it gave me a desire to write also — She had evinced a wish to see thy watch and I gratified her in that: — The more I see of Miss Donathan, the more I like her. She is very aimiable and not ugly, believe me — Mr Gordon had my Bonaparte's Birds carried to Dr Trail to whom I had promissed a view of it — I dined, as thou hast already been informed by Bill of Fare, at 2 o'clock in Company with the American gentleman of Charleston =

I remained Too long at table — I dress^d afterwards, pack^d up Harlan's Fauna neatly for Mrs E. Rathbone and having taken my cane, push^d for the institution, where Mr Munro[55] was to be to escort me to Mr Wm Roscoe S^r, where I was to take tea. No Mr Munro, but I found his wife and some Little children clean and pretty enough to be Kiss^d so I Kiss them. Fatiqued of waitting I am under way, have delivered the packet for Mrs Rathbone to a servant at her Door — and passed the Botanic Garden — entered Lodge Lane and Mr Roscoe's Habitation. — It was full of Ladies and Gentlemen, all of his *own familly*, and as I k[n]ew almost the whole, I was soon at my ease — Great deal said about Lord Stanley, his Birds and my Birds. — I was ask^d to Imitate the Wild Turkey call, and I did to the surprise of the whole [MS: all] circle, hooted like the Barred Owl, and cooed like the doves — I am glad really that I was not desired to Bray! —

"Why"?

Why! — because an ass is an ass, and it would have been rude, even in an ass, to Bray in such Company — Lucy, remark my position. I sat

54. Lucy Audubon's sister Eliza had married Nicholas Berthoud of Shippingport, Kentucky, in March 1816.

55. In the September 12 entry, Audubon identifies "Mr. Munro" as "the curator" of the Liverpool Royal Institution.

rather reclining, my legs extended before me at the upper end of the room between Mr Wm Roscoe and his son Edward fronting the whole of the aimiable circle before me — and have to answer to questions after questions as fast as I dare answer — Mrs E^d Roscoe has raised from her seat Twenty times to come and ask me questions about my style of Drawing —

The Good Old gentleman and myself retired from the Groupe into — the Dining room to talk about my Plans = He strongly advised me not to Exibit my Work without remuneration — He repeats his wish that I may succeed and desires that I should Take Tea on Tuesday evening with him when he will give me Letters for London =

Tea is [MS: his] presented and I take one Cup of Coffee! A Beautifull young lady called *here a Miss* is at my side and asks with the volubility of Interesting youth and enthusiasms [MS: anthusiasms] many many questions about America — but they all appear very much surprised that I have no wonderfull Tales to relate — that, for Instance, *I* so much in the woods have not been devoured at least 6 times by tigers, Bears, Woolf, Foxes or — a rat. — No — I never was troubled in the woods by any larger annimals than Ticks and Musquitoes and that is quite enough — Is it not, Dearest Lucy?

I must acknowledge, however, that I would like to have rode a few hundred miles on a Wild Elk or a Unicorn — or an *Alligator*.

"Alligator!!!! who in the known world ever heard of such things?"

Heard, Lucy, I do not know; but I am sure hundreds of Persons have *Read* of the like having been performed by a man just about the size of Common Men[56] —

"Come, come"

But, indeed, it is a fact the ride was taken by an Englishman — Now I am sure thy wonder has vanished for thou knowest as well as myself and much better to[o] how many many Wonders and Wonderfull things *they* have performed. —

56. Charles Waterton (1782–1865), an eccentric but much-traveled naturalist, published *Wanderings in South America, the North-west of the United States, and the Antilles in the Years 1812, 1816, 1820, and 1824* in 1825. Waterton met Audubon and Audubon's enemy George Ord in Philadelphia in 1824 and helped Ord thereafter discredit Audubon at every opportunity. Audubon regularly ridiculed Waterton's tales.

Well, it is Later; Son after Son with each a sweet wife under his care bids me and their Venerable Father *Good Night.*

Lucy, the well bred society of England is sublimity of manners. Such tone of Voices I never heard in America except when with ~~~~ Thee, my Wife! — Gentlemen are — no, it is impossible to be more truly polite. — A Gentleman at church this morning who knew me for a foreigner [MS: Stranger] handed me Book after Book, the book that contained the Hyms then sung with the page open, and with a gentle bow pointed the Verse with a finger covered by a beautifully white Glove — Have I not resons to Like England thus far? — Indeed, I have —

I bid good night myself and accompanied by a young man came all the way to Norton Street where I stop^d to rest and talk to Mr Gordon about my views of the Exibition of my Drawings for *Nothing* — He is of my way of thinking. We talk^d also about thy Relations in England, &^c &^c &^c and being now 6 minutes past 12 I will bid thee Good Night, My Love !!!! —

My Dearest beloved Friend[†]

It is now Three long months since I pressed thy form to my bosom. It is three long months since thy voice vibrated my ear with the sound that none but a Wife can Issue. Absence from thee, my Lucy, is painfull believe me and was I not living in Hopes to be approaching the long wished for moment of being at last well received in the learned World and being also likely to be remunerated [MS: renumerated] for my labours, I could not stand it much longer, no really, Lucy. I could not. I am now fonder of thee than ever in my Life. The reason is simply this: That I hope shortly to gain the full cup of thy esteem and affection. God Bless thee. My voyage was long and painfull in the extreme. It lasted 65 days. I wrote to thee twice during the time by way of Havanna and Boston from the Gulph of Mexico, yet I arrived safely, was sea sick at times, yet drew 4 none Descript. Thus, my Lucy, I am in England, thy native Country. Oh: England, continue to be prosperous. I have been received here in a manner not to be expected during my highest anthusiastic hopes. I am now acquainted, I will say cherished by the most prominent persons of Distinction in and near Liverpool. I have been feasted day following day in a manner truly astonishing. The more as it has been done in that refined amiable manner that alone can reconcile me to society. The letters of Vincent Nolte have proved of extreme benifit and I owe him much. — Clay and Clinton[57] have insured me a respect due to our greatest men. The famous Will[iam] Roscoe, Sismondi of Geneva and hundreds of Persons have been kind to me. Indeed, I cannot describe my feelings to thee. I feel Elevated from my painfull former situation and no longer have about me that dread felt in the company of some of those ostentatious persons with whom I have been obliged through my will to follow my Pursuits on the other side the Ocean *to Live*, but, Lucy, how is my Dear Dear son John Woodhouse Audubon? What a space divides us. May God grant our meeting again and his will be done.

My Drawings have been exibited at the Royal Institution here and 413 persons rushed in 2 hours. My fame reached distant places so quickly that the 3$\underline{rd}$ day persons of wealth arrived from Manchester to view them. I have been presented to one of the noblest and oldest Peers of England, Lord Stanley. He, Lucy, kneeled down on the rich carpet to examine my style closely. This renouned scientific man received me as if a School mate, shook Hands with me with the warmth of Friendship and wished me kindly to visit him often in Grosvenor [MS: Grovener] Street, London. I dined with him and he spent 5 hours looking at my drawings and said "M$\underline{r}$ A, I assure you this work of yours is Unique and deserves the patronage of the Crown."

My Plans are now as follows. I leave this in a few days for Manchester, where I may remain 4 days, to Derbyshire there 8 days to be presented to diferent noblemen, — to Birmingham, to Oxford — to London, there 3 Weeks, to Edinburgh 1 Week — back to London or perhaps at once to France to Paris, 2 Weeks there, and to my venerable kind mother — 2 Weeks — from thence return to England by way of Valenciennes [MS: Valenciences] & Brussels.

I am advised to do so by men of Learning and better Judgment

57. Audubon carried letters of introduction from both Henry Clay and DeWitt Clinton. Henry Clay (1777–1852) was one of the most influential politicians and statesmen of his day. He served as congressman and senator from Ashland, Kentucky, and as commissioner to the American-British peace negotiations in Ghent, Belgium, in 1814. He made his first bid for the presidency in 1824, after which he was appointed secretary of state by John Quincy Adams. DeWitt Clinton (1769–1828) had served in the New York legislature and the United States Senate. When he wrote his letter for Audubon, he was governor of the state of New York.

who say that my Work must be known quickly and in a Masterly way. — This will enable me to find where it will or may be published with greatest advantage. I have many comfortable nights at gentlemens seats in the neighbourhood, and the style of living is beyond all description. Coaches call for me and waiters in livery are obedient to me as if I myself was a Lord of England — I hope this may continue and that the end of all this may be plenty of the needfull.

Now, my beloved Wife, Thy Watch. Ah, Thy Watch is as good & as handsomely trimed as any Dutchess's Watch in the 3 Kingdoms. Accept it from thy Husband, Lucy, and wear for my sake The Broach that is with it. I will speak of the price another time. Mr Roskell the maker, a man of real worth and to whom I was presented by a particular person, assured me no better Watch was in England. I send thee 4 changes of glasses. I shall not send thee anything more from Liverpool but will fill thy lists in London and Paris. Thy Sister Ann Gordon is well. She exclaimed on se[e]ing thy Watch and mine "Oh: how beautifull. Mr A. this is rather Extravagent." Mine, Lucy, cost 80 Guineas. My seal [h]as 3 faces engraved and cost 15 Guineas. The chain 23 Guineas. Mr Swift bought one from Mr Roskell also, of less value yet very good. He saw thine and mine. He is now in Ireland. He was well. Let his Friends know this. He was very good to me during the passage.

I will have from this place Letters of great Importance for me, Amongst which will be The Baron de Humbolt, G^l Lafayette, Sir Walter Scott, Sir Thomas Lawrance, Sir Humphrey Davie, Robert Bakewell, Maria Edgeworth, Hannah Moore[58] &c. &c. &c.

I wish my Victor could have been with me. What an oppertunity

<hr>

58. Audubon is promised letters of introduction to General Lafayette (1757–1834), who was adored by Americans for his help in the American Revolutionary War and whose return to the United States in 1824–25 was much celebrated; Sir Walter Scott (1771–1832) was a poet, novelist, naturalist, folklorist, inventor of the historical romance, and the most revered Scottish writer of his day; Sir Humphrey Davy (1778–1829) was an accomplished and celebrated chemist, long connected with the Royal Institution of London, where he became known as a brilliant lecturer and as a researcher whose experiments led to many practical improvements; Robert Bakewell (1767–1843) was a geologist who lectured throughout the British Isles and whose textbook *An Introduction to Geology* (1813) was influential; Hannah Moore (1745–1833) was at the end of a remarkable career as a writer, dramatist, poet, early advocate for women's education, celebrity among London's literati, abolitionist, and philanthropist.

for him of se[e]ing The Highest Circles of the Learned and Nobility of This Island and of the Continent. Perhaps no Ordinary Individual ever enjoyed the same reception. If I was not dreading to become proud I would say that I am in Liverpool a shadow of Lafayettes wellcome in America.

I would have wrote sooner, but I disliked to do so untill something was done that might in some degree be worthy of thy attention. It was not, thou knowest well, either want of Inclination or affection. I found at the Royal Institution persons who knew me well and knew the existance of my work, particularly the President, The Famous Dᴿ Trail of this City. I hope Louisianna has been healthy. Present my best regard to Mʳˢ Percy and the Famally with my sincere thanks for her kindnesses, also to Charles Middlemist [MS: Midlewith] and tell him that he may Judge of what can be done with the *Flora Americanses*.⁵⁹ Should I succeed, my Lucy, [you] will be expected as early as possible in either England or Ireland. My style of Drawing is so admired here that many Ladies of Distinction have begged lessons of me. One Guinea I could get for an Hours attendance, drove to and fro in the Employers Carriages. My Drawings of the Dove is worth 25 Guineas, as well as a dozen of Eggs, with you 6 pence. Remember me to my good kind Friend Bourgeat and Wife and the whole of their connections at Pointe Coupee, to that aimiable young man Ruffian Sterling. To Judge Randolph and Gˡ {Joove}, to Dr Pope, Virginia Holl & her husband. I expect to see his mother shortly. I like England better than he did. If thou were fond of kissing *young Ladies*, I would request thee to do so with my best love to all thy sweet Pupills, particularly my little Woman Christianna whom I hope is quite well recovered. If thou shouldest prefer doing the like with my Friend Robert Percy, do so & present him my best wishes for his happiness. I have forwarded all the letters I had from Mʳˢ Percy by mail except those for Mᴿ Middlemist [MS: Midlewith] on whom I shall call soon after I reach London. The Ladies here wear their Watches out of sight, merely shewing the chain, but they have exquisite [MS:

59. Charles Middlemist (copied here by Audubon's scribe as "Midlewith") was the brother of Mrs. Jane Middlemist Percy, who owned the Beech Woods plantation near Bayou Sara, Louisiana, where Lucy Audubon had maintained a school for local girls since early 1823. Middlemist was visiting his sister in 1822 and planned to illustrate an American flora.

exquisitite] way of looking what the time is and in doing this often exhibit the whole. I have been astonished at beholding the plainness of Dress in Large Circles. No first rate Ladies wear any *Fandangos*. I am as usual admitted Free at all Public Institutions and Exibitions. I am at one of the first Hotels in Dale Street called the Commercial.[†] I have wrote to N. Berthoud and requested him to send thee either the Letter or the Copy by our Victor —

Farewell sweet beloved Friend and Wife
Farewell — believe for ever Thine most truly
   Thine J. J. Audubon

7 Aug.[t] 1826

My Dear Nicholas

The interest that I have known you to take towards my wellfare prompts me to write to you from this renouned Isle. I hope it may reach you and find you and all yours well and happy. More than two months at Sea, uncomfortable of thoughts as well as body, rendered me almost disconsolated and I approached the Land of England with a Heavy Heart on the Eve of Bowing to the World with my humble performances in my hand and a few Friendly letters. I reached the shore and felt it under foot with a sensation too dificult for me to describe beyond the saying that it was painfully accute.

I have been in Liverpool Two weeks and, although not a scrap from my Lucy has yet reached me, my feelings this day are as bright, light & comfortable as they were at my arrival Dark & Gloomy. I have been most kindly treated by all respectable persons and honored beyond the most sanguine expectations I had ever pictured to myself in those moments of peace & quietness that, like trancient dreams of Happiness, have sometimes during my life touched my heart. I will approach the truth still nearer and say that I have been feasted on kindness. The second day after my landing, I presented some letters of Vincent Nolte of New Orleans, of Dewitt [MS: Dewith] Clinton of New York, of Clay from Kentucky, of Bonaparte now in Philadelphia that threw the Doors of the first persons of Distinction in this busy City open for my reception —

The famallies Rathbones, Hodgsons, and Roscoe, so renouned throw Europe and America, procured for me all my heart desires connected with my views in visiting England. 250 of my drawings were exhibited at the Royal Institution, and my Fame as an ornithologist and Artist has flown from mouth to mouth with a rapidaty that has quite astounded me — Persons have come from Manchester to view these Collections of mine, Undertaken in my youthfull playfull moments of contentedness, and compleated with a heart allmost broken down by Deepest sorrows. Nay, they have had already compliments paid them by one of the most Learned Peers of England. I have had the pleasure of being presented to Lord Stanley, an eminent naturalist and most aimiable man, who kneelled on the Carpet to examine my work. I dined with this Influencial man and am to see more of him in town (this means throughout England the famous City of London).

My Dear Nicholas, I now have[†] some hopes of success at last and should I not succeed, I will return to my Beloved America, My Wife & Children with the conviction that no man will hereafter succeed. To give you an Idea of the crowd that rushed to the Institution during the Six hours, 2 each day for three days, that my drawings were in view (about half 250) at one sight, hung on a purple cloth ground for the purpose of exhibiting Paintings of greater merits. I will tell you that 413 persons entered the Hall in 2 Hours, and I had to stand the view and liston to the plaudity of each Individual. At the request of very many of my acquaintances here, I suffered the Exibition to be general and opened from 10 untill dusk, and it has been kept crowded. I will proceed slowly towards and to London, Edinburgh and most of the Principal Cities of this Improved Garden of Europe and proceed to Paris to shew them there also. My wish is to Publish them in London if possible, if not, in Paris, and should I through the stupendiousness of the Enterprise and publication of so large a work be forced to abandon its being engraved, I will follow a general round of remunerating [MS: renumerating] Exhibition and take the Proceeds Home. I have seen Sister Gordan and her husband. They are well. I have purchased a Watch for Lucy that I have given to Mr G. to forward to her.

Be so kind to send her either this or a Copy of this letter by My Dear beloved Son — Assure him that I will take an early opportunity of writing to him and forward him some music and be so good also as to request him to Draw at his leisure hours in *my* style as much as possible and on that subject to read a long letter I sent him from Louisianna.

Now, my Dear Nicholas, kiss they sweet famally for me, my Beloved Sister Eliza — and believe me to be sincerely and truly Thy Friend

John J. Audubon

Liverpool 7 August 1826.

When you write, direct to the Care of the American Minister, London. He will always know w[h]ere I am. Mr Gallatin[60] is the present one.

P.S. As you may wish to know whom I am likely to become acquainted with shortly, I will say, The Baron Humbolt, Sir Walter Scot, Sir Thos. Lawrance, Sir Humphrey Davie and as the Venerable Roscoe was pleased to say "It would not be a wonder, Mr A., if our King might wish to take a peep at the *Birds of America* and it would do no harm." Should my Lucy receive this, may God grant her health and Happiness. Yes, may she fare well untill we meet again — Lucy, God Bless thee.

I had no dificulty worth mentioning at the Custom House.

LIVERPOOL AUGUST 7$^{\underline{TH}}$ 1826. —

I am just now from the Learned Doctor <u>*Trail*</u>!! and have enjoyed 2 hours of his Interesting Company = to what perfection Men like him can rise on this soil of Instruction =

I have had a great deal to do this day in way of Exercise, I assure thee = I visited first the Panorama of Venice, a fine Painting but not to be

60. Albert Gallatin (1761–1849) was the Swiss-born American politician appointed as secretary of the treasury by Jefferson in 1801, a post he filled until 1814. After helping negotiate the Treaty of Ghent in 1814, he held several diplomatic posts, including minister plenipotentiary to Great Britain in 1826–27.

compared with the Chapel of Holy Rood[61] $=$ Then I Called on a Great Amateur of Paintings and promiss^d him a View of Some of my Drawings Tomorow — He told me that a Mr Thornely of his acquaintance Knew me well in New York 20 Years ago — so that I am rapidly Improving towards being acknowledged a *True one.*

I ran to our good Consul Maury's office, saw him, and promiss^d to Call tomorow for Letters to London — ran to my room and Wrote to thee and to N. Berthoud. I had the Letters Copied for me by a Young man recomended to me — to save time — I dined and Ran to the Institution for a Guide to Mr Edward Roscoe to whose [MS: whom's] Lady I wish^d to shew my way of Drawing — Mr Munro politely offered his services and we reached the Park where they Live $=$

I soon prepared every thing and Drew a flower for her and a Miss Dale, a fine artist $=$ talk^{ed} a Good deal of Bayou Sarah, St Francisville and the Country around thee as well as of thyself and our children and Walk^d to Liverpool with Edward & xxxx Roscoe[62] — with Miss Lane — I admired this afternoon the daughter of E^d Roscoe very much — She is a Roscoe Compleate — the fine Nose — the fine Eyes, the fine mouth — the fine form — aye! the sentiment of her grand Father exists Throw out her expressions, her look, her movements! She is a beautifull child.

Now, some sad Critic who might fall upon my Journal might say "Why that poor fool praises every Individual he meets," but there the Critic would be Mistaken for I would try to {tr**ese} him for his {*ile} heart and art besides whilst I would Continue with pleasure to Write of Nature Naturally, i.e. as I meet it!

We passed throw a Kind of mound thrown up Artfully and with taste, from which, a fine extensive view of the City and the Country around may be had $=$

61. From 1825 to 1827 Louis-Jacques-Mandé Daguerre (1789–1851) exhibited in Liverpool his diorama *The Ruins of Holyrood Chapel.* A diorama presented scenes painted on large semitransparent linen screens that were illuminated in ways that created illusions of movement and depth. A panorama was a painting of a landscape that was either arranged on a cylindrical wall with the viewer at the center or rolled between two drums to pass before the viewer.

62. Audubon seems to have forgotten the name of the other Roscoe walking with them, but since he links Edward's name with the forgotten one, it seems likely he has forgotten the name of Margaret Lace Roscoe, the botanical illustrator and wife of Edward (see n. 19). Ford's speculation that the person is Jane Roscoe, Edward's sister, is possible, but there is no basis for this conjecture. Ford also significantly rewrote this passage in the journal, omitting entirely the "xxxx" (*Journal*, 128n38).

Called at Doctor Trail and his absence threw me towards my lodgings, where I was anxious to see how my Coppyist performed — I am satisfied with his hand write but he writes perhap too slow = Again to Dr Trail and, as I told Thee before, met him and his Lovely children — Two sweet Daughters, perhaps 13 & 14 Years old, sat with us whilst we talk^d Natural History over — Tomorow I am to receive what he calls a Budget of Letters from him =

I feel Grieved that I have not been able to reach Green Banks to night to enjoy the Company of my good Friends Rathbone and the Comfort of Peacable Country. I hope they will not think me rude —

W^{am} Rathbone Esqr indited [MS: Indigted] me several Letters of introduction, which I received at Dinner — I would like to write more but Indeed I am wearied. I must have batered the Pavements this day full 20 miles, and that is equal to 45 walking throw the Woods — sweet Friend, Good Night —

LIVERPOOL AUGUST 8TH 1826. —

Note forward^d to W^{am} Roscoe Esqr of Lodge Lane — Augt 9th 1826 —

My Dear Sir —

I Called on my Friend A Gordon Esqr last evening after I left your house, and, having shewn to him the drafts you had made to announce the reexibition of some of my Drawings, I also beg^d for his opinion when the following was as near as possible his answer: "M.^r A, no person in my opinion can advise you better than Mr Roscoe, and his polite attentions to you prove the great desire he has that you should succeed, and I think that, all diferent advises ought to Fall before his"! so that, my Dear Sir, I hesitate no longer, and will now exibit my Drawings, If I receive permission from this day's comitee at the Royal Institution, with a feeling entirely Clear^d of the clouds that I dreaded before now, might have thick^d and put a stop to my Carreer.

Can I beg of you to be present at the Comittee this morning? Your Influence is such, you know, that all dificulties would be levelled before you! —

Permit me to be for ever yours much oblig^d and ob.^t S.^t, J. J. A. — Wednesday morning —

Although I am extremely fatigued and it is past 12 o'clock I will write —

This day I forward^d one letter for thee and one for N. Berthoud per Packet — copies annex^d here — Call^d on Mr Maury and received [MS: Re^d] Two Letters of recomendation — for Mr Gallatin and Welles of Paris — shew^d my drawings to several persons and saw Mr Thornely, who knew me well in New York 23 years ago — I wrote a Note to Mrs Rathbone at Green Banks to beg her Pardon for not having Call^d to see her and familly — I walk^d to Lodge Lane to take Tea at Wm Roscoe's Esqre but stop^d at the Botanic Garden where I drank the Botanist's health in a glass of Excellent Port Wine, being his Birthday. He presented me with a Bottle of Gooseberries for thee —

I found at Mr Roscoe, besides himself an Artist of Merit in the Landscape Way Call^d Austen,[63] and shortly afterwards came in Mr Harding[64] of Kentucky, the renowned!!!! —

3 sons of Mr Roscoe and a Lady besides M^r R's daughters were there — Mr R. spoke a great deal about my reexibiting my Drawings for Money and advised me so Earnestly and Fatherly like to do so that I promised to see Mr Gordon on the subject this night and that if he thought of it well also, I should decline any further opposition. — Mr R. drew a Draft to be Inserted in the Papers and after my having spent a very agreable afternoon there, I went to Mr Gordon —

But I must not forget to tell thee that Mr Yates[65] met me at the Institution and gave me several Letters —

Mr Gordon has removed 3 Doors from the corner of High Street, near Hedge Hill Church, where I found the Trio at Tea = I shew^d them the Bust of Mr Roscoe that he had kindly presented me with — thy gooseberries, and open^d the subject, or my subject —

Then it was decided that I should follow the advises of Mr Roscoe

63. Samuel Austin (1796–1834) was a watercolorist who exhibited mostly landscape paintings, coastal views, and architectural views of Liverpool and North Wales. He was associated with the Liverpool Academy beginning in 1815, serving as secretary from 1824 to 1827 and again in 1830.

64. Chester Harding (1792–1866) had become one of the most renowned portraitists in the United States. Like Audubon, he had traveled with his family on a flatboat down the Ohio River. He painted both William Clark and Daniel Boone. Harding had been in England since the fall of 1823 and was on the verge of returning to the States when Audubon met him.

65. Seven letters from a James Yates of "Dinglehead near Liverpool" appear among the letters of introduction copied into the journal (see app. B).

— Mͬ Gordon accompanied me some distance toward Liverpool and I reach[ed] my Lodgings, where I found my Clerk just about going and Mͬ Munro Waiting patiently for me — He handed me a kind note from Dͬ Trail, who had been so exceedingly carefull of my Bonaparte's Book that he requestᵈ Mͬ Munro not to deliver it to any one but me! —

I talkᵈ a good Deal to Mͬ Munro and read a little to him — Drank some ale with him, and he left quite pleased that my Drawings were to be up again and that I might do well with them =

I Never had any desire not to be remunerated, quite to the Contrary, but I wishᵈ it done in a most Honorable Manner — and as [MS: has] Mͬ Roscoe says that it is by no means disgracefull, I will now shew them for a Shilling with [MS: when] open heart and purse, and May I be so fortunate as to receive plenty of them =

My Eyes positively give way. Farewell, Good Night —

LIVERPOOL 9ᵀᴴ AUGUST 1826. —

So poor Audubon, thy Birds will be seen by the Shilling's worth, and Criticized no doubt by the pound. The Fruits of thy Life's labour ought now to ripen [MS: rippe] fast, or thy Winter may be yet spent without the embers [MS: ambers] — thou [h]ast been used to, during thy Happy Youthfull Days — I am almost sorry for it. Indeed, I have more than once felt vexation at heart on the occasion and yet perhaps with all, it may prove Best. As to me, rest for ever assured that it will never in the least diminish the affectionate regard and Estime that has been felt by me ever since I found thee for the first time reclining at the foot of a Magnolia, thy Eyes humid with the watters of admiration casted on the Beauties of thy *resplendissant* Friend Nature! No, Audubon, what ever may become of thee (speaking in a Phisical way) will never hinder [MS: ender] me from speaking of thee, and thinking of thee, as I con-ceived thee to be then, ever since then, and Now!! — then for ever thy Thine. xxxxxxxx

My Beloved Wife, the above Note, (the hand writting of which as well as the Composition thou knowest well) acquaints thee as quickly as all the Liverpool papers that my Birds of America (about one half, by the bye, for the — Port folio Nᵒ 1 is yet sacred) will be seen Next Monday at the Royal Institution not *Pro bono Publico* but for the benefit of *E Pluribus Unum.*

So much is to be said on the subject that I will mend my pen and write slow — although it be now half past Eleven. How many at this moment with a heart diferently framed are carousing, cheating, cheated, ah, perhaps a thousand times more disapointed after all than I ever yet have been in my humble Life —

I put the pen on my right thumb, and nipped it with the Knife thou hast given me. The pen is not very good, yet in some hands how well it would write —

Oh, Venerable Roscoe, that I possess^d thy sublime powers and could animate the coldest sense of feeling as well as thou art able! — Lucy, this excitation has allmost congealed the Black fluid and my quill works now as if I had done wrong — In attempting to express my opinion of that great man. I have daubed a Canvass that nought but a Milton was ever fitted to outline and the God of the sacred Mount to finish!

I was forced to resort to my 16 shilling umbrella this morning to take my walk. The sky and my heart were much troubled alike; the Clouds went and met, as my thoughts contraried and agreed. To be engaged is a usefull object on such occasion, and I went full 6 miles about to my breakfast at my Lodgings again — wrote a note to W$^{\underline{m}}$ Roscoe Esq$^{\underline{r}}$, Lodge Lane, walk^d fast to the Institution, and M$^{\underline{r}}$ Munro took it to be delivered. Fast to D$^{\underline{r}}$ Trail — "Sir, the Doct$^{\underline{r}}$ is not in" — fast to M$^{\underline{r}}$ Hinks, "Sir, M$^{\underline{r}}$ Hinks is not at home." However, having given my name, I was told letters were ready for me and M$^{\underline{rs}}$ Hinks politely (Thou mayest be sure) gave me 3 — I went as if i[n] pursuit of a New Specimen about the streets, pulling out and looking on my Watch's Dial to see it mark 10 with much Impatience — It is 10 and I am in the Entry room of D$^{\underline{r}}$ Trail — A Lady begs that I will wait and taking from the shelf *La beauté des Champs*![66] I try to be for a moment in the Forests! —

An other Lady, ah, it is M$^{\underline{rs}}$ Trail — My eyes naturally fall. The Lady, with an English Lady's Voice, asks that I will put my name on a Book she gives me, and whilst doing this, her mouth pays me a Compliment —

I bowed, Lucy. It is unfortunatly all I can do tolerably — She disapears. I open the Folio — a Poem! W$^{\underline{am}}$ Roscoe['s] Name — Oh, my heart, support me! — Had it not been a Lady who handed [MS: ended] me the Book Like M$^{\underline{rs}}$ Rathbone or Hodgson or Roscoe's Lady,

---

66. I have been unable to find a book with the title *La beauté des Champs*. It is appropriate, however, that the American woodsman would chance upon a work of nature writing.

I would have felt miserably vexed, but I remembered imediately that
I was in England and that all here is Genuine with good Hearts and
aimiable sensibility — I at once scratch^d the following Lines and Close^d
the Album with a Blush:

If my wanderings thro America to me so Dear!
If my warmest desires to offer to others in an humble Manner the
pleasures of viewing Nature's warbling Brood!
If the Gratitude my heart feels toward the Friendly hands so
Kindly inclined to guide me on can entitle me to write on this paper
my Name? Then I do it with all my Heart —

Had Byron the Famous been [MS: being] near me (and I wish he
had), what a slap he would have administered my Hot cheek for the 3
successive If's that I wrote there — Ah, indeed he might have given me
3 blows and I would no doubt have undergone the Evolutions of right,
Left, Front, however Byron was not there (although he was in the House
& close by) and I did not study the tacticks from under his hand —
Rapp — rapp — How is Dr Trail? What a Fine Friendly head,
ah! and heart to[o]!! — "Here is the Budget for you — Have you
breakfasted? Come in and set with us, do" = Lucy, our most
hospitable Kentuckians such as our Friends G^l W^{am} Clark's Father and
Major Croghan[67] were not Kinder = I see Two Daughters, a son with

67. Audubon's reference to "G^l W^{am} Clark's Father" as having been hospitable to him and Lucy
in Louisville is puzzling and must be an error, since John Clark, William Clark's father, died in
1799, eight years before the Audubons moved to Louisville. Audubon may have intended to refer
to the hospitality of the father of his friend George Croghan, Maj. William Croghan, an Irish
immigrant who served in the American Revolutionary War and claimed to have met Audubon's
father during that conflict. William Croghan and his wife, Lucy Clark Croghan (sister of George
and William Clark), certainly would have entertained the newly arrived Audubons at their farm,
Locust Grove, which was a short distance from Louisville. William Croghan's son, Maj. George
Croghan (1791–1849), a nephew to the Clark brothers, had enjoyed gunning with Audubon
in 1807, the year the Audubons moved to Louisville to set up in business. Croghan served
with distinction during the War of 1812, after which he resigned from the military and became
postmaster of New Orleans. Alice Ford's rendering of the reference as "General William Clark's
daughter" is also puzzling (*Journal*, 141). The manuscript clearly reads "Father," and William
Clark did not marry until January 5, 1808, and thus had no daughter in 1807. In a footnote Ford
asserts that William Clark was William Croghan's father-in-law (*Journal*, 141n48); he was instead
Croghan's uncle.

hair of the color I admire in men most — and M͟r͟s͟ Trail breakfasting —
My eyes view the whole, my Heart feels more. — I am shewn many fine
Curiosities and having open͟d͟ the subject of my Exibition to the Doctor
— having told him that the situation of a Naturalist at Heart is very
diferent to that of an exibiter of Drawings, he shook his Head and said
"It is unfortunatly too true, my Dear Sir" ⹀

Well, I am at the Institution and find the following note:

My Dear Sir

I am glad M͟r͟ Gordon agrees with me in the opinion as to the
expediency of Exibiting your Drawings to the Public, & will
endeavour to be at the Committee this morning in order to
promote that measure; believe me

Most Faithfully Yours
W. Roscoe

Lodge Lane, Wednesday Morning
J. J. A. Esq͟r͟ —

My good friend R͟d͟ Rathbone enters and as usual asks me to go to
Green Banks, is so Kind as to apologise for his not having seen me —
Now, Lucy, who is the Debtor, thinkest [MS: thankest] thou? — †

The Trial is approaching ⹀ I am Walking about the Rooms, the
Committee is sitting — The Keeper of the Institution say's "Sir, the
Gentlemen of the Comittee wish to see you" ⹀ I am in their presence
and all Eye me with Kindness!!

It is resolved that the comittee pass an order to request me to Exibit
my Work — This, I am sure, will and must take off all discredit attached
to the whole of this tormenting endurance of thoughts, and as it Comes
under such a Commanding Honorable View of the subject, I agree to
do so —

W͟a͟m͟ Roscoe shakes my Hand, appears not very well. He announces
me the Illness of his son Edward and Leaves me all wonderment ⹀
Then I shall not go to dine at M͟r͟ Roscoe ⹀ and M͟r͟ Lyons, who so

politely Invited me this morning, I Hope will know that I did not refuse
him without a true reason should he meet me in the streets. —

The secretary is Busy Instructing Mr Munro: — The reading Rooms,
— Steam Packet, Hotels, and news Papers must now all be acquainted
with my Birds Creation & entrance into this Busy World, and I: must
try to visit Wales whilst the Gentlemen and Ladies of Liverpool visit
the Institution next week ═

As I returned to Dale Street, I already thought that most of the
people I met pointed at me with a Sneer as they look^d at my poor Head
and broad pantaloons — What a Fool I am ═

"My Dear Husband, thou art not a Fool, and all who know thee
at all, will agree with me there — It is true the want of a regular
Classical education is much against thee as thy Nature has Induced
thee to Admire Nature; but thy Heart is Good and, believe me, Many
Learned Men have very little of that to boast of. Give me a Kiss and be
satisfied" —

Ah, Lucy, thy Kindness renews my faculties. Thanks, my Beloved
Wife, thanks to thee!!! —

Harrassed as I was, I walk^d to sister Ann, saw Mr Gordon off to
London — Walk^d again to this my room, — found my Young Man at
Work — dismissed him for the day, have wrote this, look^d at the Moon
as she silently Inclines towards the Western World and ~~~~ Good
night, God Bless Thee!! —

LIVERPOOL 10TH THURSDAY AUGUST 1826. —

Why should my feelings be so dampened to night? Why, because
it rains and I have just reach^d the Commerical with a wet Coat, wet
wais[t]coat, Shirt and Skin — Had it not been for this natural incident
in a Country where I was told I never would see the sun shine, not a
portion of my "tout Ensemble" would have been in the least moist.

However, this rain was not a deluge such as we often experienced in
our warmer latitude — It does not stop a man from walking on. Quite
to the contrary, it Invites one to walk faster, unless he is provided with a
16 shilling Umbrella in his Hand and open, when he may take it leisurely
— not like me and mine to night. It was dosing silently in the corner of
my room close by the washing stand & I walk^d fast, believe me!

The morning was beautifull, Clear, pleasant — I was on the Mound by times, and saw the City plainly and the Country beyond the Mersey quite Plain also —

When first I left the Inn, the watchman watch^d me and perhaps thought that I was an Owl caught out by the day as I moved not like a meteor but like a man either in a Hurry, or a Flurry, or Crazy —

The fact is that I thought of Nothing but the Exibition — Nothing else could scarcely have entered my Confounded [MS: Confiund] brains.

The wind mills are very diferent here from the few I have seen in America, and so are the Watchmen. Both are, I think, taller and fuller about the Waist — I do not like 4 square angles breaking on the fore ground of a Landscape, and yet I was forced twice to day to submit to that mortification — but to counterpoise this, I had the satisfaction of setting on the Grass and to watch 4 truant Boys rolling marbles with great Spirit for a good full half hour — How they laughed, how briskly they moved, how much they brought from far again my Younger days = I would have liked them better still at this Innocent avocation had they been decently Clean, but they were not so, and I raised after giving them enough, to purchase a Shilling's worth of marbles —

I had and have still some Idea of Leaving Dale Street and remove nearer to the Institution — Mr Munro Conducted me to examine a House and a *Landlordess* that I Liked well enough — The price was just about Suitable to my means, and I only requested to be suffer^d to think of it untill Tomorow —

I began to feel most powerfully the want of occupation at Drawing and Studying the Habits of the Birds that I saw about me, and the little Sparrows that hop^d in the Streets, although very sooty tinged by the coal smoak, attracted my attention greatly — Indeed I watch^d one of them throwing about him the manure of the street with as much pleasure to day as I recollect in far diferent places I watch^d the jinglings of the mellow thrush so Clear — All this Enticed me to prepare myself — I Bought Watter Colors and Brushes of Mr Hunt and paid Dearer than in America. I made a note for Pastelles and give it to W^{am} Rathbone Esqr to forward to London — I saw him, the Intelligent Swiss and R^d Rathbone there =

I must say that I felt sorry that the Eye of the Swiss convinced me that *he* was not pleased with the Exibition; I was the more sorry because I thought so much of his Talents and amability of Caracter —

I am strolling away towards the Park because I received the following when I return^d to the Inn:

Park, Thursday morning

Dear Sir

It will give us much pleasure if you will dine with us to day at 4 — I am sorry we were prevented seeing you yesterday — believe me your Truly

Edwd Roscoe —

Lucy, as you go to Park Place, the View up and over the Mersey is extensive and rather Interesting, although it is not form^d with any of those Gigantic Dashes of Extraordinary Mountains, Cataracts and Dark Valeys to be met with in the Alps — yet this afternoon it afford^d a calming moment of repose to the Eye from the Bustle of the Street on the silent fainting far away Mountains of Wales = Steam Vessels moved swiftly in all directions on the Mersey, but they are not to be compared with Ours of the only Ohio! No, they look like Smoaky floating dungeons, and I turn my sight from them —

Almost Imediately opposite the Dwelling of E^d Roscoe Esqre is a small pond [MS: pound], and as I neither have seen or heard a frog in England, I surveyed its banks and its watters as Closely perhaps as a Winter Falco[68] might have done had he been *here* also — but not a Frog, no, none of that grand Wildness that surrounds our swamps and marshess, no Imitation of the Surly bull's belowing to be heard here, no Macasson, nor Copper headed Snake; not even a Dozen of the Snowy White Heron to be seen Streching throw the Grasses their Neck and Watching the Intruder's motions — not a Garr Fish basking on the surface, nor an Alligator dosing in the rays of the Sun — No! The rose Colored Ibiss and her Friend the Roseate Spatula never were

68. Audubon's "Winter Falco" is the red-shouldered hawk (Plate LXXI). He is thinking of the painting of this species he made four years earlier in Louisiana in which he depicts a male lifting off heavily from marsh grasses with a large bullfrog in his talons.

[MS: where] here wild and charming — The Sprightly trout was not seen Shooting arrowlike from her grassy retreat towards the silvery fry — No, no Vulture soared over my head waiting for the spoils of my Hunt, not an Eagle was seen, perched in gloomy silence on the Dreary aspiring top of the Decaying mornfull Cypress, no — The warblers attracted not my senses with their notes to me so pleasing — The minute hum Bird crossed not my Eye. Ah, my Lucy, I was in England, not in America!! —

Yet, Lucy, England has its charms! Yes, the Creator in his Matchless works has bountifuly granted to each portion, as he has given to each attom of his Creation, a full share of Sweets — We only throw our Errors misconstrue his meanings and understand him not! —

I am received by the Beautifull Daughter of Ed$^{\underline{d}}$ Roscoe — How lovely and lively also — Her Hair light and Airy naturaly devide and in playfull Curls fall some on her neck whilst others are viying [with] the Beauty of her Circling Eye Brows =

She touches the Ivory of her Piano — Her fingers move as if accidentally and the sounds reach my ears and my heart! — Lucy, I merely told her that I like^{d} music, and like a sylph she moved towards the musical Instrument — How pleasing when compared to the Absurd "Sir, I dont play — I cant play" and all those *sordid inclined ways* of the Coquette's affected disposition — A moment with such an Angel can never be forgotten —

Her mother Comes. She is all amability — and the chat is all Drawings — Her Husband Comes, and his gracefull look fills [MS: feels] me with admiration — Lucy, there is really "un Certain Je ne sais quoi" in the Roscoe familly!!!!! —

Our dinner is simple, consequently healthfull — so the desert — so the wine — Two females enter the room and a young Gentleman also. Some receive Kisses, some do not, and I am of that unfortunate number Lucy — I say "unfortunate" because, was I even to ask thy sister Ann to accept of a Brother's Gift, she would Blush like a Rose and say ~~~~ nothing, Lucy.

Ladies riding habits are quite strangers in appearance to me — They are so cumbersome (I speak of those I saw) that the wearer must be compleatly occupied in holding the surperflous Cloth up with both hands to save them from Inevitable falls and give to the fairer sex of

England a good deal of what I conceived to be the walk of Chinese Bells, for I never was in China, that thou knowest well, and the Little Knowledge I have of that Country has been throw the perusal of *Lord McCartney's Faux pas.*[69]

The Ladies of whom I here speak are sisters of Mrs Roscoe, and thou knowest as well as myself that sometimes sisters are alike —

Tea is announced — It is a singular fact that in England, dinner, Desert, wine, chat along with the Wine and Tea Drinking follow each other so quickly that, was it not necessary to partake of this last to remove from one room to another, it would be a Constant repast — No matter, it is very Agreable and I am coming round fast, I assure thee, to this good English way of living — I read to the Matched paire a paire of My Days in Liverpool — bid them good Night, was accompanied by the Husband towards High Street a good Ways, and am Lessening to musical sounds from the Botanical Garden — but before I proceed, let me say how Shocking it is to my Eyes whilst running across the Fields to see — "Any person trespassing on these grounds will be pursued with all the rigour of the Law" — This must be a Mistake Certainly. This cannot be English Liberty and freedom surely — Of this I intend to know more here after, but that I saw the printing on the Board there is really no Doubt —

But let us return to the musical sounds from the Botanical Garden — Flutes, Hautboys, Clarinets and clarions [MS: Clairans] — Horns, Drums, Bassons & Cymballs all in perfect Unison gave to my understanding "God Save the King." Aye, I say so and more than so — God save every Good Man besides the king [MS: Kind]!!! — The sound is fainting and, indeed, I myself have very nearly fainted walking too fast towards Hedge Hill Church, but I have reach^{d} the 3rd door from the Corner of High street and seen the Interesting Miss Donathan thro the Window — have walk^{d} up the Stairs and am Resting opposite her Eyes — In Comes sweet sister Ann — I drank 2 Tumblers of Watter

69. Audubon would have read of "*Lord McCartney's Faux pas*" in John Barrow's *Some Account of the Public Life, and a Selection of the Unpublished Writings of the Earl of Macartney* (London, 1807), where it was reported that the failure of George Macartney, first Earl Macartney (1737–1806), to develop more advantageous trade relations with China occurred because of his unwillingness to bend to Chinese ways and to accept his being treated as a lower-class envoy. The actual causes were more complicated, but this was the popular perception.

and a Distant relation of Thine, perhaps no relation at all, comes in — Ah, the Man has tallent for Painting! It is Imprinted just over his Eyebrows — His name, Lucy, is the same that Thou wert so kind to abandon for mine —

Ten o'clock, pairs and plumbs and wine have been tasted but none of the Nectar that flows on thy sweet sister's Lips — No, I would not kiss her, Lucy, for all the World —

"Ah, Indeed — and why, pray? — Thou wert fond [MS: found] of kissing her formerly. I have many a time seen her on thy knee looking at thou with a kind eye."

Yes, tis all true but, Lucy, Time Effaces Time and those times of yore are, I fear, never to be felt again — Mr Bakewell as we walk along speaks artist's like, and I know must be like an artist in many other way[s] — but Good My Friend — Good Night —

SUNDAY 13$^{\underline{TH}}$ AUGUST 1826 —

Thou wilt not call me either lazy or Careless for my not having wrote as usual every night this poor Journal, when thou knowest the fact that effectually prevented me — Last night and the night before the last when I entered my room full intent to do so — after having thrown off my Coat, open^d my watch to Judge of the Time, and hung my Cravat on the arm^d chair on which I allways set to write this pitifull Book; my Ideas flew sudenly to America so forcibly that I saw thee, dearest Friend!! — Ah, yes, saw thee: covered with such an attire as completly destroyed all my powers — The Terror that ran through my blood was chilling and I was like stupified for a full hour — No — I could not have made a pen had the Universe been at stake. Both nights I undressed slowly, mour[n]fully, and bedewed my pillow with bitterest tears — Is it [MS: It is] not strange — Not a Line from thy pen has yet reach^d me — Vessels one after one have arrived from the Dear Country that Bears thee, and not a consolatory Word has yet reach[ed] my ear to assure thee [art] — Well and Happy. —

The Further Distant, my Lucy, the more I need this consolatory act of Friendship and of Love — Oh, do write or *I shall not be able to write at all* —

To one less fixed on distant objects, these Days would have been quite pleasant — nay, happiness in a Land of Strangers! — but although I felt happiness, it was like the lash of a Sharp Whip Striking the Slave Iron^d on Distant shores, who, thoughtless about all but his far Gone Country and Friends, feels not the Blows —

Even now to night after having been before My God to pray for thy sake, happiness and Salvation at the Blind's Asilum Church — spent the remainder of the day at my old and kind Friend W^{am} Roscoe — seen thy Sister well and the Sun setting Cloudless; still I cannot write and am forced to Drop my Pen — Ah, my Lucy — how art thou? Does superstition pray on me now as [MS: has] it did on the 4th July last when, so dull did I feel at sea that I believed then, some great and dismal event was taking place on our Eastern Shores — Oh, may God preserve thee still — and may he = Oh, my Lucy, the Death of Jefferson and his Friend[70] have filled me with Dire Apprehension — Do write to me? —

LIVERPOOL AUGUST 14TH 1826. —

Now that my spleen is gone with the Breese, (I can hardly tell where for the wind does not take it toward America) — I can set and write and think of thee, Hoping thee well. =

I have spent a Good, nay, a Happy half day, at the Green Banks of Mr Rathbone = It is however a fact that although I was well aware that it was the Place most congenial to my feelings at all times, when far away from thee; I felt, that shamefull Bashfulness that so distracts my life so much that, although I was anxious to go there — I reluctantly and without knowing positively why, put it off day after day, glad to have a tolerable true excuse to offer any one of the members of that Hospitable and Friendly Habitation — but, Lucy, I dined Yesterday with Mr Roscoe S^r, with part of his familly, and spent the day well there also — I merely say this now because I was too miserable last night to write it, or write any thing else Indeed =

70. At some time after arriving at the mouth of the Mersey River on July 20, Audubon learned that both Thomas Jefferson and John Adams had died on July 4. At the end of this entry for August 13, he is affected by these deaths. Because the ink here matches closely the ink used to insert the note of his premonition on July 4 above (see p. 23 and the textual note), it seems that he added that note on this night, August 13. Whether he is manufacturing the premonition or simply recalling what he neglected to record earlier is an interesting question.

"But why, my Dear Laforest — shouldst thou be so low spirited — when so kindly treated?"

Indeed, Lucy, to Thee I can make no other apology than this. I thought — I dreaded — this exibition of my poor Birds, and now that they were to be positively pointed at with the finger of the Venomous Critic who criticks merely for the worth of his Shiling — I dreaded to encounter even my best Friends and Wished Myself in the depth of our most Gloomy and retired Cypress Swamps —

But now that I have this day reconciled, I hope, those Good Friends of Mine — that I have seen Benevolence, charity — Hospitality and Comfort, all hand in hand wishing me Welcome, I feel diferently — so does the soldier that is urged by the true spirit of his Commandor, to meet even Death with a meek Countenance and a Heart free of reproach! —

It is best, however, to tell the Truth; when I reached the Avenue leading to my good Friends — I felt as if sufocating, doubted if I should proceed or retrograde, or indeed if I should sink down on the spot — Any one but thyself would think me pussilanimous and all would wrong me — Have I not met and defeated the Wild Voracious panther, the active Bear $=$ attacked the Wolfs during their slaughter, and defied the Wild Cat's anger? — Ah, yes, and again and again for such deeds I feel myself fit: but, Lucy, to wound the Heart of *Man* is beyond my Courage and there I acknowledge myself vanquished [MS: Vanshished] and Outdone! —

Well, my Lucy, I at last went forward and met a female Angel on the door. It was the Eldest daughter of Richard Rathbone, beautifull in all her purity! Perhaps 10 years old. Oh, how I did wish to kiss her, but I did not and do not know why: unless, indeed, it was fear that she might Blush, and feel worse than I $=$

The venerable Baucis received me next to her son R$\underline{d}$ but both (although Kindly) said that they had allmost given me up. I trembled least it might prove so — but no, they are still kind and the gloomy sky, instead of sinking my spirits, raised my Gratitude and, oh, yes, my Beloved Wife, I prayed God to Bless thee to the full edge of this Golden Cup —

Then I am Happy! I am seated with Beewicks Book on quadrupeds in my hands — one eye viewing that Friendly Creature the Dog, and the other that Lovely child my little Friend Bazil at his Play — Our Woodhouse, my Lucy, under thy care and affection, did study the first elements of Nature's Beautifull Arrangements = the same with the Little Friend Bazil — The Mother with an Eye just as blue as thine has a Book of Insects before her and although Intent on an other Book, she cautiously attends on her Fruit: anxious that it should grow full of Suavity! —

The sister is writting a letter, I believe = The nephew examining the Minutious Pistills of a Floweret — *Baucis* has her Heart set on a Book full of True religion, and another Nephew negligently reclined on his seat is also engaged on a work beyond my Comprehension =

Lucy, thou knowest with what pleasure I enjoy those Scenes of entire peace and quiet — Thou knowest also how quietsome they are to the mind —

The Busy World of Liverpool like the troubled Muddy Watters of our Missoury, with its whirlpools and Contrary Currents, is probably at this moment each on each Individual encroaching and like the greedy Currents undermining each Contiguous object to force an unfairly obtained Course, whilst *I* am gazing on the placitude of Green Banks =

Wert thou to see the Kindnesses of thy Fair Country Women again, Lucy, thou wouldst return to thy Native Land with a Heart filled with Devotedness toward them. —

I neither can write, nor sketch or Draw or Paint to my Liking, but I am sure I can easily say that Mᶦˢ Rathbone is looking over my work and fastening with the broach that a moment since fastened the gause over her fair Bosom — the Paper before me to stop the Breese from disturbing of my Black Lead the Touches whilst I am making a light sketch of the scenery.

How I have gaized on these *Green Banks*. How much I have thought of English Hospitality and compared it with that of our Independant brave, full Hearted Kentuckians and Virginians and every other member of our Happy Union = and said to myself, with a wish that the World might proclaim it to the Universe, that never ever exceeded the Briton's in reality! —

We have dined — I have rambled through the grounds — the Green
Houses and *Jardin Potagers*[71] — Lead by the aimiable and Complaisant
Nephew — I express my wish to return to Liverpool again and — Lucy,
I am walking most Happily bearing the gentle frame of Miss Rathbone
through and across the fields and along the road that ultimatly leads
us to W͞a͞m Roscoe — I see the learned po[r]tion of his Head — and
conduct Miss Rathbone to Miss — Benson's & C͞o͞ — return to W͞a͞m
Roscoe and discover that Miss Jane is employed taking her Greek
Lesson ═

Ladies here are learned and aimiable. That is a whole [MS: all] word
more than the Ladies of our Continent are entitld to — yet I will
acknowledge that all our Ladies are fully provided with either the one
or the second qualification ═

Now I am moving 6 miles per hour untill I meet R͞d͞ Rathbone quite
in my front — We talk. We part. — I, never to part with him in my
Heart, believe me! ═

The wind Blows quite a Cold blast — It is quite like November all
round me except at my Heart. This is not Cold — I Hope to receive a
Letter from thee — Vessels have arrived from my America — I Hope
soon to kiss thy signet and — oh, my Wife, Lucy, Dearest Friend —
God Bless thee! ah Yes, — good Night —

I raised sudenly thinking that M͞r͞ Munroe had just left my room when
he kindly came to give me an account of the Exibition, and I must go
to sleep with the thoughts that I am Debtor to the Liverpool people 64
Shillings — Now Good night —

GREEN BANKS 3 MILES FROM LIVERPOOL —
TUESDAY AUGUST 15͞T͞H͞ 1826. —

This morning, Lucy, I ought to have been at the Dwelling of the
Venerable Roscoe by 5 o'clock; I had last evening promised to do
so and to leave at his Door a dozen of *Sword Beans* that I had also
promised to that good Generous Gentleman — But Judge of my
surprise when, after having ransacked my Trunk and thrown out of it
all my Chattels and apparells on the Carpet, I had the mortification
to discover that I had parted with all of them — I have given perhaps

71. *Jardin Potagers* are vegetable gardens.

a dozen to that Friendly Man, but I regret very much he has had no more as he appeared quite pleased with the Idea of rendering them Indigenous to this Country =

No Letters from thee, Dearest Friend, no, not one word — The wind Blew quite a Breese. It rained during the early part of the morning and it was not untill 12 o'clock that I reached this *enchanted Spot*. M⁰⁰ Rathbone, the benevolent Mother, the queen Bee of this honeyed mansion received me alone — and alone I had the pleasure of contemplating her mien and of lessening to the heavenly gifts of her Heart throw her Conversation =

How gratifying it is to be able to believe that not all our Species has yet felt of the fault conferred on Man at its Creation, that there yet exists spotless, matchless divine beings to adore, to venerate, to look up to as the resemblance of the Omnipotent God that gave them Breath!! — Yes, Dearest Lucy, such are the heavenly gifts that are to be seen under this Roof, and so warming with purity are the powers of this Happy being that all around glows with calm contentedness and truly parental affection — I have been here perhaps one hour, perhaps more, perhaps less; I felt not the time passed; I panted for more to enable myself to bring my understanding under the rays of her whom, I never can cease to Admire and respect!! I saw gradually the familly enter, and I feared not this day to Kiss all the sweet children of my Friend's Wife =

How pleasing it was for me to Contemplate these dear Little Ones peaceably engaged in reaping the benefits of a good Education — Seated on their little benches, in diferent parts of the Room, each held a Book and each held their eyes on the Book before them = The Botanist is in — and also Miss Hanna Maria — We are all employed again, for I myself have taken my Bewick & am looking on the carefull Sarigue nursing, guarding her tender young.[72] =

How tranquil even my Heart in such situation — We dined as Yesterday: the afternoon is blustery, windy and all together [fit to deepen] the feelings of the American Visitor that is now within =

72. *Sarigue* is the French word for a South American opossum, *Didelphys opossum*. Thomas Bewick's woodcut of a female nursing her young and his account of the species appear on pages 395–97 of his *A General History of Quadrupeds* (London, 1792).

yet it is [well known]† that I am fond of much exercise and of Nature's contemplation. Then a walk is proposed me. The Dog that came from the Kamchatkan [MS: Kamss*katack's] shores is loosened for me to look at. Miss Rathbone is ready and accompanied by the Nephew. We three Depart — Ah, how I did wish that *I* could have conducted them towards the Beech Woods rendered by Thee so Dear; and shewn them our Wild Scenery of the Woods of America. But, no, it could not be and we walk^d between dreary Walls contenting ourselves with the distant objects without the sweet privileges of moving freely to & fro to right or Left or to advance towards any particular object that might with a wish attract the Eye — Thus we reach^d the Mersey and, I saw the Free Gull floating on the Breese, checking her Course, falling on the Watters and seize [MS: scease] her prey: I saw the busy brisk Little Sanderling searching cautiously the Lesser bivalves: I saw — the same objects on the shores of my Distant Country's Streams and Wished to be possessed for a while of the Powers of the Eagle's nervous pinions that I might at one flight sail to thee, Dearest Friend, and acquaint thee of these English Friends that every moment become dearer to me —

We are seated and feasting on the rarefied Breese our lungs — our Eyes on the distant scenery = Now on our return we proceed. =

It is not very Shocking that whilst in England, all is Hospitality within, all is Aristocratic without their Dwellings — No one dare *trespass*, as it is called, one foot on the Grass — *Signs of Large Dogs* are put up to infer that Further you must not advance. Steel Traps and spring Guns are set to destroy you should you prove Fool Hardy, & to finish our exercise we were forced to walk in files on the narrow portion of a wall fearing the rebuke of the Landlord around the grounds of which we had a desire to ramble: — but, my Lucy, this is all a Trifle; read on — Beggars in England are like our Ticks of Louisianna — They stick to one and sting our better feelings every moment — England is now Rich with poverty, gaping aghast, which ever way you may look = Good Honest People are forced here to beg, not money, Lucy, but ~~~~ ah, yes, Bread — Bread, the Beggar says. "Not for me. I am strong yet but for my poor famished little one" —

"Stract not my Heart thus, My Dear Husband, do [not], pray; thou certainly is not aware how thou grievest me" —

No more then, but only join in this Prayer *May our Heavenly Father have Mercy upon them*!!! —

Lucy, look at R$\underline{d}$ Rathbone seated with his Mother on the same chair, look at them. Dost thou feel the Heavenly power that acts around us? Dost thou hear the suavity of their reciprocal proofs of adoration? Dost thou see the Group improving with Daughters, Friends & Nephew and Younger children, almost clinging around her? Lucy, my Heart is bursting with delight. I also will adore her!! —

Gradually the day has vanished; the stormy night seems to rally all Friends together and — I am, Lucy, going to open my Heart to these Good people. I am going to read of Thee and Myself & of our Dear Children and of my feelings — Lucy (*hony soit qui mal y pense*!!!)[73]

I am attended. M$\underline{rs}$ R$\underline{d}$ Rathbone who was reposing on a sopha has approached the Table. All are listening to me. My eyes are burning. Then conceive the situation of my Heart! — but Dearest Friend, they call my totering essays at giving thee the thoughts that act upon my senses during my absence from thee quite agreable to them — I am not now so much choaked. I drank and I read on — perhaps half a dozen [MS: dz$\underline{n}$] of my Days. Ah, Lucy, could they hear of my nights at this Distance from America: from all that God gave me to render Life Dear — but, no, I will not make *Thee* Miserable — read on —

A Port Folio has been brought on the Table, by the mother who will not thro her Kind affection suffer neither son or Daughter to go for it, and out emerged Roscoe's Soul!! — I read. I lessen. Alas, I can but admire. Ah, I do more. I Live with the Surety that Roscoe will never die!!! —

Friends! Dear Friends, Good Night. May our God Bless us! Lucy, thank them for the good health they just now all wished thee and my Friends here & in America. My Ennemies, if I have any, to all Good Night. Good Night to my own Venerable Mother, to my children, Good Night to thee, the Soul of my Powers, Good Night —

I have [reached]† the same chamber w[h]ere I rested before. I have in my hands both R$\underline{d}$ Rathbone's Hand[s] and we feel mutual pressure of hands — He talks of his Mother as I wish every Son would do — gives me with his blessings a Letter and we part to meet again — Lucy, Good Night —

73. Audubon quotes the motto of the British Order of the Garter, "honi soit qui mal y pense," as he declares that he is going to open his heart to his hosts. The motto translates as "shamed be he who thinks evil of it."

Well, my sweet Friend, I am for once again writting in the
chamber where [MS: ware] I have slept free from the bustling noise
of the City =

I walk^d early to Liverpool. I was anxious to see if my happiness might
be improved by reading a letter from thy hand. I reach^d [there] so
[early] that my breakfast was over by seven o'clock and I took a long
walk again along the diferent Docks to pass the time and employ my
mind and Judgment.

I saw a Vessel undergoing the reinforcing action of Coppering =
The weather being very beautifull, I looked with pleasure on the active
scenery about me — remarked the enormous size of the Horses that
here can singly in one Cart draw as many as 16 Bales of Cotton — They
look well, fat, sleek and suficiently active for the purposes intended for
them to perform = I called at the Post office but no letter. —

I went to the Institution and Wrote there a good deal, saw Dr Trail
and we spoke much of my plans — I found the Doc^r Highly scientific
— We examined 3 Egiptian momies = Many persons peep^d at my
Birds as I peep^d at them — however how many English Shillings were
received I cannot tell. I did not enquire — I took Tea at M^r Ed$^{\underline{d}}$ Roscoe
and rode in M$^{\underline{rs}}$ Lace's Carriage close to this Place, where I descended
from it and walk^d the remainder of the way —

I felt Happier to night than I have done for months. The good Ladies
were at work when I made my entrance and the time passed away very
agreably — I read again to them — My Friend R$^{\underline{d}}$ and others were
absent. The moon shone beautifully, and I Hoped that thou might be
gazing on its silvery Robe as I was also with eye bent that way — We
walk^d and chated all ease — The Remainder of the Friends all arrived
and found us all seated fronting the Timid yet brightest ornement of
the night = How pleasing music would have been to me then, ah,
music from Thee — We returned Home, and I am just finish[ing] a
day not Complex with Incident but one very hapily spent. All I long^d
for was for thee: Miss Rathbone kindly presented me with Roscoe's
poems; Lucy, God Bless thee. I have just shook my Friends hands —
Good night —

My spirits are low to night Lucy — I am in Dale Street, not at Green
Banks — My Eyes are Cast (indeed perhaps sullenly) on the angry
looking Clouds that chafe [MS: shafe] the full Moon — not as they were
last evening when, seated in the rocky alcove of my Friends Grounds,
they were cast^{d} on the same Sublime Object with diferent thoughts —
My spirits, my Dear Wife, are Indeed very low — The Winds impart
dismall tokens in their howlings [MS: hawlings] — and the Voice of
a public Crier at an au[c]tion room not far enough distant from me
finishing the Front but very uninteresting ground of this Evening's
Miserable Picture — but let me return to Green Banks and Start like a
Lark from my Nest at the dawn [MS: down] this morning and rove thro
the Dews and watch the Timid Birds motion that flies from bush to
bush before me — Let us return to the Mersey and look on the country
in Wales, on the Calm serene sky and lessen to the voice of the quail
here so shy — Ah, yes, walk with me on the tide beaten beach and watch
the Solan Goose[74] in search of a retreat from the cruel destroyer Man —

Seest thou the Smugler how he runs away — how Little he suspected
that Goldsmith's Burchell[75] was after him. Yet I must acknowldege he
made me pant — before I reached him — I have regretted all day my
adventure of this morning, and I am sorry to think now how cruel it
was in me to frighten the poor Fellow so —. Lucy, I had my Sword
Cane and the moment the stranger drop^{d} his Bag and ran from me, that
moment I drew the dangerous blade and, Crying unmercifully *Stop
Thief*, made way towards him in a style that — I am sure he never had
seen used by the Gentlemen of the Customs that no doubt were now
rather drowsy — Poor Fellow, had he known me as I know Thee and
as I am known to thee, his Eyes would not have started from his head
as they did, nor his heart swelled with apprehansion — There he was
begging for mercy, said it was the first time and only some rotten Leaves
of Tabocco.

74. The solan goose is the gannet.

75. In Oliver Goldsmith's *The Vicar of Wakefield* (1766), Mr. Burchell is thought for a while
to be an enemy of the protagonist's family, only to be revealed later as the man who restores the
family's fortune and happiness. The expletive "Fudge," which Audubon occasionally uses in this
journal, is a characteristic expression of Mr. Burchell.

I positively did wish he had had all that I once purchased for Richd Atkinson of Richmond[76] — The Boat that had landed him quite in my view, although {I} was not seen by the smuglers on Board, Instead of landing and defending their Companion fled by rowing like Cowards —

I was astonished at such Conduct from Englishmen — I told this poor being to raise and bring the bag — He did so — No, Lucy, there is much said here about the abject state of Slavery in our Truly United States, but I never beheld there a thing shaped like a Man so completly subdue[d] by fear of punishment —

He walk[ed] to the bag and brought it — I told him that a smugler was an enemy to his Country and that he deserved severe Punishment (recollect, my Sword was all ready to defend me). He cries and says "Oh, for God sake, save me, take the tobacco [MS: Tabocca]" — Poor fellow, I never even smoaked, and that Thou knowest well, a single cigar =

I could stand this no longer — I dreaded that some real officer of the Customs might appear and Interfer in a very diferent manner — I told him to clean himself and to be carefull he never should do such outrage again — I had one of my Pockets disagreably laden with Copper stuff that the shop keepers give here and Call pennies [MS: penny] — I gave them all to him, told him to look at my face well and go — He did look, Lucy, with Eyes that I cannot either describe or understand. He pray^{d} aloud for my Salvation and made for a thick hedge [MS: Edge], where he disapeared from my view —

I Look^{d} on the River. The Boat was out of my sight — I would say that this poor Fellow had perhaps 50 or 60 pounds of fine Virginia Clean Leafed tabacco in the bag and Two Pistols, which he said were not Loaded — Of this I am not quite sure — but Cannons in the Hands of him who fears either the Laws of his country whilst acting against them fears not God but fears Men! —

I thought as I scraped the mud from my boots that I had been rather too rash and thought also that if the man Had been an accustomed Vilain, he might have Shot me Dead on the spot —

I have thought of this event all day — I thought for a while that I had seen this very man amongst the Crowd of Pilots that boarded us in the Irish Channel — He was dressed precisely Like them and, as well as I

76. Presumably, a merchant Audubon once dealt with.

Could see, every one on board the Yawl that plyed away from one single man against 5, had they Landed — What a pretty figure I would have made with my small Sword against men that were apparently full as stout as myself =

Now I am neither a Canning nor a Gallatin[77] but, Lucy, I Cannot think that Canning with all his Cunning is Equal to our Gallatin —

"Hush, my Husband, Come, No Politics, I pray" —

Well, be it so — I walk^d towards the Green Bank again thinking of the Smugler untill I saw over a wall a man digging potatoes — They were small and indiferently formed — The season has been uncommonly dry — and Hot also, the English say — For my part, I am allmost freesing —

I saw one of the famous Dogs spoken of Yesterday, but it was still worst than the Smugler. I could out run him on account of his being too fat — Now, perhaps the Smugler might have outran a Custom house officer thro the same Cause —

I have done a great deal this morning and yet it is only seven o'clock — I reach Green Banks and as no Body is up I start again an other way, not at all anxious to Imitate the Trusty officers of his Britannic Magesty — I have laid on the Grass and am Lessening to the rough rude voice of a Magpie = It is not the same Bird, I am quite [sure], that we have in America's Norwest Portion, but this I will detail when my Arkansaw Magpie Comes to view thro my Publication[78] —

I see that it is 8 o'clock, and towards the House I make again — I now enter. The Domestics are Cleaning and I open a small book Elementary of Botanical Instruction — Miss Anna Maria is come dressed in a

77. In 1826 George Canning (1770–1827) was the vigorous and eloquent British foreign secretary; he served in that post from 1822 to 1827.

78. Audubon's reference here to his "Arkansaw Magpie" is to the common magpie (Plate CCCLVII), which was first reported to Audubon as being found near the "head waters of the Red River in Louisiana" (OB, 4:408). His certainty that the common magpie of America was a species distinct from the European had softened considerably by the 1838 publication of his essay on the species (OB, 4:408–13). Of the three magpie species Audubon drew, only the common magpie was discussed in relation to the European magpie. Ford's note to this reference seems confused: "Presumably Columbian Jay (American Magpie: Folio Plate XCI)" (Journal, 159n55). The Columbian magpie, or jay (Plate XCVI), was never considered the same species as the European magpie, nor was it called the "American jay," which is the name that appears on Plate CCCLVII, the common or black-billed magpie.

Green silk riding Habit — Lucy, she is a very Kind good Girl, quite the Child of M{rs} Rathbone — She is writing — A stranger would say "What, the man cannot be reading with attention Certainly," but I will answer Yes and prove it, for the Letters are directed from Amelia to Constance — It is the Mother's wish that the Daughter Should study Botany during her sister's absence &{c} &{c}[79] — but thou knows as well as M{rs} xxxxx what an observer I am with the use of only one Eye —

I hear — I see, I kiss the sweet Children — The breakfast Bell is ringing and we are round the table seated — To Town M{rs} Rathbone and I are going, but before this, Lucy, Look at my Friend how he Kisses his Wife. Happy pair — ah, happy familly all — Never, never have I seen such regularity of kind dispositions and feelings =

But, Lucy, I am now really rolling in the little Carriage with the *Queen Bee* of Green Banks, and now I am presenting my respects to M{rs} W{am} Rathbone, whom thou Knowest well [h]as Auburn eyes and black Learned Eyebrows — The Lady of the Pocket Book —

I hear that my Pastells have not Come yet and am rolling in the Little Carriage again to the Institution —

There, have I not had a good morning's work done before the 7/8 of the good rich People of Liverpool have open{d} either their Eyes or their Heart on the poor that in greatest patience are in waiting at their Door?

I shewed Thy Face to day, Lucy, to all my Friends and M{rs} W{am} Rathbone is, she says, just thy age — Then she is not old, nor thee, nor any aimiable woman besides ye both, had you each of you doubled Each day You have spent in this World Twice —

I received the following note from M{r} Austin and 3 Letters from E. Roscoe Esq{re} who was so kind to call on me here — I answered to M{r} Austin — and this afternoon began a painting of the Trapped Otter with Intention, if well done, to present it to my Good Friend's Wife[80] —

I then proceeded to W{am} Rathbone and spent there a most agreable

79. Books designed to introduce children to botany were popular and numerous in the late eighteenth and early nineteenth centuries. They were frequently designed as a series of letters or dialogues between siblings. The situation in the book Audubon drew from the Rathbone shelf involved the absent Amalia writing home to her sister Constance to instruct her in botany, in accordance with their mother's wish.

80. This image, which Audubon painted several times in oil, eventually became Plate LI of *Viviparous Quadrupeds of North America* (1842–46).

peaceable evening — A quaker Lady named Abigail,[81] a Cousin of R$\underline{d}$ Rathbone and I believe from Manchester; made me straiten myself a little at first glance, but it was only momentary — She spoke so plainly that my understanding was not embarassed $=$ We talk^d mostly on the present situation of England — her Poors, her Institutions &$\underline{c}$. It grieved me to hear say that a Non Intercourse between the U. S. and the British West India Island had taken place.

I should now Conclude that their Government has really a Wish to Emancipate Both White & Black slaves — here for want of Bread and there also when all will raise *en Masse* and exibit to the world again the Horrors of a Revolution[82] $=$

But bless me, I have trespassed & have entered a Wrong path — one that I neither have a Wish or right to follow —

The Intelligent Swiss I thought extremely kindly Invited me to dine with him and some young French Gentlemen Saturday Next at half past 5. — I said particularly kindly because I think that he perceived how low spirited I felt. Consequently he was doubly kind —

I discovered this Evening the benevolent actions of M$^{\underline{rs}}$ Rathbone rather singularly — M$^{\underline{rs}}$ Abigail told her that her husband had Lost very little Indeed by lending [MS: Landing] to Honest poors at Manchester in sums of not exceeding 10 £. M$^{\underline{rs}}$ R. repeated this to her Husband

81. Abigail Benson Dockray (1783–1842) was a cousin of the Rathbones. She married David Dockray of Manchester in Liverpool on August 29, 1805; they had six sons and four daughters. She was a Quaker minister (beginning in 1822) involved in the antislavery and prison reform movements.

82. On July 26, 1826, England closed the West Indian ports to American vessels, effective December 1. President John Quincy Adams retaliated in March 1827 by restoring past restrictions on trade with England. The result was that no vessels could trade directly between the West Indies and the United States. This affected Liverpool merchants by diminishing the market for West Indian sugar, thereby making it even more difficult for British planters in the West Indies and plantation owners living in England to make the profits needed to keep operating their slave-labor sugar plantations. Audubon would have heard much about the issue of slavery in Liverpool. Parliament had agreed in 1823 to the emancipation of slaves on the condition that slave owners would be compensated. These issues were actively debated in England between 1823 and 1833, when Parliament passed the Slavery Abolition Act. Quakers, of course, were a major force in the British antislavery movement.

Audubon was born on his father's slave plantation on the island of Saint-Domingue (today's Haiti) and knew of the violent slave uprising that occurred shortly after his father sent him to France in the spring of 1789.

and the truth Came out that Mrs Rathbone herself follow^d the same principles and had Out run the same terms, between 50, and 100 £.

Children here are forced by their Parents to Collect during the Course of one day a Certain amount by begging or Stealing, or Murder perhaps, or undergo a severe punishment on the return home — There it is Home sweet Home — but a Hell it must surely be — The Tricks resorted to by these Miserable wretches are numberless and in some Instances very Curious — The News papers abound with them — ah, and are filled mostly with accounts of Murders — Hangings — Thefts — and more abominable acts — I can scarce look at them.

A person followed me 3 Squares to tempt me to purchase a Watch worth 4 shillings for 8 pounds — A neat young Girl stop^d me in the Midle of a principal street and delivered a paper to me of a most Extraordinary nature — I cannot really mention its Contents to thee — but, Lucy, 2 Children watch my going to the Institution every day — I for some time gave them pences, but, finding them more troublesome the more I gave — I took it in Head to carry some Bread & Meat to them and was shock^d to discover that they were not hungry — Since then I pay no attention to them, and their Calling me "Good Captain" does not Steer their Vessel into my Port —

I reach^d my Lodgings and, my Dear Wife, the number of most abandoned and Daring Prostitutes is Wonderfull — What a World. Good God! — Good night — ½ past one.

LIVERPOOL AUGUST 18TH 1826. —

I told thee that I had began a Painting of the Trapped Otter — I had outlined it and to day nearly compleated it = Of course, I have nothing much to say untill I reach *sweet Sister Ann's* house in Hedge Hill — She is well, Miss Donathan is well = Mr Gordon has not returned. = Ah, there are 2 Extra females — "Miss Duff's, Mr Audubon" — a Dark Complected face and a negative face are in View — The first is possessed of Eyes and Eye brows and understanding of a superior Cast = The second I discover is anxious to reach the merits of her Sister = The Conversation is good — The music is good and pleasing to me, thou knowest well — Miss Duff sings and plays quite Decently = I accompan^d them (not on the Piano) but to their House in Great George

Square, full one and ½ mile I think my Legs called it — but my mental faculties were quite refreshed by the Controversy that arose between Miss Duff and thy Husband about that "Lazy Horse Genius" — The Miss was against thy Husband but thy Husband was against her — Of course we parted as we had met, very good Friends I Hope —

I am now again in Dale Street. I have been 3 times to the Post Office in vain to day, and I go now to my bed in no pleasing mood, I assure thee — My Beloved Wife, do write to me — for Ever Thine, Good Night —

GREEN BANKS AUGUST 19TH 1826. —

The days, the nights, the time all passes away and I am still as destitute, desolate and alone as if *Thou* hadst never existed — Must I then bear sorrows forever and feel the pangs of absence still severer — Am I to Live without even hearing from thee, my Lucy — Ah, no. — no — no — In a few moments I will be down on a bed Intended for me to repose, but it can only be to bear my body untill the morning's dawn — Rest there is none without thee and sleep none but in Eternity —

Unfortunate *by Trade*, this day again, or better say yesterday, I commited an other error to add to the thousands that have so motled my Life that, did I not believe in God, I would scarce now care if I Lived or Died —

"Ah, My Laforest, thy unfortunate mood again. Do for my sake drop these gloomy Ideas and think of my Love for thee, of our Dear Children, of the exertions that at thy hands we need yet; that!!!["] —

Well, my Lucy, I needed but a sentence from thee — My Heart is lighter, my spirits are also beguild and I will merely relate facts ⹀

I painted this morning untill I could paint no more — My work was too wet to proceed, and I put it aside — Yesterday Mrs Rathbone's nephew went into Wales supposing (or rather let me say expecting) that I had gone also — It was thro kindness for me and mere complaisan[ce] that led him ⹀ This neglect in me vexed me [more] than If I had Lost 50 pounds — I will make no apology. I must only repent — I remained much of my time at the Institution. *I* expected to see there Sister Ann and her Compagnion with the Miss Duffs, but after having waited untill past five, I was obliged to go to my Appointment of Dinner with Mr A. Melly and I wrote the following note to Ann —

My Dear Sister — You must excuse the paper, the pen and the writter — The fact, however, is this; my painting was not suficiently dry to proceed toward its Atchievement — Of course, you will not see it to day; but it will not go beyond Hedge Hill without your Viewing it = Then, my Dear Ann, try to content your Friends and yourself with a small portion of *American produce*. Remember me, pray, to your aimiable Compagnion and believe me sincerely Yours for ever — J. J. A — †

I reachd Mr A. Melly's House in Greenville Street rather before him — He came, pulled off his Wigg, and made me at home in a moment — I had quite a pleasant time there — The Guests were Swiss, Genevise, Italians and Germans =

The *Moore Game*,[83] however, was highly *tainted*, the True Flavour for the Lords of England = Common people, or persons who have no title *Hereditary*: Those who are not *Heritics by Birth* have to write a very particular note of thanks for every paire of Rotten Grous they receive from a Fatten^d Friend — Now in America *Freedom is Hereditary*!!! — Grous and Turkey, the Elk, the Bufaloe or the *Venaison* reach^d the palate of all Individuals without a Sigh of Oppression —

"Politics again — I would be enclined to believe that thou hast a Tendency towards such matters" —

No, my Dear Wife, I merely wish the world well —

Our Dinner was quite *a la Francaise*, all gayety, wittiscisms and good Chear — Mr Melly Drove me in his Gig to Bid good evening to my Otter and afterwards to Green Banks = It was then that R^d Rathbone, having asked me if I had seen any thing of his Cousin that had gone to Wales that I felt so mortified with myself —

We had much music on the Pianno and Two flute[s] = I did itch [MS: Hitch] to take a Part but dared not, fearing the making of a False note or loosing the time by Loosing my senses thro fear — but I Lessen^d with pleasure and Turned the Leafs for the Performers —

At Eleven o'clock the moon nearly full was Inviting for a Walk, and the good old Lady took a Long one with me under my arm purposely to give me pleasure — Miss Hanna Walk^d some distance behind us

83. The *Moore Game*, that is, game birds shot on the moor.

with her Cousin and, I Assure thee, My Lucy, I heard not a word of *their* conversation — Mrs Rathbone spoke of the Heavens — of the powers of our actions, of the sources of those Powers, of the Deep Curtain that for ever must lay between our understanding and Faculties whilst we view and feel but cannot Conceive =

It was Sunday morning when we returned; I felt the want of Rest and was Conducted by my Friend to a new chamber, w[h]ere again and again I was ask^d to Come and Stay — Good People — My Lucy, Good Night =

LIVERPOOL SUNDAY 20TH 1826. — AUGUST —

I remained in bed 4 hours. How much I slept must not be known — I was at the Mersey before sun Rise when Nature was as Calm as if yet asleep = So Calm was all about Nature herself the noise of the Padles of a Steam Boat running down the River Dee then 8 miles Distant could be heard Distinctly — "I knew by the Smoak that so gracefully Curled" that a Steam Boat was the cause producing the Sound[84] =

This morning I was quite surprised to see Persons out so early = I saw Two men hunting with a Dog without Guns — The Dog was a Shabby looking setter but moved well — I thought the men redened as I approached them, but they stood Still and saw me go bye = Another man was Catching Linnets with Bird Lime — Others were Searching Clams and other Shell Fish along the Shores = I also examined some Large Baskets with mouths up Stream to Catch Fish as the River flows toward the Sea — I walk^d a great Distance to Green Banks again — It was 8 o'clock but no sound was heard. All were yet reposing — I read on the Grass — and the sweet Children soon came to me to be kissed and to wish me well —

Mr Melly took me to Town again and I breakfast^d with him at 10 o'clock with 6 young Gentlemen like those of Yesterday. Afterwards he read to the whole an excellent Sermon — Then I went to the Blinds church — then ran to my Lodgings to Dress and off to Russel Street N$^{\underline{o}}$ 60 to Dine with Mr Austin the Artist, and here I am — Looking at

84. Audubon is echoing and playing off a very popular poem by the very popular Irish poet Thomas Moore (1779–1852). The poem's title is "Ballad Stanzas," from *Epistles, Odes, and Other Poems* (1806), 286. The second line is "Above the green elms, that a cottage was near." It is a light romantic reverie of love and a cottage in unspoiled American woods.

Watter Color paintings done in a Style altogether new [MS: Knew] to me — possessing rich Effects without the {L**ast} finishing — The Imagination here must supply that and Conceive hands, faces, feet — Dogs or Horses, as the Case may be — Lucy, I have said this to be ahead of all the Critics around me. I assure thee they *Finish* with a vengeance all they begain —

We dined well, although I could have drawn a Line 2 miles Long between this Dinner and [*****]† I have partaken of at the Rathbone's — or Roscoe's — How much there is in the Breed, particularly in England!

I saw there a Doct.ʳ Cooke, a man of much Information — I went to the Blind church again with the Music Master of that Establishment and was placed Close by the Organs. It is really surprising how well the Blinds do perform — The one that Touched the Keys was an excellent Musician and talkᵈ to me as if he saw in my eyes how much I Love good Music =

I saw one of the female performers pressing gently the arm of an other female and then pressing her more to Direct her tone of voice and Keep in Time as she sang a Solo =

I have had 3 sermons this day. They were not from a Scolding wife, My Dear Lucy. Of Course, they all did me good — I went to bed early = not, however, without wishing Thee well and bidding Thee Good Night —

LIVERPOOL THE 21ST AUGUST 1826 =

I painted a good Deal this day, finished my Otter or Rather M.ʳˢ R.ᵈ Rathbone's Otter = It was viewed by many and admired = I received a Gross of Pastelles from London for which I was charged more than Double what they cost in New York — and all entirely Too soft =

I was Invited to remove to Green Banks altogether during the Time that I may stay here — but declined going untill I have painted the Wild Turkey Cock for the Royal Institution = say 3 Days = I retired early to my rooms, began a letter to thee and laid down in my bed at ½ past 10, went to sleep after wishing thee well but really do not know when ~~~~

Having not been able to write for many days, I am now obliged to resume without date to overtake the present date, able only to write the principal facts that have taken place, few of which, indeed, are worth relating but still here they come like a set of beggars, each anxious to be served first — I think then that as a good Supper is a good thing, I will serve this first = I had it at Doct^{r} Trail in Company of the French Consul with Two other gentlemen Frenchmen. The Conversation *of Course* was ornithological and I [L****t^{d}] a good deal = I was much encouraged & requested to visit France Imediately = A Young Lady there gave me some delightfull music and Mrs Trail some excellent Conversation along with good wine =

As suppers are such nice things, let us have another — Well, no objections — I received a Polite note from Mr Molineux[85] and I reach^{d} his House at 8 in the Evening. In a few minutes, seventeen persons were assembled in a Chorus — Untill 12 my Ears were indeed feasted = I do not recollect ever before in my whole Life having lessened to so many men's voices so truly well managed. The diversity was as great as it was agreable — Mr Clement[i][86] & Tomlinson from London were [MS: where] present — At half past one when Supper was just finished (and it was a very fine one), each person at table being desired to Turn his plate saw in doing this the Lord's Prayer printed on the back of it and Mr Molineux having began to sing it, each person in succession entered in action and that Chorus was divinely true =

Mr Austin came in a moment, but having seen 2 Brothers of the brush, I saw he was not at ease. It proved so. He soon retired = Being very Late and perceiving that the streets had more Ladies of rank than watchmen watching, I took to [the] first of those Latters and beg[ged] for his Company to my Lodgings. He acquiesced at once and we walk^{d} safer from the aprehensions of being caried off by force *of arms*. On Knocking at the *Commercial's* Door, a voice from above enquired who was there = The Watchman answered N° 11 — The number of my room previously given to him by me as we walk^{d} the streets lessening to the many curious night occurences of the streets of Liverpool — N^{o}

85. Ford identifies this Mr. Molineux as the French consul mentioned in the preceding paragraph (*Journal*, 167).

86. Muzio Clementi (1752–1832) was the Italian-born musician and composer noted for his contributions to the rise of the pianoforte. He traveled extensively but lived most of his adult life in London. When Audubon met him, Clementi was one of the most famous and accomplished composers in Europe.

11 was admitted, and I went to sleep for a few hours, for by six the next morning I was at work on my Painting of the Wild Turkey Cock =

As usual I was with my Neck uncovered, my sleeves up to my shoulders, my Hairs all flowing and the Colors also on a Canvas of 4 feet $^8/_{12}$ by 5 feet $^8/_{12}$ that I Covered Compleately in 23 hours time = Mr Melly, Dr Trail, Mrs W^{am} Rathbone and many other Persons were in my Painting Room during the while talking and wondering how I manage to Conceive & finish this fast, and I believe their presence made me work still faster & better — The fact is that on the 2^{d} day after I began this Large and beautifull Painting, it was framed and hung in the Exibition room = I call it beautifull, Lucy, because every body called it so before me, and thou knowest well *que la Voix du Peuple est la Voix de Dieu*[87] =

At Last I removed to Green Bank, the delightfull Green Bank, and was hailed with the same kind reception. The Good Lady requested that I should conceive myself at Home, and the Many nice attentions that I received there were convincing proofs that I was truly wellcome = I had the Study of Mr Theodore Rathbone[88] alloted me for my Drawing room = I Cannot tell how much Knowledge the Gentleman took with him to the Continent w[h]ere he is now travelling with *his* Lucy, but I found an astonishing quantity all around me in his Library — Portfolios, Casts of antiques — &^{c} &^{c} &^{c} =

Now, this is not all what troubled me. No, I am not, indeed, troubled by Knowledge myself but very much so at the Idea that Mrs Richd Rathbone should refuse to accept my Otter — I took the opportunity of her being absent and having wrote a Line to Mr Munro of the Institution. The Picture was Varnished and taken to her House with a note from me to that most aimiable Lady† = She soon saw it and sent her Brother to bring me in his Cariage, but as I well knew that either thanks or compliments or both would be the fruits of so an early visit, I declined it and beg^d to be excused — I felt Happy that the piece deserved the acceptance and this relieved me of a heavy Burthen =

When afterward I saw her; She appeared more aimiable than ever.

87. That is, that the voice of the people is the voice of God.

88. Theodore Woolman Rathbone (1798–1863) was the sixth child born to the "Queen Bee" and William Rathbone. He was the younger brother of Audubon's favorite Rathbone, Hannah Mary.

Her sweet little Bazil laid on her bosom and presented a Picture fit for the Gods to study and for men to wonder at = Her good Husband 2 days after wrote me a most kind letter of thanks worth 20 such Paintings as I gave his Lady =

Drawing every Day, and dining every Sunday at Mr Roscoe = I gave a Lesson of Drawing to Mrs Rathbone and one to Mrs Ed^d Roscoe — was really busy = I wrote to Thee, to N. Berthoud, to Victor, to Charles Bonaparte and forward^d thee *Thy Watch* by the Packet Ship *Canada* bound to New York thro the Care of Messrs Rathbone & Co =

I made a Drawing for Miss Hanna Maria Rathbone, another for Mrs W^{am} Rathbone, another for my venerable and most kind Friend Mrs Rathbone the Mother Bee — another for Mrs Roscoe and another for Young Henry Chorley[89] an aimiable fellow who plays on the Piano delightfully =

My Time in fact was most Happily spent. I needed only thee, my Dear Friend = All my Sundays have been alike, Breakfasting with Mr Melly & Friends and going to church at the Blinds Asylum: every one is surprised at my Habits of Early Rising, and all also say that I eat nothing — I raise very early to be sure and eat very much also, I am quite sure =

My exibition at the Institution Continues and pays well. I visited there occasionally = A few Days since, Mr Roscoe Dined here with his Daughter Jane. I had just finished a Drawing for Mrs Rathbone — Young Charles, the brother of Henry Chorley, a most Interesting and aimiable Young Man, a Classical scholar, was so kind as to transmit my thoughts into verse in a delightfull manner and I wrote 20 well match^d Lines under my work = Mr Roscoe's eyes grew Larger than ever and so did the fairer eyes of Miss Jane grow Larger — They Both believed I believe that I was the Composer, but, alas, no. My Poor Brains never measured Time appropriately yet, nor ever will. = But I wished to have a piece of Mr Roscoe's poetry, and I thought that this might tantalize him to set to — He frequently repeated that the Lines were beautifull, and I was glad of this as I thought so myself —

---

89. After Jane Wilkinson Chorley's husband died, she moved her family to Liverpool to help tend to an ailing cousin of the Rathbones. Two of her sons, Henry Fothergill Chorley (1808–72) and John Rutter Chorley (1806–67), were long-term regulars at Green Bank, and both befriended Audubon. Under private tutors, they both excelled in literary studies. Henry would become a well-known book reviewer and the leading music journalist in England. John would become a poet, essayist, and scholar of Spanish literature.

The Young Gentlemen that visited the House were desirous of taking early Walks with me, and I had them up with the Lark when ever they requested it — but it was only for a Day, and the next I walk^d alone with only my thoughts about me =

My receiving no Letters from thee rendered me very sullen at time[s], and Every night when I went to try to rest, I pray^d more fervently for thy safety, Health & Happiness than ever = One Night I awaken^d sudenly praying thus quite aloud and dreaded to have been heard and taken for a maniac. =

Vincent Nolte arrived from the U. S. — but I was so unfortunate as not to see him, although I tried much = I had all my Journal Copied for thy sake to send it thee — I forward^d thee and N. Berthoud each a Bundle of News Papers — and wrote again to thee = Mr Gordon who had absented to London made some Enquiries for Letters for me but none were to be found =

GREEN BANK. 6TH 1826. SEPTEMBER. — †

I forwarded thee this morning a full Copy of this Book per Brig *Isabella* bound to New Orleans, with it all the Papers that I could procure. May thou receive all in goodly Happy Mood! =

When I came to Green Bank this last time, I had been breakfasting with Mrs Ed^d Roscoe and Daughter, to whom I gave advise about drawing; I walked fast and had a Little Basket lent me by Mr Munro that contained some clean linens, a Small red port Folio, my Journal and the Drawing for Mrs Rathbone framed in an Oak frame as plain as could be, all under my arm and hands — The familly were still at breakfast — As usual each Individual rose to come and meet me = All were well = I was told that Lady Isabella Douglass,[90] the sister of Lord Selkirk, former governor of Canada, was in the house a visitor = I was told that she

90. The identity of this "Lady Isabella Douglass, the sister of Lord Selkirk, former governor of Canada" is unclear. Thomas Douglas, fifth Earl of Selkirk (1771–1820), had three sisters, none of whom was named Isabella, and while he was famously involved in establishing settlements in Canada, he was never a governor general of Canada. His son, the sixth Earl of Selkirk, Dunbar James Douglas (1809–85), was also never governor general of Canada, and, while he had a sister named Isabella (1811–93), she was only fifteen in 1826 and so not the lady Audubon met at Green Bank.

was now unable to walk and that consequently she moved about in a rolling chair from spot to spot, confined, however, to a very small area for daily exercise =

The name of Lady Douglass startled me considerably — I had found Lord Stanley an extremely Polite Kind unasuming Man, but what diference there might be between him and Lady Isabella were quite matters of conjecture = I concluded that as she was a Friend of Mrs Rathbone, *she could not* be very unmercifull because of her being Lady Douglass =

I went to my work and drew a very Short time — I could not work to my wish — The weather was Inviting. I therefore invited John Chorley Esqr to ramble with me a while = On returning to Green Bank, I saw & met Lady Isabella — Her features are regularly formed, her complexion fair and her countenance of a Happy composition — I look^d at her well and, although she spoke not to me after being Introduced, I *guessed* that she knew pretty well who was the man with the Long Hair and sheepish aspect =

"Shame, my Laforest. How canst thou speak of thyself in such words — I really do not like it — Few men are better formed, nay handsomer than thou art, and I am sure thy aspect (if aspect it must be called) is quite favorable in all points of View" =

Well, my Beloved Wife, I "owe thee one" =

Lady Douglass sat next me at Dinner and I between her and the *Lady Rathbone* — She spoke but seldom, and I chewed my food as rapidly as if I had stolled it = In the afternoon I had again the opportunity of seeing her Ladyship and after some conversation was much pleased with her acquaintance = She was apparent[l]y allways in good Spirits and, as I did not call her Lady D. or My Lady, I felt quite reprieved = She admired my Drawings on account of the Novelty of the style. I found her possessed of excellent taste and regularly *Clever*. The broad

....

Ford's note that "Alice Jaynes Tyler used this passage to implement her thesis that Audubon was 'the lost Dauphin'" is in error (*Journal*, 171n62). Instead, Tyler uses passages from two letters she claims to have inherited from Maria Audubon written by Audubon from Edinburgh and dated March 15, 1827, and October 9, 1828 (*I Who Should Command All* [New Haven CT: Framamat Publishing Company, 1937], 36).

Scotch accent that accompany's each word she speak[s] sound[s] agreably to my ear and soon sends my Ideas to Gai Ma[u]ndering[91] =

M͟r͟s͟ Rathbone wished her to see more of my work, but Lady Douglass disliking to appear in Public, *I* went to the Institution in M͟r͟s͟ Rathbones Cariadge and brought upwards of 20 Drawings for her to Gaze at = She liked them = D͟r͟ Trail gave me a singular Drawing to make this morning. It was neither more nor less than a *Pebble* about the size of Large Pigeon's Egg that had been extracted from an unfortunate Suferer of that terrible disease, the Gravel[92] = I made it during the absence of the familly and returned it with the Drawing the same evening —

In returning to Green Bank from Liverpool, I stopped at Woodcroft, the Seat of M͟r͟ Richard Rathbone, to take the good old Lady[93] who [MS: whom] had stop͟d͟ there and started my Young Man on forward to wait for the Port Folio to take it back to the Institution again = There I found M͟r͟ Shepherd of the Botanic Garden[94] engaged at disposing some Grounds in good Taste for my Friend Richard R. M͟r͟s͟ Rathbone wished to take him home herself, and we had him in the Cariage in a short time and at his House at the Public Garden — He promised me some letters for Manchester =

Now we return positively to Green Bank. The Postilion raises as the Horse he rides trots each step and I can see the Landscape as his xxx[†] escapes the bounce it would receive was he to ride solidly between his sadle and his well rounded, well formed and well buff leather covered xxx —

We are at the outer Gate. M͟r͟s͟ Rathbone desires to see a servant Call͟d͟ xxxx Imediately — He imediately came — *I* heard her say "have

91. Audubon plays with the Scottish phrase "to gai maundering," meaning "to go wandering aimlessly."

92. The Gravel, or kidney stones. Dr. Traill has asked Audubon to make a drawing of a large kidney stone.

93. Although Ford identifies "the good old Lady" here as Mrs. Richard Rathbone (*Journal*, 173), the context does not make clear whether Audubon refers to her or to Mrs. Rathbone of Green Bank, in whose carriage he is traveling.

94. John Shepherd (1764–1836) became the first curator of the Liverpool Botanic Garden at its opening in 1803. With William Roscoe, the driving force behind the garden, Shepherd laid out its plan and helped shape its character and maintain it for over thirty years. The index of Ford's edition misidentifies this "M͟r͟ Shepherd of the Botanic Garden" as William Shepherd, who wrote letters for Audubon to friends in Manchester; one of those letters appears in appendix B.

something for him to eat quickly" — *I* heard no more but I *Guessed* again that I discovered the wish of this wonderfully kind Lady = It was for my Young Man expressly — She heard me say that he had walk^d and took the hint — I heard speak of eating quickly and took the hint also — but, Lucy, this gives thee an Idea of the Nicety of Care that moves along with each step of this wonder of Females = and wert thou to see her Daughter Hanna, who has undoutedly the most brilliant and yet mild Black Eyes I ever beheld, with a contemplative smile over her visage, rising from Table Ten times during the repast to offer a nice morsel to her *Mamma,* or to see her peal an apple or a Pear or a Peach and hand it to her — to see her with a vase of wine beg of her *Mamma* to take a little more and, wert thou to see her Blush as Ingen[u]ously as I have seen her do when she thinks that she is remarked, Thou wouldst admire her,[†] I am quite sure, perhaps still more than I do, and I believe it would be a puzler for any other Persons than thyself to do =

The day has been uncommonly disagreable Out of Doors — It is quite Winter like — The blast comes from East and the rain that accompany's it is quite Cold — Fortunately, I procured a Bird to Draw and drew nearly 2 to day — Lady Isabella kept me company in my *Laboratoire* and promised me a Letter for Edinburgh for a Nephew of hers and politely Invited me to call and breakfast at her seat 5 miles from London when I reach that city as often as I may make it Convenient =

I gave to day my Journal to read to Miss Hanna, who did so to her Mother — They read from my arrival at Liverpool — Do not be alarmed, my Lucy — They are *safe persons,* I assure thee — They will not make Ill use of the favor =

Now, Lucy, that I have been a good while in this delightfull familly, let me tell thee the cause of my particular attachment to its members = The very first day that I visited Green Bank, Thou recollects that I was brought here by Mr R^d Rathbone & Lady & Mr Pyke in company [MS: comp*g*]. Whilst here and moving from the Library or setting room into the Loby or Entry to Examine the Collection of Stuff^d Birds there, *I* heard Richd Rathbone say to someone, whom I did not see then but whom I now believe was Mr Reynolds S^r, that *I* was "*simple Intelligent.*" I was struct with the power of the truth — I was quite sure that what was then said was really thought and as I knew myself to be positively very *Simple* and yet somewhat Intelligent, I was delighted and thought of Richd Rathbone since that moment as I would do of an excellent kind Brother =

Every circumstance since then has Improved my conclusions, and now I feel the wish that either he or his Brother or his Wife or his Sister, or his Mother or all of them could Judge for a moment how much I Estime, admire and venerate them all Individually and as the most truly Parentally Inclined Alliance I ever saw & probably ever will again —

Once more, my Dearest Friend, I must bid thee good night far far away from thy sweet form and sound of voice — The sun rose beautifully fair this morning. Birds all chirup[d] to his appearance with delight = Now all Nature is Angry — It is a night fit for Hopgoblins & believers to enjoy =

How Long must it be before I can again press thee to my Bosom and with a kiss bid thee Good Night? —

M[rs] Rathbone[†]
Woodcroft

My dear Madam,

At the offering you a specimen of my humble powers of painting, I feel twofold embarrassed. I dread to torment your better "taste," and still more lest you should receive it merely through that power of amiability and natural kindness of heart so plainly observable in all your actions. Yet I feel the desire of presenting to you this *amiable Otter* — because I feel a wish of proving to you my gratitude and the high respect with which I hope you will permit me to remain, my dear Madam,

Your most humble Ob[t] Ser[t]
John J. Audubon

Green Bank Aug. 1826 — Tuesday morning.

GREEN BANK 7TH SEP[R] 1826. —

I have drawn all day and finished *The Intelligent Swiss*'s Piece. It consists of 2 Watter Wag Tails and 3 Butterflies[95] — I hope he will like it — Lady

95. Audubon inscribed this drawing in pencil as follows: "presented to A. Melly Esq[r] by his Sincerely Obliged Friend John J Audubon Sep[r] 1826." Richard Keynes published it in *Country*

Douglass expressed some anxiety yesterday at se[e]ing the whole of one Bird drawn in her presence. Therefore, to day I drew Butterflies untill The Lady issued from her chamber. It was nearly 2 o'clock. The Ladies of the House had returned from meeting. I had been with M͏ͬ Chorley taking a little exercise on the Pond and Dinner was served =

When desert was served, a Beautifull white Pitcher containing cream was handed me. I admired it very much. It remembered me of thee, Lucy, Young & Beautifully modest, all the flowers of Virginity about thee, and I might, ah, yes, I will say all sweetness Like the cream in the little Pitcher that now is Thine — Yes, My Lucy; Hanna Rathbone gave it me and it shall go to America!! — After Dinner, Miss Greg,[96] the sister of M͏ͬͩ W͏ᵃᵐ Rathbone (the Latter of whom I presented a Drawing on her Birth day, the 30͏ᵗʰ of August, with a few lines from John Chorley under the Little Robin of the Red Bosom —) followed me in my little Laboratoire, that now might be styled as mine was at the Beech Woods, the "Academy of Fine Arts" — Lady Douglass came in next and next M͏ͬͩ Rathbone with a cup of Coffee in one hand and a sugar basin in the other — The first was for thy husband. Miss Greg sweetened it — Lady Douglass, as a Lady is wont to do, hear[d] me ask for India Rubber, sent for her Desk and presented me with 2 nice bits inserted in a tube — My Drawing finished, Miss Hanna hearing that I was going to Liverpool, met me with a Glass of White Wine (the name here for Madeira). I looked at her Eyes, drank the wine and thought of thee =

Off to Liverpool, walking, however, very slowly part of the way having Young Chorley with me. When we parted, I put out forth my powers and moved at my usual rate of 5 miles = M͏ͬ Munro was not at the Institution — M͏ͬ Melly was not at Home, my Trunk was not in my room in Dale Street! No — the room was given to some other person and my Bagage was in the Entry = I walkᵈ to Green Bank again and

....

Life, April 6, 1951, 1011. It was in the possession of his father, Sir Geoffrey Keynes, and is listed as item 132 in *Bibliotheca Bibliographici: A Catalogue of the Library Formed by Geoffrey Keynes* (London: Trianon Press, 1964), 16–17.

96. Elizabeth and Ellen Greg were two of the thirteen children of the Manchester cotton manufacturer Samuel Greg (1758–1834) and his wife, Hannah Lightbody (1766–1828). Elizabeth (1789/90–1882), the eldest of the Greg children, married the second William Rathbone (1787–1868) in 1812. The Greg family home was Quarry Bank House.

found there the aditionnal source of pleasure, Richard Rathbone and Lady — I read a letter on my Birds, the title: the chimney swallow —

Again, Lucy, read and be surprised — R$^{\underline{d}}$ Rathbone wishes me to paint a Large Picture to bring my talents to public view in a more forcible and stronger light. He wishes more. He wishes that I should remove to his House — with Brushes, Canvass & Colors and men to set for me and men to Prepare my Tints!! — It will, he says, give great pleasure Both to him and to his Wife = M$^{\underline{rs}}$ Rathbone herself repeats the Invitation. =

Lucy, what shall I do? It is easy to Paint the Picture and to be *Blasted to the Roots* and *Mortified to the Marow of my Bones*. When exibited it may be laughed at = but to remain perhaps more than 30 days at a house where nothing besides peace and tranquility resides, Dabbing a Picture that could not go out of it without being distended and of Course must be perfectly dried, a thing that might take months at the rate I put on Colors, would not do — No, Lucy, it would not do — The Picture *Shall* be painted, but I do not well yet know where — The Generous man speaks of my Talent in a way that positively renders me quite uncomfortable and yet I forbid saying so to him, because I am quite sure that he speaks his thoughts and wishes me really well —

The weather this Evening is Beautifull — The Cariage of R$^{\underline{d}}$ Rathbone has taken him and his Beautifull wife away — Lady Douglass, without bidding good night, has rolled herself off = I have shook hands with all,[†] rather more *brotherly* than usual with kind Hanna, and now God Bless Thee, Good Night —

W$^{\underline{am}}$ Roscoe Esq$^{\underline{r}}$
Lodge Lane. *My Dear Sir —*

I have taken the liberty to roll up a little drawing made by me with the wish that it may not be disagreable to you to receive it — I wish sincerely that it was more deserving of your attention: my Fate will force me on Sunday morning to leave Liverpool and all the kind persons with whom I have had the Honor of becoming acquainted, but I hope it will also be my good fortune to be enabled not to forget them as long as I live! — Please present my remembrances to Your Aimiable Daughter — Please to believe me also and for ever Your most devotedly attached Friend, J. J. A —

Green Bank Liverpool Sep$^{\underline{r}}$ 8$^{\underline{th}}$ 1826 —

I must now tell thee that tomorrow I will positively leave the enchanted Spot and move towards Manchester. My Heart seats Heavy — I am about leaving good Friends. It reminds me of Parting with my own familly again — When I left America I did not feel more —

Yesterday I drew a good deal, had the Company of Lady Douglass by my side — I was obliged to Copy my own face for Miss Hanna[97] =

In the afternoon 3 Carriages left Green Bank and moved toward Liverpool to pay a Visit to my Drawings at the Royal Institution — We arrived there about 5. Lady D. was caried up the stairs and remained in the Large room for upwards of 2 Hours and was aparently very much pleased = She complimented me very considerably — At 6 o'clock I was dressed and in Abercromby Square at the House of Wᵃᵐ Rathbone, where I dined in Cᵒ of Dʳ Trail, A. Melly, Mʳ Foster[98] &ᶜ — and several Ladies — It was late when we retired — I remained the night at Wᵃᵐ Rathbone, presented him with a copy of Fairman's Engraving of Bank Note Plate[99] —

97. This clearly Byronic self-portrait is currently housed at the University of Liverpool's Victoria Gallery and Museum. Beneath the image Audubon has written, "Audubon at Green Bank / *Almost* Happy!! — / Sepʳ 1826." In his journal Audubon leaves no doubt that he and Miss Hannah enjoyed a genuine regard for one another and that their friendship occasionally grew quite flirtatious. It also is evident from Audubon's inscription on the back of a drawing of a robin he drew for Hannah (perhaps the drawing referred to in the entry for August 21) that there was a limit beyond which she would not permit the charismatic artist to advance: "It was my greatest wish to have affixed on the face of this drawing my real thoughts of the amiable Lady for whom I made it in Poetry Divine! — but an injunction from Hannah Rathbone against that wish of my Heart has put an end to it — and now I am forced to think only of her benevolence! of her Filial love! of her Genial affections — her most kind attentions and friendly Civilities to all who come to repose under this hospitable roof — " (D. S. Bland, *John James Audubon in Liverpool 1826–27* [Liverpool, 1977], 11). The inspiration for the robin drawing was the living bird mentioned in the entry for September 10 as semitamed by Mrs. Rathbone and Hannah. The drawing is kept at Greenbank House, which was donated to the University of Liverpool in 1944.

98. This is possibly John Foster (1787–1846), the prominent Liverpool architect of this time. He was also a founding member of the Liverpool Academy of Arts and known for watercolor views of Liverpool.

99. According to Maria Audubon's edition of Audubon's journals, he wrote on July 12, 1824, "I drew for Mr. Fairman a small grouse to be put on a bank-note belonging to the State of New-Jersey; this procured me the acquaintance of a young man named Edward Harris of Moorestown, an ornithologist" (*Audubon and His Journals*, 1:56). Gideon Fairman (1774–1827) was a young bank-note engraver in Philadelphia beginning in 1810. Edward Harris became one of Audubon's most loyal supporters and friends.

M͟r͟ Foster promised me a Letter that would procure me a personal
Introduction to Sir Thomas Lawrence — I slept in the same [room]
with a young M͟r͟ Greg and Left him in the morning, hours before he
had any thought of awakening, and walked to Green Bank again where
I made a Small Drawing for M͟r͟ J. G. Austin before breakfast. Afterwards
I visited M͟rs͟ Ed͟d͟ Roscoe, who had finished a Beautifull Drawing in my
Style; she presented me with a Copy of Cowper Poems. I felt a very
great pleasure at this as I really knew very little about him[100] —

I called on M͟r͟ Roskell and settled my Bank Business with him —
paid my debts to M͟r͟ Hunt — My Bill at the Inn in Dale Street where
they charge for every day as if I had been living there — It made only
a diference of £ 3, in the quantum of my Purse — I wrote a Letter of
thanks to Both the Brothers Rathbone and Inclosed a £ 10. to pay for
the chalks they had purchased for me and the residue to pay for
Postage &͟c͟ =

I returned to Green Bank once more, dined there, made a Likeness
of John Chorley and walk͟d͟ to see M͟r͟ Roscoe in Lodge Lane in C͟o͟ of
Miss Hanna Rathbone — She was so kind to give me a very beautifull
Pen Knife and a Piece of Poetry copied by her own hand — I found M͟r͟
Roscoe at home with his sons and Daughter. He gave me 4 Letters of
Introduction — One to Miss Edgeworth particularly Beautifull =

He was quite astonished to see me eat some raw Tomatoes. So were
the Ladies — and yet how simple was the act — I had bid farewell to
all in Town and allmost all in the Country — I Called on R͟d͟ Rathbone
but he was absent — I was met cheerfully by his sweet Little flock
of children and his aimiable and beautifull Lady = She requested
that I should write to her when absent, and I promised to do so with
inexpressible pleasure —

The Evening was quite Stormy. It lightened some and I could see
the Effect on the features of the sweet female in whose company I was
sitting = I at last reached Green Bank and thought that I had finished
my days work but, no — A Note from M͟r͟ Austin came and announced
me that M͟r͟ Munro was distracted at the Institution, and I wrote to M͟r͟

100. Mrs. Edward Roscoe was motivated at least in part to bestow a volume of poems by
William Cowper (1731–1800) on Audubon because of the poet's vociferous opposition to slavery
"as human nature's broadest, foulest blot."

Munro a very rude rough Note and now am Pining and repenting about my conduct towards that good man =

Mͬ Joseph Chorley has copied my Letters of Introduction. We have had our cheerfull Supper, Drank thy Health, sweet wife, and now, ah [MS: ha], now I must go and bid thee Good Night —

LIVERPOOL SEPͬ 9ᵀᴴ 1826

Messͬˢ Wᵃᵐ and Richᵈ Rathbone —

My Dear Sirs —

Please to accept my sincerest thanks for your generous reception of me — on the outset of my entering in a World that I may truly say was quite new to me, your kind attentions have been powerfully felt — Never can I for *a Day* (even in the distantest portions of the World to where my avocations may lead me) lay my head to receive repose without thinking of you and the Whole of your famillies — Never will I cease to pray for your Health and Happiness — Never will I cease to be Yours most truly devoted obedient Obͭ — Friend — John J. Audubon

P.S. The Bill Inclose[d] will repay Mͬ Wᵃᵐ Rathbone 5.7.6 advanced for me for Colored chalks, the residue please memorandum to the Credit of the expenses you will be at (I Hope) paying Postages for me from America or Elsewhere — J. J. A.

———

3

Manchester

10TH SEP^{R} 1826 —

MANCHESTER COUNTY OF LANCASTER, ENGLAND —
38 [MILES] FROM LIVERPOOL —

Before I mention my arrival at this Place, I cannot help, my Beloved
Wife, to speak more of Green Bank to thee ═

I had bid my adieu last evening to each Member of the familly and
Calculated on leaving this sweet Spot by 8 o'clock with Hanna Maria
Rathbone, who proposed walking with me to Liverpool — but when 8
o'clock came, the weather was Blustery and inclined to rain; therefore it
was arranged that we should go in a Cariage ═ Mrs Rathbone sent me
an Invitation to see her in her own room and I did so — I thought I saw
her eyes wetted by a Tear — She requested that I should write often to
her and others of her familly — I saw her husband's Portrait, that of her
Father and Brother and also that of Lord Selkirk, with whom it appears
the familly has long been Intimately acquainted with ═

The Little Robin that She calls her own and that when shooting she
particularly requested I should not kill, was hopping about the room
and flying in and out perfectly free from either fear or Danger — I saw
there a gem [MS: Jem] in Painting — It was a small Vase of Flowers,
all White ═ Her Table, her Books, every thing about this repository
exibited the Tendency toward studying the Best Works by the Owner
═ I took a Cup of Chocolate, handed H. M. in the Cariadge and
bid My good Old Friend farewell — Mr Austin came with us — I
stop^{d} a few Minutes at Woodcroft and had the pleasure of meeting
R^{d} Rathbone & his Beautifull Wife at Breakfast ═ I bid them adieu
also — Mrs Rathbone said "Mr Audubon, you must write to us woman
kind" — Ah, yes, my Heart desired not a more agreeable favour. Yes, to

woman Kind I will write when I have written to the Kindest, to Thee, My Wife!

Miss H. Maria had me deposited at M̲r̲ Melly w[h]ere I had an agreable breakfast enough, but my head was all full of the Rathbone[s], and the Intelligent Swiss's Companions appeared all Dull to me this Morning ═ M̲r̲ Melly proposed that we should go in a Post Chaise together and divide expenses. I agreed to do so as some dificulty had been made to take My N̲o̲ 2 Port Folio in the Public Coach — However, the arrangement proved us[e]less as Thou wilt see by the sequel ═ I reach[ed] the Institution about 11, made my Peace with good Munro in a moment and walk̲d̲ with him to D̲r̲ Trail, met M̲r̲ W̲am̲ Lawson, the treasurer of the R. Institution ═ D̲r̲ Trail gave me with a Letter for Heywood Esq̲r̲ of Manchester[1] the {Lean} of taking with us M̲r̲ Munro for 2 Days, and I returned by Way of Dale Street to the Institution — I mention Dale because the Waitter at the Commercial had refused to give up my Linen, saying that the servants must be paid each something — I felt rather emflamed and, having proved [to] the Lady that I had done quite enough for the Servants, She politely beg̲d̲ excuse, denied having heard of the Transaction, and I March̲d̲ off with my Goods — D̲r̲ Trail told Me Never to give the Waitters any thing until I Leave an Inn or Hotel — I shall remember it, believe me ═ My seats were [s*a***d] at the Stage office — my Port Folio Man[a]ged, and I was Closing the Drawings and packing my Trunk by one o'clock ═

I went to bid adieu to thy Sister Ann, and shamefull as it is for me to say it, she for several Minutes refused to Kiss Me — My Mortification was extreme — I cannot bear Prudery — To be *Simple, Natural, truthfully Kind* is my Motto — and I cannot well bear any other Conduct — I, however, took a Glass of Wine and Drank to the Health of *her Sister* in America — I had the great pleasure of hearing of thy being well on the 24̲th̲ of July Last by a Letter of thy Little Friend Briggs to M̲r̲ Gordon — I met this latter Gentleman in the Street and perhaps may see him in Manchester tomorrow ═ returned to the Institution, saw M̲r̲ Melly and wrote the following Note to my Venerable, Hospitable, Kind Friend M̲rs̲ Rathbone of Green Bank:

1. Benjamin Arthur Heywood (1793–1865) was one of Manchester's leading bankers. He was known as a pious man interested in providing for the education and welfare of the working classes. His family home was Claremont, near Manchester.

My Dear Madam —

The very particular Interest that you have so evidently proved
to have towards my future Happiness, prompts me to Inform,
that during this morning's visit to Mrs Gordon, I received *regular*
Intelligence that My Lucy and My Dear Boys were quite well on
the 24th of July Last, that Letters had been forwarded to the Care
of the American Minister at London, and that some must be *there
now*! — Will you please ask the favour of your sons here to forward
them when received by them with all the speed that a *Husband* needs
after so long a lapse without news from those he holds so Dear to
his Heart — I leave in the coach for Manchester accompanied by
Mr Munro (whom Dr Trail has been so good as to let me have) at 5
o'clock this afternoon = Please Present my humblest respects to
Lady Isabella Douglas — to all and each of your familly Circle and
believe me for ever, My Dear Madam, Most Truly Your Devoted
Respectfull Ob^t Servt,

J. J. Audubon

This Note was taken to Green Bank by the Intelligent Swiss, whom
I saw at the Institution where he comes accompanied by his Cousin to
Study Enthymology and arranged his beautifull Collection of Subjects
connected with that Interesting Science = Mr Munro and I went to
the Coach office, arranged the Port Folio snugg in the Cariage; I paid
One Pound Sterling for our Inside Seats, no charges for Baggage —
having Left my Trunk at the Institution to be forwarded me by M^r
Munro per Steam Boat packet = I took an other View of the Shipping
on the Mersey, Look^d on the Vessells bound to America with anxiety
and thought of Louisianna, and Thee, My Kind Wife, and our Dear
Children —

At a Minute of the appointed time for our Departure, we entered
the Coach, arranged our two selves copiously at ease (being alone)
and the Instant that the Words "All right" Issued from the Clerk
attending the departure of Coach N° 11335, off we moved briskly over
the pavement = The pleasure that in many other travellers would have
been anticipated with the Idea of Visiting Manchester, One of [the]

Principal Manufacturing Towns of England and perhaps of Europe, had no effect on me = I wished some accident might take place that would retain me to Liverpool and Enable me to go once more to Green Bank to View from That Enchanted Seat the Sun about to set that was really Magnificent this Evening — but, no, it was not to be — I saw the sun seting from the Coach, and the Idea that I had no one to participate My thoughts to, and admire with, the *resplendissant* Orb, as it made way to the Placid Silvery enchanter of the night, was far from giving me either animation or Spirits to gaze on the Landscape that was fainting from my Eye with the Light of the day =

Yet M⁚ Munro did all in his Powers to Interest me. He Made me remark Lord Stanley's Domaines — and I Looked on the Hares, the Partridges and other game with a thought of aprehension that the apparent freedom & Security they enjoyed was very transient — I thought it more Cruel to permit them to grow gentle, nay, quite tame and sudenly and by Frisks murder them by Thousands than to give them the Fair Play that our Game [h]as with us in our Forests of being Free, ah [MS: ha], yes, Free and as Wild as Nature made them to Excite the active healthfull pursuer to search after it and pay for it thro the pleasure of Hunting it downe against all dificulties. =

My astonishment was great, and I was aroused from my sullenness at the sight of a Lad perhaps 12 Years of Age that ran swiftly along the side of the Coach and sudenly Tumbled 5 or 6 times repeatedly heels over head, exibiting this feat to procure a few half pence — I amply rewarded him, and I was glad that Many Coppers Made their Way from the Passengers Pockets on the Toss to the ground from where they were pickᵈ up with alertness by the Little Mendicant — M⁚ Munro assured me that these Boys are frequent and that a Letter thrown out of the Coach with a few Pence is taken by them and Conveyed to its directed office or House with great security =

We passed thro a small Village Called Prescot, the streets extremely narrow — The Coach stopᵈ, I thought frequently, to renew the Horses. We travelled about 7 Miles per Hour — where ever we stoptᵈ, a neatly dressed maid, sometime quite handsome and with a side glance, would come and offer Cakes, ale or other refreshments with a good English grace — grace in my Opinion equal to any I have seen yet —

M⁚ Munro & I drank some Brandy & Watter = I was made to remark

Little shrubs growing in many Parts of the Meadows that Concealed traps for Moles and served as Beacons to the persons who caught these Annimals = The Hare[s], that sometimes were not more than 20 steps from the Coach, paid no attention to us and fed as if confident of their security —

The Road was good but narrow, the Country, as much as [I] could see of it, handsome and in a High degree of Improved Cultivation — We crossed a Canal conducting from Liverpool here — The sails moving thro the Meadows Cut to form the Canal brought me quickly to Rochester in New York — I saw the falls of the Gennessee again in my Imagination — I thought of Dewitt Clinton and at Last again of thee — Ah, how much of my Blood would I suffer myself to be deprived of to have thee with me and also our Dear Sons — Ah, when Will we Meet *Never to part again?* —

I am then at Manchester, 38 Miles from Liverpool and Nearly 6000 from thee — with a Pocket book containing a Pack of Letters of recommendation, and tomorrow a New set of Faces must see Mine, and I, feel awkward again. It is really terrible for me, and yet as I came from America for thy Sake, for thy Sake I will suffer these dificulties and wait with patience for the only reward I Long for — a Sweet Kiss from thy Lips, My Lucy! —

I paid 2 shillings to the Coach Man (a thing of Course in this Country where the Traveller must conceive them destitute of any other remunerations [MS: renumerations] than the generosity of the Traveller for the trouble they have driving and waiting on all passengers) — In a few Minutes I was lodged in the Little room w[h]ere I am now setting writting this, and disturbed only by the Watchman's cry of "Past 12 o'clock" — The Moon shines yet. Ah, My Lucy, God Bless Thou, good Night —

The above, my dear Mᵣˢ Rathbone,[2] gives you an account of my Progress since I left you = I had the pleasure of se[e]ing to day severall members of the Greg familly, and I am Happy to be

2. Audubon wrote this paragraph at the end of the day of his arrival in Manchester, apparently intending to copy the September 10 entry or have it copied and sent to Mrs. Rathbone. For an unknown reason, Ford moves this paragraph to follow the September 11 entry.

enabled to Inform you that they were all well $=$ to have had also
the satisfaction of Shaking the hand of the Intelligent Swiss was a
great relief from my Hard Laboring $=$ I have taken the liberty of
Forwarding a Blank Book to M꞊ Roscoe and my other kind Friends.
Do me the Honor, pray, to write your own name on one of its Sheets
— Beg for me of each member of your familly to do the same and
believe me Most truly & devote[dl]y &ᶜ &ᶜ J.J.A.

MANCHESTER SEP꞊ 11ᵀᴴ 1826 — MONDAY —

I was up early enough, I assure thee, this Fair morning. The Noise in the
streets last night, after I had closed with my habitual good night to thee,
Increased but did not Improve — It was most disagreable, to say the
least of it, and I doubt if I was permitted to Close my Eyes. I am rather
Inclined to think that I did not —

Well, we had our Breakfast. It was neither such as I was used to, at My
Fathers, or Thy Fathers, or at Henderson or New Orleans, or Natchez,
ah, not even such a Breakfast as the Beech Woods of Louisianna have
frequently afforded me, and to Compare it with the Breakfasts of Hanna
Rathbone or my Good Friend the Intelligent Swiss would be absurd $=$
Yet we had enough of Beef Stake, of Coffee, Tea and Toast and Butered
Bread, but, my Lucy, I eat it alone, yes, quite so in thoughts, and I
remarkᵈ several times that M꞊ Munro perceived that *Something was
wanted* —

My Letter gives thee an account of how the day was spent — I
visited, however, the Academy of Natural Sciences — paid 3 Guineas
for a weeks rent of the Exibition room — and was accompanied a
great Portion of the Day by one of those uncomfortable Busy Bodies
that think of all other persons affairs in Preference of their own, a M꞊
Bentley,[3] a Dealer in Stuffed Specimen, and there ends his History — I

---

3. Walter Horton Bentley moved from Stafford to Manchester, where he kept a successful boot
and shoe shop near St. Mary's Gate. He also dealt in animal skeletons and mounted specimens.
He was remembered as eccentric but ingenious. When a popular elephant named Cluny in the
Royal Menagerie in Exeter Exchange went mad and had to be shot, he purchased the remains
in order to display the full skeleton in Manchester. Audubon's negative first impression soon
changed, and Bentley proved to be very helpful to Audubon.

wished him at Hanover or in Congo or New Zealand or at Bombay or in a Bomb Shell in his route to Eternity — but turn over and I will tell thee 2 Curious Occurences differing broadly from each other —

As I walked the streets with Mͬ Munro in search of the House of the Revᵈ James Tayler[4] in Faulkner Street — Mͬ Munro enquired of a Man where it was = The Stranger said he would accompany us and, whilst I entered the House to deliver my Letter — the Stranger askᵈ Munro if he knew who I was — Mͬ Munro said no (I know not why). The other then told him that I was a most *Eminent Artist* and a most *Extraordinary Man.* — It does not take much to compose and form the Latter, but the *Eminent Artist* discomboburated my Nerves very much and, although I tried for some minutes to Imagine that I might be one — I gradually fell back to my real Ideas of myself and walkᵈ on briskly again —

THE MISTRESS AND HER SERVANT —
A TRUE STORY.

The Environs of Liverpool are adorned by numerous Seats where in many persons of the Highest Distinction reside of Good Manners, of Benevolent dispositions and Good Heart. — The Traveller who retires for a few Hours from the Tumult of the City and reaches one of those Seats, laying about 2 and ½ miles South East as if he wishᵈ to go thro Wattery, cannot help remarking a Sweet delectable Mansion, in all appearance secluded from the World, and yet filled with a World of Generous Beings = The Building is Gothic. Ever-greens run along its Walls, and seem to wish to Hide from Public view = Remarkable Instances of Hospital[it]y & of actions worthy the admiration of the Universe: — A Small piece of Watter slowly moves across the foot of the gentle slope on which it stands — Many Trees embellish the Grounds around, and I recollect myself having seen a Few Sheep grazing peaceably in their shade — There, my Lucy, the Mistress lives there! And her servant has lived there also 35 Years! — They are both raising towards Heaven as they are both growing old!! —

4. John James Tayler (1797–1869) in 1826 was the young intellectual Unitarian minister at the Mosley Street Chapel in Manchester. He had trained for the ministry at Manchester College, where he also served as a tutor in classics. He had married Hannah Smith of Icknield in January 1825.

The Misstress one day (cannot tell when) called for her Maid and told her that her wages must now be augmented, that her work must be diminished!! — The Maid Weaps, trembles, fears that her Lady wishes her off from under her roof and begs to know the true meaning — Then the Mistress explains and the servant refuses to accede to any such alterations, indeed says, that if her wages are augmented she will positively depart — The Lady insists on keeping her on her own Terms — The servant Leaves the rooms and is [MS: his] taken violently Ill imediately — Her M^{rs} runs to assist with her Care and, having ascertained that the Indisposition was the Effect of her Intended Generosity, abandons the Idea of doing more than Good, and begs of the servant to remain with her. All is well again, and I have no doubt all will be well between them for Ever!!!! =

Such, My Beloved Lucy, are the acts of my kind Friend Mrs Rathbone of Green Bank. I was told this by a Young Friend who estimes her with one and all those who know her, not as much as she deserves, but as much as is in our Powers to do. —

Mr Gordon had promised me to be at Manchester and to Give me Letters of recommendation — but Mr Munro hunted every Public House of Note and, of Course, I Concluded he came not = 3 of the sons of Mrs Greg^5 called on me at the Exchange and were extremely polite. They were anxious that I should have gone to their Country Seat, but my Business would not allow it = About 20 persons came to see my Birds — of course called them very Beautifull, &^{c} &^{c}. I had to stand the Brunt of all this, and the Eyes of the Ladies again I perceive were searching the Lines of my face and the Ondulation of my Locks — but my Style puzles all — Not a Soul can even guess how I proceed — a great Proof that a simplicity of a thing proves the dificulty of its discovery —

I Gave Good Mr Munro 3 pounds, 10 shillings for his troubles — Good Fellow, he deserved more but I am not rich and I gave

---

5. Samuel Greg (1758–1834) was one of the most successful of Manchester's cotton merchants and manufacturers. The Quarry Bank cotton-spinning mill began operation in 1784 and by 1832 had become the largest in England. Greg built Quarry Bank House in 1796. His children were raised Unitarian, and he was a member of the Manchester Literary and Philosophical Society. The expansion of Greg's businesses accelerated dramatically throughout the 1820s.

accordingly — I paid our Bill at the Tavern and removed to a M̲ʳ̲ˢ̲ Hedge
[MS: Edge] in King Street, where she keeps a Circulating Library —
Here I have more quietness, Pay 12/— Per week for the use of a Parlour
and a neat Bed Room —

M̲ʳ̲ Munro Left me at 10 o'clock this Evening and took with him
my Letters for thee and M̲ʳ̲ˢ̲ Rathbone = He gave me his Basket —
Hammer and Foot Rule — He goes in the 5 o'clock coach Tomorow
morning — I sent a Blank Album by him to receive the Names of my
Liverpool Friends —

MANCHESTER 12ᵀᴴ SEPᴿ 1826 ENGLAND — †

"Yesterday was spent in delivering my letters to the different persons
to whom I was recommended. The American consul, M̲ʳ̲ J. S. Brookes,[6]
with whom I shall dine to-morrow, received me as an American
gentleman receives another, most cordially. The principal banker here,
Arthur Heywood, Esq., was equally kind; indeed *everywhere* I meet a
most amiable reception. I procured, through these gentlemen, a good
room to exhibit my pictures, in the Exchange buildings, had it cleared,
cleaned, and made ready by night. At five this morning M̲ʳ̲ Munro (the
curator of the Institution at Liverpool and a most competent help),
with several assistants and myself began putting up, and by eleven all
was ready. Manchester, as I have seen it in my wallks, seems a miserably
laid out place, and the smokiest I ever was in. I think I ought not to
use the words 'laid out' at all. It is composed of an astonishing number
of small, dirty, narrow, crooked lanes, where one cart can scarce pass
another. It is full of noise and tumult; I thought last night not one
person could have enjoyed repose. The postilion's horns, joined to the
cry of the watchmen, kept my eyelids asunder till daylight again gave
me leave to issue from the King's Arms. The population appears denser
and worse off than in Liverpool. The vast number of youth of both
sexes, with sallow complexions, ragged apparel, and downcast looks,
made me feel they were not as happy as the slaves of Louisiana. Trade is
slowly improving, but the times are dull. I have heard the *times* abused

6. Audubon identifies the American consul he spends time with in Manchester as Samuel R.
Brookes in the October 17 entry; that he is from Boston appears in the September 13 entry. Maria
Audubon identifies him only as "J. S. Brookes" (*Audubon and His Journals*, 1:117).

ever since my earliest recollections. I saw to-day several members of the Gregg family."

I Engaged a man well recomended and named Crookes to attend as money receiver at the Door of my Exibition Room — I pay him 15/ — per week. He finds himself[t] and Copies Letters for me =

M[r] A Melly, whom I had the Pleasure of se[e]ing Twice, gave me the following kind Letter. Before I Copy the Letter I will say that I deposited in M[r] Heywood's Bank 244 £ for which he gave me a receipt =

My Dear Sir —

These lines will be presented to you by my Friend M[r] Audubon of Louis[a], of whom I spoke to you this morning. I need not say much on his account, having no doubt, but that when you have an opportunity [MS: opp.[y.]] of speaking with him, you will thank me to have procured you his acqua[i]ntance —

The Talent with which he has delineated the diferent specimen of Natural History which he will exibit in your Town is so far superior to what I have yet met with, that I shall only desire you to Judge for Yourself, and add that M[r] A's Intelligence, Information in Natural Sciences, and mind do not fall short of his Talent — I will be much obliged by the attentions you will show him and have no doubt but that you will not find fault with me for having given you a Farther Opp.[y] — of Confering other obligations on, My Dear Sir, Your very Truly *A. Melly*

Manchester 12th Sep[r] 1826
George Murray Esq[r]
Ancoats Hall
Manchester

During this day, the 12th, 2 men came to the exibition and Inquired if I wished for a Band of Music to Entertain the Visitors — They were Italians by their Noses and Large Mouths — I thank[d] them. My Exibition being neither Egyptian Momies or Deathly looking wax figures, I do not conceive it necessary in the company of so many Songsters as I have, and if my Songsters will not sing or be agreable by themselves, other music would only diminish their worth =

I made some diference here in my mode of shewing my Birds; I Exibit them at once to the Public for money, and will depend more on their real value here than I did at Liverpool, where I *Know* I was supported by very numerous and particular Friends —

It is Eleven o'clock and I have this moment returned from the Consul Brookes's Dinner. The Company was principally Composed of M<u>r</u> Loyd, the wealthy Banker, M<u>r</u> Garnet[7] &<u>c</u> &<u>c</u>. Judge of my Surprise when on the 3<u>d</u> removal of Plates, I saw on the Table a *Mess* of Good Indian Corn, nicely boiled purposely to please me — To eat it buttered & Salted, held by my Two hands as if I intended gagging myself with the ear, I took was matter of much wonder to the English Gentlemen that did not even like the vegetable in any way — I found the Consul, who is from Boston, an Intelligent, agreable and very polite man — We had an English Dinner Americanized, and the profusion of wine Drank was rather uncomfortable to me — The Gentleman that sat next below me proved to be a good Naturalist and an Observer of my sort. (I mean out of the Closet.) I am satisfied that he Studies Nature properly, not *a la Watterton*. Much, of course, was said of my Work and Charles Bonaparte's also — The conversation was mixed with many good Jests and smart reparties. Some Politic was Introduced and M<u>r</u> Brookes and myself (the only 2 Americans present) ranged ourselves and Fronted *Our Ennemies in War* but *our Friends in Peace*! I am particularly fond of a man who speaks well of his Country, and the peculiar Warmth of English men on the Subject is quite admirable =

During the day I saw a Gentleman who said that Lord De Tabelay[8]

---

7. This may be Jeremiah Garnett (1793–1870), cofounder of the *Manchester Guardian*, May 21, 1821.

8. John Fleming Leicester Warren (1762–1827), first Baron de Tabley, was an art collector and patron, especially interested in promoting British painting. His interest in natural history was particularly strong for birds and fish.

was extremely anxious to see Both my Drawings and myself and that I must go to his Domaines 14 miles Distant on my way to Birmingham =

I perceived the familly Touchet coming up the Stairs of the Exibition room and I hid myself and made my escape. I had just a glance of Mʳˢ Touchet (I suppose) and saw her very beautifull = I could not bear meeting that familly in such a place for the first [MS: 1ˢ] Time =

Mʳ George W. Wood Invited me to Dinner for tomorow, 2 miles, and will call for me in his Carriadge at 4 — I remarkᵈ that many persons who visited the Exibition Investigated my Style more closely than at Liverpool, and the Surface of the work was nearly properly understood by a Young Quakress that had Eyes much like those of my kind Friend Hanna Rathbone =

A Dʳ Holme[9] spent Yesterday and to day several Hours looking at them = I was [asked] 4 diferent times if they were on Sale = I found when at Liverpool the street full of annoyances at night but, compared with this Manchester, it is nothing. I thought that the Gentleman that accompanied me from Picadilly to King Street and myself would be caried by force off the Pavement — Groups of those abandoned females of from 20 to 30 stood watching for prey at all the corners we passed =

The appearance of the feminine Sex is not so prepossessing here as it is at Liverpool — The women in the streets have none of that Freshness of Coloring nor the fullness of Breasts that I remarked at the Sea Port = I conceive this is the result of the Confinement they have to undergo in the manufactories [MS: Manuefa{tries}] =

I walked to J. Brookes Esqʳ along the Turn Pike about 2 miles from the Exchange. The Country, however, is not verdant, nor the Seats Imediately around the Town so Elegant and Clean Looking as *Green Bank*, for Instance — The funels raised to carry off the smoake of the Manufactories appear in hundreds in all Direction[s], and as you walk the streets the wirring sound of the Jennies[10] is constant on the Ear. =

9. Edward Holme (1770–1847) was known as a very learned physician in Manchester. He was cofounder and first president of that city's Natural History Society. Throughout the 1820s, he was one of the leading forces in Manchester's literary and scientific societies.

10. "Jenny" is short for spinning jenny, the cotton-spinning machine on which most of England's textile industry depended.

Now, my Lucy, good night. I hope to receive some letters from thee in a day or Two, and I Hope that thou art on the Eve of hearing of me also — God Bless Thee, Good Night =

Copy / —

My Dearest Friend —

Although I wrote to thee only the evening before last, I set at it again — I will not say much. I am quite well and well doing = I am received here as kindly as at Liverpool, putting betwen as diferences those existing from Individuals in Trade and those who are not —

I dined with the American Consul yesterday. He entertains a fine Company. The Famous Banker Loyd, one of the wealthiest in England, was Introduced to me — I dine out again to day 2 miles out of the Town with a M͟r George W. Wood. I only know him thus far thro Letters of recomendation. I will copy the Letter from M͟r Roscoe to Miss Edgeworth, and a Sonnet of the Daughter of that Great Man, wrote to my praise[11] — I Hope it will give thee pleasure — Do write, my Lucy, do write. It is all I can enjoy when far from thee — Not a word have I yet received —

Kiss our Johny. Tell him that he must exert himself at Drawing — I

11. Jane Elizabeth Roscoe published "To J. J. Audubon, Esq., on Beholding His Drawings" in the *Winter's Wreath* for 1832:

Is there delight in Nature's solitudes,
    Her dark green woods, and fragrant wilderness,
In scenes, where seldom human step intrudes,
    And she is in her wildest, loveliest dress?
Is there delight in her uncultured flowers,
    Each ripened bloom or bright unfolding dye,
Or in the tribes which animate her bowers,
    And through her groves in living beauty fly?
Then, on thy canvas as they move and live,
    While taste and genius guide the fair design,
And all the charms which Nature's works can give
    With equal radiance in thy colours shine;
Amidst the praise thy country's sons extend,
    The stranger's voice its warm applause shall blend.
(Herrick, *Audubon the Naturalist*, 2:xxiv).

wish he would begain a Collection himself of Drawings in my Style.
Birds, Plants &^{c}, every thing is valuable here that is *corectly true*. It
may prove to him of Immense benefit as I am opening such a fine
road for him here —

God Bless thee and all about Thee,
for ever thine, most Faithfully
J. J. A

to Lucy Audubon
Sepr 14$^{\underline{th}}$ 1826 — here follow^d the copies mention^d in my letter to thee
— Manchester

When walking the streets, I have been much amused with the
appearance of young men waring the Uniform of Foot men, mounted
on fine Horses and going at the full rate of 10 miles per hour as if the
safety of their necks depended on the speed of their Horses — I would
think that the reverse might be expected, but their epaulettes, looking
like 2 Brass stewing Pans, and a Bonnet that might save the purchasing
of an umbrella, a Red Jacket tightly bottoned, Pantaloons more than
double the width of Mine, whiter than snow; spurrs full 4 Inches in
length and a Black Leather Strap holding the chin from falling in action
gives the best Idea of all that must be as disagreable to the comfort
of the Bearer as it shocks [MS: chocks] the Eye of the unacustomed
Stranger — However, as I am Inform^d, that many of these Youths being
the Descendants of the Lords of the Nation can live without paying
their Debts either to the Taylor or shoe maker, or the Tavern Keeper or
the xxxxxx, I have no doubt that *they* are quite Happy —

MANCHESTER SEP$^{\underline{R}}$ 14$^{\underline{TH}}$ 1826, THURSDAY.

To day I had for the first time since here the pleasure of Touching a
female's hand — During the morning one of the Miss Gregs came with
a Brother and chatted a long time with me = I feel, however, the want
of a Familly Introduction extremely. Without female society I am like a
Herring on a Gridle =
The only Familly where I expected to enjoy ease of conversation
is out of Town (This is the Touchets), and I have seen nothing of M^r

Heywood's Sister — I visited the Academy, where Dr Holme was extremely polite: at 4, Mr Wood drove me in his Cariadge in Company of 4 Persons, all strangers to England, to his House about 3 miles from Manchester — Mrs Wood is extremely tall, but cannot be called handsome; her conversation seemed to be chosen and without the freedom of that of her Husband, who is certainly a Superior Man =

A very severe Cold that I now enjoy in all its Glory renders me dull and the time Passed but Pass^d heavily = One of the Visitors was from Mexico and well acquainted with the Country. He spoke of the mines in a very entertaining manner — Another was [from] La Guaira [MS: Laquira] — another from Constantinople — the Last from Sumatra [MS: Sumatrass] — They all were men of Information, Visiting England for their Pleasure, apparently =

The Door w[h]ere the Tea was handed round resembled a Book Seller's Shop so much that any one unacquainted with Mr Wood would have supposed him deeply engaged in the Business = This Evening had the appearance of Frost and Yet Mrs Wood had just made 100 Bags of Black Gauze to Inclose so many Bunches of Grapes to enable them to ripen without being destroyed by Wasps = A Controversy arose as to the benefit of black over any other Colors as a Conductor or retainer of heat — It ended as it begone, each defendant fixed for ever on his own opinion =

The changes in the weather here are really remarkable — At day light this morning it rained Hard, at 12 it was fair, & to night has the appearance of a very severe frost — That may yet melt away, and was the Sun to Shine in one hour (that would be [MS: being] 12 o'clock) I would not think it extremely wonderfull after all that *Watterton* has performed.

I believe I have forgot to say to thee that I have engaged a Lad of about 12 Years of Age to receive the Tickets at the exibition for 10 shillings per weeks — His name is John Willson — the son of George Willson, late [of] T. Kearsley,[12] Fustian Manufacter, Riding Court, St Marys Gate, Manchester — I am now quite sure that, shouldst thou meet either the Father or the Son or the Gostt of either of them, thou

---

12. Several generations of Kearsleys manufactured fustian in Manchester.

shalt know no more about them or their condition than I did before I left America —

My Cold is so bad that I can hardly hold up my head — God Bless Thee, Good Night —

I Cannot Sleep, and I have got out of my Bed, Dress^d & washed myself, and walk^d the room for upwards of one hour to try to be benefited by Franklin's advice;[13] but all this wont do. I cannot sleep — A man awake and alone in a bed is a most stupid annimal in Creation — What the feelings of females are on such occasions, it will be best for thee to say — Thus I am writing again for, although I am lodge[d] at a Circulating Library, the Books below will not come by themselves to my assistance, and I cannot in good conscience call the House up because I alone in it cannot sleep — but I will give thee an account of the True Business Inclination of allmost all Individuals at Manchester = A man whose name I know not, advised me yesterday morning in a very cordial manner to have a large Sign painted with Birds &^c to be affixed at the Street Door of the Exchange to attract the Eye of the Passengers: — Was I to paint a Sign, no doubt the Manchester Gentry would stop to look at it. More I fear that, was the sign painted by thy husband, they would gaze at it so long that they would forget that 200 Drawings are waiting to be examined for the mere trifle of one shilling — This Engages me to have no Sign =

It is half past 2 and, sure enough, the rain is battering my window — It is a sound that allways operates kindly on me when Wakefull — I will try to sleep now, and now, my Lucy, as I hope thou art Happy and composedly enjoying rest — God Bless & Preserve thee —

MANCHESTER 15TH SEP^R 1826 —

My Dear Sir —

I was as Happy at receiving your too short letter of Yesterday as I was surprised when I read that I had omitted writting the direction

---

13. If this is not an allusion to Franklin's aphorism "Early to bed and early to rise make a man healthy, wealthy, and wise," it is likely that Audubon refers to "The Discontented Pendulum," a moral fable written by the British children's author Jane Taylor (1783–1824). The moral of the tale is that one should make use of every moment to achieve one's goals. It was widely reprinted, and Audubon encourages his son Victor to read it in his letter of October 31 below, where he also notes that it was sometimes attributed to Franklin.

on my Wife's Letter — To a man of Business, it would appear
no doubt bordering on the wonderfull; to me it proves for the
Thousand and one time that I never was Intended to be one — A
former occurance of the like want of strict care is now forced on my
recollection, and if you will permit me I will relate it —

During my desired apprenticeship at the Mercantile Business
in New York (about 25 years ago, I think), I was in the employ of
an agent of the House of Guest & Banker of London, and was
the Cashier — A remittance being ordered to be made to the
connected House in Philadelphia, I drew a Check, had it signed^d,
received the amount at the Manhattan Bank (10,000 $) and having
Inclosed the whole [MS: all] in a Letter that I did not *forget to Direct*;
I put it in the *Post Office Unsealed*! — Having occasion to go to
Philadelphia the next day, Mr Banker or Mr Guest (I really do not
now recollect which) spoke of the error in such kind terms that I
felt the mortification of having acted wrong Ten Fold, and thought
frequently, that I would try during my future life to think of Only
One Thing at a Time — Now, my Excuse to you can only be this: The
Letter, although wrote for my Wife with good Intent, was *so far from
the Object I thought of* when finishing it, that the true Object made me
forget the Letter =

Now, should I ever Err thus again, please allways direct to M^{rs}
Audubon, St Francisville, Bayou Sarah, Louisianna —

Hoping that all is well in Aberc[r]omby, Woodcroft, Green Bank,
Great George Street, Lodge Lane, St Anne S^t &^c &^c &^c, permit me
to remain, my Dear Mr Rathbone, for ever Yours Obliged Ob^t Ser^t
J. J. Audubon

W^{am} Rathbone Esqr
Liverpool —

MANCHESTER SEP^R 15TH 1826. — FROST —

Well, my Lucy, the weather is just as I represented it; I slept about 2
Hours this morning, and at 5 o'clock the Houses were Covered with
Frost and I felt uncommonly Cold and disagreable =

My Exibition was Illy attented, but those persons who came were highly pleased — A Mr Hoyle, a very Eminent Chemist, brought with him 4 Daughters, with little Grey Satin bonnets, Grey Satine Spencers[14] and beautifully plain white peticoats — Their Eyes Search^d my mode of work, but I am sure would sooner reach the heart of any Man — I became acquainted with a Mr Freeman, Artist in Miniature, and his Lady, both Americans, the latter truly Beautifull with all the coloring of the Fair Sex here — I saw also a personnage battered by much travelling, who had been [MS: being] with Baron de Humbolt 2 Years in America — Mr Heywood, the Banker, came also and Invited me to dine with him on Sunday next — but the most curious Incident was that I received a note drawn in the style of a Puffing Paragraph, anonimous, merely saying at the end of the preamble that Mr Audubon might make use of this or destroy it — The American Consul being with me, I shewed it him, and he simply assured me that it must be some Friend to the science that felt it too much to pay for and wish^d me to have it Inserted in the Tomorow's paper = Singular act of = Courtesy this —

Another no less Curious Incident took Place. I received a few Lines from my Good Friend W^{am} Rathbone Informing me that the Last letter I Inclosed to him for thee was undirected — I answered him Imediately with the one thou seest above this — My time passes very Dully. I have not yet a familly w[h]ere I can go and chatt in a Friendly manner. Manchester feels very diferent Indeed so far from Liverpool =

I spent my Evening at the Revd James J. Tayler in Company of his Wife and 2 Gentlemen, one a Parisian = I cannot again help expressing to thee my surprise at finding the People of England, Generally speaking, so unaquainted with the Customs, habits & Localities of our country — The principal conversation about it allways turns on Indians and their ways as if the land produced nothing Else = Mrs Tayler, having visited that Portion of the European Continent that is amongst this nation called fashionable, is extremely agreable of conversation, not Handsome, yet quite Interesting by her polite manners — The Parisian is well versed in the knowledge of his Country — The other Gentleman was and is yet, I dare say, an Entymologist =

14. A spencer was usually a short, close-fitting jacket or bodice.

Almost every Lady Draws well in England in Watter Colors, very many much better than I Ever will do, and Yet few of them dare shew me their productions — It is perhaps because I have such a quantity of it against one or 2 pieces of theirs =

I retired at ½ past ten — The Evening beautifull. What the morning of tomorow may be I cannot Tell — I cannot Imagine why no letters from thee have reached me yet — God Bless Thee, Good Night —

MANCHESTER SEP$^\underline{R}$ 16$^\underline{TH}$ 1826. —

Miss Rathbone
Green Bank, Near Liverpool

My Dear Miss Hanna

If Manchester is a dull Town of itself, I can now boast that it contains at least one Happy Individual at present! — This morning I had the pleasure and Comfort of reading Two long Letters from my Beloved Wife. My familly was all well thirty days after my departure. I have been longing to write to you ever since I left your delightfull Green Bank, but my Spirits were low, and even the beautifull, sharp, neat little Knife that was so kindly given me by a Particular Friend, that I Hope is now quite well under your roof, would not cut a pen to my liking untill now.

I Cannot bear Manchester — with the exception of two of the Miss Greg's, I have not seen any ladies yet with whom I have been enabled to chat without either blushing, or trembling as awkwardly as ever — I am sorry to say that M$^{\underline{rs}}$ Touchet's Familly is absent and that I fear my visiting Your Friends, the Greg Familly, at their seat will be of very short duration; unless I should abandon the plan of going at the end of next week to Birmingham to hear some good music — Oh, how much I would Enjoy this beautifull evening if near Your Kind Mamma & you. With what pleasure I would see the little robin pick from the plate before the window a few grains for his supper, or look on the thrushes hiding themselves with bills furnished with a sprey [of] mulberies, or lesson to the sweet sounds expressed by my Friends John & Henry Chorley; or take a full pinch of Snuff from M$^{\underline{r}}$ Austin's Box, and again perhaps from Your Brother Richards or the

Intelligent Swiss's — None of those can I enjoy; therefore I will think doubly of the kind privilege you have allowed me to write to you.

My little son John Woodhouse inclosed me from America a couple of small essays of his on rice papers.[15] I have taken the liberty to put one in this with Hopes that perhaps you would give it a place in the little red Port Folio: I Hope sincerely that he may have the Honor of thanking you himself for such an acceptance — I will not apologize for the want of merit in the Drawing. John is only 12 Years old and is *My Son*.

The Sun is now set. I see you all at Tea kind to each other as ever you were — I alone am speaking only with my Pen, have just drank a Glass of Wine to the Health and Continual Happiness of all the inhabitants of Green Bank. Many, many such will I wish again if a longer life is granted me: =

I shall not breakfast with my Intelligent Friend tomorow. Neither will I lessen to a French Sermon — Indeed, I can scarce now Tell to what church I will go: had I not my Beloved Wife's Letters to read and read again Tomorow, tomorow would be dull, indeed, although I have to go to Mr Heywood to Dine, and that I dread still more than the dullness of Manchester itself. My letter is composed of diferent effects of feeling, please to excuse it — but between the pleasures of having heard from Home and the disagreable sensation of being 38 miles from You, It would be Impossible for me just now to collect one better deserving your attention =

I wrote to your Brother Wam last evening; please to remember me to both his familly and Mrs Rathbone's of Woodcroft, to whom I will take the liberty of writting next =

Do not *Forget* to write your name in full in my Blank Book, I beg of you — Believe me with the sincerest Sentiments of highest respect, My Dear Miss Rathbone, for ever yours truly Obdt Servt
J. J. Audubon

(I know not why I have not received my Trunk &c from Mr Munro. I thought he promissed to send it to the Care of Misss Greg —)

---

15. Audubon refers to drawings his son has sent, which are "essays" in the sense of "efforts" or "attempts."

My Dear Mr Sully,

Your kind letters of March 15th of this present Year reach^{d} me this morning at this place; I am sadly vexed at the loss of the letter you were so good as to forward me for Sir Thomas Lawrence, to whom (although I have Letters of Introduction from Eminent men in this Country) I would have liked to present myself with more *American Colors.*[†]

You will be glad at hearing of my Hospitable and highly gratifying reception at Liverpool and at this place now on my way to London: at Liverpool it would have been Impossible for me to desire more. The President of the Royal Institution of that Place, Mr Roscoe the ex President, and all the members greeted me with a wellcome that perhaps no one person of humble merit ever received — I was solicited to Exibit my Drawings Publickly. The Room alloted by the Institution for the artists exibition was politely offered me *Gratis* and even the advertisements &^{c} &^{c} were all paid by the Institution — The result was that I received 100 £ for the short time I remained there and collected a bag full of Letters of Introduction for allmost all parts of the Three Kingdoms =

Having received the advise of men better Judges than myself of what is best for me, I will Continue exibiting in the diferent Large towns throw out the whole Country =

I presented a Large Painting in Oil of a Wild Turkey Cock &^{c} to the Royal Institution and it was received with great applause =

I shall undoutedly call on your Friend Robt Sully at Warwick &^{c}, but I would feel so proud of having a letter from the best artist in America to the best in England that if Thomas Sully will write one again for me, I will thank him with all my Heart = Do so, if you please, my good Friend, and Inclose it to the care of my Friends Messrs Rathbone Brothers & Co, Liverpool — I will not reach London untill the 1st of March next as I am advised that untill then I can do better else where. My Work will be published at Last to the great dismay, I take it, of my Friend Ord, the academician =

I have just received Letters from my wife and feel in good

Spirits — with sincerest and best wishes of my Heart for your
Wellfare and the Hope that you will remember me to Mrs Sully, the
Young Ladies & Sons, believe me for ever yours most truly, John J.
Audubon

Thomas Sully Es^{qr} artist

   Philadelphia —

MANCHESTER 16TH SEP^{R} 1826. — SATURDAY —

This morning my Lucy I received thy 2 Letters of May 28th and June
3^{d} — Oh, how much relieved my anxieties were $=$ I recollect daily our
last parting and my blood was often congealed at the Idea that perhaps
I might never see thee again $=$ Thanks, thanks to thee, my Dear Wife,
for thy kindness to me!! —

It is not worth while to say here what I did this day in the way of
writing. The Copies of my letters to Miss Rathbone, and to Thomas
Sully are suficient — Then, to the day — I visited early this morning
a charity School Instituted about 200 Years ago in a Building erected
nearly 400 Years past — The antique Gothi[ci]ty of the structure was
quite new to me $=$ Some Boys dressed in Large Gowns of coarse
Blue cloths, close sheared heads, and feet kept from the damp by large
shoes ornemented with large brass Buckle[s], exibited the curiosities
Conntained here and in kind of nasal Song explain^{d} quite a loud, I
assure thee, the meanings or names of all the stranger saw $=$ The
Library is Immense but so old that many of the Books here appeared
better fit for food for worms than men $=$ 80 are the Boys in number.
I understood the Teacher principa[l] was unwell — The kitchen of
Immense size was particularly neat and the servants attendant very
Polite $=$ The Bread Room, as it was termed, contained many large
loafs in Substance much like those distributed to soldiers on their
marches $=$

I spent nearly all my time at my Exibition room, saw some ladies
who spoke a good deal to me — but my cold rendered me still very
uncomfortable — I read thy letters frequently and sighed for thee many
times, I assure thee $=$

Mr Tanetti, an Italian who has a large establishment of Paintings and
fancy objects on Sale, gave me advises about my Exibition and told

me that, if well managed, it must be a fortune — May God Grant it
= How often I wish^d for an Impossible thing this day, that is, to be at
work in America and have my Drawings exibiting here = I conceived
the Idea of having my Son Victor here to attend to it and I to return to
America to draw more and on a handsomer Plan Still — for what is my
Life Intended for if not to tract for my Sons the way to Industry and
consequ[en]tly to Happiness =

I thought of writting to N. Berthoud on that Subject and have his
Ideas about it = I retired early and wrote late and late wished thee
Good Night, my Sweet Beloved Wife —

MANCHESTER SEPT 17TH 1826 — SUNDAY.

Copy. *My Dearest Friend*

I at last received Two letters from thee yesterday morning, and
although they both are of extremely old dates, the 28th of May & 3 of
June, they have relieved me from much anxiety. Thank thee, Dearest
Lucy, for them and their contents. I have wrote now very frequently
to thee since my arrival. Indeed, This is the 3^d time during one week,
but I will nearly repeat all that I mentioned in all of them in substance
in this one: =

I have been most kindly received at Liverpool by all those to whom
I was introduced either by letters from America or Subsequent
means, and I feel that the name of Audubon has left no disgrace
behind him = There are at Liverpool 3 Families of the names of
Rathbones, to all whom I am particularly indebted and towards
whom I never can cease to feel the highest sentiments of Gratitude.
Thro them I formed the acquaintance of all the best famillies, and
by their recommendations abroad, I cannot fail but continue to
be received with all the kind Hospitality that renders a Stranger
Happy far from his Friends & relations: — To Dr Thomas S. Traill,
the President of the Royal Institution of Liverpool, and Mr Roscoe,
a most Eminent person, now known over all the world, I also owe
a great portion of my Success: My Drawings were exibited for 4
weeks without a cent of Expense to myself and produced me 100
£. My time was spent during the while at painting & drawing to
present pieces of my work as slender marks of my Gratitude — I
gave to the Institution a Large piece of a Wild Turkey Cock — M^{rs}

R^d Rathbone one of the Otter in a trap, Mr Roscoe, a Robin, and to Each of my other Friends also a Drawing: Mrs Rathbone, the mother of all these Friends of mine, a most Venerable Lady, having invited me to her House, I spent 2 Weeks there enjoying all that can be enjoyed far from thee, My Lucy — When I left Liverpool, now one week precisely, the President sent the Curator of the Institution to wait on me and help me here to arrange my Collection for Exibition, and I am again known here by the most distinguished Persons of Manchester and its Environs —

My plans will be now fixed unless altered by accidents or Circumstances as follow — It is my Intention to travel thro England & Scotland very Slowly, exibiting my work untill the 1st of March next, when I wish to reach London and there Exibit on a Larger Scale and for a Long time = During my travels I am determined to apply at Painting in Oil and drawing pieces of Large Birds and quadrupeds to make part of my Exibition: Should I on the contrary discover that my exibition does not continue to produce as much as I conceive it ought, say 4 times the amount of my Expenses, I will go to Paris or London Sooner and Publish my work and Establish myself under the Patronage of some Person of Importance. It would be dificult for me at present to say more of more of my movements =

Now my Beloved Wife, I would wish thee at the end of thy time at the Beech Woods to remove either to Nicholas Berthoud at Shippingport or to New York City. The latter I would greatly prefer, viewing the quickness of comunication with this Country: or the thing still more preferable: for thee to come over with John only and travel with me or with me remain either in London or Paris, where I think now I may reside a long time: if remaining at New York or any other part of the United States that thou wouldst prefer, I would remit there punctually [an] amount suficient to keep thee well comfortable, but in such a case, our Son John must come to me as, Situated as I will be, I wish him to make rapid Strides in the World: if I succeed even as I have done, I can afford you all, all the comfort that I Hope would be thought suficient, and thro my Friends in Liverpool would be able in course of time to procure a good Situation for our Victor, should he prefer being nearer his Father and Mother — I have allways assented thee the following of thy wishes in all things, and I again entreat thee to do nought but thy pleasure respecting the offers now adverted to =

In the mean time I earnestly entreat thee to *Speak French and think in French* if Possible — I also Entreat thee that my Son John Should Spend a great Portion of his time at drawing from *Nature Only*, all the size of Life, and to Scrupulously keep every Drawing he makes — and if it is possible, for thee or him to remember what Plants, or Birds, Snakes, Fishes or Insects &ᶜ &ᶜ — that I have not Drawn, to attend more particularly to those, but to draw all he can = Do also Insist on his taking Lessons of Music from thee on the Piano = I wish I had brought him and thee also along with me. = I certainly have brought with me my Collection that is considered as the best of the kind in Existence, but I wish I had remained Two more Years at Close Work in the woods of my Beloved America: =

I shall take thy advise respecting the Beech Woods, I assure thee. Yet should I return to America and to Louisiana, I would go to my Good Friend Bourgeat with great Pleasure without trespassing one foot north of his Line[16] —

The letter inclosed in thine that thou ought to have openᵈ is from Mʳ Sully, who says that he sent me one directed to New Orleans for Sir Thomas Lawrence — I would like to receive it — I have wrote to him this day =

Thy watch is gone long ago by way of New York. I have sent thee and N. Berthoud packets of News Papers and will continue to do so — I think it not worth while to send thee any other things untill my future life is more ascertained or thy own Plans known to me — Now farewell, my Dear Lucy, my Beloved Wife, write often.

Kiss my Dear John for me — It is very doutfull if I do call on Miss Gifford at all. I may, however, see her should I be presented to the Duke of Devonshire, at whose domaines she goes sometimes — Farewell, God Bless thee, and grant thee Happiness — I have seen very little of thy Sister Ann. They see no Company and I have been

16. Mrs. Percy of Beech Woods had banished Audubon from her estate following his emotional outburst at her when she disagreed with how the artist was painting her daughters. The Bourgeats were her neighbors.

in a constant round of it — Again, God Bless thee. Thine friend &
Husband, J. J. A

(Charles Midlemist's Wife shall receive her money as soon as I reach
London, he may rest assured —)
    I have wrote to H. Clay for a Letter of Introduction Especially to G.ˡ
Lafayette: *I wish thee* to write to him also and ask him to send me one
to the care of the Minister at London =

My Dear Beloved [ms: D.ʳ B.ᵈ] Son John — I am truly glad to have
received the 2 watch papers[17] you sent me in Mamma's letter — Do
continue to Improve — Draw, my Dear Boy, and study Music. You
will soon now be able to assist your Father very much in rendering
our good Friend, your Mamma, quite comfortable. Oh, what
Pleasures you will feel then — Copy this letter and send as much of
it as Mamma may wish, to your Brother Victor — I send you some
chalks and colors in a few weeks. God Bless You — Affectionately,
Your Father, J. J. A.

MANCHESTER SEP.ᴿ 17.ᵀᴴ 1826 — SUNDAY —

I wrote this morning a long Letter to thee, my Lucy, and Inclosed it to
Mess.ʳˢ Rathbone to be forward.ᵈ —

His Excellency Dewitt Clinton
Governor of New York &.ᶜ &.ᶜ —

My Dear Sir

    The extremely gratifying reception that I met with on my arival
at Liverpool, attained in a very great measure by the presentation of
your Letter to me and to Joseph Sabine Es. qʳ of London, make me
now take the Liberty of adressing you again —
    The President of the Royal Institution of Liverpool, D.ʳ Traill, the

---

17. A watch paper was a paper disc used as a protective pad in the outer case of a watch. It was
often inscribed with an ornamental design, a poem, or a drawing.

well known W͟a͟m͟ Roscoe, and many other persons of distinction, amongst whom were [MS: where] Lord Stanley, Thos Stanley B͟r͟ and Lady Isabella Douglass, Sister of Lord Selkirk, did me the Honor of Pronouncing my Collection of Drawings fully worthy the attention of their country — exibited a kindness towards me quite unexpected by an Individual of such Humble merits =

I will now proceed slowly towards London, visit Edingburgh and all the other principal cities of the Three Kingdom[s] and afterwards go to France, where I wish extremely to see our Great General Lafayette —

Will You Honor me so much as to answer this Letter of mine, and Inclose one also for me of Introduction Expecially to Gen͟l͟ Lafayette? The Gratitude of an American who holds his country's right dear to his Heart is all I can offer in return to you, but his Gratitude, I assure you, will never cease —

With highest sentiments of Respect and Estime, permit me, my Dear Sir, to be for ever yours most truly devoted and much obliged Ob͟t͟ Serv͟t͟, J. J. Audubon

Please direct to Rathbone Brothers & C͟o͟ Liverpool —
The same as the above nearly Copied for M͟r͟ Clay, Secretary of State &͟c͟, Washington City

SEPTEMBER 17͟T͟H͟ 1826, MANCHESTER SUNDAY.

Having closed my Letters to thee, to Thomas Sully, to Dewitt Clinton & Henry Clay; I shaved, washed, dressed myself and heard the Town Clock stract 2 rather Aprehensive that I might be too late at M͟r͟ Heywood for Dinner = I walk͟d͟, however, Gently down Bridge Street and followed the Great Road toward Liverpool — I was much pleased with my walk; for nearly a mile going off from Manchester the road lays on an Elevated, apparently made-up mass of earth [MS: Hearth], giving an extensive view as well as an interesting one of the Country for many miles = A small Creek orneients the fore ground, and the Vast number of pretty English women [MS: woman] bound to afternoon church service fed my Eyes amply, although my stomach grumbled all the while at my lingering movements towards Claremont $=$ I followed the new instead of the old road, and there by arived at the Younger M$^\text{r}$ Heywood. I was about sufering an *hey Ho!* to Escape when the Gate Keeper, or Porter, or Centinel, for the person might be called by all or any of those names, told me that "I might walk thro the grounds, turn to the Left and reach the old Gentleman's seat without returning" — My stomach thanked the man with a very Indecent sort of a Grumbling noise I thought; and I Hurried on $=$ Leaped over an English 5 bar Gate and was in the Presence of, who dost thou think, Lucy? — Not Waterton's snake, nor his Alligators, no, Indeed, it was Miss Heywood Senior, I guess$^\text{d}$ $=$

Yes, I Guess$^\text{d}$ that she was Miss Heywood senior because one older could not exist and be a Miss — My steps at once became balanced. They could have been counted [MS: compted] a mile off without a telescope — My face cooled also, and my speech was adapted to the *tournure* of Miss Heywood $=$

"This way, Sir." I Jump$^\text{d}$ and open$^\text{d}$ another 5 bar Gate — "You have seen many Indians, I dare say, Sir" — Now, Lucy, I dare say that *I have!* "Pray, Sir, are there [MS: they] not very many Snakes in America" — I was so near laughing that I *dare say* Miss Heywood saw my situation and spoke of her Brother $=$ but, Lucy, as I am fond [MS: found] of Ladies, read here Two Descriptions $=$ My Landlady, M$^\text{rs}$ Hedge, is Low and Miss Heywood is High — M$^\text{rs}$ Hedge is fatter than Miss Heywood, and both do not weigh more than 450 pounds avoir dupoids. My Landlady's Hams, if *Cured well*, would make extraordinary Hams indeed. Those of Miss Heywood would turn out still more extraordinary bacon — My M$^\text{rs}$ Hedge borders on 50 and the Maid of Claremont has settled 70 springs aside, without enumerating those that now creak most vehemently in her well set corset — The Woman of King Street is kind, so is the Lady of Claremont $=$ The former charges me 2 shillings for a Dinner, and to Dine with the other, I must ware 3 shillings worth of Boots —

"Stop, Stop, for goodness sake stop. Why, My Laforest, this is most tiresome and absurd. I cannot bear it" —

Well, well — I have reach$^\text{d}$ a Beautifull Garden, and far in the Distance M$^\text{r}$ Heywood & one of his nephews are perceived — We meet and we shake hands — The fat maid leaves us and we are talking about

American Bugs!!! — Fine Conversation to be sure. I would like to know what the Entymologist Thomas Say[18] Es^qr Academician &^c &^c &^c &^c &^c &^c would say on such an occasion — *American Bugs*!!! — Watterton only saw *one* — I have seen millions, and Thomas Say has described the same specie over and over again probably hundred millions of time[s] =

"Mr Audubon, this is a Most Destructive Insect. It kills all my Beech Trees" — I look and I see the Little beautifully white flies that ornement our beech woods, here before me, and wish myself in America =

The Grounds of Claremont are fine and on a much larger Scale than those of Green Bank: but the Style is utterly different = The House is too Large ever to be *filled with Friends*. However, I was receive[d] as kindly as any other man as well recommended would have been: — *Mr Heywood seems to feel the great weight of his purse*, yet he talks plainly and put me at my ease in a few moments; there was no company from abroad. 2 Nephews, Miss Heywood, and another Miss perhaps. I am quite as old [as] were all that sat round the table with me = The Dinner was plain, much more so than any at Green Bank. The wine was not handed me with Hanna Rathbone's kindness — No, it was poured here in each persons Glass by the waiters — The Ladies left us early, and we the Gentlemen soon after them left the table = We talk^d of America again and principally of the Battle of New Orleans, that seems yet to be a great rough bone in their throat = In the Library where we had sat before dinner, we retired to drink Tea, and the Port Folio of Drawings of Birds of Miss Heywood shewed itself to me as I entered, and said quite aloud to my senses — "Audubon, be merciful" = Who would not be, when looking at Beautifull Drawings under the fair hands of a Fair female? = Stuffed, by Washington! Yes, stuffed specimen, and the Drawings *Stuff also*! —

"What do you think of them, Mr Audubon?" Now, my Lucy; if kindness ever entered thy Heart — if the disconsolate brought an involuntary tear to thy Eye, if thou ever hast pitied the Culprit as he

18. Thomas Say (1787–1834) was just beginning to publish his three-volume *American Entomology, or Descriptions of the Insects of North America* when Audubon arrived in Philadelphia in 1824.

passed thee, with down cast looks of agony, take pity on thy Husband and answer for him == I took up the Drawing, looked at it side ways, brought it close to my Eye, glanced a sight at the proper distance to exibit the Effect and ~~~~ Well, shall I tell thee what I said? — I said — upon my word, I do not recollect what I said — I pass^d drawing one after another to the last, and my Heart was Glad as well as my eyes were relieved when several sheets of Blank paper appeared together without drawings — The Book is closed, and I will Close the subject with the trifling observation that I will address to Parents Generally ==

If you please, good Friends all; do not Tease the Stranger's eye, with the daubs that Your conceits bring as equals to Raphael['s] Designs == Be not deluded at First, and you will not find out the truth when too late to repent —

I took my Coffee — answered to all the questions put to me about Snakes, Indians, Mr Watterton, John Hunter and myself untill, perceiving that my Good Host Mr Heywood had fell asleep, I felt Inclined to do the same and as Gently as Possible bade the Circle good night ==

The moon was high, the clouds large, Dark and portentous of a stormy night — The navigator I knew was preparing to reef all Sails and to double the Helm — the dull dashess of light[n]ing in the north only augumented the Growing Horrors of the expected scene of Death — Here the people, each on each pressing forward Like the multiplied sheep of our vast Plains when flying before the famined Tyrant of the woods, hurried towards Manchester to Escape the rain that now Drop by Drop fell heavy on the Ground and raised each a little cloud of Dust — As I walked faster than these good Citizens, I plainly could hear the heaving breasts^† of the fair maids thro the rustling of their Silky Gowns, and as they lean^d and hung for support on the arm of their lovers, their looks were most Interesting ==

Where is my Lucy now? Is there a Storm about her or is she *herself alone*? — calm! Serene! Beautifull and Happy!!

I am in, and in a few moments will blow my Light — The Storm has past over merely as a rufled thought of anger Iritates the Countenance of man, and now all in nature is beautifull and calm again — Such is the weather at Manchester — Now, my Lucy, Good Night —

The weather being Beautifull, I took a good walk: had to day more persons than usual at my Rooms — a Mr Railton of Felton Fold, Cheatham Hill, who brought a Handsome wife & 3 sweet children, spent a good deal of time and, giving me a card, Invited me extremely kindly to his Cottage to spend either the day or night whenever it would be agreable or convenient = I know not Mr Railton any other way than thro this mark of extreme Politeness and will try to make some return — A Party from Mr Heywood also came, and Miss Heywood I Hope saw some *Drawings of Birds*.

I Received my Trunk &^{c} from Liverpool and a Packet of Letters from R^d Rathbone — a Note of Invitation from Mr Saml Greg to go and spend some time at Quary Bank, 14 miles from this =

The Invitation I had received from Mr Sergeant was not forgotten, and he came for me at half past three to shew me the way to his House — Let me tell thee before that I had the pleasure of meeting Mr Murray at my Rooms, and he was very kind to me also —

I have been delighted with the acquaintance of Mr Sergeant — and his House, and his Books and his Pictures, and his Guns and his Dogs — and very much so with a Friend of his from London who also dined with us = We chatted very friendly — made experiments with percussion [MS: precussion] pieces and drank some good wine untill half past 10. I offered him Harlan's fauna, and he promised me a good blooded Pointer — He gave me a small box of brass containing brass medals of all the great victories of England — Amongst the Letters that came for me, I have one of thanks from the Secretary of the Liverpool Royal Institution for my Wild Turkey =

Receiving no letters from Mr Alexander Gordon, I wrote the following to him — I felt some anxiety to see how he would express himself towards me in his recommendations —

My Dear Sir

I have now been here a week and after Constant and strict Enquiries, I am forced to conclude that your intended visit must have been Postponed —

The Good People of Manchester have received me with great

marks of attention, and I am going on much as I did when at
Liverpool = From this Place I will go to Birmingham — Oxford, &c̲
as I told you when last I had the pleasure of se[e]ing you, and as I do
not at all like travelling entirely thro this country without the Letters
that you promised me, I ask you again for Some — Please remember
me to M͟r͟s Gordon and Miss Donathan and believe &c̲ &c̲ &c̲ J. J. A

A. Gordon Es͟q͟r
Liverpool —

It is now become quite necessary to Inform thee, my Beloved Wife,
that that Portion of my wardrobe not unfrequently called Shirts is fast
giving way; therefore I looked at some Linens this Day and probably
will buy some tomorow — God Bless thee, Good night, my Love — It
is raining now like fury —

MANCHESTER TUESDAY 19͟T͟H SEP͟R 1826. —

I saw M͟r Melly this morning at the Exchange. He had just arrived from
Liverpool — had gone to my Door Keeper and, having examined
the *Book of Income*, he told me when we met that he was sorry and
displeased at my want of Success and that my Exibition would never
do — He advised me as he allways had done before to go either to
London or Paris, but to Paris in Preference — to return to Liverpool
first and see my Friends there and receive more Letters — Altogether
he so much reduced my Spirits that I felt sick and I am sure must
have changed my Countenance extremely = He wished me to go &
dine with him at M͟r George Murray with some French Persons of his
acquaintance, but when I told him that I contemplated going out at 4 to
Quary Bank to pass the night, he engaged me by all means to do so. We
parted for a short while, for at 4, whilst I was taking a cup of coffee with
Miss Helen Gregg in Fountain Street, in came my Intelligent Friend
who turned quite Pale at meeting the very fair and aimiable companion
I was with — The fair maid did not turn pale, no — She blushed as if
a blooming rose, and her dark eye lashes for a while robbed both the
Intelligent Swiss and I from the pleasure of looking at her Eyes. = Now
the query is, does he or she Love most the other? That they both love, *I*
have not the least doubt, and may God bless them! =

Mr Saml Gregg, the Father of the large familly, came in and met me as if he had known me 50 Years = The Brothers Saml & William also came — The Carriage was ordered, and I was soon Seated precisely fronting the Fair Maid = Her Father was next to her, and off we went pushing for the Country as if moving off from Evil Spirits =

I think that on a moderate Calculation I looked at the objects *before me* one hundred times more than I did on any about the Country we traversed, and had we not crossed a River nearly 50 feet wide! I would have look^d one more [time] at them in the same given time = but this River I did look at and positively stared when I was *told* that it was a stream of Great Importance. The name I have forgotten, but I know it to be 7 miles from Manchester in the way to Derbyshire =

The land I remarked is Improved by an Immense quantity of Lime to grow Wheat principally = The Aspect of the Country extremely Improved and many of the Buildings really beautiffull — We at last turn[ed] quickly to the Right and moved slowly down a declivity when I saw *Quary Bank*, a most enchanting spot — situated on the Edge of the same river we had Crossed;[19] the Grounds truly Pi[c]turesque and Improved as much as improvements can be =

I was Introduced to 3 Ladies that I met Drawing, reading & writting — The Misses Mary Ann — &^{c} &^{c} and I kissed there the second Daughter of my Friend W^{am} Rathbone = We had Tea, & drawing being continued, I made a sketch in black chalk of a Dog, & rub^d it with cork to give an Idea to the Ladies of the Improvement over the Common stumps usually used =

Then I accompanied the 2 Brothers present, who had come home on Horseback, to a discussing Club instituted on their premises for the advancement of their workmen = Going there we Passed the Chapel — a long line of Cottages for the Workpeople and at last entered the School Room where about 20 men had assembled and waited the arrival of their young Masters = The question presented cons[i]sted of ascertaining the superior advantage between the Discoveries of the *Compass* or the art of *Printing* — Had our Franklin been there, he could have told something on both sides the question well worth relating,

19. The Quarry Bank mill is on the river Bollin.

but the Illustrious man lays at the corner of 4th & Mulbery streets in Philadelphia — and we did without him —

I, Lucy, delivered a Lecture this Evening! Now, do not laugh so. I assure thee I understood the subject well, and that is more than one half of Lecturers can assert with a clear conscience. I spoke of Birds, alligators, Beavers & Indians and marched back to the company of the Ladies at nearly 10 o'clock = took a Glass of White Wine — looked at Miss Helen, bid the 3 other sisters good night, shook hands with the Father and the Sons, entered a Room for me that night, undressed in a thrice and bid thee at Leisure good night =

My thoughts were very Gloomy; uncertain of the future, undeterm[ine]d because uncertain, I turned over and over in search of ~~~~ thee, my Lucy, but all in vain, and at last I closed my eyes, impatient to see the next day —

QUARY BANK. 12 MILES FROM MANCHESTER,
WEDNESDAY SEP^{R} 20TH 1826 —

The Clock from Mr Gregg's Mills made me think of raising, and although the weather was bad, cloudy & rainy, I took an Immense walk, down and up the River, thro the gardens, along the Ponds, about the woods, the fields & the meadows = saw a fine flock of Partridges, some Jays [MS: Jia*ys] &^{c}, and at half Past 8 I had nearly finished daubing a Picture of an Esquimaux drawn in a Sleygh by 4 Dogs =

The Conversation of the Ladies during the whole [MS: all] morning was extremely animated and Interesting. We all talked about [the] Primitive state of Nature in our kind and discussed if or no it was preferable to the present state of acting = I know that I astonished the Ladies with my odd ways and my curious expressions, but all this could not be help^{d} and I enjoyed *them* most certainly —

The sight of the Partridges in the morning and of those that were on the Dinner table made me offer a Shooting party for the afternoon; I expressed my wish to see some Pheasants and to Draw some — All is soon arranged and the pleasure is augmented by the arrival of Mr Shaw, the principal Game Keeper of Lord Stamford,[20] who obligingly proffers

20. George Harry Grey, sixth Earl of Stamford (1765–1845), on whose grounds Audubon went gunning that afternoon.

to shew us many Birds (so are partridges called). Here we are with guns no longer than my arms — 2 good Dogs and plenty of Land before us ⹀

Pheasants are not to be touched in this Land of Freedom untill the 1st of October, and I dare venture to say that, had we seen none, we would not have infringed the Laws of the goodly Country, but somehow or other (as a Kentuckian would say it) I positively saw one tilt over tail after head untill down to the earth [MS: hearth] he came, I believe, as dead as if shot any time next month — Beautifull Creature — His eye was yet all life — his chops all crimson, his Coat all brilliancy ⹀ Presently again another was brought down; Indeed, I had so compleatly forgotten to think of October that every bird that flew brought the gun to my Eye, and I would have played the pheasants a bad trick had not the Game Keeper Interfered in their behalf ⹀

We had a fine walk and a fine Hunt, killed some partridges and saw the Hills in Derbyshire ⹀ The Hills amongst which my Lucy was born — Oh [MS: ho], how I thought of thee, of Matlock, of England, of America and of Thee and the Hills before me ⹀ 40 miles from w[h]ere my Lucy received light and Breath!! ⹀

Mr Shaw pocketted 5 shillings and we, the Pheasants and Partridges — Thus I have hunted once on British grounds — on Lord Stamford *Demesnes*, w[h]ere every tree that we would scarcely call a Saplin is marked and numbered and, for all that I know, pays either a Tax to Government or a tythe to the Parish ⹀ A Partridge that crosses the river, or a road, or an [h]edge and alight on other grounds than those of Lord Stanford are as safe from his attacks as if they were in Guin[e]a ⹀

We returned to Quary Bank well fatigued and Enjoyed our Tea drinking well, I assure thee — The evening was beautifull, of course. Thou seest that it has rained and clear^{d} up since I got up ⹀ We talk^{d} much about Mr Sim's views of the Interior of this earth [MS: hearth][21] ⹀ The whole company were much Interested, and the rapid improvements of our country was also a subject brought forward ⹀

21. John Cleves Symmes, Jr. (1779–1829), was known for his theory that Earth is hollow and its interior accessible at the poles. Audubon had met Symmes in 1820 when he worked at the Western Museum in Cincinnati, where he also drew Symmes's portrait for the *Western Magazine* of 1820. The original sketch is held in the Museum Collection of the New-York Historical Society.

I again look^d at Miss Helen very much — I could not well help it —
She is so very attractive of Looks and Manners — and so Polite, and so
~~~~ God Bless thee, my Lucy, Good night =

MANCHESTER 21ST SEP^{R} THURSDAY 1826 —

About 6 o'clock I set to drink some Cocoa, eat some bread and butter
and pack^d my male Pheasant snugly to take it to Manchester to draw it
= I was soon mounted on Dicky the Pony and moving slowly toward
town again — holding the basket in my hand and kicking Dicky to
force him to trot = and he troted and I Jump^d, for Dicky trotted hard
and I would not ride *a L'Anglaise.* Of course, my Posteriors were sadly
hurt at my stuborness = but Dicky, after 3 hours of consideration, took
me direct to his stable in Chancery lane, not by chance but by solid
raisonement — He was glad of being released from my weight, I dare
say, and I was glad to be on foot again =

I reached my Exibition Room and received *Miserable accounts* — I
saw plainly that my Expenses in Manchester would not be repaid and,
of Course, that I must move shortly =

I wished to Draw the Pheasant, but my hands refused to act —
and therefore I put my brains at work = I called on Dr Holme and
represented my situation — told him that my Expenses were enormous
and my returns did not meet them — He walk^d to the Academy of
Natural History and ordered a Comittee to meet on Saturday to see if
a room could not be provided for me *Gratis* = Mr Hindley,[22] to whom
Mr Shepherd had given me Letters, promissed me his assistance =
I hunted for another room to remove my Drawings to should I not
succeed with the academicians and should I conclude to try sometime
longer in this Place = This employment did me some good =

I took Tea at Mr Bentley, who has a fine Daughter also = Lucy,
remark that I do not miss a Miss if fair w[h]ere ever I go = He gave me
some wires, procured me a Board to fix my Pheasant, and I came to my
Lodgings in better humour than I had left them this morning = I have
mounted my Bird. All is ready for work tomorow = Will my Works

---

22. This may be the Manchester Orientalist John Haddon Hindley (1765–1827). He translated
Persian works in both prose and verse.

answer my Intentions or will they not? Oh, my Lucy, how dull I feel without thee — good night —

MANCHESTER 22ᴰ FRIDAY SEPᴿ 1826 —

I have drawn all day and am fatigued — I have had only 20 people to see my Birds = sad work this = The Consul, Mʳ Brooks, came to see me and Invited me to dine at Mʳ Loyd, Banker, at 1, next Sunday — advised me also to have a subscription Book for my Work &ᶜ &ᶜ. It is easy to have advisers, but to strack at a good one is very dificult indeed =

I am fatigued as I told thee before and too Low in spirits to write even my thoughts to night = Then farewell, god bless thee, good night —

MANCHESTER SATURDAY 23ᴰ SEPᴿ 1826. —

I could not write last evening because I felt fatigued and was rather low of spirit; therefore I went to bed early, perhaps at 9 o'clock; however, a Gentle rapp at my Door made me bid to "Come in" = and thro the dark I recognised the voice of Mʳ Bentley — called for a light and was up in a moment = We chatted a while, read some, Drank some; and as he went down the stairs bound home, I entered my bed room bound to bed for the 2ᵈ time, and the last this last night barring *all accidents* =

My Drawing this morning moved rapidly, and by 11 o'clock I was ready to Dress myself = I walked to the Exchange and met Doctor Holme with several other Friends who told me that the Comittee had voted unanimously to grant me a room in their Institution *Gratis* to exibit my Birds = Of Course, I thank them as it lessened my Expenses 13 shillings per week = I saw Mʳ Samˡ Greg Senior and three of the Daughters; one Miss Sarah was amongst them = I had many Ladies and I felt more gratified than I had been previously this week =

I went to dine with the familly Greg in Fountain Street = I had sent the Pheasant killed last Wednesday to Robt. Greg's Esqʳ Counting House and saw him at the lodgings of the Father = I gave the Miss Gregs 2 dozen Black chalks and 2 dozen 6 inch Corks to draw with, for which I paid the extraordinary price of 8/6 — more than 4 times as much as in Philadelphia = England is so overdone with duty that it is allmost past the Power of any one in it to do his duty much longer; and I feel Inclined to think that some period hence will bring forth Combustion = but, as I said, I felt in better spirits and *I* hoped that my changing Rooms would be of some good result to me and, more over, as I determined on doing with one Person only Instead of 2 for my Exibition here after ═

Now then that I feel fully at par with the weather, that, for a wonder, is much like myself fairer than usual *for this World*, let me give thee slight descriptions of the remarkable objects a man may see in England ═

Primo — a small man (an Englishman) bearing under his left arm a large setting spaniel — in the right a Nosegay not quite so sizeable as the dog, on his legs and over a red pair of breeches, Buff Colored Chamey Gaiters, that so completly seem to [h]amper this little man that an American Woodsman would conceive the whole a cari[ca]ture of our Specie, with a fair specimen of the Canine Creation; and a fairer specimen still of the stores of the Goddess Flora; now, Lucy, just look at the red Potatoe Nosed little man and his sugar loaffed hat, and lessen to the Inch wooden souls of his brass buckled Shoes on the pavement nearly kept in a constant state of Cleanliness by the square flaps of a coachman's surtout and thou wilt have the fairest Picture of one of thy *Country Men* I can give. ═

From this I Jump into Picadilly and turn in Murray's Street and enter George Murray's Es^{qr} Cotton Mills where 1500 souls are kept, not only from a pure state of starvation, but also from dissolute and Extravagant outrages when without either food or Employ ═ rather Natural Circumstances ═ These Mills consist of a compleat Square area of about 8 acres builded with houses 5, 6 & 7 stories high ═ and having in the center of this square a large basin of Watter received from the Canal that flows thro the Town ═ 2 Engines of 40 & 45 Horse powers are kept a going from 6 to 8 o'clock each day and are condensed from the basin mentioned ═

Mr Murray himself accompanied me about and I saw — a general Black smith shop ═ turning &^c &^c &^c — spining threads of Cotton that grew in Louisianna, N°s 200 & 250 ═ I saw the Gass forming furnace ═ the pressing machines for the cotton hanks and all that Mr Murray dare[d] show me when he discovered that I knew something of mechanics ═

This is the largest establishment owned by one single Individual in Manchester ═ Some others belonging to Firms or co-partnerships [MS: copparternships] of several have as many as 2500 working hands, as poor miserable abject wretches [MS: wrtetchess] as ever worked the mines of Golconda[23] =

But, Lucy, Mͫ Gregg's Mills at Quary Banks are rendered more comfortable = I have been assured that during the time of need and scarcity, Mͫ Gregg kept his Hands *paid* if not employed, and may God give him credit for so doing = but, Lucy, whilst I am speaking of Mͫ Gregg's Mills, let me say also something about his manners = He adresses his children in the most Partiarchall style I ever heard and with a kindness only equalled by my Friends of Green Bank = His son Robert, a man maried who has at least one child, dined with us and the old Mͫ Gregg scarcely ever spoke to him without calling him "My Love" = He asked his eldest daughter Mary Ann to drink a glass of wine with him as if with all the anxiety to receive the boon of a mistress = and when she refused, he appeared quite chagrin[ed], and feared that she was not well = yet there is a bluntness in his speech at time[s], regularly, however, a compleat Gentleman. I prefer this bluntness to any of the false Hipocritical phrases of the Fops as much as a beggar prefers a good dinner to starvation —

I was asked to go and spend next Monday night at Mͫ Robͪ Hyde Greg, the son that he called his *Love*, at Summer Place, Higher Hardwick [MS: Ardwick], but as I had been offered a Ticket for a Concert previous for the same night, it is doubtfull if I will go =

I felt inclined to write much when I begun and I see that I have really spun it out pretty well — yet I have not done = I took tea at Mͫ Bentley again and promissed to write to thee on his behalf for the Bones of an Alligator of a good size — Now, we will see if he gets one as quickly as Dͫ Harlan Did?[24] =

I Concluded to day, to have a *Book of Subscriptions* open, to receive the names of all persons Inclined to have the *best American Illustrations of Birds of that Country ever yet transmitted to Posterity* — and *I* will do so = I have also thought of a Plan to procure lookers on by putting up

23. Golconda was a city in southeastern India famous for its diamonds as well as the enslavement of its mine workers.

24. Shortly before he left New Orleans for England, Audubon satisfied his Philadelphia friend Dr. Richard Harlan's request for an alligator to study. Audubon sent him one in "a hogshead of spirits," the story of which he narrates in "Observations on the Natural History of the Alligator," *Edinburgh New Philosophical Journal* 2 (October–April 1826–27): 270–80.

a few drawings of mine in the most Conspicuous Shops here, to Invite
the Public to call upon me with each their shillings, and perhaps out of
20 a name for my support in Publication — Indeed, I feel as Inclined
if not more so to do all in my Power to push forward at a round pace
and prove the test [MS: Text] of my Value from the penny worth to the
Capital now in the Bank of England!! — Now, my sweet Wife, God
Bless thee; Good Night ⹀

MANCHESTER SUNDAY, 24$\underline{^{TH}}$ SEP$\underline{^R}$ 1826.

I drew at my Pheasant untill precisely 11 o'clock — the weather cloudy,
& wind warm, much like rain ⹀ M$\underline{^r}$ Bentley came in and sat with me
perhaps an hour ⹀ Then I had that most disagreable and fatiguing Job
to perform: shaving, washing, Brushing coat and brushing Pantaloons;
combing & cleaning my long locks and, in fact, making ready to walk
to M$\underline{^r}$ Loyd the Banker ⹀ I perform^d the whole of this in 20 minutes
and marched out of King Street, through S$\underline{^t}$ Ann Square, passed the
Exchange, up Fish Market, the old Church and Cheatham Hill, my cane
in one hand and the other holding both my Gloves as clean I will say as
any man in England ⹀

I pass$\underline{^d}$ a Turnpike gate where, having given a six pence, I received
5 back again and a small ticket, my full tittle to go thro on my return
⹀ This is a way in this country that prevents cheating to an Eminent
degree and no doubt most Improved the perquisition of the Keeper
very considerably ⹀ I then proceeded along this turnpike a good
2 miles, having, however, only a very imperfect view of the country
surrounding me ⹀ The servant maids and men waiters were most
plentifully in view; all neatly dressed, rosy cheeks and gay in all their
movements ⹀ Nature, however, seems to be Inclined to change her
verdant dress and I remarked that the foliage was deeply colored with
autumnal tints ⹀ The season is finer and longer as summer than usual,
and I may say with safety that I am viewing England in her best Garb
⹀

I have just passed the 2$\underline{^d}$ Gate and stop^d, as I told thee some 10 days
ago, on the right of the road and entered the House of our Consul S.
Brooks Es$\underline{^{qr}}$, where the first object after him seen was a plaster cast of
an Eminently marked cranium possessed of all the faculties belonging
to our Race either towards the bad, the indiferent or good Propensities

= We talk^d a little on craniology, comparative anatomy, and walk^d a few hundred yards to Mr Loyd's house, also close by the Turnpike and still on the right side of the way =

Before I enter this House, let me tell thee, my Lucy, that Mr Loyd is a Banker worth the comfortable amount of 400,000 pounds sterling = only Two millions of Dollars, quite a trifle in this country and less still with Columbus when he discovered America, but an amount very scarce, I assure thee, even in England except with a Banker like Mr Loyd =

The Gentleman himself receives us most kindly and politely at the Entrance, and we set for a short while in a delightfull room w[h]ere I saw a chair made in London that would be or might be called a Sopha any where = Did I know what it cost, I would tell thee, but really I do not, of course. I will abandon the task, and please follow me into the Grounds and the Gardens and the Hot Houses = The Grounds are laid on a declivity affording a far view of agreable Lan[d]scapes = The Gardens are most beautifully managed and provided with all the comodities that this wonderfull *Islet* affords, and the Hot Houses contained aboundant suplies of Exotick flowers, fruits and shrubs = The Coffee Tree was bearing = The bananas [MS: Ananas] were ripening under the Juicy Grapes of Spain & Italy. The little sensitive of Kentucky[25] shrunk humbly at my touch, and the multifloras were mingled over head with Cucumbers & other rampent growths, mixing all perfumes together — How thou wouldst Enjoy this = How much I wished my Victor with me, or our Dear John! =

Art here supercedes, nay, I might say helps Nature to produce her richest treasures at will, and Man in England may be called the *God of the Present day* = Flowers after flowers were plucked for me, and I again remarked how very much our superiors Englishmen are, in those simple attentions to strangers that at once can make them feel contented in defiance of nationnal prejudices, should any exist =

A Bell is heard; it is the summons for Dinner. We have now been Joined by Mr Thomas Loyd and Mr Hindley and we move towards the House again = Now for the second time I see Mrs Loyd, another Lady,

25. Probably the wild sensitive plant (*Sennia nictitans*), the leaves of which fold somewhat when touched.

and 2 Daughters of the Banker's. = Books are laying about the table; all is rich, comfortable, pleasing to the eye, to the mind, to the body = A second summons to dinner gives Mr Brooks an opportunity of taking under his arms the 2 Daughters = to Mr Hindley that of feeling the weight of Mrs Loyd and to thy Husband that of escorting the fair unknown =

Now I have rather an Idea of describing to night = and so here comes a Dinner. Please set down and partake = Three servants (all males I believe) dressed in livery trim^d with red on a white ground move like Keeldeers = The American Visitor is next to Mrs Loyd and Mr Hindley [MS: Findley] opposite him = Next the Woodsman, a Miss Loyd and the Consul next. Mr Thomas L^d fronts him &^{c} &^{c} = Some eat soup and I eat *Sole* [MS: *Soul*] = Mr Loyd offers a Glass of wine to thy husband, and we each bow respectfully to each other without a word and drink the wine = This in England is quite a signal & challenges follow challenges with the quickness of Communication given by Telegraphy = I ought to have ask^d Mrs Loyd to drink with me. This would have been *Bon ton*; however I did in Course, and, next her, every other person round the table =

At such dinners the waitters perform every duty = No Individuall attempts to help directly any one and, although next to Mrs Loyd, my Plate was allways handed most carefully by the waitter next her, who also put the stopper on the Decanters &^{c} &^{c} = We have at such Dinners 3 services, all aboundant, and choiced of their kinds, and conviviality moves with the wines round & round the table again untill the Ladies raise & retire = Now, Lucy, their health is Drank and thine also = Perhaps I take a paire or a few grapes and fill my Glass with Madira as regularly as the Bottles go their rounds = no more healths, however, unless some one should absent (thro necessity), when invariably his health is Drunk whilst he is doing all in his power to Improve it in the next room, from which he reappears quite relieved & improved and ready to receive again from Bachus a full Bumper — Now Politics; or Localities, or of other countries and talk of America, for Instance, and as I like it both as a *Subject* and an American, I rather swell my tone and enjoy the conversation =

The waitters have retired. We are a multiplied *tête a tête*, and they only come in to bring Old wines in fresh bottles = It is, however, quite dark and we have been no less than 5 hours at this dinner — We raise, we xxxx and are in the Library with the Ladies, who no doubt know all the Last proceedings of this closed door business as well as Any of its Members = Coffee & Tea & Books & Talks = and after another hour, a good night is bid to all, & brings me arm in arm with Thomas Loyd Es^{qr} — in the Turnpike again following the Consull to his house, where we part from him = The Flora (a coach), newly Instituted, called for Mr Hindley. We are in Manchester once more, and Mr Loyd has just left me to rapp most desperately 5 or 6 times at Mrs Hedges Door =

Thus has been spent this Sunday, without going to church, but not without praying my God to grant thee Happiness & Comfort = I heard some singular accounts of the wonderfull fortunes accumulated in this Country by men begaining with no more than Industry could bring forth — some really wonderfull but, my Lucy, I must go to bed & bid thee good night again with all my heart =

MANCHESTER MONDAY 25TH SEP^R 1826. —

Who would come this morning in my room about 7 whilst I was busily finishing [MS: finished] the grounds of my Male Pheasant? A Handsome Quaker, perhaps 30 years of age and very neatly dressed = "My friends are going out of Manchester before thee opens thy exibition rooms — Can we see thy Collection at 9 o'clock?" — I ask the stranger to set — answer Yes to all he asks, and shew him my Drawing: Now, were all the people in this good Land of England Quakers, I might perhaps have some encouragement, but really, my Lucy — my Times are dull, heavy, long, painfull and Harrass my mind allmost too much =

5 minutes before nine I was standing waitting for the Quaker and his Friends in the Loby of the Exchange, when 2 persons standing also held the following discourse = "Pray, have you seen Mr Audubon's Collection of Birds? I am told it is well worth a shilling. Suppose we go now."

"Puh — it is all a Hoax. Save your shilling for better use. I have seen them. Why, the fellow ought to be Drumed out of Town" =

Did I Blush, Lucy? No, I turned pale and dared not raise my eyes least

I might be known, but, depend upon it, I wished myself in America again =

The Quakers, however, made all up again, for they praised my Drawings so much that I *blushed then* in spite of my old age = Now, Lucy, comes in 2 Cards of Invitation for the Concert, one from Dͬ͟ Holme, the second from Mͬ͟ Loyd the Banker = I also received a short Letter from Mͬ͟͟ˢ Ed͟ᵈ Roscoe all about drawing = but I am rather, Indeed, I will say, [a] good deal surprised that I have not a word from either Miss Hanah Rathbone or Mͬ͟ Gordon — and that I have not heard a word about my album =

I took my Drawing of the Pheasant to Mr Tanetti's shop [MS: Chop] and had it put in a good light, to prove to the good People of Manchester that I really did wish to see more of them = There, Lucy, I purshased 25 yards of good Linen for £ 4.3.4, being 3 & 4 pence per yard, and I will have in 10 days a fresh supply of Comfortables =

The old dog that attends the rooms of the Exchange, gave me due notice that my Time was out and that I must clear my Birds because an Exibition of Deaf and Dumbs must take place = I have no objection, far from this — I have already made arrangements for my new place in King Street and Hope to do better there next week — At 5 I took down 240 drawings and packed them ready for removal in Less than one hour = I am quite sure that a stranger might have thought that I was about escaping to save being really drummed out of Manchester —

Now for the Concert = It was 6 o'clock and raining very agreably when I left my room for Fountain Street, where already Carriages and foot people had accumulated to a great number. I, by elbowing, arrive at the entrance and present my Ticket — am asked if a stranger and requested to write on the back my name & Residence = no objections again and J. J. Audubon, Louisiana, America is wrote just as handsomely as Napoleon himself would have done it when pressed by time =

The Room is full of Red, White, Blue, & Green Turbans well fitted to the handsome heads of the Ladies that already are seated all attention = I Glide modestly on one side and settle myself w[h]ere I conceive, that my Heart, my Eye and my Intellects may be well satisfied and suplied in course without being myself observed = but no, it would not do, my Long hairs are seen and the bearer pointed at in such ridiculous Manner that I needed to recollect that I was an Honest plain man and ranked as high as any other in the eyes of God, therefore stood the brunt [MS: bront] and lessoned to the Music = It was fine but it sunk my spirits and, could I have left the assembly, I would certainly have done so = Many Ladies were richly Beautifull, several old dames twiged[26] at me with their Lorgnettes and I wish[ed] them Younger in unisson with themselves on that score, but a remarkably Elegant woman who set on the bench before me turned so frequently round to examine (I suppose) the shape of my Nose, that I took several times within my fingers to torment this Fair one = I have passed many uncomfortable evenings in Company, and this may be added — At last "God save the King" came and I went squeesing myself side ways, pocket handkerchiefs [MS: Hdfs] in side Pockets, Coat Buttoned, one hand on my Watch and the other ready to seize on any rascal who might dare to attempt to steal from me — I soon reach[d] home with the Head ache, and have wrote this = Tomorow this time I intend being at Liverpool again = so, my Sweet Wife, good night —

QUARY BANK TUESDAY 26TH SEPR 1826. —

Well, my date here above clearly proves to thee that I am not about taking my rest for the night in Liverpool, and the reason is just in the sequel = Whilst very engaged at putting up my Drawings in my newly Granted appartment, 2 of Mr Gregg's Sons entered and, after a Hearty and friendly shake of the Hand, gave me the following kind note from their Mother =

My Dear Sir —

We are all very solicitous to see you as early in this week as possible, on *many accounts* — but more Especially because we shall lose Mr Professor Smyth[27] before the end of it — He talks of leaving us entirely on Saturday.

It will make us all very happy to be able to render Quary Bank

26. "To twig" is to watch, look at, or inspect.

27. William Smyth (1765–1849) became Regius Professor of Modern History at Cambridge in 1807. He was a fine conversationalist and a noted poet, and he cultivated an eighteenth-century manner and appearance.

comfortable or agreable to you, as often as you can favor us with your Company during your abode [MS: above] in Lancashire — Yours very sincerely

H. Greg
Hanna

My Husband & Children desire to unite me in kind regards —
Monday Night 25th Sepr —

Now, Lucy, the call of a Lady was allways heard by thy Husband, and if the Lady be such as Mrs Gregg, neither Watter, fire or precipitous Leaps could stop me a moment — Again Professor Smyth ran into my Brains as a Deep, Cool, Immensely powerfull stream of Knowledge, of Benevolence, of real Goodness, above all of Liberality = Again, Lucy, the Beautifull Dark Eyes of Helen Gregg — again the delightfull enjoyment of the Company of all the sisters, Muses like — and again the Brothers & the good old Paire themselves, all were Iresistible temptations =

The coach is forgotten — I am ready to dine again in Fountain Street and, after having Lessend with many large mouthed Yawns to a Mr *Ashton*, a Great Cotton Weaver, I again seated myself precisely fronting the fair Helen of Quary Banks = Her Father slept by the way, but I did not. No, I kept up a vivid Conversation about my own beloved Country — *Our Progress* in all points tending towards Improvement, and at last felt the hands of Mrs Greg welcoming me to her House = The Tears flew from her Eyes as she kissed her Husband and he, Lucy, acted Lover Like!!! —

On[c]e more I am surrounded by Peaceable gentleness and presently am forced to remark = more Dark Eyes, more Dark Eye brows, a Darker complection, ending at last in speaking to an Italian Lady = but mark, Lucy, here comes the stranger — Tall, fresh, Ruddy, the Compleat Gentleman walks in and, with an ease only known by Gentlemen, bows and meets first the Ladies and then thy Husband = Yes, it is he, the Professor of Cambridge. All about him is knowledge accompanied with agreable Gay[e]ty = What a Leap from the Council's bluffs on the Missoury to Quary Bank! What contrast betwen the Natives of either country! — There the Red Man with nought but simple Nature lays spread on the earth [MS: Hearth] and receives the stranger without Courtesy and yet affords you security and warants it by the mere presentation of his Pipe == Here the Pow[d]ered headed Man,[28] nearly silkened [MS: silke**ed] over, gives his Hand and his Eye and gradually his heart with affection, with regard, with Esteem and in Course is quite as powerfull a Friend == Pray, where does the Diference lay? ==

We dine, the Professor opposite the Woodsman == the Father betwen his Eldest & Youngest Elen — The Mother divides both Knowledge & Country affections from the professor & thy Husband — An oblique Glance gives me a Correct view of the Fair Italian female, and sons & Daughters Intermix^d fill the rounded Table ==

America again the Subject == Englishmen & I may say Ladies also are fond of hearing of it and I fonder still of Praising it — of giving its true light == Our Washington and the Napoleon of France are weighed (as they ought to be) in very diferent Scales — Our Habits and those of Europe come next and vary in Value quite as much and after many witty pros & cons (from the Professor, recollect), we raise to go & see the Ladies that have prepared Tea for us ==

This professor, Lucy, is a Happy Man; he possesses the extraordinary talent of Teaching Comfort & Pleasure as he goes where ever he stops == and I may safely say that one Evening spent with him and the fair, kind Circle at the Quary Bank is worth a hundred such Concerts as I heard last Evening ==

Lucy, when I related our receiving our noble & worthy Genl Lafayette both in New York & Philadelphia, I saw the Tears Trickle down the cheeks of the good Mr Gregg with a weight of feelings better understood by me than easy of description == These Tears, Lucy, proved to me that many men were born alike and might have been Washingtons! ==

Mr Gregg, my Dear Wife, is a Lover still of Wife, of Children and of Friends!!! == I saw & kissed the Eldest daughter [MS: daughett] of my Good Friend W^{am} Rathbone —

28. If Audubon did not intend "Powdered headed," the awkward phrase "Powered headed" may echo the French "C'est une tête puissante," literally, "It is a powerful head."

To night, my Lucy, my bed was narrow but comfortable. I was led into my room by one of the Sons, and whilst I undressed myself I lessen^d to the Heavy drippings of the rain with sorrow, thinking that my early morning's walk would be less Comfortable by far than the Evening I had just spent = Wife & Sons & Friends, God Bless you all — Good Night =

MANCHESTER WEDNESDAY SEP^R 27TH 1826 —

My walk was Long, wet, fair, rainy again & fair again, all in 120 minutes laps[e] = Strange state of atmosphere = worse than Louisianna by half = My return to the House at about 8 — brought me in the Company of 4 of the sisters, all drawing in the Library, that in this Country is generally the setting room = then the well arched Eye browed Italian — then the Professor — then 10 o'clock and we all arose and went to Breakfast = aye, 4 hours later than we used to do at Natchez = What odds!! — Again "Mr Audubon is the most Abstemious man I Ever saw" — I answered that the Ohio had raised 60 feet at the foot of the Falls of that River, and every one Wondered, and yet how true = Then of Duels with us — of my Friend Clay & Crazy Randolph — or wearing Daggers and of our Murderous son of the Governor of Kentucky[29] = All here, my Lucy, is known about our Country but is known Imperf[ect]ly = so much so, Indeed, that I dread to Talk about it — for the English themselves say that *Truth is not Creditable* =

Now, Lucy, I am advising about Drawing and I am quite sure that my old master David[30] never [had] an Easier Task = but I, Lucy, foolish, conceited, yet anxious to Please (my only apolo[g]y in cases of this kind) attempted a sketch of the Professor and made one of M^r

29. Henry Clay's April 8, 1825, duel with the bizarre and feared John Randolph of Roanoke was not his first. Randolph spared Clay's life. Joseph Desha (1768–1842) was governor of Kentucky from 1824 until 1828. In 1825 his son Isaac B. Desha was convicted of murder, but, in a politically contentious period of Kentucky politics, his conviction was overturned, and plans were being made to retry him for the same murder. The Desha case had been a sensational news event for some time when Audubon spoke of it.

30. Audubon claimed several times to have studied in France under Jacques-Louis David (1748–1825), "First Painter" to Napoleon at the height of his power. The claim is generally dismissed as a fabrication.

Priestley[31] *Instead* — Fatal Error. — yet better off than those who work altogether in Vain. I thought my[self] Lucky that if I had not Imitated one Great man, I had revived a far distant one —

We eat a Lounch = The Pony Dick is again ready — M͟r͟s Greg [h]as said *in English* to the Fair Italian that a bunch of Grapes will be given her for a walk thro the Garden — I have all the Notes for Liverpool in my Packet — pressed all hands that pressed mine = mounted the sadle and, armed with a whip, Trot off towards the Smoaky City again —

Dick is a Pony of Knowledge and, of Course, wishes to Impart and to Improve others = Of course, he brought me by a new Road quite to Manchester again — and here I am = positively bound to Liverpool tomorow — have paid my Faire on Top, because my Companion M͟r Bentley is not an American = Yes, tomorow I Hope Most sincerely to be 38 miles nearer to thee and most probably in the Company of the benevolent & aimiable familly Rathbone = I must look for Clean Linen — pack up — have all ready and then, my Lucy, I will wish thee, as I Hope I may allways be able to do, a Good Night =

31. Audubon jokes that his sketch of Smyth looks more like one of Joseph Priestley (1733–1804), who was known for his identification of oxygen and other gases, but he was also an outspoken advocate for the liberal reform of British society and theology. Before William Bakewell, Audubon's father-in-law, moved his family to America in 1802, he had been a friend of Priestley; Bakewell's advocacy of Priestley's liberal views may have cost him a post as justice of the peace and led to his decision to immigrate.

4

Return to Liverpool

Perhaps at 5 this morning I left Manchester and all its smoak behind
me; but I left there the Labours of about 10 Years of my Life, fully
one half of my Collection. I had had my place [in the coach] taken by
Young W<u>am</u> Greg inside, but finding the weather fine, and an English
gentleman, very solicitous to make sure of the weather and the extra
comfort betwen being on Top or in, prevailed on my feelings so
much that I gave my situation and took his = The weather, however,
proved that I was still in the vicinity of the Manufact[ur]ing Town.
It rained hard and the wind followed us = I soon found my skin
wet and, although I wrapped well up, my Great Coat about me, and
held my umbrella [MS: umblella] strongly, I could not save my Ears
and sometimes my Eyes and frequently my Neck from being very
disagreably tickled with the gatherings of the umbrellas [MS: umblellas]
that surrounded me = The condition was uncomfortable, but I felt
too much foolish pride within me to recall my Inside seat and the good
Gentleman too snugg in his situation to have the least Idea of disturbing
himself.

I saw nothing of the Country and very little of my fellow travellers,
none of whom seemed the least incline[d] to chatt but look^d very
Inclined to Cry = Thus, Lucy, I was brought to Bright Liverpool again,
and as I bounced on the pavement I felt not as if being in a Land of
Strangers but in [MS: on] that of Friends and good Friends! = Stop
a moment. Let me tell thee that the Englishman or Englishgentleman
did not even offer thy Husband the diference of Price that I paid for
the Inside seat — a trifle of 5 shillings only, but I must remark that I
thought it rather a strange Occurence and again that perhaps another

time an *EnglishGentleman* would not meet the Like Courtesy from
me =

Now I am at the Institution; Mr Monroe is glad to see me and I am
pleased to meet W^{am} Rathbone Es^{qr}, Mr John Foster and Mr Pillet,[1]
who all wellcome me as if glad to see thy Husband again — The streets
of Liverpool looked very wide, very clean, very well lined with very
handsome Buildings and, although I was compleately drench^d by rain, I
felt it not = so glad was I at being in Liverpool again =

Breakfast at the Institution, dressed there and marched towards
St Ann Street; meeting by the way Dr Rutter and there the 2 young
Chorley's, who ran out from their house and shook hands as if Brothers
= From them I received an Invitation to some music tomorow, and
as I well know that my Hair will not be ridiculed, I believe I will go =
Dr Trail is at home and Mrs Trail and the whole [MS: all] familly are
well = What shakes of the Hands; the sleves of my Coat tapped my
wrists with the rapidity of one of the Cutting Machines of Manchester
— My being at Liverpool is soon explained, the Doctor refers me to
W^{am} Roscoe Es^{qr}, and after a good talk and the promiss of Breakfast
with him tomorow, I am off towards Lodge Lane — Ah, Lodge Lane
on the very way to Green Bank = With Hopes to see my Good Friend
Richard Rathbone and his Beautifull Wife and sweet little Bazil = I
am quite sure that I was not walking slowly when Miss Donathan came
across the street with a smile on her Lips and her fair arm extended to
ask me how long since in Liverpool, if well &^{c} — What pleasure for me
to be so remembered — I pressed her hand gently and my feet felt not
the pavement = Abercromby Square is deserted by Mr Rathbone's
familly — They all are at Green Bank = but the Intelligent Swiss I am
told may be found here = Not at home = the Botanic Garden — M^r
Shepherd not in, Sir = Lodge Lane, Mr Roscoe; even the maid that
opens the door smiles and answers to my wishes = Once more I see
that Venerable, Generous, Good man at study and at work — His large
eyebrow bent over his mild eye is once more before me, and in an
Instant I hear him speak = Good man, the Noblest work of God —
God Bless him = My Business is brought forth, and he will attend to
my wishes =

1. This may be the French nobleman and banker Michel-Frederic Pillet-Will.

I see Miss Jane, we dine, and talk of Manchester, of Allkolm,† of
Professor Smythe and bye & bye, I having asked for my album, it is
given me = Not Blank now, no, Lucy, the names of Roscoe will lead it
thro worlds of time and those of many many more Friends I Hope will
color it for thee to peruse =

Now towards Green Bank; I can already discern the new Residence
of Good Richard, and I soon have before me and seated by my side his
aimiable Consort: I had not the pleasure of se[e]ing my Friend Richard,
and the sweet little Bazil would not kiss me = Again I am forwarded
and am positively at Green Bank. Yes, my Lucy, I have the consolation
that, if from thee and from my own Home, I have a Home at M^r
Rathbone =

The evening is spent as usual — Mrs W^{am} R. is forming {paths}
of Constellations for the *Bazar*, and I read them part of my time at
Manchester = W^{am} Rathbone reads fine Poetry for my pleasure, and
the venerable Queen Bee needles a well colored Carpet = Again I
am in the Prophet's chamber and in bed and — God Bless thee, Good
night, my sweet wife =

GREEN BANK SEP^R 29TH FRIDAY 1826. —

I did not tell thee, my Lucy, how surprised I was during the course of
last evening at se[e]ing that Gentle being Hannah Rathbone, after a
short absence from the Library, return with a beautifull frame of Rose
wood and a drawing, asking me to arrange both to each other; I look^d
at a Drawing that I had entirely forgotten. Yet it was a Good likeness of
thy husband, and I framed it = surrounded by his newly [acquired]
habillements of English manufact[u]r[e] he look^d well and I am sure
that thou wilt be glad to hear it =

It rained during the night and nearly all the early portion of this
morning; the Curator of the Botanic Garden, Mr Shepherd came in
early, and I breakfasted by the side of Hannah Rathbone, although I
had promised to be at Dr Trail by ½ past nine and to call on M^r W^{am}
Roscoe on my way = W^{am} Rathbone took me to the latter's house in
his Gig = There I was told that nothing could be done in the way of
forming a Prospectus for my work without more knowledge of what
it could be brought out for. I was refered to Dr Trail again & there I
went —

It happened that a M.ʳ Bohn [ms: Bhoon][2] from London, an Immense Book seller (not publisher) was in Liverpool and, being a man to be depended on, as an excellent person, from whom truth and truth only might be expected, being also a very particular Friend of D.ʳ Trail, this Latter had Invited him to meet for the very purpose of giving me Light and advise respecting my Publication =

I was Introduced to this mighty Book Ware House man, who has 200,000 volumes as a regular stock, and saw a handsome well formed Young Gentleman possessing all the ease and good manners requisite to render him fit for his situation = His advises to me were as follows = to proceed at once to London and thro my Introductions to form acquaintance with the Principal Naturalists of the day, and by their advises to see the Best Engravers, Lythograph[er]s = Colorists — printers, Paper Merchants &.ᶜ &.ᶜ with a Memorandum Book and Note down on the spot all required to give a tolerably fair Idea of what could be expected = then to go Imediately to Paris thro Bruxells and at Paris with the assistance of good Letters to proceed in the same manner and thereby becoming able to Judge of the advantages & Disadvantages attached to either country to determine myself, where, when & how, the work would be undertaken and begun = to be during this Lapse of Time & thro the medium of those able and connected corespondant[s] with scientific Societies be announced to the World in some of the most read periodical publications = "Then, M.ʳ Audubon, Issue a Prospectus, & bring forth a Number of Your Ornithology, and I think that you will succeed and do well, but remember my observations respecting the size of Your Book and be biased by this fact; that, at Present, Productions of Taste are purchased with delight by Persons who receive company particularly, and that to have Your Book, to be laid on the table as a Past time Piece of Entertainment is the principal use made of it, and that if in Compass it needs so much room as to bring shame on other works, or encumber the table, it will not be purchased by this set of People who

2. Although Audubon identifies this Mr. Bohn as the London bookseller John Bohn (1757–1843) in his October 1 letter to Lucy, he must be mistaken. He described Bohn in the September 29 entry as "a handsome well formed Young Gentleman," which better fits the elder Bohn's son Henry George Bohn (1796–1884), who at this time still worked with his father traveling extensively throughout the world of the European book trade.

now are the very life of the trade = If Large Public Institutions only,
and only a few Noblemen, will have it, and Instead of a thousand Copies
that may be sold if small, perhaps not Exceeding one hundred will find
their way out of the shops of my Brothers in Business = The size must
be suitable for the *English Market* (such was his Expression), ought not
to ex[c]eed double that of Willson" =

This conve[r]sation, Lucy, took place all in the presence of D͟r Trail.
I repeated it to my Good Friends here, and all are convinced that it will
be prudent to follow this Plan = M͟r Bohn [MS: Bhoon] told D͟r Trail
in my Presence that my Exibiting my Drawings, would not do well, that
I might be in London 12 Months before I would be known at all there,
but that thro the *scientific periodic monthly* productions I would be well
known all over Europe in the same time, when probably my 1͟s͟t number
would have found its way even to America = As to N͟o of Copies he
said that Paris would take 100 —

$$
\begin{array}{llll}
\text{London} & - \text{ " } - \text{ " } - & 250 & - \\
\text{Holland} & - \text{ " } - \text{ " } - & 100 & - \\
\text{Russia} & - \text{ " } - \text{ " } - & 100 & - \\
\text{America} & - \text{ " } - \text{ " } - & \underline{450} & - \\
\text{In all} = & & 1000 &
\end{array}
$$

He strongly advised me to have the Work at the whole [MS: all]
published and finished in Paris (where he think[s] it is best for me
to undertake it) brought over to England, say 250 Copies, to receive
its form and have its Tittle Page printed, to be Issued to the World of
England as English Genuine production, an astonishing advantage in
matters of this kind = to do the same with all the other portions of
the Number of Copies and that although the undertaking was greatly
Laborious, My Drawings being so very superior, I may rest assured that
success would ultimately crown my undertakings =

Then, my Beloved Wife, I will follow this Plan and no other untill
I find it impossible to succeed, and I will follow it with the same
perseverance, that since 25 Years I have continued to wish to come
at the completion [MS: complexion] of it, and for thee and for our
Childrens ultimate good may it succeed, and *God's will be done* =

Having determined thus, I will return to Manchester after a few more days spent with these Dear Good Friends from whom it is sorrowfull to part; Visit thy native Matlock; gaze on the Tomb of the Friend of thy Youth, the sensitive Darwin,³ lose my steps amongst thy cherished former Paths of Derby's Wilds, and enter into London with a Head humbly bent, but with a heart Intently determind to Conquer or to die ═

I was anxious to meet the Intelligent Swiss to afford him the pleasure due to a person by whom I have been so kindly treated [MS: treaded], to assure him that now in full unisson with all other Friends I was going to do what *he first* wished — but he had left for Manchester; nay, not Manchester. I Hope he is now Enjoying the Company of Quary Bank and has seen the sweet Helen that so richly ornements that lovely spot ═

I Called on thy sister Ann and dined with her and Drank thy Health ═ Mr Gordon I was told is extremely engaged and will leave for the Continent in a few days ═ In returning to this abode of Peace & repose, I was overtaken by a Gentleman (who was not on foot, thou knowest well) but in a Gig, unknown to me quite, but who, offering me a seat by his side, I thanked, accepted, and learned very shortly to be Mr Dearman; not so Dear a Man, Lucy, as the English one who took my seat inside the Coach was to my pocket, no, and Yet I assure thee much Dearer to me altogether.

At Green Bank Mr Shepherd was still, and I thought the Venerable Lady enjoyed a good portion of good spirits. The evening came [MS: come]. It was truly like at Home at Henderson, each busily employed and conversing with mildness, Learning and that spirit suficient to bring the American to a Pause of thoughts, and Contemplative mood delightfull and necessary to relax the bent bow of his morning['s] abstracted business ═ We were Joined by Mrs Rathbone and her Husband Richard, and I again admired the warm, well lighted Picture, of Friendship, of Benevolence & of real merit, that laid before me. ═ Now, Lucy, Dear Friend, Good Night ═ †

3. Erasmus Darwin (1731–1802) had been a friend of the Bakewell family in England before their move to America. Darwin's grandson Charles Darwin would be in attendance at the meeting of the Wernerian Society in Edinburgh in December 1826 when Audubon read his essay on the turkey vulture.

I bid that God might grant thee rest and Happiness from under the roof of R$\underline{\text{d}}$ Rathbone, the most lively {reality} of what is known by the name of the true English Gentleman and am quite Sure thy Friend, although thou art yet unknown to him =

I did not leave Green Bank this morning untill nearly 12. I was extremely anxious to possess a few lines from the very pen and hand of M$\underline{\text{rs}}$ Rathbone, the Queen Bee = and something also from each member of the familly = It required to be Audubon, my Lucy, to have this granted, and now that I possess this Jem in my Book, the more persons will write on it, the more will be Honored by having their productions in the company of this truly wonderfull Lady — M$\underline{\text{rs}}$ E. Rathbone wrote, but I could not prevail on my Miss Hannah. She turned her wishes another way and covered the Book to save all its contents. I then took it to D$\underline{\text{r}}$ Trail, who promised to add to it this day, but who, however, amid a great deal of other things to attend, did not remember the album = I tried to meet M$\underline{\text{rs}}$ Edw$\underline{\text{d}}$ Roscoe. She was absent and I must be contented [MS: contended] that I kissed her lovely child. I visited the Institution. I was Glad to see the American Hills in the Ground of the Wild Turkey = but, my Lucy, I felt an extra fatigue about my body. My Head felt heavy and the bones of my legs ached; I was not well, and the Idea of being Ill far from thee tormented me dreadfully =

I, however, went & dined with D$\underline{\text{r}}$ Trail. We had only the familly and a M$\underline{\text{r}}$ Finy; D$\underline{\text{r}}$ Trail entertained me very much. Indeed, a man of so extensive a knowledge of all things cannot fail to be agreable if he will only talk. About 8, having previously declared that my wish was to go to Woodcroft, the D$\underline{\text{rs}}$ Son took me in a Gig at a round rate and I was soon with M$\underline{\text{rs}}$ R$\underline{\text{d}}$ Rathbone and 3 Quakers, of whom 2 were females = The conversation was Natural History, and the Ladies were well versed in such matters — My Friends Wife produced a beautifull and good Microscope and thro it the Diamond Beetle[4] shone in all its sp[l]endor = My Good Friend R$\underline{\text{d}}$ did not Join us untill 10, fatigued from

4. The boldly colored, jewel-like diamond beetle (*Curculio imperialis*) was a favorite object to view under a microscope.

his Saturday's Labours, and we set chatting after the Quakers had left us untill 12. I was sorry to discover that he did not know how to Swim, and still more so that I could not have the pleasure of Teaching him a thing so easily done in one hour's time. My Good Friend, with manners quite beyond my Powers to describe, accompanied me to my chamber, felt if the bed would be comfortable and pressed my hand with a pressure felt at heart. We parted. His Wife was in the next appartment and thou, my Beloved Lucy, fully 6,000 miles from Laforest. I notwithstanding wished thee quite *aloud* Good Night =

LIVERPOOL OCT<u>R</u> 1<u>ST</u> ROYAL INSTITUTION 1826 —

My Dearest Beloved —

I return^d here from Manchester a few days since by the advise of my Friends & learned acquaintances, with a view to confer with them respecting my Publication of the Birds of America = For that Purpose the President D<u>r</u> Thomas S. Trail invited me to meet at Breakfast at his House a M<u>r</u> Henry George [MS: John] Bohn of London, perhaps the most extensive *Bookseller* (not Publisher) in that Immense City = This Person has on hand a stock of 200,000 Volumes; travels constantly thro this Country, and the Continent, is well versed in all matters relative to the subject, and exceptionable for Veracity and Candor = so much so that D<u>r</u> Trail assured me that I might with great Confidence disclose all my views, ask all questions and expect answers full of truths = His advises have been amply given, and so full of prudence, care, and knowledge have I found that Gentleman to be possessed of, that, I now will proceed with a firm resolution to attempt the *Being an Author*. It is a Terrible thing to me, far better fitted to study & delineate in the Forests than to arrange phrases with sensible gramarian skill = However, my efforts will only equal my faculties, and with this I must & will be satisfied if remunerated suficiently to enhance thy Comfort and that of our Dear Boys =

Then, my Dear Friend, my exibiting Publickly my work will be laid aside for a while at least. *I* Hope for ever =

I visit next week or early the week following that, thy Dear native spot and kiss & Bless that earth [MS: Hearth] that bore thy sweet

form, Youthfull, Gay, lovely & destitute of Care = I can hardly
Yet tell thee if it will be mostly a Jaunt of Pleasure or a pilgrimage
of Sorrow: but I long to feel either — under the Happy round of
Circumstances that, after a Knowledge of thee, of full Twenty five
Years have passed, and filled me with that sense of Gratitude towards
thee, that I Hope our God will enable me to feel and enjoy untill we
meet *never to part again*! — Yes, I will see thy Matlock, thy Derby,
thy Hills, dales, mountains, cataracts & valeys, and see amid the
morning dews the light tract of thy steps and see thee, my Lucy, as *I
Love thee*!

I will visit our Cousin[s] Gifford & Bakewell[5] & thro them make an
effort to see & speak to the Duke of Devonshire — pass thro Oxford
and reach the Metropolis sometime this month — There, Lucy,
from street to street will I move and examine all objects connected
with my views, make regular memorandums and try *once more* to
become a *Man of Business* = I must know from the best Engravers
or Lythograph[er]s their prices & executive powers = the same
from the Printers, Paper Makers, &c &c, all I can discover; I must try
to become acquainted with men of Eminence as Naturalists and of
Standing in Society = sound all and each & every night weigh well
the diferent Parcels of advises & Judge for myself at Last —

What a task, my Lucy! How dificult to please one self and yet how
much more so to please many = With my Book of Memorandums
made all on the spot & time, I will leave *la Belle Anglettere* and go
to Paris to compare the advantages of these two mighty Countries
= I feel, however, a certain predilection that beyond my Venerable
Mother, my kind sister, and their familly Circle, I shall not like France
as I *now* do England = and I sincerely Hope that this Country will
deserve the preference that, by Interested motives, I must ultimately
give to the one best suited to meet my Endeavours at doing well
= Then I will enter my own old Garden on the Loire and with
trembling steps reach my Mother! Our Mother, my Lucy — ah —
Then we must part — May it be to *meet again*.

5. Euphemia Gifford was a wealthy cousin of Lucy's father. Robert Bakewell (1767–1843)
was a geologist best known for his *An Introduction to Geology* (1813). Audubon carried a letter of
introduction to him.

As betwen this day and the time that I will determine at Paris what will be considered best to be done, I hope to be able regularly to write to thee again & again, I will now bid thee farewell = and I will speak of my Good Friends here =

My Letter of the 2ᵈ of last month said that I *wished thee*, to have cut and forwarded to New Orleans as soon as Possible, 6 Segments of 1 Magnolia, 1 Yellow Poplar, 1 Beech tree, 1 Button [MS: Botton] Wood or sicamore, 1 sassafras, 1 oak each of about 7 or 8 Inches in thickness of the Largest Diameters that can be procured in the woods about thee = Try to have the whole [MS: all] avarage 6 feet — Of course, six segments only are wanted = to have each segment carefully handled to save the Bark, and names painted in oil neatly on one face with the Hight of the tree = to direct them to the care of who thou may think will be most attentive to have them shipped as soon as Possible, all directed to & for the Liverpool Royal Institution, care of Messʳˢ Rathbone Brothers & Cᵒ here =

I wish thee, my Dear Wife, to be at some trouble and expense to bring this to a good Conclusion =

It is probable that Dᴿ Pope would feel a pleasure at doing this, being favorable to scientific pursuits, or our good Friend Judge Mathews, to both whom I beg thou wilt remember me. As the least Carriage by land will be best — perhaps some might be found at the Bayou near the Mississipi or on the Very Bank, and floated to the steam Boat where particular request must be made to the Captain that they are not barked or Injured in any way = Recollect, those are troubles that I have given thee to repay troubles that I have given in exchange to others. Advise me as soon as possible = I conceive the whole [MS: all] can be managed in one week with a little attention and John could see about it =

Kiss him, my Lucy, and remember me to all about thee. I will see Mᴿ Midlemist's wife as soon as I reach London. God Bless thee and Protect thee for ever, thine Husband & Friend — J. J. A —

The freight from America here will be *paid here* — Cotton is raising in value and business bears a better face = Give this to Mʳˢ Percy and my Good Friend Bourgeat, who perhaps will enter in the segment Business if not already shipᵈ =

I slept more than usual and, although the morning was bright & fair,
I did not leave my Friend's House untill nearly 6. — The air felt more
rarefied and I filled my lungs with pleasure — I reach[ed] this sweet
spot in a few minutes and wrote in the Library whilst the mirth of the
Young Rathbones above Indicated their being gamboling about the
nursery =

I soon returned to Woodcroft to breakfast and did not see my Friends
here = I had the pleasure of riding to Liverpool by the side of M^{rs} R^d
Rathbone, most aimiable Interesting Lady — Dr Trail had not wrote
in the Album, and I went to the Institution where I wrote the letter
to thee now annexed before this sheet = Visited Mrs Ed^d Roscoe
and found her as usual devoted to Study and anxious to Improve; she
promised to put something in my Book also, and I came then to Green
Bank to enjoy during this afternoon that silentness & quiet [MS: quite]
connected with devotion =

Speaking of America, the Immense of the Watters, the numerous
Steam Boats, Immense trade & traffic, I told W^{am} Rathbone that N.
Berthoud kept an account of the whole and that, if he desired it, I
would write for a Copy to our Victor = He wished it and I wrote =
The same Gentleman ask^d if I should wish to [be] a Coresponding
Member of their Philosophical society and to that I answered Yes =
but, Lucy, the strangest and most curious event of this Evening was that
after service had been read, and supper over and bidding good night
was passed, I found Mrs Rathbone leaning on her children in the Loby
waiting apparently for me, and with a smile that I never saw before she
ask^d me with a modesty just as scarce if I would make a sketch of a Wild
Turkey for her, that she wished a seal with one engraved on it = For
a moment I innocently thought it was to be all for her, and I felt elated
at the thought of presenting her one from the hands of Roskell's best
artist, but she smiled again, and I then discovered my Simplicity, for she
begged that I would give her the Sketch only = Then *she*, Lucy, wished
to give me the seal, and I thank^d her with all my Heart — Who could
not wish to admire such a kindly, delicate, worthy woman?

My night was bad, my cough very rough, and I thought that I had caught the Whooping dicease = I scarcely slept and I thought of thee, Dearest Wife, untill day.

My Cough, as I told thee, was bad. I did not raise untill late and had scarcely time to write a page before my sweet Kind Friend Hannah made her appearance and, with a Smile and the gentle pressure of her hand, bid me good morning =

My principal objects to day were to attend on Mʳˢ Rᵈ R. and to sketch the Wild Turkey — I rode to Liverpool with Wᵃᵐ Rathbone Esᑫʳ and went again to Dʳ Trail for my Book. I waited a short while on the way at Mʳˢ Chorley, the mother of my Young Friends John & Henry, saw their sisters and their Portraits — had my Book from Dʳ Trail and walkᵈ to the Institution very slowly with John Chorley, who gave me some kindly advises and spoke much of the habits of his Countrymen =

I sat opposite the 23 hours Picture and sketch[ed] it the size of my Thumb's nail in less than 23 minutes. If the Engraver does his duty, the seal will be beautifull and in such a Case the Wild Turkey will revisit America, his Country. I sent my album to Mʳˢ Eᵈ Roscoe and walkd to Woodcroft — The sweet children were all a little Indisposed except my Little Darling Basil⁺ = I gave a lesson of Drawing and received one of Pleasure = My acquaintance in this kind family has fortunately been of so propitious a nature that we can talk of our feelings without fear, risk or Danger =

I dined and took my Friend Richard's Seat = a thing I disliked even at my own Home. = Whilst desert was on the Table, the calls of a Younger little one reachᵈ the mother's ear [MS: hear] and heart, I dare say, and *sans* ceremony she bid me farewell, and went to nurse her sweet little Benson. Once more, my Lucy, I had the sweetest of Pleasure at hand — I attended on 4 Little ones, devided paires and pealed them, gave them the fruit and kissed them =

I left this little group and reach[ed] Green Bank where, being in Pudding time, I sat to table again to receive from Hannah a Glass of wine and from her mother a Bunch of Grapes = I gave the Wild Turkey and, as they please to admire all I do, they admired that also = It was nearly 5 when I walkᵈ to Liverpool, reach[ed] the Institution, saw

Mͬ Munro, who is so good to see that the little quantum of Linen that I brought from Manchester will suffice, and reach^d my Friends Chorley in good Time to have a good deal of chat with his mother, sister and Brothers before the flutes and the Piano were brought to unisson —

I saw the son of Mͬ Gilpin of Brandy Wine Creek,[6] America = My Father had been well acquainted with his = I had seen this Young Gentleman at Dͬ Meaze[7] in Company of Bonaparte, and I felt quite gratified to be known by my own Countryman = The Evening passed most agreably = I told them how shockingly annoyed I had been the last concert I had been at and they all were sorry for it = Mͬˢ Rathbone['s] servant & Gig arrived for me and against all Entreaties I left about 9: the Evening Clear, but quite Cold, the frost now in heavy dew was falling. The servant was surprised that I would not make any use of a Great coat brought for me = How little he knew how often I have laid to rest, wet, hungry, Harrassed & full of Sorrow with millions of Musquitoes buzzing me awake, lessening to the chuck wills widow, the Horned owl, and the roaring Bullfrogs = Impatiently waitting for the return of day to enable me to hunt the Forests and feed my eyes on their beautifull Inhabitants =

I thought of all this and then moved the scene to the Hunters Cabin, again wet, Harrassed and Hungry, felt the sudden warmths of a "Wellcome Stranger," saw the Busy Wife unhook dry cloth[e]s from the side of the Logged Hut, untie my mocassons — {uncach} my Indian dear skin Dress, and give me a warm draft of Whiskey with looks that Insured my Life free from Danger, and bid me expect more comfort = I saw the Athletic Husband wipe my Gun, clean the Locks, hang the whole [MS: all] over the aboundant fire, call his eldest [MS: heldest] son to rise, to see about more wood, some Eggs and some *Venaison*, whilst my ears were greeted with the sounds of the hand mill crushing the Coffee that was to enliven my spirits = I saw, Dear Lucy, many Little

6. John Gilpin of Brandywine Creek in Chester County, Pennsylvania, had claimed discovery of a lead vein on the grounds of Mill Grove before Audubon came to America.

7. James Mease (1771–1846) was a Philadelphia physician and naturalist who had visited Fatland Ford numerous times to observe William Bakewell's agricultural experiments. As curator of the American Philosophical Society in 1824, when Audubon went there for support for *The Birds of America*, Mease introduced Audubon around and advised him.

ones roused by the strangers arrival, peeping from under the Robe of the Buffaloe, and Turn over on the Black Bear's Skin to resume their rest = I saw all this, my Dear Wife, and arrived at Green Bank to see much the same on a larger Scale =

The Squater is rough and true, my Friends here polished, aimiable & Benevolent = The first gives all he has freely, and here the stranger has about him all he wants, and he who during the Comfortless storms of Life can reach of either such a spot may say before he dies, that he felt Happiness During the while =

Sweet Friend, God Bless thee, my Lucy, Good Night =

GREEN BANK OCT^R 3^D 1826 TUESDAY =

I have been to the Jail of Liverpool to day, my Lucy, and will try to give thee some partial description both of its buildings and manners within = The situation is fine. It is placed at or near the mouth of the Estuary that here is called the River Mersey, and from its walls an extensive view of the Irish Channel may be had, drawing the eye on the Country & Mountains of Wales = The area altogether occupied by this Institution consists of about 8 acres, and the arrangement within the walls are. ~~~~ but permit me. I think a slight sketch will describe faster and better than my poor Pen.

Now, A is a large handsome building in front, forming a Court House of quarterly sessions with all the Conveniences appertaining =

B is the General Entrance for Strangers of all descriptions, even for those, My Lucy, who go there to receive sentence of everlasting banishment =

C is a large entry lined on both sides with the offices of the Governor, assistant Governor and diferent Turnkeys that are well secured from communication from the Culprits, should they attempt at Escaping =

D and all the plain Grounds are used as Walks but only by visitors and members, properly speaking, of the Institution —

E a piece of Watter with the Tree emblematic of Sorrow in its center.

F an office of Distribution & Guard House.

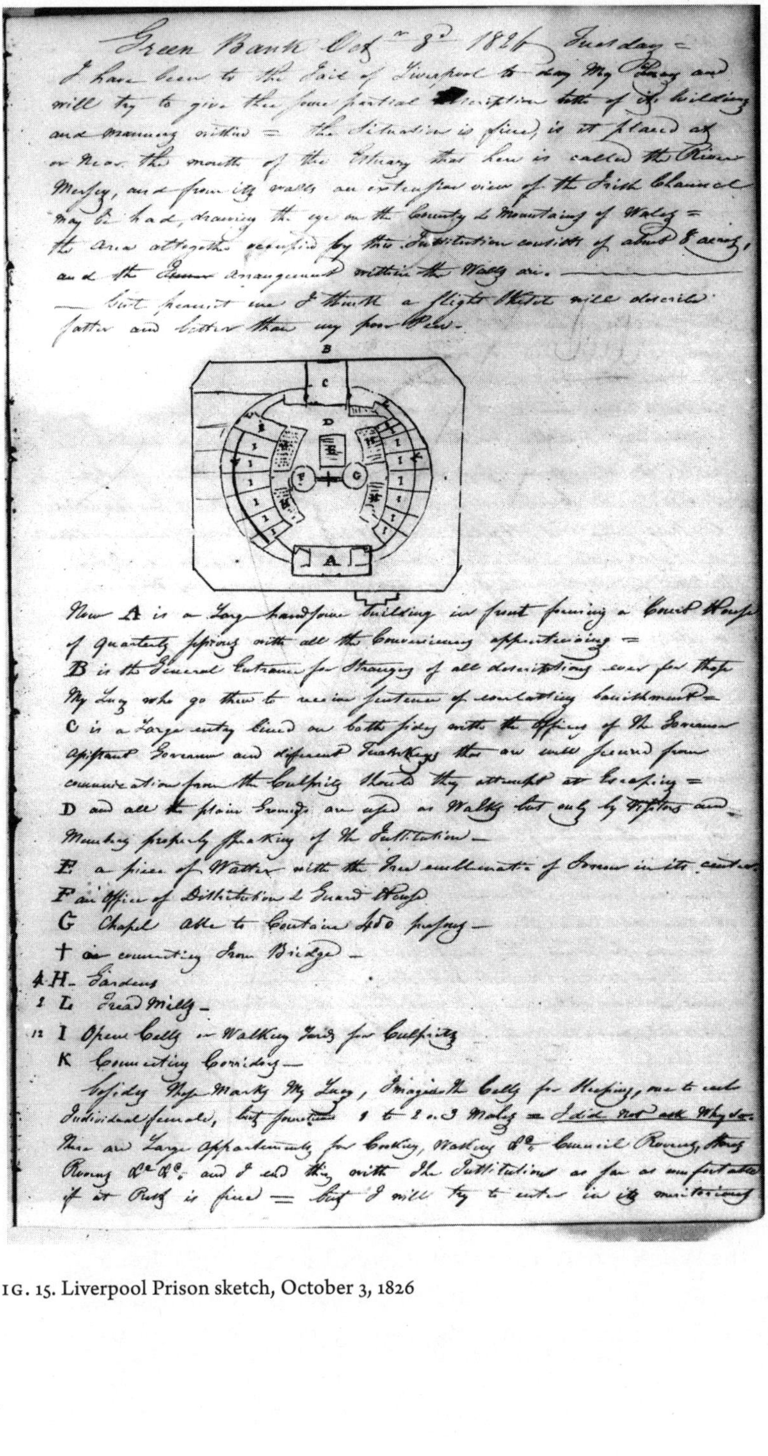

G Chapel able to Contain 450 persons —
+ a connecting Iron Bridge —
4 H Gardens
2 L Tread Mills —
12 I Open Cells or Walking Yards for Culprits
K Connecting Corridors —

Besides those marks, my Lucy, Imagine the Cells for sleeping, one to each Individual female, but sometimes 1 to 2 or 3 Males = *I did not ask why so*. There are large appartments for Cooking, washing &^{c} Council Rooms, stores Rooms &^{c} &^{c} and I end this with: the Institution as far as comfortable if at Rest is fine = but I will try to enter in its meritorious Intentions =

I Consider the Tread Mills as Infamous. Conceive a wild squirel in [a] Round Wheel working [MS: worcing] himself without progressing = The Labour is too severe and the true motive of Corection destroyed as there [MS: their] are no mental resources attached to this Laborious Engine of shame only if view^d by strangers = Why should they not each Individual be taught diferent trades enabling them, when thrown again on the Vile World, to Support themselves more honestly and save them from the temptations that thro necessity they must ultimately resort to (knowing naught [MS: not] but Walking up hill) and be dragged again and again to the Tread Mill = to transportation or to Despair. — Trades would be more profits to the Institution 4 folds than the mere grinding of Flower that is done here, and the principle would be more Honorable and more Worthy the true Intention of such an Institution = Thus I do condem the tread [MS: trade] mills not only as machines of Labours without benefit either General or personal, but also as extremely prejudicial [MS: prejuciable] to health = Think of those Poor Miserable beings obliged either to Weigh heavy on one padle or raise their o[w]n weight to the Next, which is the same Labour as Walking up Constantly a steep Hill for 4 or 6 Hours, making an average of 5, whilst the same man might make a Good paire of shoes, cut nails, be a Hatter or a Watch Maker — or any other usefull Business =

The Wheel is only 6 feet in Diameter. Therefore, the Motion is accelerated. Therefore, each step must be performed in quick succession — and as I know that a quick short step is more fatiguing

than [a] Long one and destroy[s] soon and ultimately the power of
the General frame, I say it is condusive to destruction, and the sallow,
withered, Emaciated, thin visages & bodies of the men at work proved
this to my Eyes as well as to my powers of Calculation = The Wheel
forces 30 steps to a rotation, and, as I say, they are steps going up hill
more than equal in length and labour than those on Level Grounds. I
will calculate them at 2½ feet for each, and as the Wheel goes round
once per minute, I will call the single movement 75 feet, the Hour 4500,
the Labour 22,500. This repeated Twice per day gives 45,000 [***].

But, Lucy, the circulation of free air is wanted. Each man receives the
breath of his neighbour in Exchange for his and, as this is accompanied
with most debased Conversations, both the body & the mind are
sufering = I would write more, but I am not W^am Roscoe; therefore
I close the subject = I was sorry to find the female deportment more
dificult to manage than that of the men = and to give thee an Idea of
the force of Habits kept in this place, sufice it to say that thro want of
Tabacco the *Ladies* there smoaked their *Peticoats*. Yes, when I entered
the rooms the smoake was {fist} and most disagreably so — Each
female Hid the cause in her bosom = Lucy, did Nature intend the
female Bosom the receptacle [MS: receptable] of a filthy pipe? Come —
no answer, heigh —

Lucy, I felt glad when, after writing my name in the Governor's Book,
I Issued with my Companion from this abode of Misery = Now that
I am as free as ever I have been, know that my Companion's name is
Mary Hodgson, a Quaker of great benevolence, smartness and solid
understanding, part of a Comittee that attends every day & per week
to superintend this Institution, purchase & Dispose of all articles
necessary or for sale &^c &^c —

I dined with her and her sister, who is a poet, and with her Brother
who is a merchant in Partnership with Messrs Benson, Cropper & Co
= I took a long walk with Friend John Chorley — had seen M^rs R^d
Rathbone a moment this morning, Mrs W^am Roscoe, had seen the
Engraver of the Wild Turkey, had thought of thee so often and so much
that I forgot to call on Mr Roscoe, who will think me Rude and, after
all this, reach Green Bank to Enjoy handsome prints — Handsome
Ladies, good wine & good Conversation and bid thee Good Night,
Dearest Friend =

I heard last night that perhaps the Intelligent Swiss would be with us
to breakfast, but he came not. I called several times at his office but no
Mr Melly. I visited Mr Foster, Mr Lawson, the familly Chorley &^c &^c,
bidding my farewell as diligently as possible. I called on Mr Gordon,
who Invited me both to Dinner & Breakfast for Tomorow and, as
the Latter generally comes first, I accepted of the opportunity to see
once more thy sister, Lucy. I saw the Engraver of the Turkey = I saw
Mr Munro and spent time at the Institution = I took a Long walk
with John Chorley, spoke of the *Bataille* of Tipocanoe and my being
a Midshipman when a Boy — I gave a long lesson of Drawing to my
Friend R^d R['s] Lady = Called on Mr Roscoe, whom I feared would
be offended, having been so stupid as not to go near him since the 2^d
day after my Return to Liverpool — I Received a Present of a *Snuff
Box*. —

"A Snuff Box! Why, my Laforest, thou astonishes me, not going to
suffer a Vile habit to encroach on thee, I hope"? =

No, my Lucy — John Chorley presented me with a Snuff Box to
hand to my Friend Snuff takers, and I assure thee I have some Worthys
among them — I, Lucy, will not take much, I assure thee = I called for
my Album at W^{am} Roscoe J^r, but it had been forward^d to Mrs Foster and
I must go there for it =

There are various ways of begging in England, but the following
deserves thy Notice. A man of midle age sat on the Edge of the street
walk and writes with a beautifull hand that he is "a poor man, out of
Employ, turned away from the Manchester Mills on account of the hard
times and solicits the charity of Passengers" = He had a few Pamphlets
for sale. I gave him the value of one, and as I proceeded faster I saw thro
a window many {**ry} efforts of the Pencil consisting of several dozen
of small attempts at Portraiture, all miserable, under which "Apprentices
are Wanted" was wrote in Immensely Large Characters — As I walked
I wished the person had been in need of masters Instead of apprentices.
It would have suited the Latters best =

I returned early, felt very fatigued, spent a most agreable Evening,
saw the signatures of many Great men, and retired Early — Sweet Wife,
Good Night. =

I felt extremely fatigued when [MS: with] I returned here in this afternoon, but se[e]ing Hannah reading this Book to her Sister Mrs W^{am} R. gave me pleasure, & refreshed me quite as much as the wine that was handed me = I read to them untill the Company arrived for Dinner and — but, my Lucy, I am rather forgetting myself = I Breakfasted with thy Sister this morning — She and her Husband gave me some Letters and a Commission to purchase for them 10 Guineas worth of Engravings in France: — I called on Mr W^{am} Laneson, upper Islington N° 53, and saw some wonderfull Paintings of Wouvermann's[8] &^{c} &^{c} &^{c}, and I think the finest oil Landscape I Ever saw from the Pencil of a Liverpool Lady, the name of whom I regret I have forgotten — This Gentleman was unusually polite, and I spent full 2 hours with him — His travels over the European Continent enable him to amuse and Interest the Visitor to a very gratifying degree — I can only regret that I did not see as much of him as I wished = I also outlined the Turkey compleatly for Mr Gifford, the Engraver, on the very peble Itself — I felt more satisfied about it. Although Mr G. Certainly engraves well, his Knowledge of Birds is not quite so extensive as mine = I walk^d in the *Baazar* of the *Fair of Charity*, but it was too crouded. I saw very Little and the air was quite disagreable = I spoke a few words to Mrs Trail and some other Ladies who knew me better than I did them = I had bid farewell to Dr Traill before = to John Chorley towards whom and his whole familly I felt a great attachmen[t], had received my Album from Mrs Maria Foster, the wife of John Foster Es^{qr}, to whom's farewell I wrote a few lines =

I visited the Institution once more and, accompanied by the Good Munro, I made sail for this spot = Mr Roscoe, his Daughter Jane, Mr Pillet of Paris & the son of another Banker of the same City dined with us = I was not very prepossessed [MS: prepossed] in favor of the Latter because he openned the conversation at table on Horse Races whilst Mr Roscoe & I were talking of the miseries of treadmills [MS: Trade Mills], another kind of Race quite as disgusting in its effects but towards the abolition of which Mr Roscoe & I were Intent, whilst the Banker's son

8. Philipp Wouvermann (1619–68) was a Dutch animal, landscape, and genre painter.

seemed willing the continuation of the first should be Improved =
This Gentleman, however, gradually changed his Grounds and I liked
him better. I gave some particular details to the Company after the
Ladies had retired (amongst whom thy good Friend Mrs Rathbone did
not make her appearance) of the Navigation of the Mississipy &^{c} &^{c} =
R^d Rathbone and his Lady came and the Evening was quite Chearful
= W^{am} Rathbone thinks much of the cleverness of his Wife, and she in
return is very good to him = They have here now 3 Interesting Little
children, the youngest a fair Simile of a Rose bud =

I bid adieu to R^d Rathbone and his Lady with a feeling of uncomfort
more than disagreable. I could not accompany them to their Carriage
= About 12 o'clock the Ladies bid us good night — Mr Saravey [MS:
Parawa] (the Bankers Son)[9] wrote a Letter to his Father and, giving it
me, said that I would receive at his House all the Hospitality that I had
met with in England = I thought this a good deal in a few words, but
recollected that he was a Frenchman = I have no wish, my Lucy, to
Infer that Frenchmen are not very kind. I merely say that *generally* their
kindness is more transient and that I prefer a *growing acquaintance,* one
that Improves as it grows, and like the live oak stand[s] the storms of
life thro all Kinds of Circumstances —

The Venerable Roscoe was extremely kind to me. He requested I
should write to him often and, depend on it, I shall, and never will
forget him and his attentions to me = Lucy, Tomorow I go again to
Manchester. I would anticipate the Journey and write more, but I must
bid thee Good Night =

9. The manuscript clearly reads "Parawa," but Alice Ford discovered a copy of the letter at
Yale University's Beinecke Library (*Journal,* 249). It is dated October 5, 1826, from Liverpool and
recommends that Mr. Saravey's father extend to Audubon in Paris all the help and hospitality
that Saravey has received in England. The letter is in box 7, folder 391, of the Morris Tyler Family
Collection of John James Audubon; its listing, however, mistakenly renders the name "Paravey"
and the date 1836.

5

Return to Manchester and
Travel to Matlock and Bakewell

I could not bear the Idea of leaving either this Place or Liverpool
without having previously seen the Intelligent Swiss = I knew how
Generously he had acted during my Exibition at the Royal Institution
and many Pounds Sterling had been added to the regular amount of
those received in Concert with some other Friends (the names of
whom I will not speak now) and I felt as if I saw that he had towards me
a peculiar Interest.

Well, then, with this all before me and scarcely day light suficient to
see to dress myself, I Issue[d] from my bed where I had not been more
than 4 hours, arranged my Clothes about me as snug as the Opportunity
would allow and again with my boots in one hand, I turned the latch
gently and on tip toe moved along the Passage down the stairs and out
of Doors finally in† sight of waking nature. It was one of the mornings
when, not suficiently cold to effect a Frost, the dew lays in large masses
on all objects, weighing down the Points of every leaf, of every blade
of Grass, and runs in startling streamlets about the Larger objects.
The Heavens were Cloudless, all breeses were hushed and the only
intervening twiterings of the Red Breasted Warbler broke on the silence
that Nature at this spot seem[ed] willing to Enjoy. I Cast my eyes around,
perceived the Blackbird mounted on the Tall Larch waitting anxiously,
wishing to Salute the reddening [MS: rededing] horizon [MS: orison]
with his melow notes — The Thrush stood on the Grass & by the
Mulberry Tree, quite errect, well spotted, her cunning large eye watching
the movements of one she knew was a stranger, and the Lark unwilling to
bid farewell to the last days [of] summer had sprung, and raised and with
a swelled throat was trying to recall the pleasures of spring =

Lucy, I also had raised early, and this sight of Magnificence and Peace made me wish to recall my youthfull days, to see again in reality the pleasures of our early Life and again to regrow together = The bright light of the Sun now colored the upper foliage of the Trees around, the sheep walked under, and eat the fallen fruit, the rooks voice Joined that of the Magpie, I saw a Stock Pigeon[1] swiftly pass over me and recollected my errand to Liverpool = I walked Swiftly and never met a Person untill I reached Abercromby Square, and that Person neither thee nor any other Person could know [MS: no] a word of was I not about telling thee that, after having closely examined every name on the Doors of Chatham Street and other surrounding Buildings, I was forced to procure Information by knocking at the House of W$^{\underline{am}}$ Rathbone to know where the Swiss resided since his removal = Then, Lucy, the person that I met first this morning was a young female, scarcely dress^d, with Rosy cheeks and Eyes that had not been made to sleep for ever = I begged her Pardon, gave her my name, and at a quarter of 6, the sun brightly risen, enabled me to see the Head of Mr Pillet, who from an upper window, was giving me notice that he had heard my repeated pulls of the Bell =

I would not have wrote so much about a morning, the like of which I have had for full 30 Years, but I had nothing else to do and to have been Idle might have created evil wishes, ending probably by hanging myself, as many [a] man has certainly done for want of other much better employment =

Mr Melly openned his Eyes as I opened his chamber Door, and with [MS: well] his usual *"Eh, bien, Papa"* received [me] with great cordiality, although as I sat on his bed side I felt fully convinced that I had been the cause of the Head Ache of which he complain^d during the Conversation by disturbing him before *his* accustomed time = What Powers habit gives! but what Powers does not habit destroy? His Partner was perhaps better, still very Ill, and as I might forgett his name, know, my Lucy, that it is *Schmidt*: —

On my return I met M^r W$^{\underline{am}}$ Roscoe J^r with a straw hat, taking he said an early Walk = The straw hat struck me more than the walk — For several days past the last Swallows had flown towards the south, several

1. The "Stock Pigeon" is the European wild pigeon, *Columbaaenas*.

Frosts had altered the primitive tints [MS: taints] of Foliage, and this mornings chillness engaged me to rubb frequently my hands & fingers together as I walk[ed] along. There habit exibited herself rather against me, I must say = "A fine warm morning this, M͟r Audubon." "Yes," I answered, "Just such as brings on half a cord of wood to the squaters fire in Latitude 32."[2] — We parted, I walking fast to warm myself, and he slowly to enjoy the effects of an English Oct͟r morning = It is not to be wondered at if Englishmen with so much warm Blood about them, are *warm hearted* =

At Green Bank all was still yet except the maid that gives light to the House by opening it first in the morning when I am not there = I had done much by this early time, had walked 5 miles, seen my Friend, had a book in hand and Lessen͟d to the 7 of the Clock anxious for my breakfast = Soon the Little ones came down to kiss me, and then ran after flowers to their own Garden = I felt as if [I] only wanted thy Presence and a kiss from thy Lips to afford me all the Bliss is earth [MS: hearth] can produce — but that only kiss was wanted, and all that Bliss with it and I reclined on the Sopha =

I saw W͟am Rathbone and his Clever Wife and aimiable and her Benevolent Mother. We breakfasted — The Carriadges drew up. The first paire and their Children bid us all adieu = Our Turn came and by 10 o'clock we were on the Road towards Manchester = I look͟d at Green Bank unknowing if it was for the last time but wishing its Inhabitants all well & Happy = Hannah sat next me, her mother beyond, and thus compactly arranged three on the seat of the Chaise we passed thro *Wavertree* = The silence lasted during this while. Each thought no doubt of their most Imediate concerns, friends & relations. Judging for myself, this must have been the Case = Conversation soon, however, found its way and from one topic to another, either by change of objects

2. In this friendly exchange with Roscoe, Jr., Audubon seems to allude to a story he told of squatters that he would expect Roscoe to recall. The 1834 published version of the story, "The Squatters of the Mississippi" (OB, 2:131–34), narrates the difficult migration of a Virginia family west across the southern states to the Mississippi River, where the "hoar-frosts" of October cause them to cut firewood. Latitude 32 would place the family just north of Natchez, a region Audubon knew well. We see here that many of the "Delineations" interspersed throughout the first three volumes of *Ornithological Biography* were developed orally over many years of storytelling.

in view or in recollection. The time passed most agreably = Hannah
had requested that this my poor Book would be given her, and from
time to time she open^d and read in it =

We changed horses perhaps 12 miles from Green Bank. It was done in
a moment. A new Postillion mounted and again we proceeded = Did
I ever when in the Forests of America dream or think [MS: thought]
of travelling in the Chaise of one of the best Ladies of England at her
particular request accompanied by her kind aimiable daughter, both
feeding me with the most obliging and unremitted attentions merely
because I brought a single Letter of Introduction from a Friend of
mine from New Orleans and after an acquaintance of only a very few
weeks? No, that I never did — I can scarcely now realise it — It is all
wonderfull to me and whatever receptions, no matter how diferent
my Country men have had, in this Land, I can only say that mine far
surpassed all my most Sanguine Hopes = May God forbid that I
should ever be ungratefull, and may he Bless those who have so kindly
received the Naturalist of Louisianna =

But, my Lucy, I have almost forgotten that I was travelling towards
Manchester = We frequently spoke of thee, of our Children, and
sudenly my Venerable Friend said that she had an Inclination to be
hungry! — Each of us had his little table made of our Knees, each a
Little Cloth, Little plate, knifes & Plenty of provisions = The wine
was handed round and, although it seemed as if anxious to escape the
Glass before reaching the lip, it at last produced the effect intended =
Our desert, Lucy, consisted of a Melon and some Grapes & some paires
& some apples, and I at last doubted if coffee was not coming = We
were all gay — I never saw my Miss Hannah more so. Her Dark Eyes
were more beautifull than ever, and the smile around her mother's Lips
proved to me how much can be felt when the Heart is at peace with the
Mind =

Thus we rolled and reach[ed] the smoaky Manchester, gradually
passing from street to street, Halted at the Door of the Academy of
Natural History, pressed the Hands of my Good Friends and, thrusting
myself into the Building, felt an end of my Pleasure = How changing
the scene = again in Worldly engagements — My Door Keeper
proved Insane. He certainly had an oreplus of spirit within him. I do
not wish to Pun, Lucy; the Man had positively taken quite too much

Irish Whiskey to Look with care on American Birds $=$ Seldom in my life have I felt more vexed $=$ I, however, coolly begged of him to come to my Lodgings where I Balanced accounts with him and, opening the Door quite broad, gave him a full opportunity of breathing at Leisure, of cooling himself and of Looking for a new Situation for the next day $=$

I Returned to my Birds and Looked at them very Closely — They were fresh and as gay in appearance as their originals in our Woods — I determined to have only the Young Son of Mʳ Willson to take charge of them and pushed thro the streets again to seek Mʳ Bentley $=$ I saw him — I received my Income that was rather slender and in time retired to my appartment $=$ There, my Lucy, in the World and yet compleatly divided from it, I thought of thee, of the time spent in England since my arrival, of the acquaintances I have formed — of the many kind attentions I have received, of the Proba[bi]lities of my ultimate success $=$

My Good Friends had proceeded to Mʳ Dockrey about one mile Distant — I thought of them $=$ I was not fatigued, yet I felt the wish that I might sleep quickly. I felt as if my situation was not suited to enliven the dullness of my present Ideas and, after my Super and glass of wine dranked in desire that my Health might be good and thy Happiness compleat, I wished thee again, again and again Good night! —

QUARRY BANK SATURDAY 7ᵀᴴ 1826 OCTᴿ —

I arranged many letters this morning for my good Friend Mʳˢ Rathbone and, having promised her one of thine, I gave her thine of the 9ᵗʰ of May Dated Beech Woods $=$ I had also promised one of Charles Bonaparte to her Daughter in Law, Mʳˢ Wᵃᵐ Rathbone, and this I also put by for her $=$ My time was spent walking, visiting my acquaintances with a wish to procure more letters of Introduction and, whilst I was resting in front of my Drawings at the Academy giving some Idea of the Habits of some to some Lady who seemed to possess a good knowledge of Ornithology, Mʳ Robᵗ Greg and his mother came to me and with so much openness and friendly manners desired that I should accompany them this evening to their Country seat that, although I had rather obligated myself to spend the evening with Mʳ Rathbone at Mʳ Dockrey, I could not refuse the Invitation. Then thanks to this good Lady, I will be peaceably in the country again to night and tomorow

= I arranged colors, chalks, paper & Linen suficient and walked to
Fountain Street at 3 of the afternoon — Conceive my astonishment and
momentary disapointment & confusion when told at the Door that the
Carriage was gone — Yes, gone — With my Colors, chalks, &ᶜ, I made
for the office of the Son and, being told there that Mͬ Gregg expected
me at Mͬ Dockrey, I pushed towards Picadilly to procure a Coach = It
is not every man who knows where Picadilly lays in this smoaky town
of Manchester; therefore I applied to the first man that I thought could
Instruct the Woodsman — "Sir, I am walking that very way myself and
will do myself the pleasure of conducting you to the place" —

This, Lucy, would have been true English politeness had not my
present companion been *guided* himself by Interested Motives = I had
my new Coat *shaped* and Called after Lafayette — Never untill now had
I dared to ware it and it was quite as new to the gentleman by my side
almost as to me = He saw with a Conoisseurs's Eye that *I* was not a
Manchester man, asked what Countryman I was with [MS: will] all the
ease of one of our brave Yankees and, per my answer, begged to know if
I wished to purchase Umbrellas for America!

The weather certainly did look as if one might be wanted and
although mine was again snug at my Lodgings, I smiled and told him
that I delt not in the article generally — "No offence, Sir, I Hope. If you
follow this street, turn to the right and then to the left, any body will
show you the Way to Picadilly."

Thus, Lucy, from an umbrella maker or merchant, to a Cotton Dealer
and then to [a] fop, I collected all Information needed to bring me in a
few minutes more opposite a Coach Just at the Entrance of Picadilly —
"Take me to Mͬ Dockrey, Hardwick" — "A Quaker, Sir?" "Yes" — Up
the Driver Jumps and, rounding his Horses, I was in a moment at Mͬ
Dockrey = There my Friends were, all, yes all. I cannot help calling
them all Friends who are so truly kind to me = I was chid for not
having come to Dinner or to breakfast, and betwen the 3 parties it was
dificult to tell with whom I would spend the time to come —

I saw the very Lady Abigail with 9 children of Diferent ages — all
Lovely = but, my Dear Wife, the reception of Mͬˢ Rathbone exceded
perhaps all I had ever experienced from her. She positively appeard to
think that I was one of her own Sons; I could not help feeling rather
disagreable for a while. The more I saw, the more I was surprised; I

really think that I was ask^d 3 distinct and different times if I had dined; and altho I certainly had, I could not refuse a Glass of Wine brought to me by kind Hannah = Mrs Rathbone spoke of going to *Mattlock* with me in such a manner that I thought it might [MS: make] be and, oh, how I did wish it. We soon bid adieu. I handed Mrs Gregg in the Carriage, her husband filled the further seat, and after the last nod of adieu we rolled most easily snug — We were now at Summer Place, the seat of Robt Gregg Es^qr where, whilst I was admiring a Laughing Girl of Sir Joshua Reynolds and some fine drawings of Vernet, a Tall female figure entered the room and gave me a powerfull Idea of the Inferiority of Art when in contact with beautifull Nature — I forgot Reynolds & his Girl, Left Vernet at the Field of Moscow[3] — and after a timid Glance on the well featured Mrs R. Gregg, gradually bent my head and at last made a most awkward bow, I have no doubt = She, Lucy, has blue eyes and is very aimiable and, I doubt not, very Clever, but I really Like the fair Helen of Quarry Bank better, and the Dark eyes of Miss Hannah also =

This House is agreably situated about 2 miles from Manchester and from it a very extensive view is obtained and a Circulation of air that ensures [MS: ansures] Health and pleasure = Again in the Carriage, Mr Greg soon went to sleep and Mrs Greg help[ed] me to a good quantity of most agreable Conversation = Lucy, Mrs Gregg is one of those rare exemples of the superior powers of Thy Sex over ours when education and Circumstances are combined = She is most aimiable, Smart, quick, witty, positively Learned, with an Incomparable Memory, and as benevolent as Woman can be = Her and her Husband form the finest picture of Devoted, tender and faithfull attachment I Ever met with, and I have look^d on them and their *familly circle* as being probably as happy a Compound as would be found in all America, for Instance. = Well, Mr Gregg is awake, I give him a pinch of Snuff, and we turn again quite short to the right, move slowly down the Hill, and I am leading Mrs Gregg to her House — Thus from Green Bank to Quarry Bank, but from one pleasure to another, not like a Butterfly that Skips from flower

3. Sir Joshua Reynolds (1723–92), a cofounder of the British Royal Academy of Art, was one of the most successful and prolific portraitists of the eighteenth century. His portraits of children were some of his most popular works. Carle (Antoine-Charles-Horace) Vernet (1758–1835) was a French painter known for his idealized historical battle scenes.

to flower and merely sees their beauties, but more, I Hope, as a bee gathering Honied knowledge for older times! —

I am soon amongst that flock of females, the daughters of my kind *Irish Gentleman*; therefore, I am soon at ease — One Academician would Stupifie me whilst 20 such fair objects as surround me now have no other tendency than to augment the ease I am so fond [MS: found] of = The Italian makes her appearance. She is more Magestic. Her Eye brow is more regular, darker, her nose more Angular, but her Voice is delightfully sweet, her expressions glide into the remotest Intercesses of the Mind and give a good Idea of the Superiority of Language adapted for Conversation —

My Cold was really disagreable and I sneezed so constantly that it was no Joke to me, I assure thee, and had I followed the kind advises of the familly I would have felt still more like Sneezing the next day for the[y] wished me to *"do something for it"* — that is to say, to take some Phisic — This I never do, thou knowest well, unless quite Ill =

Our Conversation was animated respecting the Superiority of Women over our Sex and Miss Annah Mary (I believe) proved the superiority of her knowledge, understanding and eloquence in a very few minutes = Dispersed about the Room as we were, some singly, others by Twos, I Look^d at the whole when Mr Gregg, with a smile that reached the Eye {whilst} it was on his Lip, pointed to his Lady and pronounced her his Superior also! — The Ladies all worked at Light things. I look^d at them all and returned, allways with more Satisfaction, my eyes on the Fair Helen =

I went to rest Early. I had been obliged to open this Book to shew a sketch of the Flying Fish. All eyes were fixed on the Drawing for a while and when, after I had answered to their questions that it was my Journal, they said that no doubt it must contain some Curious things. The Hint was not Likely to take, however — I remembered well my Promiss to thee, and the Observations of some other Friends and shut it quietly: Now, my Love, Good Night =

SUNDAY OCT^R 8TH 1826. — †

I went to church at Mr Gregg's chapel, sat by the side of his Fair Daughter and prayed that she may be as Happy as she is Beautifull = The Sermon was good, delivered by a Young Man. I sung amongst the

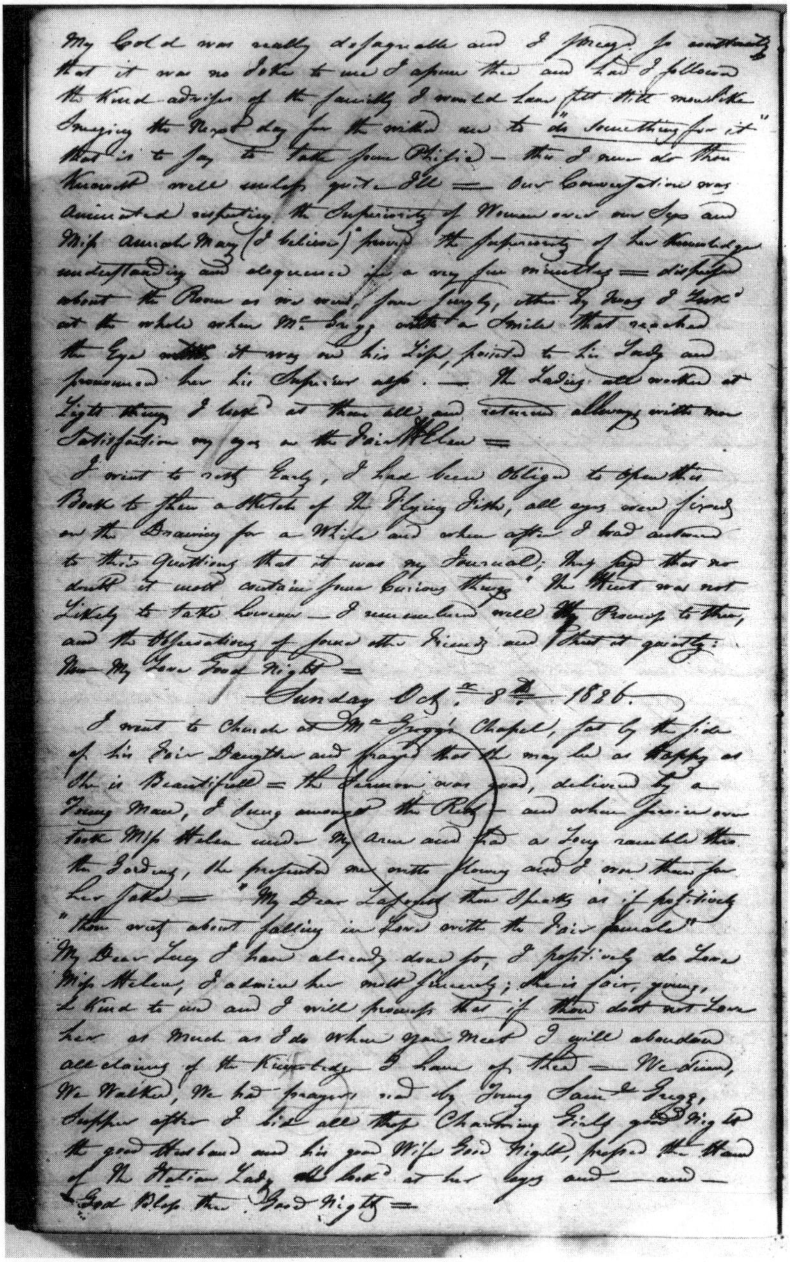

FIG. 16. The height of flirtatiousness, October 8, 1826

Rest — and when service [was] over took Miss Helen under my arm and had a long ramble thro the Gardens. She presented me with flowers and I wore them for her sake =

"My Dear Laforest,[4] thou speaks as if positively thou wert about falling in Love with the Fair female."

My Dear Lucy, I have already done so, I positively do Love Miss Helen, I admire her most sincerely; she is fair, young, & kind to me, and I will promiss that if *thou* dost not Love her as much as I do when you meet, I will abandon all claims of the knowledge I have of thee =

We dined, we walked, we had prayers read by Young Sam[l] Gregg, Supper. After,[†] I bid all these charming Girls good night, the good Husband and his good Wife Good Night, pressed the Hand of the Italian Lady & look[d] at her eyes and — and — God Bless thee, Good Night =

QUARRY BANK MONDAY 9TH 1826 OCT[R]

As soon as possible, this day a male chaffinch was procured and I sat to draw it to give an Idea of the Style, as the Artist calls it, of my work = Helen Gregg ask[ed] me with a smile that would penetrate Cold Marble for a Pin, and as I had none about me she presented me with a little Cushion made flat for the Waistcoat Pocket, well furnished, and *Hoped* I would not refuse it = Refuse it? No, I would just as soon think of Dranking Poison. Refuse it, not I. I snugged it in my waistcoat and thank[d] the fair maid with a *good Portion* of my Heart, Lucy. =

The chaffinch was outlined, daubed with Watter Colors and nearly finished in *My Style* when Two Youths made their appearance. They were Introduced, but I scarcely saw them; they were some Lord or other's relations, and as the Language they used was *exceedingly exquisite*, I kept my thoughts confined and my eyes bent on the Chaffinch — The Young Ladies I thought cared not for them. I heard that they had called to pay their respects to the Fair Italian, and as she had not appeared since breakfast, the Gentlemen after tapping the fair tops of their boots smartly with their smart whips, arranged their Cravats a little and walk[d] round my seat to View my Locks, my Coat &

---

4. Audubon seems to have adopted the additional name "Laforest" in 1805 while he and his future wife were courting. Lucy used it thereafter as a pet name for her husband.

my Performance, made an *exceedingly exquisite* bow and departed $=$
May God Bless them and help them and render them both rather more
Simple! Yes, Simple! $=$

Mr Gregg, not so well aware as W^{am} Rathbone that I prefer wine
when handed me by a Lady, brought me a glass himself $=$ This
proves how apt we all are to do contrary to our Likings, but I am quite
Persuaded that Mr Gregg himself is blessed with the same wish of being
[MS: been] help^d to such things *as Wine*, for Instance, by a Lady as ever I
was or ever will be $=$

Doct^r Holland[5] came in. I was pleased with him and, although I
am neither a Phisionomist or Cranaologist, the moment he talk[ed]
I within myself pronounced him a Good Man $=$ We dined most
chearfully. I was glad that Dr Holland had come. It gave me the
opportunity of sitting opposite my Favorite Helen and to see her Wild
Eyes moving as if they Loved and yet feared all $=$ The Doctor had
come to see Miss Gregg. She had a cold also; the Doct^r no doubt will
cure with time; time will cure me without the doctor, and as I dislike to
trouble more Individuals than is really necessary, I am glad to confide
entirely in the Latter's ability —

Now the Gamekeeper of Lord Stamford is again waiting for the
Young Gentlemen and me, and to my great regret we leave the Table
and Company to enter the fields and commit murder — We had a long
walk; the Grass was very wet — I killed a Pheasant & a Hare, and M^r S.
Gregg killed a Hare also $=$ This walk did me much good. The weather
& Drawing had kept me close within the walls of Quarry Bank, and I
needed exercise as well as time to Cure my Cold: $=$

It was with dificulty that I escaped the Physic Intended for me this
Evening. Mr Gregg said that wine was bad for me and I must not touch
it $=$ I pleaded that it would warm my Cold and swallowed a Glass
with quite as much pleasure as Ever $=$ This evening was delightfull.
Mr Gregg was in high Spirits, so was his Lady, and all the Starrs shewn
brightly also; much entertaining Poetry was read and repeated. We had
a little music and a great deal of Interesting conversation — The Map

5. The young and brilliant George Calvert Holland (1801–65) was in his last year of medical
studies at Edinburgh when he and Audubon met. By 1826 he had become an enthusiastic
phrenologist.

of the U. S. was laid before me, and they all were astonished to discover how Little the Particular[i]ties of that country have been mentioned by Writers $=$ I wish^d I could write. I would delight at giving my Country Fair Play $=$

Well, Lucy, I went to bed and did not forget to bid thee Good Night —

MR DOCKREY NEAR MANCHESTER

TUESDAY 10TH OCT^R 1826 —

The Ladies were all up at Quarry Bank very early. The weather was sad — I work^d at some oak Leaves for the Miss Greggs much in a Hurry $=$ I gave my Fair Pupil my Brushes and she gave me some Excellent Indian Ink & Chinese white $=$ but, Lucy, I positively forgot the Little Pin Cushion, a full proof of the Diference betwen Loving as I do Miss Helen or Loving as I do thee. — Mr Greg generally goes to Manchester every Tuesday. I wished to return with him, anxious if the weather should alter tomorow to visit Matlock $=$ I pack^d up half my Chalks, anxious the Ladies should try to work with the other half and, after an early breakfast, I found myself Close on the right side of Miss Helen, who divided me from her father.† Assending slowly the Hill that Leads from Quarry Bank, thinking of Manchester, I Cleaned my nose and took a pinch of Snuff, moved sideways not to encumber the fair companion and opened the conversation on Cotton, Corn Laws, Taxes here and in America $=$ begged Miss Helen to send me the Little Pin Cushion and arrived at 11 on Fountain Street. $=$

I soon reach^d my Birds all well. I found a Card from Mr Bohn on my Table: Saw my good Friends M^{rs} & Hannah Rathbone, the familly Dockry, to whom I promissed to dine with, and pushed out to discover Mr Bohn $=$ I found him at the Stare Hotel by the help of Mr Bentley, who I may say has been of great Service to me in Manchester $=$ We returned to the Academy together and, after examining my Drawings a long time, he advised me to publish them the full Size of Life and that they [MS: them] must pay well: may God grant it $=$ Mr Bohn advised me strongly to clear off from Manchester; assured me that in London I would be cherished by the Nobility and could not but succeed with my talent. He was going to add *"and agreable manners"* when I stopped him short by putting a question to him $=$

Lucy, the Boy that attends my exibition is named John Willson. When I returned with Mr Bohn, he came and showed me a Sovereign and said the Lady who had read a Letter to me this morning had given it him and said that the amount over the number of her Company was for him == I did not mention that Mrs Rathbone had read to me a part of her Daughter's Letter of Liverpool, but I am very sure that thou hast guessed before this *She is the Sovereign* Lady == What am I to do; to ever return all the *gifts*, attentions and motherly kindnesses of this good Lady? ==

I reached Mr Dockrey['s] House about 2, was not directed the way first to the right and then to the left by the Umbrella Manufacter, but I was positively conducted by a good neatly dressed woman who walk^d on Pattins quite as fast as I did without and would have accompanied me to the very door had I not begged of her not to do so == I felt a great desire to give her a shilling but, remarking again her figure and neat dress, I dared not least I might offend her —

I am at Mrs Dockrey, Lucy, but I am not able to Describe her beyond this, that she is a Quaker, a Lady and a most kind & benevolent woman — has a Large Interesting familly and a Husband resembling W^{am} Penn == My Letters are returned me, but a Port folio has been made by one of the Daughters to keep them safer from Cutting: I read a few short Passages of this Book at the request of my Good Friend Mrs Rathbone — show how to rub the Chalks, sketch an Egret for one, a Wild Turkey for another, speak of America, write with my Left hand, drank I think rather too much Wine, enjoy my Miss Hannah's Dazling eyes, and at 11 o'clock am conducted with many apologies to a nice small chamber where, after praying for Our Sakes and that of *all our species*, I lay to sleep and *bid thee good night*, Dearest Friend —

BAKEWELL OCT^R 11TH 1826 — WEDNESDAY ==

I am at last, my Beloved Wife, at the spot that has been honored with thy Ancestors name; I am at Bakewell and I can neither describe my feelings nor the place; it is dark, rainy and all promises a wet tomorow == I have just returned this moment, 15 minutes of nine, from a walk in the very church Yard of the Village == Singular place to resort to, is it not? but being on an errand with Hannah Rathbone, say shopping [MS: choping], she wished to see some portion of it and attracted by the Gothic ancient appearance of the Church, we gradually approach^d it and finally walked round it. I positively know very little either about the church yard or the church, but I am quite sure that I and Hannah Walkd around it, she leaning on my arm and I supporting her, neither very Happy nor very sad, perhaps feeling a sort of vacancy about me, an undetermination, a kind of restless dreaming Illusion like, that now made me doubt if I lived, & walked?, If I saw & felt?, if Thou wert present or not?, if the Place was called Bakewell or Audubon? but since I have reentered the Inn and seen my Good Lady Rathbone and her niece Mrs Dockrey & Lessened to the light touches of Hannah Rathbone on the Piano, I have awakened and know, Yes, positively know, that Audubon possesses a Bakewell!! But I have not come here accidentally, that thou knowest well = It must be some Twice 10 years since a View of Bakewell was desired, and when I think how frequently since my plans have been defeated and my voyage to Europe postponed, it is no great wonder if I should feel more at a loss than usual when seated here & finding it dificult to tell thee precisely or in the most Interesting manner how and under what Circumstances I have reached it at Last =

Know then, my Beloved Wife, that at breakfast this morning Mrs Rathbone spoke of going to Matlock and in a few minutes it was all arranged that her, Daughter & niece and several of the children in Two chaises would leave at 12. The Weather was then fair = Elated, I walked with Mr Dockrey and viewed all his works with pleasure, perhaps the more so on account of his extreme politeness in giving to my view all the most Interesting details = He procures wool rough from the sheep and disposes of the Cloth when finished. Betwen 60 & 70 weavers were at work = The Engine made her returns silently and smoothly = I saw the Dying apparatus &^c &^c and walked to Dirty Manchester to put up my Birds, I thought — however, the limited time did not permit me to do this, and I only packed some to shew Mr Gifford & others willing to view them = I saw Mr Railton, who extremely kindly Invited me again to his House = Dr Holme appeared disapointed that my prospectus was yet to be prepared = I begged of Mr Bentley to see to my Drawings and, the Coach being waiting with Mr Dockrey, I thrusted my Body, My Bundle, My Book & my thoughts into it and off we whirl^d to Hardwick [MS: Ardwick] =

Now, my Lucy, It was decided that I should have the pleasure and the Honor of riding to Matlock with my Good Friends = to Matlock where Doct^r Darwin has Nursed thee on his Knees. What shall I be in body or mind when I reach the *Bijoux of England*? I know not at present =

See us arranged in 2 chaises, 7 of us, one servant, and 2 Postillions peeping to the right & left, hungry with curiosity, passing objects one after the other, finding [MS: finder] the one before us allways the most Interesting because perhaps the Newest, untill we reach^d Stockport, Wellington North Road, a manufacturing [MS: Manu*faring] Town Laying betwen the 2 elongated sides of Hills and where we entered in Cheshire = We changed Horses = again at Chapel-en-le-Frith [MS: Chapel La Frith], 20 miles from the point of Departure = I had by this time taken my station on the *Dicky* behind and had for Companion the Younger Daughter Sarah Dockrey, who entertained me very much with her Innocent, well regulated observations = again with the Eldest who spoke much to my satisfaction on many Subjects = I saw a good deal of thy England that I admired very much; the Rail Ways were New to me, many buildings were resembling those of Pennsylvania, but the approach of the Mountains dampened my Spirits, the aridity of the soil, the want of Hedges, of course of Birds, of course of good music, the scarcity of catle and the super aboundance of shakling stone walls cutting the Hills in all kinds of distorted ways were quite too tending to recall me to America and probably made me a very unsociable sort of Companion to Miss Rachael! —

When we arrived here, I was pleased to see how comfortably we were at the Inn; the Room where our Tea & supper was drank & eat, many good Prints ornemented it, and thou Knowest that a Piano was there = Our Circle was all gayety and being so Contiguous to Bakewell, raised my own spirits and I now with the help of several glasses of Wine feel quite Enclined to wish thee as Good, Happy, Blessed a Night as I ever did since I knew thee, either by the name of Bakewell or that of Audubon, so may God bless thee, Dearest Friend, my sweet wife, Good Night —

Stop. Only conceive how foolish I found myself when about a mile from Mr Dockrey I discovered that I had forgotten my Letters to Mrs Gifford, and more over that instead of Matlock being, as I thought it, thy Birth Place, I look^d at thy memorandum and plainly saw that it was

Burton upon Trent in Stafford Shire! — and why all this? Because I was bound towards thy native spot —

MATLOCK, DERBYSHIRE THURSDAY OCT$^{\underline{R}}$ 12$^{\underline{TH}}$ 1826 —

I Certainly slept well last night. I felt comfortable although so very far from thee: my bed was sweetly clean, and the name of Bakewell was so connected with all about me that I laid my head on the Pillow contented [MS: contended], Imagining thee well and most Certainly wishing thee so = Day made its appearance. My eye lids aware of it, consciously opened: I sprung up Anxious to see all about this delightfull Country = I called my young companion, David Dockray. His Youth, the Peace of his heart, and the tenderness of his body all joined in reluctance, and it was not untill I had warned him several times that it was quite light, that he sliped from his slumbers and after my Example dressed quickly =

Again I saw and walked around the church, remarked its decaying state, and that of all the Thatched roofs of the Humble cottages that surround this religious Asylum = The sky was cloudless; one might have easily believed that all above us was silently admiring the opening of Nature & morning Twilight = I saw, I thought close by my side, a little child, a female, dimpled Cheeked, smiling with loveliness, light footed, lightly moving, gazing with that anxiety that nothing but youth can genui[ne]ly enjoy, bec[k]on to me, and bid me follow path after path and turn and wind from Lane to Lane and Impercept[ib]ly lead me thro this village Called after thy name; I watched the bewitching child, and the more I saw of her, the more I saw in her my sweet little Lucy — so young, so beautifull, so Joyfully gamboling thro the Bakewell grounds = So well persuaded did I at last believe thee near me that I concluded to have thee [MS: me] most Especially for this Day's Guide, and with thee will I now go and ramble from this thro Matlock, and as I have come here under the beneficial escort of Benevolence, Friendship, and Sweetness of amability, let me Introduce thee to my Good Friends M$^{\underline{rs}}$ Rathbone & Her Hannah, M$^{\underline{rs}}$ Dockray and her Rachael and her 2 younger children = Come and walk with Hannah, Rachel & David, and let us take our course over the bridge that Crosses the winding River Wye [MS: Why], and assend with us the Hills that look upon the Village with complacency. From the bridge,

234   RETURN TO MANCHESTER

look and see the sprightly trout, how gaily it leaps at the skiping fly =
Look now how sweetly the old church emerges thro the smoake to
receive the rays of the Morning sun, and see how playfully the Villas are
arranged amongst the Hills and along the ornemented Valey = Now
that we have assended quite to the summit, watched the sun's light, how
it clears for us the horizon [MS: Orison], how plainly we see the road
that we followed last night and the one that we will survey to day =

Did[st] thou ever taste of the Watter of this spring or plucked the
violets that growed under these [h]edges? Hast thou ever rambled thro
this shrubery and seen the Beautifull sights up the river before us? =
Let us return to the Rutland Arms Inn. Hast thou rested in it with thy
good Father and thy Botanical Friend? and seen & felt the comfort
that along with good Friends one can Enjoy there? — It is nearly seven
o'clock, and it is the time appointed for us to proceed. Young as thou
art, walk by thyself, but I pray thee be close at my Elbow whilst I help
our Friend Hannah = Pretty place this, my Lucy, very quiet, peaceable
and Happy Looking — No Manchester this — no hamerings = no
heavy blows either to the Heart or the eye! Come, this way and let us
walk up and make ready = Now we are arranged and we go = The
Weather is fretfull. I doubt if it will be fair all day = Ah, here is Haddon
Hall, beautifull! It looks still better now, and now still more so — The
road is really very good and this valey truly charming. How contented
those Pheasants appear by the side of that wood, how safe from all but
the will of the Lord! —

Hey day, what have we here? The very duke of Devonshire's Groom,
what whiskers! Mustachios and strange looking spotted Horses, going
tandem too = At what rate he goes = This Gentleman['s] seat is
pretty. That Cipress is large and well Leafed. Ah, Lucy, what beautifull
brake of High Hills, what delightfull fern [MS: Furn] and well shaded
little stream, surely we must be nearing some Enchanted fairy's
boudoir!

"Ha, what now?"

What now, my Friend! *Matlock*: opening before thy wistfull eye in
all its beauty. Seest thou the spotted mountains nearly all over with
sweetest cottages, and gentlemen's seat[s] = The Autumnal tints
diversifying the Landscape and enriching bountifull Nature — How
pretty, yet how grand. Is it not very much like thy America on the River

called the Clear Juniatta? = Watch and remark the Cleanliness = Here is the Old Bath, the Museum = the little shops [MS: chops] that dispose of the Sparry productions[6] = This pond [MS: pound] they use to wash the Post Horses, and now that we have left the course of the River and are rising slowly and Gently, we approach the new baths where thy Friends wish to spend the day = Thank thee, Dearest Friend = Remark the Large New Foundland Dog = His name is Neptune = quite Comfortable a House this = How well our [MS: hour] friends do look. I cannot help remarking their anxiety to please thee! = Mr Saxtons is our Landlord, it seems, and here is breakfast ready.

Well, it will not do to be Idle and looking at our Empty Coffee Cups, on with Bonnetts and umbrellas and let us proceed and, as thou hast visited this so frequently, fly to America and look at our Dear Sons = I will visit all and compare Notes with thee when we meet again: farewell, be Happy.

"My Dear Miss Hannah, which way?"

"Let us go and visit the museum first. I am anxious to gather a little assortment to send to America and will thank you for your tastefull Judgement = I will take these Boxes & smelling Botles and this vase, and I would like to have this beautifull Inkstand. Pray, accept of this Little Box for Little John. Matlock is nicely engraved on it; send it him."

Thank you — Here is another shop [MS: chop], cheaper to be sure but no[t] well assorted; however I will buy here 16 shilling worth & here 11 and — "I will not buy any more" =

Now let us take a good long Walk, assend those Hills and, as this man offers to take us into a Curious Cave, let us follow him = Now, my Lucy, we walked slowly up a very steep Hill. On turning to view the Delightfull scenery, I saw either a good Husband or a good Brother or a well recompensed Lover, bearing in his arms either his Wife, his Sister or his young Mistress, as Heartily as I have done Myself hundreds of Times: with my Wife, my Sister or my Lovely Mistress = The weather had now become quite rainy. We reached the Entrance of the Cave; Hannah was fatigued. I dried a portion of a Bench, spread a portion of my umbrella and my handkerchief [MS: Hdf] for her to set, but her

6. Spar calcite is a lustrous white mineral that can be cleaved and polished to produce attractive objects.

FIG. 17. Saxton's new baths at Matlock

genuine politeness on se[e]ing the female stranger made her bid of me
to offer the seat prepared for her == I did so; the Lady accepted but
in a moment we were all under way towards our Visitation into the
Earth's [MS: Hearth] Bowells == Hannah went in only a short distance,
returned and walked about the Door untill our Incursion (If I may thus
call it) == We proceeded, each of us with a light in hand, and saw all
the diferent Caves containing most rich minerals & sparrs the Country
affords == From one Natural Chamber we reach another, and the Last
and Lowest I squeeze myself into with the guide only, scarce able to
maintain my hold and expecting that every other stone I took by the
Hand would give way with me and find the bottom faster than I was
willing == That chamber was, however, superb == The whole [MS: all]
shone [MS: shun] like burnished steel and dazled my eyes compleatly ==

Again out, I bid the Fair Stranger good bye, bowed to her senewy
partner and, leading our Groupe, we walked and saw all the views
that render this enchanted Matlock so desired by every traveller: We
again felt our steps lengthening and went down hill after Hill untill we
found ourselves on the first level == A single Door and a single Woman
troubled us == The first could not be passed without a Toll of 6 pence
each (having passed the private grounds) and the Latter would not give
up guiding us without a shilling == Again at the Inn, my Bountifull
Friend having heard me mention the Black Spar Inkstand, Hannah
was requested to purchase it for thee, and it was == Now, Lucy, how
much art thou in Debt and how much are both of us in Debt to this
Wonderfull Woman? ==

I saw the Turning of Sparr from the Crude State and was rather
astonished at the very great alteration perceivable when any portion
is put under the Influence of a *Red heat.* == I thought of Gathering
Leaves, Plants and all other such trifles that might give thee a moments
pleasures by reaching America == Some of [the] objects that probably
met my ears with most pleasure was the repeated Notes of the Jack
Daws that constantly flew from hole to hole along the stupendous
declivities of the Rocks about us — The wind blew fresh — Each tree
turned each Leaf as if anxious to shew thy Husband positively all about
Matlock == I will not dwell upon our Dinner. I have not time when
the Country so much calls on my attention and so reminds me of thy
youth, and thy Loveliness == Our Dinner, my Dinner, Lucy, was Good

FIG. 18. "View of Path & Road Cut thro the Lock about 1 Mile below Matlock on the Right Bank of the River Derwent"

= Trout, Mutton & Rabbits, vegetables and many Hearty Healths were Drank & eat =

Now, my Lucy, we all did wish to ride on the *Derwent*. We all set off from the Inn for that Purpose but, the rain falling again, the aunt and niece returned and we, the remainder, seated in a Boat Rowed by thy Husband, went down the stream of the pretty River, and down that of our Lifes! — We reach[ed] a Dam and a Fall, Landed, Looked at the Fall — Walk^d thro the woods, gradually rised to Hill tops again; gathered all kinds of mosses for thee, saw some Hares; heard a Kestrell just as if in America = entered our Boat again and Rowed up the stream = reached our Inn = eat & Drink & Enjoyed a most lively Evening, saw my sweet friend Hannah quite Happy, all about me quite Happy, wished thee quite Happy and bid thee Good Night quite Happy!!! —

MATLOCK DERBYSHIRE OCT^R 13TH 1826 — FRIDAY =

The rain did not put a barrier to my Inquisitive desires = We got up early and walked down the River. I saw a particularly handsome spot affording just the makings of such a sketch as I thought would give fresh Ideas of the Vale of Matlock = I made it on a card for Hannah Rathbone, very slightly and here for thee closely drawn during the morning. We entered part of the Grounds of Sir Thomas Arkwright, saw his Castle, his church and his medows = The Rooks & Jackdaws were by hundreds over our heads = The Steep Rocks that border [MS: bordern] here the right side of the Valey, as we followed the course of the Derwent, were pleasantly aspersed with clumps of shrubby trees = The Castle on the Left and on a fine Elevation is Large, and too regular to be called (by me) adapted to the Rich Natural Scenery about it = We passed along a Canal, by a Large Manufactory, a Coal Yard, and returned to breakfast thro *Crumford* =

Nearly the whole of my Day was employed at Drawing = I purchased more sparrs for thee = Having reached the *Hights of Abraham* I seated myself in full sight of the whole [MS: all] of Matlock, Hills & Vale & River, below me and there I made a General Sketch = David Dockray took that of the Castle and his Sister followed me and worked by my side = I found her a very Interesting child = Dinner over, I returned quickly to the spot with David and betwen him and I it was finished about sun set = Rachael Dockray accompanied me thro the Rutland Cave. I was highly gratified; it surpassed all my expectations = The Natural chambers sparkled with brilliancy and to enhance the value of the sight, lights were rised to the very summits to reflect the richness of the whole [MS: all] = The way into all the parts was easy = I saw there some little Fishes that had not seen day light for 3 Years and yet were quite sprightly: a certain portion of the Roof represented a very good Head of a Large Tiger = We were going out intent on returning to David Dockray when our Good Friend Mrs Rathbone, her Daughter Hannah and Abigail presented themselves to our view = They went in also. I soon followed to Imitate the owl's cry and the Indian Yell = This Latter music never pleased my fancy much, and I well know the Effects it produces previous to an attack, during an attack, and whilst the scalping Knife is at work =

We had a pleasant walk back to the Inn. The Moon shone brightly, the evening was quite Calm, and Matlock and my Friends were all purity —

Our Tea was soon over, and the night so truly Inviting that in a Body we made for the River, entered a Boat and seated ourselves to

FIG. 19. "Matlock from the Hights of Abraham," October 14, 1826

Contemplate the Placitude around us = I rowed and I sung, up, down
& up the Derwent again, again on shore and again at the Saxton's Bath's
= I had all thy wares nicely packed up and, fearing that I might forget
the contents, I will now put down the whole —

1 Fruit Bowl —	£1.6.0
1 Bell Vase —	1.0.0
5 Boxes 4 bought by me —	1.16.0
1 Waffer Box —	1.2.0
19 Smelling Bottles —	1.19.0
10 Locketts —	<u>1.10.0</u>
	4.13.0

1 Inkstand given thee —
1 Salt Stand ditto ditto [MS: Dᵒ Dᵒ] —

We have now eat our supper and talk^d of our Departure of Tomorow
= I have seen thy Matlock and repeat it: it is most Beautifull!! = God
Bless thee. Good night, my Dear Wife =
I have no wish to forget that I bathed in the watters of Matlock =
The Baths are situated imediately under our setting room. That is the
Eastern one with a Large bow window thro which we could see the

stupendous rocks accross the River = The baths are built of White Marble and Vaulted. I thought them compleatly secure from my noise and splashes, but when I returned to the company, I was told that I was heard all over the House = a great proof, Indeed, that walls are no safeguard for secrecy =

Our Lady Hostess came last night to bid us all farewell and thank^d Mrs Rathbone very gentlewomanly = I Liked this =

MANCHESTER OCT^R SATURDAY 14TH 1826 —
MR DOCKRAY'S HOUSE HARDWICK =

Several times during last night I wished to get up, dress & ramble thro the Hills of Matlock, but the frost was too severe to enjoy such walks alone and I patiently waited untill I thought I might wake my little Friend David = We were running down along the Derwent by five o'clock. Nature was positively enclosed in a veil of sparkling congealed Dew = The Fog arising from the little stream only permitted us to see its watters where they, rolling against a rock, formed a Ripple. The vale was all mist and had we not known our positive situation & heard the Notes & the wings of the Jackdaws above us, we might easily have conceived ourselves travelling thro a Large Subteraneous avenue =

The strength of day gradually abated this {fainting} Curtain, and gradually the tops of the Tallest Trees, the Turrets of the Castle, and the church pierced thro and stood in our eye as if suspended and detached from all objects below = All was calm & pure untill a Bell struct our ear and we soon saw the long files of little Girls, Sisters & Mothers moving in a procession towards the Mills of Arkwright = We had but little time allowed us, and I returned to the Inn to write a few lines in my Yesterday Sheet =

Judge of my Dismay when after a close search for my Little Knife, I could not find it = pockets, Baskets, walks, the Boat of last night, we all in vain researched = I knew that I had mended this very pen with it during the writting of this Book, and that was alas all that could be known of it = Hannah Rathbone said in such [a] cold, uninterested manner that it was not worth pining after that I felt quite Irritated and again sorry fearing she might think that I ought to have been more Carefull = The Knife was lost and by me very much regretted = At seven we all were underway, and I passed the last Cottage of Matlock thinking of thy young days, of the sweetness of the spot, and of the great pleasure we would have had if thou hadst been *more positively* of the Party =

Anxious to see well, I & Sarah Dockray mounted in the Dicky but regretted it. The Cold was too severe for me and, notwithstanding the beauty of the scenery that accompanied us, I was heartily Glad when we reached Bakewell and still more so when we entered the well furnished, well warmed Room of the Rutland Arms. There a good breakfast soon reinstated us all, and had I had my little Knife in my Pocket, I would have felt quite well — I felt towards that knife a kind of Sentimental attachment. Indeed, I allways prefer objects like those given by a sweet female Friend, than all that money can purchase out of my own purse =

Travelling thro Bakewell I still liked its ancient look, its peaceable quietness and the simplicity of its Cottages, crowded together as if needing the support of each others = The Ivy, the wall Flowers and the little Boxes of *Reseda*[7] before the little leaden glazed windows made me wish to reside under their Mossied Roofs to feel the Happiness of the owners = We changed our rout and made for the well known Wattering place of Buxton, still in Derbyshire, the principal portion of which belongs to *his Grace* the Duke of Devonshire = The Country here is barren, Rocky but so Pi[c]turesque that the want of Trees is well balanced by the Grand beauty & Frisks of Nature displayed along the whole road = This winds along a very narrow Valey for several miles, bringing a vast variety of Detached bits of views extremely agreable to the sight = The natural Scantiness of vegetable matter forces the vagrant Catle to risk much to obtain their food, and now & then, when se[e]ing a Bull on bent knee with a streched neck putting out his tongue to nib the few grasses hanging over the precipices, made me dread for their safety = The Hawk here sails in vain; after many repeated rounds he is forced to abandon the Dreary Stoop, having only espied the swift King Fisher that in full security gives chase to the little minnows [MS: minoos] of the deep seated rivulet =

7. *Reseda* is a genus of numerous popular flowering plants common in the Mediterranean region and cultivated elsewhere. The best-known species are the mignonette (*R. odorata*) and the dyer's weed (*R. luteola*).

Here the view is quite Close. A high wall of shattered [MS: chattered] Rocks seems to put an end to our Journey, yet the chaise runs swiftly down the hill and, suddenly Turning a sharp angle, affords delight to our eyes by opening a new Prospect, quite as Wild, quite as diversified and Interesting as before = We all alight and walked to view more at Leisure the beauties around us = The Mosses are examined, the finest gathered and we see now before us the Pretty Village of Buxton. We all reach the large Building properly called the Crescent [MS: Cressent], and we meet the American Consul and Friend Maury = The Baths are all visited, in company with the Consul, but his age not admiting of his moving at the anxious rate needed on such occasion, when curiosity forces the body & mind onward with all its power, I felt anxious to be alone. My kind Friend Hannah knew this and procured an opportunity by advising me to accompany David Dockray to the Bath, and I flew on the wings of Extasy toward the Crescent again.

For one Shilling a man procures the Comfort of cleanliness in the Public Baths = for 3, in a private one, and for 2, Two persons have a room that admits of no greater numbers = They all are Comodious, Clean & well attended, but I found the heat of the atmosphere uncomfortable thro a want of Circulation of air = Mr Maury has visited this Place regularly each year for 25 past and has during that Lapse spent Just 2 full years of his time at Buxton = I saw his Lady = The beauty of this Place is not of that Nature that Interests me. One Day there and Twelve months at Matlock would suit me =

I heard of the Duke being gone to Russia to pay his respects to the Emperor. Thus god knows if I will ever meet him = We had what Travellers usually call a Luncheon. I thought it an excellent dinner. We left at Two = It was perceivable that since Bakewell we had been gradually descending. I had the pleasure of Hannah's Company in the Dicky untill the Drizle that is usually felt on these Hills made us exchange our Seats and we parted, I to enter the Carriage of her Mamma, & her, that in which Mr Dockray was = This Good Hannah gave me most excellent conversation and some advise and desired me particularly to see Mr George Barclay when in London =

As we drew again towards Manchester, the air became gradually thick with coal smoake, the population encreased, the Carts, the Coaches & Horsemen gradually filled the road = The female faces became less clean, less rosy, and the children had none of that live[li]

ness found amongst those of the Derbyshire Hills $=$ I involuntar[il]
y felt the general Diference opperate and gain on my thoughts, & I felt
the Cariage turn into Har[d]wick regretting, Mattlock, the Country,
the loss of my little knife and the approaching moment when I must
leave these excellent Friends about me. Lucy, during this most agreable
excursion I became more Intimate in Two Days with the aimiable
familly Dockray than ever I have done with any other in so short a time
— I called the Eldest Daughter "The Little Lady" and spoke to her as I
do to *Thee* $=$ The Mother, I assure thee, is one of the *Fairest* Specimen
of English female and most aimiable & kind. To view the Groupe I have
been in is enough to refresh from Years of Labour.

I wished to go and see how my Birds were: Mrs Dockray put around
my neck & wrists comfortables of her knitting and presented them
to me in a way that admited not of a refusal $=$ Am I not fortunate,
my Lucy, to possess such Friends in England $=$ Manchester is not
altogether a Umbrella Man Manufactory, and it is easier to find the
House of the Dockrays than to leave it when found $=$

My Drawings all safe, I returned here. My Friends in Liverpool
were all well. The good Mother had heard from all her children. The
kind Hannah mended my Gloves most neatly, and during the while I
finished for her the Little Sketch I had began on a card yesterday $=$ We
were all Happy. Mr Dockray enjoyed our return $=$ We supped and I
wish thee a Happy good night, my Lucy $=$

MANCHESTER OCT^R 15TH SUNDAY 1826 —

I went to Uniterian Chapel in Moseley Street for the purpose of hearing
a good Sermon delivered by the Revd John Tayler [MS: Taylor] $=$
However, he was gone into Derbyshire and I was obliged to content
myself with one from Mr Carpenter, but it was not quite as *practical* a
Sermon as I am fond of $=$ I saw Mrs Tayler [MS: Taylor], who with a
Smile Invited me to see her at her House that She would give me Letters
for Edinghburgh &^{c}. I also saw Mr Ewart & familly[8] $=$ Mr Maury
Invited me to go & spend the evening with him, but I felt no Inclination.

8. Peter Ewart (1767–1842) was an engineer who entered into a partnership with Samuel
Greg in 1793. After that partnership ended in 1811, Ewart developed another mill in Manchester,
where he investigated the mechanics of moving forces and published influential papers thereon.
Audubon carried a letter of introduction to Ewart from William Rathbone (see app. B).

I did not like to have perhaps to wait untill quite too late to Return to
my Friends at Hardwick = I returned towards my Lodgings, Enquired
for Parcels &ᶜ but was sadly disapointed. My Hopes that a Letter from
thee would have been there were ended = I reached Mᵣ Bentley,
Dined with him and familly, and was glad to find him and all about him
so kind to me & to each of themselves = When I reached Ardwick
[MS: Hardwick], Mᵣ Robᵗ Gregg was there & told me that he had sent
2 Parcels for me to my room = & that they were from Liverpool =
I pushed for Town, enquired again at my room, at Mᵣ Bentley's, all in
vain. I had no hopes to see the Parcels untill tomorow. I returned with
my little Friend David to Harwick quite Sick at Heart, and what ever
figure I made this Evening amongst my Friends, I cannot well tel[l], but
frequently I felt as if Tears were rushing from my eyes, and a Lowness of
Spirits so overcame me that I scarcely spoke to any one = My having
so few Letters from thee was very trying at this great Distance = I went
to bed early, I scarcely heard what was [MS: was what] read at prayers =
I thought of my Little Pen Knife over & over and Concluded that, even
amidst my kind Friends, sorrow made its way to me in spite of all their
best endeavours = yet, my Lucy, I bid thee good night!

MANCHESTER MONDAY OCTᴿ 16ᵀᴴ 1826. —

I left Mᵣ Dockray's early this morning intent on getting the longed for
Parcels. I went to the Exibition room and found, instead of Letters
from thee, my Album with a note from Mʳˢ Wᵃᵐ Rathbone and another
from Miss Agnes Greg — I felt myself fainting at the disapointment,
and to force my sorrows again I determined to do a great deal of
work by calling on almost every one I knew and ask for letters = I
was very fortunate at this and walkᵈ so much that it relieved me very
considerably. I was vexed that one of the Printers who had Inserted
some advertisements for me about my Birds had called during my
absence several times without receiving his Pay. I have no doubt the
Poor Fellow wanted it bad enough = I had promised to dine at
Hardwick to see my Good Mʳˢ Rathbone & her Hannah before their
going to Quary Bank = I read the notes from Mʳˢ Wᵃᵐ Rathbone
& Miss Gregg, that thro disapointment & sorrow I had put in my
Pocket without having scarcely glanced at either of them — They were

both kind notes and the little Pin Cushion from the Fair Ellen was carefully put up in my pocket book, fearing that it might share the like misfortune of my sweet Hannah's little knife, that came across all I did & thought of constantly = Whilst walking the streets this morning, I saw her Twice, but she did not see me. I was as busy as she was herself = I bid good bye to her mother, to all around the Table and herself, and moved towards the Door with Mr Dockray = Hannah rose from her seat and, coming to me, ask^d if my Knife had been found — I felt a blush, answered no, and was going to bow again to her when she gave me another Knife, My Lucy = I took it, scarcely look^d at her, and walk^d off not even making the Intended bow — but, Lucy, as I went, I Look^d at the Knife, and if I have not it whenever I meet her, I agree now never to use a Knife again =

I reached Mr Bentley by 4 of the afternoon. It had been agreed that he would accompany me to the Reverend John Clowes at Broughton Hall, 3 miles from Manchester on the Cheat[h]am Hill Road; we entered a Coach Known here by the name of The Flora and were going chatting together pretty generally when the Coach stop^d, the steps thrown down, and a Tall Figure of a Flora with a child in her arms came in & seated herself opposite me, and the child was put [by] my side = Her light colored hair hung more loosely about her forehead & neck than is generally seen now — The fairness of her Complexion & the placid blue of her large eyes attracted my eyes & my thoughts; I dare[d] not look at her again, and had not Mr Bentley been [MS: being] there, no doubt that I would not have even open^d my Lips = The Lady arranged herself Comfortably in her seat & the rustling of her deep purple silk Gown almost electrified me = Mr Bentley talk^d, however, and I answered to him. The conversation brought on many names of Persons about and in Manchester and, having said to Mr B. how much I admired the Familly Greg, the Lady ask^d me with an angelical voice if I was personnally acquainted with the Miss Gregs — I bowed an affirmative when she again spoke and told us that she had been a school mate to them, spoke of their aimiable qualities = of the goodness of their Father, of the Cleverness of their Mother in such delightfull manner that I felt as great a desire to thank her, for expressing herself so much to my wish as I ever did on such an occasion = I gave the little child by my side a few Pomfrets,[9] and dared ask if the Lady had seen Mr Audubon's Drawings. She replied no, but that she had a great desire to do so; then, my Lucy, as a Manchester Man, I Composedly took my Pocket Book out, & handed the Lady one of my Cards — She read my name, but all Her face so redened that I dreaded my having committed a very rude & Impertinent action — I was soon relieved from my aprehensions when she said she was very Happy to have the opportunity of se[e]ing me and paid me so many Compliments that at last thro diferent motives from the first, I wished my Card in my Pocket and my name unknown =

The Coach stop^d opposite her Door. She told me her name and I wrote down in my tablet Mrs Haihg, Cheat[h]am Hill = A man servant in Livery took the child and I lost sight of both in a moment. Her curtsy [MS: Cursie] proved to me as well as her language that she was an accomplished Lady altogether —

We soon reached the Lodge of Broughton Hall, ordered the Coachman to call at 7 & went in the Lodge. It rained and I had no wish that my Port Folio should feel the dampness — Every thing here was snug & Clean, chairs were handed us, umbrellas look^d for whilst I watched the Bubling Tea Kettle overflowing its spout = The weather is so changeable here that by this time, it was quite cleared up and we walk^d towards the Hall = entered a Garden, saw a Swan, an Eagle and at the Door of the Entrance, the Thermometer marking 53 of Farenight = The Master had walk^d out. Good Paintings ornemented the Lobby and the setting room, a little table was richly prepared for the Master's dinner, we seated ourselves on a Sopha where I thought, quite at Leisure, of the astonishing distinctions amongst men of Fortune, of Talents, of Power, and the miserable wretchess that pine thro the World in want of Nourishment = How much could this Gentleman, for Instance, might spare to help others; how much pleasure could he feel in doing so? — but, Lucy, a man 6 feet high with a square set body, a large hooked nose covering a good portion of an angular red face came in and I was Introduced to the Reverend J. Clowes of Broughton Hall =

9. "Pomfret" was short for "Pontefract cake," a licorice confection named for the town of Pontefract in Yorkshire, where it was originally made.

"I am not much of a Frenchman, ah ah ah ah" —
"A blustery evening this Sir, ah ah ah ah" —
"Take a walk in the Garden, Talk English, ah — he he he he."
"Fine eagle this, no watter this season, he he he he" =
I look^d at this wonderfull Laughing man untill I became so very
serious that I walk^d by his side more like an automaton [MS: otomatum]
than a Living Friend of Nature —
"Have dined, he he he he — walk about and come in bye & bye. I'll
to dinner, he he he he" —
I now thought this still more wonderfull. Had I come alone to
Broughton Hall, had I not had an Invitation from the Reverend J.
Clowes, I would have turned about face and reach^d Picadilly, I am sure,
without asking the way notwithstanding the Politeness expected from
the umbrella Manufacters = So here we were gazing at the objects
around —
I could not help remarking the structure of the old hall, the rookery,
the Pudle; I even visited the stable w[h]ere I found more fat on Two
horses ribbs than could be seen on those of a hundred of the spinners
of Manchester: — We reentered the hall much against my good will
= The Gentleman bid us take seats with a well fed set of ah ah ah's and
offered us wine & fruit — I drank, and I lessen^d, I saw & I thought, I
fairly shut up myself within myself wondering at the strange personnage
before me = Sometimes I met his sharp, fine eye. I saw penetration in
his glance, and his whole head signified much within of knowledge. He
spoke cleverly, is a good botanist and knows something of Birds, but it
would puzle him to guess what I thought of him = He told me he had
no acquaintances any where particularly, that he made Friends as he
moved along thro the World — I was on the point to say that, untill this
evening I myself had been as fortunate, but my tongue fortunatly laid
quiet & cool and I did not offend him —
He saw Clay's Letters. Dewit Clinton he knew not — He read aloud
a few words of Bonaparte's Letter to Baron Temminck[10] and, probably
perceiving the extreme composure and coldness of my manners, put an

10. Coenraad Jacob Temminck (1778–1858) was a Dutch zoologist. While serving as the
first director of the Rijksmuseum van Natuurlijke Historie in Leiden, he became a pioneering
biogeographer.

end to his fits of laughter and met my eye more frequently $=$ I at last heard 7 and bid him well. He did not ask me to call again and, depend upon it, I will here after know more of a Hall before I enter one $=$

Why should he have been so anxious to see me and receive me in this way? With thy knowledge of the World, my Dear Lucy, answer me —

The Bugle sounded a Call but we reached the Gates too late. The Flora had gone and I realized the great superio[ri]ty of manners betwen the Lady Haihg and this wonderfull new specie of clergiman $=$ We walk^d & talk^d of our reception. Mr Bentley had been disapointed but, as he knows the Reverend J. Clowes better than I ever will, he alone pleaded his defence $=$ I reach^d Manchester, supped with Mr Bentley and retired to my little room early $=$ I turned my Ideas over & over and could not conclude which of the Reverend Sir or thy Husband had appeared the most original to the very kind Mr Bentley $=$

MANCHESTER OCT^R 17TH 1826, TUESDAY $=$

I had my Trunk repaired Compleetly this day, purchased a neat Box of Razors and had a neat Comb neatly arranged in a case to be able not to borrow where ever I go $=$ I wrote a Letter to the Consul Saml R. Brookes of Thanks $=$ and prepared myself to go to Mr Robt Gregg to spend the night. I intended going to Quarry Bank tomorow when I was told that a Gentleman was now waiting to speak to me at Doct^r Holme — I went and Doct^r Holme himself proved to be the person — He Invited me in such a lively manner, so very kindly, to dine with many of his Friends, all Invited on my account, that I concluded to accept his offer and to write an apology to Quary Bank by adressing my Generous Good Friend Mrs Rathbone and I wrote the following —

My Dear Madam

I Intended fulfilling my promiss of se[e]ing you, your kind Daughter, and the aimiable familly at Quary Bank Tomorow, but an express Invitation from Dr Holme, that I would meet & Dine with several of his Friends, will force me to remit the pleasure to Thursday $=$

As you are best able to frame and offer an apology in my behalf, will you please to do so for me to M^{rs} & Mr Greg? To present my remembrances to the General Circle, and to believe me, my Dear Madam for ever your most obliged & most humble Ob^t Ser^t, J. J. Audubon

Mrs Rathbone Quary Bank —

I had scarcely finished this when I found that I was engaged to go & spend the Evening with the *Buxton Gentleman*, who had been at some trouble to procure some musical Friends to amuse me = What was to be done? I know not the *Buxton Gentleman* but he is very polite. I wish to go and again how shamefully I will treat Mr Gregg, whom I have now disapointed several times —

I took a shilling out of my Pocket and, whirling it up in the air, I left it to chance, giving Mr Greg the face of the King and the Buxton Gentleman the Arms of England. Those came uppermost and now, my Lucy, what will Mr Gregg think who knows, I am very certain, nothing of all this?

I had excellent music, vocal & Instrumental, Enjoyed the Evening extremely and went off at ½ past 12 just thinking of Mr Molineux's party at Liverpool, of the diference of this evening and that of last day = of Mr Greg and went [to] beg a bed at Mr Bentley, sure that my Lodgings must be shut up = His large familly and his little house were, I knew, just fitted to meet their number, but I knew him so good that I dreaded not giving him the extra trouble = All was arranged in a few moments, and he and I laid in the same bed = I told him that I prayed aloud every night and bid thee good night aloud also — What he thought of this I do not know but without any further ceremony I did bid thee Good night, my Love =

Yesterday, my love, Mr Bentley presented me with [a] Beautifull specimen of art & persevering patience — He gave me for our Dear Johny a Beautifull model of a 74 Gun Ship compleatly rigged, mounted with guns, under full sail, in a glass Case altogether 3 Inches long & about 2 broad = It was obtained at a Lottery for the benefit of a Poor French Officer at the Cessation of the last War and was then valued 30 Guineas — I Hope it will sail safely across the ocean and remind Johny, if he ever visits England, that this Land produces many Good Men, truly benevolent & kind to Strangers who behave as Good men of all nations ought to do — Again, sweet Wife, God Bless thee =

MANCHESTER WEDNESDAY OCT^R 18TH 1826 —

MANCHESTER WEDNESDAY OCT<u>R</u> 18<u>TH</u> 1826 —

I Breakfasted at M<u>rs</u> Dockray. Having much writting to bring up, the quietness of the place attracted me = I wrote untill about one o'clock whilst her Daughter and son drew by my side = I returned to Manchester where, with the assistance of M<u>r</u> Bentley, I accomplished many small undertakings = I reach<u>d</u> Doct<u>r</u> Holme's at 4 but was so surprised to find the setting room filled with Ladies & Gentlemen that I felt awkward for a moment = I offered to shew them some Drawings and about half past 5 we proceeded, each male bearing away a female to the Dining room; this novel way of taking a Lady under the arm is by no means disagreable. She frequently sets next to you and you feel a mutual Desire to please that brings allways a relaxion from the Custom of being stiff, unsociably carefull in the use of words, and allways makes me believe that I am before a high Tribunal of Justice than at a table to partake of good food & good cheer =

Amongst those names that I was told, I recollect only that of the Brother of Professor *Smyth* — his Wife, his Daughter and a Miss Harrison = Miss Smyth is extremely well looking, and the Young Gentleman who sat next her knew this fact quite as well as myself or any body present = I thought that the Ladies next & beyond her did not gaze at her with quite so much pleasure. We had already dined, the Ladies had retired and the Wine and Witt was {flowi*lly} going round when a servant entered and told me that 3 parcels had just arrived from Liverpool — Thinking of scarcely any other object than thee — I hoped to have Letters from thee, made a gentill excuse and went to my Lodgings —

The first Parcel was Directed for M<u>rs</u> Rathbone. The second contained 4 Flannel shirts for thy Husband and the third the Box of Sparrs that I purchased at Matlock for thee = My arms insensibly crossed each other and my eyes cast on the last parcel. I wished myself a Sparr ornement to be forwarded and bound to thee = I Could not return to Doct<u>r</u> Holme. I had no wish for Company — I went to bed very early, but before I bid thee good night, I must not omit to transmit no doubt the best act I did this day. — Whilst writting at M<u>rs</u> Dockray a poor woman, who no doubt is a constant visitor, called and soon made her

252   RETURN TO MANCHESTER

errand good — I saw with great Pleasure the mother ask the Daughter, who was purse bearer that day, to come to the entry — I heard the jingling of the shillings with a shaking, quick beating pulsation at my heart and got up, Joined the group, where humility was honestly bowing and Honestly without pomp giving — I also, Lucy, gave and returned to my writtings much better pleased than I was before = I will put up my old Clothes and send them to my good Friend Abigail Dockray and she will give them to the poor woman — Now with a good Heart, sweet Lucy, Good night —

QUARRY BANK 12 MILES FROM MANCHESTER,
THURSDAY OCT^R 19TH 1826. —

At six, my Cane in hand, and a small bundle under my arm, I made my way from Manchester bound and on foot to Quarry Bank; the morning was pleasant. I enjoyed my Walk very much untill I found myself quite out of the way leading to the spot I wish^d to reach; therefore instead of 12 miles I measured 16 — When I arrived, I was warm and hungry — Several of the familly were still at Breakfast. It was 10 — I shook hands all round the long table but, as I allways have done, felt pain that my venerable Friend Mrs Rathbone as well as the rest should get up from her seat =

My Hannah was well, the Fair Ellen and *La Belle Estrangêre* also = Indeed all were well = Mr Gregg was making love to his Lady as usual and as usual received me very kindly = I long^d for a walk with Hannah. I wished to talk to her alone but the weather altered. It rained and I rambled by myself after a Beautifull Rose that died on her Bosom —

I was soon put in requisition at Drawing and Drew the whole day — Those days spent amid such female groupes allways bring a calm to my mind delightfull to enjoy. I wish the parting at night might not come at all —

A nephew of Mr Gregg arrived from Ireland [in] time to Dinner — a Tall, Firm built youth of about 20 — The afternoon was spent first at sketching a Portrait of Mr Gregg. Mr Rathbone and his Lady sat opposite him, the chalk moved fast and I was quite satisfied of my work, but it was not so with every body Else. Faults were found and I Enjoyed the Critiscisms very much — It was however concluded to be finished the next day =

The weather fairer, a walk took place and I entered an English

Cottage = All about it was sweetly clean and regularly arranged — The Dairy especially = A short Distance from this another was visited. It was that of a Poor Silk Weaver. All, however, was well arranged & comfortable, and I saw there for the first time since I left France the weaving going on = We returned quite in the Dark — but enjoyed the evening exceedingly. The Ladies read & wrote Poetry for me and I Drew for them — La Belle Madam Grabant of Leghorn retired early. She had received a mandate from her husband to Join him at a short distance and all regretted her approaching departure = I gave Mr Gregg accounts of the Planting of Cotton, and wrote for him the names of many of our best Planters.

I was Induced to remain the night, finding myself so Happy & Comfortable and very desirous of finishing the sketch of Mr Gregg for his aimiable Daughter, Mrs W^{am} Rathbone = I then was accompanied to my little Chamber, bid thee good night and slept well =

QUARRY BANK OCT 20TH FRIDAY —

This day again was mostly employed at Drawing but, Lucy, I was most surprised at being presented by Mrs Gregg with a beautifull Pen Knife of 8 Blades and almost Imediately again another from Miss Agnes, and a beautifull Pin Cushion with a large Parcel of Pins for thee from the fair Ellen = Another gave me a little Book of Ridles and I at last found my Pockets literally filled with diferent articles = The pretty little plants on this sheet[†] were given me by the Sweet child of W^{am} Rathbone, her name Elizabeth = Mrs Rathbone was mortified that she had not the Turkey Seal for me yet =

We had a long walk and again visited a beautifull Cottage where, to my great surprise, I saw 2 Cases of well stuffed Birds. I had the kind Hannah under my arm nearly all this morning and also Miss Gregg (Hannah Mary), *a clever* Lady, I assure thee — possessing a commanding eye and a benevolent Heart = Fair Ellen had in the morning, before breakfast, lead me with her Sister Agnes to their Farm, where I saw the Finest dairy and handsomest Catle I have yet met with in England =

I finished Mr Gregg's sketch quite to my satisfaction — It was shewn to many of the servants, work people &^{c} — the observations of many of whom I felt exceedingly pleased at = *La Belle Italienne* had left us, was

accompanied to her carriage by all present — Her beautifull dark Eyes
wept with gratitude and those of the young Ladies with sorrow — The
Young Nephew gave me his Card and a pressing Invitation that I should
call upon him if ever I was lead to visit Ireland — He lives near Belfast,
his name Saml Gregg — Young W^{am} Gregg had wrote a pretty piece in
my Album and bid farewell to the familly and my Generous kind Friend
Mrs Rathbone = Hannah promiss^d to walk with me on the road to
Manchester — again, and Miss Agnes promiss^d to accompany her = I
retired to my room quite late and bid thee as usual Good Night =

MANCHESTER OCT^R 21ST 1826 SATURDAY —

As soon as I had swallowed 2 Cups of warm Coffee and a few slices of
Buttered bread, I left Quarry Bank. The 2 fair Companions had already
preceded me. I Joined them a few hundred yards from the Valey and
with one under each arm, three Roses in the upper button hole of my
Coat, we walk^d lightly on. The weather was pleasantly warm, the rich
tinted Leaves fell languid to the earth, the clouds had much of Wildness
in their Distributions, and the sun was as bright as in Louisianna.
Perhaps three miles had been reviewed when my Friends spoke of
parting = Miss Agnes bid me well and Happy and shook my arm
with Friendship ardour = I Turned to Hannah, met her brilliant black
eye, felt my heart swell, pressed her hand fervently and fervently said
"May God Bless You" = We parted. She wished me well [I] am sure
— Good Girl, how I admire her, how kind has she been to me — Dear
Hannah, may thou be for ever Happy = Thy Mother, thy Friends and
all about thee! —

I button^d close, put on my Gloves, sunk my hat deeper on my head
and Hurried towards Manchester — Arrived, I breakfast^d fast — called
on Mr Bentley, paid for my Trunk's repair £ 2.14, called on Mr Heywood,
took my money from his Bank, had a Letter from him to Professor
Jameson of Edingburgh = called on Doct^r Holme, who wrote three
more to Diferent persons, paid 20 visits and dined with Mr Bentley,
with his assistance pack^d up my Birds safe & snugg, walk^d to 20 more
places and felt so uncommonly fatigued that I determined to go to
Hardwick to stay the night with the Dockray familly — I found them
all well. I paid £ 2.10.4 for my flannel shirts and was again surprised
at my receiving a large Book purchased for me and presented me by

my Generous Lady Rathbone — Will this good Friend adopt me for one [of] her sons, I wonder? — For positively there is no end to her generosity —

I was thinking of what I have just wrote and what was to be written when I recollected suddenly how mortified I have been to day, when a Letter from Edward Roscoe was brought me from M̲ͬ Gregg's Office, to find that a small paper was Inside it with a Bill of Postages = I imediately sent John with a Sovereign, who brought a receipt of £ 0.17.4 but I felt mortified that M̲ͬ Greg should have *a Clerk* that was so far from possessing the *feelings* of his Employer =

M̲ͬ Bentley, to whom I am (I repeated) under many obligations, presented me with a nice foot rule for the Pocket — my name Engraved on it by the side of his — Lucy, M̲ͬ Bentley is a Brother Mason!! — I received at his house from a Gentleman who saw me exibit to his Daughters my little pack of Penn knives [MS: Knife], a most Superb one — the most beautifull I ever saw and as good as can be manufacterd = The handle made of Cocoa Nut shell; the whole strong, and made for Service = We chatted a Good Deal — "The Little Lady" thanked me for the silver port Crayon[11] I had given her = I drank several Glasses of wine with the good Quaker Dockray, his Wife and Benjamin Watterhouse and went to bed in a Superb room where, if I mistake not, my Friends M̲ͬˢ & Miss Rathbone slept whilst here = I prayed for thy Health, bid thee good night and went to sleep without a remorse at Heart =

A. DOCKRAY, HARDWICK, SUNDAY 22̲ᴰ 1826.

My Dear M̲ͬˢ Rathbone —

I write to you now, not only with a wish to thank you for the usefull Book that I found here for me — but for all your kind attentions — At your hands, under your roof, and thro your Introductions, I have now felt in England all that generous Hospitality, benevolence and warmest Friendship can bestow = I speak from the Heart. Never have I felt more; never did I expect it, so strong & powerfull is the reality impressed on the whole of my feelings, that I blush least I may

11. A porte-crayon is a split metal tube that can be tightened by a sliding ring around a drawing pencil or crayon.

never suficiently feel Gratefull to you and to the whole [MS: all] of your familly =

I arrived at Manchester after a delightfull walk, dressed my familly in their red coats, buttoned them all tightly and put over them a good slip of well oiled silk to preserve them from wet = I paid all my visits, and I Hope all my Debts, but felt so fatigued that I concluded coming here to rest and to write the whole of this day = I felt extremely mortified yesterday whilst packing my Manuscripts, when my eyes accidentally glanced over that portion of the week mentioning the Flight of Birds, at the astonishing mistake I made when I wrote down for you their velocity = Please to destroy the Memorandum and instead accept it more correctly now =

Swallows 2½ miles per minute, Wild Pigeons when travelling 2 miles per minute — Swans D⁰ 2 miles per m. Wild Turkey 1¾ D⁰.

My Body feels now quite a *superficial* degree of warmth = The familly Dockray is all well — Pray, remember me to all your Sons & Daughters — Again accept my thanks and believe me for ever with Highest Consideration and Estime Your Most Humble Obliged and Obedient Servant, J. J. A.

Mʳ Rathbone, Green Bank

My Dear Friend —

I could not bear the thought of leaving this Dirty Smoaky Town and removing to Edingburgh without leting you know that since I left you, I have enjoyed life in the most agreable, congenial manner Possible — My Journey to sweet Matlock with good Friends, the Ladies Rathbone & Dockray, is yet like a dream of enchantment. *One more female* would have made it Home to me quite —

Then, my Dear Friend, the time since spent at Quary Bank has been no less interesting: I left that last place with a pocket Literally filled with Pen Knifes given me not to {saver} friendship, but to mend pens — Permit me to mend mine now and take [a] pinch of No 37¹² = Now I want from John Chorley a little poem about those

---

12. Manufacturers of snuff numbered the different varieties or flavors. The numbers of the more popular ones would be familiar references among snuff takers.

same pen knifes — They are in one Pocket — all claiming supremacy and delirious to prove how much one might be prefered, more than the other — Hannah Rathbone's gift has powerfull demands on my feelings — It has 2 blades and is mounted in silver bright — Quary Bank is engraved on another and came to me from an Agnes — It has two blades also, but a round mass containing 8, the former property of Mrs Gregg, swears that he will cut & clash most Cruelly if not suffered to have his way first = A modest other, of cocoa nut handle, large, usefull, firm & Elegant, says that was he not in his opinion quite a *Gentleman,* he would demand the first cutting [MS: calling] of my goose quill — Now what is to be done, is best known to you — so set to, stir up the brains in the pan on your shoulders and send [MS: sent] me soon the desired object =

The silver pheasant (as if discon[ten]ted) attempted to fly the other day, positively started from his ground but fell imediately and I luckily caught him. I cannot think that he ever will again try such a prank. I positively had him nailed thro the body and held him faster than ever =

Remember me to Friends all — to Mother, to Sister, to Uncles & Brothers and rest assured that with Estime I am and Hope to be for ever Yours most attached Friend, J. J. Audubon.
John C. Chorley —
Liverpool —

My Dear Sir —

Will you permit me to Honor my list of Subscribers with your name and ask of your father in Law[13] if I may also his = I hope you will not feel offended. I have no wish to Call as a mercenary, but positively for the Honor of enriching my list with those names — I have some Hopes of forwarding my first number (size of Life, 20

13. Charles-Lucien Bonaparte married his cousin Zenaida, the daughter of Joseph Bonaparte (1768–1844), elder brother of Napoleon. After the banishment of the Bonapartes from France in 1816, Joseph eventually made his way to the United States, where he was living at this time on an estate near Bordontown, New Jersey.

Engravings) in about 4 months — You would oblige me much if you will send me a Copy of all Your observations on the Birds of Willson, your sinopsis &^{c} and a Copy of your Second Volume = Should you please to do so direct the whole to Messrs Rathbone Brothers & Co Liverpool — Pray, remember me to *our* Friends of Philad^{a} and believe me, my Dear Sir, Yours Truly Obliged Ob^{t} Servant — J.J. Audubon

(The same nearly to Dewitt Clinton, H. Clay, G^{l} Andrew Jackson, G^{l} W^{am} Clark)

My Beloved Wife —

I leave tomorow for Edinghburgh. My time at Manchester has not been productive = I visited Matlock in Company of my Generous Friend Mrs Rathbone, who made a Party purposely on my account, took me in her carriage and nursed me with Kindnesses = Matlock is beautifull truly — We were there 2 full days — passed & repassed thro Bakewell, & returned by Buxton = I have some sketches for thee and send thee now a Box of beautifull Sparrs = Some Plants collected about thy favorite Hills, and an Inkstand presented thee by Mrs Hannah Mary Rathbone = The Little Black Box, marked Matlock, is especially for Johny from Miss Rathbone, to whom I request he will send as quick as possible *a very small beautifull Drawing* = I forward him all my chalks. I Hope he will use them fast — The ship is for him and is beautifull. It is a present from Mr Bentley, who has been uncommonly [MS: uncomly] kind to me — He will write to Johny and I Hope Johny will meet his view = It may turn out quite an advantageous thing for John — The Plaster head is that of W^{am} Roscoe — The Piramid is the *Rock* of Gibraltar; the Pins & Little Cushion from Miss Ellen Gregg = The Gooseberries from the Botanic Garden, Liverpool — I will write to thee a Long Letter a few days after I reach the great seat of Learning = No Letters from thee, My Dearest Friend, and I cannot conceive why = I Hope thy watch has reached thee by this — The White Pitcher is from my Friend Miss Hannah Rathbone = I would like thee to write to Mrs Rathbone, for my sake, a kind Letter of thanks for her attentions to me. Remember that the familly is of the first Distinction, and extremely aimiable & Learned = Mrs R. is particularly desirous of knowing thee — The services she has rendered me can never be repaid — Direct Care of her Sons Messrs Rathbone Brothers & Co Liverpool and if thou canst accompany thy Letter with dried Plants, or a small keg of good nuts, large acorns, seeds &^{c}, she will receive those most gratefully = Farewell, my Beloved Lucy. Be Happy, be well, and believe me for ever Thine — J. J. A.

Remember to Mr Bourgeat
Mrs Percy's familly &^{c} &^{c}
I will be in London in a fortnight from now —

I have been writting all day, my eyes ache = I forward^{d} all the Letters to Richd Rathbone and Inclosed 5 pounds to him = but I have not the strength of Copying the note = I forward^{d} the Letter for Charles Bonaparte to W^{am} Rathbone = I took Tea at Mr Bentley, Dined at Mrs Dockray, but really cannot say more. Sweet, Dearest Friend, Good night =

MANCHESTER OCTOBER MONDAY 23^{D} 1826 —

This day was absolutely spent at Packing & making all ready. The great Confusion of my Letters & Papers required some time to put them again under a sistematic order. Mr Bentley, with whom I breakfasted, was of great service at such a work = My Box of Sparrs &^{c} was also well packed and directed to Mr Munroe to be forwarded from Liverpool thro the care of my Friends W^{am} & R^{d} Rathbone. Then my Trunk & Effects were all arranged, my seat in the Coaches taken and paid £ 3.15.0 to Edingburgh. I Intended calling on the Dockray familly but I found it [MS: founded] Impossible, and I merely wrote a note of thanks & apology =

Having found in my Trunk 2 of the Damask Sword beans, I thought the best present use that could be made of them would be to present them Inclosed to the reverend J. Clowes, whom I thought had received me so very civilly that no one else would be better entitled — I paid all my Debts, I believe. My Bill at Mrs Hedge [MS: Edge] was £ 5.2.0. I had only I eat a few breakfasts there; Poor Woman was sadly sorry at loosing me for I discovered that my Bill had maintained her and her children — I spent my Evening with Mr Bentley & familly; gave the young ladies each a handsome Pin Cushion, and they in return gave me a knife just one Inch long & young night thoughts — The coach is [MS: Coache's] leaving [MS: Living] before 5 tomorow. I went to sleep at the Inn to be called at the moment, thinking all done. I have only to regret that I left Manchester much Poorer than I at first entered it — May my Friends in it and about it be Happy — Sweet Wife, good night =

CARLISLE ENGLAND TUESDAY 24TH 1826 —

At 5 I had left Manchester, the morning was Clear & beautifull, but as no dependance can be placed on the weather in this Country, I thought but little of it — I was rather amused at the observations made about my Folio at the stage office = A Clerk there Laughed allmost as much as the Reverend J. Clowes, but the poor Fellow Lived *in Manchester* and consequently had not heard of either the owner or his Works =

I was alone in the Inside of the Carriage (for truly Coaches in England are very good) and had been there for some time lamenting myself and feeling much dissatisfied at having no Company when a very Tall Gentleman came in from the Top and said that he wished to sleep. He turned on his side *and* I look^d at him and envied his condition. Could I have slept also, I would certainly have preferred this to being now the Companion of a Drowsy Man = We rolled on, however, and arrived at the Village of Preston, w[h]ere breakfast was swallowed as quickly and with as much avidity as our Kentuckians usually do = Coaches were exchanged, baggage transferred &^c and I entered the Carriage to meet 2 New Gentlemen; their appearance was goodly, and to break on the silence I offered both of them a pinch of N° 37. It was taken by one and smelled at by the other — The Chat began and in less than 10 minutes we all had travelled thro America, part of India, Crossed the Ocean in New York Packets, discussed the Emancipation of Slavery and reach^d the point of [the] Political starvation of the poor of England & Ireland, the Corn Law — tranquilly going, peeping frequently thro each window — I saw little Girls running along the side of the Coach with nosegays Loosely fastened to a long stick and offered to Passengers for a Penny. I took one for a 6 pence and again resumed the chat =

At a little Village where the Horses were changed, it was discovered that a shocking [MS: chocking] smell existed on the Top of the coach. The man [who] is called the Guard spoke of it and told us that he could not keep his seat — I felt anxious to view the Country when still and got out to mount up and behind, but the smell was so Insuferable and the appearance of the man near whom I would have seated myself so far from being pleasing that I Imediately Jump^d down to take my Inside seat =

Judge of my Dismay, Lucy, when I was ask^d if *My Trunk belonged to me* and if it did not contain a Dead Body intended for Dissection at Edingburgh = I answered no, thou may be sure = The Guard smiled as if quite sure my trunk contained such a thing and told my companions that he would Inform against me at Lancaster; I bore all this very well. I was Innocent! I offered to open my Trunk and would have certainly done so at Lancaster but whilst we were proceeding, the Guard came to the door and made an apology, said the smell has been removed, and that it was positively *attached to the Inside parts of the Man['s] Breeches* who was on the seat by him = This caused much Laughter and many Course Jockes; *my subject* was a source of Conversation when every thing else failed = I became quite pleased with all my Companions. My being a stranger was suficient to be well treated by them, and Indeed what better mark of Superior Politeness, is it not, over all other countrymen = The English Gentlemen are Gentlemen at all points and in all Circumstances =

The approach of Lancaster is beautifull. The view of the well planted Castle is commanding. The sea seen from this also was agreable as it is bounded by Picturesque shores = We dined at Kendal, having passed thro Bolton & Burton, but before we dined at a stage before whilst the Horses were changing, my Companions were left behind and had to run for nearly one mile to overtake the Coach; this caused many altercations betwen the Gentlemen and the Driver & Guards, and one of the Proprietors, a Mr Saunders, who Interfered and who was unfortunately *rather* Drunk, made matters much worst. A Complaint was lodged against the Driver and he received no more shilling[s] from my Companions =

I saw & heard all very peaceably. Mr Walton, the Tall Gentleman who had slept so well during the morning, was extremely attentive to me = but the Messrs Pattison [MS: Patisson][14] from *Cornwall* were still more so. The Father Kindly gave me his Card and beg[ged] that I would call on him if ever I travelled in the south of England =

We now entered a most Dreary Country, poor beyond Conception, Immense Hills rolling one by the other in constant succession, spotted here & there with miserable Cotts, the residence of poor shepperds — No game was seen, the weather was bleak & rainy, and I cannot say that I enjoyed the ride at all beyond the conversation of my Companions. We passed thro Penrith and arrived at Carlisle at ½ past 9, having rode 122 miles = I was told that in hard winters the road became at times Impassable, choaked with snow, and that when not entirely obstructed it was necessary to see some Posts placed every 100 yards and painted black at top to be guided surely =

We had a miserable supper but good beds, and I enjoyed mine for I felt very wearied, my Cold & cough having very much Increased by my having rode some 20 miles outside to view the Country = I was praying and wishing thee well when Two female voices struct my ears and I discovered that the noise was close by my door = A conversation was kept low and undistinguishable for some minutes, when one of the persons began weeping and continued Increasing untill it became most piteously Hideous = I felt a strong Inclination to raise, to open my Door and to enquire into the cause when I recollected that it could not be about me and that consequently it was not my Business to Interfer, a part of conduct in man that I allways strongly will recommend to our Beloved Sons = The females at last retired into a room next me and the noise subsided. I felt fatigued and bid thee Good Night full of thoughts of apprehension for the future =

14. Alice Ford's identification of Audubon's Mr. Pattison as the physician Granville Sharp Pattison (1791–1851) is an error. The physician was from Glasgow, not Cornwall, and he had no children.

6

Edinburgh

We breakfasted this morning at Carlisle, Left there at 8 — but I was
sadly vexed that I had to pay 12 shillings for my Trunk and Portfolio as
I had been positively assured at the Coach office at Manchester that no
further charge would be made = I paid it, however =

For perhaps 10 miles we passed thro an uncom[e]ly flat Country,
meandering a while along a River, passed thro a Village Called
Longtown and entered Scotland at 10 minutes before 10. I was then just
6 miles from the spot where runaway matches are rendered Lawfull[1] =
The country changed its aspects; it became suddenly quite woody. We
ran along & 4 times across a Beautifull Little Stream, quite a miniature
of the Mohawk with us. Many little rapids were formed in its abrupt
windings. The foliage was about to die and look^d much as it does along
our Magestic streams of the West — This Lasted, however, only one
stage of perhaps 12 miles and again we came to the same Dreariness of
yesterday. Now & then a tolerable Landscape of Nakedness was open
before us, but the want of objects beside mere burnt mountains was
very uninteresting = The number of sheep grazing on these Hills was
very great and they all look^d well, although of a very small species, many
of them with Black Heads & Legs with all the Body White without
Horns = another species with Horns & some colors, and a very small
other called here the Cheviott = The shepherds were poor, wrap^d up

---

1. The Marriage Act of 1753 abolished common-law marriage and established strict rules for all
marriages in England and Wales. Parental consent was required for those under twenty-one, and
the marriage ceremony had to be conducted in a church. Since Scotland was exempted, young
lovers regularly traveled to the border village of Gretna Green for their nuptials.

in a thin piece of Plaid, and possessed none of that noble race so well painted by Walter Scot =

I saw the sea again to day = We dined at Hawick on excellent Sea Fish. There I [for the] first time in my life drank Scotch Whiskey = I suspected young Pattison wished to surprise me and make me drunk — I told him of this and the Father replied that probably it was to try if I would in such a case be as good natured as I was without — I thought this quite a Complement and forgave the son, but soon discovered that Scotch Whiskey was too powerful for my weak Head. I felt it for some time afterwards. I found the taste extremely agreable; some Scotchmen who were at table with us drank glasses of it pure as if watter — So much again for habit — We passed thro Selkirk, having during nearly the whole of this day travelled thro the Dominions & Estates of the Duke of [Buccleuch],[2] a young man about 20 who passes his days shooting Black Game[3] and his nights — Indeed, I really do not know how! — He has something like 200,000 pounds per annum = Some of the poor shepherds on this astonishing Estate have not probably more than 200 pounds of oat meal, miserable contrast; perdition of man in moral & Phisical points of view. Will this stand thus long? —

But, Lucy, I past so near Sir Walter Scot's place or seat that I raised from my seat and streched my neck some Inches to see it, but it was all in vain. I did not see it, and who knows if ever I will = We pass'd a few miles from Melrose. I had a great wish to see the old Chapel and the Gentleman to whom Dr Rutter had given me a Letter, but the coach rolled on, and at 11 o'clock I entered the Splendid City = I have seen yet but a very small portion of it, and that by Gass light, yet I called [it] splendid City — but this is not the time to say why —

The Coach Stopt^d at the *Black Bull* Hotel, but the Hotel was so filled with travellers that no bed could be procured — We had our Baggage taken to the Starr = The Clerk, the Guard, the Driver all swore at our Baggage and said that had we not paid at Carlisle, he would have

2. Walter Francis Montagu-Douglas Scott (1806–84) was thirteen when he became the fifth Duke of Buccleuch. His extreme wealth led him to impose a nearly feudal control over his tenants and their votes. Audubon leaves a blank space here to fill in later when he got the spelling for "Buccleuch."

3. The black grouse (*Tetrao tetrix*) was known as "black game."

charged me particularly 10 times as much as I had given $=$ Now, it is true that my trunk is large and heavy and so is the Port Folio I cary with me, but to give thee an Idea of the charges & Impositions connected with those coach owners & attendants, remark that *primo* I paid £ 3.15.00 — at Carlisle for baggage 12.00 — and during yesterday & to day to Guards and Drivers 18.6 Making — £ 5.5.6 for two days travelling from Manchester to Edingburgh — It is not so much the general amount, although I am sure it is quite enough for 212 miles, but the beggarly manners used to obtain nearly one half of it — To see a fellow with a decent coat on who calls himself an Independent free Born Englishman, open the Door of the Coach every 10 or 12 miles and beg for a shilling each time is detestable and quite an abuse, but this is not all. They never are satisfied, and if you have the appearance of wealth about you, they hang on and ask for more $=$

The Porters here were porters indeed, carrying all on their backs, the first of the kind I have seen since in this Island $=$ At the Starr we had a good supper, chatted a good Deal. The Messrs Pattison [MS: Patisson] were with me, but Mr Walton had made another course, perhaps never to meet again — It was more than one o'clock before I went to bed $=$ I thought so much of the multitude of Learned Men that abound in this Place that I dreaded the delivering my Letters tomorow $=$ I wished that thou hadst known at this very moment that I was positively bidding thee good night in Edingburgh $=$

THURSDAY OCT^R 26TH GEORGE STREET —

It was Ten o'clock when I breakfasted because I wish^d to do so with the Messrs Patisson, being so much pleased with their company $=$ During the breakfast I could not help observing the bombast and Impudence of some of the persons who were seated and walking in diferent parts of the room $=$ Some blowed their noses violently to attract others to view them; another whistled, whilst two more laughed to burst their lungs, and another again with an acquired phlegmatic air stirred a lump of sugar in a large Tumbler of watter $=$ each pleased and proud of himself, I have no doubt, all keeping the waiters skiping about with all the nimbleness of a Dormouse, but to Business —

My Companions who knew all about Edingburgh offered to accompany me in search of Decent lodgings and we proceeded; soon turned and enter^d the 2^d door in George Street (perhaps the most beautifull here) and in a moment made Bargain with Mrs Dicky for a fine Bed Room and a fine well furnished setting room = I am to pay here one Guinea per week. I considered it very low. The situation is fine; I can see from where I now am writting the Firth [MS: Frith][4] and the Steam Boats plying about = I had my Baggage brought here by a man with a tremendous beard who Imposed on me most Impudently by bringing a brass shilling which he said he would swear I had given him = I gave him another, threw the counterfeit in the fire and promised to myself to pay some little attention hereafter what kind of money I receive or give away =

I walk^d to Professor Jameson's[5] in the Circus, not at Home = James Hall,[6] advocate, 128 George Street, absent in the Country = Dr Charles Henry of the Royal Infirmary[7] was sought after in vain; Dr Thompson[8] was out also — & Professor Duncan[9] could not be seen untill six

4. The Firth of Forth is the estuary or arm of the sea at the mouth of the river Forth, on the south bank of which Edinburgh is situated.

5. After Robert Jameson (1774–1854) had studied natural history in Germany under Abraham Gottlob Werner, he became chair of natural history at Edinburgh University and remained so until his death. With David Brewster he cofounded and coedited the *Edinburgh Philosophical Journal* in 1819. Jameson continued as sole editor after 1824, when the title changed to the *Edinburgh New Philosophical Journal*, in which Audubon would publish two of his earliest natural history essays. When Audubon met Jameson he was under considerable criticism for exhibiting in the natural history museum only those specimens that supported his theories.

6. James Hall (1800–1854) was the younger son of Sir James Hall (see n. 61). Although he did not practice law after having studied it at the University of Edinburgh and being admitted to the Faculty of Advocates in 1821, he continued to identify with the faculty. In 1826 Audubon would have known him as an aspiring artist.

7. Dr. Charles Henry of the Royal Institute might be William Charles Henry (1804–92), the son of William Henry (1774–1836), the Manchester chemist. In the October 31 journal entry, Audubon refers to the letter that "Young Dr. Henry" will write to Thomas Allan. The letter is in appendix B; while it is directed to Allan at the "Royal Infirmary," it is signed "W. B. Henry."

8. John Thomson (1765–1846) was professor of surgery at the College of Surgeons in Edinburgh from 1804 until 1821 and professor of military surgery at the University of Edinburgh from 1806 until 1832, when he became professor of general pathology. He was known as an assiduous student and researcher.

9. Andrew Duncan, Jr. (1773–1832), became the first professor of forensic medicine and public health at the University of Edinburgh in 1807. As editor of the *Edinburgh Medical and Surgical Journal*, he was influential in shaping developments in public health and other matters of medical policy. He was known throughout Europe and maintained an extensive foreign correspondence.

o'clock = I only saw D.ͬ Knox[10] in Surgeon's Square and professor Jameson at the College = This latter received me I thought lightly — said that Sir Walter Scott was now quite a recluse, much Engaged with a Novel and the Life of Napolean and that probably I would not see him. = Not see Walter Scot, thought I — By Washington I shall if I have to crawl on all fours for a mile! — but I was a good deal surprised when he added that it would be several days before *he* could pay me a Visit, that his Business was great and must be attended to — I could not complain. I was precisely bent on doing the same towards myself, and why should I expect any other line of conduct? Why, my Lucy, because the World goes all against the streams and very crank sided besides; each needing help, and more anxious to receive than to give — yet not so with all: Look at my Friends The Rathbones — The Benevolent Familly, how I have been treated by them all! =

Doct.ͬ Knox came to me with only one eye; dressed with an over gown, and bloody fingers — He bowed, washed & wiped his hands, read D.ͬ Traill's Letter and, wishing me well, promised all in his Power, appointed tomorow to see me and my Drawings, and said he would bring some good Friends to Science to be Introduced to = Now, my opinion is that D.ͬ Knox is a Phisician of great merit and M.ͬ Jameson a Professor of great merit also, but that they act on Diferent principles, I am quite sure — The former does not deal in Birds but the Latter does, *I Guess*, although his principal study, I am told, is Mineralogy = but I have perhaps met him at a bad moment — I will draw no further conclusions untill I know more positively more of him =

I walk.ᵈ a good Deal and admire this City very much. The great breadth of the streets, their good pavement and foot ways, the beautifull uniformity of the Buildings, their Natural Gray coloring and wonderfull Cleanliness of the whole [MS: all] perhaps was felt more powerfully coming direct from Dirty Manchester = but the Pi[c]turesque *tout Ensemble* here is wonderfull, a High Castle, here, another there, on to a Bridge Looking at a Second City below, here a Rugged Mountain and there beautifull Public Grounds, Monuments, the sea,

10. Beginning in 1825, Robert Knox (1791–1862), an anatomist and ethnologist, was conservator of the museum of comparative anatomy and pathology at the College of Surgeons of Edinburgh. His lectures in anatomy were in great demand.

the Landscapes around, all wonderfully managed indeed. It would require 50 diferent good views at least of it or of its parts to give thee a true Idea, but I will try day after day in my humble way of writing to describe more particularly all that I may see either in the old or new part of this Town =

I could not spend the day without having a peep at my *own handy works*. I disengaged my Birds and look^d at them with pleasure and yet with a considerable degree of fear that they never would be published = I felt very much alone again and longed for some one to dispose to of my Ideas. Whilst at my Dinner, how much I thought of the Country that I have left behind, and of thee particularly. Some dark thoughts came accross my mind. I feared thee sick, perhaps lost forever to me and fell deadly sick — My Dinner was there cooling fast whilst each part I swallowed went down slowly as if choaking. I felt frequently tears about my eyes, and I forced myself out of the Room to destroy this painfull Gloom that I dread at all times and that sometime I fear may do more =

After a good walk I returned rather more at ease and looked at the paire of stuffed Pheasants on the large Buffet that ornements my present seating room; at the sweetly scented Geraniums opposite them, at the Black Haired Sopha, the armed chairs; the studying little cherubs on the mantle piece, the Painted landscape on my right, the Print exibiting Charity well appropriated by Free Masonry, and my own face at last in the mirrow in my front = I saw in it not only my own face but such powerfull resemblance of that of my venerable Father that I almost Imagined it was him that I saw = The thought of my Mother flew about me; my sister was also present, my young days. Those I have enjoyed with thee and those I have spent miserable from thee all were alternativly at hand and yet how far away — Ah, how far is even the last moment that is never to return again = but, my Lucy, such reflexions will not do. I must close my Book, think of Tomorow, yes, of the future that allways as we reach it evaporate[s] and becomes a mere yesterday, not thought of but with regret, if passed either right or wrong =

My sweet Beloved Lucy, God for ever bless thee. Good night —

EDINGBURGH SCOTLAND OCT^R 27TH 1826. FRIDAY —

I visited the Market this morning, but to go to it I first Crossed from the New Town into the begaining of the Old over the North bridge; went down many flights of winding steps, and at last reached the desired spot = I was then positively under the Bridge that no doubt has been built to save the trouble of descending & mounting from one side to another of Edingburgh, which is mostly built on the slopes of Two long ranges of High broken Hills = The Vegetable Market were well arranged and looked well, as well as the Fruits & Meats, but the low situation and narrow kind of Booths in which the whole was exibited was not agreable and, Compared with the Famous New Market of Liverpool, Nothing = I ascended the stairs leading to the New Town and seeing before me, after turning a little to the right, the monument in Honor of Nelson, I walk^d towards it and reach^d it — Its elevated situation, the Broken Rocks along which I went made it very Pituresque, but a tremendous shower of rain accompanied by a Heavy Gust of Cold wind made me hurry from the spot without being quite satisfied = and I returned *home* to Breakfast =

I was struct with the relative appearance of the woman of Lower Class with that of our Indian Squaws of the West. Their walk is precisely the same and their mode of Carrying Burthens also — They have a Leather strap passed over and poised on the forehead attached to Large Baskets without covers, and wadle thro the streets with Toes Inward just as the Shawanées, for Instance = Their complexion, if Fair, is beyond rosy, partakes indeed of Purple; its cold and Disagreable — If Dark they are dark Indeed = Many of the men wear long Whiskers & beards, are extremely uncouth of manners & still more so of Language =

I had eat my breakfast when Messrs Patisson came to see my Drawings and brought with them a Miss *Ewart* whom Mr P. senior said Drew *uncomonly beautifully*. I thought that according to Johnson this, if well applied, must mean a great deal, and I open^d my Book with a certain portion of reluctance — I thought I could soon discover if she *thought so herself* — Several drawings were looked at — She remained mute. Mr P. pronounced them surpassing all he had ever seen — I watched the Ladie's eyes and the Coloring of her fair cheeks. She look^d closer and said with a Smile that it seemed America would certainly surpass all the Countries in point of Arts & Sciences in less than another Century = Now, I shall not be alive then, neither my name recollected, and I still longed for an acquiescence from the mouth of the fair stranger — I thought that perhaps a Picture of Lovers would bring my wish to bear $=$ I turned untill I found my Doves and held them in a good light —

"How beautifull, Exquisitely beautifull! — How delighted Sir Walter Scot will be to see Your Magnificent Collection!" —

Now that I found the steam was High, that perhaps some exploxion might be produced, I exibited the Rattlesnake attack[d] by the Mocking Birds[11] — This had the desired Effect — The Lady was pleased & I was satisfied that she drew well $=$ M[r] P. said that M[r] Selby[12] never would publish another Bird was he to see mine $=$ We parted all Friends; I having begged of each of them to bring or send any of their Friends to View my Work any morning from 10 untill 12 $=$

I called again at D[r] Thompson but, Monsieur Tomson not being at Home, I left the Letter and my Card $=$ The same at Professor Duncan, and walked to Fish Market Close [MS: clloce],[13] High Street, Old Town, where I found Patrick Neill Es[qr][14] at his Desk, after having passed betwen 2 long files of Printers at their work $=$ At first the Gentleman (if I mistake not) believed that the Letter I handed him was an advertisement for Insertion, but after having read it, he shook hands Cordially, offered me his services & proved to me in a few words that he was a Gentleman and a very Clever one $=$ gave me his adress at Home, promiss[d] to come and see me, and accompanied me to the street, Begging of me not to Visit the Museum untill Professor Jameson had sent me a General Ticket of Admittance. He said the Professor would feel Hurt at my paying for it &[c] &[c], and I felt towards M[r] Neill a great deal of Estime $=$

Now it was one o'clock; I returned to my Rooms, eat a Lunch, Drank a Tumbler of Scotch Grog, and, determined to see a good deal,

11. This drawing became Plate XXI of *Birds of America*.

12. Prideaux John Selby (1788–1867) was an ornithologist and illustrator; his *Illustrations of British Ornithology* would be published in nineteen parts between 1821 and 1833. Selby was in the beginning stage of his collaboration with Sir William Jardine that would produce *Illustrations of Ornithology* (1836–43).

13. In Scotland a "close" is a passage or entryway that leads from a street to houses, stables, or the different floors of a building; by extension, "close" can refer to a court, lane, or alley to which the entryway leads.

14. Patrick Neill (1776–1851) was a printer and travel writer with extensive interests in botany and zoology. He held memberships in scientific societies to which Audubon aspired.

proceeded toward the Port of Leith, distant not quite 3 miles — Having missed my way, I reach^d the Firth [ms: Frith] of Forth at *Trinity*, a small village on that Bay from where I could see the German Ocean's Watters. Opposite me the shore of Fife was Distant about 7 miles, Look^d Naked & Hilly (Fife happen[ed] to be the name of my Landlady in New York in 1823 —)† — During my Walk here, I frequently turned round to view the Beautifull City back of me, raising in Gradual Amphitheatres most sublimely and back^d by mountainous Clouds that Improved the whole really Superbly = The wind was high, the watters beat the shores violently, the vessels pitched on their anchors, all was grand! On Enquiry I found that this was no longer an Admiral's station, and that in a few more weeks, the steam boats that ply betwen this & London & other Parts of the Northwest of this Island would stop their Voyages, the Ocean here being too rough during the winter Season =

I followed along the shores and reach^d Leith in about 20 minutes. I saw a very pretty Iron suspended Jettée of 3 arches, at the extremity of which steam Vessels & others land their Passengers & Freights = Leith is a Large Village apparently mostly connected with Hamburgh and other sea Ports of Holland; much Business was going on = I saw there a great number of Herring Boats and the netts, for capturing the Fishes = also some curious Drags for Oisters, Clams & other shell Fish = The Docks are small and contained mostly Dutch Vessels of small sizes = An old one is appropriated as a chapel to mariners =

New Heaven,[15] & not that New Haven planted on the shores of the Conecticut River ornemented with diversified colored buildings of wood where thou first put thy foot on the Happy continent of America and gamboled around its famous Colege and thro its extensive salt marshes — not the New Haven where thy Father Lost his Large Brewery by Fire and where each youthfull Girl has cheeks better colored than even the Peach blossom. No, my Lucy — it was only a Place bearing the same name but possessed of not one of its embellishments — a small village only of white stones & not very clean, built there one would think to remind the traveller that he will

15. Newhaven is on the west end of the Port of Leith on the Firth of Forth. Its fish market was the heart of a fishing community.

not allways meet with such a Place as Edingburgh or the sweet village on the Sound[16] — †

Gradually again I approach[d] Edingburgh, was walking slow and viewing the beautifull scenery around when a Woman extremely well Dressed accosted me, and with good Language & a soft voice told me that she was very poor and much in need, offer[d] to do any thing for me for a little money — I thought this a stranger way of craving charity than any thing I had seen yet — I told her that, being a perfect stranger and without change, I beg[d] she would not either stop or follow me, and went away fast — yet not quick enough, for I heard her *Damn me* as plainly as could be = This is a Lesson I shall not forget, depend on it. I after this knew well what sort of a woman this wretch was, and how guarded I must be in my Generosities =

The sun was set. I returned to my Lodgings to Inform my Landlady that I was going to the theatre and that I wish[d] not to be shut out = She answered politely that she would wait my Convenience and, having left my Purse, my Watch, my Pocket Book & even my Pocket handkerchief [MS: Hdf], I took my Sword Cane, and off I went to see Rob Roy. The theatre not opening untill ½ past 6 precisely, I entered a Book sellers shop, ask[d] for Prints to look at, and purchased for thee a Map of this Town ornemented with 18 Views of the principal & most Interesting objects about and in it = I gave an order on M[rs] Dicky for 5 shillings and forward[ed] it to her = I read accounts of the Palace & Chapel of Hollyrood and also of Roslyn Castle and was at the Door of the Pitt[17] at the Lawfull Instant = It was crowded by Gentlemen & Ladies, for, my Dear Lucy, Ladies of the 2[d] class go to the Pitt — the Superior Class to the Boxes and those of neither, unfit to be classified, way above — The House is very small but well lighted; many handsome females ornemented it = God Save the King was the overture, when everyone rose uncovered; I Wish we allways had

16. New Haven, Connecticut, is situated on the north shore of Long Island Sound. Lucy's father moved their family from Burton upon Trent, England, to New Haven in the fall of 1802 because he had invested in an ale brewery with his brother. Although the brewery was lost in a fire, it is evident from Audubon's tone that Lucy had pleasant memories of her first home in America.

17. The "pit" is the main floor of a theater.

Hail Columbia Happy Land, with us, or Washington's March on such occasions. It would almost daily Impress the mind of our Citizen[s] of our Noble Institutionial Constitution = but to Rob Roy =

It was represented as if positively in the High Lands, the characters [MS: Caraters] were good and Natural, the scenery perfectly adapted, the Dress, the Manners & Language quite true — I may safely say that I saw a good Picture of the Great Outlaw, of his Ellen, and of his unrelenting Dougal, as ever could be given = I would, were it Possible, allways see "Rob Roy" in Edingburgh = "Le Tartufe" in Paris and "She Stoops to Conquer" in London = The first exibited, if in America, is quite a Burlesque; we do not even know how the Hardy Mountaineer of this rigid Country throws on his Plaid or wear[s] his Cap, or his front Piece, beautifully made of several tails of the red Deer — neither can we render the shrill tone of the Horn bugle that hangs at his side; the merry Bag Pipe is wanted also and also the scenery = I would Just as well be punished with the 2ᵈ in broken French by a strolling company, as to see the first again as I have seen it in Kentucky, for Instance = It is allmost to be regretted that each Country does not keep to its own productions — To do otherwise is only Infatuation and leads to Inforce on minds, Ideas as far diferent from truths as Day is to Darkness =

I did not stay to see Rosina[18] — Although I liked Miss Stephens[19] pretty well, she is by no means equal to Miss Foote. Her Appearance is too attempted, her voice is not sweet but much affected, and I left her & the House at ½ past 10 extremely pleased with Rob Roy — his Ellen, his Dougal, the Magistrate and his Matté —

It is now late and very Cold. My Landlady has brought me some warm watter to make a Glass of Grog again. She says it will do my Cough good — God knows = Dearest Friend, Good Night =

18. *Rosina* is a two-act afterpiece by William Shield (1748–1829) consisting of spoken dialogue and numerous balladlike songs.

19. Miss Stephens is probably Catherine "Kitty" Stephens (1794–1882), a London singer and actress who performed throughout the British Isles during the off-season. Her brother, Edwin Maxwell Stephens, whom Audubon mentions meeting with Miss Stephens in the November 5 entry, traveled with her and acted as her manager. Ford identifies Miss Stephens as "Jane Stephens (1808–1850), popular actress" (*Journal*, 311n12) (for Maria Foote, see n. 45, chap. 2).

I have Just time to Copy the following before I go to deliver it to the Dread of all Writers, the famous Francis Jeffrey Es^{qr} — .[20]

45 York Place 28, Oct. 1826. —

My Dear Sir —

I take the Liberty of Introducing to you Mr Audubon, who has come to Europe with a most magnificent & truly Scientific collection of drawings of The Birds of North America — His Letters of Introduction are of the Strongest description & from what I have observed, he seems deserving of them — I have no doubt that you & your Friends will be highly gratified by seing the Productions of his Pencil.

I remain yours most Truly —
Andrew Duncan Junr —

Francis Jeffrey Es^{qr}

My Dear Mr Bentley —

Although I have positively but little to say, I set to to write this more to fulfull my promiss and to have the pleasure of enquiring how you all are than persuaded of its being either very agreable or advantageous to yourself =

My Journey here was pleasant. I had Good Company in the Coach and fared well — I was pleased with some portions of the Country, but since in this Island I have seen nothing to compare with this Beautifull Edingburgh = I have done nothing yet in my way of Business and, although I regularly delivered all my letters, only one of the Persons has called on me. The setting in of the Lectures &^c

---

20. Francis Jeffrey (1773–1850), famous for his unrestrained and often savage literary reviews, was cofounder and longtime editor of the enormously influential *Edinburgh Review*. He was also known as a vocal Whig and an attorney who actively exposed abuses of executive power.

renders all the professors too busy to come and see only the Birds of America = I now send you a list of such Birds as I think my son John can procure for you =

Pray remember me kindly to your Young Ladies & M̲r̲s̲ Bentley and believe sincerely Yours truly obliged Friend, John J. A. — Here followed a *whole letter*

M̲r̲ W. H. Bentley
S̲t̲ Mary's Gate, Manchester —

My Dear John —

I now write to you from the place where I wished most you could have been educated — It is a most beautifull City, perhaps the most so I ever have seen. Its situation is delightfull, not far from the sea, running on Two parallel Hills, ornemented with highly finished monuments and guarded by perhaps Impregnable Castles = The Streets are all laid at right angles in that portion of it that is called the New Town = are built of fine houses of 4, 5, 6 & 7 stories, are cleaned and well paved and all lighted by Gass Lamps =

I have been here now Three Days. I came from Manchester in a public Coach that carried 4 Inside Passengers and 10 outside, or rather on the top, besides a Guard and a Driver and all the Luggage of the parties = I sometimes stay^d in and sometimes rode outside to have beter views of the Countries I travelled thro — Now & then I saw some fine English pheasants that you would delight in killing = and some curious small sheep with black heads & feet only, the remainder being white, and some of those pretty little poney's that you are so fond of = I wish I could send you one =

Before I left Manchester I visited Mattlock, Bakewell & Buxton, all Wattering Places, in the carriage & company of an old Lady named Rathbone & her Daughter and several others, all Quakers and all extremely kind to me = The daughter of M̲r̲s̲ Rathbone purchased & sends you a beautifull little Black Box of Mattlock Marble or Sparr, and her Mother, a beautifull Inkstand of the same materials for your

Good Mamma — I forwarded them with great many others and also diferent things for you Both the day before I left Manchester = to the care of Mess.rs Gordon & Forstall, New Orleans —

I was very much pleased with all the places I saw and wished very much that you and Mamma had been with us to enjoy the Journey; we all spoke frequently of you both & brother Victor = To day I have visited the Royal Palace of Holyrood compleatly — was in Queen Mary of Scots rooms and saw her bed, chairs, tables &.c. I look.d at my face in the mirror that once was hers, and I was in the little room where the murder was comitted — It is very curious — I also saw the chapel where the queen was maried and the spot where she prayed = also Paintings of all the Kings famillies of Scotland = the appartments where the present King of France resided during his Exile and the fine rooms w[h]ere the King of England, George the 4 was four Years ago when he visited this Country =

The women of the low class who labour hard for their living here carry burthens Just as our Squaws do in Louisiana in a Large basket behind and a Leather strap coming from it to their foreheads =

I bought for you & Mamma 18 views of diferent Parts of this City that I will send when I make up another Box from London = In a day or 2 I will see Roslyn's Castle and afterwards go to Melrose to see the chapel there and call on Sir Walter Scot, the great novelist = I hope you will be good to your Dear Mamma and do all she bids, Draw [a] Great Deal and study Music also, for men of talents are wellcome all over the world =

Talk about all your little affairs when you write to me and send me a Long Letter and tell Mamma she does not write often enough. I have only received 2 Letters from her since I landed in England =

M.r Bentley of Manchester will write to you to send him Bird Skins &.c. If you do it well, he will send you what ever you please to write for, either Books or any thing Else = Remember me to all the young Ladies = Little Charles, Bourgeat &.c &.c and believe me for ever Yours most affectionately Father & Friend — J. J. A.

And thou, my Sweet Wife, I Hope thou art well and Happy = I will write to thee as soon as I have seen more of my learned Acquaintances here = for ever thine and may God Bless thee, thy

Husband & Friend $=$ I will send thee my Journal up to my arrival
at London. It will be there Interesting — I have more over ask^d
if I might or not write to Mrs Percy — Keep directing to Messrs
Rathbone Brothers & Co Liverpool.

My Dear Madam —

As I stood this evening quite late, silently & lonely looking from
within at the shattered [MS: chatered] remnants of Holyrood chapel,
I could not help remembering my pleasure I felt at Liverpool when,
guided by You and your kind Husband, I saw there the powerfull
beauties that pencils well tutored can render — I compared the
Efforts of [the] arts of Free Masons at their early age, with those of
the Painters of the Present day and Lost myself in a Labyrinth of
uncertainty, not knowing whom I ought to give preference, either as
regards Taste, Powers of comprehension — or those of Execution $=$
Those thoughts caried me back Instantly to Woodcroft and reminded
me of how much I was indebted to you & your Husband, and the
pleasure I would feel by thanking you this evening for the Pretty
black chalk sketches [MS: scke*t*s] you have been so good as to send
me in the Album $=$ The Album again convinced me that I ought to
have wroten especially to thank my Good Friend Mr Rathbone for
the many usefull hints contained in his piece $=$ Please assure him for
me that
    "England although once unjust to my Country
    "England has not been unjust to me"
will never be forgotten $=$ Then I again Look^d at the little boy
praying, and thought how well you would draw, could a Mothers
attentions to a lively brood be put aside a short while daily $=$
    I have found Edingburgh far more beautifull than I expected.†
Its Cleanliness almost equals that of our Philadelphia, and its
picturesque site far surpasses it. I allways was fond [MS: found] of
plain appearances, and the Greyish *Friendly* color of the Buildings
here is very much more congenial to my feelings than either red
painted bricks or the sooty [MS: sutty] overcast that hangs about
Manchester, for Instance $=$ There is a wildness expressed in all of

its component parts as well as its *tout ensemble* that agrees precisely with the Ideas of a Man of the Woods. I can ramble here in company with grand Nature, and cast an Eye of admiration on the powers of man so very alternatively that more pleasure accompanys me in my Excursions in and about this City than ever I yet had felt on like occasions. It brings to view many Groupes of diferent figures so well managed in one large picture that you are pleased at each of them, attracting singly, as well as when, with a cool Judgement, no fault can on the whole be found = (Such a hand I do write that, notwithstanding a compleat assortment of beautifull knifes, not a Pen can I make that will mark legibly —)[+]

T'is no wonder indeed that the Scotch Kings sought the spot = None other could be better suited either to protect them or afford them repose,[+] and how the round Monarchs of France must have fattened on the sweet Black headed sheep that ramble over the Heath = I was also very much delighted when, on my way here from Manchester and about 15 miles from Carlisle, I entered Scotland following the meanderings of a compleat miniature of our Mohawk river = Many little rapids ornement its abrupt windings, and the Foliage about to die look[d] much as along our Magestic streams of the West — It remainded me of the most agreable tour your Generous Mamma procured me to, about & from Matlock; I was admiring Nature here, and the goodness of her heart in her every movements when sudenly entering amongst high, bleak, naked Hills, I found myself *quite alone*, rolling fast away from the best Friends I ever had [away] from my Home =

Two aimiable Gentlemen of the name of Patisson from Cornwall, one accompanying the other (his son) to this Place, were polite & very kind to me, either in the coach or where ever we stop[d]. We soon understood each others, and since here they have rendered me valuable services, but this reminds me that I ought to tell you that near Lancaster I was on the Eve of being arrested, and my trunk open[d] & examined on the suspicion that it contained a dead subject for anatomical researches going to the learned of Edingburgh — My poor *chevellures*[+] went against me [so] that every one said I was an eminent Foreign Phisician = I offered to open my trunk, but one of the outward passengers having left us shortly after this, the

Insuferable odor complained of went with him and apologies were made me =

I liked the appearance of the Castle at Lancaster but sets a {Pa***e} for those within. On the whole my Journey has been suficiently agreable = The Colleges will soon be in *full bloom*. Students are arriving from all parts of the World, and in a few weeks this town will be seen at her best in point of society. I would prefer, I must acknowledge, the atmosphere warmer by 30 degrees than it will be either then or now, for altho wrap^d up as carefully as a sufering Infant, the cold enters me at every pore =

I am extremely agreably lodged at N° 2 George Street, where some of the first People here have already visited the Birds of America = Unfortunately for me, however, a Letter from my Good Friend Dr Traill proved to be adressed to an eminent man who is himself engaged in a Publication of an ornithological nature and *Consequently* (I am Told) received me not very warmly = I, indeed, fear that he will not even call to see my Drawings — Yet I never made them with a view to offend any one, but with a great wish to please all.

The pleasure of writting to you, or as you were please[d] to say, to "*Woman-Kind*," has kept me at it, untill I fear your patience will suffer. Then, my Dear Madam, permit me to beg of you to present my sincerest and most kind remembrances to your good Husband, to your Mamma, Your sister Hannah and Mrs E. Rathbone: to your brother Mr W^am Rathbone, and to Mr Theodore Rathbone, my humble good wishes. The pleasures you all must have felt at his arrival I can partly conceive, and that of his Conversation I would like, in company with you all, to enjoy. =

If you please ever to grant me the honor of an answer, will you remember that I was once bid to expect a Joint one — Sweet Little Bazil and all his little relations are, I Hope, quite well = Wishing you & yours, my Dear Madam, Health, prosperity & a continuity of the sociable pleasures I have seen you all enjoy — I remain for ever most Respectfully Yours much obliged & very obedient Ob^t humble Servant J. J. A^t

Mrs M. H. Rathbone
Woodcroft =

Dr Thomas S. Trail.

My Dear Good Sir —

I do not write to you because I have much matter on hand, but because I began feeling ashamed of not having done so before: When at Manchester I saw Mr Bohn, and he examined my Drawings Closely. What will you think and say when you read here that he is of opinion now that the work ought (if at all) to come forward, *The Size of Life*? — He said more, for he offered to publish it himself if no one else would undertake it, but as I *need the needfull,* I did not Jump at his offer = *He again desired that I should* see him in London and I certainly shall = I am anxious and will try very much to have a few lines from Sir Walter Scot to some one of note in the Metropolis and will be there after having spent a few days with Mr Selby: Professor Jameson is, I find, Engaged with this Gentleman and others in a large publication, and Mr Edd Roscoe, to whom I will write this morning, advises me to Connect myself with them =

Will you write me Imediately and give me your views on this subject? — I must acknowledge that my Independent spirit does not brooke the Idea with any degree of Pleasure, and that I think that if my work deserves the attention of the Public, it will stand on its own legs as firm as if joined to those of men who are no doubt far my superiors in point of education and literary acquirements, but not so in the actual courses of observations of Nature at her Best — in her Wilds! — as I positively have done. = Yet, as I am but an Infant entering the Great World of Man, I wish to be submissive to its ways and not stubornly raise mountains betwen my connections with it and my own Interests.† It is for that very reason that I beg your opinion as one that I look upon as extremely valuable =

Please present my humblest & best respects to Mrs Trail & familly = Remember me to our Good Friend Wam Roscoe, the familly Rathbone and all others who have been so very kind to me and believe me, my Dear Sir, Yours Much Obliged Friend & Obld Servt — J. J. A.

Please direct care of Patrick Neill Esqr —

It is very perceivable, my beloved wife, that as I Copy allmost every scrap of Letters or Note, that I write purely for thy own sake when absent from thee, that as my corespondance Increases, so must my mannual Labours == It is now Sunday night, and at the Exception of a few minutes walks taken to carry my Letters to the Post office, *I* have been as busy as a bee all day ==

Yesterday at 10, Messrs Patisson brought 12 Ladies & the Messrs Thomas & John Todd of this City to see my Drawings; they remained with me a full 2 Hours == Professor Duncan came in during the Interim and is truly a kind Friend == Mr Patisson proved that I was right about Professor Jameson, for this Latter is most positively engaged and connected with many others with ornithological publications — never the less I will have fair Play if I deserve it, for although there exists heavy taxes on Windows in this Country, still I, being a free man, will have my share of the Sun when shining ==

After my company had left and I had been promised several Letters for Walter Scot, I took a Walk and Entered a Public Garden, where I soon found myself a Prisoner and from where, had I not found a pretty maid who took pity on my *Etourderie*[21] and praised my Curled Locks and called me the Handsome Stranger, I certainly would have felt very awkward as I had neither pocket Book or any Letter to show == This proved to me that Women were most undoutedly Intended for the comfort of Men and in that Instance again superior, for this one had the Key that gave me Liberty! —

I then went in search of the richest Scotch [MS: Scocth] Peble that could be found but saw none suficiently superior to be bought for thee. One for an Instant attracted my fancy, but a child in the shop [MS: chop] said his Father could *make another* still handsomer — I open^d my Eyes and made way towards the street. I wanted not Pebles made by Man == I wanted them the result of Time and of Natural Invention — As I was going off, the man of [the] shop went out also. I watched him turning a corner and returned to this house to inquire how handsome pebbles were made. Without hesitation the Boy answered *"by fire heat,"*

21. An *étourderie* is a careless mistake or instance of thoughtlessness.

and whilst the pores of the pebles are open, colored Infusions are Impregnated frequently with a surprising Effect — Now what will not man do to deceive his Brother?

This account of the Pebble Maker made me forget to say that Mr Jeffrey was not in, that he comes from his Hall 2½ miles off, every day, from 2 to 4 o'clock of the Afternoon. Therefore, I entered his *Sancto Sanctorum*, sealed the Letter and wrote on my Card that I would be Happy to see him = What a mess of Books, papers, Letters, port Folios & Dirt; Beautifull Paintings, Engravings & Casts, with such parcels of unopen^d packets all Directed Francis Jeffrey Es^{qr}. Why, Lucy, the People are crazy when they say that I have done wonders to produce so many Drawings, and what have I done? compared with what this Man has, and has to do! — I much long to see that Famous Critic to watch his penetrating Eye measure the depth of my understanding = All knowledge now seems tending to the knowledge of the Head, by outward appearances of the composition within = I wish more Philosophers would examine Hearts and try to Judge of and Improve them =

My Letter to John shews thee that I Visited the Palace of Holyrood, its every room and antichambers. What a round of Diferent Causes have brought Kings after Kings to that spot, what horrors have been comitted there. The General structure is not of a defensive Nature. It Lays in a Valey now dividing the Old from the New Town and has simply its walls to guard it = I was much surprised that the small stairs by which the Conspirators arrived at the little chamber where the murder was comitted, communicates at once, with the open Country and without any means of defence. Could it have been merely to afford the queen opportunities to receive friends at once to her Imediate Bed Chamber? or give her free admittance to walk abroad? — I was also surprised to see that her Mirrors were positively much superior to any of the present day in point of Intrinsic purity of reflexion. The Plates cannot be much less than ¾ of an Inch in thickness = The furniture is all decaying fast as well as the Paintings that are all Incrusted into the walls =

The Great room for the Kings audience contains a Throne by no means coresponding with the Ideas of the *Luxe* that I thought moved along with his magesty where ever he goes = The whole, however, being hung in bright scarlet cloth had a very warm Effect, and I thought more than once during my stay, that it would be a capital Room for my Drawings to be exibited!!!

From there, where I paid 5 shillings to 5 Ladies who attended me, and called out names of every articles I saw = I asscended a long high Hill untill I had a splendid General view of the whole City, country & Sea around for miles. The more I look on Edingburgh, the better I like it = On returning I ransacked much of the Old Town where the Colleges, Museums &ᶜ are and where the great Portion of Business is done =

To day, as I told thee before (Sunday, 29ᵗʰ), I have been at my room constantly, received this morning Doctʳ Knox and a Friend of his who pronounced my Drawings the finest in the World (it is no triffling Praise this. I wish it was worth 10,000 £ but unfortunately it is only a Light Puff). However, they promised to see that I should be presented to the Wernerian Society, and talkᵈ very scientifically, indeed, quite too much so for the Poor Man of the Woods — They assured me that the work on Ornithology now about being Published by Messʳˢ Selby, Jameson, Sir Somebody & Cᵒ was a Job Book = It is really amusing and distressing at the same time to see how enimical to each others Men of Science are, and why are they so? = I will no further trouble thee. Good Night, friend of my Heart —

EDINBURGH OCTᴿ 30ᵀᴴ 1826, MONDAY.

I waitted most Impatiently to day untill one o'clock, getting up from my chair and looking down in the street thro my window to see some one coming to view my work; but all my anxiety & my Ill humor availed not, and to vent it I took my umbrella and Marched direct, rather stifened, to Fish Market Close [MS: Cloce], and passed the files of printers in Mʳ Neill's office as if the World was about being convulsed. I reachᵈ the owner of the establishment & all my pomposity evaporated and dispersed like a morning's mist before the Sun. I became at once as quiet as a Lamb and merely told him that I regretted very much my not deserving the attentions of those for whom I had Letters, and that, if so, I must off to London = He gave me good words and in such [a] calculated cool manner, that none but an ass could have resisted his *reasonement*; he accompanied me Instantly to one of the most scientific men, who, after looking at me as I Look at the Eye of a Bird as it looses its brilliancy & I fear to Loose its caracter, he noted down name & residence, and promised to send *amateurs*. Mr Neill, not satisfied any more than myself, took me to a Mr Lizars[22] in St James Square, the Engraver of Mr Selby's Birds, who at once followed me to see my Work == He talk^d of nothing else (as we walk^d along under the same umbrella) besides the astonishing talent of his Employer, how quick he drew, and how well, had I seen the work &^{c} &^{c}, untill having ascended the stairs of my lodgings and entered my room, his Eye fell on my Port folio and gave him some other thoughts, I am quite sure == It is a doubt with me if I open^d my Lips at all during all this; I slowly unbuckled the straps, and putting a chair for him to set, without uttering a Word, I turned up a Drawing! — Now, Lucy, poor Mr Selby was the suferer by that movement — Mr Lizars, quite surprised, exclaimed, "My God, I never saw any thing like this before" — Now, Lucy, Lawson the *Philadelphia Brute*[23] never gave an Inch and to this day swears that I know nothing about Drawing, that Willson did more with one Bird than I ever will with thousands! ==

Mr Lizars was so astonished that he said Sir Somebody must see them, that he would write Imediately, and so he did == that Mr Selby must see them, and to him also he wrote and, going as it grew dark, he called it seems on a Mr W. Heath,[24] a great artist from London, who came Imediately to see me == I had, however, made my exit [MS: Exett] in search of a handsome peble for thee, and missed him then == I called at the Post office, but it was not open — shocking arrangement for a Traveller, that if in town for a few hours only cannot be told if, or not, there are letters for him; I found it the same case in England ==

I returned and found 2 lines from Mr Heath and, not knowing who

---

22. William Home Lizars (1788–1859) was the superb Edinburgh copper engraver who engraved and printed the first ten plates of *The Birds of America*. In the summer of 1827 the colorers who worked for Lizars would strike for better pay, and Audubon would arrange for Robert Havell and son, a London engraving firm, to take over the work.

23. Alexander Lawson (1772–1846), the Philadelphia engraver, came to the United States from his native Scotland in 1794. In 1798 he developed a friendship with fellow Scot Alexander Wilson, for whose *American Ornithology* he became the chief engraver. Lawson and George Ord successfully opposed Audubon's attempt to find an engraver for his work in Philadelphia.

24. Mr. W. Heath may be William Heath (1794/95–1840), a London artist known for his illustrations, portraits, satirical caricatures, and landscapes. He was known to be in Scotland in 1825 and 1826, but further evidence is wanting.

he was, I posted to go and see who he might be = N° 4 Sᵗ James Street
— up 3 paires of stairs (*a L'artisan*), met a very dark Brunette who
acknowledged herself to be the better half of her Husband, who in a
moment after, shewed me two Enormous Mustachios on his upper Lip,
and great many various Drawings & Etchings — I will not say that they
were without faults, as thou knowest there are faults in every thing — I
thought some of them very good = He will come tomorrow = I met
accidentally this day my 3ᵈ Companion from Manchester, Mᵣ Walton.
I was glad to see him and he reciprocated my feeling very amicably =
Tomorow he also comes. =

LETTER TO VICTOR AUDUBON — FALLS OF THE OHIO —

Edingburgh, my Dear Victor, where I am now since 4 Days, is the
most beautifull, Picturesque & romantic City probably in the World
— I am delighted with every portion of it — but as I am a very poor
Describer, I will refer you to Morses Gazetteer[25] for a General outline
and tell you only that its streets are broad & Clean & well lighted
with Gass, its Public squares regular in all their shapes, difering
from *squares* by their being Octogons, hexagons [MS: Exagons], full
Circles, Cressants, pentagons &ᶜ. The Monuments are many and well
errected = The especial one to Nelson is superb and mounted on a
Rock Commanding a fine View of the German Ocean = The Castle
I should conceive Impregnable. 2 sides of it are protected naturally by
an almost perpendicular Rock 300 feet high — It looks like an Eagle
perched on a bold naked Cypress ready to fall and crush all about
below = The 2 Hills that run parrallel, one of which is covered by
the Old Town & the other by the New, are connected by Immense
bridges, under which a third city may be said to exist. To reach this,
stairs are made winding easily from either side [of] the declivities,
and lead from diferent parts of the Great Street verging the Two
principal Towns =
   The public buildings are immense and, as the whole City is made

25. A likely edition of Morse's gazetteer would be Jedediah Morse and Richard Morse, *A New Universal Gazetteer or Geographical Dictionary, Containing a Description of the Various Countries, Provinces, Cities, Towns, Seas, Lakes, Rivers, Mountains, Capes, &c. in the Known World*, 4th ed. (New Haven CT: S. Converse, 1823).

of fine well cut white stones, it has a modest, chaste appearance quite agreable to the traveller's eye. The markets are Extensive & well suplied, their contiguity to the sea being very advantageous[†] == The palace of Holyrood and its decaying Chapel are objects deserving the attention of all strangers — The ancient furniture and beds of Queen Mary of Scot are real curiosities, and I sought in her Mirrors for traces of her beautifull Visage with anxiety & concern as I knew how tormented her life was == The little table and room wherein she supped the night of the Murder, are perhaps in best repair. The armour of the Conspirators I saw, and went down the stair case that help[d] the Introduction of the Villians == The Paintings of all the diferent families of the Stuarts are decaying fast == The rooms that were inhabited by Louis 18th during his Exile here are in good Order, yet not to be compared with the appartments kept for the King of England, who visited this Palace now four years ago & laid the foundation stone for a new Cathedral at the same time that he ordered the rebuilding of Holyrood Chapel ==

But, my Dear Victor, Scotland generally is a Barren poor Looking tract. The mountains are merely covered with heaths [MS: Eaths] and the shepherds the most abject beings I ever saw. None but the rich here seem to enjoy life, and was it not my Interest to remain here some weeks to form a Close acquaintance with all the great men of this portion of the World, I would leave its rigid Climate and poverty behind me tomorow ==

Since I left Liverpool I remained at Manchester and its Environs about 4 Weeks, formed there very Interesting connections, particularly with a familly of the name of Gregg 12 miles [from Manchester] on a seat called Quarry Bank, where I Enjoy[d] a Circle of aimiable young females with the company of a most happy Father & Wife == Courted for my Talents, my time was uncommonly agreable == There my Friends mother, M[rs] Rathbone of Liverpool, who had brought me in her carriage with her Daughter to Manchester, gave me again a most delightfull ride of 120 miles to Bakewell, Matlock & Buxton. The whole of that familly has treated me with a kindness never experienced before by me under any circumstance, and that I am debtor to my Friend Vincent Nolte, who never sufered either opulence [MS: oppolulence] or poverty to pray on his Generous feelings ==

My time at Liverpool was wonderfully spent, I can safely say. My Pocket was furnished and my body fed most Luxuriantly $=$ Tomorow I will visit Roslyn Castle, where I have an excellent Friend in Mrs Fletcher, a scientific Lady[26] $=$ Afterwards I will go to Melrose to see the Chapel there and present my Introductions and myself to Sir Walter Scot $=$ Then I shall go into the High Lands, after having seen Glascow, & Inverness $=$

I am forced to travel a great deal to open the Gates of renown to my work, that now proves superior to any thing of the kind in existence — I never before this knew what felt [MS: feft] pride was, but I am confident that I no longer fear to shew my head or my Drawings $=$ That all this may end well and that I may return to my Beloved America with rich stores of wealth & fame is to be Hoped — I shall spare neither [MS: neih] time nor attention or perseverance to reach my ends, I assure you $=$

In the course of next month I will pass thro London, Bruxelles, Valenciennes, Paris & reach my mother's House in Nantes, and may my God Grant me the favor of Kissing her once more — I expected long ere this to have had at least one letter from your Uncle Berthoud and also from you. Certainly time is not so scarce with you — I do with 4 hours sleep and keep now a great Corespondance, yet copy all my Letters myself, even this one, and my Journal keeps a Pace with all, and my Letter Press for my Birds is allmost ready $=$ My Boy, pray read the Discontented Pendulum from Doct^r Franklin, or some one Else[27] (for the World is at { Ja**ies} about the authorship) and see how much can be done if time is not squandered $=$ It would give me much pleasure to receive from you some token of your still thinking about drawing or music or your natural talent for Poetry $=$ Talents

---

26. Elizabeth Fletcher (née Dawson) (1770–1858) was encouraged from her earliest years to pursue her intellectual and literary interests. After her marriage to the Edinburgh attorney Archibald Fletcher (1746–1828) in 1791, she cultivated the acquaintance of many writers, with an affinity for the Whig writers of the *Edinburgh Review*. She had published a blank verse closet drama, *Elidure and Edward*, in 1825. She was known as an animated and unaffected conversationalist.

27. "The Discontented Pendulum" is a children's fable by Jane Taylor (1783–1824) (see n. 13, chap. 3).

will lay dormant in man if by exercise he does not cultivate them and he dies unaware of his faculties.

I have an Album that contains many beautifull pieces from very Eminent men and, as I travel, I gather! $=$ I was at the theatre the other night & saw Rob Roy —

Here follows what I [thought] of it a few sheets previous —

This reminds me that the Labouring Class here carry their burthens just as our Squaws do, and was I to Judge by the present appearances here, fashion will soon put aside Razors & Scissors, that You Know I seldom use myself when away from your Mother $=$ but, my Son, amongst People of solid understanding, outward appearances have no weight, and my Locks are not even here Sneered at — I find myself in Company where persons from all parts of the Globe [are] all attired diferently and yet all reasoning very much to the purpose $=$ In fact, it is not the coat but either the Mind or the Heart that connects Man to Man.

I sent a fine soft assortment of Colored Chalks to John $=$ Should you feel Incline[d] to draw in my Style (and for your own sake you ought to do so) request him to forward you an exact half $=$ corect measured outlines, precise tints, and a little Life given makes a Picture $=$ My Works in Oil are now no more despisable, and a few Lessons from Thomas Lawrence will enable me to send you my own Portrait worth the remembrance $=$

During my Publication I will visit Spain, Italy, Holland & Germany, of course Switzerland, where I have at Geneva, a most powerfull friend in the Baron of Sisimondi, who Introduced me to Baron Humbolt.[28] My Letters for Paris are Good Stock & Cash on hand $=$

I have heard that your aunt Sarah was maried, to whom, Pray? At her age she would better not have done so (if I may give my allowance of advise) — Your aunt at Liverpool said that my sweet Sister Eliza has proved a *Mother again*! Your Uncle TWB. is now a Citizen of Cincinati, if not a Cincinatus — Pray, Inform me how the world busy's about you — Is Your Uncle, the Duck Killer, married

28. That is, Sismondi wrote a letter introducing Audubon to Humboldt, whom Audubon never managed to meet.

yet?[29] — I thought when I saw him that his Eyes glistered with affection for some unknown fair one to me — Has my sweet little Mary grown well? and what has been done with Friend Gibbs? who also I heard had some Ideas of Kneeling to the Goddess of love — Is Poor Bainbrogh still alive? At this distance, a step in thought but thousands of miles in Measurement, all details are agreable, and were you to set to with you[r] Uncle and write to me for one week, I would thank you Both == Now, may God Bless you, keep you well & Happy, and convince you that I am and for ever will be Yours most affectionately, Father & Friend J. J. A.

Direct to the care of
Mes[srs] Rathbone Brothers & C°—
Liverpool

I forward[d] this Letter in one to W[am] Rathbone Es[qr] — to whom I spoke about the sketch of M[r] Gregg — on the 30th of Oct 1826 Too much fatigued to Copy it — it being 2 o'clock at night — [†]

EDINGBURGH SCOTLAND OCT[R] 31ST 1826 — TUESDAY —

So, at last Professor Jameson has Called on me! That warm hearted M[r] Lizars brought him this morning just as I was Closing my Letter to Victor — He was kind to me, very kind, and yet I do not understand the man Clearly. He has a look quite above my reach, I must acknowledge; but I am to breakfast with him tomorow at 9 == He says he will announce my work to the World with my Permission, bring his Lady & Daughters &[c] &[c], and who knows after all if I, myself, am not mistaken and if *he* may not prove an Excellent Friend! — But really he & M[r] Lizars did praise my Drawings so highly, so astonishingly so, so

29. In this passage Audubon is soliciting a mélange of family information from Victor. Lucy's sister Sarah married Theodore Anderson and lived in Baltimore; in 1826 she was in her midthirties. Victor's "Uncle TWB" was Lucy's brother Thomas Woodhouse Bakewell. Victor's other uncle, the "Duck Killer," is Lucy's younger brother William Gifford Bakewell. Both Lucy's sister Eliza and brother Will had moved in with the Audubons during late 1814 in Henderson, Kentucky. Young Will had enjoyed shooting excursions with Audubon. Eliza, known as the family beauty, married Nicholas Berthoud in March 1816.

much above all I ever heard that I cannot help thinking yet that some quizzing [MS: Queezing] must be about the affair and the Entre[***].

Doct.ʳ Thompson's sons came in tall, slender and well looking; made a decent apology for the Father and Invited me to Breakfast at 9, Thursday next — Young D.ʳ Henry also came and wrote the above note† and again, having called this Evening when [I was] absent, left his card and a note of Invitation to Professor H. Hibbert [MS: Ibbert]³⁰ to breakfast tomorow — This I cannot do; a M.ʳ Symes who lives 63 Great King Street and who besides is called Patrick,³¹ but who I am quite sure is a learned Scotchman, was with me a long time, and Entertained me very much =

My morning was Indeed quite an agreable one within, although it rained and the thermometer never rose up to 35 this day = I called at the Post office — all fudge = and again, my Lucy, Edingburgh is surprisingly Grand, Beautifull, most Picturesque & Romantic!! — I eat fish for my dinner to day because my Landlady (may God bless her) said that she heard me cough last night and that light food was best for me = God knows — I never heard myself cough, nor am I very sure about light food being so very advantageous, but Women being Men's Superiors, I will not medle in contradiction with them; for although they suffer us to hold the reins, they will for ever lead for us the way! —

I have looked on thy likeness, sweet wife, very Intently to day and felt such an Inclination to kiss it, that my lips became burning hot and ~~~~ Oh, sweet wife, when will we meet again? —

I Called again this evening on M.ʳ Lizars, who seems very favorable to me — He shewed me some of his work, and Judge how abashed I felt when I discovered him to be a most wonderfull artist = He has Invited me to call on him at 8 to spend the *Evening* with him; now I call it much more as if going to spend the night there — His wife is lively, very affable and has fine large well colored Eyes, with Burnt umber, or

30. Samuel Hibbert-Ware (1782–1848) had been a minor member of the literati in Manchester before his father's death in 1815, when he moved to Edinburgh and developed as a geologist and antiquary. Among his friends were Walter Scott and David Brewster.

31. Patrick Syme (1774–1845) was an Edinburgh naturalist, a flower painter, a member of the Royal Institution, and the official artist of the Wernerian Society. He had helped found the Scottish Academy a few months before Audubon met him. Syme was also the uncle of John Syme, the portrait painter.

perhaps Vandyke Brown — yet they may be [a] better color. I am not quite sure as it was just during this Twilight when I saw her, and eyes then render objects Not allways as they really are — On the whole [MS: all], however, I cannot commit any mistake by saying that she is beautifull! and she is the first lady to whose House I have yet been and received kindly. I will here after Call her Lady N° 1. Remember this, my Beloved Wife —

Now, my Lucy, I have just returned from Mͬ͟ Lizars — It is just 11 o'clock, His younger brother accompanied me. Of course I came without any risk or Danger = My Evening has been extremely pleasant. I have had many good advises given me. I have seen Mͬ͟ Selby's *Original Drawings*, and *Sir W͟a͟m͟* Jardine's, and as I conceive my Johny can do as good, I feel quite proud = Lady N° 1 had a sister of her's there, a very agreable woman — another Brother, a good Doctor. [They] wish[ed] me well and all together we Drank thy good health all round = I hate late hours. I have to be up, Lucy, long before day to write, & so may God for ever Bless thee, Dearest Lucy, my Love, Good Night =

EDINGBURGH SCOTLAND NOVEMB͟ᴿ 1͟ˢ͟ᵀ 1826 WEDNESDAY.

Well, my Good lovely wife, I breakfasted with *Professor Jameson!*, a most splendid House, splendid every thing, a good Breakfast to boot! The professor wears his hair [in] three distinct diferent courses; when he sets fronting the south, for Instance, those on the upper forehead are bent westwardly; towards the East, those that cover both Ears are In[c]lined, and the very short sheared portion behind mount directly upwards, perhaps somewhat alike the stifer quills of the "fretfull Porcupine." But, Dearest Lucy, notwithstanding all this curious economy of the outward ornemental appendages of his scull, the sense within is Great, and If I mistake not, it feels of the suavity of a kind Generous Heart = Professor Jameson to day is no more the man I took him to be. He accosted me most friendly, chatted with an uncommon degree of cordiallity and promised me his Powerfull assisstance so forcibly, convincibly that I am quite sure I can depend upon him =

I left him and his sister at 10 as we both have a good deal to do besides drinking hot, well creamed Coffee — The separation, however, was short, for when the Clock struct 12, he entered my room (then filled with fair females) accompanying a Notable Baronet and perhaps a couple more Gentlemen = *He*, Lucy, made them Praise my Work — said he would call again, and I saw him pull my Door after him quite sorry, for as I said Just now, Professor Jameson is quite the Man for me now = ah, and M.ʳ Neill also, and M.ʳ Lizars and D.ʳ Hibbert and D.ʳ Henry, and D.ʳ Knox, and for all I know a full score doubled twice —

At 4 o'clock I was still turning very patiently drawings one after the other, holding at full arms length, the Larger ones — and pushing quite under the delicate beauties noses, the small ones to give their fair Eyes all kinds of opportunities [MS: opp.ᵗⁱᵉˢ] (and yet God Knows how all this will end) when I felt very fatigued — My left arm once, I thought, had some Idea of revolutionizing. I thought once that my left fist was about assailling my own so well formed Nose — I took the hint and save[d] both —

I walkᵈ out and was lookᵈ at by many = As I passed one, I could hear [MS: here] — "That's a German Phisician, I know" — I answered *low*, Fudge! — another "That's a French Nobleman." I answered *low*, bah! — took plenty of needed exercise, Enquired in Vain after chalks, called in vain at the Post office = thought often of my Good Friends of Green Bank, and of thee, and at last {peepᵈ} [MS: pupᵈ] in at M.ʳ Lizars just as he was about {putting} [MS: pupping] several Cups of Tea into his {putting} [MS: pupping] in Place⁺ — Well, I could not remain quite a blank the while — M.ʳ Lizars uncorked a bottle of warmᵈ London Porter, Lady N.º 1 handed it me with a smile, and I handed it to my mouth with thanks! — Whilst down in his counting room I Expressed the wish to purchase a sett of Views of *Superb Edingburgh*.³² The Book was brought upstairs for me to look at — He ask[ed] me to Draw a Vignette for him and wrote on the first sheet of his Book the exact following transfer of Properties in fee simple thus —

"To John J. Audubon as a very imperfect expression of the regard entertained for his abilities as an artist, and for his worth as a Friend, by Will. H. Lizars, Engraver of The Views of Edinb[urgh]"

Any Kentucky Lawyer who would pretend not to acknowledge the whole *un bona fida* I would knock down; but as our advocates are all

32. *Picturesque Views of Edinburgh*, drawings by J. Ewbank, engraved by W. H. Lizars (Edinburgh, 1825).

of the *Good Clay Kind*, I neither fear the contestation nor that of being conquered by Phisical Power in such an encounter =

Now we walk^d and Purchased chalks — Yet: for 3 pounds and one shilling & 8 pence I took home 3 Boxes of Crayons, 2 brushes of sable hair, and 2 handles of God knows the Genera or the species of the wood =

I had seen some artists of Mr Lizars, coloring by Gass Light, printing on Copper &^c &^c for the 1st time of my life = How little I Yet know. My God, how Ignorant I am! —

Well, I went to bed after reading untill I was so pleased with the book that I put it under my head to dream about it, like children are wont to do at Christmass Eve, I believe — However, my senses all operated another way. I Dreamed of the Beach Woods, of a House there! of a female there! of ~~~~ God bless thee, sweetest Friend, Good Night.

EDINGBURGH 2^D NOVEMBER 1826 — THURSDAY —

As punctual as an *Artist*, I drew the Bell of the Door at N° 80 George Street Just as the Great Bell of St Andrews church struct slowly 9. Whilst I was blowing my Nose & taking off my Gloves, I examined how well the name of Doct^r Thompson was Engraved on a well polished & well brightened piece of Brass, 8 by 5, not feet, Lucy, the more common Measurement of *Extraordinary Paintings*, no, Inches — Well, the Scotch Waitter came and Introduced me to his Scotch Master, a Good, and very Good looking man. Kind, extremely kind, he said to his wife "Mr Audubon, my Dear" — Happy man who can thus to day, at Breakfast, wellcome a stranger and present him to a sweet Wife, the company of whom he has enjoyed ever since and every day, since *I*, poor Exile from American shores, can only remember that I also have had the pleasure of doing the same — Ah, my Lucy, every Woman brings me more allied with thy good qualities, the more aimiable they, the still more aimiable thee! — We sat to, to Breakfast, a Daughter entered, then the son of the other day, then another young Gentleman, and when my second cup of Coffee, held carefully, ah, and gracefully by its Delicate handle, was asscending among its perfumed smoake, a Certain Doct^r Fox entered also & sat to, like an old acquaintance, fine Young man — speaks well, has been 17 Years in France, of course speaks that well also — wishes to see my Birds — most willingly —

After [MS: hafter] having talk^d somewhat about the scrubiness of the Timber here, and its lofty Magestic existence in my Country Dear, I left them to come and shake Hands with lady N° 1, who came in as tall and as Lovely as Ever, with her Husband and some other persons. — Mr Lizars had not seen one of my Largest Drawings. He had been enamoured with the Mocking Birds & Rattlesnake but, Lucy, the Turkey — her Brood — the Cock Turkey, the Hawk pouncing on 17 Partridges — the hooping Crane devouring Alligators newly born, all were, he said, Wonderfull productions — according to his say so, I was a most wonderfull Compositor — He wished to Engrave the Partridges, but when the Great footed Hawks came with bloody rage at their beaks ends, and cruel delight in the glance of their daring eyes, he stop^d mute for an Instant, perhaps his arms fell (if so he was not queezing me), then he said, "*This* I will Engrave and Publish" —

We were then too numerous in the Room to *transfer* Business — and the subject was adjourned = A Gentleman offered to pay me a certain amount for the use of my Drawings for Exibition — but more of this bye & bye — Fatigued again at 4, I walk^d and paid my Respect to Young Dr Henry at the Royal Infirmary — a nice Young Man —

At 5 or thereabouts I was positively again in the presence of Lady N° 1 & her Good Husband first gave me a Glass of Good Wine and, let me see, one, two, yes, three, Glasses of warm Scotch Whiskey Tody. I requested him to advise as to size for a Picture of Turkeys in Oil = We spoke of the Exibition when, having mentioned to him how kind & Generous the Institutions of Liverpool & Manchester had been and that I had a Letter of Thanks containing the Order & Invitation of the Comittees — he started at once with me and we marched arm in arm to Mrs Dickie's = He read the Letter, and off he went to Professor Jameson. Then again he returned but had given my Letter to the Professor to make (he said) good use of it = [I] shewed many many Letters of recommendation and he said, "Mr Audubon, the People here don't know who you are at all — but depend on it, they shall know" — We talk^d of the Engraving of the Hawks and it seems they will be done =

Then, Fame, extend [MS: expend] thy unwearied Pinions, and far, far, and high, high soar away!, yet smoothly Circle about me wherever [MS: whe eve] I go and call out with musical mellowness the name of this

Child of Nature, her humble, but true Admirer. Call out, call out, Call out — Loud, *Loud, Loud, Audubon*!!!! —

Now, sweet wife, should this Lady positively put it into her head, by puting the mouth of her trumpet first into her Mouth, to name Audubon as worthy [of] public Patronage, depend on it, Audubon's Industry & Perseverance would soon be able to procure the Needfull — yet that Dirty Trash Money —

But why thus anxious?

Why! Do I not love thee and my children? Have I not the most ardent desire to give them a Good & more sound Education than I ever will have? Do I not wish the Comfort of You all? Yes, by Heavens, I do! —

Then must I, as the World goes, have this Trash called most Judiciously and with most accurate veracity the Needfull. I'll try so much to dream about it that perhaps dames Fame & Fortune may think it pleasant, to lay under my Pillow, a good many scores of long, strong, woorsted hose, of ample dimensions filled with Gold, amethists, Rubys, Diamonds and what now shall I wish for? — Wish, Aye — UNE PRUNE!!! —

EDINGBURGH 3ᴰ NOVEMBER 1826. FRIDAY —

Instead of *une prune* this morning, I had most positively Two boiled Eggs for my Breakfast — I was not very much surprised at the diference. November is not a Month for Plumbs. It is too late then for my expectations this Year. Perhaps next June, in Paris, I may be suplied: because better prepared, and because more seasonably *apropos* —

My Birds were visited by many persons this day, amongst which several female Artists of fine features and good Taste were, and amongst the numerous males a Mͬ Professor James Willson,[33] a Naturalist of pretensions, an agreable man who Invited me to dine at his Cottage next week — I received a Letter from Mͬ Bentley of Manchester Informing me that Thy Box of Sparrs, Letters &ͨ had been received at the Royal Institution, Liverpool — but I must say that I am quite

33. James Wilson (1795–1856) would become one of Edinburgh's most diversified and accomplished zoologists. He was already much traveled and had been publishing in *Blackwood's Magazine* since 1816. His *Illustrations of Zoology* would appear in 1831. He was a younger brother of John Wilson, who wrote for *Blackwood's* under the pen name of Christopher North.

Surprised at not hearing from M.̲ Monroe or any of my Liverpool Friends — M.̲ Lizars, who certainly is here *mon bon Cheval de Bataille*, is exerting himself in my behalf most Manfully. At ½ past 3, Good M.̲ Neill came whilst I was dressing — and we soon together walk.̲ towards his little hermitage. Sweet spot, quite out of Town — nice garden, house, with Exotics and House Walls peopled by [a] Thousand sparrows secured in the Luxuriant masses of Ivy that only here and there suffer the eye to see that the Habitat is of stone — The Herons sharp lance laid on his downy breast, his shoulders surmounted his watchfull Eye, and balanced on one leg, he silently stood motionless! The Skua [MS: Kua] Gull Yelped for food; the Cormorant gredily swallow[ed] it, whilst the wadling Gannet welcomes her master by biting his foot: The little Bantems and the Great Cock leaped for the bread held out — the faithfull Pigeon cooed to his timid mate, and the Great Watch [dog] rubbed against his master with Joy! We enter the House, the Library, the Parlour, all neat and gracefully sistematic. The Friends have Encreased, I compt amongst them Bridges,[34] Combs,[35] Lizars, Symes[36] & others and, full of Gayety, we all set to a sumptuous Dinner. The wine augments the fecundity of Wit — The eyes around sparkled with Knowldege, & sense and the health of Audubon [was] Drank in unisson — Then thine, sweet Lucy — Then our Noble Host & then Peace for ever!! M.̲ Comb has a head quite like our Henry Clay and is an extremely fine Man = My neighbor Bridges is all Life and the pleasantest Companion I ever met, but, Lucy, after a few observations

34. David Bridges (1776–1840), as Audubon wrote on December 3, "goes every where and knows every body." He had a famous art collection and cultivated relationships with many artists. He was a close friend of John Wilson (the Christopher North of *Blackwood's Magazine*) and — as were many of the "Blackwood wits"—was a fellow of the Dilettanti Society. He had a clothier's shop on High Street in Edinburgh (where Audubon bought cloth for a coat on December 9). Alice Ford's identification of Bridges as a newspaper editor seems in error (see *Journal*, 335n25; JJA).

35. George Combe (1788–1858) was an Edinburgh lawyer who became a well-known lecturer and writer on phrenology and a collector of skull casts of persons he met. In *The Constitution of Man* (1828) Combe presented phrenology in the context of a system for governing social, political, and economic morality.

36. John Syme (1795–1861) was an Edinburgh portrait painter who would soon paint the first portrait of Audubon. He studied under Sir Henry Raeburn and was a founding member of the Scottish Academy. Audubon thought the portrait was a "fine picture" but the resemblance deficient. It is now part of the White House collection in Washington DC.

concerning the Birds of our Woods, *he* retires to let the World know
that many of them are arrived to Scotland =

What thinks thou when it is unanimously agreed that I must set
for my Portrait to M͟r͟ Syme — and that Friend Lizars must engrave
it to be distributed abroad? Even so, and next week there will be
Two Audubons in Edingburgh. I wish, for my happiness, that one of
them was Named Lucy! — Well, my Love, this is the way, much *a la
Liverpool*, and if I mistake not, it will end well; 4 Link͟d together, I am
accompanied to my Lodgings — have brought some native bread for
thee, & chesnuts and Walnuts & Paires & Apples, all natives and rather
bigger than Green Peas! Tomorow I am to see Lord Somebody and
Miss Stephens. She was called such [a] *delicious* actress so frequently by
my Learned Friends that I reverse my Judgment, or at least will suspend
it [MS: suspended] untill I see more of *hers* — Wife & Friend of my
Heart, God Bless Thee, Good Night —

EDINGBURGH 4͟TH͟ NOVEMBER 1826 — SATURDAY —

Now, had I the Inexpressible faculties of my Good Friend M͟r͟ Bridges,
and therefore was I able to write all that I feel towards him and the
Good People of the Romantic Edina's academic [MS: acamicic] halls,
I would set to and post up most merveillious accounts of what I have
Enjoyed this day, but alas, poor me can only scrat[c]h a few words next
to Unnintelligible and very simply say that I know that they are good,
Great & friendly! —

Full [was] my little room, of Noblest Individuals all day — exibiting
my Wonderous Works (as they are called). I am quite wearied to night
— so, sweet wife, only know as quick as possible (for it be now ½ past
1) that if I dined at Home, I supped abroad, yes, abroad most deliciously
at D͟r͟ Lizars — w[h]ere music, beauties, wines and conviviality all in
hands Joined to proclaim health to thee! To America health & Peace
and by thy Husband the "Spirit of Noble Scotland." Lady 1. & her
husband *supported* me here — I felt the warmth of her arm and thought
of thine —

I Rec͟d͟ a delightfull Letter from John Rutter Chorley and the Poem
on [the] Knife and — yes, and — went to bed praying for thee and our
Dear Ones! =

I begun painting very early this morning with Hopes that I would go deep into my Picture of Wild Turkeys — but no, by 10 o'clock my room was full of Visitors — Friend Bridges, I will please to call him, came and stayed a long good Time $=$ Miss *Stephens*, the Actress, & her Brother also paid me a Visit $=$ The Lady who, I am told, bears well in the respectable World had my album sent her, and I am to have in it some produce of her fair hand. The day past but I did little at my Work, for Friend Bridges having Invited me to dine with him, I walk^d to his House at 4 and never perceived that I was in my slippers untill I reach[ed] the Port of Destination $=$ A Mr Howie [MS: Howy] dined with us $=$ Mrs Bridges is one of those stately good featured ladies [MS: Lady]. We had quite *une Dinner de famille* that pleased me exceedingly. I saw quite a stock of Paintings, well selected by my knowing Friend. I returned home early, found a note from Mr John Gregg and waitted anxiously their coming — They brought me a *Scrubby* Letter from Charles Waterton [MS: Watterson] the Alligator *Maquignon*[37] and a sweet little sketch from Fair Ellen of *Quarry Bank*. I was very glad to see them. It seemed like old [MS: all] times to me $=$ They were desirous that I should go to Mrs Fletcher's with them, but as I cannot leave Town, I wrote a note to that Lady promising to call on her next week and must try to do so $=$

I am by no means in spirit to write — It seems to me as if thou hadst entirely forgotten that poor Audubon *who* never ceases to think of thee — Ah, my Lucy, this is severe, indeed, and how long it will continue I cannot even Guess — yet I cannot go to rest without wishing thee as much as Ever a Good Happy contended night $=$

MONDAY 6TH NOVEMBR 1826 — .

The same to day, very little work and a great deal of trouble $=$ I was glad, however, to see those who came. I had one [MS: I] *Lieut^t* Colonel *Faithfull*, extremely interesting. Mr Walton, my Coach Companion from

---

37. A *maquignon* is a horse dealer. Audubon is disparaging his enemy's claim to have ridden a caiman of some ten and a half feet in length (see n. 56, chap. 2).

Manchester, also called and Invited me in a very friendly manner to see him often =

It snowed this morning. It was quite new to me, for I had [not] seen any for about 5 Years — I think —

I do not feel well, my Lucy. I am quite dispirited about thy silence or better say at my not receiving the letters that I know thou must certainly have wrote = The papers give such accounts of my Drawings and of Myself that I am quite ashamed to walk the streets = I would not be very surprised If I exibit my drawings here again — †

SUNDAY 19TH NOVEMBER 1826 —

I do not know when I have thus pitilessly put away writing day after day for just Two Weeks — My Head could not admit of it I am quite sure and that is the only excuse I can now bring forth —

I must try to *memorandum* now all I have seen — What I have felt and feel at this present moment is quite too much for me to write down — Yet, my Beloved Wife, not a night has been spent without praying for thy Health and Happiness, and may God for ever Bless thee!

Every day I kept exibiting my Drawings to all who came recomanded — I had many noblemen, amongst whom Sir Patrick Walker, and†
Inumerable numbers of Ladies & of Artists and, I dare say, of Critics = At last the Committee of the Royal Institution, thro the astonishing perseverance of some unknown Friends, Invited me to Exibit Publickly in their Rooms *Gratis* — Then *I was no longer at home* — My Book was shut and I painted from Day to Night closely and perhap[s] more attentively than I Ever have done before — The Picture was Large, contained a Turkey Cock, a Hen, and 9 Young all the size of Life =

Mr Lizars and his aimiable Wife visited me often. I often spent the Evenings with them — Mr David Bridges — Mr Cameron and several others had regular admittance, and they all saw the *Progress* of my Work — All apparently admired it — I dined at many Houses, was every where kindly received and certainly enjoyed the time Happily as far as my Isolated situation could admit — It was settled by Mr Lizars that he would undertake the Publication of the first Number of my Birds of America, and *that* was Enough to put all my Powers of acting & of thinking in a High Paroxism of fever =

The Papers also began to be eulogists of the merits of myself and

Productions, and I felt quite dazled with uncertainties of Hope and of Fear = I Received Letters from Miss Greg, from Mrs W^{am} Rathbone, Mrs M. H. Rathbone and one most Precious from the Wonderfull Queen Bee of Green Bank, accompanied with the Beautifull Seal of the Wild Turkey Cock surrounded with *America My Country!* — I saw Miss Fletcher and liked her very much — The Young Miss[es] Greg Visited me often, and at last my Exibition was open^{d}.

The Professors of all denominations saw them and spoke well of them — I forwarded by the Penny Post 75 Tickets of Free Admission to the Principal Persons who had been kind to me and to those also from whom I needed further assistance, and to *all the Artists of Edingburgh!* I sat on[c]e for my Picture, but *my* Picture Kept me at Home ever since afterwards =

I saw, dined, & dinned again with Sir W^{am} Jardine Bar^{t}, became acquainted with him and like him very much — He visited me frequently and sat and stood looking at my Painting during his stay in the City = The famous Phrenologyst Geo. Combe, visited me also, spoke much of the Illustrating Powers exibited about my Poor Skull, of the truth of his Theory, beg^{d} that I would suffer a Cast of my Head to be taken &^{c} &^{c}, sent me a Card of admission to his Lectures for the Winter = The Famous Professor Willson,[38] *the Author* of Blackwood's Magazine, visited me also and was quite kind to me — Indeed, Lucy, every one was kind, most truly so =

How proud I felt that in Edingburgh, the very Vitals of Science, Learning and solidity of Judgement, Thy Husband was liked, well thought of and thus treated and received most kindly — How much I wish^{d} thee to see all this — to partake of it. That our Dear Sons should also have enjoyed it all would have rendered each moment an Age of Pleasure —

I wished to write to thee, to Victor, to N. Berthoud, to W^{am} Roscoe most especially, and yet nothing of the kind could I conclude to send after I read what was done. I burn^{t} 4 Letters, all for thee, because they

---

38. John Wilson (1785–1854), one of the most influential and controversial critics of his day, wrote for *Blackwood's Edinburgh Magazine* under the pseudonym of Christopher North. Two months after meeting Audubon, Wilson published the first biographical sketch of the man whose work he would continue to praise in print.

did not please me and wished to see more of my Way before I could set to in real Earnest =

I have now determined to remain here untill my first Number is Compleated, when I shall go to Liverpool again to procure with *proofs on hand* Subscribers — I will forward a N̲o̲ to John Quincy Adams — to H. Clay, James Barbour,[39] Andrew Jackson, Joseph Bonaparte, the King of England — Sir Walter Scot, the King of France, Emperor of Russia & Young Napolean and 2 to thee, Dearest Beloved — I will keep painting here the While and Watch the Progress of my Engravers & Colorists — 2 Drawings are now under the Gravers, and God Grant me success for thy sake and that [of] our Beloved children —

I have not written to my Dear Miss Hannah once since I pressed her gentle hand at Quarry Bank — I will try to find time to go and spend one week at Jardine Hall and some days at M̲r̲s̲ Fletchers and write to all my Friends this week Coming —

EDINGBURGH NOVEMBER 20̲T̲H̲ 1826 — MONDAY —

Whilst my breakfast was preparing and day light improving, I sat to at my little table to write a notice of descriptive import about my Painting of the Wild Turkeys, that now Leaned against the wall of my room *finished!*[†] — My breakfast came in, but my pen caried me on the Arkansas River, and so much did I feel of my beloved Country, that not a morsel could I swalow, and for the 1̲s̲t̲ time since in England, 9 o'clock had come and I was neither shaved or cleaned — but still I wrote — M̲r̲ Bridges, who generally pays me a daily Visit, happen^d to come in Just then. I read my composition and told him my Intention of having it wrote down in a neat hand to lay on the table of the Exibition room for the use of the Public — He advised me to go to Professor Willson to have it put in English and, taking my Hat, undressed as I was, slippers [MS: sleepers] on, I push^d to his residence — I thought of the fine dwelling[s] I passed, of a multitude of Learned beings they contained — wished for Knowledge also and reached the door of the Author of Blackwood's Magazine as it was about 10 =

39. James Barbour (1775–1842) was a Virginia-born legislator and statesman who served as John Quincy Adams's secretary of state from 1825 to 1828.

I did not ask if the Professor was in — No, I ordered the man waiting to tell his Master that Mr Audubon from America wish[ed] to Speak to him — In a moment this person returned and conducted me in a room where I wished that all that ever was written in it was my own — I did not [wait] long before a sweet child, no doubt a Happy Daughter of this great man, with her hair all yet confined in fairly white paper, beg^d that I should go up stairs, that her Papa would be with me in a moment — Could I have gone upstairs? Could I have intruded undressed and in sleepers into the heart of such a familly? Not I — I shrunk, I am sure, very considerably from my usual size and, apologising very awkwardly — I scarce had done speaking and the fair child scarce turned away from me when the Professor came in with freedom and kindness at Hand, Life in his eye, and benevolence at heart — My Case was soon explained — He took my Paper, read it, and said he would send [it to] me in good time =

Off again to my Lodgings and, hungry by this time or rather say cooled after walking, I breakfasted most Heartily — and now let me say I wrote to thee Last night after all and send thee several copies of the puffs contained in the News papers about my Drawings and one of my cards of admission to my own exibition. I then felt much relieved, my painting finished, I dressed and walk^d to the Royal Institution and was pleased at seing there a good deal of Company — It produced to day £ 6.3.0 — and 17 shillings of Catalogues sold — Young W^{am} Greg was at my room when the Ticket Box arrived, and he complemented me on my Success — but, my Lucy, my most disagreable part of this day is yet untouched — I had to go to dine at Professor Graham[40] in Great King street, N° 62 — It was six o'clock when I reached there — Ladies after Ladies came in and each with her brought a gentleman, my outlandish name was called out, and I entered the Saloon also — I was Introduced only to Mrs Graham and I bowed to the rest of the company — Then, Lucy, I stood up — Yes, stood up motionless as if a Heron, and gazed about me when I dared, at all that surounded me — Still I stood still, and thought of the Concert at Manchester, for I saw many fair sets of

40. Robert Graham (1786–1845) was a physician and had been a professor of botany at the University of Edinburgh since 1820.

Eyes cast upon me — not, however, rudely, no. I felt better here. I knew that I was in perfectly polite Company and waited more patiently for a change of Situation ═

The change came — A Woman, Aye, an Angel, spoke to me in such a way that I walk^d at once towards her and sat at her side. As I spoke or rather answered to her, I could not help thinking how much her little foot was shaped like thine, and how much like thine it rested in a well fitted enclosure of Blue Satin — She moved it too, a little up and then down, then side ways, just as females do when they talk with Interest or, when not so kind, they exibit a little of what is usually termed temper — In 5 minutes more I was at ease; the shrill ringing of a Bell ordered us to Dinner. I accompanied the Blue Satin Ladie (for her name I may never know) and sat by her, opposite another Young Daughter of Venus ═

The sumptuous Dinners of this Country are quite too much for me. This is not with friend Bourgeat on the *Flat Lake* roasting the orange fleshed Ibis, and a few Sun Perch. Neither is it on the heated Banks of Thompson Creek on the 4 of July swallowing quickly the roasted Eggs of a Large Soft shell Turtle — Neither was I with my Lucy at Henderson at Good Doc^r Rankin[41] lessening to the howlings of the Wolfs in full security eating well roasted & Jellied *Venaison* — No, alas, it was far from all those Dear Spots — In Great King Street N° 62 at Dr Graham, professor of Botany &^{c} &^{c} &^{c}, by the side of the Blue Satin Lady — most sumptuous dinner, well eat —

I found here an acquaintance of our Doct^r Dow of New Orleans — I would have staid late, no doubt, if I had wished, but I long^d to rest one good night quite thoughtless if Possible, and I bid the party all good night at 10 o'clock — I reach^d [my rooms] safe. Edingburgh I found much clearer of those servile wretches that Infest both Liverpool & Manchester at these hours, and I bid thee Good night, longing to hear from thee and still more so to press thee to my Heart — God bless thee —

41. Adam Rankin was the generous physician of Henderson, Kentucky, who (with his wife, Elizabeth) invited the Audubons to live on their Meadow Brook Farm in 1811 and 1812. Lucy was invited to help educate the Rankin children. Rankin continued a friend of Audubon for many years.

My Dear Good Friend[†]

I have just this instant received your favour of the 21ˢᵗ Instant and, engaged and harassed as I am, I know that the present moment is the best to answer to it.

I am really happy and very much relieved from much anxiety at seeing that your Dear little ones are all on the recovery and quite safe from ultimate danger.

I have indeed received the seal from your kind Benevolent Mother. I am certainly pleased with the powers of the impression, But, my Dear M.ʳ Rathbone, the short note th[at] accompanied it in that very hand writing of that excellent friend of ours is far far more valuable to me — The Golden present is and always will be precious, but the note is a gem not to be purchased — One I begged for but never expected it and now is placed in the first sheet of my Album — I felt inclined to write to you[r] Good Mother and sat to do it twice, but my heart failed me. All I wrote was trash and I destroyed it — but it is my Duty to thank her personally, and I shall certainly do so in a few days. Pray, tell her so and beg of her to excuse me for having defered daring doing it.

I must now enter on a subject that I assure you is perhaps of more consequence to me than any event save my mariage that ever has hapened me — It is positively the publication of my Enormously Gigantic Work, but to do this I must lead you gradually back to my arrival here and give you several of the most Circumstantial details, that have brought [me] to the present moment Connected with that mighty Business. The 3 first days after my arrival here were spent dismally and quite by myself — The different Letters I delivered I thought were of no use, and I had determined to leave Edinburgh for London *uncalled upon* when a friend of D.ʳ Trail, Patrick Neill Esq, on whom I *called again*, left his Business to see about mine and introduced me to M.ʳ Lizars, the Gentleman who is now occupied at publishing my first number. He came to see my Drawings (not without some small degree of reluctance) but was so very pleased with them that to him, I may safely say, I owe the vast many attentions bestowed on me since. I sent persons after persons to view them, untill some of those to whom I had delivered Letters let a little of their Scottish fearfulness and also came and since have [MS: has] proved good solid substantial friends —

The Royal Institution offered me their magnificent Rooms to exibit my Drawings, and the newspapers all resounded their praise — The Exibition itself has been doing well, averaging about 5 Pounds per day clear of expenses — M͇ Lizars gradually evinced a wish to publish my Work, and my anxiety to see it proceed has made me acced[e] to his offer. I would have sent you a prospectus sooner, but I really felt awkward about it, fearing that you should think yourself bound to subscribe your name to it thro a friendly way of acting. Your letter, however, has relieved me, and I now enclose one with great pleasure. It is not so fully expressed as I intend to have one, but sufficiently so I hope to obtain subscribers — My Plan is to publish *One number* at my own Expense and risk, and travel with it under my arm & *beg my way*. If I can procure three hundred of good substantial names of persons, or bodies, or Institutions, I cannot fail doing well for my family, altho I must abandon my life to its success, and undergo many sad perplexities and perhaps never see again my own beloved America — The Work from what I have seen of M͇ Lizars execution will be equall to any thing in the World at present — My vanity and wish to do better might prompt me to say that it will surpass all, and I think it is best to let the World Judge for itself; however, I shall Superintend it myself, both Engraving, Colouring, and bringing up, & I hope my Industry will be kept in good repair thereby — In about six weeks, some numbers will be ready to leave this place to difuse themselves — and the very first will go to my own beloved wife, with a wish that the whole may suceed and render her happier still.

In the meantime, I will certainly beg of you to procure me as many subscribers as you can — difuse of the enclosed prospectus as you please for the same purpose. I would be pleased that Lord Stanley and Sir Tho͇ Stanley should subscribe, also perhaps the Liverpool Royal Institution may think it fit to do so. Although the whole [MS: all] amount is certainly great, the number of years that must elapse before it is ended, render it an easy task, and as I often have thought, I must try — If I do not succeed — I can return to my woods and there in Peace and quiet [MS: quite] die with the thought that I have

done my utmost to be *agreable* if not usefull to the World at large
— Some of my good friends, particularly Dr Trail, is much against
its being the size of life. I must acknowledge it renders it rather
Bulky, but my heart was always bent on it, and I cannot refrain from
attempting it so. I shall publish the Letter Press in a seperate work,
got at the same time with the Illustrations, and it is well that you
should know that [the letterpress] will encompass many Localities
in anecdotes Connected with my Eventfull life — I would beg of you
to be so good to instruct me whenever *One* Subscriber is procured
and how many numbers over the quantity subscribed I might send
to you to be depossited where ever you please for Inspection, at the
Atheniaum or the Institution —

I have painted a large Picture of Wild Turkeys and can only say that
instead of 23 hours, I spent 16 days closely at it. It is now at the Royal
Institution, where it will probably remain for ever =

I have formed the acquaintance of all the Principal people here and
am treated with great kindness, Yet never will I forget the Dealers
in Pounds, Shillings & Pence of other places, no never. Sir William
Jardine, who is now at the head of a large publication on General
Ornithology, has spent many hours at my side, seeing me work and
enquiring *about my knowledge*. I am to spend some weeks at his
hall about 80 miles from this and probably will be cosseted [MS:
couseted] with the whole tribe of Scotish ornithologists shortly.

This has been a tolerable long talk, and I will close with wishing
you most happy. — I have not heard from my Lucy since I left
Manchester, and I assure you it bears hard with me, and the many
immense Parties where I go are only dreary reflections of Past times.
Remember me, pray, to all your family and our friends and believe
me for ever your most sincere friend.

sig.^d J. J. A.

Willm Rathbone Esqr
Abercromby Square
Liverpool

Edin^b 24th Nov. 1826.

My Dear Good Sir

As you are a man of Business and my friend, I therefore will not
apologize any farther, than saying that, with all my good will and
great wishes to write to you long since, I have defered it untill the
present moment because I disliked to write about nothing — . I
heard thro our kind friend, Mr Rathbone, of your dissapointment
at not going, to Allcome, at the intended time, but I heard that your
health was good & that your spirits were also very good. — My great
work is at last under way, but how long it will be able to bear itself
up is a matter of much doubt and concern to me == It is publishing,
however, here by Mr W. H. Lizars, an immin[en]t Artist and a man
of most excellent Character and great personal amaibility — It will
come out in its best dress only life size [MS: li — s—], all Coloured
and in the very handsomest style. That is promising a good deal in a
few words and perhaps presumptuously speaking, but it is really my
wish and intention that it should prove so. I have some hope that I
shall not disappoint either my friends or the World at large —

My prospectus is a very humble one, and I send it you now in its
nakedness that you may clothe it (if you please) as you may best
think fit — To tell you all my feelings would be quite impossible. My
head can scarcely be said to be on my shoulders. I never before felt
so wild, and at a loss to speak or to act, as I do now == I may perhaps
become reconciled and habituated to all my present perturbed
situation, but I scarce can conceive it possible, and I fear often that
the Woods only were intended for me to live in. I have wrote a long
letter to my friend Mr Rathbone, that I wish you to read, as it contains
more than I can possibly say now —

Should you, as chance may happen, procure Subscribers for me,
will you advise me?

Please assure your son Edward and Lady, that I am quite ashamed
that I could not send them a drawing. I found that shop I intended
for them was [MS: were] in London and have remitted day after day
writing them so — Remember me kindly to all your amiable Family,

your daughter Miss Jane particularly, and believe me, my Dear Sir, for ever your most Obliged & Ob.^{t} humble servant,

(sig.^{d}) J. J. A.

William Roscoe Esqr

Edin.^{b} 24.th Nov. 1826

My Dear Miss Hannah,

Night after night my Journal has counted [MS: compted] an increase of days spent without speaking to you until they have accumulated to precisely thirty. I have wished frequently to write to you, but really my poor head has been so employed with Business that I have been forced to relinquish the pleasure one day after another, untill shame and the fear that you might think me neglectful, brings me now to it. So truly busily engaged have I been, that I have not forwarded the letter you gave me to Professor Stuart, because I spared his making an appointment that I must have been forced to decline, as I have not been able to absent myself from this City one hour yet. I have frequently thought of the delightfull Journey of Matlock, and longed for one of those peaceful nights that I have spent at Green Bank, often willed that I could for a few moments walk by your side, and enjoy your and your dear Good Mamma's Conversation, but every time the turmoil that now surrounds me Calls me off untill my poor Head aches [MS: Hakes] and I am ready to faint. Will you, untill I can summon up myself to do so, thank your Benevolent Mother for her tokens of esteem? Then Please read the following and the long letter I have written to your brother William. Remember me kindly to all about you and believe me for ever your most devotedly and most sincerely attached and ob.^{dt} humble servant. sig.^{d} J. J. A.

Here followed the poem on Knives —

I have not had the pleasure of seeing Mrs Fletcher yet. Miss Fletcher was so good as to Call on me with the Misses Greg when I gave sight of my drawings at my Rooms. I have formed the acquaintance of two extremely agreeable Ladies where I at

Evenings go to relax from the Labours of the day. You must know the phrenologists are about having my poor head Plaistered to take an impression of the extraordinary Bumps that are, they say, all about it. My Portrait is also just now Painting for the good of the Public, and I am told I soon will be a *fellow* of higher rank than I am at present expecting. Sir Walter Scott will be here shortly, and I shall have the Pleasure of being Presented to him by Proff. Wilson, the Author of Blackwoods Magazine, an extremely agreeable man. Would you like to see the different sights of Edinburgh? I have had a superb present made me of 51 Engravings in one vol. that also contains accounts of this beautiful City. I intend sending it to my Lucy, and would send it to you first with great pleasure if you wish, only say so. Will you please to write to me? I perhaps ask too much, but I cannot well help it, you have been so good and kind to me. May you be for ever happy. Most respectfully yours sig^d J. J. A.

Miss Hannah Rathbone
Green Bank

EDINBURGH NOV^R 25TH 1826 —

I have been Drawing all day at some *Wood Pigeons*, as they are Emphatically called here, although Woods there are none == Young Greg called upon me as usual == The day was cold — wet, & snowy — Mr Lizars brought me a Doct^r Brewster,[42] an Eminent Man — I Expected a Visit from Mrs Fletcher and her Young Ladies but was disapointed and therefore disapointed my Portrait Painter, Mr Syme == I received a Note of Invitation from George Combe Es^qr — the Phrenologist, to sup with him on Monday next and, having also received one from Young Doctor Henry telling me that he could not accompany me to Dr *Monroe*,[43] *Craiglockhart* near *Slateford*. I had

---

42. Sir David Brewster (1781–1868), the natural philosopher and editor, had been editor of the *Edinburgh Encyclopedia* for eighteen years when he met Audubon. He was also coeditor, with Robert Jameson, of the *Edinburgh Philosophical Journal*.

43. Alexander Monro III (1773–1859) began to assist his father as professor of medicine, surgery, and anatomy at Edinburgh University in 1800, moving into the post himself upon his father's death in 1817. He was a much-published anatomist.

declined going there to Dinner, but M͏ʳ Lizars and Doct͏ʳ Brewster advised me to the contrary, so much so that I dressed and sent for a coach that took me there 2½ Miles from my Lodgings for the Moderate sum of 12 Shillings =

As I rolled along quite alone, my thoughts were multipl[y]ing fast and perhaps would have perplexed me still more than I was already — when I found that my purse must again be pulled out of Pocket to pay one shilling Toll = a Dear Dinner this — I arrived, however, and Entered a House richly furnished; 3 Ladies & 4 Gentlemen — the formers, M͏ʳˢ Monroe, Miss Maria Monroe and M͏ʳˢ Murray — Amongst the Gentlemen, the Aimiable and Learned Staff Surgeon Lyons I recognized and was Happy to meet. The remainder I knew not, neither will I probably ever know them —

M͏ʳˢ Murray I found a Woman of most extraordinary Powers = Voluble, aimiable and most atracting — It is a querey with me if her Eyes are not quite as brilliant as those of my Sweet Friend Hannah Rathbone = She sat by me and Entertained me much as well as the whole [MS: all] company very much — I need not tell thee that the Dinner was Sumptuous — for I meet no other kind here — D͏ʳ Monroe was more agreable than I had anticipated, and his *Rosy Dressed* Maria, quite an aimiable child of 5 and Twenty — a perfect Musician, anxious I thought that I should look at her, but I could not. I thought too much of Home, of thy sweeter self, and my beloved Boys — quite comfortless [MS: comfortabless] at not hearing from thee — The Evening passed and I came away alone again in my coach, reached M͏ʳˢ Dickie at 10 and sat to write this very fatigued and very cold — Snow lies about all the Hills that suround this Enchanted City — I was astonished to see to day all the Gass Lamps let loose by 3 o'clock A.M. Just as light gave way and I was forced to abandon [MS: abandonned] my Work = God Bless thee, Good Night —

EDINBURGH SUNDAY 26ᵀᴴ NOV͏ʳ

I had been Drawing constantly and I will add assiduously all the morning; snow laid thick on the Ground, all look͏ᵈ forelorne and dismall in my room *except my Picture* — I had got up on my chair and put the Work on the floor to study the power of Effect at a good distance — I had thought a thousand times of thee; my chagrine was greater than usual — I could not well understand why no tidings from thee reach^d me — Oh, how much I thought of the Dear Wife, the Dear Sons, the Dear Woods, all in America — I walked in thought by thy lovely figure, kissed thee, pressed thee to my Bosom, heard I thought thy sweet Voice but, good God, when I positively looked around me and found myself in Edinburgh, alone, quite alone — without one soul to whom I could open my own heart — my head became dizy and I must have felled to the floor for when my senses came again to me, I was strecht on the carpet and wet with perspiration although I felt quite cold and as if recovering from a long fit of Illness =

It was about that time that the Interesting figure of Lady N° 1 made her appearance in my room — Her husband and herself had come to Invite me to Dinner with them on Roasted Sheep's Head (a Scotch Dish) and I was glad to accept, for positively I now felt as if afraid to remain alone at my Lodgings =

Last November I Twice per week had my ride to Woodville, but Twice per week I could kiss thee and gaze on thy features with delight = run down with thee to the Bayou Sarah and again to the *celebrated room* where many of the Birds of America had been look^d at before they flew to this mighty Land of Learning & Science =

At 4 I reached James Square and dined with those good people without pomp or Ostentation — found the Sheeps head delicious and spent the evening most agreably — A letter from Sir W^{am} Jardine was read to me — *He* enquired if *My Turkeys* were Sold &^{c} — I told Mr Lizars that I would prefer selling them to him for 70 Guineas than to any other person for One hundred, which was the case — and Mr L. wrote him so — I was shewed many beautifull sketches from great Masters and Two plates of my Birds well advanced — At Ten Mr L. accomp^d me home — He was anxious to see my Work — He gave me some advise about the ground and I altered [MS: alter*rund] it Imediatly although in Oil =

The weather was intenselly cold — When turning a corner the wind cut me almost down — and although wrapte up in flannel shirts & Drawers I felt it most acutely — This morning it was scarce light at ½ past 7, and the lamps were yet all lighted —

God for ever Bless thee —

As soon as up, I was at Work and finished my Drawing quite before breakfast — Mr Syme came to see me and was not a little surprised to find it *done* — I had also outlined an Otter in a Trap, my very favourite Subject, and that he pr[a]ised also — At 12 I went to *Stand up* for my Picture, and sick enough of it I became by 2 — Mrs Lizars and her husband saw *me* and it in the Wolf Skin Coat — As it is to [be] Engraved, I sincerely Hope it will [be] a strong Likeness — Mr Lizars brought a Mr Key, an artist to thro a Sky over my Drawing, and the Gentleman did it in a handsome style =

I dinned at home on Herrings, Mutton chops, Cabbage, & Fritters — received 5.11.6 from the Money Man of my Exibition, saw W^{am} Greg a moment and, as I am going out to sup with the famous George Combe Es^{qr}, the great Phrenologist, I will stop and write tomorow morning what I may hear there to night, but, my Dearest Friend, Professor Jameson sent me this day a Card of Admittance to the Museum — I have not seen the Professor for these 3 Weeks —

I left my room and went to watch the Engravers at work at my Birds — I was glad to see how faithfully copied they were done, scarcely able to conceive the great [ad**it] required to form all the lines in a sense contrary to the model before them — I took a Cup of Coffee with Lady 1 and her husband and Daniel Lizars, a Brother Bookseller[44] — Again I went home to Dress and at 9 was again with Mr Lizars — He was so kind as to accompany me to George Combe Es^{qr} in Brown Square and I entered the Dwelling of Phrenology! — Mr Scot, the president of that Society,[45] Mr Stuart,[46] Mr Pritchie, McNalahan, Dr Combe and many others were there — and also a German named

---

44. Daniel Lizars (1793–1875) was business partner and younger brother of the engraver William Home Lizars. In 1827 Audubon would appoint Daniel as his Edinburgh sales agent.

45. William Scott (1782–1841), a distant relative of Sir Walter Scott, was president of the Phrenological Society at this time. He had cofounded the *Phrenological Journal* in December 1823 and was one of the most active contributors to the society.

46. Only one Mr. Stewart, not otherwise identified, is mentioned in the minutes of the Edinburgh Phrenological Society between 1820 and 1827. Ford's identification of the "Stuart" Audubon met at Combe's home as Professor Dugald Stuart (*Journal*, 356n37) seems unlikely, since he rejected phrenology.

Charles N. Weiss,[47] a great musician, Compositor &^{c} — but, Lucy, neither the musician or myself had been seen by the President Scot — George Combe, before the president entered, ask^d if we had any objection that our Heads should be *looked* at by the President — Both having answered negatively, we were seated on a Sopha and Mr Combe, as the President entered, said I have here Two Men of Great Talents. Will you please to tell us what their Natural powers consist in =

The President came up, bowed and, looking at Mr Weiss, pronounced him possessed of the Musical faculties — He then look^d at my forehead and said, "There cannot exist a moment of Doubt that this Gentleman is a great Painter, compositor, colorist [MS: colororist], and I would add a very aimiable man, but he might take this as a compliment!" There's Phrenology for Thee, sweet Wife! Our heads were then gently touched. The company was highly gratified.

We had supper — A Miss Scot and a Miss Combe were there, neither of them by any means handsome — Mr Weiss played most sweetly on the Flute, Mr Scot sung Scotch airs, and at one o'clock Music & Painting, lock^d in arms together, left the company — I soon reached my lodgings — Mr Weiss [MS: Mr N.] gave me a card for his Concert — and left me at the corner of Rose Street = Mrs Dickie, who had sat up waiting for me, said she had Good News for me and brought me a Ship Letter which she Hoped was from Home — Ah, my Lucy, how I did Hope it myself — but alas, no — It was from Governor Dewitt Clinton, inclosing one of Introduction to G^l Lafayette — It was dated just 30 day[s] from Albany and as [MS: has] it came to the care of my Friends at Liverpool, I expect now some from thee shortly — I am quite mad of Disapointment — Yet may God Grant thee a good Night — God for ever Bless Thee —

TUESDAY 28TH NOV^{R}

I forwarded this morning, as soon as I could see to write (say 9 o'clock on account of the damp fog), 5 News Papers, each one to W. Rathbone, R. R., Mrs R., Dr Trail & A. Gordon — with [the] wish that they should

---

47. Charles N. Weiss (1777–?) was the British-born son of a German flutist who had been principal flutist for King George III. Weiss lived in London and had performed his own compositions in Italy and Switzerland.

all go to America — I put the Drawing of the Stock Pigeons in the Institution, framed superbly, and they look^d well, I thought — very little company there, this day being quite too dark — I sat for my Portrait 2 dreadfully long hours, but it Improved and I Hope to see it a good one — Whilst yet in my hunting Dress M^r _____ sent me word that Sir Walter Scot was in the rooms of the R. Institution and wished to see me — Thou may depend, I was not long measuring the distance and reach^d the Building quite out of breath — It was, however, to no purpose — Walter Scot had gone to preside upstairs and, [it] being now quite dark, he neither could see my work or my Drawing and I abandoned the thought of seing him this day —

I dined with Mr Lizars & Lady 1. and saw, my Dearest Wife — the first Proof Impression of one of my Drawings — It look^d pretty well and, as I had procured one Subscriber, Dr Meikleham of Trinidad, I felt well contented — Imediately after my good Dinner, I wrote the following note to Mr Professor Wilson —

My Dear Sir — It is full 15 Years since I first felt a great anxiety to shake the hand of the Great Sco[t]ch *Well Known* — I have heard this afternoon of his being in the City, and my heart has been positively Aching with aprehension — Will I or can I have the Honor and the pleasure of being Introduced to him? Will *You* provide the means of such a meeting? Appoint whatever time or Place you like and you will confer a very great favor, I assure you, on Your M. H. O. S., J. J. A.

Mr Lizars also wrote to Mr Professor Jameson about my notice of the Wild Turkey — Intimating that I was not so hard run for support as to beg for such an account to be Inserted in a Journal without its being ask^d for — Then, Sweet Wife, we all walk^d a long distance in Gilbert Street to a Mr Moule, where we spent the Evening extremely agreably — I saw there Two as Beautifull Young Boys as, I assure [you, I ever] saw — The little wife is also extremely interesting, *particularly at this Period when Ladies are at their best* —

Mr Moule is a man of good Information — We talk^d much of America — I learned there that Mr Professor Jameson was Jealous and

extremely shy of Comunication — It was Twelve o'clock when we left
and it is now ½ past one — God bless thee, Good Night —

THURSDAY 29TH 1826 —

The day was Cloudy. I received no answer from Mr Professor Wilson
and was not a little surprised at this = I hope I did not hurt his feelings
by asking a favor that perhaps I am not entitled to — Setting for my
Portrait has become quite a arduous [MS: harduous] piece of Business.
I was positively in *Durance Vile* for 2 and ½ hours — and *par Surcroit de
Malheur*,[48] Mrs Fletcher sent for me Just as I was setting to my Dinner
— Ladies, however, having the right to Command, I went imediately
and saw a Woman not handsome but Good Looking, more charaterised
in her features than Women are generally — Her Eyes were penetrating
and her words powerfull. I was struct with the strength of all she said.
Although nothing seemed to be studied, it certainly was and is the
fruits of a long, well set round of General Information. She, of course,
praised my Works, but I scarce thought her candid — Her eyes reached
my very soul, and I feared her presence. I knew that at one Glance she
had discovered my Great Inferiority — The groupes of children she
had with her were all Gentil Looking but not so properly subordinate
as those of the Beautifull Mrs Rathbone of Woodcroft — She ask^d me
kindly to go to her house near Roslyn, but her Cariage was not offered
as that of the delightfull Mrs Gregg —

Lucy, I feared her probably too much to like her — I felt her elevated
mind bearing on my feeble Intelligence more & more forcibly the
longer I tried to steal a Glance at her face, but this was not permitted.
She positively rivetted me to my blushes, and never before have I felt
more stupid. I was glad I had met with her and yet still better pleased
that I was at liberty to go —

The Doct^r from Trinidad relieved me — His fair Wife and Wife's
sister (I suppose) open^d a conversation with me not so scientific but
more pleasant, and I pressed their beautifull hands as they went off with
more warmth than I did that of the female Ma[e]cenas[49] —

I returned to my Dinner and swallowed it down in a hurry — Then

48. In English, "in addition to these miseries."
49. That is, a wealthy patron of the arts.

I went to Mr Lizars to talk and take a Cup of Coffee — I forwarded from his house News papers for thee, Victor and Governor Clinton — wrote a Letter to my Friend W^{am} Rathbone and heard that the Doct^r from Trinidad had a wish that I should draw 400 Birds for him for a Publication of the Birds of the West Indies — I reach[ed] home early and wrote a Long Letter to my Good Friend Mrs Rathbone of Green Bank — but, Lucy, before this I received, answered and received again a Note from Mrs Isabella Murray Inviting me to go and see her and some fine Engravings at her house, and I shall do so on Friday =

I went to bed late and bid thee Good Night at about one o'clock, very distracted about not hearing from thee —

Edinburgh 29th Novr 1826[†]

My Dear Good Mrs Rathbone

I have postponed writing to you day after day in hopes that I could do it as I longed to do. I mean much better than I am able, and more as I thought the occasion required, but it is all a vain attempt and I am at last reduced to thank you in humble words for the beautifull "Token of Esteem" you have sent me. Yes, I most sincerly thank you for the "Token" and the 'esteem' that you have so kindly expressed towards me in your precious note; those favours neither can or ever will be forgotten and, if you will permit me, suffer that I should say with all my heart: warmest wishes, may God Bless You.

The first Impression of the seal was sent to my beloved wife the very night I received it from the hands of Professsor Duncan, and it has given me much pleasure to hear some of my learned acquaintances here praise the workmanship and the Donor — It is not, I assure you, of little consequence to me here that the knowledge of the kind attentions received by you has been diffused through the medium of unknown friend[s] of mine. Where ever I go I am told "You became acquainted with the family Rathbone at Liverpool, Mr Audubon," but, my dear Madam, I dare not say any more. I know your gentle temper too well, and I will remove to other subjects.

I supped on Monday last at George Combe Es^{qr}, a renounded Phrenologist, and to give you some Idea of the authenticity of that

Gentleman in the pursuit of his Ideal Science, I will copy you the time as spent there from my Journal.

"Again I went home to dress and at 9 was again with M͏ͬ Lizars — He was so kind as to accompany me to George Combe Es͏ͬ in Brown Square, and I entered the dwelling of Phrenology. M͏ͬ Scott the president of the society, M͏ͬ Stewart, M͏ͬ Clairre, D͏ͬ Combe and many others were there, and also a Gentleman German named Charles N. Weiss, a great musician, compositor &͏ͨ but, Lucy, neither [MS: nhether] the musician or myself had ever been seen by the President Scott. George Combe before the president entered asked if we had any objections that our heads should be looked at by the president and, having answered negatively, we were seated on a Sopha, and as the president entered G.C. said "I have two men here of great Talents, will you please to tell us what their natural powers are best in." The president came up, bowed and looked at M͏ͬ Weiss, pronounced him possesed of musical faculties. He then looked at my forehead and said "There cannot exist a moment of doubt that this gentleman is a great Painter, Compositor, Colourist, and I would add a very amiable man, but he might take this for a compliment." There! Phrenology for there I was {Wise}!! Our heads were gently touched, and on the whole the company was full convinced that M͏ͬ Weiss could blow the flut[e] and I quite able to soil Brushes —

I am not very fully convinced that M͏ͬ Scott did not know previously who we were. Neither can I ever be convinced of the truth of his assertions as far as I am connected with them, but if those men have positive proof to support what I call only a theory, away goes my Ideas concerning the very existence of†   M͏ͬ Combe says that my poor skull is a greater examplification of evidence of the truth of the systeme than any he has seen except Napolean, Molière, Garrack &͏ͨ &͏ͨ, and positively I have been so tormented about the exuberances of my head that my brains are now, I am sure, very nearly out of sort ═ but this is not all, my eyes will have to be closed for about one hour, my face and hair Oiled over, and plaister of Paris poured over my nose to form a mould of the whole. Then a Bust will be made and then, my Dear M͏ͬˢ Rathbone, I will be as I hope always to be only "*Simple and Intelligent Audubon*," as your good son Richard was pleased to call me. And on the other side, the artists quite as crazy and silly inclined, have said that my head was a perfect Vandyke's, and to establish that fact my portrait is now growing under the pencil of the ablest Artist Advocate of the Science [to be] had. It is now a strange looking figure, [***lly] in fact with Gun, trap and Buckles, and eyes that to me are more those of an enraged eagle, than mine, yet it is to be engraved, and that being the case, I shall take the earliest oppertunity of letting you be judge of the whole for yourself —

I have been thrown into a constant round of parties, Suppers, & Dinners ever since my birds were seen, which, by the bye, was not untill 3 days after my arrival, but the late hours it forces me to keep are distressfull and very wearisome, yet I paint during every moment I can steal from company and have done much work. I have been [called] on in a very friendly way by several of the nobility — Sir Walter Scott arrived yesterday from Paris, saw my drawings a moment, and I hope to dine with him tomorrow, with the comittee of the Antiquarian Society at the Waterloo Hotel, where an annual feast is given ═

My work is proceeding in a very good and superb style. Proof impressions have already been struct, and in a couple of days, coloured plates will be at the exhibition rooms, and the different Booksellers shops ═ I this day had a subscriber from Trinidad — M͟r͟s Fletcher, on whom I never yet had time to call, came to see me herself. I have been very much pleased with the Interview, and also with a short visit I received from her daughter ═ but with all this bustle and hopes to succeed, my heart is heavy, yes, very heavy — I do not hear from my dear friend, my wife, and cannot imagine the reason or the cause. Could it be possable that [a] letter should be now at London for me? I will not be ready to leave this place untill the necessary lessons for cording and hanging up of the plates so as to be able afterwards to absent myself. I have undertaken this at my own risk but have calculated closely, and if in twelve months from this date I can procure 300 subscribers, I will do well for my children, although I will probably have to bid eternal adieu to my Beloved America, the very thought of which just now fills my eyes with bitter tears ═

My Exhibition has been thus far attended quite beyond my expectation and the papers have been all constantly support[ing] the man of the woods — I have taken the freedom of forwarding some to you and will continue to do so, if you have no objection, from time to time, from [where] ever I may chance to go. I will be glad that, after you have read them, they should be forwarded to my Lucy or my son Victor. I have been very much afraid that our good friend William Roscoe has felt offended at my not writing sooner to him than I have done, but realy to write to such a man is not easy, and I am foolish enough to feel anxious, not to be laughed at for the want of knowledge in such matters. If he is at all offended, pray cap[i]tulate in my favour with him on any terms that will bring back his kind wishes for me =

The weather here is dull, moist, and disagreeable, cold at times. The short duration of day light here is shocking. The lamps are lighted at ½ past 3 o'clock A.M. and are yet Burning at ½ past 7, and [I] never can enjoy walking or staying in Bed, and I have to sit moping by my fire untill Breakfast time. I am agreeably lodged in a street called George at No 2 at a Mrs Dickie, a good sort of a woman who is extreamly attentive and kind in her way. An American lady called Campbell also lodges in the same house, and is pleased to chat with me sometime. A Mrs Murray call[ed] Isabella besides, who has visited the European Continent frequently, is also extremly kind to me. The familys of Professor Wilson, Munro, Brown,[50] Jameson, Dr Thomson and many others have afforded me much pleasure, yet since here I have thought a thousand times at least of Green Bank, of Woodcroft, Abercromby Square, Lodge Lane, Matlock, Quary Bank, the Dockray Amelia, my kind friend Miss Hannah, little cherub Basil, and all others connected with you. I long to see you all again, and am anxious that my first number should be finished to afford me that pleasure, for then in two days I will be rolled to Liverpool and walk to Green Bank and press your hands and enjoy your sight and feel happy! Fare well, my Dear Madam, may God Grant you health and

50. Andrew Brown, DD (1763–1834), had been professor of rhetoric and belles lettres at the University of Edinburgh since 1801. Alice Ford's identification of this Professor Brown as "John Brown (1784–1859)" is in error.

pleasure. Remember me to all about you and believe [MS: bleave]
me for ever yours much attached Devoted and respectful friend and
humble servant. Signed J. J. A —

EDINBURGH NOV^R 30TH 1826 —

My Portrait was at last finished to day. I cannot say that I thought it a
very good resemblance, but it was a fine Picture and the Public are the
best Judge as to the other part — The weather being fair, the exibition
was well filled — I did not feel quite well this morning. My head achked
a good deal; however, it went off. To be Ill far from thee would be
dreadfull — Who would nurse me with thy kind care, kiss me to repose
and do more for me in a Day than all the Doctors in Cristanndum can
in a Twelve month? — I visited my Rooms for a few minutes. I would
like to go there oftener, but really to be gazed at by a Crowd is of all
things the most detestable to me =

W^{am} Gregg called on me at 4 o'clock and in a few minutes, having
told me that his money had run out, I offered him some and went
for a bundle of Bank Notes to my Trunk — He, however, would only
accept of 5 Pounds — Mr Bridges and an acquaintance of the famous
Alligator Rider came, and I was told that Mr Watterton said that
Joseph Bonaparte Imitated his Brother Napoleon's manners & habits
constantly — That is much more than I know or saw —

My Invitation to dine with the Antiquarians of this City was not
forgotten — I was at 5 at Mr Lizars when, having already found M^r
Moule, we proceeded to the Watterloo Hotel — The setting room
was soon filled. I met many that I knew, and a few minutes after the
Earl of Elgin[51] had made his entry, I was presented to him by Mr Innes
of Stow[52] — He shook hands with me and spoke in very kind terms,
complimenting me at the same time about my Pencil's Productions —
At 6, I suppose, we walked in couples to the Dinning room — I had the

51. Thomas Bruce, seventh Earl of Elgin (1766–1841), was the army officer, diplomatist, and
antiquarian who brought the "Elgin marbles" from Athens to London and sold them to the
British Museum in 1816. The Elgin home is Broomhall in Fife near the Firth of Forth.

52. Gilbert Innes (?–1832) of Stow was a deputy governor of the Royal Bank of Scotland
known for his great wealth and civic engagement.

arm of my Good friend P. Neill — M⁣ᴿ Lizars sat on one side of me and
M⁣ᴿ N. on the other, and there I was helped from a sumptuous dinner,
Indeed = It at first consisted Entirely of Scotch Messes of old Fashion
— such as Marrow Bones — Cod fishes heads stuffed with Oat Meal
and Garlick — Black Puddings — Sheeps Heads — Trachey of the
same and I do not know what all —

Then a second Dinner was served quite *a L'Anglaise*. I finished with
a nice bit of Grous — Then, my Lucy, Came on the Toasts — Lord
Elgin, being President and provided with an Auctionneering Mallet —
brought all the company to order by rapping smartly on the Table with
this Instrument. He rose and simply said "The King, 4 times 4." Every
one rose, Drink to the Monarch's health, and the President saying "ip ip
ip," sixteen cheers [MS: shears] were loudly called out — The Duke of
York, of Clarence and many others had their healths. Then Sir Walter
Scot (who was not present to my great discomfiture), then one and
then an other untill, my Lucy, thy Husband's Health was proposed by
M⁣ᴿ Skene [MS: Skin],[53] the first secretary to the Royal Institution, of the
Antiquarian Society &ᶜ &ᶜ — Whilst he was engaged in a handsome
Panageric, the swet ran down me, I thought I would faint, and I was
seated in that situation when Every body Rose and Earl President called
out "Mr Audubon" — I had seen each Toasted Individual rise and
deliver a Speech. That being the case, could I remain speechless like
a fool? — No, I summonned Resolution and for the first Time in my
Life addressed a large assembly thus, "Gentlemen, my Powers of voice
are as Humble as those of the Birds now hanging on the walls of the
Institution. I am truly obliged for your favor. Permit me to say, may God
Bless You all and may this Society Prosper" — I felt my hands and they
were positively covered with Perspiration. I felt it runing down along
my Legs, and M⁣ᴿ Lizars, seing how I was, poured out a Glass of wine
and said "Bravo, take this" —

The Company went [on] Toasting — A Delightfull old Scotch song
was granted us by M⁣ᴿ Innes. The refrain was "put on thy Cloak about

53. James Skene (1775–1864), an Edinburgh lawyer and antiquarian, was one of Walter Scott's
closest friends. Scott relied on Skene's travel journals for several fictional backgrounds and
contexts. Alice Ford's identification of this "Mr. Skin" as "William Forbes Skene (1782–1850)" is
in error; he was the son of James Skene, and his actual years were 1809–92 (*Journal*, 364n39).

thee." Then M̲ Donald gave us an other. W̲a̲m̲ Allan Es̲q̲r̲, the famous Painter,[54] told a beautifull story — then rose and Imitated the buzzing [MS: busing] of a Bumble bee confined in a room and followed it as if flying off from him, beating it down with his handkerchief [MS: Hdfs] &̲c̲ most admirably — At 10 the Earl Rose and bid us well — At ½ past 10 I proposed to M̲r̲ Lizars to go and we did —

I was now much pleased of my having been there, particularly as Lord Elgin expressed a wish to see me again — I went to M̲r̲ Lizars w[h]ere I took some Scotch Grog and return̲d̲ home well = The lad that Copied my Letter to M̲r̲s̲ Rathbone was yet at work. He took the Letter to the office and I took myself to bed — It is again one o'clock, Sweet Wife, and another day has Elapsed without a word from Thee — God Bless Thee, Good Night —

I forgot to say that I visited M̲r̲ Allan the artist in the morning and saw there a most superb Picture of his own Pencil —

EDINBURGH DECEMBER 1̲S̲T̲ 1826 —

My Portrait was at last hung up in the exibition rooms. I prefered *it* to be gazed at than the *Original* from whom it was taken — M̲r̲ Lizars thought pretty Good =

The day was shockingly bad, wet & slippery. I had to visit Lord Clingertie and his Lady[55] at 12. Therefore, I went; I met M̲r̲s̲ Murray, her children and the Daughter (Eldest) of D̲r̲ Monroe — M̲r̲s̲ Murray began a speech about her Grand Father, Lord Strange, the famous engraver[56] and, Strange to tell, the speech continued for half an hour. The details of the Stuart's familly and the kings of England to this present day were all in rotation Introduced, and I would probably be there yet standing, motionless like a Heron, merely saying *yes* from time to time to help my

54. William Allan (1782–1850) was a much-traveled painter of primarily historical subjects who was also well known as a mimic and entertainer. Beginning in 1815, Allan's work had been regularly represented in the annual exhibitions of the Royal Academy in London. He would be knighted in 1841.

55. Alice Ford identifies Audubon's "Lord Clingertie" as "Richard Le Poer Trench, second Earl of Clancarty, first Viscount Clancarty (1767–1837), and diplomatist" (*Journal*, 365n42). Since Clancarty had retired to county Cork in 1823, however, corroboration of this identification is still needed.

56. Sir Robert Strange (1725–92) was a world-renowned line engraver who was also involved in political disputes between the houses of Stuart and Hanover.

breathing, if a Lucky message that the Earl of Elgin desired to see me at the Institution had not come — but it did so happen and, bidding Lord Clingertie and his Black eyed Isabella a good morning, I trotted off, remarking how tall and well formed Miss Monroe was —

I soon reach^d the Institution, for the Lord I had Just left resides in Charlotte Square at N° 17 — I Cast my Eyes on the Immense and singularly situated rock on which stands the Castle and reached the Institution in a Jiff — I met Lord Elgin in the Academy of Arts room in company with Mr Secretary Skin and Mr Hall, the advocate, nephew to Lady Douglass — My Interview was extremelly pleasant and, although I never said *Lord* to the Noble Earl, he spoke to me with all the Kindness Imaginable. We spoke of my Travels, my Work, my Drawings, and he complimented me much, indeed —

Mr Hall Introduced himself, and it gave me an opportunity long^d for to send him the letter I had for him from Lady Douglass, my Card, and one of admittance — but, Lucy, perhaps the best thing to relate to thee is my Breakfast at & with that wonderful man David Bridges — I was at his house, N° 27 Dundas [MS: Dundar] Street, at ¼ before nine — A Daughter was practising the Piano, the son was reading, the wife was well Dressed and sewing [MS: sawing] — The little Girl played with my Watch Seals,[57] and I stood with *my front from the fire* looking on the Pictures about the room — Thus was I looking & thinking when my friend came *en robe de Chambre* — shook my hand and, taking his pocket handkerchief [MS: Hdf] out of his usual abode, he began wiping, chimney mantle, Tables, Desk &^c, to my utter annoyance — for I felt for the wife whose fault was thus exposed and felt much, for it brought me home to thee — I saw thee so sweetly clean, and all about us thro thy constant Care so delightfully sweetly Clean, that I kissed thee in Imagination and Bless^d my God for having such an Angel for a Wife! —

We walk^d to see my Picture and to Criticise it — both Mr Lizars and Bridges are capital Connaisseurs = I dined at Home, took Coffee with Lady N° 1, visited Mr Howe, the Editor of the Courant — and having received an Invitation again from Mr Bridges to go to the Theatre to

57. Watch seals were engraved pieces of flat stone or colored glass used to seal letters; they could be attached to a watch fob or worn elsewhere.

see Wairner perform Tyke in the School of Reform,[58] I went to meet at the Rainbow Tavern w[h]ere he and his son were Enjoying a Glass of Punch — The Theatre was thinly attended, but I was delighted with the piece and the Performance — At 9 we left the House and went to Weiss's Concert in the assembly Rooms in George Street a Couple of Squares from my Lodgings — very few, Indeed — Saw and spoke to Mrs Innes of Stow — and several others — The flut[e] Player was admirable both in point of Execution and softness of Tone — We returned to Mrs Dickie's at ½ past 10 and Mr Bridges Supped with me —

It is now again one o'clock. I am quite worn out. I wish I could spend some time with thy sweet self in the Country to rest my poor head on Thy Bosom and Enjoy that sweet composing repose that I never can expect any where else — Oh, my Lucy, God Bless Thee, Good Night —

EDINBURGH DEC^R 2^D SATURDAY 1826 —

The weather was a sharp frost untill evening, when it rained. 15 pounds sterling were collected at my Exibition. I was busy painting an Otter in a Trap and never put my foot out of Doors untill I went to Dine at Dr Brown the professor of Rhetoric — Mr Bridges called on me and said that, the weather being bad, a coach must be taken and that he would be glad if I called on him in time — Of Course, a Coach was taken, and I called for Friend Bridges. We travelled together quietly enough — He told me that Professor Willson had prepared a notice for Blackwoods Magazine respecting myself and my work[59] but that I must Keep the secret — that Professor Willson had read it him in confidence — I said quite elated that 12 Copies must be had to forward to America; this my Friend thought very proper, and assured me that If I paid his Coach fare this night, he would amply repay me by purchasing for me the Pamphlets at a Lower rate than any Individual could do =

58. *The School of Reform, or, How to Rule a Husband* (1805), by Thomas Morton (bap. 1764, d. 1838), featured the popular rustic Yorkshire character Robert Tyke.

59. Wilson's praise for his "friend Audubon's Exhibition" was unqualified: "He is the greatest artist in his own walk that ever lived" and "full of fine enthusiasm and intelligence [...] and esteemed by all who know him for the simplicity and frankness of his nature" (Christopher North [John Wilson], "Noctes Ambrosianae No. XXX," *Blackwood's Edinburgh Magazine* 21 [January 1827]: 100–107 [*sic*], quote on 112–[13]).

I *Swallowed* this as a man thirsty [MS: Thursday] in the Wilderness, forced to drink from the filthiest pudle or perish — and we arrived at last at Doc.ᵣ Brown = I think that the servant who called out my name when I entered the saloon must have received a most Capital Lesson on Pronunciation, for seldom in my travels did I hear my name so clearly, audibly and well pronounced — Two Miss Henderson's — Professor of Greek Dunbar⁶⁰ and his Lady and Professor⁺ of Military Surgery formed the company along with the cool, reserved Professor Jameson — We had quite an agreable time of it — Dᵣ Brown is one of those most aimiable and Clever men who possess the talent of making all comfortable about them at once — Such a dinner would be acceptable every day to me — We retired in goodly time, and now that it is for [the first time in] a long time only ½ past ten, I will go to rest with hopes of hearing from thee tomorow — Sweet Wife, Good Night —

I forget, as I am often apt to do, that Sir James Hall⁶¹ and his Brother called on me this afternoon — The former wished to receive some information respecting the comfort that may be expected in travelling thro my dear Country and said that he would bring a map and write down my observations —

EDINBURGH SUNDAY DECEMBER 3ᴰ 1826 —

My Good Friends Mᵣ Lizars and Lady Nᵒ 1. came to pay their regular visit at ½ past one — Mᵣ Lizars thought more of the Otter painting than of that of the Wild Turkeys — I nearly finished to day to the great astonishment of Mᵣ Syme and Mᵣ Cameron, who came to announce me the decision of the Institution that the rooms should be mine untill the 20ᵗʰ Instant = "No Man in either England or Scotland could paint that Picture in so short a time" — Now to me this is all truly wonderfull; I came to this Europe fearfull, humble, dreading all, scarce daring to hold

---

60. George Dunbar (1777–1851) had been professor of Greek at the university since 1806. He was known as an assiduous lexicographer.

61. Sir James Hall of Dunglass (1761–1832) was an accomplished experimental geologist who helped the theories of James Hutton prevail against the Neptunist theories of Werner and Jameson. He was also the father of Basil Hall and James Hall. Because Basil Hall later presents Audubon with a map of America and many questions (see the entries for December 14 and 16), Ford mistakenly suggests that this reference to Sir James's brother is to his son Basil (*Journal*, 369).

up my head and meet the glance of the Learned, and I am now praised so high — It is quite unaccountable and I still fear it will not last — this — Good People certainly give me more merit than I am entitled to. It is only a mere glance of astonishment or surprise operating on them because my Style is new and diferent from what has preceded me —

I had to dine with Mr Witham of Yorkshire[62] in Great King Street N° 24, but I did not know him at all — I had mistaken^d him for Sir Patrick Walker in the street and addressed him as such a man — He had invited me on such an occasion and I made ready to experiment on human propensity to please — Mr Bridges, who goes every where and knows every body, lead me to the House — Dr Knox, the Daughter of my Host, his Wife and his Wife's sister were all [the company] — I discerned in an Instant that this Gentleman was a Gentleman, Indeed, quite wealthy, polite and versed in all courteous ways — We dined, we drink Coffee, we supped at 11 — At 12 the Ladies bid us good night. I wished and long^d to retire, but it was Impossible — Mr Bridges talk[ed] much — We all talk^d much, for I believe the good wine of Mr Witham had a most direct effect — It was determined by Dr Knox to propose me as an Honorary member to the Wernerian Society — Our Host said he would second the motion =

It was determined that to satisfy Mr B., Mrs W. would set for her Portrait to Mr Watson Gordon[63] and at ½ past one, after having been dubbed [MS: daubed] a great Philosopher and an extraordinary man — thy health Drank &^{c} &^{c} = I retired with Dr Knox but left Mr B. and Mr W. at their Whisky Toddy — The Doctor as we walk^d together spoke by no means very favorably of reserved Mr Jameson — said he was of the old school and that perhaps he was the only person who might bear against me at the Trial for Ellection —

It is now ½ past 2 o'clock — What hours I do keep. Am I to lead this life long? — If I do I must receive from my Maker a new suit of strength and a better constitution or I shall not be able to stand it — Lucy, Dearest Lucy, Good Night —

62. Audubon notes in the entry for December 18 that "Mr Witham Subscribed to my Work." Witham is listed among the European subscribers to the *Birds of America* as "Henry Witham, Esq. of Lartington, Durham" (OB, 5:649).

63. Sir John Watson-Gordon (1788–1864) was an Edinburgh painter of portraits and historical scenes of rising importance in the 1820s.

I gave early orders to M$\underline{\text{rs}}$ Dickie to have a particuarly good Breakfast ready by 9 o'clock because M$\underline{\text{r}}$ Whitham had offered last night to come and partake of such with me — I then took to my Brushes and finished my Otter entirely — I Just had been 13 hours at it, and had I Laboured for 13 weeks more I could not have bettered it —

9 and Ten o'clock sounded, no M$\underline{\text{r}}$ Witham — The good Wine of last evening made bad work with him, I dared say — He was to accompany or rather lead me to D$\underline{\text{r}}$ Knox's Lecture on Anatomy — I was hungry, thou mayest suppose — however, he did come at last, well balasted with a probably much better fare than I could afford him, and allowing me to perform mastication in 10 minutes, I gave him some letters to read and sat to at a round rate — We then walk$^\text{d}$ to the lecture room in the Old Town. The weather was beautifull but extremely Cold — We reach$^\text{d}$ the place, asscended the stairs and, on Entering the room where probably 150 students were already assembled, a beating of feet and clapping of hands took place that quite shocked [MS: chock$^\text{d}$] me — We seated ourselves — Each person who entered the room was saluted as we had been, and during the Intervals a low beating was kept up resembling by its great regularity the footsteps of a Regiment on a flat pavement = The Doct$^\text{r}$ came and all was hush$^\text{d}$ as if silence had been the principal study of all present =

I am not an Anatomist — No, unfortun[ately] I know scarce more than nothing. Yet I was much [Inte****d] in the Lecture — and the words Larinx, Clavicles, Spinal Bones, Rotulas came to my ears with pleasure — The Lecture lasted ¾ of an hour — The Doct$^\text{r}$ felt also the effects of London Griffith's Claret of 105 pounds per 20 dozens — He said his head ached most confoundedly and he was by no means well — I would have lik$^\text{d}$ to have seen Friend Bridges this morning. I will be bound he was not up as I was at 6 nor painting at 7, the dawn of the present days — but Instead of seing him, I saw the Anatomical Museum and preparations of M$\underline{\text{r}}$ Bell of London — This sight was extremely disagreable — The Venereal Subjects were shocking [MS: chocking] beyond all I ever thought could be — I was glad to leave this charnel [MS: charner] and breath again the salubrious atmosphere of the streets of Fair Edina —

I accompanied M.ʳ Witham to my exibition. It was well ornemented with many Ladies. I was much gratified that it so well bore the test [MS: text] of all description of Judges — I gave him a ticket for his familly and went home ＝

I was engaged most certainly to dine out but could not recollect where, and I was seating predicamenting when the Reverend W. J. Bakewell, thy first Cousin, being the son of Rob.ᵗ Bakewell the Zoologist and famous Grazier of Derbyshire,[64] came in to see me and to say how pleased he was at the sight — He was Thin and Tall but being a Unitarian said he was not liked &.ᶜ &.ᶜ. He told me of having seen Thomas Bakewell when in England for Glass Blowers[65] — He said that his Father spoke oftener of thine than of thy Uncle Benjamin of Pittsburgh and ask.ᵈ me if I had known D.ʳ Priestley — I remember having seen him at Fatland Ford[66] and also that he paid me a visit with thy Father at Mill Grove before Our Mariage ＝

He gave me his card, Invited me to see him often, and to Dine with him the next unengaged day, which will be next Monday week —

I saw M.ʳ & M.ʳˢ Lizars and told them that, as I could not remember my Engagement, I would dine with them and I did so ＝ I received a Letter from M.ʳ Monroe of the Liverpool Institution in answer to my last. I was Glad to hear that he had forwarded the little figures to John and thy Box of Sparrs — He also said that he thought I was elected a member of the Literary and Philosophical Society of Liverpool ＝

My time at M.ʳ Lizars is allways agreable. They are both kind to me

64. Lucy's cousin William Johnstone Bakewell (1794–1861) was a Unitarian minister in charge of congregations in Chester and Edinburgh. He would later immigrate to the United States and settle in Pittsburgh. His father was Robert Bakewell (1767–1843), a geologist; his *Introduction to Geology* (1813) was widely read and saw several editions. In 1813 he moved to London, where he continued to lecture and write books in the natural sciences. Audubon's references to him as a zoologist and grazier of Derbyshire seem mistaken.

65. Thomas Bakewell (1792–1866) was the son of Lucy's father's beloved brother Benjamin. In his youth Thomas had studied the natural sciences, especially chemistry. When his family moved to Pittsburgh in 1808, Thomas assisted his father in his glass factory. In 1815 he traveled to England to recruit skilled glass workers, which was legally risky because of laws prohibiting some skilled workers from emigrating. Thomas had been a partner in his father's glass firm since 1813.

66. That is, Audubon remembers having seen the Reverend W. J. Bakewell at Fatland Ford, not Priestley.

and both very aimiable and appear to live quite Happy together —
They were both very much pleased with my Portrait =

It was concluded that the Wild Turkey Cock should be the Large
Bird of my first Number to prove the necessity of the size of the Work.
I was glad to retire at a goodly hour. I felt fatigued of being up every
night untill one or 2 o'clock, and now that it is a quarter of Ten, I will
go and lay down, rest and think of thee, of our sons, America and my
very Extraordinary Situation at present in Edinburgh, look^d upon with
respect, receiving the attentions of the most distinguished Caracters
and supported by all men of Science — It is really Wonderfull. Am I
really deserving all this? — God Bless Thee, sweet Wife —

TUESDAY DECEMBER 5$\underline{TH}$ 1826 —

After I had put my Otter in the exibition — I met Mr Syme and
with him visited Mr Nicholson,[67] Portrait Painter — I saw there,
independant of his own work, a Picture from the far famed Snider[68]
intended for a Bear beset by Dogs of all sorts — The Picture had great
Effect — fine Coloring and still finer finishing, but the Bear was no
bear at all and the Dogs we[re] so badly drawn, distorted mingled
Caricatures, that I am fully persuaded that Snider did not draw from
specimen put up in real Postures in my way — I was quite disapointed,
so much had I heard of this man's Pictures of Quadrupeds —

I thought of Dr Traill who, although well acquainted with Birds, had
never remarked that the Engraver of Willson's work had allways put
both legs of each Individual on the same and off side — This made me
discover how easy man can be Imposed on his better Judgment with
artificial beauties — for really this Picture so much admired by every
one else had no merit in my Estimation —

Mr N. *is only an Artist.* We then proceeded to Messrs Watson. I saw
there better work and one or [two] very handsome and good Pictures
— I again Proceeded to Miss Patrickson in Great King Street — a good

67. William Nicholson (1781–1844) was a prolific painter of portraits and landscapes. In May
1826 he had cofounded the Scottish Academy of Painting, Sculpture and Architecture.

68. Frans Snyders (1579–1657) was a Flemish painter known especially for his boldly colored
depictions of game animals, hounds, and foods.

soul, I dare say, but a pupil of small attainments — her mother quite a Lady!

I returned to the Institution and had the pleasure of meeting Cap$^{\underline{e}}$ Bazil Hall of the Royale Navy, his Wife[69] and Lady Hunter — They were extremely kind to me — spoke of the Greg familly and my good Old Friend M$^{\underline{rs}}$ Rathbone in terms that delighted me — The Captain ask^{d} if I did not intend to exibit by Gass Light, when I replied that the Institution had granted me so much favor already that I could not take it upon myself to speak of it — He promissed to do so at once and told me that he would write me the answer of M$^{\underline{r}}$ Skin the Secretary —

I received their Cards and must, of Course, call upon them soon — I dined at home, Lucy, for after all I found that I had forgotten again that for this day I had no Invitation, and I was heartilly glad of it — I saw the Friends Lizars and took my usual Cup of Coffee from the hands of Lady N$^{\underline{o}}$ 1, as I liked so much to do from those of that delightfull Girl Hannah Rathbone a Glass of Wine — How much I would like to see her fine eyes just now or thine, or hear thee or her talk and her dear mother, or my Johny or Victor or thy sweet lovely sister Eliza — Ah, nothing but a deep sigh answers to me, and my poor pen goes on scratching wishes quite in vain, but God Bless you all —

I returned home full intent on writting to thee, but my heart is positively giving way and I must wait and feel better for it. I must perhaps wait untill I hear from thee first — I wrote the History of my Picture of the Otter and with a note to Professor Wilson sent him for Corection — May God grant thee Health, Lucy, sweet Lucy, good night — †

EDINBURGH DEC$^{\underline{R}}$ 6$^{\underline{TH}}$ 1826 — WEDNESDAY

My Breakfast over, I paid a visit to Professor Jameson and proposed to him to give him an account of the habits of the Turkey Buzard instead of the Wild Turkey — He appeared anxious to have either — I spoke to him about the presentation to the Wernerian Society. He then again

69. Basil Hall (1788–1844) was a British navy captain, travel writer, and fellow of the Royal Society. He had retired from the navy in 1823 and in 1825 married Margaret Hunter, with whom he would tour the United States in 1827–28.

said it was quite necessary, that it would attach me to the Country, and that he would give me all his assistance —

I visited Cap⁵ Bazil Hall of the Royal Navy. He lives now in S⁵ Colme [MS: Cholm] Street N⁰ 8, where I had the pleasure of finding him *at Home*! As I assended the stair case, I heard distinctly the sweet sounds of a Piano well fingered. I entered the room and saw Both the Captain and his very Interesting Lady, the performer on the Instrument — Few Women ever attracted my notice more forcibly at first sight, although by Nature Thou knowest well I am dearly fond of aimiable ones — but something more than common was her fine face, and the spectacle [MS: spectable] she wore had a Power that I cannot describe to thee — Her Youth & form all were in great unisson to engage a Liking — Her husband received [me] with great true Politeness and a degree of Kindness far difering from usual on such slight acquaintance — I spent there an hour very agreably — They spoke of visiting the United States, and I engaged them strenuously to do so — Cap⁵ Hall, a man of Extraordinary Talents, a great traveller and a rich man profering friendship towards thy Husband, was very acceptable, thou mayest be sure — If I am a *Phrenologist at all*, they are a most happy couple, and I derived this conclusion from the Lady telling her husband, as I bid them good morning, to accompany me down stairs quite low and in such a tone as I am sure she never thought I heard — He told me that I would be received an Honorary Member of the W. S. with acclamation —

I made for Friend Neill's Establishment in the Old Town to see by what time my Memorandums must be ready for the Press — To my astonishment I was told that Tomorow was the last day, and I ran home to scrible — Professor Monroe called on me with a friend, asked me what I would charge to draw Skulls for him &ᶜ. Then M⁵ Syme brought an Engraver to consult with me on the subject of my Portrait being Immortalized — Young Gregg paid me a visit, and at last, in a great Hurry, I dressed and ran to M⁵ Lizars to know the way to M⁵ Ritchie, where I had to go & dine — I saw M⁵ L's sister Just arrived — M⁵ L gave me a Young Man to accompany to Great George Square in the Old Town, and I reachᵈ the spot appointed just one hour and half too late — I dined, however, and dine[d] well — M⁵ Weiss was there, Miss Comb, Miss Scot and several others, but after wine drinking, when the Gentlemen ascended to their Tea Room, a Crowd of Ladies and

Gentlemen not before seen were in waiting to see the *Great Unknown* of America[70] — I think, Lucy, I may well call myself thus just now — We had music & Dancing, and I left them at ½ past nine, all at their pleasures, to come & write more — Mr Weiss again accompanied me =

I must tell thee that yesterday some *greater unknown* than myself gave a false note of one Pound at my Exibition and, therefore, I paid him well to go & see my Birds = A man who met me to day at the doors of the Institution and who was not a *Phrenologist* ask^d^ me if they were very well worth seing — Dost thou think I said Yes? — Not I, I positively said no, and off he went — but a few yards off I saw him stop & talk to another man and again he returned, when I saw him go in, when I dare say he paid his shilling — Sweet Wife, God Bless thee, good night —

THURSDAY DECEMBER 7TH 1826 —

I wrote as hard as I could untill 12 o'clock, when I finished copying the Letter to Professor Jameson on the habits of the Vulture. I went with the last sheet to the Printer — received a short note from P. Jameson desiring that I should put the University of Edinburgh as a Subscriber for my Work. I was highly pleased with this, [the university] being a powerfull leader. I saw in this day's paper that Charles Bonaparte had arrived in Liverpool in the Canada from New York. How I longed to see him. Had I been sure of his remaining at Liverpool a few days, I certainly would have gone there by the mail — How surprised I am at the same time at having no letters either from thee or any one in America, not even One from the familly Rathbone =

I saw to day 2 of my Proofs of Drawings compleated. I was well pleased with one of them, more so than with the first =

My Dinner at Mr Howe's, the Editor of the *Courant*, was agreable, but we had no females to render the conversation less rude — Mr Allan, the Artist, came after 9 when his Lessons were just ended at the Academy of Arts — an extremely agreable man, full of gayety, wit and good sense,

70. When Sir Walter Scott began publishing the Waverly novels, he preserved his anonymity with great success. The phrase "the great unknown" became the common way to refer to the author of these phenomenally popular novels. Audubon's application of the phrase to himself shows that his confidence has risen since the day he feared association with John Dunn Hunter (see the entry for July 28).

a great Traveller in Russia — Greece, Turkey &^{c} &^{c} == I went to M^r
Lizars's house with him, had there some sweet music from his Wife['s]
Sister Miss *Ann Wilson*, took a Glass of Scotch Tody and returned
home at 11. — I am positively quite done, Harassed about thee. So
apprehensive am I that I cannot enjoy any thing, not even a few hours
repose at night — God Bless Thee, Lucy, God Bless Thee —

EDINBURGH FRIDAY 8<u>TH</u> DEC<u>R</u> 1826 —

Men and their Lifes are very like the diferent growths of our Woods.
The Noble Magnolia, all Odoriferous, frequently sees the teazing nettle
[MS: neetle] growing so near its large trunk as to be sometimes touch^d
by it == Edinburgh, my sweet Wife, contains a Wilson, a Jameson, and
with many others, all great men, a Walter Scot, but it contains also
many teazing netles of the Genus Mammalia amongst which *Men* [h]
old a very preponderent station —

Now I run into one of those curious aerial flights of the mind that
puzles thee quite, I know, but, as I [am] never fond of distressing thee
long at a time, I will go bluntly to Work and say that a Drawing of
Mine was *Gently purloined* last evening from the Rooms of the Royal
Institution by some one teazing Nettle who had certainly strong
propensities for Drawing == So runs the fact: perhaps a few minutes
before the close of the Doors, a Somebody in a large Cloak paid his
shilling, entered the Hall, and made his round *Watchman* like with
great Caution — took a Drawing from the Walls, rolled it up carefully,
and walk^d off carefully also — The Porter and Men attending missed
it almost imediately — and this morning I was ask^d if I or Mr Lizars
had taken it to his house to be engraved — No — no such things — I
Imediately Informed Mr Lizars, we Enquired for advise of Mr Bridges,
went to the Court, and Cap^e Robeson, who by the bye was at the Battle
of New Orleans — Issued a Warrant against a Young Man Deaf &
Dumb of the name of Ingles, who was unfortunately strongly Suspected
== Mr Lizars & I had called on a friend of this Youth, who told us that
he would sift the business and could tell all about it during the day —

I went to the Exibition whilst Mr Lizars and a Constable went to a M^r
Henderson in Kilrick Street, and there [*****] — I met on the stairs a
beggar Woman, with a child in her arms but passed her without much
notice beyond pitying her in her Youth — reach^d my door and seeing a

Roll of Paper there, I pick^d it up, walk^d in, open^d it & found my Drawing of the Black Poll Warbler! ═

Is this not an Interesting tale this? The thief, who ever he may be, God grant him pardon, had been Terror Struck, had heard we conceived of our steps, and taken this method of returning the Drawing before detected — I was in time to stop the Warrant, and the affair was silenced — The wonder of all this is that the lad suspected is the Son of Sir Henry Raeburn [MS: Raiburn],[71] a distinguished familly ═ During the afternoon I was called on Twice by Cap^e Bazil Hall, who was so polite as to present me with a Copy [in] 2 Volumes of his Work on South America[72] with a remarkably polite note — and an Invitation to Dine with him Thursday next at 8 o'clock — His note was this,

8. St Colm St Friday E,3 —

Dear Sir

I beg you will do me the favor to accept a Copy of a work which I published some time ago on South America — This is a very feeble method which I take to express the admiration I feel for your wonderfull Collection. I remain Your most O^b S^t, Basil Hall

You will not forget to come to us at 8 o'clock Thursday the 14th —

Now it happened that Cap^e Hall was the supporter of Young Ingles and was heartily pleased that the affair had had no further effect — but I assure thee that the *Effect* it had on *me* was tremendous. I ran about to & fro to proceed to business — became wet to the skin, fretted to my very heart and wished the business, the Drawing and the Nettle at the ~~~~

"What?"

What, the Devil, to be sure —

71. Sir Henry Raeburn (1756–1823) had been one of Edinburgh's most important and influential portraitists. Ford identifies Ingles as an illegitimate son of Raeburn (*Journal*, 377n52).

72. *Extracts from a Journal, Written on the Coasts of Chili, Peru, and Mexico*, 2 vols. (Edinburgh, 1823).

The weather was miserable and I had only 30 persons at the Exibition
— but another very strange thing took Place — I was Invited to
Dinner by M͞r Bridges at M͞r Bridges — M͞r Bridges was to call on me
to accompany me but M͞r Bridges came not and I, at last reduced to
all extremities, eat all in the House, where nothing is provided for
me when I say that I dine out — I spent my Evening pleasantly at M͞r
Lizars's and now have come to bid thee well, Happy and a Good Night,
my Love —

EDINBURGH SATURDAY 9TH DEC͞R 1826 —

The Principal Incident of this day was that I purchased Cloth for a
Coat from M͞r Bridges and wrote Closely during all the morning from 6
o'clock untill 12 — Without either having washed, comb[ed] or taken
away my night Cap for, Lucy, I wear such things now — My Landlady
was frightened for my health's sake that I wore no caps, and I, to save
her from falling into a swoon about it, told her to procure 2 for me,
which [she] did for 6 shillings — but I was thus writting and fretting
because I had no news from thee, when M͞r Hall came and handed
a note from Lady Hunter requesting the Honor of my Company on
Saturday next to dine at 6 — He look^d at me with Surprise and thought,
I dare say, that I was the strangest looking Author of the day =
    I had much running about, with Professor Jameson to the Printer
&͞c — Took my M.S. to M͞r Lizars, who took it to Professor Brewster —
We visited the Museum Together — called on a M͞r Wilson, where I
saw a most beautifull dead Pheasant that I long^d to have to paint, went
to Doct͞r John Lizars[73] lecture on anatomy and saw him operate on a
beautifull Dead body of a female quite fresh = but afterward I went to
the disecting rooms, where such horrible stench [MS: staunch] existed
that I thought I would sufocate — I soon made my escape, I assure
thee, and went home —
    The day was extremely wet — yet I had upwards of 100 people to see
my Birds; therefore, to day paid the Expenses of the week, which has

73. John Lizars (1791/92–1860) was an innovative and successful Edinburgh surgeon and
brother of William Home Lizars. He had been a fellow of the Royal College of Surgeons in
Edinburgh since 1814. His brother had engraved his five-volume *A System of Anatomical Plates of
the Human Body* between 1822 and 1826.

not be[en] so good as the preceeding one == I spent my evening at M.ᵣ
Lizars — talking on all sorts of Subjects == We heard that M.ᵣ Selby
would be here on Monday night next —

Now, my Love, God Bless thee. I shall write to thee a long Letter
tomorow that I hope will reach thee well and quite Happy —

EDINBURGH DEC.ᴿ 10ᵀᴴ 1826 — SUNDAY[74]

My Beloved Wife —

After postponing day after day for the last Two weeks writting to
thee, full of Hopes that each new day would bring some tidings of
thee, or of some one connected with me in America, I am forced to
set and write filled with fears and sorrow ==

Many of the vessels I have wrote by have returned from America
with full Cargoes, but nothing from thee — It is the more surprising
because, a Fortnight since, Dewitt Clinton answered a Letter of mine
dated Manchester and Inclosed one of recommendation to Gen.ˡ
Lafayette: ==

My situation in Edinburgh borders almost on the miraculous,
without education and scarce one of those qualities necessary to
render a man able to pass thro the throng of the learned here; I am
positively look.ᵈ on by all the Professors and many of the Principal
persons here as a very extraordinary Man — I brought from
Liverpool 13 Letters of most valuable Introduction == After I had
delivered them and my Drawings had been seen by a few of those
persons, I requested them to Engage all their acquaintances to call
on me and see them also. For that Purpose I remained each day
for a week at my lodgings from 10 untill 2, and my room was filled

---

74. There is some puzzlement about the date of this entry because the manuscript letter edited
and published in Howard Corning's *Letters of John James Audubon, 1826–1840* is dated December
21 (7). However, the date in the manuscript journal is clearly December 10 and occurs between
the entries dated December 9 and December 11. Audubon's opening reference to his not having
written to Lucy "for the last Two weeks" is not borne out by the manuscript evidence. The date
of December 10 is also supported by Audubon's statement that "[i]t is now a month since my
work has been begun by M.ᵣ W. H. Lizars," who agreed to "undertake the Publication of the
first Number of my Birds of America" (according to the entry for November 19) shortly after
November 8—that is, about a month before December 10. Alice Ford's claim that the date should
be December 9 seems in error (*Journal*, 386n55).

constantly by persons of the first rank in Society — After that, the comittee of the Royal Institution having met, an order was passed to offer me the Exibition Rooms *Gratis* for some weeks. My Drawings were put up in the splendid Room, all the news papers took notices of them in a very handsome manner, and have [MS: having] continued to do so constantly; the rooms have been well attended when the weather has in the least permitted it — Last Saturday I took in 15£. It will continue open to the last of Christmas week, when I will remove them to Glascow 50 Miles from here, where I expect to do well with them — I have had the pleasure of being introduced to several Noblemen here and have found them extremely kind, Indeed =

About a fortnight [MS: 14ᵗ] since, Sir W. Jardine came to spend a few days here purposely to see me. He was almost Constantly with me. He and Mʳ Selby are engaged in a General Ornithological Work, and as I find I am a usefull man that Way, it is most likely that I shall be connected with them, with a good share of credit and a good deal of Cash. They both will be in in a few days, when the matter will be discussed over at length and probably arranged.

It is now a month since my work has been begun by Mʳ W. H. Lizars of this City. It is to come out in numbers of 5 prints, all the size of life and on the same size Paper of my largest drawings, that is called double elephant — They will be brought up and finished in such superb style as to Eclipse all of the kind in existence. The price of each number is two guineas, and all individuals have the privilege of subscribing for the whole or any portion of it — Two of the plates were finished last week. Some of the engravings colored are now put up in my exibition Rooms and are truly beautifull — I think that the midle of January the first number will be compleated and under way to each subscriber — I shall send thee the very first, and I think it will please thee. It consists of the Turkey male — the Cuckoos on the Papaws, and three small drawings that I doubt thou dost not remember but, when thou seest them, I am quite sure, the little Drawings in the Center of those beautifull large sheets, have a fine Effect and an Air of Richness and Wealth that cannot help ensure success in this Country: =

I cannot yet say that I will ultimately succeed, but at present all bears a better aspect than I ever expected to see. I think that under the eyes of the most discerning People in the World, I mean Edinburgh, if it takes here, it cannot fail any where — It is not the naturalists that I wish to please altogether, I assure thee: it is the wealthy part of the Community — The first can only speak well or Ill of me, but the latters will fill my pockets — The University of Edinburgh having subscribed, I look to the rest of them, 11 in number, to follow — I have here strong friends who interest themselves considerably in my success of the work who will bear me a good hand — but I cannot do wonders at once — I must wait patiently untill the first number is finished and exibit that, for, although my Drawings are much admired, if the work itself was Inferior, nothing could be done, and untill I have it I cannot expect many subscribers — as soon as it is finished, I will travel with it over all England, Ireland & Scotland & then over the European Continent, taking my Collection with me to exibit it in all principal Cities to raise the means of supporting myself well and would like most dearly to add thyself and my Sons also, but can I or can I not expect it? Alas, it is not in my power to say. It does not depend on me or it would soon be accomplished —

The first Professor of this Place, Mͬ Jameson, the conductor of the *Philosophical Journal*, President of the Wernerian Society [MS: P. W. S.] &ͨ, gives a beautifull announcement of my work in his present number, along with an account of mine of the Turkey Buzard = Dͬ Brewster also announces it with my Introductory letter to my work — and Professor of Natural Philosophy John Wilson also in *Blackwoods Magazine*. These 3 Journals[75] prints upwards of 30000 copies so that my name will spread quickly enough =

I am to deliver lectures on Natural History at the Wernerian Society [MS: W. S.] at each of its meetings whilst here, and I will do the same in all the Cities where I will be received an Honorary member — P. Jameson, who also is Professor of Natural [MS: P. of N.] History, told me that I would soon be a member of all the

---

75. Jameson published anonymously "Mr. Audubon's Great Work on Birds of the United States of America," *Edinburgh New Philosophical Journal* 2 (1826–27): 210–11. Brewster published anonymously "Mr. Audubon's Ornithology of the United States of America," *Edinburgh Journal of Science* 6 (1826–27): 184 (see n. 59 for Wilson's notice).

Societies here — and that it would give my Work a great standing thro out Europe =

In the event of ultimate success, I must have either my sons or some other persons to travel for me to see about the Collecting of Payment for the Work and to procure new subscribers Constantly. As I conceive my Victor a well fit man for such business, and as it would at once afford him the means of receiving a most compleat education and a Knowledge of Europe surpassing that of probably any other man — In case, I say, of success, I will write for him Imediately, when I hope no more constraint or opposition will be made to my will = I am now better aware of the advantages of a Familly in unisson than ever, and I am quite satisfied that by acting conjoinetly and by my advise, we can realize a handsome fortune for each of us — It needs but Industry and perseverance = Going to America is a mere song, and I now find that most Valuable Voyages could be made by procuring such articles as are wanted here and most plentifull there: —

It is now about time to know from thee what thy future Intentions are — I wish thee to act according to thy Dictates but wish to know what those dictates are = Think that we are far divided and that either sickness, or need may thro one into a most shocking [MS: chocking] situation, without either friend or help, for as thou sayest thyself, "The World is not Indulgent." Cannot we move together, and feel and enjoy the mutual need of each other? Lucy, my Friend, think of all this very seriously. Not a portion of the Earth [MS: Hearth] exists but will support us amply, and we may feel Happiness any w[h]ere if Carefull. When you receive this, set and Consider well. Consult N. Berthoud, Thy son Victor, or such a Person as Judge Mathews, then Consult *thyself* and in a long plain, explanatory letter, give me thy own kind Heart entire!

In this Country John can receive an Education that America does not yet afford, and his propensities are such that, attached to me, he would be left at my Death Possessor of a Talent that would be the means of his support for his life — I earnestly begged of thee in all my Letters since I discerned that I was advancing in the world, to urge him by all means to set to and begain a Collection of drawings of all he can = and not to destroy one Drawing, no matter how

Indiferent — but to take all from Nature — I find here that altho I have drawn much, I really have not drawn half enough — Tell him to employ my method of putting up Birds before him &$^{\underline{c}}$, to Draw fishes, reptiles — Eggs, trees, Landscapes, all, all he can draw — It will be most valuable to him. If he was Industrious and work well & Closely, by the time he comes of age, he would be quite able to have a Collection that would be a little fortune for him to begain upon =

I was much surprised at hearing of Charles Bonaparte in Liverpool last week — He arrived in the very Vessel that took thy watch to New York, the Canada —

The diference of Manners here from those of America are astonishing. The great round of Company I am thrown in has become fatiguing to me in the extreme, and does not agree with my early habits — I go to dine out at 6, 7, or 8 o'clock in the evening, and it is one or Two in the morning when the party brakes up, then painting all day, with my corespondance that Increases daily. My head is like a Hornet's Nest, and my body wearied beyond Calculation, yet it has to be done. *I must* not refuse a single Invitation —

(Here I spoke of the rev. Wm Bakewell —)†

Edinburgh must be the handsomest City in the World. Thou wouldst like it of all things, I think, for a Place of residence —

When I send thee the first number of the Birds of America, I will also send a Book given me containing 51 Views of the Place — In the event of You all removing from America, keep those things, I beg = Finding that I was not going to London for some time, I forwarded the Letters I had for M$^{\underline{rs}}$ Middlemist from here and request her to let me know where Charles's wife resided, that I could have the money paid her thro the secretary of Legation at London — I have [been] and am yet most surprised that C. M. should not have answered my letters to him when I conceive it of the very greatest Importance to his future Welfare — How is he and what does he do now? =

I regret extremely my not having brought Barrels of Reptiles of all sorts with me. I could get fine prices, I assure thee, and also for rare birds skins — seeds of Plants, but I thought I had enough to attend to —

I very frequently spoke to thee respecting the very great kindness I have experienced from the familly Rathbone of Liverpool. This kindness they continue to me so constantly and in such a manner that I feel quite anxious to repay them thro our humble means: W^am^ R. is one of the principal members of the Royal Society of Liverpool [MS: R. S. of L.] and one of the wealthiest merchants there. I wrote thee from his Mother's House, dated Green Bank, to forward him some seeds, Dried flowers, leaves &^c^ and some segments of the largest trees = I Hope that thou wilt attend to these things, for in the event of thy coming to England, thou wouldst land and come to their care — and they would be as kind to thee as they have been to me — The seal with which I now close all my principal Letters, was given me by Mrs Rathbone, the mother of that excellent familly, and accompanied by a letter that would honor any man living — Keep always directing thy Letters to them, and write to Mrs R. herself. She will be a most valuable friend to thee —

Since here I have painted 2 Pictures in Oil, now in the Exibition — One contains 11 Turkeys with a landscape. The other is my Otter in a Trap. My success in Oil painting is truly wonderfull — I am called an astonishing artist &^c^. What diferent times I see here, courted as I am from those I spent at the Beech Woods, where certain people scarcely thought fit to look upon me — I have written to Mr Bourgeat — Dr Pope — Judge Mathews — N. Berthoud — Victor — W^am^ B., all to no purpose so far it seems —

I must now close this and bid thee adieu for a while — I have to copy it, as I do all I write — The task is an arduous one, but the consolation of seing what I say to thee from time to time compensates amply =

I very frequently forward thee the news Papers. Each of them contains my name — I dined at the Antiquarian Society and was toasted by Lord Elgin — Thou wilt see it in the papers I sent thee — I would have forwarded thee Books and other objects but, uncertain if thou wouldst not come to Europe as soon as my Plans are *Solidly* fixed, I thought best not to do so — but I assure thee, I cannot at present conceive a failure on my part — and may God grant that it be true. If I can procure in the whole of 2 Years 300 Subscribers, we will be rich, Indeed — God for ever Bless thee — Remember me kindly to all about thee — Kiss my Sons and believe me for ever Thine husband & Friend, J. J. A.

I wrote & Copied this Long Letter to day — but I felt as If I was writting in vain — I saw thy form move about me in such sickly appearance that I again was almost afraid to remain alone in my room so distracted was I with the Idea that some most shocking [MS: chocking] accident had befallen thee or one of our Dear Boys — Oh, my God, destroy that suspence — Let me know if my sweet Lucy is well — for thy sake, amen —

I wrote also to Mʳˢ Rathbone and to Charles Bonaparte under Cover of the Professor Drapier of Bruxelles and was not a little surprised that I was charged 4ˢ and 6ᴾ Sterling for the Inland Postage of this last. Young Gregg called on me. He was as much astonished at not hearing from home as I was at not receiving a word from Liverpool =

I spent my Evening at Mʳ Lizars, talking on our mutual Business — but my eyes were heavy as my heart, and I came home early to bid thee a Good Night —

MONDAY DECEMBER 11ᵀᴴ 1826 —

I had raised quite as dull as ever this morning, had walkᵈ out to the Institution and gone to see Mʳ Lizars without shaving or dressing and probably would have remained in that uncomfortable way the whole of this day had I not found on my return to my Lodgings a Letter from Mʳˢ Middlemist containing Two precious ones from thee. How I read them! Perhaps never in my Life were Letters so well wellcome — and they were such sweet Letters, My Lucy! Thy being quite well, and anxious that I should be so was all thy Laforest could wish — to hear that on the 14 and 27ᵗʰ of August, the most sickly time about thee, both John & thy sweet self had escaped Illness rendered me quite Happy — I kissed thy Name and a hundred of Times blest it with thee — I felt a new life, and braced to encounter any dificulties. I rushed out and ran to announce my pleasure to the familly Lizars, who take so much Interest about thee and our Dear Boys — I determined to answer thee next Sunday —

Now, my Love, thou knowest the great Interest I have for C. Bonaparte — Whilst eating my luncheon, Mʳ Stokoe,[76] whom I had met in Philadelphia with Charles, came to my lodgings and told me that he

76. John Stokoe (1775–1852) was the British naval surgeon who tended to Napoleon on St. Helena from June 1817 to September 1819.

had received a Letter from him dated London requesting that he should present me his best remembrances. I was highly pleased at this although thought [it] rather strange that he, Charles, had [not] wrote direct to me —

Now, my Lucy, about my New Coat — A Taylor who had been spoken to and who was supposed to be an Expert, came to me to assure me that *he* could not undertake it — A second still superior in Skill acknowledged also his Ineficiency, but at last a third, a German, was shewn [MS: shewn**e] into my room that undertook the Business, and I Hope I shall not [be] troubled about it any more —

I dined at thy Cousin the Reverend W<u>am</u> J. Bakewell — and dined well — His wife is [a] very aimiable woman with 3 little ones, the last 5 weeks old called Robert = A D<u>r</u> Gardner was there, who is a clever man. I left at 7, having engaged to M<u>r</u> Lizars to go with him to the Antiquarian Society — There I met many of my Friends = Doct<u>r</u> Russel[77] engaged me to sup with him on the 18, at ½ past 9 = I saw a Gun Barrel found on the sand of:[†]   that had belonged to the Armada of Spain that tryed to Invade England & Scotland in 1527 — heard [a] very curious and Interesting account of that Event read by D<u>r</u> Hibbert — and saw the Scotish Antiquities collected by the Society — Six or seven persons were presented to be received Honorary members =

At ½ past nine I was again at M<u>r</u> Lizars, w[h]ere I supped and left there at 11. Now, my Lucy, with feelings utterly diferent from those of last night, I will go to bed and dream of thee = May God Preserve thee and bless thee for ever — Good Night, my sweet Wife —

TUESDAY 12<u>TH</u> DEC<u>R</u> 1826 —

I Took one of my Manuscripts Imediately after breakfast, i.e. 10 o'clock, to D<u>r</u> Brewster. I found him writting in a large room where several fine Pictures hung around — He received me very politely and in a few minutes, having blown my nose, and put my neck in a good attitude to suffer my lungs to operate freely, I began reading my letter on the manners of the Carrion Crow — *Vultur Attratus* — when about mid

---

77. James Russell (1754–1836) had been a fellow of the Royal College of Surgeons of Edinburgh since 1777; he was also professor of surgery at the university and fellow of Edinburgh's Philosophical Society and Royal Society.

way my respiration becoming encumbered, I rested a moment to breath when the Doctor took this opportunity to say "that it was very Interesting" — I soon resumed and went thro, thank God! — He who has all his life been [MS: being] an Auctionneer or brought up in the Green Room of Covent Garden Theatre for Instance, with all his Knowledge of Business and of Man, Knows nothing about the feelings that agitate me on such an Occasion. Thou art probably the only one, sweet wife, that ever analised them as I felt them = a man who never look^d into an English Grammar, and very seldom, unfortun[a]tely, in a French or a Spanish One — a man who has allways felt awkward and very shy in the presence of a stranger — one habituated to ramble along with his thoughts allways bent on the beauties of *Nature herself.* — This man, *me*, in Edinburgh to be seated opposite Dr Brewster reading one of my puny efforts at describing habits of Birds that none but an Almighty Creator can ever know = was so ridiculously Absurd in my estimation, during all this while, and whilst I felt the riveting looks of observation of the Learned Personnage before me, that to say that a Cold sweat ran over my body much worst than when I dined with the Antiquarians and that to say this to thee, is only giving thee one of the thousand tormenting thoughts that crossed my mind whilst my Eyes & mou[th] were Reading = However, a Large Black Dog not altogether of the New Found Land Breed came in, caressed his Master, and chassed my most dismall agitations =

I was afterwards Introduced thro a sliding partition into a large Drawing room and presented to the Doct^rs Lady = Again I repeat it: the well bred People of this Country are uncommonly kind to strangers, and I must add, my Lucy, that thy Sex possesses here the most astonishing power of rendering *me*, for Instance, in an Instant, quite at my Ease —

I left = A proof sheet was to be sent me tomorow. I was told that I would be Introduced to Sir Walter Scot on Monday Next at the Royal Academy = Poor me — Far from Walter Scot I could talk to him. Hundred[s] of times have I said quite Loud in the Woods, as I looked on a silvery streamlet, or the sickly swamp, or the Noble Ohio, or on Mountain tops loosing their peaks [MS: picks] in Grey mist — Oh, Walter Scot, where art thou? Wilt thou not come to my Country? Wrestle with Mankind and stop their Increasing ravages on Nature &

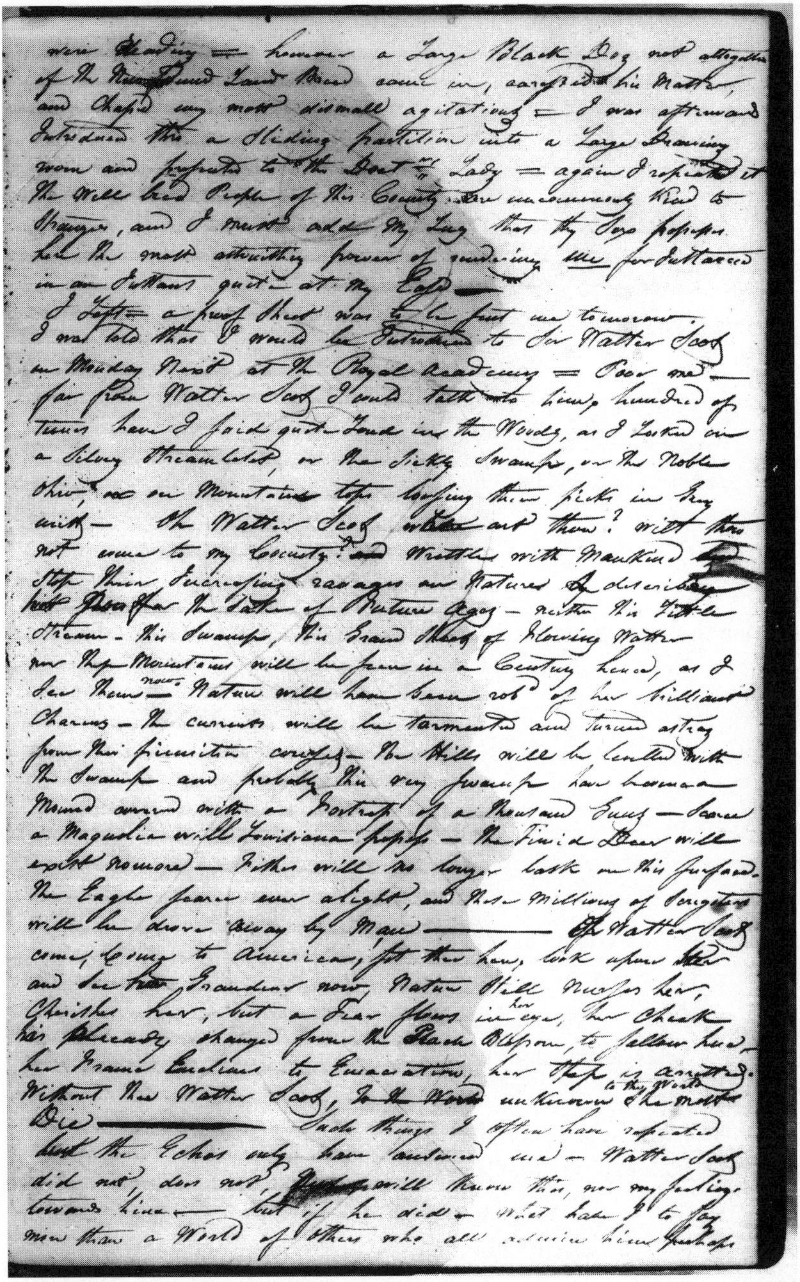

FIG. 20. Audubon's December 12 plea to Sir Walter Scott

describe her Now for[†] the sake of Future Ages — Neither this Little stream — this swamp, this Grand sheet of Flowing Watter, nor these Mountains will be seen in a Century hence, as I see them now. Nature will have been rob^{d} of her brilliant charms — The currents will be tormented and turned astray from their primitive courses — The Hills will be levelled with the swamp and probably this very swamp have become a mound covered with a Fortress of a thousand Guns — Scarce a Magnolia will Louisiana possess — The Timid Deer will exist no more — Fishes will no longer bask on this surface, the Eagle scarce ever alight, and those millions of songsters will be drove away by Man — Oh, Walter Scot, come, Come to America! Sit thee here. Look upon her and see her Grandeur now. Nature still nurses her, cherishes her, but a Tear flows in her eye, her cheak has already changed from the Peach Blossom, to sallow hue — Her Frame Enclines to Emaciation, her step is arrested. Without thee, Walter Scot, unknown to the world she must Die —

Such things I often have repeated, but the Echoes only have answered me — Walter Scot did not, does not, never will know this, nor my feelings towards him — but if he did — what have I to say more than a World of others who all admire him perhaps more than I do because, more enlightened, they are better Judges of his Worth —

Ah, Walter Scot, when I am presented to thee — my head will droop, my heart will swell, my limbs will tremble, my lips quiver, my tongue congeal. I shall be mute, and perhaps not even my Eyes will dare turn towards thee — Great Man; nevertheless will I feel Elevated that I was permitted to touch thy hand, and I shall Bless thee within in spite of all the deadness of my Phisical faculties ═

Lucy, Walter Scot resides the Next Door from Dr Brewster in Coats Cressent N° 11.

My Exibition appeared to have been abandoned, and I ordered the News Papers to say that it would Close Saturday next — Mr Skin had advised me to do so — and he also told me this morning that he would present me as a member to the Antiquarian Society at the Next Meeting —

I Expected to have seen Mr Selby and Sir W^{am} Jardine, but neither came to town —

I went to Mrs Welbank, N° 41 Albany Street, to Dine with W^{am} Gregg — Dr Gardner was there — Mrs Welbank has a Red Nose, Lucy — Now, when I say red, I do not mean to say that it is covered with that soft downy, velvety light substance that I often have seen and felt on thine, composed of a Bloom of pure White, with a thought of vermillion — Not I — I Infer that the strongest decoction of the little Insect called *cochenille*[78] would only be a very poor color compared with the Truly red colored Nose of the Lady here mention^{d} — This redness extends from the center of the ridge, off and over the cheeks, the forehead, & the chin in rich profusion, and along with the Cap, the Ribbands and the Dress, I thought that Nothing so very red had ever met my Eye before = She is aimiable, however, and so are her Daughters and so, Lucy, never mind the Color! —

I had promised to accompany Young Gregg to a Society where he was going to deliver a lecture on the Mental Powers of the *Annimal Creation* — I knew what he ment, because I felt it, and would have gone — but I was too old for Such a Society; and having a great anxiety to see Mr Selby, I made an apology and left at 7 — I arrived at Mr Lizars — He was busily Employed assorting Mr Selby's Plates for 11 numbers. I was glad to see how very Industrious he was — An apointment called him from home, and I was left with the Ladies — but I became very sleepy — I felt a great contentedness this Evening — I thought of thee and was so pleased with thy Letters, that I begged their pardon and have now come to go to bed, where I think I will sleep better than I have done since in Edinburgh — God bless thee, My Wife — Good night, my Lucy —

WEDNESDAY. DECEMBER 13TH 1826. —

Although it is late, I am not the least drowsy or sleepy this evening. I have spent the greater portion of this day in the company of Mr Selby, the Ornithologist! Probably thou wilt feel alarmed at my being brought in Contact with a man of such Genius, but really thou needst not — Mr Selby is a Gentleman Naturalist — not in the least resembling

78. In English, "cochineal" (*Dactylopius coccus*), a scale insect, the females of which are used to make a common red dye.

the Venomous Tallow Chandler of Philadelphia,[79] the possessor of 3
Greek words, 7 of Latin, none belonging to his what ought to be his
usual Language, and the Describer of Objects unknown yet to the
Almighty. M̲r̲ Selby is not a man that would say at a large meeting of
the Wernerian Society that *he* would be damned rather than to give me
a favorable vote of Election — He is not a man who would say that I
knew nothing about Drawing, nor the habits of Birds. No, my Lucy, M̲r̲
Selby is not an Hipocritical Fool, I assure thee =

In appearance he resembles N. Berthoud very much Indeed, is
nearly the same complexion, perhaps a little taller, well formed, plain,
polite, Clever but unassuming, and such a person I conceive M̲r̲
Selby to be that I would open my heart to him as freely as I did to my
Benevolent Friend M̲rs̲ Rathbone. I was more than 2 hours with him at
the Institution — He was greatly pleased with my Drawings, wishes to
understand the Style, and he shall —

I dined with him at M̲r̲ Lizars in C̲o̲ of M̲r̲ D. Lizars; we talk̲d̲ all
Ornithology — I wish I possessed as much knowledge on the Scientific
part of that study as he does — I read to the whole my Letter on the
Buzard, and he was again quite pleased, took it with him to read it to Sir
William Jardine, to whose [MS: whom] Hall he goes tomorow to return
on Monday next =

About 2 o'clock Lord *Clengertie* and M̲rs̲ Murray called on me in their
Carriage but, being absent, a card was left and has cut me so much
more to perform tomorow, when it would be impolite not to return the
Visit = Then Doctor Brewster came, and brought me the proof of the
Carion Crow — He read himself. We corrected it together and, after
having thank[ed] me for it — he told me that it was a question if or not
I could be made a member of the Royal Academy — for 30 foreigners
only were alloted by Law and they had already infringed on it and had
now 33, but that perhaps this might operate favourably for me —

This evening when I returned, I found a very kind note from [Doctor
Brewster] thanking me for my M.S. and giving me Intelligence that Sir
Walter Scot wished to see me and my Drawings — and that he would
certainly present me to him on Monday next at the Royal Academy =

M̲r̲ Bridges sent me a few lines to Invite me to go and dine with him

79. Audubon refers to his nemesis George Ord, who entered his father's ship-chandler
business in 1800 and continued there until 1829 (see also n. 33, chap. 1).

to a Mr Grime — but, Lucy, Mr Bridges had promised me a notice in the Scotsman[80] which, since a week, has never made its appearance, and I shall think tomorow about the Invitation =

Doct^r Charles James Fox, to whom I was Introduced at Dr Thompson, wrote desiring that, having been very Ill, I would be so good to go & see him, at the Meadows — and here I am, my Lucy, at 2 George Street, come to Bless thee and to wish thee a good night —

THURSDAY 14$^{\underline{TH}}$ DEC$^{\underline{R}}$ 1826 —

I paid my Visit to Mrs Murray this forenoon with little trouble, for the Lady, although at home, was not Visible to poor Audubon — I hastily put my hand in my left side pocket, took my pocket book and out of it a beautifull card on which could be read with much ease "Mr Audubon, 2. George Street" and give it to the slender Youth who stood before me looking at my Hair Like an Ass on a fine Thistle, and made off quickly to Dr Brewster. My Business was before him in an Instant. I wished not to be Introduced to Walter Scot in a Crowd, and he promised not to [do] so — Thus relieved, I went to the College University to see Dr Andrew Brown, Professor of Rhetoric, who had called twice on me — What a bore [MS: Boor] it is to be obliged to return Calls that are merely fashionnable — He also wished that I would write for him, Manners of Indians &^{c} &^{c}, but writting this way is very Irksome and of no benefit to me whatever. I must think of this before I proceed much further in my Authorship = Yet, my Lucy, whilst I was speaking thus (to myself, recollect, for the Doct^r was gone), I arrived at home and sat down Imediately to Write a long set of Memorandums respecting a Journey in America for Cap^e Basil Hall, and I wrote untill my head ached [MS: Hacked] =

I saw M^r & Mrs Lizars, thou mayest be sure not a day passes without — and heard that Mr Howe, the Gentleman Editor of the Courant with whom M^r L and I dined this day week, had Absconded to the West Indies — This did not signify much to me, but his poor Sisters, how dreadfull to them must it be — left unsuported and God knows perhaps without Talents to support themselves — Mr Daniel Lizars procured me Two Cats to paint and Invited me to Dine with him on Friday at 3

---

80. The *Scotsman* had been Scotland's national newspaper since 1817.

o'clock — Now, that suits me to a T, very diferent from to day, for it was 5 minutes past 6 when I reach^d St Colm Street and N° 8 where Cap^e Hall resides, but, my sweet Wife, I had on beautifull New Pantaloons, New Splendid Lafayette Coat, and over all this my own face to embellish the whole — The Company was precisely what the Cap^e had promissed me — Mrs Hall, this Interesting Mrs Hall, had her beautifull Babe in the room — a Rosy fat Little female Urchin — a Mrs Hunter and Daughter — Young Hall, the Advocate — Mr Hall's brother in Law and Wife — Dinner was soon announced and I lead a Lady to it downstairs — We dined in perfect *Bon ton*. I was saved the great trouble of asking any one to Drink Wine, a thing in my opinion detestable quite — a compleat fopish act that I cannot bear — I wish every one was permitted to Drank as he likes and when he likes and not when he Dislikes it —

The Ladies having left, the American Atlas was put on the Table — I read my Notes and the Cap^e follow^d the Course with a Pencil from New York, My Lucy, to New Orleans — Having visited Niagara — St Louis — Nashville and a Hundred other places — we talk^d of nothing Else but a Voyage to America, and Mrs Hall appears quite delighted with the Idea — The Cap^e Wishes to write a Book, and he spoke of it, Lucy, with as Little concern as I would say "Dearest Girl, beloved wife, I will Draw that Duck" — He Engaged me to write what [MS: was] I have seen and make a little Book — How could I make a little Book when I have seen enough to make a Dozen of Large [ones]? — And in such a case, knowing how badly Large books go off, I will not write at all — It [is] 11 o'clock. The Cap^e has accompanied me to the street Door — He says that he [is] glad of having formed my acquaintance — I Bless him within for his good attentions and having walk^d here — and Mrs Dickie having complimented me about my fine Clothes, and my Day now wrote down, I kiss thee in thought — pray God to Bless thee and wish thee Good night —

DECEMBER FRIDAY 15TH 1826 —

My Sweet Wife, I have just returned from the theatre where I saw for the first time The Beggars Opera and the Lord of the Manor[81] == They were both badly represented, certainly — Only one female did her part and could sing — It was most truly a Beggars Opera ==

81. *The Beggar's Opera* is John Gay's popular musical play, first produced in 1728. *The Lord of the Manor* was presumably a play now forgotten.

I went to the Theatre, because I dined at M͟r͟ Daniel Lizars, with his Wife's Brother, and they were all desirous to see a M͟r͟ S͟t͟ Clair perform [MS: performed] = but I really think that M͟r͟ S͟t͟ C. had drank too much Brandy this day — M͟r͟ Lizars has been extremely kind at procuring Cats for a Picture that I will try to begain tomorow = He has a great wish to go to America to live, has an aimiable Scotch Lady for a wife, and a Daughter 6 Years Old who [s**ed] better than all the performers at the Theatre to night to my wish =

I did little more than saunter about all this day — I thought I would use it to refresh me from the constant round of hard work I had been at since here — The weather was very Inviting — and as pleasant as in Louisianna at this season = I visited My Exibition Twice — Upwards of 200 people were there. The Idea of its Closing tomorow had roused the dormant Curiosity of the public = M͟r͟ Lizars procured a Subscriber this morning — I saw him but an Instant =

M͟r͟ Stockoe called whilst I was absent and left word that he wished to see me, that he heard from a friend of mine, and I suppose it must be Charles Bonaparte = M͟r͟ Stockoe, Lucy, was formerly a Phisician of Eminence in the British service — When Do͟r͟ O'Meara was taken away from S͟t͟ Helana, where he acted Phisician to Napolean, this Gentleman was first in line — but *would not* answer the views of his barbarous government and was also called off and dismissed [from] the service with a trifling pension — but he already was liked by Napoleon, and when he returned to [England] he was employed by Joseph Bonaparte to attend his Daughters from Rome to Philadelphia = I saw him during his stay in America with Charles B. at Do͟r͟ Mease = So pleased was Joseph with his Conduct that [he] is now one of his *pensionnaires* and his general agent in Europe =

I wrote to day to M͟rs͟ Middlemist at London and Inclosed a 6 £ note payable to the order of M͟r͟ Charles M. — but not a word from Liverpool yet. Young Gregg, whom I met this morning, has not heard either. It becomes quite a matter of Surprise to us both — God Bless Thee, Sweet Lucy, oh, a Kiss, my Love, and Good Night —

SATURDAY 16ᵀᴴ DEC͟R͟ 1826 —

I have really done much to day, my Lucy. Just read and see and Judge for Thyself —

At ½ past nine, after securing a good breakfast to front the

Intemperance of the weather (it rained hard all day), I went to M.ͬ
Stokoe, N.º 42 Lothian Street in the Old Town. I passed over the
Bridge, look.ᵈ at the Curious portion of the Town below — passed
by 2 side[s] of the College, regretting that such [a] memorable and
valuable monument was quite buried among the antiquated Dismal
houses and narrow streets that surround it — then Wrung the Bell at
M.ͬˢ Robertson's Lodgings, and in a minute was admitted to M.ͬ Stokoe's
room where he was yet snug asleep — so that *I* had enjoyed 3½ hours
of Life during his extra quantum of Sleep =

He wished to see me, he said, because Bonaparte had wrote to him
again and had commission.ᵈ [him] to mention several particular things
to me — that If I wrote this morning to the *Prince of Musignano* [MS:
Lusignano] at London, Care of Mess.ͬˢ Sampson & Battard & C.º &.ͨ &.ͨ
&.ͨ, my letter would probably reach him there = I was obliged to M.ͬ
Stokoe, Invited him to call on me, and left him to snore longer if he
chuse =

I returned home — had begain my letter to Charles Bonaparte
when I received one from my Friend W.ᵃᵐ Rathbone that, I assure thee,
was far from being an agreable one — He feared my Work would not
succeed — &.ͨ &.ͨ &.ͨ; his Mother refused me the pleasure of naming a
Bird after her. The whole made me feel Dismal but Yet not in the least
disheartened about my Enterprise — Since Napoleon became from
the Ranks an Emperor, why should not Audubon be able to leave the
Woods of America a while and Publish and sell *a Book*? — No, No, I
will try, by Heavens, untill each and every hair about me will have dropt
from my body dead, Grey from old age!! —

I Composedly finished my Letter to Charles — took both to
M.ͬ Lizars and read them both — He was not dismayed either and
promised me that *he* would see that *I* should not be ruined = I took
my Letter to the Office and wished it good speed.

Now my Business = I purchased a Tame Pigeon — Killed it —
packed up all my Wires and Hammer — and at one o'clock, having a
Coach, *I* was put *in it* with my *Position Board* to go to the Wernerian
Society at the University — Lady Morton, however, stop.ᵈ me for a
while. She had sent for me from the Institution; therefore, there I
ordered the coach — M.ͬ Skene presented me to a small, Handsome
woman who adressed me in excellent French, shook hands with me

cordially — of course, praised my Drawings and told me that Lady
Douglass had wrote to her from London about me = She ask^d my
residence, took my Card and I, Lucy, bid her farewell, excusing myself
on account of the Engagement at the W. Society — She hoped to see
me at her Hall &^c &^c —

Now, Lucy, I have called for Mr Lizars, and we are both arrived
with all my Apparatus at the College = We enter the Room of the
Wernerian Society of Edinburgh! What a Name in America! The room
is a plain oblong Square, Two Tables — one chimney — many long
seats and a chair for the President were all I saw there at the Exception
of a Sword Fish *stuffed* on the Table for examination that day — Several
persons were already present — I unrolled my Drawing of the Buzard
for them to look at = Professor Jameson came in — the secretary Neill
— Mr Witham I knew — Professor Russel &^c — The first object was
my Letter on the Buzard, read by P. Neill — not very well — Professor
Jameson rose, made quite an Eulogy about it — about my whole [MS:
all] Works and Lastly *Myself* — I had the thanks of the Society &^c — I
then shewed them my manner of Putting up my specimen for Drawing
Birds &^c — This they thought uncommonly Ingenious — Professor
Jameson then Rose and offered me as an Honorary member to the
Society when Every one there clapp^d Hands and stamp^d the Floor in
mark of Approbation — Then again the Professor desired that the usual
Law of sufering the Ellection to be tried for months should be infringed
upon and that I might be Ellected at the next meeting — The same
acclamations took place and the society disolved — I promised to read
at the next meeting a Letter on the Habits of the Alligator =

Now I returned Home in a Coach again — I had paid 2/6 for going
and 1/6 for returning. Thus money was refunded to the good people of
Edinburgh —

I found a note of Invitation from George Combe to Dine on Monday
next, and I answered it imediately —

Now, my Lucy, my Dinner at Lady Hunters — I dressed all new
again, and at precisely six of the Evening, I took Coach for N° 16 Hope
Street — I was shew[n] up stairs and presented to Lady Mary Clark,
who knew both General Wolf & Montgomery, a most aimiable English
Woman of 82 Years of age — Lady Arbuthnot [MS: Arthbunot], Young
&^c — Lady *this* — Sir *that*, Lord *this other* untill I reach^d the Interesting

M̲ͬ̅ˢ Hall, with whom I was too stupid not to shake hands — A Post Captain was there — the rich M̲ͬ & M̲ͬ̅ˢ Harvey &ͨ &ͨ and Young Gregg — I had the pleasure of leading M̲ͬ̅ˢ Hall to the Dinner and was seated next her Mother, Lady Hunter and Lady Clark — We Dined — I did not feel so uncomfortable as usual. This nobility is so uncommonly kind, affable and truly well bred — Lady Hunter & Lady Clark quite nursed me — Capͤ Bazil Hall had the other end of the Table — Young Gregg was next him — I could see M̲ͬ̅ˢ Hall quite well from my seat. I took frequent opportunities of doing so — Little wine was Drank. About 9 the Ladies rose and Capͤ Hall *attacked me* about America again — hundreds of questions were put me by all those noble Folks and I had to answer to all but, as all I said was very plain Truths, I had no dificulty except of feeling choaked from time to time thro my natural Deffect of awkward feelings in Company — When we reach[ed] the Lad[ies] perhaps 11, I was quite delighted to see M̲ͬ̅ˢ Hall making Tea as simply as I have seen thee do it. Without any apparent pomp or Fudge — Lady Hunter brought a Cup of Coffee — a little Girl one of Tea saying she knew that "American Gentlemen liked it" —

The Company had not augmented to a great number and several still were coming — Miss Monroe came in — M̲ͬ̅ˢ Hall, from whom I begged a little music, played swe[e]tly for me on the Pianno — Card tables were prepared — Some set at those — others played at chess, some Examined Prints — some stood talking in Groupes, others *Tete a Tete* — and I, my Lucy, my Head supported by my hand, my Elbow on a rich Table, was Lessening to the sounds of the Piano, had my Eyes watching the whole for observation sake and my Heart full of thee, Sweet Girl — How I longed for thee = This very Bustle thou art fond of. It suits thy Lively Spirits and thy acquirements but not mine — I prefer more solitude in the Woods by thy side — or at Home by the fireside or in† by thy Bosoms side. Such are the Treats for me —

Well, my Love, I left at Last with young Gregg but left all the rest behind me — all busily enjoying themselves this Rainy Sunday morning, for it is now long long after 12 — and I, Lucy, have come to my Lodgings to comit *Murder* = Yes to Comit *Murder* —

My Canvass was ready and the Cats M̲ͬ Daniel Lizars had sent me were ready to be Killed! — I ask̲ᵈ the Son of M̲ͬ̅ˢ Dicky to help me —

We hung the Poor Annimals in 2 minutes each, and I put them up in fighting attitudes ready for Painting when day light would Come —

Now either good night or good morning. It is 2 o'clock. God bless thee. I must have my poor bones a little rested, Good night —

SUNDAY 17TH DEC^R 1826 —

I painted all day, my Lucy, that is, during all the time I could see — and I was up at 6 this morning writting by Candle light that I could not put out untill 9. Mr Bridges called on me for a wonder, for the man is now getting scarce — I dined at home on Fried Oisters and Vinegar stewed Scotch Herrings — sent an apology to W^{am} Gregg and went in preference to Mr Lizars — fell allmost asleep there — but Wash^d my Head, took some Coffee, saw some miserable Drawings of Birds by the renowned Mr Pelletier,[82] and Mr Lizars came to see my Cats that would have been finished this day had I had 4 hours more day light — God Bless thee, Good night —

EDINBURGH MONDAY 18TH DECEMB^R 1826

My Painting of the Cats fighting like Two Devils for a Dead Squirrel I finished at 3 o'clock, having been 10 hours at it = This is Turning out Work of the hands as a Journeyman Carpenter would do =

I received a delightfull letter from my Friend Thomas Sully Dated 9th of last month Inclosing one to Sir Thomas Lawrence to Introduce me = How strange that Dr Mease should now advise me not to cut my Locks when he was so strenuously desirous to have me do so when in Philadelphia.

I dressed and took my painting to Mrs Lizars to shew it her as it rained all day and [she] had been prevented from coming to see me — I was at 5 at George Combe where I dined — the conversation positively Phrenology — George Combe extremely agreable Companion and wittie =

I left them all at seven, called for Mr Lizars and went to the Royal Academy meeting = Two of my Plates were laid on the Table = Doc^r

---

82. Mr. Pelletier is probably the French engraver Laurent-Auguste Pelletier de Chambure (1789–1832).

Brewster and M.̲ Allan wished the Society to Subscribe for my Work, and the comittee retired to act on it and other Business, no doubt =

The meeting *was very Numerous* and, no doubt, [a] very learned one — Thou knowest I cannot well say — but according to M.̲ Ord *who is Learned and an Academician*, I suppose each member here quite as much so at least as M.̲ *George Ord* =

Sir W.ᵃᵐ Jardine and M.̲ Selby arrived and came in a little before the seating of the whole = The door of the Hall was open [MS: ohpen], and we all marched in and seated ourselves on well dressed hair clothed seats = The Room is rich and beautifull — It is a large oblong lined with brilliant scarlet paper imitative of Morocco = The ceiling is devided in large Oblong Compartments raised from the ground of it, painted [in] imitation of Oak = The Windows are Imensely large, decorated with borders resembling those of the Ceiling and had thin Green Jalousies = Two sets of Lamps, each composed of 6 large globular ground Glass preserves,[83] hung from above and lighted with Gass, gave a light in every part of the Room suficient to Read by =

The President sat in an Immense arm chair lined with Red Morocco, and after the results of the last meeting were read — Professor† gave us a long, tedious, laboured Lecture on the origin of Languages, their formation &.ᶜ — It was a very poor mess, I assure thee, although I ought [not] to say so who am not an Academician — Now, my Friend Ord would have swallowed it whole with delight, no doubt, but I could not make either head or Tail of it =

A few fossil Bones of a Mammoth were offered to view and, thank God, we raised the Siege = Sir Walter Scot sent D.̲ Brewster an Apology for not coming this Evening. I saw the hand writting but not the contents =

Sir W. J. and M.̲ Selby had brought Birds with them from Jardine Hall and wish to see my style tomorow, and Tomorow they shall —

M.̲ Witham Subscribed to my Work, but I went away with M.̲ Lizars at 10 without knowing the result from the Comittee, who sat much latter — I had to go to Supper at Doc.̲ & Professor Russel — in

---

83. "Preserves" is a rare Scottish term for a glass lens used in eyeglasses designed to "preserve" one's eyesight. Audubon appears to use it analogously here for the larger lenses of the lamps he is describing.

Abercromby Place = I entered a set of 2 large Rooms upstairs, well furnished and exibiting much Wealth in the Owner. Some Pictures were about the Walls (this is of course [customary] in this country it seems) — but, Lucy, I Entered with as much ease as if I had been going to work at Home = I walked about and chatted with several of the Academicians that had also come and was rather surprised to find that many, although Great men in that way, knew nothing of America beyond her Laws or the Situation of her Principal Cities =

We went down to supper at about 11, every thing magnificently rich — I look^d on each Tart and wished myself by thy side. I felt quite worn out — at work since 6 o'clock, either writting or Painting or Thinking hard — Dining here — going to the Academy — Supping at this house, I felt quite sick of the Whole, and when the Company rose at ½ past 12, I was glad to leave and run here — In 3 minutes I will be in bed, and may God Bless thee, Good night —

EDINBURGH TUESDAY 19TH DEC^R 1826.†

My writting generally takes me full Two hours every morning, and as soon as finished this day, I dressed smart to go to breakfast with Sir W. Jardine and Mr Selby at Barry's Hotel, Prince's Street, where I believe they allways take their abode when they visit Edinburgh — It was just 9. The morning was pure and beautifull — The sun was about raising higher than the line of the Old Town — The horizon [MS: Orison] was all like burnished Gold — The walls of the castle, white in the light and allmost black in their shade, along with many of the detached buildings in the distance, had a surprising effect on my feelings = I thought of the Grandeur of the scene = of that Power of the great Creator that formed it all with a thought, of the Power of Imitative Man, and was launched in deepest reflexions when a child, bear footed, ragged and apparently on the eve of starvation, shook my views and altered my whole devotion. I gave him a shilling. The poor child complained so of want that, [had] I dared, I would have taken it to Sir William and made it breakfast at the Hotel = but thinking how Novel such an act might appear, how little I yet knew Sir W., and how strange the world is, I told him to come with me — I returned home = took all my clothes from my Trunk and, having made an Honest parcel of all my linen I had, that I resolved at the moment never to wear again — I gave it the child. I gave 5 more shillings — I gave it my blessings and I felt — oh, my Lucy, I felt such pleasure — I felt as if God smiled on me! —

Now, I soon reach^d the Hotel and was in a moment with my new Friends = They had brought — Ducks, Hawks and other Birds to Draw after my Fashion — I breakfasted well. The thoughts of the little mendicant gave me an appetite not felt for some days past — We then came to my Lodgings — I shewed the Ornithologists how I put my specimen, squared my paper &^c, and had them both Intently Occupied drawing a little squirrel — They call^d this a Lesson — Is it the first, my Beloved Wife? It was to me like a Dream that I should have come from America to Teach Men so much my superiors =

They work^d very well, Indeed, although I perceived at once that Mr Selby was more Anthusiastic and work^d therefore faster than Sir W., but this one finished Closely as he went so that on the whole it was dificult to give to either the Supremacy = They were delighted — Of course, Mr Selby more particularly so = He already cut out much work to himself for, said he, "I will paint all our own Quadrupeds in oil for my own house" = They remained with me untill we could see no more =

I read them my letter of the *Carrion Crow*, but Dr Brewster had altered it so much that I was quite shocked [MS: chock^d] at it — It made me quite sick — He had Improved the style and destroyed the matter —

I dined at Major Dods, 19 Pitt Street, with a compleat set of Military Gentry — Colonels & Cap^es & Majors and G^ls = I found there to my great astonishment Young Pattison, my companion in the coach from Manchester here — He was cousin to Mrs Dods — Major Dods is the Uncle of John Crawford, who was the clerk of N. Berthoud — I retired early. I did not like the Blustery Talk of all those Warriors — I went Direct to Mrs Lizars and, having found the Ladies by themselves, I felt as if enjoying a pleasant bath after a days march of 50 miles — Miss Annah offered to play on the Piano for me — I felt delighted at this mark of kind attention, and I compar^d her at once to my sweet good Friend of Green Bank — from whom I fear I never will have an answer to any of my letters to her =

Mr Lizars came in with Sir W^am & Mr Selby and announced that I was Ellected by acclamation a member of the Society of Arts of this City. Thus I possess one Tittle in Foreign Lands! —

We talk^d a great Deal about Ornithology — My Work, their Work &^c,

and at ½ past 10 we all three came away Linked closely together untill
we reach^d their Hotel — I am again at my Lodgings and find a kind note
from Cap^e Basil Hall of thanks &^{c} and Inclosing one to Cap^e Campbell
of the R. N. at Glasgow — Now, my Beloved Wife, I feel extremely
anxious to set up all night and write a dozen long letters, but then, If I
do, I fear that I will suffer tomorow and so may God Bless thee for ever!
= Good night, my Love.

WEDNESDAY 20TH DEC^R 1826 EDINBURGH.

Phrenology was the order of this morning. I reached Brown Square at
9 and breakfasted most heartily on Mutton, ham and good Coffee with
Geo. Combe Es^{qr}. The cloth was [*e**] and we proceeded up stairs
into his *Sancto Sanctorum* = A Beautifull Silver Box containing the
Instruments of Measuration was open^d. This was a neat present from
the Ladies who have attended [MS: attented] his Lectures these Last 2
Years =

I was seated fronting the light — Doctor Combe acted as Secretary,
and George Combe thrusting his Fingers about my Hair began to
search for Miraculous Bumps! My Skull was measured acurately as I
measure the Bill or Legs of a new Individual, and all was duly noted
by the Scribe — Then with most exquisite sense of Touch, each
protuberance was found as numbered by Phrenologists and also put
down according to their respective sizes = I was astonded when they
both said that I must be a strong and Constant Lover and affectionnate
Father — that I had great Veneration for High Talented Men — that
I would have made a Brave General — that music was not to be
compared with Painting in me — that I was extraordinarily Generous
&^{c}. Now I know all those to be facts, and how they discovered them
to be so is quite a Puzle to me — I was made to sign my Name and
Residence on one Copy whilst the other was handed me — I was asked
to have Leave to Expose this to the first Lecture — I consented and
came off full of wonder at the singularity of this science =

Geo. Combe gave me a note for a Mr Simpson,[84] the advocate, and I
was accompanied to the court in search of this Gentleman by a Clerk
— I saw Mr Simpson and a Hundred other advocates strutting with

---

84. James Simpson (1781–1853) was an author and advocate who helped George Combe
establish the *Phrenological Journal* in 1823.

their Raven gowns and powdered curled wigs — M.ʳ S. was to Introduce me to *Francis Jeffrey*, but he was not in Court and I pushed off =

I called on Friend Bridges. He was preparing a *Puff for me*. M.ʳ Lizars took me to see Doct.ʳ Greville[85] to know from him the scientific Botanical names of some plants = This Gentleman is tall and handsome = had a Green silk night cap on and has been unfortunately confined to his House for some time, being asmatic — He look.ᵈ at the Drawings and search.ᵈ for names, but I discovered at once that he studied more in his closet than in the Woods — He gave me the names wanted — Invited us to breakfast on Tuesday next, and we bid him good morning at 3 o'clock A.M. —

Neither Sir W. nor M.ʳ Selby came to Finish their Drawing, but M.ʳ Selby sent me 3 most Beautifull Pheasants, and tomorow I begain a Large Painting of these Birds attacked by a Fox for the Exibition in London next March =

I received a polite note from the Earl of Morton[86] to go & spend a day and a night at his Hall — and that his Carriage would call for me on Wednesday next, one week hence —

Then, my Lucy, I wrote an apology to Young Gregg and went to Dinner to M.ʳ Lizars, where I had a most agreable time of it — The company was formed of Bankers, all lively fine fellows — I was betwen the Two Sisters and we all Dranked thy health, my sweet Wife — At 9 I felt an Itching to Write Letters, and I came here for the purpose of setting up all night, but I find I cannot. I am wearied out — I have written 2 — 1 to N. Berthoud & the other to T. Sully, and now I will go & rest a while — God for Ever Bless thee, good night —

Edinburgh December 20ᵗʰ 1826†

My dear M.ʳ Sully — It is quite impossible for me to say how truly delighted I was 2 days ago at receiving your kind letter of the 9ᵗʰ of

---

85. Robert Kaye Greville (1794–1866) was an independent botanist who had been a member of the Edinburgh Wernerian Society since 1819. He had been publishing volumes of his *Scottish Cryptogamic Flora*, which he illustrated, since 1823.

86. George Douglas, sixteenth Earl of Morton (1761–1827), as Audubon points out, had been "great Chamberlin to the late Queen Charlotte." He lived near Edinburgh in Dalmahoy House, the seat of the Earls of Morton.

November enclosing the one for Sir Thomas Lawrence dated 20th of same month.

It is in my present extraordinary situation quite an easy matter to procure Letters of Introduction not only to the President of the Royal Academy but I believe to any person I wish to see during my present wonderful Tour of Europe, but it was the one I now possess from T Sully I longed for, and I assure you it is the only one I shall present to Sir Thomas Lawrence.

My work is positively now under fair way of Publication in all the splendour I have so long wished to see it come forth — I have here valuable friends who have and do take a most earnest interest in its progress and, I may safely add, my Welfare.

Edinburgh, this Queen of Cities, has greeted me with a welcome far superior to that experienced in Liverpool — The Royal Institution presented me with their magnificent Hall to exhibit my Drawings — The Newspapers, the People, the Nobility all have paid me homage due only to very superior men, and to tell you that I feel greatly elevated is only a slender way of expressing the grateful feelings that swell my heart towards all those good persons with whom I am daily in contact — I am thrown into a vortex of business that I never conceived I could manage and also into a round of most agreeable Society — The Professors of all classes are pleased to call me a valuable man to Society. I am Courted by the Nobility, and if I do not become a proud fool (and God forbid) I cannot help but succeed — Think of my painting oil pieces of 11 Wild Turkies estimated at 100 Guineas finished in 10 days work — Conceive what my feelings must be when the famous Professor Jameson is pleased to request that I should write & furnish the Philosophical Journal with a Letter on the habits of some Birds — of my portrait being taken to be engraved at their request — of my being elected member of different Societies by Acclamation and *off hand* — What will my friend Ord say to all this when he sees those Journals — the Papers, and hear[s] of all those wonderful events — Yet with all this, believe me, a dear thought never leaves me a moment. I think constantly of my beloved America and of my friends there — of you most especially who have honored me so much and in whose company I have felt such delight.

I am truly glad that your amiable Daughter has met with *half her match*. May God bless her and her good Husband — Why did you not say a word about your Daughter *the Artist*, my sweet Pupil? Where is your eldest son now? — Believe me, besides hearing that *you* are doing so well, I long to know that each individual of your family is likely to prosper — Present my respects to Doctor Meaze — My locks are still flowing and, I am happy to say, are by no means disagreeable to the eyes of the *learned Public*, who in all countries pay but little regard to outward appearances. Not even my regular upright collar stops me from being introduced to Walter Scott — As soon as my first number will be finished, say one month hence — I will forward you a copy. I have to beg of you that you will take the trouble of presenting it in my name to that Institution who thought me unworthy being one of their members — There is no malice in my heart and I wish no return from them — I am determined now never to be a Philadelphia member of *that* association — Merely let them know (if you please) that humble talents *ought* to be fostered first in one's own Country — I take the privilege of forwarding you from time to time Newspapers that I hope cost you nothing and I shall also write to you from different parts — I wish you would write to my dear wife and have my Letters copied — At this distance she cannot write to me too often — She lives at Sᵗ Francisville — Bayou Sarah, Louisiana. I gave today a Lesson of Drawing Birds to the two famous ornithologists of England, Sir William Jardine & Mʳ Selby —

May God Bless you and yours & grant you the happiness you deserve — Write to me, pray, I beg, always directed to the care of Messʳˢ Rathbone Brothers & Cᵒ Liverpool and believe me for life your friend, J. J. A.

Remember me to Mʳ R Haines — Titian Peale[87] &ᶜ, & kiss all your children for my sake — I may yet listen to their voices and to your sweet flute.

---

87. Reuben Haines (1793–1834) was a Quaker naturalist and corresponding secretary of the Academy of Natural Sciences in Philadelphia; he had not joined Ord's opposition to Audubon. Titian Ramsay Peale (1799–1885), youngest son of the Philadelphia naturalist Charles Willson Peale, was a naturalist and artist whom Audubon had originally met in Cincinnati when Maj. Stephen H. Long's expedition to the upper Missouri passed that way in 1820. Audubon met Peale again in Philadelphia in 1824.

N. Berthoud Esq Louisville Kentucky
Edinburgh 20ᵗʰ December 1826

My dear Nicholas — That you should not answer my letters is rather strange and most painful to me —

I have wrote to you often, for I am no more lazy now than I was at Shippingport — I do with regularly 4 hours sleep and I hope yet to see my family derive the benefit of my labours — Why does not Victor write to me regularly every fortnight? — I have heard but twice from Lucy since my landing — yet letters from Dewit Clinton and Thomas Sully have reached me in Answer in 42 days here — I wish you would send me copies of your daily Journal of the weather and water and all kind of observation and suffer me to present you as a corresponding member to the Philosophical Society of Edinburgh — Make Victor draw at all leasure hours any thing from Nature and keep all his work no matter how indifferent in his eye or yours.

Collect Fossils from the falls for me or for you. I will send you a copy of my 1ˢᵗ Number and a Prospectus in January — Curious Birds preserved in spirit would be valuable to me or to you — Send a copy of this to Lucy — Kiss your lovely children for me — Tell your sweet Eliza that her Brother still hopes to see her again — Urge Victor on to Business, reading, Music &ᶜ and believe me for ever your friend, J. J. A.

Keep directing to Messʳˢ Rathbone Brothers & Cᵒ Liverpool

THURSDAY 21ˢᵀ DECEMBER 1826 —

Weather Clear with sharp frost — I thought as I saw it what a number of Wild Ducks I could have brought down from their wings with a little powder and plenty shot = but I had other Fish to Fry. I put up a Beautifull male Pheasant in attitude and outlined it on coarse Grey paper to *pounce it* in its proper situation on my Large Canvas — I had Sir William J. and P. Selby Esqʳ drawing in my room a good portion of the day = Mʳ Selby finished his piece — but not Sir William =

My time being now so taken up and day light so short, I Engaged Mʳ D. Lizars's Brother in law to copy letters for me, and he also sat in my room at work = Mrs Lizars and her Sister paid me a Visit, found us all engaged and brought a piece of Linen for me to look at and that I took to make me more shirts, for I am frequently obliged to dress Twice a day, the greatest bore [MS: Boor] Imaginable to me — The piece cost 5£ =

Doct^r Charles Fox came to see me — [The] poor fellow looked, indeed, as if he had been in the grave. Mr Simpson, the advocate, who lives 33 Northumberland Street came, tried to see me and Invited me and Mr Selby to a Phrenological Supper, but, Lucy, the morning passed away and no canvas came for me = I looked at the Beautifull Bird before me, admired it much, thou knows — long^d to have him under my pencil and waited most Impatiently hour after hour = I went to Mr Swinton the Seller = It was all vain promises and I did not receive it untill ½ past 8 this evening = So I had lost a most precious day. That is a vast deal in a Man's Life Glass — I wrote, however, to W^am Rathbone, Mrs Gregg and John Chorley, and when a ¼ before nine had come and brought Mr Selby, we both went to the Advocate Simpson =

It was really a Phrenological party — Nothing else was talked of. Jeffrey's letters and Combe's answers — Mr Simpson compared Selby's head and mine — I had more Coloring, he said, but when we had all been seated at table digesting the long gone supper, I was attack^d in the formation of Colors at such a round rate that I let loose and proved to the whole set that if they knew the value of protuberances, I did that of prismatic composition = They were not adequate to what they wish[ed] to seek, and I would have willingly abandonned the Field, for I was very sleepy. I saw there a Brother of David [MS: D^d] Bridges and his Lady, a nice fat bit of English composition. This is quite another sort of paire =

At last 12 o'clock came. The company rose *en masse* and proceeded to the street, where I was glad to feel the rarefied pure frosty air of this fine starr light night — Mr Selby and I walked off together = I think him, my Lucy, one of those aimiable rare Characters, that come on the Earth [MS: hearth] only at very distant period[s] to prove to mankind how good some of our species may still be found = He Invited me in the kindest manner to go to his house and beg^d that I would write to him when ever I wanted Pheasants — We parted at my door. I pressed his hand with great pleasure and bid him well and Happy from my heart =

Now I have come to my lodgings again and will go to bed — for the poor Girl servant who waits for me at night and will have to raise in 4 hours to make the fire for me is not quite so *tough* as I am and cannot do with as little sleep = Dearest wife, God Bless Thee, Good night =

FRIDAY 22ᴰ DECEMBER 1826†

Continued from 10ᵗʰ Decʳ

Thou hast here a copy of my letter because it contains much of all sorts — but, my sweet friend, the very morning that I forwarded thee the original, I had the pleasure of receiving two kind letters from thee, forwarded me here from London by Mʳ Middlemist — I need not say how grateful I was and how happy I felt at knowing thee quite well and our dear sons also — I sincerely hope thou wilt continue thy rides on Horseback every fair day and walk a great deal besides in the rich Magnolia Woods about thee — I never felt so much in my life the want of a glance at our Forrest as I now do — Could I see thee but a moment there — hear the mellow Mock Bird or the Wood Thrush, to me always so pleasing, and be able to give thee a kiss of affection, Oh, my Wife, how Happy I would again be — Since I received thy letters (they are dated 9ᵗʰ & 27 August) I have felt delighted at the idea of thy probably coming to Europe sometime next summer — But, my Lucy, we must not hurry too much. I wish to found all well and be perfectly assured of the general ultimate success of my work —

The Engravings are proceeding apace and are thought beautiful — My Exhibition closes here on Saturday next, and I will remove it either to Glasgow or New Castle on Tyne, but this place will continue my residence until my first number is quite finished — I received a kind letter from Sully a few days ago, dated only 29 days [before], enclosing one to Sir Thomas Laurence — I continue to be well with every body for an astonishing round of Company — I will have copied here for thee some of the invitations I received. It will give thee an Idea of the Circles I move in — I was elected a member of the Society of Arts & Sciences a few days ago by acclamation — and when I was presented to the Wernerian Society (this is the Natural [History] Society) for an Honorary member, I had the same acclamation and no doubt I will be elected next meeting, for the President told the Committee that on such Occasions the usual time waitted for consideration must be laid aside — I have the honor of being at the Royal Academy meeting — The Halls are beautifull indeed — The Great British Ornithologist Sir

William Jardine & Mr Selby have spent two days with me drawing in my style. I am much pleased with both and would have gone to Jardine Hall to spend a week but I am really too much engaged at present —

I have forwarded to Mrs Middlemist the 30 Dollars of Charles in a post note payable to her — I wish I could see John to tell him to draw all he can for his and my sake — I expect to hear from thee now very shortly thro' Messrs Rathbone, to whom always direct at Liverpool — I want to know how thou art pleased with thy watch & Mattlock Spars — I hope thou wilt like the Book I now send thee. It will give thee an idea of the Beauty of Edinburgh — Do not forget to collect acorns of all sorts and all other kinds of seeds & send them to Mrs Rathbone at Liverpool — Send a great quantity, and all the Noblemen are pleased to have some & I will have them from here. I send thee very frequently parcels of Newspapers. They all contain my name somewhere & it will be a pleasure for thee to read them —

I wish thou wouldst write every week & enter in any little details thou likes. Tell Friend Bourgeat that I will send him a pair of the best English Hounds when I go to Liverpool again in about 6 weeks — I think John might use my Gun if he would be careful of it & keep it particularly clean. Does he play on the Piano now? Send me some of his Drawings. I wish to see what Charles Middlemist has made of him — I feared myself that he would not be quite as good a Teacher as I wished and for his own Father hoped he might be —

I will now again bid thee farewell — Do take especial care of thy sweet self for my sake — Thy health is uniformly drank wherever I go, and at Mr Lizars it is expressed thus: "*Mr Audubon, let us drink Mrs Audubon and the Bairns.*" I have not dined at my lodgings for upwards of a fortnight one single day — My Journal would amuse thee — I here in send thee the results of Mr Combe the Phrenologist about my Skull. It proves to resemble that of Raphael very much, and I have been astonished at the merit of the Science thro some particular observations this Gentleman and others have made about my propensities and faculties — Mr Selby will take me to the Duke of Northumberland when I call on him at his house on my way to Newcastle; he will, Mr Selby says, subscribe to my work. The number allotted *to Scotland* is now filled and I bid fair to have more, but I will take nothing for granted until within my Grasp — I will exert myself much, depend on it, to ensure success, and may God grant that I may reach it — I want thee to send me by first opportunity as much of thy Hair as will make me a Cord for my watch. The Silver one that I wear now measures 3 feet & is about the size of that[†] but a mere thread in thickness will content me much, as I wear a guard besides — I have come to fine dressing again — silk stockings and pumps I have every morning & sometimes dress twice aday. My Hairs are now as beautifully long & curly as ever and, I assure thee, do as much for me as my Talent for painting. I began this morning a Painting in oil of 14 Pheasants on the wing attacked by a Fox that I wish to finish for the exhibition of the Royal Academy at London in March when I will be there myself — Read this to Johny for my sake more than once ═

To His Excellency Albert Gallatin Envoy Extraordinary of the United States &ᶜ &ᶜ London
22ᵈ Decʳ 1826

Sir — Having had the honor previous to leaving the United States of receiving from our Secretary of State Letters of Introduction to your predecessor Ruffus King Esquire — I took the liberty to ask of my friends to send their letters directed to his care — It was my intention to have reached London long ere this and indeed daily so till this very moment — Having now, however, engaged in the publication of my Ornithological Work in this City & having this moment received a letter from Chas. Bonaparte Esqʳ informing me that parcels for me were now under your care, I take the liberty to beg of you to forward them to the care of W. H. Lizars Esqʳ, Edinburgh, & please inform me if any charges have been incurred. I will take the earliest opportunity to refund them. In hopes of having the pleasure of seeing & presenting you with my respects early in the spring, I remain with sentiments of high esteem Your very obedᵗ humble servᵗ, J. J. A.

William Rathbone Esqʳ
Messʳˢ Rathbone Brothers & Cᵒ LiverpoolEdinʰ 21 Decʳ 1826

My dear Friend

Your friendly letter has reached me — I am sorry that you should conceive my case so very shocking as to be afraid that thro the publication of my work, I must be ultimately ruined — I am far from joining you in that thought. I must tell you most confidentially that one Hundred subscribers will cover all my expenses. The number I long for is 300. If I meet in each City in this Island of the same reputation of Edinburgh with the success & support felt here, I must do well ultimately. I had calculated on Scotland for 10 subscribers — That number I have already secured, and I am proud to say I will have more — The University, The Royal Academy &ᶜ have put down their names as leaders. Mʳ Selby has assured me that when he presents me to the Duke of Northumberland, I will have him also & *there are several Noblemen* in this neighborhood who will very probably join. Had Charles Bonaparte been a second Napoleon, he would have spoken differently of my Enterprise — When I wrote to you I felt myself rather alarmed, but could I have laboured as I have to be dormant at last & dread to encounter farther difficulties? — No. I am determined to Conquor or Die in the field. It is not my Talents I look to. They are humble, but it is my patience, Industry & perseverance that will enable me to surmount obstacles — I shall have many difficulties, I am quite sure, but I am prepared to meet them & if I do not succeed, as I said I believe before, I shall have tried all in my power and will retire still contented —

I will leave Edinburgh with Letters for all parts of the World & I will not suffer a stone to lay unturned — My spirits are not damped even by difficulties — Did you know all the severe attacks that my mind, my fortune & my body have had to contend against, you would believe as I now do that I can meet more with a calm eye and a free heart — Twenty times at least when with Your Brother Richard, yourself & excellent Mother, has my heart been on the eve of opening itself entire to you all and let you enter into secrets that would probably make you look at me with astonishment, but sensations that I cannot describe did Keep me silent and I cannot now confide to paper what I regret I have not said to you on the subjects I now allude to.

I am sorry, very sorry, that I should receive any more cold baths, particularly when I hear that Dʳ Trail is quite of your opinion because both you and him are men of the world & dealers of Wor[l]dly affairs — I will on next Sunday forward you a Package by the Coach which, please to open it, will contain several letters & Papers differently directed and that I beg you to be so good as to forward to America — The Views of Edinburgh please to look at and shew them to your sister Hannah & Mrs Rathbone — Did they receive my last long letters & did also your good mother receive an extremely long one? — I do not wish to intrude in the least on her enjoyments or cause her a single moment of pain, God forbid, but it would be a great satisfaction to me to be suffered to address her & Miss Hannah from time to time — And if I expect no answer from either of them, could you not just say they were received? — The little flycatcher of my first number will bear a humbler name. It is called Muscicapa Lucia.[88]

I would be glad that you would read the present number of the Philosophical Journal and also the one by Dr Brewster. They contain each valuable notices of my work — I was presented by the President of Wernerian Society as an Honorary Member and a general acclamation ensued — A few days ago I was elected, offhand, member of the Society of Arts — This is not money, it is true, but operations conducive & agreeable to a man who never expected such Honors — I will be presented to the Antiquarian Society also — The different Professors are all equally attached to me and seem anxious that I should succeed — I will read different articles to each Society at all their meetings during my stay here — My Exhibition closes on Saturday & will be removed to Glasgow & afterwards to New Castle, thence to Cambridge, Oxford &^{c}.

I am *obliged* to go to the Earl of Morton to spend a short time — I have found the acquaintance of a valuable friend Cap^n Basil Hall here and that of his Mother in law, Lady Hunter — I am now so truly engaged Painting, Writing &^{c} &^{c} that I am obliged to confine myself to 4 hours sleep only each 24 —

Sir Wm Jardine & Mr Selby have been drawing in my room all day to study my Style — They are most amiable men — I have received intelligence from Charles Bonaparte who now has assumed the name

88. In this flurry of letter writing on December 21, Audubon seems at first to have considered naming the bird in Plate V for his wife ("Muscicapa Lucia"), but in his letter later the same day to Mrs. Rathbone, he asks permission to name it for her ("Muscicapa Rathbonia"). Soon, however, he would decide to name it for Charles Bonaparte ("Muscicapa Bonapartii"), to whom he also wrote a letter this day. .

of Prince of Musignano — the Pictures belonging to his Uncle all left this city for London a few days since — Their friend Dr Stokoe called on me several times. I have had the great satisfaction of receiving two Letters from my beloved wife. All was well and I think in a few days more some will come thro' your care — The letter you forwarded to me was from my good friend Sully, enclosing one to Sir Thomas Lawrence — I dare not say a word respecting my good friend. Mostly I am truly sorry to hear of his misfortunes. Remember me to your good lady, your dear Mamma, Brother & Sisters and all who are kind enough to think of me sometimes & believe me for ever your poor friend & devoted servant, J. J. A.

Would your Lady have a letter of Dewit Clinton? I can give her one now.

Mrs Gregg   Edn^h 21 Decr 1826
Quarry Bank near Manchester

My dear Madam — Your son William has just this moment left me and as he told me that all my friends in England were chagrined and fearful of the success of my ornithology, I have been tempted to address you for a moment — I would not intrude had not you and each member of your family been so truly kind to me whilst at Manchester and your delightful Quarry Bank — My spirits are altogether good and I look forward to the Completion of my enterprisse with a degree of pleasure & surety that ten years since would have afforded me comfort infinite.

The number of subscribers that I need to pay all the expenses of the Publication is not great, and how many persons of either fortune or rank are now existing in this Island who can afford 20 Guineas per annum for a *Solid pleasure*? Upheld as I am now in the very centre of Judgement of Talents, learning & Carefulness of conduct so characteristic to the citizens of the beautiful Edinburgh, I am inclined to believe that I cannot fail elsewhere. Indeed, I look on the reception I have had here as a conductress thro the world.

Many persons are terrified at the sound of 180 Guineas for 3 large Volumes, but when they know that these 180 Guineas will be drawn out of their purses so very slowly that in Eight years, five will still be in it — The brow becomes less irritated & they either put down their names or will me to do so.

I have here very valuable subscribers and will have more, & when I travell thro England with my first number under my arm, I think I will exhibit a book of so much magnitude that many will be willing to contribute towards the welfare of the humble author.

Will you please present my best respects to your Good Husband, all your amiable Daughters & sons & believe me, my dear Madam, with Highest sentiments of regard Your truly obliged & obed^t serv^t, J. J. A.

Mr John Chorley St Anns Street LiverpoolEdin^h 21 Decr 1826

My dear Charles — It is reported that all my English friends take it for granted that I am a gone dog because my Book is the size of the originals — Whatever men may think on this score, I say they are wrong — They might as well condemn the first author as to condemn its humble imitator — but this is not what concerns you and I.

I am most gratefully thankful to you for the lively piece of Poetry you were so kind to forward me red hot from your press — You no doubt guessed long ere this that I wanted it to send my gentle Friend, the kind Miss Hannah of Green Bank — I have done so & hope no offence to your honor, but I assure you that I never have heard a word in reply — Indeed, I hope my friends about Liverpool are not about forgetting me, but I assure you that it looks much like it — Are you and friend Henry quite well now? How does the World proceed towards you? — Here I am truly afloat. Mr Audubon here and Mr Audubon there. I hope they will not make a conceited fool of Mr Audubon at last — I would have wrote long before this, but it is a dry fact to say that I positively could not find time, and was it not past 2 o'clock and such a night that no one dares run the chance of life and death to call on me, this bad day would not even now have had a chance to do so — It is you who must write long epistles by the bye — You are not yet quite an Author altho' you are a Poet. Poor me is an Author, aye, an Author over head & ears. I hope I will not stick & yet how dangerous the mire — I am painted to be engraved, head plastered to be cast in clay — Member of the Society of Arts & Sciences — deliverer of lectures at the Wernerian Society — Seated myself once at the Royal Academy, am quite well & not sorry that I came to Edinburgh — My Exhibition has brought some guineas, believe me, & I have painted 11 Turkeys on one canvas, one Otter in a Trap, 2 Cats fighting like Divils for a squirell & have begun a picture of 14 Pheasants all on the wing attacked by a fox. God bless you, good night. I cannot stand writing at present any longer. Yours for ever, J. J. A.

Account of Letters Wrote since I left the Beech Woods —

4 to Lucy in May & the last from on board the Hercules =
1 to Victor Audubon May, New Orleans —
1 Charles Bonaparte May,   D°   D° —
1 Lucy 7 June Gulph of Mexico per Brig Andromache for Boston
1 N. Berthoud 7ᵗʰ June D°   D°   D°
1 Lucy 16 June Gulph of Mexico Brig Howard for Havanna —
1 R. Currell   D°   D°   D°   D°
1 E Costé   D°   D°   D°   D°

Mʳˢ Rathbone — Liverpool

My dear Madam

Three of the plates for my work being now completely finished and some impressions having been taken & colored to my utmost desire, I have a great favor to beg of you.

Each of my Numbers are to contain a nondescribed individual. Consequently that one must receive a name to enable it to be well known in future — Will you permit me to honor it with the name of your family & style it the Rathbone Flycatcher Muscicapa Rathbonia? I made choice of a Flycatcher in this my first number because I heard your amiable & kind Daughter Hannah speak with pleasure of some little Grey ones that were frequently in front of your sweet Green Bank — My Letterpress is ready and I will wait with greatest anxiety your answer to enable me to act — It will be too seldom alas that I will have opportunities granted me to return your kind attentions — With Hopes that you and your whole family are well & Happy & that I will very soon receive a *kind* answer, I remain with the Highest regard, my dear M͏ͬͦ Rathbone, your truly obliged and very ob͏ͭ humble serv͏ͭ, J. J. A.

Charles Bonaparte Esq͏ͬ &͏ͨ &͏ͨ, Bruxelles

My dear Sir — I by mere accident heard of your lately [having] landed at Liverpool and also that you would pass thro' Bruxelles on your way to Italy — I am truly anxious to forward you a copy of the first number of my Birds of America that will be finished in whole [MS: all] January, and now that I do not any longer know where or how to direct it, I beg you will inform me.

I wrote and forwarded to you a letter & large case of Bird skins from New Orleans in May last, have written several times from England to you without a single answer. I sincerely hope that I have not incurred your displeasure or merited this long silence — The overplus of work that I now have on hand, the great anxiety I have respecting my yet *floating* enterprise render this a very short letter — but I know you have had the same to {meet} and therefore Hope that you will excuse me for the shortness of this. It is my intention to forward to your Cousin, the son of the Great Napoleon, a copy also. Will you please to say how I am to act that it may reach him safely. May you be blessed with health & happiness for ever, your most obliged & sincere friend, J. J. A.

EDINBURGH DECEMB͏ᴿ 22͏ᴰ FRIDAY 1826 —

I painted a good portion to day although it was quite dark before 3 o'clock this afternoon — Oh, how I long for the fair days of May, June, July and August.

My room this day was a compleat Levee — I really thought several

times that it was a Burlesque kind of quizing me = However, I
received every one as politely as I could, having my night cap, night
shirt, slippers [ms: sleepers], and no coat on — I walk^d with pallet and
Brushes in my hands and conducted each in his turn to the Door. Thus
was I disturbed from my Work 25 times, and I shaved and dressed in a
hurry as soon as my light had given way to escape more. I was, however,
extremely glad to see some of those and, indeed, all, for no matter how
humble I am, I like such attentions as well, I dare say, as if I deserved
them more =

Sometimes I hope that I deserve what I receive, but again the Instant
that dificulties arise in my Composition, or Coloring or finishing, I
droop at once and fear that the good people of Edinburgh are not quite
awake — Mr Stokoe came in early to see if I had received a Letter from
Charles Bonaparte, and I have, my Lucy, a very kind friendly Letter,
dated London = I wrote this morning to Mrs Gregg, John Chorley and
N. Berthoud and added much to my letter to thee = My Young Friend
Mr Hamilton was copying for me all day. I supped with Sir William
Jardine — Mr Lizars and a Mr Mole, uncle to Sir William, at Barry's
Hotel on Oisters cook^d & Raw = had much talk about Fishes and
Fishing, for we were all sportsmen — I left at 12 this Evening, anxious
to rest well, for tomorow I must Paint away — God Bless thee, Good
night, dearest Friend —

SATURDAY THE 23^D 1826 —

I had to grind my own colors this morning. I dettest that. It makes me
hot, and fretfull and, I am convinced, has a bad effect on the mind of
any Artist —

However, I work^d close, but the days are shokingly short. I cannot
see before ½ past 9 and I am forced to stop at 3. However, this is the
shortest day of the Almanach and I will be patient —

My Exibition Closed this day and here follows the account:

		Cash received	Catalogues (1,101)
November	14th	£ 3.18	17.6
	15	3.3	12.6
	16	2.6	9.6
	17	3.12	16.6
	18	4.17	15.6

	20	6.3	17.6
	21	5.12	13.6
	22	5.5	15.6
	23	3.3	6.6
	24	4.4	11.6
	25	8.4	18.6
	27	4.16	15.6
	28	2.2	7.6
	29	1.18	5.6
	30	6.5	14.6
Decem.ʳ	1	1.1	4.6
	2	13.2	1.12.6
	4	7.7	17.6
	5	4.14	6.6
	6	2.4	2.6
	7	1.4	4.6
	8	1.10	2.6
	9	5.10	4.6
	11	2.3	11.6
	12	2.5	2.6
	13	2.8	3.6
	14	4.5	6.6
	15	8.2	5.6
	16	8.8	1.5.6
	18	1.3	19.6
	19	2.12	3.6
	20	1.8	2.6
	21	4.11	8.6
	22	2.19	4.6
	23	<u>11.2</u>	<u>9.0</u>
		£ 152.18.0	£ 20.12.6
			<u>20.12.6</u>
		£ 173.10.6	
		$770.	

Thou seest here the amount I am indebted to the good people of
this City, a returning Memorandum of my past Labours — As soon as
the amount of Expenses has come in, I will give it thee — It is heavy,

I know, although I paid nothing for the Hall — The Door Keepers, {pl[a]card} Bearers and sweepers of the street's. Expenses during the Exibition has been just 30 £. Good Night, God for ever bless thee —

Mrs Rathbone Liverpool⁺   Edinh 25 December 1826

My dear Mrs Rathbone

I take the liberty of forwarding you the following, thinking it will afford you some pleasure. It is by Mr Simpson, an eminent Phrenologist of Edinh & was sent to Mr Combe the Lecturer here on that science (copy of letter)

You will see, my dear Mrs Rathbone, that these good Phrenologists has formed of me a very curious compound that unfortunately does not say much in my favor and how true the Almighty Creator only knows for I am not able myself to say. Present my humblest respects to Miss Hannah & all of your family & Believe me forever with sentiments of the highest regard, your most obedt & most obliged humble servt, J. J. A.

The 24th and 25th I remained closely at my Work painting. On the 24th My Drawings were all taken down and my paintings also — I wrote to the President & members of the Royal Institution and presented them my large Painting of the Wild Turkeys and, I may say, I lookd on this as giving them *Something* to remember me by as I could have most certainly had 100 Guineas for it from Gally the Picture Dealer, but I was glad to return the politeness of such a Body in a handsome manner and regretted only that the Painting given [MS: giving] to the Royal Liverpool Institution was so Inferior ＝

I purchased this morning a Broach for thee, My Lucy, that I send thee as a Christmas gift. Now, if in return my Christmas present had been a kiss from thy sweet Lips, how Happy I would be at this moment. My confinement at work brought a Heavy sad head ache. I felt quite Ill all the night, but to day I went to Mr D. Lizars to dine and feel much better now. I got up several hours before Day light to write for Cape Bazil Hall and am glad it is over — I paid for the pin I send thee 7 Guineas — God Bless thee —

My painting all day so assiduously and my mind agitated by thousands [of] Ideas of my future prospect brought on me every evening now a weariness that I could not surmount or command — This is, I think, the first Instance in my whole life when *if needed* I could not rouse myself from sleepiness and Jump up, shake myself and be ready for action in an instant, but it is now as I tell thee, and I will Illustrate the fact with this evening's Exemple =

I left work and my room imediately after my dinner. Capᵉ Hall and his Brother having called on me to thank me for my notes to him and invite me to dine with him next Thursday: I had also received a Letter from the Secretary of the R. Institution acknowledging receipt of mine of Yesterday to their Body, and thanking me in good Words for my painting of The Wild Turkeys. Then, my Lucy, as I said before, I left my room about 5, for I felt a necessity to breathe air from out of the house = The Gass Lights were dimly shining thro the thick warm, moist fog that filled the atmosphere. I could scarce discern the Lights in the *Old Town* and persons within 30 yards were quite hid from my view — I reachᵈ the bustling Princes Street and soon was at James Square № 3 w[h]ere I found Lady № 1 and her sister Annah busily engaged, cutting out the piece of Linen for which I paid 5 £ this morning to make me some shirts — Here, after welcomes and how do you do are Exchanged and hands are pressed, I set myself in a Large well stuffed Black armed chair, Lay one hand on each side of me, Lean my back to touch the reclining back of the seat, push my feet forward and, being perfectly at my ease, I ask for some music, as I would ask for it of thee = Bye and bye, Tea comes, I take my Coffee — We chat to supper, eat that, drink thy health, and I come to my bed at ½ past 10. This is all very well and very agreable, is it not, Wife? —

"Indeed, My Laforest, it is, and I am glad to hear of this" —

But, Lucy, this Evening I went to sleep in spite of all my best endeavours 15 minutes after my arrival — I took some hot Coffee, but it would not answer — The charm was Iresistible, and at last I only could beg pardon and make my Escape with Intention to go to bed at once and rest well — Walking restored me to life again, but when at home, the drowsiness came on anew. Recollecting that Mͬ D. Lizars was to call at 8, I threw myself on the Sopha, rolled my Cloak about me and went to sleep, giving orders to be wakened at 8. — This came, but no M.ʳ Lizars — At 9 I went positively to bed. I was just praying for thy safety and thy happiness to our God, when M.ʳ D. came — I Jumped up, dress.ᵈ at once, and in 3 minutes was with him — He was holding a candle up to my work looking at a Pheasant. He said his Lady was at the Shop — I begged he would go for her — He returns with her and her Brother — Things are ordered, we are eating — drinking and chating again all very merry. It is 12 o'clock. They are gone, and so is my sleepy fit —

Yet I will go now to rest and rest late in the morning, for Tomorow, was I to go to sleep at the Earl of Morton, what would they say of me? But that would be quite Impossible, for I will feel abashed, and awkward, and my blood will be all alive, I have no doubt — Sweet Wife, God Bless Thee, Good Night —

My beloved Wife†   Edin.ʰ 27 Dec.ʳ 1826

I send thee as a Christmas Gift a Broach that may be worn either on thy bosom or on thy fine hair — I hope it will reach thee all safe & find thee well & happy. May God bless thee for ever, thy Husband & friend, J. J. A. — As soon as the New Year's books appear, I will send a present to Victor & John, God bless thee.

DALMAHOY THE SEAT OF THE EARL OF MORTON
8 MILES FROM EDINBURGH,
DECEMBER WEDNESDAY 27ᵀᴴ 1826 —

There's a data for thee, sweet wife! Thy husband has leaped from America to Liverpool, & from thence to Manchester, Bakewell, Matlock, Buxton, Twenty other places besides, then to Edinburgh, and now is seated at a sweet little table, in the *Yellow bed Chamber* at the Earl of Morton! — but in this fine room, I am quite alone *I believe* and will write for thy sake and that of our Dear Sons [a] regular account of this day —

After my breakfast, not anxious to begin an other Pheasant, I called on M.ʳ Lizars, who was much engaged. I saw the Ladies and bid them farewell for one day — The morning being *longer than usual*, I called

on the Mess.ʳˢ Symes, the Painter[s] — One was unwell, & the other
being absent, my visits extended only to my walks to their doors, and
I returned to my lodgings, to make ready to pay a Visit to an Earl and
some Countesses — All this did not go on without thinking of thee
a good deal — Indeed, I thought of other people beside thee; my
Good Friend M.ʳˢ Rathbone was about me and so her Dear Annah, the
Quarry Bank familly and the Dockrays, all visited me whilst my razor
was smoothing my chin — but I thought of thee most! — I had to
pack a Box for thee, containing the Views of Edinburgh, the Broach,
some curious Lamps M.ʳ D. Lizars sent thee, the travels of Cap.ᵉ Hall,
all the diferent cards I had received here, with as many News papers as
possible — I did all this assisted by D. Lizars and brother, and wished it
a good voyage to thee —

Now we three had a Luncheon, some fried Oisters, some Drink
and some cake, and were still all at work thus when M.ʳˢ Dickie open.ᵈ
my room Door and said, "Lord Morton's Carriage, Sir" — Well, I was
ready. We shook hands all round — My *Porte feuille* was taken off and I,
after having washed my hands and ~~~~ walked down stairs, touched
slightly the arm of the Waitter who opened the carriage door and
Jumped on a large soft seat lined with purple Morocco — The Carriage
moved — Yes, my Lucy, the Carriage moved, but upon my word I never
moved in such before — The ship that under easy sail glides slowly
on an even Sea, has more fatiguing motion, and had [I] not been fully
persuaded (being awake) that it was a Cariage I was in, I would have
thought myself gently wafted thro the air in a swinging hammoch — It
passed the castle — thro Charlotte Square — thro Coats Crescent and
along the Glascow road for 8 miles so swiftly too, that my watch had just
changed the hour to another when the Porter pushed open the Gates of
Dalmahoy —

I now began thinking of my Meeting a Man who had been great
Chamberlin to the late Queen Charlotte, for I was not so terrified
at meeting the Countess. Her eyes the days I had seen her at the
Royal Institution spoke softness and amability of disposition, but the
Chamberlin I could not help dreading to encounter —

"And why, my Dear? I would not" —

No, thou wouldst not because thou art a well bred woman — but
I do because I am a fool — All this did not stop the carriage from

proceeding smoothly round a Great Circle; neither did it stop my
eyes from seing a large square, half Gothic Building with Two Turrets
in front ornemented with Great Lyons and all the signs of heraldry
belonging to the Great Lord within =

The cariage has stoped. It is open[d] — a bell wrung — a man in livery
unfolds a large door, and I walk in giving my Hat and Gloves and my
American stick (that bye the bye never leaves me when I do not leave
it myself) — Now I am lead thro this Hall and upstairs, my name is
given, and I Enter the Drawing room of the Earl of Morton! — The
Countess[89] runs to me, then returns to her Lord and presents *him* to
me, My Lucy — Yes, him to me! — I look — I stare, I am astounded
[MS: astonted] that I have not before me another Richard *coeur* [MS:
caeur] *de Lion* — for positively I had expected nothing less. I had
formed an Idea that a Chamberlain and an Earl must be a man able to
Cleave Worlds in two — Oh, my Imagination, where doest thou lead
me? Why, my Dear Wife, I saw a small, slender man, tottering on his
feet, weaker than a new hatch[d] partridge welcoming me to his Hall
with Tears almost trickling from his Eyes — He held one of my hands
and attempted speaking, but this was dificult — His Good Lady was
rubbing his other hand — I saw at a Glance his situation and beg[d] he
would be seated. This was done, and I was relieved — The Countess
of Buller [MS: Boulear] Introduced also, and I at last seated my body
on a Sopha that I thought would swallow me up, as this down swelled
around me =

Now I am looking fearfully around — What a room! = full 60 feet
by 30, all hung with Immense Paintings on a rich purple Ground = All
was purple about me = The Table[s] were covered with various Books,
& Instruments — Telescopes, Drawing apparatus with thousands
of ornements = The queen of England fronted Marie of Scots — a
chamberlain was here, a Duke there, and in another place I could see a
beautifull head of Rembrandt — Claude Loraine had some Landscapes
here also. Vandike has not been forgotten and Titian gave a Lustre to

89. Susan Elizabeth Buller married the sixteenth Earl of Morton in 1814. The year of her
birth is unknown, but Audubon suspects she is about the age of Lucy, who was born in 1787.
Her mother, Elizabeth Lydia Hallidat Buller-Yarde-Buller (ca. 1774–1851), was the "Countess of
Boulear," Audubon's apparent misspelling of "Buller."

the whole [MS: all] — I rose and took a closer view — The Countess
explained all to me — but conceive my surprise when on looking thro
the midle window, I saw at the horizon [MS: Orison] an object that
was no less attractive [MS: attractif] than any about me — The Castle
and City of Edinburgh, a compleat Miniature 8 miles off making its
way to the mind thro avenues and over pieces of watter and fields
Innumerable! =

Now, my Lucy, I am told that Luncheon is ready — What, said I to
myself, Luncheon again? — I am sure that if my friends complain of
my not eating much, they must at all event[s] allow that I eat suficiently
often — Well, to Luncheon we go — The Countess of Buller [MS:
Boulear] rolls Lord Morton in his castored chair, and I give my arm to
Lady Morton = We cross a large antechamber [MS: entichamber] and
enter a Dinning room also quite rich in Paintings and at present with a
sumptuous repast — I eat again and drink again and in the midle of all
this — Three Gentlemen make their appearance = They were visitors
at the Hall also — a M͏ͬ Hays, Ramsey — and a young Clergiman —

This Luncheon over, we had to see my Drawings — The Lord was
rolled into a good situation for light, and I again unbuckled the *great
Book of Nature*. I am not going to repeat praises again, my Lucy, for
I am quite sickened at the sound — The drawings seen, we adjourn
to the drawing room again. The Countess desires to receive a Lesson
of Drawing from thy husband Tomorow and I acquiesce with great
satisfaction = Conversation becomes now general. I gradually feel
[MS: fill] at ease and all goes on smoothly —

The Countess is about *thy age*. Thus I save you both from being called
old as you are both quite Young enough to delight a Husband = She
is not what men call handsome, nor beautifull, but she is good looking,
has a good form, fine clear fresh skin and Eyes, Lucy, that I dared not
meet, they were so dark! — Her conversation is frequently interrupted
by a natural Impediment, but it gives more spirit to all she says, and
she is certainly a very superior Woman = As Ladies are sometimes
concerned about another's Dress, the Countess, I will tell thee, was
then enrobed in a rich crimson Gown — Her Mother was dressed in
black Satin —

Now, Lucy, it had become 6 of the afternoon. I had taken a short walk
about the grounds with the Gentlemen and returned to this Hall when

I was asked by the Countess if I wished to see my room — I knew that this meant that to dress for Dinner was now necessary, and I followed a Gentleman waiter to this Room who, on hearing his M^rs say the "Yellow Room," pointed the way to me — When I came in, a good fire of *wood* was lighted = My Linen was warming in front of it, my shoes had been [MS: being] unpack^d as well as my night apparels, and all was snug and delightfully comfortable — I beg^d to be left alone — and I look^d around me — All was truly Yellow in this Yellow Chamber — It might well have been a parlour in some other Countries — The bed for me this night was ornemented with crowns and was large enough to receive 4 of my size = A Sopha was at the foot of it — Large armed chairs on each side the fire — a Table containing a writting desk with all ready and all that I never use every w[h]ere —

My Toilette is soon over, thou knowest, for in my opinion it is a vile loss of Time, that spent in arranging a cravat with as much care as a hangman does his Knot — and I was down again in a moment — "Ring the Bell, Mr Hays" said the countess — A Waiter came and dinner is ordered — It is now seven and I again lead the Countess under my arm, who now is dressed superbly in white satin & crimson turban,[†] and the Earl is again rolled in his Chair =

I set by the Mother's side — Mr Hays officiate[s] as Master, and I dine again for the third Time this day — The Waitters, Lucy, are all powdered and dressed in rich Red Clothes all liveried over excepting one who has Black clothes on and who gives plates by handing them with a neat napking without touching them *positively*. After one hour the Ladies and the Lord retire, and we the Gentlemen Visitors set to to talk and Drink Wine = We talk^d entirely of Antiquities — Mr Hays is a deeply learned Man, an original besides and quite Interesting in his manners —

At 10 we join the Countess again, but the Earl has retired for the night, and now that we have been looking at the Signatures of the Kings of Old — of Marie — Henry, James &^c &^c — and examined a Cabinet of ancient Coins, and 12 o'clock is come, the Ladies bid us good night by shaking all our hands — We are then left alone and to settle the Coffee that we have drank, we drank now Madeira wine — What a Life — Oh, my Lucy, I could not stand this. I prefer my primitive woods after all — but as I Hope this life will enable me to enjoy them at a future period,

I bear it patiently — I leave the Gentlemen at their wine and cakes and have come to my Yellow Chamber =

Now, Lucy, I have prayed on my Knees my God to grant thee well, and I will go to bed — Sweet Friend, Good night =

— Day light came, my Lucy = and I got up, for a bed when awake and without a Wife is very stupid — I opened all the Yellow Curtains and visited my room by day = Three Doors besides that of my entrance were in sight and the *démangeaison*[90] of seeking new adventures prompted me to open one = Singular! — A neat little closet, lighted by a high narow slip of a gothic window was before me, and in a moment I discovered its purpose — It was a bathing room = Large porcelain tubs, Jarrs of watter, drying Linens, and all else wanted laid about — but the color of the whole was quite changed. The carpet was variegated with crimson = and all appeared alike warm = beautifully contrived = I saw but touch^d nothing. I was clean enough — The door opposite lead me into another closet *diferently intended* and I merely saw its use — I was going to unlatch the third yet unknown, when thinking a moment — I made up my mind not to Intrude, for I recollected that it led back towards the Interior of the Hall —

My chimney piece was decorated with Choice shells — I saw myself in the large mirror on it and above it a painting representing a lovely young female, a true resemblance of Queen Marie =

I concluded to venture down. I say venture, for nought but the breese had yet been heard, but I proceeded and arrived at the Drawing room where Two Young Women were engaged busily cleaning = *The Youngest saw me first* and I heard her tell her companion, "The American Gentleman is down," and they Instantly both vanished = I examined quite at leisure all about me — The paintings were truly beautifull, the morning was clear and the light on them very good = The young Clergiman came in and a walk was Imediately undertaken. The Hares all started before our Dogs. From wood to wood we arrived at the stables w[h]ere I saw 4 truly well formed Abissinian Horses with tails down to the earth and legs of one sinew [MS: signew] no larger than those of an Elk = The Riding room was yet lighted and the Manage or Training of those Annimals had been performed that morning. The

90. *Démangeaison* is inflated diction for an itch or urge.

Game Keeper was unkenelling his Dogs — He shewed [us] a large Tame Fox, and thro further woods we proceeded to the Manor, now the habitat of the Great Falconer = I saw *John Anderson* and his Hawks — He had already received orders to come to the Hall at 11 to shew me these Birds in their full dress =

We visited next hanging gardens where, to my surprise, Roses were blooming most swetly — I pluck^d one for my button hole and, returning to the Hall by following the sinuosities of a brooke, reach[ed] it by 10 — The Ladies were in the Drawing room — A sweet babe was here also — It was a little nephew of the Countess, rosy with health and gay with the Innocence of his age =

Mr Hays & Ramsey had left for Edinburgh = The Earl came in and we went to breakfast — Neither at this meal nor at Luncheon are seen waiters = Now all was Bustle about the Drawing Lesson. I might positively have said that I was about receiving one for, Lucy, Lady Morton Draws much better than I do, believe me — The chalks, the crayons, and all wanted was before us in a few minutes, and I sat to give a Lesson to one of the first, or rather most ancient, Peeress[es] of Scotland as well as of England — Singular fact = Yet sometimes when in the woods I have rested and anticipated my being Introduced to the great nobles of Europe, and I am now gradually proceeding to that effect = Well, I gave a Lesson — taught how to rubb with the Cork and prepare with watter colors = The Earl saw the proceedings and was delighted at my Invention = I shewed him many of my Drawings — The Falconer came and I saw the *Falcos* ready for the chase — He held them perched on his gloved hand, with bells — and hoods and crests flowing, but the morning was not fit for a flight, and I lost the sight of that pleasure =

During one of the resting moments, the Countess ask^d for my subscription Board and wrote very legibly with a steel Pen "*The Countess of Morton.*" She wished to pay for the first number now — but this I declined. She promised me Letters for England and, I assure thee, I was pleased = I concei[ve]d a wish to have some fresh Pheasants, and she Imediately ordered some to be killed for me = Luncheon again — after which I walked out to see a flock of full one hundred brown Deer that like sheep were feeding within a few hundred paces of the Hall = I approach[ed] them pretty close; many had shed their horns. They scampered off at my sight, probably knowing well what a sin[n]ing hunter I was —

The Cariage had been ordered for me, for I was engaged to dinner in Edinburgh at Cap^e Basill Hall — I saw it come to the Hall and returned to pay my respects and did so, but it was agreed by all parties that it should be sent for me next week to give another Lesson — and spend another night — I pressed their hands and took my leave — My ride home was soon over — The Cariage moved as smooth as before — Here I found a Packet from the American Minister Gallatin — a Letter from Charles Bonaparte, some books also from him, and a Bill from my Tailor = I ran to Mr Lizars to give an account of my Journey and reach[ed] N° 8 St Colme at 6 o'clock = Cap^e Hall soon spoke of America and, strange to tell, he was a midshipman on board the Leander when Pierce was killed off New York and when, on my way from France, our Captain seing the British Vessel {wore w**ut} round Long Island and reach[ed] New York by Hell Gate —

My Port Folio was there. After dinner the crowd accumulated. I open[ed] for a moment my book, but soon closed it for I felt wearied — Lady Hunter came in and Sir W^am Hamilton[91] — I saw a beautifull sister of Cap^e Hall — The handsome Mrs Harvey and many more — but, Lucy, I made my Escape without biding adieu except to the Cap^e, and I have reach^d George Street almost broke down = See what I have again written to night, but stop — Having seen in Blackwood's Magazine a curious notice about me written by Professor Wilson, I wrote him the following note† — and there [MS: their], my Lucy, I bid thee a most happy and a most peacefull good night =

FRIDAY 29TH DECEMBER 1826 —

I painted all day and did this most Happily and chearfully for I received thy Two kind Letters of the† and 14 of Octr last = In the Evening I went to Cap^e Hall to shew some drawings to one of his sisters. I returned early, but Messrs Lizars & Brother in Law having called on me, it was full past midnight when I bid thee well —

91. William Hamilton (1788–1856) was a brilliant philosopher defeated by his underqualified friend John Wilson for a professorship of moral philosophy at the University of Edinburgh in 1820. He publicly opposed the phrenology of George Combe.

[SATURDAY, DECEMBER 30, 1826]

Saturday was much the same as Yesterday. I painted constantly and for a wonder was not disturb[d] by visitors =

[SUNDAY, DECEMBER 31, 1826]

Sunday was also spent at Painting as long as light lasted, but I had to go and dine at Cap[e] Hall again to be particularly Introduced to Francis Jeffrey, the principal writter in the Edinburgh Review = I reach[d] [there] at 6 o'clock, but did not take my watch nor any money, for I was afraid that it might be late when I would return = I was first at Cap[e] Hall. His Lady, Lady Hunter and the Young babe were all there in the setting room — but a M[r] McCulloch,[92] a great writer on political Economy, soon came in. This is a most extraordinary man and a plain aimiable Character without fudge — Then Famous Jeffrey and his Wife entered. A small (not to say little) being, with a woman under one arm and his hat in the other, bowed very seriously indeed, and so much so when he turned toward me that I conceived the personage to be full aware of his weight in society — His looks were shrewd [MS: shrud], but I thought much cunning resides over his cast of eyes, and the man talk[d] so aboundantly that I did not like him at all — but, Lucy, this is my first impression, and *he* may prove better than I now think him = His American Wife was dressy, and had a Twitch of a nervous nature that, Joined to her uncommon share of *plainliness* (for I never called a woman ugly in my whole Life), rendered *her* not extremely Interesting — There again I may form very erroneous Ideas, but I like to put down my opinions as they come at once fresh from the active mind.

If I mistake not Mons[ieur] Jeffrey was shy of me, and I was kind enough to return the compliment = Thou must know that this Gentleman has used me rather cavalierly. When I came, I received a letter of Introduction to him — I called on him and, his being absent, I left the letter — My Card and a note of mine, of which I regret much I did not take [a] Copy = When my Exibition opened, I Enclosed M[r] Jeffrey a card of admittance and my card again — M[r] J. never came near

92. John Ramsay McCulloch (1789–1864) was a widely known and respected economic journalist and lecturer on political economy.

me, and I never went near him for if *he* was Jeffrey, *I* was Audubon and
felt quite as independant as all the Tribe of Jeffreys in Scotland, England
and Ireland put together =

This Evening he thanked me for what I had done, but there I would
not return his compliment for *he* had done nothing towards me — and
notwithstanding his being a wonderfully great reviewer, I thought
he wanted a little of the polish and finished manner of *Simpler Men*
— During the dinner the conversation was various — I liked Cap^e
Hall and his Lady the more I saw of them, and I found Lady Hunter
extremely kind = Mrs Jeffrey sat opposite me, each close to Cap^e Hall.
Whenever I look^d at her, her Eyes were rivetted on my whole person
and, not finding her quite so Interesting as Mrs Hall or Mrs Harvey, I
turned my look more frequently to them — Very little was said about
America. I soon discovered that neither the Reviewer nor his Consort
knew much about it besides their reading, and I thought the subject
was carefully avoided notwithstanding Cap^e Hall['s] wish that it should
become the Topic — We went to Tea — I talk[ed] some to Mr J. and
he talk^d a little to me, a few Inquiries were made about my work, he told
me that he was glad to have met me, and at 10 o'clock I took my leave
having positively seen the Little Man that sound[s] so great abroad —
aye, and in Scotland too —

I walk^d briskly — This was the Eve of a New Year, and in Edinburgh
it is rather a dangerous thing to be late in the streets, for Vagabonds are
wont to comit many Errors at this time; Murders and other sinfull acts
take place — To prevent these the Watch is doubled = and an over
usual quantity of Gass lights afforded = I reach^d my Lodgings quite
safe — set to and outlined a Pheasant to save day light tomorow and
was about going to bed when Mrs Dickie came in and begged that I
would waite past 12 o'clock to take some Toddy with Miss Campbell, my
American boarding companion, and bid her a Happy New Year — I did
so — and had I sat up all night, and wrote, or Drawn, or sat still by my
fire and thought of any thing, I would have done as well, for the Noise so
Increased in the streets and lasted with such confusion untill morning
that I never closed my Eyes a moment — Cap^e Hall presented me with
3 volumes of his Voyages — I received a note again from the Countess
of Morton requesting that I would go to her on Thursday next when she
would send a Cariage for me. I received some Pheasants from her —

Account of Expences since April 26ᵗʰ 1826, the day I left the Habitants
of the Beech Woods near Bayou Sarah Louisianna —

paid Negro Toby of Mʳˢ Percy	$	50	cts
Dᵒ for Mʳˢ Percy's horse shoes		50	
My Passage to New Orleans in Red River		7.50	
2 flageolets		5.00	
Plants for my Wife		2.00	
Crayons for John my Son		9.00	
Cushion for Lucy to set on		3.50	
Barber, theatre &ᶜ up to Wednesday 3 May		2.50	
Sirops, Lime Juice, Liquors &ᶜ pᵈ Sapinot		16.00	
passage to Bayou Sarah & down again		18.00	
My Bill at Sapinot for Sundry Stores & board		20.00	
Bed & Bedding with hauling		9.00	
My Passage to Capᵉ Joseph Hatch, Ship			
Delos of Kennebunk to Liverpool		100.00	
1 Column of Gibraltar Rock		1.50	
Cleaning Porpoise Jaw Bone		.25	

EDINBURGH DEC. [31], 1826†

Sunday Night 12 o'clock —
and Now My Dear book, must I part with thee? Back [to] America, and
fed in England and Scotland, and at sea — go to My best Friend. To My
Wife, to my Beloved Lucy — yes, go back, return to thy own native soil
and give her pleasure a while. *She* will be glad to hold conference with
thee now — for she will look on thy sheets as the reflectors of my daily
Life. Simple, either in times of Nothing or of wondrous events, and
whilst she reads them, she will observe my very gradual advancement
into a World yet unknown, and dangerous to be known. A World
wherein I may prosper but wherein it is the easiest thing to sink into
compleat oblivion. When I open thy sheets again where will *we* be?
God only knows, and how happy or miserable shall I be — I will not
pretend, at present, to investigate — or torment my brain about [that]
— for this simple reason, that God being my Supreme commander
I am, and for ever will be, contented to act, to enjoy, to suffer or feel

whatever in his Wisdom he may think best fit for me — and so well aware do I think him right in all he does, that happy or miserable, I will enjoy or suffer, perfectly satisfied that it is all for the best at last. Go, that My Wife read this, let my children read it. Let the world know these my heartfelt sentiments, and believe me, my Dear Book, for ever thy most obliged, yes truly obliged Friend.

John J. Audubon
—Citizen of the United States of North America

Appendix A

A Page from Audubon's 1828 Journal

One page from Audubon's 1828 journal was preserved and inserted into the 1826 journal. The New-York Historical Society's microfilm shows it inserted following the page whose recto is the entry for August 13, 1826. Audubon's sketch of the French lady blowing soap bubbles was integrated into the text following the first paragraph below.

At a Balcony not far from us a rather well formed Lady made her appearance. I Judged her to be about 36, well dressed &ᶜ — a small table was at her side on which a Glass vase was seen. The Lady held a Glass tube in one hand, leaned on the balcony with the other and, —

Come, dearest Friend, what was *that Child* doing? — —

As the merry Andrew Mathews said "You give it up". — Hey dost thou give it up? — Well, the Child of 36 was blowing Soap Bubbles to the paysans [MS: Passans]!!! This is the French Caracter, Lucy, Light as air and as though[t]less as the Lamb who goes bounding at the approach of the Storm. — I drew her Position on my Pocket Book and I repeat it here with the same pencil for thy own pleasure when we meet never to part again. —

We have spent an Evening as much like the French Lady as possible, not to be thought *Outré* in France. We in fact have been Two hours at a very small Theatre to see *Punch* and his gay coadjutors for 15 sols. — and now, dearest Wife, God Bless thee for ever. — Good Night!

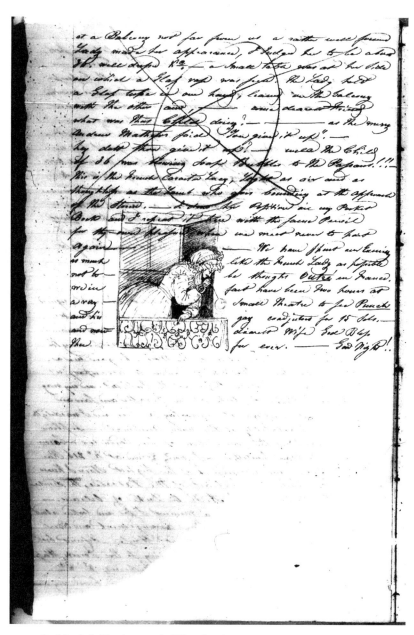

FIG. 21. Parisian lady blowing soap bubbles, October 2, 1828

I wrote to Havell to send the Duc of Orleans[1] setts; &ᶜ and I received
a kind letter from Greene. — I also had a letter from the Director of
the Expenses of the Duke requesting that I should see him and arrange
respecting the Duke's subscription. — This letter, however, reached
me too late to attend to it to day. — My day has been an Idle one; my
wishes were bent on receiving an order from the Minister and yet I
had no good reason for so doing as Ministers have too much to do to
hurry in any thing. I felt a great desire to write to Friend Wᵃᵐ Rathbone
and yet have not done so, anxious to give him as much good news as
possible at once — but if by Sunday nothing remarkable takes place *I
must* write or he will think that I have forgott all his kindnesses to me
and God forbid, = Good Night, Dearest Friend. —

SATURDAY 4ᵀᴴ

I called on Friend S.[2] after breakfast and at his request went to the
Jardin du Roi[3] to interpret for him. — We called afterwards on Geoffrey
Sᵗ Hillaire[4] and remained some time, and heard some curious facts
respecting the habits and conformation of the *Mole.* He gave me a
Ticket for Doctᵣ Bostick[5] of London to accompany us to the delivery
of the Prizes at the Institut[e]: on my way back I stopped to look at
the Giraffe and saw an Elephant employed at unrooting a Tree and I
was delighted at the tractability of this noble annimal. — He seemed
to understand the conversation of his conductor or Cornac as if a man
himself. =
   I now arrived at Nº 216 Rüe Sᵗ Honoré and asscended 4 of the highest

---

1. Louis-Philippe, duc d'Orléans (1773–1850), had been with the army of the French
Revolution but then lived in exile for twenty years before returning to France in 1814 and
recovering his fortune. He would be made "king of the French" in 1830.
   2. William Swainson (1789–1855) was a prominent London naturalist and artist who had
traveled extensively in the Mediterranean and South America. A fellow of the Royal Society, he
was in Paris to gain access to natural history collections and zoological gardens.
   3. Also known as the Jardin des plantes, the Jardin du roi was the main garden of the French
National Museum of Natural History.
   4. Étienne Geoffroy Saint-Hilaire (1772–1844) was a professor of zoology at the Jardin des
plantes.
   5. John Bostock (1772–1846), a physician and medicinal chemist, was much published in
physiology and medicinal chemistry.

stairs I know of to reach the Cabinet of M. Pascales, the director of the Expenses of S. A. R.[6] the Duke of Orleans. — As he was expected in a moment, I sat and looked about me. — Oh, Lucy, what fine arrangement and order in the management of this great House — diferent book Cases contained the papers belonging to the Forests, Horses, Furniture, Fine Arts, Libraries, Fisheries, &ᶜ &ᶜ — and when M. Pascales came in and heard my nam[e]

6. S. A. R. stands for "Son Altesse Royale" (His Royal Highness).

Appendix B

Letters of Introduction Copied into the 1826 Journal

The following three letters were copied by Audubon into the 1826 journal immediately preceding the entry for June 22.

Copy of a Letter from Mͬ͡ E[d]ward Holden

New Orleans May 16ᵗʰ 1826
George Ramsden Esq.

Dear Sir

The present will be handed to you by Mͬ͡ J. J. A. of this City, whom most respectfully I beg to Introduce to you.

The Principal object of Mͬ͡ A's visit to England is to make arrangements for the Publication of an extensive and very valuable Collection of his drawings in Natural History — Chiefly if not wholly of American Birds, and he takes them with him for that purpose. Can you be of any assistance to him by Letters to Manchester and London? If you can I have no doubt that my Introduction of him will insure your best attention & Services. — Mͬ͡ A. is afraid of having to pay heavy duties upon his Drawings. He will describe them to you, and, if in getting them entered Low at the Custom House, or if in any other respect you can further his views, I shall consider your aid as an obligation conferred upon myself. Pray, introduce him particularly to Mͬ͡ Booth; who I am sure will feel great Interest in being acquainted with him were it only on account of the desire he has allways expressed to be of service to the new Manchester Institution — to which Mͬ͡ A's Drawings would be an Invaluable acquisition.

I am, Dr Sir
Yours Truly
Edward Holden

Copy of a letter received from Mr Vincent Nolte at New Orleans Dated
May 16th 1826 —

I have ventured to put in the hands of Mr J. J. Audubon, a
Gentleman of highly respectable Scientifick acquirements, these
introductory lines for you under a persuasion that his acquaintance
cannot fail to be one of extreme interest to you. Mr A. is a Native
of the U.S., has spent upwards of 20 years in all parts of them and
devoted most of this time to ornithological Pursuits. He carries with
him a Collection of upwards of 400 Drawings, which far surpass any
thing of the kind I have yet seen and afford the best evidence of his
Skill and of the perfection to which he has carried his researches.
His object is to find a Purchaser, at any rate a Publisher for them;
and if you can aid him in this, and Introduce him either in person
or by letters to men of Distinction in arts and sciences, you will
confer much of a favor on me. He has a Crowd of letters for England,
amongst others very particular ones from Mr Clay, Mr Dewitt Clinton
and others, which will [MS: will which] do much for him, but your
introduction to Mr Roscoe and others may do more. His Collection
of Ornithological Drawings would prove a most valuable acquisition
to any Museum; or any monied Patron of the arts, and I should think
convey a farr better Idea of American Birds, than all the stuffed Birds
of all the museums put together. —
Permit me Likewise to recommand Mr Audubon to your
Hospitable attentions. The respectability [MS: respectabilitiets] of his
Life and of his familly Connections entitle him to the good wishes
of any Gentleman, and you will derive much gratification from his
conversation. I am Dear Sir with very sincere regard Yours most truly

Vincent Nolte   Simile of Vincent Nolte
Richd Rathbone Esqr
Liverpool

From the same and same dated

My Dear Sir,

Permit me to make you acquainted with the Bearer Mr J. J. A., an
European by Birth, but upward of 20 years a resident and citizen
of the U.S. He has devoted most of that time to Ornithological
researches of various kinds, and of the Pitch and perfection to which
he has carried them, the beautifull collection of Drawings from his
own pencil, with which he now proceeds to England, may afford
the Best Evidence. These Drawings or Pictures are *unique* in their
kind — Something like, *tableaux de Famille* of Birds; if Birds lived in
families, and Mr A.'s object is to find a Purchaser for these fruits of his
exertions, assiduity and perseverance. You will on seeing them, be
able to Judge yourself how valuable a Collection they form, and that
they cannot fail to prove a desirable acquisition to any museum or to
a wealthy patron of the Arts and Sciences.

If either by letters of Introduction, or personnal recomendation
you can bring Mr A. in contact with men of that description, you will
sincerely oblige him as well as myself. —

I have known Mr Audubon for many Years, and can truly say, that
the respectability of his life, and that of his familly Conection entitle
him to the particular notice and good wishes of every "homme de
bien." —

Mr Clay, Mr Dewitt Clinton, and other men of Distinction on this
side of the watters have suplied Mr A. with letters of introduction and
ample testimonials of the merit of his performances.

Excuse the freedom of my applications and believe me allways and
most sincerely devoted to you.

    I am, my Dear Sir, Yours very sincerely
                 Vincent Nolte

Adam Hodgson Esqr
Liverpool

The following letter was copied by a hand other than Audubon's in the Beinecke fragment immediately preceding the entry for June 22.

John Owens Johnson Esqre

Dear Sir

Permit me to introduce to your acquaintance & civilities my friend J. J. Audubon Esqre whose scientific acquirements are of the first order period. M^r A visits Britain [MS: Britian] with the view of completing a work on which he has been engaged for upwards of 20 years & as a Foreigner may perhaps meet with some dificulty in passing it through the Custom House, therefore as I consider that the accomplishment of M^r A's views would be of service to the Country, let me solicit for him your assistance in getting them passed. Your usual kindness & attention to M^r A will greatly oblige your friend

Randall Currell

New Orleans 16 May 1826

The following three letters were copied by Audubon into the 1826 journal immediately following the entry for June 22.

Copy of a letter received from Henry Clay Esq. dated Washington March 17th 1823.

I have known for some years the bearer hereof, Mr Audubon, a native of France, but a naturalized citizen of the United States, as an ingen[i]ous, worthy and highly respectable Gentleman. He resided several years in the State of Kentucky and has been engaged for some time past in exercising his fine talent for painting on objects connected with the natural history of the U. States. He purposes going to Europe, to avail himself of the artists and opportunities of that quarter, in executing some of his scetches and designs, so as to give them a wider diffusion—

I take particular satisfaction in recommending him to the good offices and kind reception of the American Ministers, Consuls and public agents abroad, and to the Hospitality and good treatment of all other persons.

H. Clay

Washington 17ᵗʰ March 1823

Copy of another received from the same dated Washington, 24 Feb. 1826

Sir

The bearer hereof, Mʳ J. J. Audubon, a respectable citizen of the U. States, whom I have had the pleasure to know has been, for some years, engaged in procuring drawings and preparing manuscripts in relation to the birds of America. He goes to England with the purpose of completing his work, and having it published there. I shall be glad if you would procure from Government any facilities (should any be necessary) that may be reasonably asked in a foreign Country for the tending &ᶜ of his drawings and manuscripts, and that you would otherwise shew him any attention in your power. I am respectfully

Your ob servant

Rufus King Esq[1]   H. Clay

Copy of a letter from the Governor of the State of Louisiana dated New Orleans May 13ᵗʰ 1826

The bearer hereof, Mʳ J. J. Audubon, a citizen of the United States, who has resided in this State eight years, has been for some time engaged in procuring drawings and preparing manuscripts in relation to the birds of America. He proposes going to Europe with the purpose of completing his work and having it published there. Mʳ Audubon is a gentleman of worth and highly respected for his

---

1. Rufus King (1755–1827), a U.S. politician, had served as ambassador to Britain from 1796 to 1803. He was in that position again in 1826.

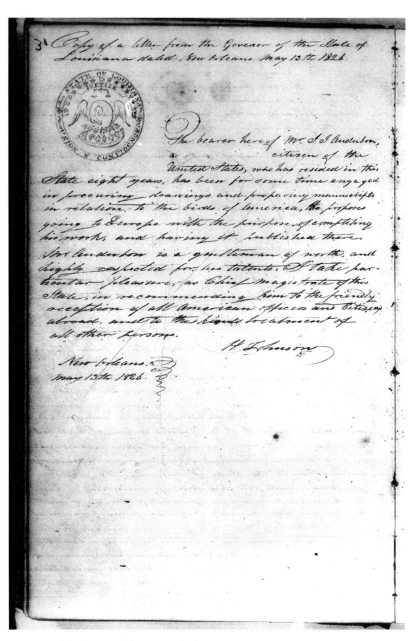

3¹ Copy of a letter from the Governor of the State of
Louisiana dated New Orleans May 13th 1826

The bearer hereof Mr. J. J. Audubon,
a   citizen of the
United States, who has resided in this
State eight years, has been for some time engaged
in procuring drawings and preparing manuscripts
in relation to the birds of America, he proposes
going to Europe with the purpose of completing
his works, and having it published there
Mr Audubon is a gentleman of worth, and
highly respected for his talents. I take particular pleasure, as Chief Magistrate of this
State, in recommending him to the friendly
reception of all American officers and citizens
abroad, and to the kind treatment of
all other persons.

H. Johnson

New Orleans.
May 13th 1826

FIG. 22. Audubon's copy of the state seal of Louisiana, May 13, 1826

talents: I take particular pleasure, as Chief magistrate of this State, in recommending him to the friendly reception of all American officers and Citizens abroad and to the kind treatment of all other persons.

H. Johnson

New Orleans
May 13$^{\underline{th}}$ 1826

Liverpool 5 August 1826.

My Dear Sir

Permit me to introduce to your acquaintance Mons$^{\underline{r}}$ Audubon, an eminent naturalist who is proceeding to London, with a large & very valuable collection of drawings chiefly of American Birds, the produce of 23 years labour in the Woods. I think you will be equally pleased with this gentleman & with his productions & therefore venture to recommend him to your kind attentions.

Believe me,
My Dear Sir
With Sincere respect
Yours faithfully
William Rathbone

To Benj$^{\underline{n}}$ Ar. Heywood Esq$^{\underline{re}}$
Bank
Manchester

The following fifteen letters of introduction were copied into the manuscript by a hired scribe after Audubon's entry for August 7, 1826.

Liverpool 5 August 1826

My Dear Sir

Permit me to introduce to your Acquaintance Mons$^{\underline{r}}$ Audubon, an eminent Naturalist and who is proceeding to London, with a large Collection of drawings chiefly of North American Birds, the produce of 23 years labour in the Woods. I think you will be equally pleased with this Gentleman as with his productions. I venture, therefore, to recommend him to your kind attentions.

Believe me
With sincere respect
Yours faithfully
William Rathbone

Peter Ewart Esqre

Manchester

Consulate of the United States
Liverpool 7 August 1826

Dear Sir

I hope this will reach [you] at the end of your journey & that the route you chose proved a pleasant one to you and the Ladies. While in this place it was my wish & intention to have presented to you Mr Audubon, our fellow citizen of Louisianna, who is the bearer of this. M^r A's object in coming to Europe is to avail himself of (as I believe) the most splended & correct collection that ever has been seen, of Drawings of Birds of the United States, in which he has been empl[o]yed *twenty two years*. He has a letter from Mr Clay to our Ministers & Consuls recommending *him* to their good offices. With great respect & esteem I have the honor to be, Your faithfull & Obedient Servant

James Maury

To His Excellency
  Albert Gallatin
    Envoy Extraordinary
      of the United States &^c &^c &^c
    London

Liverpool 5 August 1826

My Dear Tom

In mentioning Monsr Audubon's name to you, who you met at my House, I do all that is necessary to secure him the kind attentions you were obliging enough to offer to one who has unceasedly pleased on encreased acquaintance

Your Always
William Rathbone

Thomas Greg Junr Esqre
  Wainfords Court
    Throgmorton Street
     London

Mr Miller

My Dear Sir

    Allow me to make you acquainted with Mr Audubon, of the United States. He visits this country with the view of making public a Work on Ornithology which has engrossed his attention for many valuable years of his Life. With his labors I am confident you will be highly delighted. Mr A. will fully explain his views in which your advice & knowledge in such matters may be truly valuable to him & I am sure will be readily rendered.

    I hope Mrs M. & my friend John are quite well. Pray, make my compliments. I am much better than when I had last the pleasure of seeing you.

Yours very sincerely
George Godard.

I am glad to see your friend Price is to have Drury Lane. I hope it will be a public as well as private benefit.

Liverpool 27 Manestys Lane
31 July 1826

Mr Miller
  5 Bridge Street
    Blackfriars
     London

Liverpool 5 August 1826

My Dear Sir

Permit me to introduce to your acquaintance Mons.ʳ Audubon, an eminent Naturalist who is proceeding to London, with a large collection of drawings chiefly of American Birds, the produce of 23 years labour in Woods. I think you will be equally pleased with this Gentleman as with his productions. I venture therefore to recommend him to your kind attentions. Believe me with sincere respect

Yours faithfully
William Rathbone

G. M. Wood Esq.ʳᵉ
Manchester

Will you have the kindness to advice M.ʳ Audubon what course he had better pursue in the object he has in view at Manchester.

Liverpool 4 August 1826

My Dear Sir

Permit me to introduce to your acquaintance Mons.ʳ Audubon, an eminent Naturalist who is proceeding to London with a large collection of Drawings chiefly of American birds, the produce of 23 years labours in the Woods. I think you will be equally pleased with this Gentleman and with his productions and therefore venture to recommend him to your kind attentions.

Believe me
With sincere respect
My Dear Sir
Yours faithfully
William Rathbone

D.ʳ Henry
Manchester

Liverpool 5 August 1826

My Dear Sir

Permit me to introduce to your acquaintance, Mons.ʳ Audubon
an eminent naturalist who is proceeding to London, with a large
collection of drawings chiefly of North American Birds, the produce
of 23 years labour in the Woods. I think you will be equally pleased
with this gentleman and with his productions and venture therefore
to recommend him to your kind attentions. Believe me

With sincere respect
Yours faithfully
William Rathbone

John Edw.ᵈ Taylor Esq.ʳᵉ [2]
   Guardian Office
   Manchester

Edward Hull Esq.ʳᵉ

Dear Sir

Allow me to introduce to your acquaintance M.ʳ Audubon of
the United States of America. M.ʳ Audubon has devoted a great
portion of his Life to Natural History and visits this country with
the Treasures of twenty years research in the hopes of reaping a rich
harvest of reward and honor for his past labours and privations. I
have much pleasure in making you acquainted with this gentleman
for I am certain you will derive infinite delight from the inspection
of his performances being one of the few who are capable of really
appreciating merit, and it may be possible that M.ʳ A. might derive
much advantage from your knowledge of & acquaintance with
the first artists of the day. For an explanation of M.ʳ A's views in the

---

2. John Edward Taylor (1791–1844) had been editor of the *Manchester Guardian* since its
founding in 1821.

prosecution of his plans I must refer you to the gentleman himself &
remain Dear Sir

Yours ever truly
George Goddard

Liverpool 31 July 1826.
E. Hull Esqre
   North Brixton
    Surry

Liverpool 5 August 1826

My Dear Sir

Permit me to introduce to your acquaintance Monsr Audubon,
an eminent naturalist who is proceeding to London with a large &
valuable collection of drawings, chiefly of Birds in North America the
produce of 23 years labour in the Woods. I think you will be equally
pleased with this gentleman as with his Productions.

I venture therefore to solicit your kind attention to him, remaining
with sincere respect

My Dear Sir
Yours faithfully
William Rathbone

Revd J. Corrie
  Birmingham

Dinglehead near Liverpool
5 August 1826

Dear Sir

The bearer Mr Audubon has empl[o]yed a large part of his life in
executing a most admirable series of drawings of North American
Birds, whose habits he has attentively studied in their native
situations. He is taking them to Birmingham on his way to London,

and wishes some of them to be inspected there by such gentlemen as are attached to the fine Arts or to the study of nature. I do not hesitate to promise you much gratification from the sight of them and will beg of you to assist M͟r Audubon by such suggestions as may be usefull to him respecting the best mode of disposing of them.

I remain Dear Sir
Yours always
with great regard
James Yates

M͟r Hodgson
  Temple Row
    Birmingham

My Dear Sir

I take the liberty of introducing to you the Bearer, M͟r J. G. Audubon, who has been most respectably introduced to us, and whose short stay amongst us has given us a very lively interest in him and his pursuits.

He is an European by birth (or rather an Haytian of European Parents), but has been for upwards of Twenty years a resident in the United States. He has devoted most of that time to Ornithological researches of various kinds and has brought with him a beautifull Collection of drawings, which I am very anxious you should see both on account of their entrinsic excellence and the very correct idea they convey of the Birds of America. He has some idea of offering them to the British Museum, but will be guided by the advice of those friends to whom he will take letters. Among these I am very desirous to secure for him the benefit of your advice, which is one of the objects I have in view in giving him this letter. Another is to secure for Lady Inglis and the Miss Thorntons the gratification I am sure they will derive from a sight of the drawings. It was a great mortification to me to spend three days in London this spring without seeing you and my excellent friends at Battersea Rise, but one of the days I was confined to my bed and the other two, though I worked hard for the express purpose, I could not get my business completed in time to get over to Battersea Rise as I fully expected. I beg my best respects and very kind remembrances to Lady Inglis and the Miss Thorntons and their Brothers and with a lively recollection of all your kindness

I remain
My Dear Sir
Yours very sincerely
A. Hodgson

Liverpool 3 August 1826
Sir Robert Inglis Bar^t
   Battersea Rise
     near London.

Liverpool 6 August 1826.

My Dear Sir

The bearer Mr Audubon has lately arrived in Liverpool with a magnificent series of his own Drawings of Birds of North America, which have engaged his attention during above 20 years. He is going with them to London with a view, I understand, of disposing of them, and as it is important to him that their merits should be made known to the lovers of the fine Arts and of Natural History, I take the liberty of introducing him to you and requesting you will have the goodness to favor him with your advice as the best means of bringing his meritorious labours before the Public.

Believe me, Dear Sir
Yours truly
J. A. Yates

Ar. Aiken Esqre

Sec^y to the Society of Arts &^c &^c
   Adelphi

Liverpool 6 August 1826

My Dear Sir

The bearer of this, Mr Audubon, has lately arrived in this Town from North America with a most interesting and valuable series of

Drawings of the Birds of that Country. As he is desirous of disposing of them in London and with that view exhibiting them to the lovers of Natural History and the fine Arts, I take the liberty of introducing him to you, and asking the favor of your giving him your advice as to the best means of bringing his works before the public in an advantageous manner.

I am Dear Sir

Your very truly

J. A. Yates

D.ʳ Roget[3]
    Bernard Street
    Russel Square

Liverpool 6ᵗʰ August 1826.

My Dear Sir

Permit me to introduce to your acquaintance Mons.ʳ Audubon, an eminent Naturalist who is proceeding to London with a large and beautifull collection of Drawings chiefly of American Birds, the produce of twenty three years labour in the back Woods. As I feel certain that you will be equally pleased with this gentleman as with his productions, may I venture to solicit for him your kind attentions, remaining with sincere respect

My Dear Sir

Yours faithfully

William Rathbone

John Kennedy Esq.ʳᵉ[4]
    Manchester

3. Peter Mark Roget (1779–1869) was a London physician and lecturer on anatomy.

4. John Kennedy (1769–1855) was a Manchester cotton spinning mill owner and manufacturer of machinery.

Dinglehead near Liverpool
August 6th 1826

My Dear Sir

The bearer Mr Audubon has lately arrived in Liverpool with a most admirable series of Drawings of the Birds of North America, whose distinctions and habits he has studied most attentively during more than 20 years. He is taking them to Birmingham on his way to London, and wishes for advice and assistance respecting the best way of disposing of them and of obtaining a remuneration [MS: renumeration] for his extraordinary labour. If you can spare time to look at a few of them, I am sure you will be highly gratified, and Mr Audubon will be obliged by any suggestions which you may think usefull with a view to his future proceedings. Your kindness and friendship render it unnecessary for me to apologize to you for this introduction. I will only subscribe myself therefore

> My Dear Sir
> yours always most truly
> James Yates

Dr Johnstone[5]
Edgbaston Hall
near Birmingham

The following twenty letters of introduction were copied into the manuscript by a hired scribe after Audubon's entry for August 8, 1826.

Dinglehead August 6th 1826.

My Dear Sir

The bearer, Mr Audubon, has passed more than 20 years in the minute and attentive study of the distinctions and habits of the birds of North America and has prepared a most admirable series of

---

5. Edward Johnstone (1757–1851) had been a Birmingham physician since 1779; he also helped establish a society of the arts there.

drawings of them, which he wishes to be inspected by some of the friends of the fine Arts and of the study of nature in your vicinity. I can promise you a high gratification in seeing them, and you may possibly be of service of M.ͬ Audubon by your advice respecting the best method of disposing of them. I suggested to him that an exhibition of them in Birmingham at the time of the Musical Festival might be desirable. Perhaps you could furnish him with a letter of introduction to M.ͬ John Morgan in London. Believe me to remain, Dear Sir

Yours most affectionately
James Yates

Liverpool 6ͭͪ August 1826.

Dear Doctor

The bearer, M.ͬ Audubon, has lately arrived in Liverpool with a most extensive and valuable series of Drawings of the Birds of North America, which have occupied his attention during more than 20 years past. He is going with them to London, with a view as I believe of disposing of them, and as his friends are anxious that he should obtain the best advice as to the best mode of obtaining a remuneration [MS: renumeration] for his extraordinary labour, I have much pleasure in introducing him to you, and shall feel obliged by your putting him in the way of making his labours known to other lovers of the fine Arts and Natural History.

Your Affectionately Bro.ͬ
J. A. Yates

D.ͬ Bostock
    22 Upper Bedford Place
    Russel Square

My Dear Sir

I know you will excuse the liberty I take in introducing to you the Bearer M.ͬ J. G. Audubon, an European by birth but for upwards

of twenty years a Citizen of the United States. He has devoted
most of that time to Ornithological Recearches and has brought
to England a very valuable collection of Drawings which I am very
anxious you should see. It is with the double object of securing you
this gratification and of obtaining for M.ͬ A your kind advice with
regard to the best mode of carrying his views into effect, that I have
ventured to give him this letter.

M.ͬ Audubon carries with him excellent letters of introduction
from M.ͬ Clay, Clinton and several of the most distinguished men in
America, who speak on high terms of the respectability of his Wife
and familly connection, and all we have seen of him here has inspired
us with a strong interest in his favor. I wish he may be so fortunate
as to find you in Town, though on your own account [in] this hot
weather I ought hardly to wish it.

I had lately an animated letter from our excellant friend Bishop
Char. I beg you to present my best compliments to Lady Acland and
I remain

My Dear Sir
Yours sincerely obliged
A. Hodgson

Liverpool 3 August 1826
  Sir Thomas Acland Bar.ͭ M. P.[6]
    Warrens Hotel
      Regents Street
      London

Liverpool 7 August 1826.

My Dear Sir

Permit me to introduce to your acquaintance Mons.ͬ Audubon,
an eminent naturalist, who is proceeding to London with a large
and very valuable collection of drawings chiefly of Birds of North
America. As I feel certain that you will be equally pleased with this
gentleman and with his productions and when known be anxious

---

6. Sir Thomas Acland (1787–1871) was a London politician and philanthropist active in issues
of religious progress.

to serve him, I venture to solicit for him your kind attentions and service, remaining my Dear Sir

with sincer[e] respect
Yours faithfully
William Rathbone

S. R. Brooks Esqre
Manchester

Liverpool 8 August 1826.

My Dear Sir

Knowing the pleasure which it affords to Mrs Welles and yourself to patronize the Arts, I take much satisfaction in introducing to you Mr Audubon of Louisianna, whose object in coming to Europe is to avail himself of a most splended collection of Drawings of the Birds of the United States, which has been exibited here and admired by all the

M^r A is highly introduced by the Secretary of State at Washington to the notice of all our Consuls and Ministers in Europe, and I need hardly add that your attention to him will add to the many favors conferred upon yours most truly

James [MS: William] Maury

Saml Welles Esq^{re 7}
Paris

My Dear Sir

I have the pleasure of introducing to you Mr Audubon, a gentleman who has devoted the last 22 years to a very attentive study of the habits and distinctions of the Birds of North America, and who has executed a most admirable series of drawings upon these Subjects which he is now desirous of publishing. It has occurred to me that you may probably be able to assist him with your advice, and I am

---

7. Samuel Welles (?–1841) was an eminent American banker in Paris, where he had founded the banking firm Welles and Company.

sure you will be greatly pleased with him and his productions. Believe me to remain

Dear Sir

Yours most truly

Liverpool 8 August 1826   James Yates

Richard Taylor Esq[re][8]
Shoe Lane
Fleet Street
London

Mr Audubon

My Dear Sir

Inclosed are some introductions which I hope may serve to usher you to some agreeable and useful acquaintances. Your own merits will render my services of secondary importance the moment you are known in London or in Edinburgh. I shall feel gratified if my humble efforts can in the slightest degree be useful to one whose workes have afforded me such high gratification. With best wishes for your success,

I am Dear Sir

With great respect

your sincere friend

Thomas Stewart Traill

Liverpool 9 August 1826.

My Dear Swainson

By introducing to you a kindred spirit, M[r] Audubon, an American Naturalist probably well known to you by name, I know that I am preparing a treat to my *old friend of Warwick*. You cannot fail to be pleased with the Drawings of M[r] Audubon, and with his inteligence and manners. He has literally studied in the Wilds for many years,

8. Richard Taylor (1781–1858) was a London printer especially interested in the natural sciences but of broad intellectual interests. He was a member of the Linnean Society.

and the results of his labours are proportionate to his zeal and talents. He intends to offer a new American Ornithology to the World, and you will oblige me by giving him your best advice, with respect to the mode of setting about it, so as to secure to our Country the honour of being the patron of so magnificent a work. Any instructions you can give to the southern tribe of Naturalists will be gratifying to him and pleasing to your sincer[e] friend

Thos. Stewart Traill

Liverpool 9 August 1826
William Swainson Esq⁻
    Warwick or London

My Dear Sir

Permit me to introduce M⁻ Audubon an American Naturalist, whose magnificent Ornithological drawings will please you no less than they have astonished me. They are the fruits of many years investigation of the Works of Nature in her own domains.

M⁻ Audubon intends to publish a New American Ornithology on a splendid scale and he goes to London to consult with scientific men and artists respecting his intended publication, you will I think be pleased with his unassuming manners and conversation, and should you have it in your power to introduce him to some of our Naturalists in the Metropolis, you will oblige

Dear Sir
Yours very truly
and respectfully
Thos Steward Traill

Liverpool 9 August 1826
Sir James E. Smith[9]
President of the Linnaean Society
    London

9. James Edward Smith (1759–1828) was a trained physician who devoted himself to botany. He became first president of the Linnean Society in 1788.

Liverpool 9 August 1826

My Dear Sir

The bearer, Mr Audubon, is a gentleman from whose acquaintance you will receive a high gratification.

He is a distinguished Naturalist, and his Wonderfull drawings, which have delighted and astonished us here, will speak his praises far better than any eulogy from me. He is no closet Naturalist, but has spent 20 years in investigating the natural History of the United States of North America. He intends to publish a splended work on Ornithology and is solicitious to be introduced to the principal London Naturalists, who will be much pleased with both the artist and the man. Could you procure him an introduction to M^r M Leary, Mr Vigors[10] — Latham or other eminent Naturalists in your vicinity, it would I think gratify them and also

Your friend
Thos. Stewart Traill

Dr Bostock
Bedford Street
London

Liverpool 9 August 1826

My Dear Sir

I shall offer no apology for introducing the bearer, Mr Audubon, an able and accomplished American Naturalist. His numerous and in my opinion quite unrivalled Ornithological Drawings cannot fail to please you, and should you think it would be the wish of the Natural History Society of Manchester to inspect them, he will have pleasure

10. Nicholas Aylward Vigors (1785/86–1840) became a member of the Linnean Society in 1819; he was a wealthy gentleman with interests in ornithology and entomology. He argued for the quinarian classification system. John Latham (1740–1837) was a London physician and naturalist interested in ornithology and comparative anatomy. He was a fellow of the Royal Society.

in shewing specimens of his vast collection to the Members or their friends. You will, I think, like the man as well as his Works.

I am Dear Sir
Most sincerely yours
Thos. Stewart Traill

Dᴿ Holme
Manchester

My Dear Sir

Knowing your discrimination [ms: disenimnation] of fine design in objects of natural History, I shall make no apology for making you acquainted with the bearer, Mᴿ Audubon, an American Naturalist whose portfolio will astonish you no less than his manners will interest you. Any manner in which you can bring his merits before compleat Judges in Edinburgh will gratify me. Mᴿ Audubon means to publish a splended work on Ornitho[lo]gy, and naturally courts the acquaintance of those who are capable of judging of his labours. This is the cause of his visit to Edinburgh.

I think Dᴿ Brewster, tho' not, I believe, addicted to zoology, would be pleased to know Mᴿ Audubon.

I am Dear Sir
Yours truly
Thos. Stewart Traill

Dᴿ Knox   Liverpool 9 August 1826
Edinburgh

Liverpool 9 August 1826

My Dear Sir

Permit me to introduce a Naturalist of no Ordinary talent, Mᴿ Audubon, whose graphic delineations of Birds and other objects of Natural History have surprised and delighted me. You will own on inspection that they are superb. Mᴿ Audubon intends to publish a grand work on American Birds, the habits of which he has studied, like our Country Man Wilson in their native wilds, for 20 years. If through you or any of my Edinburgh friends he were introduced to the Wernerian Society, his talents and unassuming manners would secure him the notice of all true naturalists. Can you introduce him to M.r Syme your draughtsman or to M.r Greville.

Believe me Dear Sir
very truly yours
Thos. Stewart Traill

Patrick Neill Esq.re
  Secretary to the Wernerian Society
    Edinburgh

My Dear Sir

I prepare for you a high treat as a Naturalist in introducing to you my friend M. Audubon, a distinguished American Ornithologist, who has spent years in studying in the great field of nature, as his admirable drawings will readely convince you. Never have any delineations so perfect in form, life and execution been submitted to my inspection, and the manners of the Artist will not destroy the impression you receive from his works. He is highly respected in America, his adopted country, and I trust will be well received in ours. He intends to publish on a magnificient scale the result of his labours, and should he find artists capable of transmitting his beautifull designs to the block or the plate, I hope that an ornithological work will be produced in Britian capable of ex[c] iting the envy of the World. Could you procure for my friend introductions to your Scotish Naturalists, Wilson, Fleming J.r or to Sir Walter Scott, the president of *our* Royal Society, it would oblige me.

I am Dear sir
faithfully yours
Thos. Stewart Traill

Liverpool 9 August 1826
  Professor Jameson
    Edinburgh

Dear Sir

In presuming on a slight acquaintance to introduce to you the bearer, M. Audubon, I trust that one of the most eminent British Naturalists will be happy to become known to a most distinguished American Ornithologist. His great collection of Materials and his drawings, which for accuracy, life and finish surpass every thing of the kind which has fallen under my observation, will explain to you his merits better than my pen.

He intends to publish a magnificent American Ornithology and I am not without hopes that our Country may have the honour of ushering it into the World.

	I have the honour to be
Liverpool 9 August 1826	Dear Sir
Joseph Sabine Esqʳᵉ[11]	very truly yours
London.	Thos. Stewart Traill

My Dear Sir

Allow me to introduce the bearer, M. Audubon, a distinguished Naturalist, who has studied Ornithology for 20 years in the Wilds of North America. His Ornithological drawings, for high finish and most scrupulous accuracy, are unrivalled, and he intends to promote the interests of his favourite study by the publication of his labours either in this Country or in France. I feel anxious that our Island should have the honour of publishing what, from the quality of his materials and the magnificence of his designs, I believe will be the most splended Ornithological Work ever given to the World, and you will confer benefit on science while you oblige me by procuring for him introductions to the chief London Naturalists, and the president of the Royal Society.

The unaffected urbanity of his manners will not Discredit your recommendation, and you may procure a high treat to any of your

11. Joseph Sabine (1770–1837) was a cofounder of the Linnean Society in 1798, fellow of the Royal Society since 1799, and secretary of the Horticultural Society since 1816.

friends fond of Natural History by making them acquainted with Mʳ Audubon.

I am Dear Sir

Liverpool 9 August 1826   very faithfully yours

P. Roget Esqʳᵉ M. D.   Thos. Stewart Traill

Bedford Street, Russel Square

London

Liverpool 9 August 1826.

Dear Uncle

This will be delivered to you by Mʳ Audubon, the celebrated American Ornithologist, with whose name & labours in your *vocations* you are no doubt well acquainted. Mʳ A. intends to go to Edinburgh in the course of the next month & has expressed a desire to have an introduction to a Gentleman whose taste is similar to his own & whose works he highly admires. From the mild amenity [ms: aminety] of his manners & extreme information, I have little doubt but that you would be glad to shew him the hospitalities of Twisel & should be mutually agreeable & you will be able to give him much valuable information as to his best method of

You both are Birds of a Feather

P. J. Selby Esqʳᵉ   Arcades ambo[12]

Twisel House,   Yours sincerely

Bedford   Will. Atherton

Northumberland

12. *Arcades ambo,* literally, "Arcadians both," meaning two people of similar characteristics or interests; from Virgil's *Eclogues.*

Dear Madam

I take the liberty of requesting to make known to you the gentleman, M͟r Audubon who will I hope be the bearer of this. No one can better than yourself appreciate the value of his beautifull collection of drawings of Birds & made by himself in the Woods of Louisianna and which have given great gratification to M͟r Roscoe, D͟r Traill, and other friends of ours here. M͟r Martin & Frederick join with me in best respects to yourself and M͟r Corrie. I shall be happy to hear you are recovering from the effects of the late hot weather, which I was sorry to learn from Miss Corries note to Fany still seriously affected you. Fanny is staying with a friend or she would have taken this oppertunity of acknowledging Miss Cs kind note.

	I am Dear Madam
M͟rs Corrie	Your obliged friend
The Rev͟d John Corries	Fran[k] J. Martin

WoodvilleAllerton 9 August 1826
near Birmingham

Dear Sir

I have much pleasure in introducing to you M͟r Audubon of Louisianna, a gentleman who favored the Institution here, with the sight of some beautifull drawings of Birds which he made himself on the spot. From your taste for Natural History and from the value which I thought the sight of the specimans in Soho Square would be to M͟r A., I presume to request the favor of his being known to you. Last May or June I troubled you with a note requesting to know some particulars respecting the British Museum. Had I known my Brother James was in London, I should have done this thro' him, but owing to the delay of a packet of letters from my Brother to myself & M͟r Roscoe, which was detained by a private hand in Norwich, I did not

know of Sir James being in London. Mͬ Martin & my Daughter unite
with me in best respects and am Sir your obliged friend & servant

Frank J. Martin

Brown Esqͬᵉ[13]   Allerton 9 August 1826
Linnean Society
  Soho Square
    London

Dear Sir

The gentleman Mͬ Audubon, who will I hope be the bearer of this,
has been staying a short time in Liverpool and has afforded much
gratification to Mͬ Roscoe and Dͬ Traill, as well as to our less scientific
by the sight of some very beautifull drawings of birds and other
animals which he made himself in the Woods of Louisianna.

I thought the sight of them might afford you pleasure. I have written
a few lines wishing to make him known to my friend, Mͬ Brown of
Soho Square. I do not know whether the British Museum is open
to the Public at this season of the year. May I request if it requires a
personal introduction to see the Natural History Part to advantage
that you would do Mͬ Audubon this for me.

Mͬ Martin and family beg to unite with me in most sincere regard to
yourself and Mͬˢ Menzies, who I hope with yourself is in good health.

Dear Sir
Your much obliged friend
Frank J. Martin

Archͩ Menzies[14]   Allerton 9 August 1826
  6 Chapel Place
  Cavindish Square
    London
36†

---

13. Robert Brown (1773–1858) was a brilliant, accomplished, and much honored botanist who
had been with the Linnean Society since 1805.

14. Archibald Menzies (1754–1842) was a physician and botanist who accompanied Capt.
George Vancouver as naturalist and surgeon on his expedition around the world of 1790–95. His
plant collections were significant.

The following letter of introduction was copied into the journal by Audubon's paid scribe after the entry for August 13, 1826.

Toxteth Park, Liverpool
12 August 1826

My Dear Sir

Permit me to introduce to you the bearer, Mr J. J. Audubon, a gentleman of very great merit, as an artist & a naturalist who has lately arrived here from North America with a most splended collection of Drawings of Birds, the labours of his own pencil. He has been prevailed upon by the Committee of the institution to exhibit them in their Rooms, & to escape the bustle has determined to make an excursion into Wales for a few days.

I have requested him to carry a portfolio of his drawings to you, feeling assured that they will give you great pleasure & satisfaction & that the introduction will prove mutually agreeable. As Mr A. has not determined as to the publication or disposal of his collection, your extensive knowledge of the Scientific Work may perhaps enable you to offer some suggestions or introductions which may be useful to him, for which I shall feel very greatly obliged to you.

Believe me my dear Sir
your obliged very faithfully
Edward Roscoe

David Pannant Esqre
Downing.

The following two letters of introduction appear in the manuscript following the entry for September 6. They are in a hand other than Audubon's.

Gatiane September 3 1826

My Dear Miss Bent

I have much pleasure in introducing to you Mr Audubon, an American gentleman, who has lately brought over to England, a splendid collection of his drawings, with which we have all been delighted. Mr Audubon is now visiting Derby and I shall feel much gratified to be the means of giving you an opportunity of seeing these beautiful birds, and of introducing to your acquaintance a gentleman in whose society we have had so much pleasure

With our kind remembrances
I remain my dear Miss Bent
Yours very truly
M. Lace

To Miss Bent
Dr Bent Derby

Gatiane Sept. 3. 1826

My dear Sir

I have much pleasure in introducing to you Mr Audubon, an American gentleman &^c &^c (the same as above)

Mary Ann Lace

To Thomas Lee Esq —
Edgebaston
  Birmingham
Office New Hall S^t —

The following six letters of introduction were copied into the manuscript journal by a paid scribe after the entry for September 7, 1826.

Dear Sir

I beg leave to recommend to your particular attention and patronage Mons: Audubon, whose talents as an artist and a naturalist I know you are well able to appreciate. During his residence in Liverpool he was in almost daily communcation with Mr Roscoe, who highly esteems him as a man of talent and a gentleman. Believe me Yours Truly, Wm Shepherd[15]

Liverpool Sept 23^d
To Dr Holme
Manchester

John R Chorley, N° 14 St Annes Street, Liverpool
To Miss Edgeworth

My dear Madam,

I am happy in any opportunity of recalling myself to your remembrance, but the present occasion is doubly gratify[ing] to me, as it affords me the means of introducing to you the bearer of this, Mr Audubon — a gentleman who, amidst the pursuits of natural history and the employment of drawing Birds & Plants in the wilds of America, has relieved his fatigues by the perusal of your delightful writings, and on his arrival in Europe, is desirous above all things of paying his respects to the person, whom, at so great a distance, he has so long conversed with, and so highly admired. It is not, however, on account of a sentiment which he feels only in common with so many others, that I beg to introduce Mr Audubon to your notice —

15. William Shepherd (1768–1847) was a Unitarian minister long associated with William Roscoe. He was an educator and advocate for civil and religious liberty as well as a scholar of Italian literature.

Should your Engagements permit you to converse with him, you will find him both able and willing to afford you information on many subjects connected with American history and scenery in which you cannot fail to be deeply interested; whilst his beautiful delineations of Birds and plants drawn on the spot, with all the character, glow, and freshness of Nature, will recommend themselves to your Examination and secure your applause.

I could say much more in favour of Mr Audubon, but he comes here so well recommended by persons of the highest character in his own country, that I feel it to be unnecessary; and after all, his best recommendation is himself for such are his various acquirements, and such his candid, obliging and communicative disposition, that he has not failed to create for himself numerous friends here who take an earnest interest in his welfare. With the sincerest sentiments of attachment and respect, believe me always, my dear Miss Edgeworth, Most faithfully and affectionately yours, W. Roscoe. —

Toxteth Park near Liverpool 8 Aug. 1826

To Jos: Sabine Esq — Horticultural Society Regents London

My dear Sir

I have great pleasure in introducing to you the bearer of this, Mr Audubon, who has lately arrived here from Louisiana, bringing with him a collection of drawings of Birds, Plants and other subjects of natural History, executed by himself on the spot, in the most unexplored parts of America, exceeding both in truth of character and beauty of execution anything of the kind I have before seen. What his views are respecting them in bringing them to Europe, he will himself explain to you, & if after having inspected his works, you would have the goodness to allow him the benefit of your kind advice and opinion, as to the means he should adopt for availing himself of the labor of so many years of his life, you will confer on him a favor which few persons are so competent to do, and will greatly oblige — my dear Sir, Yours most respectfully & truly, W. Roscoe

Toxteth Park near Liverpool 8 Aug: 1826 —

To Miss Duckworth. Wm Duckworth Esq, Manchester

My dear Miss Duckworth

May I take the liberty of recommending to your notice Mr
Audubon, the bearer of this; a gentleman who has gratified us all
very much in Liverpool by the sight of some very beautiful drawings
of American birds & plants, executed in their native forests, and the
labour of twenty years. If you take an interest in American Scenery
or information, you will, I think, have pleasure in conversing with
Mr Audubon, whom we have found intelligent & agreeable. I have
by no means forgotten your kind attentions to me when I was in
London, and this recollection, and the knowledge of your hospitality
and goodness to strangers, have led me to wish to secure to him the
advantage of your attention and recommendation, in case he exhibits
his paintings in Manchester, which I believe it is his intention to
do. Believe me, my dear Miss Duckworth, very truly yours, Jane E.
Roscoe

Lodge Lane, Aug 8th

To Mrs Marsh, No 7, Whitehall Place.

My dear Mrs Marsh

I venture to recommend to your attention an uncommonly
beautiful collection of paintings of American birds and plants, which
Mr Audubon, the bearer of this, has been exhibiting in Liverpool,
and which are the result of the labour of more than 20 years. I beg
also to recommend to your kind notice Mr Audubon himself, who is
a very intelligent & interesting person, and has made many friends
in Liverpool who take a sincere interest in his future success. He has
been staying at Mr Rathbones, Green Bank, lately, and we have seen
a good deal of him. You will find him original, and if you are at all
interested in descriptions of Amn Scenery or character, you will have
much pleasure in conversing with him. Believe me always, My dear
Mrs Marsh, very truly yours, J. E. Roscoe

To Augustus Stolberfont Esq — Lübeck
Liverpool 8 Sept 1826

My dear Augustus

This letter will be presented to you by Mr J. J. Audubon, an eminent naturalist, who has spent nearly twenty years in the woods of America, in the collection of the most splendid set of ornithological drawings, all of them executed with his own hand, that has been ever seen in this country.

He has been a short time in England, & intends, after visiting London and Paris, to proceed through Germany to St Petersburgh. I shall feel much gratified if, on his passing through Lübeck, you can be of any service to him; as his talents, which are of the first order, as well as his amiable qualities, which I had the pleasure of observing during a visit which he paid at the house of Mrs Rathbone, where I was staying at the same time, have interested me considerably on his behalf — Indeed, I may say that I never felt so much interested in any one in so short a time as I have enjoyed the privilege of Mr Audubon's acquaintance.

I feel less hesitation in thus recommending him to your kind offices, from the conviction that any little trouble you may take in forwarding the views he may possibly have in crossing through Lübeck, shewing him anything worthy of observation &c &c will be amply repaid by the pleasure I am sure you will enjoy in his acquaintance, with very dear love I remain Your sincere & affe. Friend, J. R. Chorley

The following two letters of introduction and note of other letters in his possession were copied by Audubon into the journal after the entry for September 9, 1826.

My Dear Sir

Allow me to introduce my friend Mr Audubon, a Naturalist whose admirable delineations of American Birds will speak more in his favour than any thing which I can say $=$ Mr A. intends to publish a magnificent work on American Ornithology — and wishes for an opportunity of exibiting his designs to the Natural History Society of Manchester. He will probably afterwards publick[l]y exibit them as you may have seen by the news paper, he did here. — but I trust for the honor of Manchester, with more emolument than he did in Liverpool, where several thousands came to see them during the 3 days of their gratuitous exibition — and comparativelly few after he was invited by the Committee of the Royal Institution to make the exibition general at 1/ — for each person — In introducing him to you I request your advice regarding the best method of forwarding his objects — and I know that you will find his aimiable and gentlemanly manners, adding greatly to the accomplish^t of the artist and naturalist —

I am sure your sister will be delighted to have an opportunity of seing and conversing with Mr A. I am, my dear Sir, very faithfully Yours, Thos. Stewart Trail

B. A. Heyward Esqr —
Manchester —

Liverpool 9$^{\underline{th}}$ Sepr 1826. —

My Dear Sir,

Permit me to Introduce to your acquaintance Mr J. J. A., an eminent Naturalist who has spent upwards of 20 Years in the woods of North America forming a beautifull Series of Drawings of American Birds with which he is proceeding to London but has been recommended to shew them for a short time in Manchester.

I believe yourself and M$^{\underline{rs}}$ Touchet will feel equally pleased with this Gentleman & with his Drawings, which has induced me to Venture upon making him known to you, with best respects to M$^{\underline{rs}}$ T, believe me, my dear Sir, Yours faithfully, W$^{\underline{am}}$ Rathbone

John Touchet Esqr — King Street, Manchester —

Besides these I had the following sealed, consequently could not copy them —

R. H. Greg Esqr
35 King Street — Manchester

Mrs Touchet, King Street, Manchester from Hanna M. Rathbone of Green Bank —

Mrs R. H. Greg, R. H. Gregs Esqr, Manchester —

Revd J. Jam^s Taylor, Faulkner Street Manchester.

George W. Wood Esqr — Messrs Philip Wood & Co, 7 Sommerset Street — Manchester

A Card from the Reverend J. Clowes, requesting that I should write to him at my arrival at Manchester

The following letter of introduction was copied by Audubon into his journal following the letter to Victor Audubon that follows the entry for October 30.

My Dear Sir

Allow me to Introduce to you Mr Audubon an artist of great ability & extensive Information. He has been engaged for the last Twenty Years in forming a Collection of Drawings of American birds, which is shortly about to Publish — My Father was unfortunatly from Manchester during Mr Audubon's visit to that place or would have himself had great pleasure in making Mr A. acquainted with you. Believe me &^{c} &^{c} W. B. Henry[16] —

Royal Infirmary Octr 30$^{\underline{th}}$
Thomas Allen Es$^{\underline{qr}}$[17] —
Charlotte Square Edingburgh —

16. Possibly William Charles Henry of Manchester (1804–92), who married in 1832 a daughter of Thomas Allan of Edinburgh (see n. 7, chap. 6). Henry studied medicine at Edinburgh University and would be elected fellow of the Royal Society in 1834.

17. Thomas Allan (1777–1833) was the leading mineralogist at Edinburgh University and fellow of the Royal Society of both Edinburgh and London.

Appendix C

Front Matter in the Manuscript of the 1826 Journal

The first three pages of the manuscript contain the following miscellaneous notes.

Patrick Syme
63 Great King Street
Edingburgh
Octr 30$^{\underline{th}}$ 1826

Staff Surgeon Lyons
Dr Stephenson
13$^{\underline{th}}$ Lt Dragoons —
Mr Innes of Stow
Dr Monro
Mr Lisbon
J B Kenney

the residence of my good friend A. Hodgson: Breckfield Cottage,
   Everton.

John Crooke — recommended by M$^{\underline{rs}}$ Edge, King Street —

To the Benefit

For Commemoration
The morning — My Knife — Fog. Walk &^{c} —
our start — The Valey, The River —
Bakewell, breakfast — road to Buxton

The River, our Walks — Buxton —
Mr Murray, his a/c of himself —
battrey — the Pony & Driver — our Dinner
ride with hannah = our arrival
at Manchester, Density of Population
on approaching — work^d at Manchester
Mrs Dockray's Present — Evening =

The Brig Howard — from Boston — from Liverpool 40 days
bound to Habana spoke to us on the 15th of
June off Cuba & 50 miles of[f] Havana —
Joel Birney — Master — wished to be reported at
Liverpool =
The Ship Thealia of Philadelphia
Bound to Minorca Mediteranean, Spoke
to us on the 21st June 1826 — Latitude —
9 o'clock P.M. = Sent a Large Petrel to the
Cap^e for the Phil^a Society

Corset Laces — (motto on seals all's well) —
Trunk. p^r Excellence — with Thermometer, &^{c} — Ink stand

       hence-forth may her sorrows Cease;
       affliction's frown assail her never;
       Bless her, Kind heaven, with health and peace,
       and Joy attend her steps for ever!

       For she is my Supreme Delight;
       She can fill my heart with pleasure;
       She is most precious to my sight;
       She is Nature's choicest treasure!—

Textual Notes

A dagger symbol (†) in the body of the text of this edition indicates a textual note below, keyed to the pagination and line numbers of this edition. The miscellaneous matter included in the first three pages of the manuscript journal is reported in appendix C. The only manuscript pages that are numbered begin with page 3 and continue through page 57, with only the right-hand rectos numbered in the upper right corner. The illustrations reproduced throughout this edition are placed as closely as possible to their location in Audubon's manuscript journal. References to the "Beinecke fragment" are to a partial copy of the 1826 journal held by Yale University's Beinecke Rare Book and Manuscript Library (Morris Tyler Family Collection of John James Audubon, General Collection).

4.22 All the letters of introduction included in the manuscript, which Audubon regularly copied or paid someone to copy into the journal, comprise appendix B.

5.32 Audubon indicates by means of an X in the margin and a line drawn to a double slash mark at its correct location that this sentence ("Their flesh is firm, perhaps rather dry yet quite acceptable at Sea") should be moved from where he originally wrote it, following "suficient to extricate him" above in the same paragraph. Thus, here we see him developing a sense of the order of information he will include in his natural history essays. Throughout the *Ornithological Biography*, the author regularly placed his observations about the relative savoriness of each bird species toward the end of its essay.

6.8 Two Xs in the right margin are connected by a dark line bordering approximately the beginning of this paragraph from "You must not suppose" to "devided the Bounty." Their purpose is unclear.

6.11 "Ballocuda": I can find no other spelling or variant of "barracuda" similar to Audubon's here. He spells it "Balacuda" on his drawing of a barracuda (see fig. 2).

10.7 Audubon wrote the text in parentheses perpendicularly over the finished manuscript page. A marginal X on either side of the page near the bottom seems to indicate the point of insertion after "for some time." I have inserted the text there in parentheses as it interrupts somewhat the coherence of the passage.

10.22 This paragraph is bracketed in the left margin and marked with an X. The meaning of this is unclear. The Beinecke fragment shows the paragraph in the same place.

11.11 This sentence is written perpendicularly over the finished manuscript page.

11.29 In the right margin following "a few of them" appears "1829 =," below which is written one or two illegible words. The purpose and meaning of this notation are unclear.

16.2 The Beinecke fragment reports this illegible word as "after."

16.6 The text in parentheses occurs at the bottom of the page and in pencil rather than ink. Audubon placed an X by this passage in the left margin and an X in the left margin by the reference to the great-footed hawk. I have inserted it where the X seems to indicate and in parentheses.

16.34 The manuscript clearly reads "Kitch." The Beinecke fragment shows "Ketch." The meaning is unknown. Ford renders it "I catch" (*Journal*, 34), but Audubon regularly correctly spells "catch" and "caught."

17.2 In the space remaining at the bottom of this page, Audubon has sketched a dorsal view of a flying fish with its lateral fins outspread. On the next page of the manuscript, Audubon has sketched four views of the coast of Cuba. At the bottom of the page he has written: "Ship Delos 14$\underline{^{th}}$ June 15$\underline{^{th}}$ at 5 PM by sea account / the Bearings and distances of the principal head lands were taken" (see fig. 7). Although Ford claims that a page has been cut away from the manuscript after the views of Cuba (*Journal*, 34), there is no evidence of that, and the Beinecke fragment confirms that no material is missing here.

19.3 "This is": Ford omits this without note (*Journal*, 35). Audubon wrote this to introduce his drawing on the next manuscript page whose caption completes the sentence: "This is / our first Mate M$\underline{^{r}}$ Sam Bragdon / Reading on the Booby Hatch — / Off Cuba" (see fig. 8).

19.5 Alice Ford found a page missing from the journal manuscript dated June 20, 1826. She reproduces it in facsimile. The passage herein is my edited transcription.

20.5 The bracketed phrase is adopted from the Beinecke fragment.

20.6 Following "reposing," the rest of this entry for June 20 is taken from the Beinecke fragment. The corresponding material appears in Maria Audubon's *Audubon and His Journals* divided between the dates of June 26 and June 29 (1:89–90). Alice Ford includes these two entries from *Audubon and His Journals* in her edition (*Journal*, 41–44). The Beinecke fragment, which is in a hand other than Audubon's, has greater textual authority, however. Since Maria Audubon regularly rewrote and rearranged material in the manuscripts she worked from, her edition is fundamentally unreliable. Also, since Audubon mentions several times having parts of his journals copied, and since the Beinecke fragment corresponds very closely to the 1826 autograph manuscript in its other portions, this fragment seems to be a faithful copy. The material in question in the fragment is under the date June 20.

20.13 Following "much," the scribe of the Beinecke fragment left a space for a word he apparently could not read in Audubon's hand. Someone in a later hand wrote in red pencil "**istended" in this space. Maria Audubon gives the word as "distended."

20.32 After "My friend" there is a line across the page, following which is a copy of the letter from John Owens Johnson, for the text of which see appendix B.

22.13 The Beinecke fragment supplies words obscured by ink blots on this page: "by our" in the preceding sentence and "the" here.

22.21 Following this entry, Audubon has made a list of events and observations to remind himself of what to write about in his journal. He has drawn a line through all but two of them, apparently checking each one off as he wrote about it. Only "Our Cook" and "Explanatory Description" are not checked off:

> Large PetrelsTal[*] of the 26ᵗʰ June —
> When near the Grand Banks saw Large flocks of the above —
> Their flight, swiming &ᶜ —
> Weather here much altered, being a Foggy Mist, cold enough to wear Cloths;
>   ran in 12 days 1713 miles
> The motion of the Vessel when sailing 9 Nots extremely fatiguing —
> Read Thomson's Seasons —
> The Dullness of the 4ᵗʰ of July with us —
> Change of Clouds —
> Our Cook, singular free man of Colour from Martinique —
> History of our *hen*. Capᵉ Jellerson's mate for her —
> Explanatory Description of *Belle's Letters by a Friend.*
> Employment of time on boat by the Crew —
> Our Young Boat Passengers — Dick &ᶜ —
> Three Vessels in sight, our sailing — Whales — My Studying Navigation.

23.22 Using a darker ink, Audubon went back to this page at a later date and wrote the following sentence between the top two lines of this manuscript page: "I felt sorrowfull in the extreme as if America had lost much this day — ." Later in his journal under the date of August 13, Audubon wrote to Lucy that "on the fourth of July last" he sensed that "some great and dismal event was taking place on our Eastern shores." He refers to the deaths of Thomas Jefferson and John Adams on that day, which he would have learned about only later.

32.38 Audubon scribbled the following notes in pencil at the bottom of this page: "Larger Petrells — Northern Gale & Cold Weather / Spoke Brig Albion bound to Quebec — / Sea Sickness — / Mother's Cary Chickens Left in Latitude 44.53 / probably on a/c of the Cold Weather —." The remaining five paragraphs of this entry are written on the bottom half of a page the top half of which has been cut away. The verso of the half page was not filmed because, as Ford reports (*Journal*, 58), it is blank.

33.17 For the first time in this journal, Audubon has gone back later to add an *h* to the beginning of his usual "Orizon."

33.22 On this record of latitudes, beyond the fourth column, which gives the miles traveled each day, in the right margin Audubon also gives the main bearings of the day. He also tallies the total miles traveled through Saturday, July 15, thus:

2079
3089
5168
125
5283 [showing that his math was not perfect].

36.18 Audubon does not indicate with a new date in the heading that the July 15 entry has ended and that a new entry begins here, but internal evidence suggests that this is the case. At approximately one-fifth of the way into the entry I am dating July 17, Audubon writes, "Yesterday night ended the 9$\underline{th}$ Sunday spent at Sea." Since July 15 was a Saturday, there appears to be no entry for his "Yesterday," July 16. Thus it appears that at the end of his entry for Saturday, July 15, he expressed his plan to describe his cabin but did not return to this until Monday, July 17, when he begins by recalling his plan to describe the cabin: "Mr Swift had just Left me. [. . .] I dipt^d my Pen in the Inkhorn and swore I would describe this cabin of the Delos." He then begins his thoughts on the looking glass in his usual present tense.

40.26 At some later time, Audubon scrawled in pencil two lines of prose between these paragraphs; these lines are only partially legible.

42.14 Most of "writing" is under an ink blot. The handwriting shows that Audubon was quite tipsy by this time.

43.10 "Questions" is clearly the wrong word here. Ford was correct to substitute "greetings" (*Journal*, 71). Since Audubon frequently dropped *h*'s from the beginning of words, I emend "Oh" and "I" to "Ho" and "Hi." See also his "ho" for "oh" in the July 20 entry.

43.17 The required sense of the illegible word would seem to be "deceived" or "mistreated," humorously or ironically saying to England that your own sons ought not deceive you by tricking you in order not to pay an import duty on the

Russia duck deceptively placed as patches on the sails. Ford renders the word as "untroubled" (*Journal*, 71), which is possible but not clearly the case.

47.19 Audubon has made a bold horizontal line with seven crosshatches, probably indicating the seven letters of "Captain," similarly to the Xs used above, only here the expression seems much stronger, less restrained.

47.22 What Audubon meant by this heavily bold and double underlined "A B." is unclear, but he clearly intended something quite emphatic.

53.1 Audubon did not supply a new heading for the July 21 entry.

56.12 At this point, Audubon's handwriting begins to grow less controlled, as does his mental state. He is clearly drinking and growing steadily more inebriated as he writes on this evening of July 23.

56.23 Where "be" stands in the manuscript, Audubon originally wrote two words, the second of which is canceled and illegible. The first word is a four-letter word ending in "ill." The initial letter is illegible; "be" is written in larger letters over the original word. Ford reports the word as "tell" (*Journal*, 86). The difference between "be" and "tell" here has great implications. Audubon's reference to the same oath five days earlier corroborates the reading of "be" in this passage: "I have now to regret that I am *by Oath* no Politicician" (July 18).

59.18 In the right margin of the manuscript, Audubon has worked a six-line math sum, apparently recent minor expenses.

61.33 Audubon smeared the wet ink over most of this word.

65.32 An ink smear obscures all but the first two letters of "sooner," which is thus conjectural.

65.38 Audubon penned these notes to himself following this day's entry: "An Orange Woman / shall I describe her — / She sells sweets during day and Poisons at night — / My Cards / Call[d] on M[r] Maury — ."

67.25 On both sides of "we" a tall, thin X has been written.

68.28 Audubon left a long blank space here as if he intended to fill in this destination later.

72.25 Audubon added the phrase "my Drawings" as an afterthought at the end of this sentence.

97.17 The next six manuscript pages are in a hand other than Audubon's. He has apparently asked someone to copy letters he sent to his family members into his journal. In his August 7 entry, he explains: "I had the Letters Copied for me by a Young man recomended to me — to save time — ."

101.5 The rest of this letter is in Audubon's hand.

102.16 Audubon's scribe began this sentence with the phrase "I have." I have eliminated the redundancy.

110.19 This short paragraph is written vertically across the page and keyed by a symbol to be inserted approximately here in the text.

122.1 A black line on the microfilm obscures the phrases "fit to deepen" and "well known," reported by Ford (*Journal*, 152).

123.30 A black line on the microfilm obscures the word "reached," reported by Ford (*Journal*, 154).

132.8 A copy of this note to his sister-in-law occurs in the manuscript in another hand following the September 6 entry. The copy is not reproduced in this edition.

134.8 Smeared ink obscures this word.

136.28 A copy of this note in another hand follows the entry for September 6. Ford includes this letter at the end of the August 21 entry without comment.

138.16 Written vertically across the text of this page on the left-hand side is the following: "Forwarded up to this Day per Brig Isabella bound to New Orleans ⸗ ." Thus, Audubon had a copy of his journal made from its beginning through the entry for September 5 and directed it to Lucy by way of New Orleans. More such partial copies of his journals are yet to be discovered.

140.22 Here Audubon initially wrote six *x*'s, thus: *xxxxxx*. He canceled the final three, apparently deciding that he had a three-letter rather than a six-letter word in mind.

141.14 Following "thou wouldst admire her," Audubon wrote a line and a half that he then thoroughly struck out. This is unusual in this manuscript, indicating that he did not want Lucy or anyone else to read what he wrote about the young Miss Hannah, to whom he would give his journal to read later the same day.

142.14 Four brief letters are copied here, as Audubon explains at the end of the entry for September 9, by Joseph Chorley. The first is a copy of Audubon's letter to Ann Gordon, reproduced above in the August 19 entry. Two others are letters of introduction and appear in appendix B.

144.22 The comma following "all" is an emendation.

157.10 Maria Audubon includes the following paragraph as dated "Manchester, September 12" (*Audubon and His Journals*, 1:117–18). There is no physical evidence that it was cut or removed from the bound journal. Presumably it was on a loose sheet, now lost or destroyed. The second and third paragraphs under September 12 appear in the manuscript.

158.5 Audubon omitted the word or phrase in his head; Ford suggests "with time" (*Journal*, 189).

169.8 Across the middle of this first paragraph in large letters Audubon has written "Copy."

178.28 This word is either "breasts" or "breaths" or rather both. Audubon wrote one and then revised it to the other. Given the antic tone of this entire entry, it seems more probable that he first wrote "breaths" and then changed it to "breasts."

201.1 "Allkolm" is clear in the manuscript, but it does not name any as-yet-discovered person or place. The *o* could be an *a*. Since Audubon frequently omits initial *h*'s, "Allkolm" could be a version of "Hallcolm" or "Holcomb."

204.33 Following the entry for September 29, on the bottom half of the manuscript page, are notes in pencil in a hand other than Audubon's. They seem to summarize the entry above.

210.20 For the first time, Audubon adopts the usual spelling of this name, abandoning his earlier "Bazil"—evidence that he did improve his spelling over time.

219.16 A hand other than Audubon's has stricken out "in" and inserted interlineally "Rise early & walked out to enjoy the."

226.33 The entry for October 8 appears clearly on the bottom half of its manuscript page. It is not obscured in any way; in fact, Audubon has drawn a balloon-shaped circle over the top center of the entry as if to distinguish it in some way. Alice Ford omitted the entire entry.

228.11 In the manuscript there is no period following "Supper," and "After" is lowercase.

230.19 The period following "father" is my emendation.

254.23 The remains of a bristly plant are evident on the microfilm. Audubon attached a plant to the center of the page and then wrote around it.

273.6 Audubon as an afterthought wrote this sentence vertically in the left margin. I insert it here in parentheses. The year 1823 seems to be an error, since he went to New York in 1824.

274.2 This paragraph is written vertically over the text of this manuscript page. The chronology of events suggests that it should follow his walk to the docks of Leith and precede his return to Edinburgh and the pit.

279.28 Following "more beautifull than I expected," Audubon has written and then slightly canceled these words: "having seen sweet Matlock I thought that this Island was covered only by smoaky towns." Since the crosshatches he made are so light, it is not certain whether he intended to cancel the words. He probably intended to have written "before having seen sweet Matlock."

280.11 At the end of this manuscript page, Audubon has made a bold X to indicate that this parenthetical, which he wrote vertically up the left-hand side of the next page, is to be entered here.

280.14 Following "repose —" Audubon wrote and canceled "but I have been troubling you with details." He then inserted the subsequent comment about the "round Monarchs of France," which he wrote diagonally across this page of text.

280.35 After originally inserting "hairs," Audubon canceled that and substituted the French *chevellures*.

281.34 In the left margin near the close of this letter, Audubon has written "remember me kindly to the Intelligent Swiss."

282.27 Following "my own Interests," Audubon wrote and canceled "& Natural Ideas."

283.1 Audubon has omitted his usual heading at the beginning of this day's entry.

288.3 This sentence is written vertically down the right-hand side of the manuscript page. Audubon has drawn a line to show where to insert it.

291.16 This closing note is written vertically across the text of this letter to Victor.

292.6 The "note," a letter of introduction, is printed in appendix B.

294.22 This is a playful passage in which he uses two forms of the same word in three places. For the sake of making some sense of it, I have suggested "peep^d" in the first instance and "putting" in the second and third instances. He seems, however, to have written "pup^d" and "pupping" quite deliberately.

301.9 Following the November 6 entry, Ford includes a letter from Audubon to William and Richard Rathbone dated November 8. Since this letter does not appear in the microfilm, it is likely that Ford found it on a page not bound in the manuscript. Here is the text of the letter as reported in Ford's edition (*Journal*, 338–39):

> My Dear Sirs,
>
> Please to accept my sincerest thanks for your generous reception of me on the outset of my entering in a world that I may truly say was quite new to me. Your kind attentions have been powerfully felt — never can I for *a day* (even in the most distant portions of the world to where my avocations may lead me) lay my head to receive repose without thinking of you and the whole of your families. Never will I cease to pray for your health and happiness. Never will I cease to be your most truly devoted, obedient servant, friend, John J. Audubon
>
> p.s. The bill enclosed will repay Mr. William Rathbone £5.7.6, advanced for me for colored chalks. The residue please memorandum to the credit of the expenses you will be at, (I hope), paying postages for me from America or elsewhere. J.J.A.

301.19 Following "Sir Patrick Walker and" occurs this phrase in the manuscript, deleted here for sense: "Ladies where."

303.20 Audubon double underscored the word "finished" and drew a line across the top of the word as well, the only time he has done this in the manuscript.

306.2 This and the subsequent two letters are in a hand other than Audubon's. Thus, on November 24 Audubon wrote letters to William Rathbone, William Roscoe, and Hannah Rathbone and hired someone to copy them into his journal.

318.12 This letter is written in a hand other than Audubon's.

319.27 Following "existence of" Audubon's scribe has left a two-inch-long blank space.

327.7 Following "Professor," Audubon has left a blank space to fill in the name later.

332.26 At the bottom of this manuscript page is a faint sketch of two cats.

342.19 This is Audubon's note to himself. I have placed it in parentheses.

345.17 Following "found on the sand of:" Audubon has left a blank space to fill in the location later.

348.1 The phrase "& describe her Now for" was originally "by describing it for the." Audubon's deliberate revision removes the implication that Scott could stop human depredations by means of his writing ("by describing") about nature in America.

356.30 Following "in," Audubon has left a blank space, indicating a word he is omitting, probably "bed."

358.19 A blank space follows "Professor."

359.16 Vertically and over the text on the left-hand side of this manuscript page, Audubon has written in large letters: "Ellected a member of the Society of Arts of this City this Day —."

362.27 This letter and the following one to N. Berthoud are in a hand other than Audubon's.

367.3 This journal entry and the six letters that follow are all in the hand of "My Young Friend Mr Hamilton."

369.2 Following "that," Audubon has drawn a pattern of woven lines, five horizontal and five vertical, about half an inch long and a quarter of an inch high.

378.4 This letter is in a hand other than Audubon's.

380.15 This letter is in a hand other than Audubon's.

384.19 The clause "who now is dressed superbly in white satin & crimson turban" is written vertically across the text of this page; Audubon has drawn a dark line showing to insert it following "arm."

387.25 Audubon did not copy the note into the journal.

387.29 Audubon left a blank here, intending to fill in the date later.

390.19 Alice Ford reports this final entry as torn from the manuscript and privately owned (*Journal*, 428). It is reproduced here from her edition.

424.29 This is Audubon's tally of the total number of letters to this point.

Index

animals (*cont.*)

152, 182–83, 229; pigs, 46–47; porpoises, 7–8, 8n12, 16, 20, 27, 38, 46;
rudder fish, 8, 9; sharks, 9, 10; sheep,
265–66, 277, 280; sizes of, 60, 60n8;
sword fish, 16, 355; whales, 27, 33, 38.
See also birds

Antiquarian Society (Edinburgh), 320,
322–24, 343, 345, 348, 371

Arbuthnot, Lady, 355

aristocracy, 132, 356, 384–85; Audubon's
opinions of the, xxiii–xxiv, xxxvii,
122; descriptions of, in Manchester,
162; Lord Stanley, 90, 91–92, 139. *See
also* class consciousness

Arkansas magpie (bird), 127, 127n78.
See also birds

Arkwright, Sir Thomas, 240

Arthur, Stanley Clisby: *Audubon: An
Intimate Life of the American Woodsman*, xlii

art supplies, 112; canvas, 366; chalks,
63, 290, 295; and color grinding,
376; cost of, 112, 134, 146, 147, 185,
295; pastells, 71, 112, 128, 134. *See also*
drawing; paintings

Asylum of the Blind. *See* Blind Asylum
(Liverpool)

Athenium (Liverpool), 79

Atherton, William, 422

Atkinson, Richard, 126, 126n76

Audubon, John James: and the Academy of Natural Sciences (Philadelphia), 364, 364n87; affinity of, for
women, xii, xxxvi, xxxvii–xxxviii,
xxxix, xlvii–xlviii, 145n97, 182, 226,
228, 253, 283, 292, 305; album ("blank
book") of, 154, 157, 168, 192, 205,
209, 210, 216, 217, 246, 255, 279, 290;
anxiety of, 22–23, 43–44, 50–51,
93–94, 111, 116, 118, 267, 335, 344,
376; apprenticeship of, 165; and the
aristocracy, xxiii, xxxvii, 90, 91–92,
97, 122, 132, 139, 162, 325, 356, 384–85;
attending art exhibits, 62, 63, 103–4,
133–34, 225, 331; biographical sketch
of (in *Blackwood's Magazine*),
302n38; biographies of, xlii, xliii–
xliv; bird imitations of, 95, 240; birds
killed by, xxxvii, 11, 16; birthday of,
xix; and boredom, 14, 41, 45, 56; and
business failures, xxii, xxvii, xxviii;
cats killed by, 356–57; charisma of,
xx, xxxiii; charity of, xl, 112, 126, 253,
359–60; and children, 64, 69, 73, 88,
93, 95, 112, 118, 119, 121, 128, 133, 209,
210, 248, 316, 353; and church, 80–81,
94–95, 117, 133, 137, 168, 226, 228, 245,
388; confidence of, xx, xxvii, xxviii,
334n70; and copying of journal, 138,
153–54, 153n2, 440; critical reception of, xxx–xxxi, 112–13, 304, 307,
321, 326n59, 343, 373–74; and custom
duties, 55, 397; depression of, xxii,
xxvii, 62, 66, 101, 125, 129, 131, 167, 180,
182, 185, 205, 232, 246, 301, 354; and
drawing lessons, 100, 137, 138, 181, 196,
210, 216, 228, 360, 364, 365, 367–68,
371; and drinking, xlv, 25, 36, 42–43,
47–49, 56, 58–60, 229, 266, 296, 328,
329, 352, 438, 439; early rising of,
xxxix–xli, 60, 63–64, 84, 89, 90, 124,
127, 128, 133, 137, 138, 154, 209, 219–21,
239, 242; editing of, xxxiii; editing
of, by Alice Ford, xii, xliii–liii, 14n17,
338n74, 436–37, 442, 443; by David
Brewster, xxxii, 337, 345–46, 350,
360; editing of, by Maria Audubon,
xii, xli–xliii, xlviii, l–li, 145n99, 157n6,
436–37, 440; editing of, editing of,
by William MacGillivray, xii, xlix,
l; and education, xxvii, xxxii, 111;

expenditures of, 94, 146, 151, 153, 154, 156–57, 158, 184, 185, 192, 241, 255, 260–61, 265, 267, 268, 295, 312, 344, 366, 377–78, 390; and field observations, xxvii–xxviii, xxxii, 282; flirtatiousness of, xlvii–xlviii, 145n97; gifts from, to Lucy Audubon, 54, 64, 99, 137, 173, 240, 252, 259, 274, 278, 330, 368, 378, 380, 381; gifts from, to the Greg family, 185; gifts from, to William Rathbone, 145, 145n99; gifts to, from Abigail Dockrey, 245; gifts to, from Elizabeth Greg Rathbone, 91; gifts to, from the Greg family, 228, 230, 247, 254, 257–58, 259; gifts to, from Hannah Mary Reynolds Rathbone ("Queen Bee"), 209, 210, 215, 217, 254, 256, 302, 306, 318, 343; gifts to, from Hannah Mary Rathbone, 124, 143, 146, 167, 238, 242, 243, 245, 258; gifts to, from John Chorley, 216; gifts to, from Margaret Lace Roscoe (Mrs. Edward Roscoe), 146; gifts to, from Walter Bentley, 251, 256, 259; hair of, 60, 156, 192–93, 200, 283, 290, 357, 364, 369; and Haitian birth, 14n17, 75n29, 129n82, 409; and head cast (for phrenology), 302, 319; and hopes for *The Birds of America*, xix, xx, 22, 75, 289, 297, 339–40, 370; humor of, xxxiv–xxxv, xxxviii–xxix, xlv, xlvii–xlviii, 37–38, 61, 71, 140, 155–56, 164, 176, 184, 196–97, 197n31, 204, 220, 223, 249, 262, 294, 315, 334, 442; identity of, as "American woodsman," xxxvi; identity of, as "gentleman artist-naturalist," xxii, 84; illegitimacy of, xlv–xlvi, 74n28; illnesses of, 25, 46, 163, 164, 170, 209–10, 226, 229, 263, 275, 292, 322, 345–46, 378; journey of, to Edin-

burgh, 260–63, 265–67, 276, 277, 280–81; journey of, to England (sea voyage), 4–8, 10–11, 13–14, 16–17, 19–27, 31–47, 49–51; journey of, to Liverpool, 151–54, 221–22; journey of, to Manchester, 151–54, 221–22; journey of, to Matlock, 232–36, 238–42; journey of, to New Orleans, 3–4; and lack of letters from Lucy, xxii–xxiii, xxiv, xxix, 66, 101, 116, 117, 121, 124, 131, 138, 167, 246, 259, 278, 300, 301, 308, 313, 318, 320, 334, 337, 338; losing knife from Hannah Rathbone, 242, 243, 245, 246, 247; as a Mason, 256; and mathematics, 438; and *mauvaise honte* (embarrassment and unworthiness), xx, xxvi, xxxiii, 66–67, 67n15, 74, 93; missing Lucy, xlvi–xlvii, 22–23, 36, 44, 66, 83, 97, 116, 117, 124, 142, 151, 153, 161, 183, 205, 211–12, 234, 270, 292, 295, 313, 325, 341, 356, 381; "Observations on the Natural History of the Alligator," 187n24; and personal liberty, xxiv, xxviii, xxxvi, xxxvii, 115, 122; physical appearance of, 25, 60, 136, 156, 192–93, 200, 283, 290, 357, 364, 369; poetry of, 108–9, 310; and politics, xxiii–xxiv, xxxvi–xxxvii, 37, 49, 56, 57, 127, 129, 132, 159, 439; and portrait drawing, xxvii, 4n6, 173n16, 183n21, 196–97, 253, 254, 333; portrait of, by John Syme, 299, 314, 316, 317, 320, 322, 324; and poverty, xxii, 53; and praise, 65, 75, 82, 92, 102, 136, 144, 192, 285, 291–92, 296–97, 343, 398; premonitions of, xxii–xxiii, xxvii–xxx, 23, 116, 117, 117n70, 270, 344, 437–38; and prison reform, 214–15, 217–18; and prudery, xxxviii, 150; and publishing plan, xxiv–xxv, xxvi, xxx,

Audubon, John James (*cont.*)
xxxii, 99, 102, 172, 202–3, 206, 303, 306–8, 309, 339, 398; and reading, xxvi, 16, 24, 25–26, 41; and reading aloud from journal, 115, 122, 124, 217, 231; reputation of, xii, xlii–xliii, xlviii, 398, 399; return of, to America (1829), xxxii; and sea-bathing, 10, 17; seasickness of, xx, 5, 16, 97; and self-doubt, xx–xxi, xxvii; self-portrait of, 145, 145n97; shyness of, 65, 66–67, 73, 74, 93, 98, 117, 153, 317, 323; "simple intelligent" description of, 141, 319–20; and smuggler incident, 125–27; and snuff habit, 167, 216, 225, 230, 257, 257n12, 261; and society memberships, xxxii, 92n51, 285, 328, 330, 333, 340–41, 348, 350, 355, 360, 363, 367, 371, 374; and spelling, lvi, 441; study of, with Thomas Sully, 77n33; and "tameness" of England, xxiii–xxiv, xxviii, xxxvi–xxxvii, 115, 122, 132, 132n83, 152, 182–83; and the theater, 85, 274–75, 325–26, 352–53, 393; and time management, 164, 164n13, 289, 366; and tipping, 150; and travel plans for Lucy, xxix–xxx, xxxii, 172–73; travel plans of, 98–99, 102, 145, 172, 175, 180, 197, 204, 206–7, 289, 290, 303, 340, 371; travel skills of, xxviii; and umbrella salesman incident, 224, 245, 249; wardrobe of, 64, 180, 192, 224, 252, 255, 337, 345, 352, 359, 365, 369, 379; and watch shopping, 54, 64, 99, 146; and "wildness" of America, xxiii, xxviii, xxxvi–xxxvii, 49, 96, 113–14, 122, 152. *See also* Audubon, Lucy Bakewell (Mrs. John James Audubon); *The Birds of America* (Audubon); exhibitions; letters; letters of introduction; prose style

Audubon, John Woodhouse (son), xli, 3, 4, 98, 208; Audubon's drawing advice to, xxviii, 103, 161–62, 173, 174, 278, 341–42, 368; Audubon's letter to, 277–79; drawings of, 168, 259; education of, 341; gifts to, from Walter Bentley, 251, 259; gifts to, from Hannah Mary Rathbone, 236, 259, 277; and music study, 173, 174, 278; and travel in Europe, xxx, 172, 341

Audubon, Lucy Bakewell (Mrs. John James Audubon), xlvi–xlvii, 3, 4, 50, 93n52; Alice Ford's identification with, li–liii; and Audubon's descriptions of women, xxxviii–xxxix; Audubon's letters to, xxv, 4, 16, 17, 97–101, 137, 161–62, 165, 171–74, 206–8, 259–60, 338–43, 367–69, 380; Audubon's worries about, xxii–xxiii, xxvii–xxix; beauty of, 82; as "dearest friend," xii, 3n2; and Fatland Ford, 81n40; gifts to, from Audubon, 274, 278, 378, 380, 381; gifts to, from Hannah Mary Rathbone, 143, 238, 259; and knowledge of husband's character, xx–xxi; lack of letters from, xxii–xxiii, xxiv, xxix, 66, 101, 116, 117, 121, 124, 131, 138, 167, 246, 259, 278, 300, 301, 308, 313, 318, 320, 334, 337, 338; letters from, to Audubon, xxvi, xxix, 167, 168, 169–70, 171, 344, 367; in New Haven CT, 273, 274n16; plans ("future intentions") of, 341; and politics, xxiii, xxxvii, 37; and publication of the 1826 manuscript journal, xli; and schoolteaching, 4n7, 73, 100n59, 305n41; and travel plans, xxix–xxx, xxxii, 172–73, 367. *See also* Audubon, John James

Audubon, Maria Rebecca (granddaughter), xii, xli–xliii, xlviii, l–li, 145n99, 157n6, 436–37, 440

Bewick, Thomas: *A General History of Quadrupeds*, 118–19, 121, 121n72; *History of British Birds*, 88, 88n50

Bibliotheca Bibliographici: A Catalogue of the Library Formed by Geoffrey Keynes, 142n95

Bigors, Nicholas Aylward, 418, 418n10

"bird biographies." *See* essays

birds: black grouse, 266, 266n3; chaffinch, 228; Columbian magpie, 127n78; cormorant, 298; curlew, 38; English black bird, 84; European hawk, 38; European magpie, 127n78; frigate pelican, 13, 16; gannet, 16, 125, 125n74, 298; goldfinch, 78; great-footed hawk, 16; green heron, 13; gull, 19–20, 122, 298; hawk, 243; heron, 298; hooping crane, 13; jack daw, 238, 240, 242; jay, 182; king fisher, 243; lark, 54, 56, 63–64; magpie, 127, 127n78, 220; merganser, 42; *Muscicapa Bonapartii*, 371n88; noddy, 20–21, 22; partridge, 182–83; petrel, 10, 10n14, 16, 19, 20, 21, 23–24, 33; pheasant, xxxiv–xxxv, 182–83, 184–85, 188, 191, 192, 277, 362; pigeon, 17, 298, 354; *Procellaria*, 10–11, 10n14, 19–20, 24; red-shouldered hawk, 113, 113n68; rice bunting, 13; robin, 145n97, 149, 167; rook, 240; scarlet tanager (*Tanagra rubra*), 72, 72n22; solan goose, 125, 125n74; sooty tern, 13; sparrow, 112, 298; stock pigeon, 220, 220n1; summer red bird (*Tanagra aestiva*), 72n22; swallow, 220–21; thrush, 219; warbler, 13, 16, 219; winter falco, 113, 113n68. *See also* animals

The Birds of America (Audubon), xxviii, 22, 72n22, 363, 365; advice about, from Henry George Bohn, xxiv–xxv, 202–3, 206; completion of (in 1838),

xxxii–xxxiii; cost of, 339, 372–73; engravings for, by Robert Havell, Jr., xxxii, 286n22; engravings for, by William Lizars, xxxi, 286n22, 301, 313, 314, 316, 339, 367, 374; and Lucy Audubon, li; Mocking Birds plate in, 272, 272n11; and naming of birds, 371, 371n88, 374–75; number of plates in, xix; printing of, xix, xxx, xxxii, 207, 285–86; publishing plan for, xxiv–xxv, xxx–xxxii, 99, 102, 202–3, 206, 258–59, 303, 306–8, 309, 339, 370, 398; size of plates in, xxiv–xxv, 202–3, 230, 282, 308, 309, 331, 339, 373. *See also* exhibitions; *Ornithological Biography* (Audubon); subscriptions

Birney, Joseph, 17

black-billed magpie. *See* magpie (bird)

black grouse (bird), 266, 266n3. *See also* birds

black vulture essay. *See* carrion crow essay

Blackwood's Edinburgh Magazine, xxxii, 297n33, 298n34, 302, 302n38; and article about Audubon, xxx, 326, 326n59, 340, 387. *See also* Wilson, John (Christopher North)

Blackwood's Magazine. See *Blackwood's Edinburgh Magazine*

Bland, D. S.: *John James Audubon in Liverpool 1826–27*, 145n97

Blind Asylum (Liverpool), 80–81, 80n36, 94–95, 117, 133, 134, 137

Bohn, Henry George, xxvi, 202n2, 230–31, 282; and publishing advice, xxiv–xxv, 202–3, 206

Bohn, John, 202n2

Bonaparte, Charles Lucien, 5n11, 81, 81n41, 223, 258n13, 370, 371–72; Audubon's letters to, 4–5, 137, 375; in England, 334, 342, 344–45, 354; let-

ters from, 369, 376, 387; and letters of
introduction, 101, 249; and ornithol-
ogy, 5n111, 75, 159
Bonaparte, Joseph, 81, 81n41, 258,
258n13, 303, 322, 353
Bonaparte, Zenaida, 258n13
Boone, Daniel, 106n64
Booth, Mr., 85, 397
Bostick, Dr. *See* Bostock, John
Bostock, John, 395, 395n5, 413, 418
Botanic Garden (Liverpool), 69–70, 81,
106, 115, 140, 140n94
botany books, 128n79
Boulear (Countess). *See* Buller-Yarde-
Buller, Elizabeth Lydia Hallidat
Bourgeat, Augustin, 4, 4n8, 64, 100, 173,
173n16, 208, 368
Bragdon, Samuel L., *18*, 19, 31, 39
Brewster, Sir David, 292n30, 311–12,
311n42, 348, 351, 357–58, 419; and
the *Edinburgh Philosophical Jour-
nal*, 268n5, 311n42; and editing of
Audubon, xxxii, 337, 345–46, 350,
360; "Mr. Audubon's Ornithology of
the United States of America," 340,
340n75, 371
Bridges, David, xxxii, 298–99, 298n34,
328, 329, 335, 362; and Audubon's
cloth purchase, 337; and *Scotsman*
notice, 350–51; and the theater, 325–
26; visiting Audubon, 300, 301, 303,
322, 357; and John Wilson, xxxii, 326
Briggs, Charles, 3, 3n3, 53, 150
Brookes, J. S. (American consul in
Manchester). *See* Brookes, Samuel
R. (American consul in Manchester)
Brookes, Samuel R. (American consul
in Manchester), 157, 157n6, 160, 166,
188–89, 190, 191, 250; Audubon dining with, 159, 161; and letter of introduction, 414–15

Brooks, Samuel. *See* Brookes, Samuel
R. (American consul in Manchester)
Brooks, S. R. *See* Brookes, Samuel R.
(American consul in Manchester)
Broughton Hall, 247, 248–50
Brown, Andrew, 321, 321n50, 326–27, 351
Brown, Robert, 423–24, 424n13
Bruce, Thomas (Earl of Elgin). *See*
Elgin, 7th Earl of (Thomas Bruce)
Buccleuch, 5th Duke of (Walter Fran-
cis Montagu-Douglas Scott), 266,
266n2
Buchanan, Robert, xli
Buffon, comte de. *See* Leclerc,
Georges-Louis (comte de Buffon)
Buller, Susan Elizabeth (Countess of
Morton). *See* Morton, Countess of
(Susan Elizabeth Buller)
Buller-Yarde-Buller, Elizabeth Lydia
Hallidat, 382, 382n89, 383, 384
Burton upon Trent, England, 234,
274n16
Butler, John R., 20
Buxton, England, 244, 251, 259, 277, 288

Cameron, Mr., 301, 327
Campbell, Miss, 321, 389
Canning, George, 127, 127n77
Cape Clear, Ireland, 38, 38n29
Cape Florida songster (bird), 16. *See
also* birds
Capes of Florida. *See* Florida
carrion crow essay, xxxii, 345–46, 350,
360. *See also* essays
The Castle of Indolence (Thomson),
25–26, 25n23
Castle Rackrent (Edgeworth), 47n39
chaffinch (bird), 228. *See also* birds
chalks. *See* art supplies
Charity (painting), 80, 80n36
Chisholm, Virginia, 3n1, 4

xxxii, 345–46, 350, 360; for the *Ornithological Biography*, xix. *See also* prose style

Essays on Practical Education (Edgeworth), 73, 73n24

European hawk (bird), 38. *See also* birds

European magpie (bird), 127n78. *See also* birds

Ewart, Peter, 245, 245n8, 403–4

Ewbank, J.: *Picturesque Views of Edinburgh*, 294n32

Exchange buildings (Liverpool), 53, 54, 59, 62–63, 79n35

Exchange buildings (Manchester), 157, 160, 163–64, 166, 170, 178, 180, 184, 185, 191–92

exhibitions, 157, 192, 206, 257, 260, 302; at the Academy of Natural History (Manchester), 154–55, 156, 185, 222–23, 230, 232; attendance at, 84, 85, 86, 90, 98, 102, 156, 166, 185, 321, 322, 330, 337, 353; in Audubon's lodgings, xxx, 59, 271–72, 283, 285, 286, 291–92, 293–94, 297, 299–301, 338–39; charging for, xxii, 84, 96, 97, 106–8, 159; and copying of Audubon's drawings, 86; and counterfeit notes, 334; critical reception of, xxx, 112–13, 304, 307, 321, 326n59, 343, 373–74; onboard the *Delos*, 11, 13; at the Exchange buildings (Manchester), 157, 160, 163–64, 166, 170, 178, 180, 184, 185, 191–92; failure of, 180, 184; and gaslight, 332; money receivers hired for, 158, 163–64, 186, 222–23, 378; music for, 158–59; proceeds from, 120, 137, 171, 219, 304, 307, 314, 326, 337, 339, 374, 376–77; publicizing, 111, 166, 188, 246, 302, 326, 333, 334; for the Rathbone family, 65, 68, 75; at the Royal

Institution (Edinburgh), xxx, xxxi, 301–2, 304, 307, 314, 321, 322, 326, 330, 332, 335–36, 337–38, 339, 348, 353, 367, 376–77; at the Royal Institution (Liverpool), xxii, 72, 79, 82, 84, 85, 86, 87, 90, 98, 100, 102, 106–8, 110–11, 120, 124, 131–32, 136, 137, 145, 150, 169; and subscriptions book, 185, 187; and theft of drawing, 335–36. *See also The Birds of America* (Audubon); drawing; paintings; subscriptions

Extracts from a Journal, Written on the Coasts of Chili, Peru, and Mexico (Hall), 336, 336n72

Fairman, Gideon, 145, 145n99

Fatland Ford, 81, 81n40, 211n7, 330n66

Fauna Americana (Harlan), 70n20, 95

Fifty Years in Both Hemispheres (Nolte), 75n30

fishing, 5, 6–8, 10, 17, 22, 38. *See also* hunting; sea voyage

Fletcher, Archibald, 289n26

Fletcher, Elizabeth, 289n26, 289, 300, 310, 317, 320

Floral Illustrations of the Seasons (Roscoe), 70n19

Florida, 19–22

flying fish, 5–6, 226, 436. *See also* animals

food: and dining customs, 115, 252, 342, 352; in Edinburgh, 292, 297, 305, 312, 313, 323, 357, 376, 381, 386; game birds, 132, 132n83; on journey to Manchester, 222; in Manchester, 154, 159, 190–91; at Matlock, 238–39; at sea, 5, 8, 17, 42, 45–47; tomatoes, 146. *See also* fishing; hunting

Foote, Maria, 85, 85n45, 275

Ford, Alice: and the Alice Ford Papers, xlviii–liii; and bird names, 127n78;

Ford, Alice (*cont.*)
and "censoring" Audubon, l; diary
of, lii–liii; editorial decisions of,
xii, xliii–liii, 14n17, 338n74, 436–37,
442, 443; and index errors, 140n94;
John James Audubon, xli–xliii; and
letter inclusion, 153n2, 440; and
Lucy Bakewell Audubon, li–liii;
and Maria Audubon, xlii–xliii, l–li;
and name references, 3n2, 64n14,
70n19, 81n39, 104n62, 109n67, 135n85,
140n93, 218n9, 263n14, 275n19,
298n34, 314n46, 321n50, 323n53,
324n55, 327n61; omissions of, 441;
and proofing errors, liii; publications
of, xlviii–xlix, l–liii; scholarship of,
xliii–xliv
Foster, John, 146, 200, 217
Foster, Maria (Mrs. John Foster), 217
Fox, Charles James, 74, 74n27, 295, 351,
366
Franklin, Benjamin, 164, 164n13
Freeman, Mr., 166
French language, xii–xiii, xxxii, xxxiii,
xxxv–xxxvi. *See also* prose style
frigate pelican (bird), 13, 16. *See also*
birds
"fudge" expletive, 46, 125n75, 292, 294,
356, 388. *See also* prose style

Gallatin, Albert, 103, 103n60, 106, 127,
387, 404; Audubon's letter to, 369
game animals, xxviii, xxxvi–xxxvii, 132,
152. *See also* animals
gannet (bird), 16, 125, 125n74, 298. *See
also* birds
Gardner, Dr., 345, 349
Garnet, Mr. *See* Garnett, Jeremiah
Garnett, Jeremiah, 159, 159n7
gaslight, 79; in Edinburgh, 266, 277,
379, 389

Gay, John: *The Beggar's Opera*, 352n81
Gellée, Claude. *See* Lorrain, Claude
A General History of Quadrupeds
(Bewick), 118–19, 121, 121n72
Gifford, Euphemia, 207, 207n5, 233
Gifford, Mr. (engraver), 217, 232
Gilpin, John, 211n6
Gleaner (sailing vessel), 11, 13, 14
Godard, George, 405, 407–8
Goddard, George. *See* Godard, George
Goddard, William, 65, 81
Golconda, India, 187, 187n23
goldfinch (bird), 78. *See also* birds
Goldsmith, Oliver: *The Vicar of Wake-
field*, 125, 125n75
Gordon, Alexander, xx, 50n42, 61, 85,
95, 111, 204, 216, 217; Audubon dining
with, 81–82; and Audubon's exhibit,
84, 97, 105, 106–7, 110; Audubon's
letter to, 179–80; avoiding Audubon,
xx, 53, 55, 59, 59n6, 71–72, 77; and letter of introduction, 156; in London,
130, 138
Gordon, Ann Bakewell (Mrs. Alexander Gordon), 50, 50n42, 61, 85, 93,
95, 99, 115–16, 117, 130, 173–74, 217;
Audubon dining with, 81–82, 90,
204; and Audubon's exhibit, 131–32;
avoiding Audubon, xx, 53, 72, 76–77;
prudery of, xxxviii, 150
Grabant, La Belle Madam, 254
Graham, Robert, 304–5, 304n40
"graining." *See* fishing
great-footed hawk (bird), 16. *See also*
birds
"the great unknown." *See* Scott, Sir
Walter
Green Bank (Rathbone family seat),
xxii, 86, 110, 137n89, 149; Audubon
dining at, 87–88, 146, 147, 210, 217–
18; Audubon's visits at, xxiv, 88–89,

117–24, 132–33, 136, 138–45, 200, 204, 209, 212, 215–18; Audubon's walks to, 87, 127–28, 133; location of, xxiv, xl; paths around, xxiii–xxiv, 122. *See also* Liverpool, England

Green Banks. *See* Green Bank (Rathbone family seat)

green heron (bird), 13. *See also* birds

Greg, Agnes, 246–47, 254, 255

Greg, Elizabeth. *See* Rathbone, Elizabeth Greg (Mrs. William Rathbone)

Greg, Ellen, 143, 143n96, 182, 184, 229, 253, 300; and André Melly, 68n16, 180, 204; descriptions of, 180, 194, 226, 228; gifts from, 230, 247, 254

Greg, Hanna. *See* Greg, Hannah Lightbody (Mrs. Samuel Greg)

Greg, Hannah Lightbody (Mrs. Samuel Greg), 143n96, 193–94, 225, 226, 254; Audubon's letter to, 372–73

Greg, Helen. *See* Greg, Ellen

Greg, John, 300

Greg, Mary Ann, 181, 187

Greg, Robert Hyde (son of Samuel Greg), 185, 187, 223, 225, 246, 250, 432

Greg, Samuel, 73n25, 143n96, 179, 181, 229, 230, 245n8, 253, 256; Audubon dining with, 185; relationship of, with family members, 187, 195, 225, 226; spinning mill of, 156n5, 187

Greg, Samuel (son of Samuel Greg), 181, 228

Greg, Sarah, 185

Greg, Thomas, 404–5

Greg, William (son of Samuel Greg), 181, 199, 255, 349, 356, 372; and Audubon's exhibit, 304; borrowing money, 322

Greg family, xxv–xxvi, 158, 162, 167, 185, 288; and Audubon's visits at Quarry Bank, 181–84, 193–97, 225–26, 254–

55; gifts to Audubon from the, 228, 230, 247, 254, 257–58, 259; relationships among the, 187, 195, 225, 226

Gretna Green, Scotland, 265, 265n1

Greville, Robert Kaye, 362, 362n85, 420; *Scottish Cryptogamic Flora*, 362n85

Grey, George Harry (Earl of Stamford). *See* Stamford, 6th Earl of (George Harry Grey)

Griffies, Jane. *See* Roscoe, Jane Griffies (Mrs. William Roscoe)

gull (bird), 19–20, 122, 298. *See also* birds

Haihg, Mrs., 247–48, 250

"Hail Columbia Happy Land" (Hopkinson), 23, 23n21, 275

Haines, Reuben, 364, 364n87

Haiti, 14n17, 75n29, 129n82

Hall, Basil, 327n61, 332n69, 333, 356, 361, 371, 378, 379; Audubon dining with, 351–52, 387, 388–89; and Audubon's exhibit, 332; *Extracts from a Journal, Written on the Coasts of Chili, Peru, and Mexico*, 336, 336n72

Hall, David. *See* Holl, Diedrich

Hall, Sir James, 268n6, 327, 327n61

Hall, James (son of Sir James Hall), 268, 268n6, 325, 327n61

Hall, Margaret Hunter (Mrs. Basil Hall), 332, 332n69, 352, 355–56, 388, 389; description of, 333

Hall, Virginia, 100

Hamilton, Mr., 376, 443

Hamilton, Sir William, 387, 387n91

Harding, Chester, 106, 106n64

Harlan, Richard, 70, 92, 187, 187n24; *Fauna Americana*, 70n20, 95

Harpers Ferry WV, 37, 37n27

Harrington, 4th Earl of (Charles Stanhope), 85n45

Harris, Edward, 145n99

Hatch, Joseph, 3, 10, 11, 28, 30, 43; and fishing, 7, 8, 38; and pigs, 46; and swift patent, 27, 27n24, 29; visiting Audubon in Liverpool, 79. See also *Delos* (sailing vessel)

Havell, Robert, Jr., xxxii, 70n19, 286n22, 395. *See also* Robert Havell and Son (engraver)

hawk (bird), 243. *See also* birds

Hays, Mr., 383, 384, 386

Haywood, Mr. *See* Heywood, Benjamin Arthur

Heath, William, 286–87, 286n24

Hedge, Mrs. (Manchester landlady), 157, 176, 191, 260–61

Henry, Charles. *See* Henry, William Charles

Henry, William, 268n7

Henry, William Charles, 268, 268n7, 292, 294, 296, 311; and letters of introduction, 406, 432, 432n16

heron (bird), 298. *See also* birds

Herrick, Francis Hobart: *Audubon the Naturalist*, xlii

herrings, 33. *See also* animals

Heywood, Arthur. *See* Heywood, Benjamin Arthur

Heywood, Benjamin Arthur, 150, 150n1, 157, 158, 166, 168; Audubon dining with, 175–78; and letters of introduction, 255, 403, 430–31

Heywood, Miss, 176, 177–78, 179

Hibbert, H. *See* Hibbert-Ware, Samuel

Hibbert-Ware, Samuel, 292, 292n30, 294, 345

Hindley, John Haddon, 184, 184n22, 189–90, 191

Hinks, Mr., 90, 108

Histoire naturelle (Leclerc), 60, 60n8

History of British Birds (Bewick), 88, 88n50

Hobart (*Delos* second mate), 31, 39

Hodgson, Adam, 75, 75n29, 89–90, 93, 102; Audubon dining with, 82–84; and Audubon's birth in Haiti, 75n29, 409; and Audubon's exhibit, 85; and letters of introduction, 79, 87, 399, 408–10, 413–14; and Lord Stanley, 79, 86, 91–92

Hodgson, Mary, 215

Hogdson, Mr. *See* Hodgson, Adam

Holden, Edward, 397–98

Holiday, John, 3

Holl, Diedrich, 3, 3n1, 4

Holland, George Calvert, 229, 229n5

Holme, Edward, 160n9, 163, 192, 232, 250; and Audubon's exhibit, 160, 184, 185; and letters of introduction, 255, 418–19, 427

Holyhead port, Wales, 49, 49n40

Holyrood. *See* Royal Palace of Holyrood (Edinburgh)

Homer (sailing vessel), 43

hooping crane (bird), 13. *See also* birds

Hopkinson, Joseph: "Hail Columbia Happy Land," 23, 23n21

Horticultural Society, 421n11

hospitality, English, xxiv, 83, 97–98, 108–9, 115, 119, 122, 189, 190, 251–52, 256, 262, 346. *See also* aristocracy

Hotchkiss, John, 41–42

Howard (sailing vessel), 17

Howe, Mr. (*Courant* editor), 325, 334, 351

Hull, Edward, 407–8

Humboldt, Baron of (Alexander von Humboldt), 99, 103, 166, 290, 290n28; *Relation historique du voyage aux régions équinoxiales du nouveau continent*, 86, 86n46

humor. *See* prose style

Hunt, Andrew, 76, 76n31, 112, 146

Hunter, John Dunn, 178, 334n70; *Manners and Customs of Several Indian Tribes Located West of the Mississippi*, 74–75, 74n28

Hunter, Lady (mother of Margaret Hunter Hall), 322, 337, 355–56, 371, 388, 389

hunting, xxviii, xxxvi–xxxvii, 132, 132n83, 133, 152, 182–83, 229. *See also* fishing

Hutton, James, 327n61

Illustrations of British Ornithology (Selby), 88, 88n49, 272n12

Illustrations of Ornithology (Jardine and Selby), 272n12

Illustrations of Zoology: Wilson, James, 297n33

Ingles (thief), 335, 336, 336n71

Inglis, Sir Robert, 409–10

Innes, Gilbert, 322, 322n52, 323

"Intelligent Swiss." *See* Melly, André

An Introduction to Geology (Bakewell), 99n58, 207n5, 330n64

Ireland, 38, 38n29, 49

Irmscher, Christoph, xii, xliii

jack daw (bird), 238, 240, 242. *See also* birds

Jackson, Andrew, 259, 303

Jail of Liverpool, 212, 213, 214–15

Jameson, Robert, 268, 268n5, 282, 316–17, 321, 327, 327n61, 334; description of, 293; and the *Edinburgh Philosophical Journal*, xxxii, 268n5, 311n42, 363; and letters of introduction, 255, 296, 420; "Mr. Audubon's Great Work on Birds of the United States of America," 340n75; and museum admittance, 272, 314; and ornithology work, xxviii, 269, 283, 285; prais-

ing Audubon, xxx, 291, 293–94, 340; visiting Audubon, 291–92; and the Wernerian Society, 328, 332–33, 355

Jardin du Roi (Jardin des plantes), 395, 395n3

Jardine, Sir William, xl, 313, 350, 358, 359, 360–61, 362; Audubon dining with, 302, 376; collaborating with Prideaux John Selby, 272n12, 293, 308, 339; and drawing lessons, 364, 367–68, 371; *Illustrations of Ornithology*, 272n12

jay (bird), 182. *See also* birds

Jefferson, Thomas, 60n8, 117, 117n70, 438

Jeffrey, Francis, 276, 276n20, 284, 362, 388–89

Jellerson, Captain, 11, 13

John James Audubon (Ford), xlii–xliii, xliv, 14n17

John James Audubon: Writings and Drawings (Irmscher), xliii

John James Audubon in Liverpool 1826–27 (Bland), 145n97

Johnson, Henry (Governor), 4, 4n10, 401, 403

Johnson, John Owens, 17n19, 400

Johnson, William Garrett, 4n7

Johnstone, Edward, 412, 412n5

Kearsley, T., 163, 163n12

Keats, George, 3n3, 58, 58n4

Keats, Georgiana (Mrs. George Keats), 58, 58n4

Keats, John, 3n3, 58n4

Kennedy, John, 411, 411n4

Keynes, Sir Geoffrey, 142n95

Keynes, Richard, 142n95

Kimble, Captain, 3

Kinder, Arthur, 82n42

Kinder, Thomas, 82, 82n42

403, 430–31; from Charles Lucien Bonaparte, 101, 249; copying of, 4, 147, 276, 397, 400, 403, 412, 425, 426, 427, 430, 432; to David Pannant, 425; from DeWitt Clinton, 98, 98n57, 101, 249, 315, 338; from Edward Holden, 397–98; from Edward Holme, 255; to Edward Holme, 418–19, 427; to Edward Hull, 407–8; to Edward Johnstone, 412; from Edward Roscoe, 425; from Frank J. Martin, 423–24; from George Godard, 405, 407–8; to George Ramsden, 397–98; from Henry Clay, 98, 98n57, 101, 174, 175, 249, 400–401; from Henry Johnson (governor of Louisiana), 4, 401, 403; from Isabella Douglass, 141, 325; to James Edward Smith, 417; from James Maury, 104, 106, 404, 415; from James Yates, 106, 106n65, 408–9, 410–11, 412–13, 415–16; from Jane E. Roscoe, 429; to John Bostock, 413, 418; to John Corrie, 408, 423; to John Edward Taylor, 407; to John Kennedy, 411; from John Owens Johnson, 400; from John R. Chorley, 427–28, 430; from John Shepherd, 140; to John Touchet, 431; to Joseph Sabine, 421, 428; to Maria Edgeworth, 427–28; from Mary Ann Lace, 426; to Miss Bent, 426; to Miss Duckworth, 429; from Mr. Hinks, 108; to Mr. Miller, 405; to Mrs. Marsh, 429; to Patrick Neill, 419–20; to Peter Ewart, 403–4; to Peter Mark Roget, 410–11, 421–22; to Prideaux John Selby, 422; to Randall Currell, 400; to Richard Rathbone, 398; to Richard Taylor, 415–16; to Robert Bakewell, 207n5; to Robert Brown, 423–24; to Robert Jameson,

420; to Robert Knox, 419; to Rufus King, 401; to Samuel R. Brookes, 414–15; to Samuel Welles, 415; to Thomas Acland, 413–14; to Thomas Allan, 432; to Thomas Greg, 404–5; to Thomas Lee, 426; from Thomas Stuart Traill, 105, 150, 269, 281, 416–22, 430–31; from Thomas Sully, 169, 357; from Vincent Nolte, xxi, 54n1, 75, 75n30, 98, 101, 398–99; from William Atherton, 422; from William Charles Henry, 432, 432n16; to William Charles Henry, 406; from William Home Lizars, 286; from William Rathbone, 91, 105, 245n8, 403–5, 406–7, 408, 411, 414–15, 431; from William Roscoe, 96, 146, 427–28; from William Shepherd, 427

Letters of John James Audubon, 1826–1840 (Corning), 338n74

letters to Audubon: from Agnes Greg, 246–47; from Elizabeth Greg Rathbone (Mrs. William Rathbone), 246–47; from Hannah Mary Reynolds Rathbone ("Queen Bee"), 301; from Lucy Bakewell Audubon, xxvi, xxix, 167, 168, 169–70, 171, 344, 367; from Margaret Lace Roscoe (Mrs. Edward Roscoe), 192; from William Rathbone, 166, 354

The Life and Adventures of John James Audubon, the Naturalist (Buchanan), xli

The Life of John James Audubon, the Naturalist (Lucy Audubon), xli, lii

life-size plates (*The Birds of America*), xxiv–xxv, 202–3, 230, 282, 308, 309, 331, 339, 373. See also *The Birds of America* (Audubon)

Lightbody, Hannah. *See* Greg, Hannah Lightbody (Mrs. Samuel Greg) "the Line." *See* Tropic of Cancer

Linnaeus, Carolus, 42, 42n32

Linnean Society, 416n8, 417, 417n9, 418n10, 421n11, 424n13

Literary and Philosophical Society (Liverpool), 73n26, 209, 330

Literary and Philosophical Society (Manchester), 156n5

Liverpool, England: Audubon's arrival in, xx, 51, 53–54; Audubon's lodgings in, 54, 79, 101, 112, 143, 146, 150; Audubon's reception in, xxi, 169, 171–72, 174, 200; beggars in, 122, 130; Blind Asylum in, 80–81, 80n36, 94–95, 117, 133, 134, 137; Botanic Garden in, 69–70, 81, 106, 115, 140, 140n94; "coppering" industry in, 124; customs house in, 54–55, 103, 126, 397, 400; descriptions of, 53, 78–79, 113, 200; Exchange buildings, 53, 54, 59, 62–63, 79n35; Jail of Liverpool, 212, *213*, 214–15; Literary and Philosophical Society in, 73n26, 209, 330; population density of, 78; weather in, 56, 108, 111–12, 120, 127, 141, 146, 149, 220–21. *See also* Green Bank (Rathbone family seat); Royal Institution (Liverpool)

Liverpool Academy, 106n63

Liverpool Literary and Philosophical Society, 73n26, 209, 330

Liverpool Royal Institution, 343

Lizars, Daniel, 314, 314n44, 351, 353, 379–80, 381

Lizars, John, 337, 337n73; *A System of Anatomical Plates of the Human Body*, 337n73

Lizars, Mrs., xxxv, 294, 296, 332, 351, 357, 360; Audubon dining with, 293, 299, 316, 330–31; and Audubon's wardrobe, 366, 379; description of,

292–93; visiting Audubon, 301, 313, 327, 366

Lizars, William Home, xxxv, 292–93, 298, 314n44, 318, 319, 332, 337, 338, 344, 351, 354, 357, 362, 387; and the Antiquarian Society, 322, 323–24, 345; Audubon dining with, 299, 313, 316, 319, 330–31, 350, 362, 376, 378, 381; and Audubon's mail, 369; and colorists' strike, xxxii, 286n22; and engraving of Audubon's portrait, 299, 314; gift from, 294, 295, 342, 368, 381; and letter of introduction, 286; *Picturesque Views of Edinburgh*, 294, 294n32; and Prideaux John Selby, 286, 293, 349; and publishing of *The Birds of America*, xxxi, 286n22, 296, 301, 306, 307, 309, 313, 316, 338n74, 339; and the Royal Academy, 357–58, 360; *A System of Anatomical Plates of the Human Body*, 337n73; and theft from exhibition, 335; visiting Audubon, 286, 291, 301, 311–12, 327; and the Wernerian Society, 355

Locust Grove (farm), 109n67

London, England, 202, 203, 204, 230

Long, Stephen H., 364n87

Loraine, Claude. *See* Lorrain, Claude

The Lord of the Manor (play), 352, 352n81

Lorrain, Claude, 37, 37n26, 382

Louisiana state seal, *402*

Louis-Philippe, duc d'Orléans. *See* duc d'Orléans (Louis-Philippe)

Low, Sampson, xli

Loyd, Mr. (banker), 159, 161, 185, 188, 189–91, 192

Loyd, Thomas, 189, 190, 191

Lyons, Mr., 56, 59, 110–11

Macartney, 1st Earl of (George Macartney), 115, 115n69

MacGillivray, William, xii, xlix, l
magpie (bird), 127, 127n78, 220. *See also* birds
Manchester, England: Academy of Natural History, 154–55, 156, 163, 184, 185, 222–23, 230; Audubon's dislike of, 167; Audubon's lodgings in, 157, 164, 191, 260–61; Audubon's reception in, 259, 260; and business inclination of individuals in, 164; charity school in, 170; and cotton mills, 186; descriptions of, 157, 162, 164, 166, 175–76, 178, 181, 186–87; education in, 181–82; Exchange buildings, 157, 160, 163–64, 166, 170, 178, 180, 184, 185, 191–92; Literary and Philosophical Society in, 156n5; Natural History Society in, 160n9, 418–19, 431; and prostitutes, 160; weather in, 163, 164, 165, 178, 182, 199, 224, 244, 248, 255, 261. *See also* Quarry Bank House (Greg family home)
Manchester Guardian, 159n7, 407n2
Manchester Literary and Philosophical Society, 156n5
Manners and Customs of Several Indian Tribes Located West of the Mississippi (Hunter), 74–75, 74n28
manuscript journal (1828), 393, 394, 395–96
Marsh, Mrs., 429
Martin, Frank J., 71, 72, 423–24
Martin, Henry Bradley, xlii, liii
Mathews, Andrew, 393
Mathews, Judge, 208, 341
Matlock, England, 183, 207, 232–41, 241, 242–43, 259, 277, 288, 441; baths at, 237, 241–42; River Derwent at, 239, 242
Mattlock. *See* Matlock, England
Maury, James (American consul), 62–63, 63n12, 65, 66, 67, 244, 245; and letters of introduction, 104, 106, 404, 415
Maury, William. *See* Maury, James (American consul)
mauvaise honte (embarrassment), xx, xxvi, xxxiii, 66–67, 67n15, 74, 93. *See also* quality of mind
McCulloch, John Ramsay, 388, 388n92
meals. *See* food
Mease, James, 211, 211n7, 353, 357
Meaze, Dr. *See* Mease, James
Meikleham, Dr. (subscriber from Trinidad), 316, 317, 318, 320
Melly, André, 67, 68, 68n16, 75, 93, 129, 133, 136, 137, 150, 151, 154, 216, 220; Audubon dining with, 131–32, 145; Audubon's drawing gift to, 142–43, 142n95; and Audubon's exhibits, 84, 112–13, 180, 219; and Ellen Greg, 68n16, 180, 204; and letters of introduction, 86, 158
Melrose, Scotland, 278, 289
Menzies, Archibald, 424, 424n14
merganser (bird), 42. *See also* birds
Mersey River, xl–xli, 51, 59, 89, 113, 122, 133
Middlemist, Charles, 4n7, 100, 100n59, 174, 342, 353, 367, 368
Midlewith, Charles. *See* Middlemist, Charles
Miller, Mr., 405
"The Mistress and Her Servant" (story), 155–56
Molineux, Mr. (French consul), 135, 135n85, 251
Monro, Alexander, III, 311–12, 311n43, 333
Monroe, Dr. *See* Monro, Alexander, III
Moore, Hannah, 99, 99n58
Moore, Thomas: *Epistles, Odes, and Other Poems*, 133n84

Northumberland, Duke of, 368, 370

"Observations on the Natural History
of the Alligator" (Audubon), 187n24
oil paintings. See paintings
Old Town (Edinburgh), 270–71, 284,
285, 287, 329, 333, 354, 359, 379. See
also Edinburgh, Scotland
"orange women." See prostitutes
Ord, George, 42, 169, 350, 350n79, 358,
363; opposition of, toward Audubon's work, 42n33, 70n20, 96n56,
268n23
Ornithological Biography (Audubon),
435, 221n2; as companion to The
Birds of America, xix, xxvi, 308;
completion of, xxxiii; editing of, by
William MacGillivray, xlix; writing
of, xix, xxxi–xxxii. See also The Birds
of America (Audubon)

Paget, John, 73n25
paintings, 131, 375–76, 387–88; cats
fighting, 351, 353, 356–57, 374; as gifts,
xxiv, 128, 130, 134, 136–37, 142, 169,
171–72, 179, 308, 378, 379; for Margaret Lace Roscoe (Mrs. Edward
Roscoe), 128, 130, 134, 136–37, 142,
171–72; pheasants, 362, 365, 369,
380, 389; for the Royal Institution
(Edinburgh), 308, 378, 379; speed
of completing, 136, 308, 327–28, 329,
357; Trapped Otter, 326, 327, 329, 331,
332, 343, 374; Wild Turkey Cock, 134,
136, 169, 171, 179; Wild Turkeys, 300,
301, 303, 313, 374. See also The Birds
of America (Audubon); drawing;
exhibitions
Pamar, Roman, 4, 4n6
Pannant, David, 425
Panorama of Venice (painting), 103–4

Paravey. See Saravey, Mr.
Parawa. See Saravey, Mr.
Paris, France, xxiv, 75, 202, 203, 207,
393–94
partridge (bird), 182–83. See also birds
Pascalis-Ouvrière, Félix, 76–77, 76n32
Pascallis, Doctor. See Pascalis-
Ouvrière, Félix
pastells. See art supplies
Pattison, Granville Sharp, 263n14
Pattison, Mr., 263, 263n14, 266, 267, 271,
280, 360; and Audubon's exhibit, 283
Peale, Charles Willson, 364n87
Peale, Titian Ramsay, 364, 364n87
Pelletier, Mr. See Pelletier de Cham-
bure, Laurent-Auguste
Pelletier de Chambure, Laurent-
Auguste, 357, 357n82
Percy, Jane Middlemist, 4, 4n7, 66, 100,
100n59, 173n16
Percy, Robert, 100
petrel (bird), 10, 10n14, 16, 19, 20, 21,
23–24, 33. See also birds
Pfeil, Philip. See Phile, Philip
pheasant (bird), 277; drawing, 184–85,
188, 191, 192; hunting, xxxiv–xxxv,
182–83; painting, 362, 365, 369, 380,
389. See also birds
Philadelphia PA, xxx, 5n11, 70n20,
77n33, 92, 165, 177, 279; Academy of
Natural Sciences in, 20, 92, 92n51,
346, 364, 364n87; cost of art supplies
in, 185; and George Ord, 42, 42n33,
96n56, 286n23
"Philadelphia Brute." See Lawson, Alexander
Phile, Philip: "Washington's March,"
23, 23n21
Philosophical Journal. See Edinburgh
Philosophical Journal
Philosophical Society of Edinburgh,
345n77, 365

Phrenological Journal, 314n45, 361n84

Phrenological Society, 314n45

phrenology, 70, 70n20, 92, 229n5, 298n35, 357, 366, 387n91; and examinations of Audubon, 302, 311, 314–15, 319, 361, 368, 378

Picturesque Views of Edinburgh (Ewbank), 294, 294n32, 295

pigeon (bird), 17, 298, 354. See also birds

pigs, 46–47. See also animals

Pike, Zebulon Montgomery: An Account of Expeditions to the Sources of the Mississippi, 45, 45n36

Pillet, Mr. See Pillet-Will, Michel-Frederic

Pillet-Will, Michel-Frederic, 200, 200n1, 217, 220

pirates, 11, 13, 40

plays. See theater

politics, xxiii, 37, 49, 56, 57, 127, 159, 261, 439; and aristocracy, xxiii–xxiv, xxxvi–xxxvii, 132; and hunting ethics, xxxvi–xxxvii, 132; and slavery, 129, 129n82. See also America; class consciousness

Pope, Dr., 3, 100, 208, 343

porpoises, 7–8, 8n12, 16, 20, 27, 38, 46. See also animals

Priestley, Joseph, 197, 197n31, 330, 330n66

Prince of Musignano. See Bonaparte, Charles Lucien

printing: and The Birds of America, xix, xxx, xxxii, 207, 285–86. See also engraving

Procellaria (bird), 10–11, 10n14, 19–20, 24. See also birds

prose style, xxxiii, xxxviii; and analogies, xxxiv, 335; animal allusions, 59, 59n7, 72; and bombast, xxxiii–xxxiv,

56; and dialogue with Lucy, lviii–lix, 36, 43, 44, 56, 58, 63, 67–68, 76, 77, 87, 89, 91, 94, 95, 96, 107, 111, 118, 122, 127, 131, 132, 139, 176, 228, 235, 379, 381; and digressions, 58n5; and editing, xxxiii; and editing by Alice Ford, xii, xliii–liii, 14n17, 338n74, 436–37, 442, 443; and editing by David Brewster, xxxii, 337, 345–46, 350, 360; and editing by Maria Audubon, xii, xli–xliii, xlviii, l–li, 145n99, 157n6, 436–37, 440; and editing by William MacGillivray, xii, xlix, l; and French words, xii–xiii, xxxiii, xxxv–xxxvi, 39, 39n31, 46, 59, 59n7, 64, 66–67, 74, 75, 80n37, 85, 85n43, 114, 120, 120n71, 121, 121n72, 136, 136n87, 195n28, 280, 283, 283n21, 300, 317, 349, 349n78, 385, 385n90, 442; and "fudge" expletive, 46, 125n75, 292, 294, 356, 388; and inebriation, 47–49, 56, 58–60, 439; "Laforest" references, 89, 91, 94, 118, 131, 139, 176, 228, 228n4, 379; and Latin words, 10–11, 11n15, 94, 94n53, 107; literary allusions, 58, 58n5, 78, 78n34, 133, 133n84, 164, 164n13; and playfulness, xxxiv–xxxv, xxxviii–xxix, xlv, xlvii–xlviii, 37–38, 61, 71, 140, 155–56, 164, 176, 184, 196–97, 197n31, 204, 220, 223, 249, 262, 294, 315, 334, 442; and punctuation, lvi–lviii; and satire, xxxiv–xxxv, 25, 25n22, 260–61; and spelling, lvi, 441; and wordplay, xxxv, 26, 58, 71, 107, 132, 133, 133n84, 139–40, 140n91, 294, 442

prostitutes, 68, 68n17, 72, 72n23, 130, 160, 305

publishing plan, xix, xx, xxiv–xxv, 172, 303, 306–8, 309, 339, 398; plate order, 331; and prospectus, xxiv, 202, 307,

309; search for engraver and printer, xxiv, xxvi, xxx, xxxi, xxxii, 207, 285–86; suggested by Henry George Bohn, 202–3, 206. See also *The Birds of America* (Audubon)

Pyke, James, 64, 75, 141

Quakers, 129n82, 191, 192, 205, 215, 231, 277

quality of mind, xxxvi, xxxix–xli, 86, 88; anxiety, 22–23, 43–44, 50–51, 93–94, 111, 116, 118, 267, 335, 344, 376; boredom, 14, 41, 45, 56; depression, xxii, xxvii, 62, 66, 101, 125, 129, 131, 167, 180, 182, 185, 205, 232, 246, 301, 354; and lack of letters from Lucy, xxii–xxiii, xxiv, xxix, 66, 101, 116, 117, 121, 124, 131, 138, 167, 246, 259, 278, 300, 301, 308, 313, 318, 320, 334, 337, 338; *mauvaise honte* (embarrassment), xx, xxvi, xxxiii, 66–67, 67n15, 74, 93; and premonitions, xxii–xxiii, xxvii–xxx, 23, 116, 117, 117n70, 270, 344, 437–38; on the sea voyage, 35–36, 39, 42–43; and secret-keeping, xxxix; and shyness, 65, 66–67, 73, 74, 93, 98, 117, 153, 317, 323. *See also* Audubon, John James

Quarry Bank cotton-spinning mill, 156n5, 181, 181n19, 187

Quarry Bank House (Greg family home), 143n96, 156n5, 179, 193, 250–51, 288; Audubon dining at, 194–96; Audubon's stays at, 181–84, 196–97, 225–26, 228–30, 253–55. *See also* Manchester, England

Raeburn, Sir Henry, 298n36, 336, 336n71

Railton, Mr., 179, 232

Ramsden, George, 85, 397–98

Randolph, John, 196, 196n29

Rankin, Adam, 305, 305n41

Rankin, Elizabeth (Mrs. Adam Rankin), 305n41

Rathbone, Basil (son of Richard Rathbone), 64, 88, 119, 137, 200, 210

Rathbone, Elizabeth (Mrs. John Paget), 73n25, 254

Rathbone, Elizabeth Greg (Mrs. William Rathbone), 73n25, 95, 129–30, 143n96, 218, 221, 223; Audubon dining with, 74–75; and Audubon's album, 205; and Audubon's drawing gift, 137, 143; description of, 90–91, 128; gifts from (pocket book), 90–91, 93; letter from, 246–47

Rathbone, Hannah Mary, xxi, 88n48, 121, 136n88, 144, 210, 217, 225, 244, 253, 371; and Audubon's album, 205; Audubon's carriage ride to Liverpool with, 149–50; Audubon's carriage ride to Manchester with, 221–22; and Audubon's drawing gift, 137, 240; Audubon's letters to, 167–68, 310–11; Audubon's walks with, 132–33, 231–32, 236, 238, 239, 254, 255; descriptions of, xxviii–xxix, 88, 89, 127–28, 141, 143, 222, 440; flirtatiousness of, with Audubon, 145n97, 226; gifts from, 124, 143, 146, 167, 238, 242, 243, 258; gifts from, for John Woodhouse Audubon, 236, 259; gifts from, for Lucy Bakewell Audubon, 143, 238, 259; lack of letters from, 373; and letters of introduction, 432; reading Audubon's journal, 222; self-portrait of, 145, 145n97, 200

Rathbone, Hannah Mary (Mrs. John Hamilton Thom), 73n25

Rathbone, Hannah Mary Reynolds ("Queen Bee"), xxi, xxix, 88n48, 89, 136, 140n93, 172, 201, 221, 222, 223–25;

robin (bird), 145n97, 149, 167. *See also* birds

"Rob Roy" (play), 274–75

Roget, Peter Mark, 410–11, 411n3, 421–22

rook (bird), 240. *See also* birds

Roscoe, Edward, 70n19, 87, 87n47, 96, 104, 114, 124, 146; Audubon dining with, 114–15; illness of, 110; and letter of introduction, 425; letters from, 113, 128, 256

Roscoe, Jane Elizabeth (daughter of William Roscoe), 104n62, 120, 137, 201; and letter of introduction, 429; poetry of, 161, 161n11

Roscoe, Jane Griffies (Mrs. William Roscoe), 55n3

Roscoe, Margaret Lace (Mrs. Edward Roscoe), 70n19, 87n47, 114, 146n100, 209; descriptions of, 70, 87; and drawing, 70, 70n19, 96, 104, 137, 138, 146; gift from, 146; letter from, to Audubon, 192

Roscoe, Miss (daughter of Edward Roscoe), xxxviii, 104, 114, 138

Roscoe, William, 55, 55n3, 68, 70n19, 73n26, 86, 90, 98, 169, 171, 200, 218, 321, 427n15; Audubon dining with, 95–96, 117, 137; Audubon's drawing gift to, 144; and Audubon's exhibit, 85, 105, 106–7, 108, 110; Audubon's letters to, 105, 144, 309–10; and the Botanic Garden, 69–70, 140n94; description of, 67; letters from, 110; and letters of introduction, 71, 96, 146, 398, 427–28; poetry of, 124, 137; snuff box gift from, 216; and sword beans, 120–21

Roscoe, William, Jr., 220–21

Rosina (Shield), 275, 275n18

Roskell, Mr. (jeweler), 54, 64, 99, 146

Royal Academy (Edinburgh), 350, 357–59, 360, 367, 370, 374

Royal Academy (London), 324n54

Royal College of Surgeons (Edinburgh), 337n73, 345n77

Royal Institution (Edinburgh), 292n31, 301, 339; Audubon's exhibition at, xxx, xxxi, 301–2, 304, 307, 314, 321, 322, 326, 330, 332, 335–36, 337–38, 339, 348, 353, 367, 376–77; theft of drawing from the, 335–36; and Wild Turkeys painting from Audubon, 308, 378, 379. *See also* Edinburgh, Scotland; exhibitions

Royal Institution (Liverpool), xxii, 71, 73n26, 76, 200, 208, 210–11, 217, 307; Audubon's exhibition at, 72, 79, 82, 84, 85, 86, 87, 90, 98, 100, 102, 105, 106–8, 110–11, 120, 124, 131–32, 136, 137, 145, 150, 169; founding of, 55n3; and Wild Turkey Cock painting from Audubon, xxiv, 134, 136, 169, 171, 179. *See also* exhibitions; Liverpool, England

Royal Institution (London), 99n58

Royal Palace of Holyrood (Edinburgh), 278, 279, 284–85, 288

Royal Society, 332n69, 345n77, 395n2, 418n10, 421n11, 432n16, 432n17

rudder fish, 8, 9. *See also* animals

The Ruins of Holyrood Chapel (Daguerre), 62, 104, 104n61

Russel, Dr. *See* Russell, James

Russell, James, 345, 345n77, 355, 358–59

Sabine, Joseph, 174, 421, 421n11, 428

Saint-Domingue. *See* Haiti

Saint-Hilaire, Étienne Geoffroy, 395, 395n4

Sapinot, G. L., 3, 3n4

Saravey, Mr., 218, 218n9

Saxtons, Mr., 236

Saxton's Baths (Matlock), 237, 241–42

Say, Thomas, 177; *American Entomology*, 177n18

scarlet tanager (bird), 72, 72n22. *See also* birds

School of Industry for the Indigent Blind. *See* Blind Asylum (Liverpool)

The School of Reform (Morton), 326, 326n58

Scotsman (newspaper), 351, 351n80

Scott, Sir Walter, 99n58, 103, 269, 278, 282, 292n30, 311, 314n45, 316, 323, 323n53, 346–48, 350, 358, 420; and Audubon's exhibit, 320; *The Birds of America* proofs for, 303; home of, at Melrose, 266, 289; and letters of introduction to, 99, 283; novels of, xxvi, 49; as "the great unknown," 334n70

Scott, Walter Francis Montagu-Douglas (Duke of Buccleuch). *See* Buccleuch, 5th Duke of (Walter Francis Montagu-Douglas Scott)

Scott, William, 314–15, 314n45, 319

Scottish Academy, 292n31, 298n36, 331n67

Scottish Academy of Painting, Sculpture, and Architecture. *See* Scottish Academy

Scottish Cryptogamic Flora (Greville), 362n85

sea voyage, 97, 437; Atlantic Ocean, xx, 22–26, 31–49; and birds, 10–11, 10n14, 13, 16, 17, 19–21, 22, 23–24, 33, 38, 42; conclusion of the, 51; around Cuba, 14, 17, 17; and fishing, 5, 6–8, 10, 17, 22, 38; around Florida, 19–22; and food, 5, 8, 17, 42, 45–47; Gulf of Mexico, xx, 5–8, 10–11, 13–17, 19–22; latitude and longitude measurements, 33–35; and

measuring current speed, 10, 10n13; mileage measurements, 34–35, 438; and saints, 31–32; speed of, 25, 32; St. George's Channel, 49–51. *See also Delos* (sailing vessel)

Selby, Prideaux John, 282, 338, 349–50, 358, 359, 360–61, 362, 366, 370; and drawing lessons, 360, 364, 365, 367–68, 371; *Illustrations of British Ornithology*, 88n49, 272n12, 285, 293, 339; *Illustrations of Ornithology*, 272n12; and letters of introduction, 422; and William Lizars, xxxi, 286, 350

Selkirk, 5th Earl of (Thomas Douglas), 138n90

Selkirk, 6th Earl of (Dunbar James Douglas), 138n90

sharks, 9, 10. *See also* animals

Shaw, Mr. (gamekeeper to Lord Stamford), 182–83, 229

sheep, 265–66, 277, 280. *See also* animals

Shepherd, John, 140, 140n94, 184, 200, 204

Shepherd, William, 140n94, 427, 427n15

Shield, William: *Rosina*, 275, 275n18

Sigismondé, Mr. *See* Sismondi, Jean-Charles-Léonard Simonde de

Sim, Mr. *See* Symmes, John Cleves, Jr.

Simpson, James, 361–62, 361n84, 366, 378

Sismondi, Jean-Charles-Léonard Simonde de, 85, 85n44, 86, 89, 98, 290, 290n28

Skene, James, 323, 323n53, 325, 348, 354–55

Skene, William Forbes, 323n53

Skin, Mr. *See* Skene, James

slavery, xxiii, 129, 129n82, 146n100. *See also* politics

"tameness," English: and hunting, xxviii, xxxvi–xxxvii, 132, 132n83, 152, 182–83; and trespassing laws, xxiii–xxiv, 115, 122. *See also* America; "wildness," American

Tanetti, Mr., 170–71, 192

Tayler, John James, 155, 155n4, 166, 245, 432

Tayler, Mrs., 166, 245

Taylor, Jane: "The Discontented Pendulum," 164n13, 289, 289n27

Taylor, John Edward, 407, 407n2

Taylor, Richard, 415–16, 416n8

Temminck, Coenraad Jacob, 249, 249n10

Thealia (sailing vessel), 20, 21–22

theater, 274–75, 325–26, 352–53, 393

Thom, John Hamilton, 73n25

Thompson, Dr. *See* Thomson, John

Thomson, James, 49; *The Castle of Indolence*, 25–26, 25n23

Thomson, John, 268, 268n8, 272, 292, 295–96, 321

Thornely, Mr., 104, 106

thrush (bird), 219. *See also* birds

Titian, 25, 25n22

Todd, John, 283

Todd, Thomas, 283

tomatoes, 146. *See also* food

Touchet, John, 431

Touchet family, 160, 162, 167, 431, 432

Traill, Mrs., 85, 108, 109–10, 130, 200, 217

Traill, Thomas Stuart, xxv, xxvii, 73, 73n26, 90, 95, 103, 107, 109–10, 136, 151, 306, 308, 331, 370; Audubon dining with, 135, 145, 205; and Audubon's album, 205, 209, 210; and Audubon's exhibit, 85; Audubon's letter to, 282; family of, 105, 200; and Henry George Bohn, 201–3, 206; and kidney stone drawing, 140,

140n92; and letters of introduction, 105, 150, 269, 281, 416–22, 430–31; and the Royal Institution (Liverpool), 55n3, 73n26, 84, 100, 124, 150, 171, 174–75

Trapped Otter painting, 128, 130, 134, 136–37, 142, 172. *See also* paintings

Tread Mills (prison labor), 214–15, 217–18. *See also* Jail of Liverpool

Trench, Richard Le Poer (Earl of Clancarty). *See* Clancarty, 2nd Earl of (Richard Le Poer Trench)

trespassing laws, English, xxiii–xxiv, 115, 122. *See also* "tameness," English

Trinidad subscriber. *See* Meikleham, Dr. (subscriber from Trinidad)

Tristram Shandy (Sterne), xxxiv, 58, 58n5, 78, 78n34

Tropic of Cancer, 14, 14n17, 15

turkey. *See* wild turkey

Tuskar Rock lighthouse, 49, 49n40

Tyler, Victor Morris, xlii

University of Edinburgh, 268n8, 268n9, 304n40, 311n43, 321n50, 387n91, 432n17; and natural history, xxvi, 268n5; and subscription to *The Birds of America*, 334, 340, 370. *See also* Edinburgh, Scotland

Vancouver, George, 424n14

"Venemous Tallow Chandler." *See* Ord, George

Vernet, Carle (Antoine-Charles-Horace), 225, 225n3

Vernet, Claude-Joseph, 50, 50n41

The Vicar of Wakefield (Goldsmith), 125, 125n75

Vigée-Lebrun, Élisabeth, 62, 62n11

Viviparous Quadrupeds of North America (Audubon), 128n80

Vowles (*Delos* passenger), 25–26

Walker, Sir Patrick, 301, 328
walks: in Edinburgh, 269–71, 272–74,
    283, 294–95; at Green Bank, 122,
    132–33, 139, 143; to Green Bank,
    87, 143–44, 146, 209, 220–21; with
    John Chorley, 215, 216; in Liverpool,
    61–62, 76, 77–79, 84, 105, 108, 111–12,
    113, 124, 138; in Manchester, 160,
    175–76, 179, 188–89, 224, 246; at
    Matlock, 234–36, 238, 239–40; along
    the Mersey River, 59, 89, 122, 133; at
    Quarry Bank, 182, 196, 253–54; and
    smuggler incident, 125–27
Walton, Mr., 262–63, 267, 287, 300–301
Wanderings in South America (Water-
    ton), 96n56
warbler (bird), 13, 16, 219. *See also* birds
Warren, John Fleming Leicester
    (Baron de Tabley), 159–60, 159n8
Washington, George, 63n12
"Washington's March" (Phile), 23n21,
    275
Waterton, Charles, 177, 178, 300, 322;
    Wanderings in South America, 96n56
Watson-Gordon, Sir John, 328, 328n63
Watterhouse, Benjamin, 256
Watterton, Mr. *See* Waterton, Charles
weather: in Edinburgh, 281, 292, 301,
    312, 313, 321, 326, 353, 365; in Liver-
    pool, 56, 108, 111–12, 120, 127, 141, 146,
    149, 220–21; in Manchester, 163, 164,
    165, 178, 182, 199, 224, 244, 248, 255,
    261; at Matlock, 242, 243; during sea
    voyage, 5, 12, 16, 23, 24, 33, 35
Weiss, Charles N., 315, 315n47, 319, 326,
    333–34
Welles, Samuel, 106, 415, 415n7
Werner, Abraham Gottlob, 268n5,
    327n61

Wernerian Society (Edinburgh),
    292n31, 332–33, 362n85, 420; Audu-
    bon's membership in, xxxii, 285, 328,
    333, 340–41, 355, 367, 371; and essay
    reading, xxxii, 204n3, 340–41, 355
Western Navigator (Cumings), 37n28
West Indies, 129, 129n82
whales, 27, 33, 38. *See also* animals
Whitham, Mr. *See* Witham, Henry
"wildness," American, xxiii, xxviii,
    xxxvi–xxxvii, 49, 96, 113–14, 122, 152.
    See also America; "tameness," English
wild pigeon (bird). *See* stock pigeon
    (bird)
wild turkey, 42n33; Audubon's impres-
    sion of, 95; essay on, for *Ornithologi-
    cal Biography*, xxxii
Wild Turkey Cock painting, 134, 136,
    169, 171, 179. *See also* paintings
Wild Turkeys painting, 300, 301, 303,
    308, 313, 374, 378, 379. *See also* paint-
    ings
Willson, George, 163
Willson, James. *See* Wilson, James
Willson, John, 163–64, 223, 231
Wilson, Alexander, 420; *American
    Ornithology*, xxiv, 5n11, 42n33, 286n23
Wilson, Ann, 335
Wilson, James, 297, 297n33, 321
Wilson, James G., xli
Wilson, John (Christopher North),
    297n33, 298n34, 302, 302n38, 311, 387,
    387n91; exhibition review by, 326,
    326n59, 340; and letters of introduc-
    tion, 316, 317; and writing help, xxxii,
    303–4, 333
winter falco (bird), 113, 113n68. *See also*
    birds
Winter's Wreath, 161n11
Witham, Henry, 328, 328n62, 329, 330,
    355, 358

women, 114–15, 120, 162, 167; Abigail Benson Dockray, 231; Audubon's affinity for, xii, xxxvi, xxxvii–xxxviii, xxxix, 182, 253, 283, 292, 305; Audubon's flirtatiousness with, xlvii–xlviii, 145n97, 226, 228; descriptions of, xxxviii–xxxix, 83, 104, 118, 130, 160, 166, 192–93, 247–48, 252, 278, 290, 305, 312, 366; in Edinburgh, 271, 278, 290; Elizabeth Greg Rathbone (Mrs. William Rathbone), 90–91, 128; Hannah Mary Rathbone, xxviii–xxix, 88, 89, 127–28, 141, 143, 222, 440; Hannah Mary Reynolds Rathbone ("Queen Bee"), 86–87, 121, 122; Helen Greg, 180, 194, 226, 228; Isabella Douglass, 139; in the Jail of Liverpool, 215; in Liverpool, 55; Margaret Hunter Hall, 333; Margaret Lace Roscoe (Mrs. Edward Roscoe), 70, 87; Maria Foote, 85; Miss Donathan, 77, 95; Mrs. Fletcher, 317; Mrs. Hedge, 176; Mrs. Jeffrey Francis, 388, 389; Mrs. Lizars, 292–93; Mrs. Robert Greg, 225; Mrs. Welbank, 349; Mrs. Woods, 163; in Paris, 393, 394; prostitutes, 68, 68n17, 72, 72n23, 130, 160, 305; Susan Elizabeth Buller (Countess of Morton), 383, 384. *See also* Audubon, Lucy Bakewell (Mrs. John James Audubon)

Wood, George W., 160, 161, 163, 406, 432

Wood, G. M. *See* Wood, George W.

Woodcroft, 140, 149, 205–6, 209, 210

Woods, Mr. *See* Wood, George W.

wordplay, xxxv, 26, 58, 71, 107, 132, 133, 133n84, 139–40, 140n91, 294, 442. *See also* prose style

Wouvermann, Philipp, 217, 217n8

writing style. *See* prose style

Yates, James, 106, 106n65, 408–9, 410–11, 412–13, 415–16